"A very important guide. Gives a very clear, very factual picture. I must admit that I carry and use the book like a bible and refer to it often. Thank you *Billboard* and thank you Joel."

Hy Lit
Program Director
WSNI RADIO, Philadelphia

"For a number of years I have used a review of music from a specific year as a specialty on my radio show. In those years I've been nicknamed 'The Professor' for my history lessons on music. One of my choice sources for information has been Joel Whitburn's books. Thanks."

Scott Muni
WNEW-FM, New York

"There's nothing else like it — only Joel Whitburn could accurately track 7,269 records of the rock era. *The Billboard Book of Top 40 Hits* is worth its weight in solid gold!"

Arnie "Woo Woo" Ginsburg
WXKS-FM, Boston

"Don't stay home without it!"

Bruce Bradley
WYNY-FM, New York

"Hit records have changed the way we dress, dance, talk, and even perceive ourselves. They make us happy, sad, or just help us to pass the time. Music *is* the message, and with this book Joel has given us a firm platform to catalog those messages and memories."

Jack Armstrong
KFRC, San Francisco

"A valuable reference for oldies but goodies — we wouldn't leave home without it!"

Art Laboe
Los Angeles radio personality
President, Original Sound
Record Co., Hollywood

"Very informative—takes the guesswork out of pop music."

Joe Niagara
WPEN, Philadelphia

"*The Billboard Book of Top 40 Hits* is an invaluable aid to anyone interested in pop music."

Dick Biondi
WNMB-FM, North Myrtle Beach
South Carolina

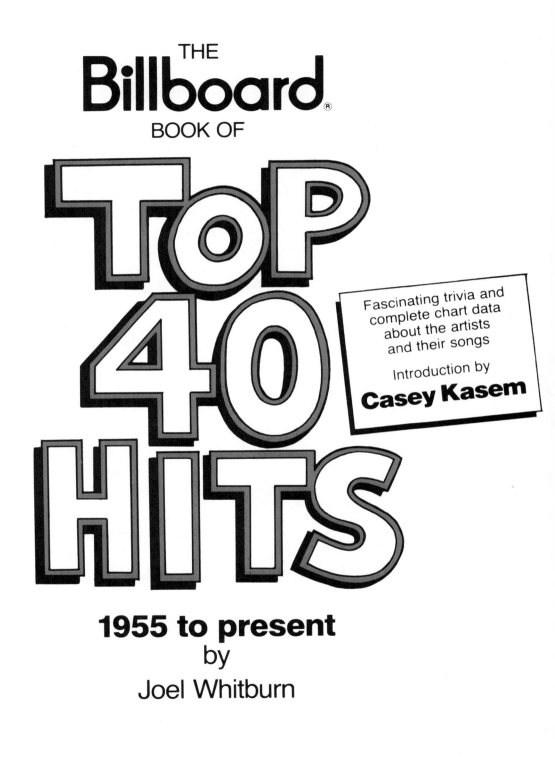

THE Billboard® BOOK OF

TOP 40 HITS

Fascinating trivia and complete chart data about the artists and their songs

Introduction by **Casey Kasem**

1955 to present
by
Joel Whitburn

BILLBOARD PUBLICATIONS, INC./New York

Photo captions by Adam White, managing editor of *Billboard*.
Picture sleeves selected from Joel Whitburn's personal collection.
Photography by Malcolm Hjerstedt of Munroe Studios, Inc.
Custom programming by Joe Buday of Effective Management Systems, Inc.
Typography by A-Line and Ries Graphics, Inc. and Intergraphic Technology, Inc.
Edited by Marisa Bulzone
Book design by Bob Fillie
Jacket design by Lee Lebowitz

First published 1983 by Billboard Publications, Inc., 1515 Broadway,
New York, New York 10036.

ISBN 0-8230-7511-7

Library of Congress Catalog Card Number: 83-71259

Distributed in the United Kingdom by Guinness Books, 2 Cecil Court,
London Road, Enfield, Middlesex EN2 6DJ, England.

ISBN 0-85112-245-0

Manufactured in the United States of America

3 4 5 6 7 8 9/88 87 86 85 84 83

This book is dedicated to
the disc jockeys,
worldwide,
who've supported my work
for the past twelve years.

The author wishes to give thanks to
the entire staff of RECORD RESEARCH:

Bill Hathaway
Brent Olynick
Kim Whitburn
Fran Whitburn
Judy Pedigo
Doug Lawrence
John Novak

CONTENTS

INTRODUCTION

Everyone who listens to my television and radio shows knows that my source—the only source—of chart data is *Billboard*. As *the* trade paper of the record industry, it's been publishing charts of every size, shape, and significance for more than 40 years, reflecting the popularity of the music and performers that have become part of our lives.

When "American Top 40" began in 1970, our staff had to thumb through back issues of *Billboard* to find the achievement records established by any artist who ever had a hit. But it wasn't too long before we became aware of Joel Whitburn's work.

Joel began collecting popular records in the early '50s, a hobby that not only turned into the world's largest collection of original, mint-condition singles, but also formed the basis for compiling and organizing the data contained in *Billboard*'s weekly surveys. Those surveys themselves are based on radio airplay and retail sales.

This book is the result. You can look up any recording artist or song title in the alphabetical listings. You can identify all the Top 40 hits of a performer's career; the date on which each debuted on the charts; and the number of weeks it spent on them.

You can, of course, check a disc's chart peak, and if it went to Number 1 or Number 2, how many weeks it spent there. Each record's entry includes label name and original record number, and also indicates which were certified gold or platinum by the Recording Industry Association of America.

But music fans cannot live by numbers alone, and that's why you'll find a truckload of trivia from the past three decades: tidbits, essential and otherwise, about the recording artists and their songs, pulled from the pages of history and illustrated with more than 300 photographs of unusual and often rare record sleeves.

For professionals in the record business and in radio, *The Billboard Book of Top 40 Hits* has a practical value that's obvious. For everyone else, it's pop music history—and pure, nostalgic fun.

Casey Kasem

AUTHOR'S NOTE

For the past two decades I have immersed myself admidst pop records and *Billboard*'s pop record charts—it seems one can hardly exist without the other—so that this book could be presented to you as a factual account of the pop music scene for the past 28 years.

If you've ever wondered if one of your favorite songs ever made the top 40, or which version of a particular song was the most popular, or just how many hits your favorite artists have accumulated and which of those made the top 10 or perhaps even No. 1, you hold in your hand the book that will give you all these answers and more. While you'll find this book can serve as a dictionary that you may refer to on a daily basis, you'll also find that it can be the hit of your next party—you'll find thousands of facts about records and artists that can serve for some great trivia contests.

This book is actually a spin-off of a larger volume, which I have been publishing and selling within the music industry since 1970. Now in its fourth edition, this larger volume details the entire history of *Billboard*'s Hot 100 charts (a weekly listing of the top 100, rather than just the top 40). In addition to the Hot 100 charts, I have also written books (most in the same format as this one) dealing with the following *Billboard* charts: *Pop 1940–1955*; *Top LPs* (pop albums); *Country (Country and Western)*; *Black (Soul-Rhythm & Blues)*; *Easy Listening (Adult Contemporary)*; and *Bubbling Under the Hot 100*. Although these books are mainly for the music professional, this top 40 volume now gives the average record/music fan a close look into a segment of America's chart history.

I chose 1955 as the beginning year for this look at the popular music scene because it was really the first year of the "rock era." While the roots of rock music go back to perhaps even a decade before 1955, it was in this year that the term "rock and roll" became identifiable to a whole new generation of eager music fans. When Bill Haley's "Rock Around The Clock" topped the charts for the first time in July of 1955, the rock explosion began. Probably at no other time in the history of popular music has such a dramatic change in musical style occurred than at that moment. And when Elvis Presley debuted on the pop charts in March of 1956, rock and roll music found a leader for millions of devoted teenagers worldwide.

Although pop music can include any form of music that captures the public fancy, from dreamy instrumentals to barking dogs, it is rock music that has been the lifeblood of the music industry for the past 28 years. Since the advent of the rock era, the music industry has risen to the top as America's number one source of entertainment. In 1955, the total sales of recorded music was 275 million dollars. By 1980, that figure had risen to over 4 billion dollars!

While critics write of stagnant periods in the pop music industry, it is fresh artists and new styles of music that always seem to pump life into an exciting and ever-changing pop music scene. I hope you will enjoy this book with as much fervor and excitement as I have had in researching and listening to all 7,269 titles included herein.

JOEL WHITBURN
March, 1983

ABOUT THE AUTHOR

Considered by many in the music industry to be the foremost authority on charted music, Joel Whitburn began collecting records as a hobby in the early 1950's. Eventually, he started to categorize his records by year according to the highest position each one reached on *Billboard*'s charts. Later, prompted by friends and colleagues who recognized the importance of his research, he published *Top Pop Records 1955–1969*, the first in a series of books based on *Billboard*'s major charts.

Today, Joel Whitburn's *Record Research* books and supplements are used worldwide, and his record collection has grown to be one of the largest and most comprehensive in the country, encompassing every title to appear on *Billboard*'s pop singles and pop albums charts from 1955 on.

Married, with one daughter, Whitburn lives in Menomonee Falls, Wisconsin. An avid sports enthusiast, he especially enjoys water skiing at his lake home in northern Wisconsin, and playing basketball—a game in which the 6'6" Whitburn excels.

For Joel Whitburn, though, there's still no bigger thrill than finding an untouched basement or back room full of old records and simply rummaging to his heart's content.

RESEARCHING THE CHARTS

Although *Billboard* began publishing in 1894, it wasn't until 1940 that it published its first weekly national pop chart. This first chart was a top 10 listing and the chart fluctuated in size from 10 to 30 positions until 1955, when *Billboard* introduced its first Top 100 chart. The Hot 100 chart, which has become recognized as America's definitive record singles chart, was first published on August 4, 1958.

From 1955 to 1958, before the introduction of the Hot 100, there were a number of charts published by *Billboard*, which were consulted by various members of the music trade. It wasn't until the Hot 100 chart was published in 1958 that the music industry settled down to consulting simply one chart as the definitive source for popular record chart data.

Here are the pop charts that were researched for this book:

Chart Title	Dates Published	Positions
Best Sellers in Stores	Jan. 1, 1955 – Oct. 13, 1958	25–50
Most Played by Jockeys	Jan. 1, 1955 – July 28, 1958	20–25
Most Played in Juke Boxes	Jan. 1, 1955 – June 17, 1957	20
Top 100	Nov. 12, 1955 – July 28, 1958	100
Hot 100	Aug. 4, 1958 – present	100

The record's *date* of chart entry is taken from whichever chart it first appeared on. The date shown is *Billboard*'s actual issue date, and is not taken from the "week ending" dates as shown on the various charts when they were originally published. The issue and week ending dates were different until January 13, 1962, when *Billboard* began using one date system for both the issue and the charts inside.

The record's *highest position* (POS) is taken from the chart on which it achieved a higher ranking.

The record's *weeks charted* (WKS) and weeks at positions No. 1 or No. 2 are taken from the chart on which it achieved its highest total.

THE ARTISTS

THE ARTISTS

This section lists, alphabetically by artist name, every single (45 RPM) record release to make the top 40 on *Billboard*'s pop charts from 1955 through 1982.

Each artist's charted hits are listed in chronological order. A sequential number is shown in front of each song title to indicate that artist's number of top 40 hits. All top 10 hits are highlighted in dark type.

Columnar headings show the following data:

DATE   Date record first made the top 40

POS   Record's highest charted position (highlighted in dark type)

WKS   Total weeks charted in the top 40

LABEL & NO.   Original record label and number

Other data and symbols:

A number in brackets next to a No. 1 or No. 2 positioned record indicates the total weeks the record held that position.

- ●   RIAA certified gold record (million seller)
- ★   RIAA certified platinum record (two million seller)

The Record Industry Association of America began certifying gold records in 1958 and platinum records in 1976. Prior to these dates, there are most certainly some hits that would have qualified for these certifications. Also, certain record labels have never requested RIAA certification for records that would have qualified for these awards.

Symbols in brackets after titles indicate the following:

(I) instrumental
(N) novelty
(C) comedy
(S) spoken word
(F) foreign language
(X) Christmas

If both sides of a record made the top 40, a diagonal symbol (/) is shown after the first charted side and the second charted side is indented. The label and number are shown only once—after the second title. In cases where both sides of a record were shown as one listing on the charts, the secondary sides are shown as above, but no date or position is given for the secondary side. Only the weeks it charted as a secondary side are given.

Directly under some artist's names are brief notes about the artist or group that may be of special interest.

Directly under some song titles are brief notes that may be of special interest, such as a record that may have originally charted at an earlier date, or one that may feature a famous singer providing background vocals. If the song is featured in a Broadway musical or film, the title of the show is given under the record title. If the record title and show title are the same, the show title is not given.

DATE	POS	WKS	ARTIST—Record Title	LABEL & NO.
			ABBA	
			Swedish: (A)Agnetha (B)Bjorn (B)Benny (A)Anni-Frida	
6/22/74	**6**	12	1. **Waterloo**	Atlantic 3035
10/12/74	**27**	4	2. Honey, Honey	Atlantic 3209
10/11/75	**15**	8	3. SOS	Atlantic 3265
3/27/76	**15**	9	4. I Do, I Do, I Do, I Do, I Do	Atlantic 3310
6/19/76	**32**	4	5. Mamma Mia	Atlantic 3315
9/25/76	**13**	11	6. Fernando	Atlantic 3346
1/22/77	**1** (1)	15	● 7. **Dancing Queen**	Atlantic 3372
6/04/77	**14**	10	8. Knowing Me, Knowing You	Atlantic 3387
1/28/78	**12**	9	9. The Name Of The Game	Atlantic 3449
5/06/78	**3**	14	● 10. **Take A Chance On Me**	Atlantic 3457
6/09/79	**19**	10	11. Does Your Mother Know	Atlantic 3574
12/08/79	**29**	6	12. Chiquitita	Atlantic 3629
12/27/80	**8**	16	13. **The Winner Takes It All**	Atlantic 3776
2/06/82	**27**	8	14. When All Is Said And Done	Atlantic 3889
			AC/DC	
			Australian quintet led by Angus Young (guitar) & Brian Johnson (lead singer) - Bon Scott (former lead singer) died 2/19/80 (30)	
10/25/80	**35**	3	1. You Shook Me All Night Long	Atlantic 3761
2/07/81	**37**	5	2. Back In Black	Atlantic 3787
			ACE	
			British quintet -- also see Paul Carrack	
4/05/75	**3**	11	1. **How Long**	Anchor 21000
			ACE, JOHNNY	
			died playing Russian roulette on Christmas Eve, 1954 (25)	
2/19/55	**17**	9	1. Pledging My Love	Duke 136
			ACKLIN, BARBARA	
8/10/68	**15**	8	1. Love Makes A Woman	Brunswick 55379
			AD LIBS	
2/06/65	**8**	7	1. **The Boy From New York City**	Blue Cat 102
			ADAMS, JOHNNY	
7/26/69	**28**	4	1. Reconsider Me	SSS Int'l. 770
			ADDERLEY, "CANNONBALL", Quintet	
			Julian died 8/8/75 (46)	
1/28/67	**11**	8	1. Mercy, Mercy, Mercy [I]	Capitol 5798
			ADDRISI BROTHERS	
			Dick & Don Addrisi	
2/26/72	**25**	7	1. We've Got To Get It On Again	Columbia 45521
5/14/77	**20**	8	2. Slow Dancin' Don't Turn Me On	Buddah 566
			AEROSMITH	
			Boston quintet led by Steve Tyler & Joe Perry	
7/12/75	**36**	3	1. Sweet Emotion	Columbia 10155
2/14/76	**6**	11	2. **Dream On** -re-entry of 1973 hit-	Columbia 10278
6/26/76	**21**	10	3. Last Child	Columbia 10359

DATE	POS	WKS	ARTIST—Record Title	LABEL & NO.
12/18/76	10	11	4. **Walk This Way**	Columbia 10449
5/07/77	38	2	5. Back In The Saddle	Columbia 10516
9/02/78	23	7	6. Come Together	Columbia 10802
			AFTERNOON DELIGHTS	
9/12/81	33	5	1. General Hospi-Tale [N]	MCA 51148
			AIR SUPPLY	
			Australian group led by Graham Russell and Russell Hitchcock	
3/08/80	3	17	1. **Lost In Love**	Arista 0479
7/19/80	2 (4)	17	● 2. **All Out Of Love**	Arista 0520
11/15/80	5	17	3. **Every Woman In The World**	Arista 0564
5/23/81	1 (1)	14	● 4. **The One That You Love**	Arista 0604
10/03/81	5	15	5. **Here I Am (Just When I Thought I Was Over You)**	Arista 0626
1/09/82	5	15	6. **Sweet Dreams**	Arista 0655
6/26/82	5	13	7. **Even The Nights Are Better**	Arista 0692
10/23/82	38	2	8. Young Love	Arista 1005
			AKENS, JEWEL	
2/06/65	3	12	1. **The Birds And The Bees**	Era 3141
			ALABAMA	
			Randy Owen, Jeff Cook, Teddy Gentry (cousins), & Mark Herndon	
7/25/81	20	8	1. Feels So Right	RCA 12236
1/16/82	15	10	2. Love In The First Degree	RCA 12288
6/05/82	18	8	3. Take Me Down	RCA 13210
			ALBERT, MORRIS	
			Brazilian	
8/23/75	6	16	● 1. **Feelings**	RCA 10279
			ALEXANDER, ARTHUR	
3/31/62	24	6	1. You Better Move On	Dot 16309
			ALIVE & KICKING	
7/04/70	7	10	1. **Tighter, Tighter**	Roulette 7078
			ALLAN, DAVIE, & THE ARROWS	
9/09/67	37	3	1. Blue's Theme [I] -from film "The Wild Angels"-	Tower 295
			ALLEN, REX	
			Western movie star	
10/06/62	17	4	1. Don't Go Near The Indians	Mercury 71997
			ALLEN, STEVE	
			founded "The Tonight Show" in '54	
12/03/55	35	2	1. Autumn Leaves [I] -with George Cates' Orchestra-	Coral 61485
			ALLISON, GENE	
3/10/58	36	1	1. You Can Make It If You Try	Vee-Jay 256
			ALLMAN BROTHERS BAND	
			Duane Allman, founder, died in a cycle accident on 10/29/71 (24) - Gregg Allman and Dickey Betts led band after Duane's death	
9/08/73	2 (1)	13	1. **Ramblin Man**	Capricorn 0027
4/07/79	29	5	2. Crazy Love	Capricorn 0320
9/19/81	39	2	3. Straight From The Heart	Arista 0618

Abba. By winning 1974's Eurovision Song Contest before an estimated television audience of 500 million, Sweden's Abba began their ascent to superstardom. They also defeated Britain's representative in the competition, Olivia Newton-John, who finished fourth.

Air Supply. Relative anonymity (quick, name one member) didn't prevent this group from becoming one of Australia's most successful exports of the '80s.

The Allman Brothers. Willie Dixon's blues classic "Spoonful" was this group's first single, released on Dial Records as The Allman Joys. Their producer at the time was country music's John D. Loudermilk.

Herb Alpert & the Tijuana Brass. Before fronting the hugely successful Tijuana Brass, Herb Alpert was a key figure in the Los Angeles pop scene. He and colleague Lou Adler produced Jan & Dean, and wrote "Wonderful World" for Sam Cooke.

The Ames Brothers. After nine top 10 tunes between 1950 and 1957 with brothers Joe, Gene, and Vic, Ed Ames embarked upon a solo career. His biggest hit: "My Cup Runneth Over."

The Angels are best remembered for "My Boyfriend's Back," such a smash in 1963 that the producers even recorded an answer disc with Bobby Comstock that same year.

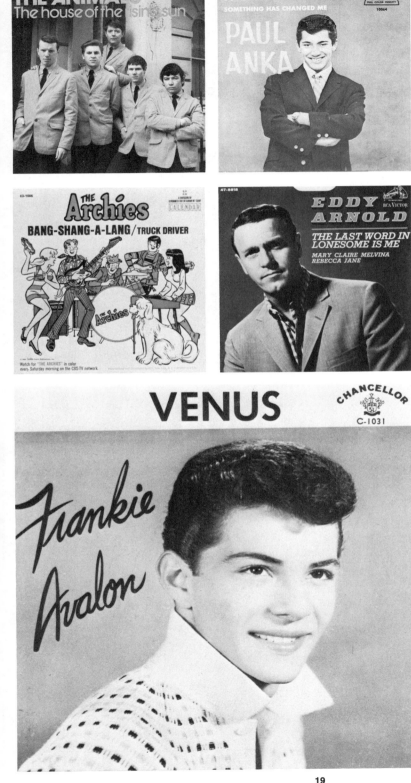

The Animals. Legend suggests that it was this version of "House of The Rising Sun" that inspired Bob Dylan to go electric the following year.

Paul Anka. His co-authorship of Frank Sinatra's anthem, "My Way," probably earned Paul Anka more royalties than all of his own hits put together.

The Archies. The 1969 chart-topper, "Sugar Sugar," featured vocals by Ron Dante, who re-recorded the song under his own name six years later, arranged and conducted by Barry Manilow.

Eddy Arnold. His most successful pop hit, "Make the World Go Away," also charted for Timi Yuro. The song was written by Hank Cochran.

Frankie Avalon. Seventeen years after he first took "Venus" to the top of the charts, Frankie Avalon couldn't resist a 1976 disco remake. The public resisted.

DATE	POS	WKS	ARTIST—Record Title	LABEL & NO.
			ALLMAN, GREGG	
1/19/74	19	8	1. Midnight Rider	Capricorn 0035
			ALPERT, HERB	
5/25/68	1 (4)	12	● 1. **This Guy's In Love With You**	A&M 929
8/25/79	1 (2)	15	● 2. **Rise [I]**	A&M 2151
12/22/79	30	6	3. Rotation [I]	A&M 2202
7/31/82	37	4	4. Route 101 [I]	A&M 2422
			ALPERT, HERB, & The Tijuana Brass	
11/10/62	6	11	1. **The Lonely Bull [I]**	A&M 703
10/16/65	7	13	2. **Taste Of Honey [I]**	A&M 775
1/22/66	11	7	3. Zorba The Greek/ [I]	
2/05/66	38	2	4. Tijuana Taxi [I]	A&M 787
4/09/66	24	5	5. What Now My Love/ [I]	
4/09/66	27	4	6. Spanish Flea [I]	A&M 792
7/09/66	18	6	7. The Work Song [I]	A&M 805
9/17/66	28	4	8. Flamingo [I]	A&M 813
12/03/66	19	6	9. Mame	A&M 823
4/01/67	37	2	10. Wade In The Water [I]	A&M 840
4/29/67	27	6	11. Casino Royale [I]	A&M 850
7/22/67	32	3	12. The Happening [I]	A&M 860
9/30/67	35	3	13. A Banda (Ah Bahn-da) [I]	A&M 870
			AMAZING RHYTHM ACES	
			Memphis-based sextet	
7/26/75	14	9	1. Third Rate Romance	ABC 12078
			AMBOY DUKES	
			Ted Nugent, leader	
7/27/68	16	7	1. Journey To The Center Of The Mind	Mainstream 684
			AMBROSIA	
			Joe Puerta, Burleigh Drummond & David Pack - from California	
7/19/75	17	8	1. Holdin' On To Yesterday	20th Century 2207
4/02/77	39	2	2. Magical Mystery Tour -from "All This & World War II"-	20th Century 2327
9/30/78	3	13	3. **How Much I Feel**	Warner 8640
4/19/80	3	14	4. **Biggest Part Of Me**	Warner 49225
8/02/80	13	10	5. You're The Only Woman (You & I)	Warner 49508
			AMERICA	
			Dewey Bunnell & Gerry Beckley - with Dan Peek thru 1976	
3/04/72	1 (3)	12	● 1. **A Horse With No Name**	Warner 7555
5/27/72	9	9	2. **I Need You**	Warner 7580
11/04/72	8	9	3. **Ventura Highway**	Warner 7641
2/24/73	35	2	4. Don't Cross The River	Warner 7670
9/21/74	4	11	5. **Tin Man**	Warner 7839
1/18/75	5	10	6. **Lonely People**	Warner 8048
4/26/75	1 (1)	12	7. **Sister Golden Hair**	Warner 8086
8/16/75	20	7	8. Daisy Jane	Warner 8118
6/12/76	23	6	9. Today's The Day	Warner 8212
8/21/82	8	15	10. **You Can Do Magic**	Capitol 5142

DATE	POS	WKS	ARTIST—Record Title	LABEL & NO.
			AMERICAN BREED	
			Chicago rock quartet - evolved into soul group Rufus	
7/08/67	24	4	1. Step Out Of Your Mind	Acta 804
12/16/67	5	12	● 2. **Bend Me, Shape Me**	Acta 811
3/16/68	39	3	3. Green Light	Acta 821
			AMES BROTHERS	
			Ed, Gene, Joe & Vic Ames - Vic died 1/23/78 (51)	
11/20/54	3	15	1. **The Naughty Lady Of Shady Lane**	RCA 5897
9/24/55	11	11	2. My Bonnie Lassie	RCA 6208
3/24/56	35	3	3. Forever Darling	RCA 6400
5/19/56	11	20	4. It Only Hurts For A Little While	RCA 6481
7/22/57	5	16	5. **Tammy**	RCA 6930
10/07/57	5	14	6. **Melodie D'Amour**	RCA 7046
3/31/58	23	2	7. A Very Precious Love -from "Marjorie Morningstar"-	RCA 7167
9/29/58	17	10	8. Pussy Cat	RCA 7315
1/19/59	37	4	9. Red River Rose	RCA 7413
2/22/60	38	2	10. China Doll	RCA 7655
			AMES, ED	
2/11/67	8	10	1. **My Cup Runneth Over** -from musical "I Do, I Do"-	RCA 9002
12/30/67	19	4	2. Who Will Answer?	RCA 9400
			ANDERSON, BILL	
5/11/63	8	11	1. **Still**	Decca 31458
			ANDERSON, LYNN	
			daughter of country singer Liz Anderson	
12/19/70	3	14	● 1. **Rose Garden**	Columbia 45252
			ANDREWS, LEE, & THE HEARTS	
12/09/57	20	10	1. Tear Drops	Chess 1675
6/16/58	33	1	2. Try The Impossible	United Artists 123
			ANGELS	
12/04/61	14	7	1. 'Til	Caprice 107
4/07/62	38	1	2. Cry Baby Cry	Caprice 112
8/10/63	1 (3)	12	3. **My Boyfriend's Back**	Smash 1834
11/09/63	25	5	4. I Adore Him	Smash 1854
			ANIMALS	
			British group whose roots began with The Alan Price Combo -- also see Eric Burdon & War	
8/15/64	1 (3)	10	1. **The House Of The Rising Sun**	MGM 13264
10/17/64	19	6	2. I'm Crying	MGM 13274
3/06/65	15	6	3. Don't Let Me Be Misunderstood	MGM 13311
5/29/65	32	4	4. Bring It On Home To Me	MGM 13339
9/04/65	13	8	5. We Gotta Get Out Of This Place	MGM 13382
12/04/65	23	8	6. It's My Life	MGM 13414
4/02/66	34	1	7. Inside-Looking Out	MGM 13468

DATE	POS	WKS	ARTIST—Record Title	LABEL & NO.
6/04/66	**12**	8	8. Don't Bring Me Down	MGM 13514
			ERIC BURDON & THE ANIMALS:	
10/01/66	**10**	7	9. **See See Rider**	MGM 13582
12/31/66	**29**	4	10. Help Me Girl	MGM 13636
4/22/67	**15**	6	11. When I Was Young	MGM 13721
8/19/67	**9**	8	12. **San Franciscan Nights**	MGM 13769
12/30/67	**15**	6	13. Monterey	MGM 13868
6/22/68	**14**	10	14. Sky Pilot (Parts 1 & 2)	MGM 13939
			ANKA, PAUL	
			Canadian-born; Paul was 15 years old when he recorded "Diana"	
7/29/57	**1** (1)	18	1. **Diana**	ABC-Para. 9831
2/03/58	**7**	11	2. **You Are My Destiny**	ABC-Para. 9880
4/28/58	**15**	10	3. Crazy Love/	
4/28/58	**18**	7	4. Let The Bells Keep Ringing	ABC-Para. 9907
1/05/59	**15**	13	5. (All Of A Sudden) My Heart Sings	ABC-Para. 9987
4/20/59	**33**	3	6. I Miss You So	ABC-Para. 10011
6/08/59	**1** (4)	14	7. **Lonely Boy**	ABC-Para. 10022
			-from film "Girl's Town"-	
9/14/59	**2** (3)	14	8. **Put Your Head On My Shoulder**	ABC-Para. 10040
11/30/59	**4**	12	9. **It's My Time To Cry**	ABC-Para. 10064
3/07/60	**2** (2)	11	10. **Puppy Love**	ABC-Para. 10082
6/06/60	**8**	9	11. **My Home Town**	ABC-Para. 10106
8/22/60	**23**	6	12. Hello Young Lovers/	
9/12/60	**40**	1	13. I Love You In The Same Old Way	ABC-Para. 10132
10/10/60	**11**	7	14. Summer's Gone	ABC-Para. 10147
2/06/61	**16**	5	15. The Story Of My Love	ABC-Para. 10168
3/27/61	**13**	8	16. Tonight My Love, Tonight	ABC-Para. 10194
6/12/61	**10**	7	17. **Dance On Little Girl**	ABC-Para. 10220
9/11/61	**35**	1	18. Kissin' On The Phone	ABC-Para. 10239
3/17/62	**12**	9	19. Love Me Warm And Tender	RCA 7977
6/16/62	**13**	7	20. A Steel Guitar And A Glass Of Wine	RCA 8030
11/24/62	**19**	5	21. Eso Beso (That Kiss!)	RCA 8097
2/09/63	**26**	4	22. Love (Makes The World Go 'Round)	RCA 8115
5/25/63	**39**	1	23. Remember Diana	RCA 8170
2/01/69	**27**	6	24. Goodnight My Love	RCA 9648
7/27/74	**1** (3)	11	● 25. **(You're) Having My Baby**	United Artists 454
11/30/74	**7**	11	26. **One Man Woman/One Woman Man**	United Artists 569
			-above 2 with Odia Coates-	
4/05/75	**8**	10	27. **I Don't Like To Sleep Alone**	United Artists 615
8/16/75	**15**	8	28. (I Believe) There's Nothing Stronger Than Our Love	United Artists 685
			-with Odia Coates-	
11/29/75	**7**	12	29. **Times Of Your Life**	United Artists 737
5/01/76	**33**	3	30. Anytime (I'll Be There)	United Artists 789
11/18/78	**35**	3	31. This Is Love	RCA 11395
			ANKA, PAUL-GEORGE HAMILTON IV-JOHNNY NASH	
12/15/58	**29**	5	1. The Teen Commandments [S]	ABC-Para. 9974

DATE	POS	WKS	ARTIST—Record Title	LABEL & NO.
			ANN-MARGRET	
			movie starlet Ann-Margret Olson	
8/21/61	17	6	1. I Just Don't Understand	RCA 7894
			ANNETTE [with the Afterbeats]	
			Annette Funicello	
2/02/59	7	9	1. **Tall Paul**	Disneyland 118
12/14/59	20	10	2. First Name Initial	Vista 349
3/07/60	10	8	3. **O Dio Mio**	Vista 354
6/20/60	36	3	4. Train Of Love	Vista 359
9/05/60	11	9	5. Pineapple Princess	Vista 362
			ANTHONY, RAY, & His Orchestra	
			trumpeter for the Glenn Miller and Jimmy Dorsey bands -- also see Frank Sinatra	
1/19/59	8	13	1. **Peter Gunn [I]**	Capitol 4041
			ANTON, SUSAN - see FRED KNOBLOCK	
			APOLLO 100 [Tom Parker]	
1/22/72	6	10	1. **Joy [I]** -based on Bach's "Jesu, Joy of Man's Desiring"-	Mega 0050
			APPLEJACKS	
			Dave Appell, leader	
10/06/58	16	9	1. Mexican Hat Rock [I]	Cameo 149
1/12/59	38	3	2. Rocka-Conga	Cameo 155
			APRIL WINE	
			Canadian rock quintet	
4/29/72	32	5	1. You Could Have Been A Lady	Big Tree 133
4/14/79	34	4	2. Roller	Capitol 4660
3/14/81	21	7	3. Just Between You And Me	Capitol 4975
			AQUATONES	
5/05/58	21	8	1. You	Fargo 1001
			ARBORS	
			group formed at the University of Michigan in Ann Arbor	
4/05/69	20	3	1. The Letter	Date 1638
			ARCHIES	
			studio group created by Don Kirshner - Ron Dante lead singer	
11/02/68	22	8	1. Bang-Shang-A-Lang	Calendar 1006
8/16/69	1 (4)	18	● 2. **Sugar, Sugar**	Calendar 1008
12/20/69	10	10	● 3. **Jingle Jangle**	Kirshner 5002
3/28/70	40	2	4. Who's Your Baby?	Kirshner 5003
			ARDEN, TONI	
6/02/58	13	11	1. Padre	Decca 30628
			ARGENT	
			Rod Argent, leader - formerly with British group The Zombies	
7/08/72	5	11	1. **Hold Your Head Up**	Epic 10852
			ARMS, RUSSELL, with Pete King & Orchestra	
			star of TV's "Your Hit Parade"	
2/02/57	22	8	1. Cinco Robles (Five Oaks)	Era 1026

DATE	POS	WKS	ARTIST—Record Title	LABEL & NO.
			ARMSTRONG, LOUIS	
			'Satchmo' died on 7/6/71 (71)	
2/25/56	**20**	7	1. Mack The Knife (A Theme From The Threepenny Opera)	Columbia 40587
12/15/56	**29**	1	2. Blueberry Hill	Decca 30091
			-originally recorded in 1949 with Gordon Jenkins Orchestra-	
2/29/64	**1** (1)	19	3. **Hello, Dolly!**	Kapp 573
			ARNOLD, EDDY	
			Country music's all-time #1 artist	
12/01/56	**22**	1	1. I Wouldn't Know Where To Begin	RCA 6699
11/13/65	**6**	10	2. **Make The World Go Away**	RCA 8679
3/12/66	**36**	5	3. I Want To Go With You	RCA 8749
6/18/66	**40**	1	4. The Last Word In Lonesome Is Me	RCA 8818
			ASHFORD & SIMPSON	
			Nick Ashford & Valerie Simpson	
10/13/79	**36**	2	1. Found A Cure	Warner 8870
			ASHTON, GARDNER & DYKE	
			British: Tony Ashton, Kim Gardner & Roy Dyke	
8/07/71	**40**	1	1. Resurrection Shuffle	Capitol 3060
			ASIA	
			British: Steve Howe, Carl Palmer, Geoff Downes & John Wetton	
5/01/82	**4**	12	1. **Heat Of The Moment**	Geffen 50040
8/14/82	**17**	8	2. Only Time Will Tell	Geffen 29970
			ASSEMBLED MULTITUDE	
8/01/70	**16**	7	1. Overture From Tommy (A Rock Opera) [I]	Atlantic 2737
			ASSOCIATION	
			California sextet	
6/25/66	**7**	8	1. **Along Comes Mary**	Valiant 741
9/03/66	**1** (3)	12	● 2. **Cherish**	Valiant 747
12/17/66	**35**	3	3. Pandora's Golden Heebie Jeebies	Valiant 755
6/03/67	**1** (4)	13	● 4. **Windy**	Warner 7041
9/09/67	**2** (2)	11	● 5. **Never My Love**	Warner 7074
2/10/68	**10**	8	6. **Everything That Touches You**	Warner 7163
6/22/68	**39**	2	7. Time For Livin'	Warner 7195
			ATLANTA RHYTHM SECTION	
			Atlanta studio musicians	
11/09/74	**35**	2	1. Doraville	Polydor 14248
2/26/77	**7**	14	2. **So In To You**	Polydor 14373
3/25/78	**7**	12	3. **Imaginary Lover**	Polydor 14459
7/08/78	**14**	7	4. I'm Not Gonna Let It Bother Me Tonight	Polydor 14484
6/16/79	**19**	9	5. Do It Or Die	Polydor 14568
9/08/79	**17**	8	6. Spooky	Polydor 2001
10/10/81	**29**	4	7. Alien	Columbia 02471
			ATLANTIC STARR	
			Sharon Bryant, lead singer	
5/15/82	**38**	3	1. Circles	A&M 2392

DATE	POS	WKS	ARTIST—Record Title	LABEL & NO.
			AUGUST, JAN - see RICHARD HAYMAN	
			AUSTIN, SIL	
11/24/56	17	7	1. Slow Walk [I]	Mercury 70963
			AVALON, FRANKIE	
			17 year old teen idol from Philadelphia in 1958	
1/27/58	7	11	1. **Dede Dinah**	Chancellor 1011
7/28/58	9	12	2. **Ginger Bread**	Chancellor 1021
11/17/58	15	10	3. I'll Wait For You	Chancellor 1026
2/23/59	1 (5)	14	4. **Venus**	Chancellor 1031
6/01/59	8	10	5. **Bobby Sox To Stockings/**	
6/15/59	10	9	6. **A Boy Without A Girl**	Chancellor 1036
9/14/59	7	11	7. **Just Ask Your Heart**	Chancellor 1040
12/07/59	1 (1)	12	8. **Why/**	
1/04/60	39	1	9. Swingin' On A Rainbow	Chancellor 1045
3/28/60	22	6	10. Don't Throw Away All Those Teardrops	Chancellor 1048
8/01/60	32	4	11. Where Are You	Chancellor 1052
10/17/60	26	7	12. Togetherness	Chancellor 1056
5/05/62	26	4	13. You Are Mine	Chancellor 1107
			AVANT-GARDE	
10/26/68	40	1	1. Naturally Stoned	Columbia 44590
			AVERAGE WHITE BAND [AWB]	
			Scottish 6-man white soul band	
12/21/74	1 (1)	13	● 1. **Pick Up The Pieces [I]**	Atlantic 3229
4/26/75	10	12	2. **Cut The Cake**	Atlantic 3261
9/27/75	39	2	3. If I Ever Lose This Heaven	Atlantic 3285
12/20/75	33	3	4. School Boy Crush	Atlantic 3304
10/16/76	40	1	5. Queen Of My Soul	Atlantic 3354
			BABYS	
			John Waite, lead singer of British foursome	
10/29/77	13	11	1. Isn't It Time	Chrysalis 2173
2/03/79	13	10	2. Every Time I Think Of You	Chrysalis 2279
3/08/80	33	3	3. Back On My Feet Again	Chrysalis 2398
			BACHELORS	
			trio from Dublin, Ireland	
5/16/64	10	8	1. **Diane**	London 9639
8/01/64	33	2	2. I Believe	London 9672
1/30/65	27	4	3. No Arms Can Ever Hold You	London 9724
7/03/65	15	7	4. Marie	London 9762
11/06/65	32	3	5. Chapel In The Moonlight	London 9793
5/14/66	38	2	6. Love Me With All Of Your Heart	London 9828
			BACHMAN-TURNER OVERDRIVE	
			BTO is a Canadian quartet led by Randy Bachman & Fred Turner	
3/23/74	23	9	1. Let It Ride	Mercury 73457
6/29/74	12	10	2. Takin' Care Of Business	Mercury 73487
10/05/74	1 (1)	12	● 3. **You Ain't Seen Nothing Yet**	Mercury 73622
2/01/75	14	7	4. Roll On Down The Highway	Mercury 73656

DATE	POS	WKS	ARTIST—Record Title	LABEL & NO.
6/07/75	21	7	5. Hey You	Mercury 73683
2/28/76	33	3	6. Take It Like A Man	Mercury 73766
			BACKUS, JIM, & Friend	
			Jim plays Thurston Howell III on TV series "Gilligan's Island"	
7/21/58	40	2	1. Delicious! [N]	Jubilee 5330
			BAD COMPANY	
			British: Paul Rodgers, Simon Kirke, Mick Ralphs & Boz Burrell	
8/31/74	5	11	1. **Can't Get Enough**	Swan Song 70015
2/08/75	19	6	2. Movin' On	Swan Song 70101
5/31/75	36	2	3. Good Lovin' Gone Bad	Swan Song 70103
7/26/75	10	11	4. **Feel Like Makin' Love**	Swan Song 70106
4/24/76	20	7	5. Young Blood	Swan Song 70108
4/14/79	13	12	6. Rock 'N' Roll Fantasy	Swan Song 70119
			BADFINGER	
			British quartet originally known as The Iveys - leader Peter Ham committed suicide on 5/1/75 (27)	
3/07/70	7	11	1. **Come And Get It** -from film "The Magic Christian"-	Apple 1815
11/21/70	8	9	2. **No Matter What**	Apple 1822
12/18/71	4	12	● 3. **Day After Day**	Apple 1841
4/08/72	14	7	4. Baby Blue	Apple 1844
			BAEZ, JOAN	
8/28/71	3	13	● 1. **The Night They Drove Old Dixie Down**	Vanguard 35138
11/08/75	35	2	2. Diamonds And Rust	A&M 1737
			BAKER, GEORGE, Selection	
			Dutch group led by Hans Bouwens	
4/11/70	21	10	1. Little Green Bag	Colossus 112
1/10/76	26	5	2. Paloma Blanca	Warner 8115
			BAKER, LaVERN	
1/15/55	14	11	1. Tweedlee Dee	Atlantic 1047
10/13/56	22	2	2. I Can't Love You Enough	Atlantic 1104
12/29/56	17	14	3. Jim Dandy	Atlantic 1116
12/28/58	6	15	4. **I Cried A Tear**	Atlantic 2007
6/01/59	33	2	5. I Waited Too Long	Atlantic 2021
5/01/61	37	3	6. Saved	Atlantic 2099
1/05/63	34	3	7. See See Rider	Atlantic 2167
			BALANCE	
8/15/81	22	9	1. Breaking Away	Portrait 02177
			BALIN, MARTY	
			member of Jefferson Starship	
6/13/81	8	13	1. **Hearts**	EMI America 8084
10/10/81	27	5	2. Atlanta Lady (Something About Your Love)	EMI America 8093
			BALL, KENNY, & His Jazzmen	
2/17/62	2 (1)	12	1. **Midnight In Moscow** [I]	Kapp 442

DATE	POS	WKS	ARTIST—Record Title	LABEL & NO.
			BALLARD, HANK, & The Midnighters	
			The Midnighters had 6 top 10 hits on the R&B charts ('54-'55)	
7/18/60	7	13	1. **Finger Poppin' Time**	King 5341
8/29/60	28	6	2. The Twist	King 5171
			-flip of Hank's 1st charted hit-	
10/17/60	6	11	3. **Let's Go, Let's Go, Let's Go**	King 5400
1/16/61	23	4	4. The Hoochi Coochi Coo	King 5430
3/20/61	39	1	5. Let's Go Again (Where We Went Last Night)	King 5459
5/01/61	33	3	6. The Continental Walk	King 5491
7/17/61	26	4	7. The Switch-A-Roo	King 5510
			BALLOON FARM	
3/16/68	37	4	1. A Question Of Temperature	Laurie 3405
			BAND, THE	
			Levon Helm founded group in Canada as backup band for Ronnie Hawkins and then for Bob Dylan	
11/29/69	25	7	1. Up On Cripple Creek	Capitol 2635
10/14/72	34	6	2. Don't Do It	Capitol 3433
			BANKS, DARRELL	
9/10/66	27	4	1. Open The Door To Your Heart	Revilot 201
			BAR-KAYS	
			4 members killed in plane crash with Otis Redding on 12/10/67	
7/01/67	17	9	1. Soul Finger [I]	Volt 148
12/04/76	23	8	2. Shake Your Rump To The Funk	Mercury 73833
			BARBER('S), CHRIS, Jazz Band	
2/02/52	5	10	1. **Petite Fleur (Little Flower) [I]**	Laurie 3022
			BARBOUR, KEITH	
11/01/69	40	2	1. Echo Park	Epic 10486
			BARCLAY, EDDIE	
7/16/55	18	1	1. The Bandit (O'Cangaceiro) [I]	Tico 249
			BARE, BOBBY	
			also see Bill Parsons	
8/18/62	23	7	1. Shame On Me	RCA 8032
6/29/63	16	9	2. Detroit City	RCA 8183
10/26/63	10	7	3. **500 Miles Away From Home**	RCA 8238
3/07/64	33	2	4. Miller's Cave	RCA 8294
			BARNUM, H.B.	
2/06/61	35	1	1. Lost Love [I]	Eldo 111
			BARRETTO, RAY	
5/11/63	17	7	1. El Watusi [S-F]	Tico 419
			BARRY & THE TAMERLANES	
			Barry Devorzon	
11/16/63	21	5	1. I Wonder What She's Doing Tonight	Valiant 6034
			BARRY, JOE	
5/29/61	24	5	1. I'm A Fool To Care	Smash 1702

DATE	POS	WKS	ARTIST—Record Title	LABEL & NO.
			BARRY, LEN	
			lead singer of The Dovells	
10/23/65	**2** (1)	10	1. **1-2-3**	Decca 31827
1/22/66	**27**	5	2. Like A Baby	Decca 31889
4/09/66	**26**	5	3. Somewhere	Decca 31923
			BARTLEY, CHRIS	
8/19/67	**32**	2	1. The Sweetest Thing This Side Of Heaven	Vando 101
			BASIE, COUNT [Orchestra]	
2/04/56	**28**	3	1. April In Paris [I]	Clef 89162
			BASIL, TONI	
10/09/82	**1** (1)	18	● 1. **Mickey**	Chrysalis 2638
			BASS, FONTELLA	
10/23/65	**4**	10	1. **Rescue Me**	Checker 1120
1/29/66	**37**	1	2. Recovery	Checker 1131
			BASS, FONTELLA, & BOBBY McCLURE	
3/27/65	**33**	3	1. Don't Mess Up A Good Thing	Checker 1097
			BASSEY, SHIRLEY	
2/27/65	**8**	8	1. **Goldfinger**	United Artists 790
			BAXTER, LES [Chorus & Orchestra]	
4/09/55	**1** (2)	21	1. **Unchained Melody**	Capitol 3055
8/13/55	**5**	12	2. **Wake The Town And Tell The People**	Capitol 3120
2/18/56	**1** (6)	20	3. **The Poor People Of Paris [I]**	Capitol 3336
			BAY CITY ROLLERS	
			Scottish quintet	
11/08/75	**1** (1)	12	● 1. **Saturday Night**	Arista 0149
2/14/76	**9**	11	2. **Money Honey**	Arista 0170
5/22/76	**28**	4	3. Rock And Roll Love Letter	Arista 0185
9/18/76	**12**	12	4. I Only Want To Be With You	Arista 0205
6/25/77	**10**	12	5. **You Made Me Believe In Magic**	Arista 0256
11/19/77	**24**	9	6. The Way I Feel Tonight	Arista 0272
			BAZUKA [Tony Camillo's]	
6/07/75	**10**	11	1. **Dynomite - Part 1 [I]**	A&M 1666
			B. BUMBLE & THE STINGERS	
			Billy Bumble	
4/24/61	**21**	5	1. Bumble Boogie [I]	Rendezvous 140
3/31/62	**23**	7	2. Nut Rocker [I]	Rendezvous 166
			BEACH BOYS	
			California quintet led by Brian Wilson, with brothers Dennis & Carl Wilson, & cousin Mike Love, & Alan Jardine	
9/15/62	**14**	10	1. Surfin' Safari	Capitol 4777
4/13/63	**3**	13	2. **Surfin' U.S.A./**	
5/25/63	**23**	8	3. Shut Down	Capitol 4932
8/17/63	**7**	11	4. **Surfer Girl/**	
9/07/63	**15**	7	5. Little Deuce Coupe	Capitol 5009
11/23/63	**6**	8	6. **Be True To Your School/**	
11/30/63	**23**	6	7. In My Room	Capitol 5069

DATE	POS	WKS	ARTIST—Record Title	LABEL & NO.
2/22/64	5	9	8. **Fun, Fun, Fun**	Capitol 5118
6/06/64	1 (2)	13	● 9. **I Get Around/**	
6/27/64	24	6	10. Don't Worry Baby	Capitol 5174
9/19/64	9	8	11. **When I Grow Up (To Be A Man)**	Capitol 5245
11/21/64	8	8	12. **Dance, Dance, Dance**	Capitol 5306
3/13/65	12	7	13. Do You Wanna Dance?	Capitol 5372
5/01/65	1 (2)	11	14. **Help Me, Rhonda**	Capitol 5395
8/07/65	3	9	15. **California Girls**	Capitol 5464
12/11/65	20	5	16. The Little Girl I Once Knew	Capitol 5540
1/15/66	2 (2)	9	17. **Barbara Ann**	Capitol 5561
4/09/66	3	10	18. **Sloop John B**	Capitol 5602
8/20/66	8	7	19. **Wouldn't It Be Nice/**	
9/17/66	39	2	20. God Only Knows	Capitol 5706
10/29/66	1 (1)	12	● 21. **Good Vibrations**	Capitol 5676
8/12/67	12	5	22. Heroes And Villains	Brother 1001
11/18/67	31	4	23. Wild Honey	Capitol 2028
1/13/68	19	6	24. Darlin'	Capitol 2068
8/17/68	20	7	25. Do It Again	Capitol 2239
4/05/69	24	6	26. I Can Hear Music	Capitol 2432
9/28/74	36	1	27. Surfin' U.S.A. -re-release of 1963 hit-	Capitol 3924
6/19/76	5	13	28. **Rock And Roll Music**	Brother/Reprise 1354
9/18/76	29	4	29. It's O.K	Brother/Reprise 1368
6/09/79	40	1	30. Good Timin'	Caribou 9029
8/15/81	12	11	31. The Beach Boys Medley	Capitol 5030
12/19/81	18	8	32. Come Go With Me	Caribou 02633
			BEATLES	
			#1 recording group of all-time from Liverpool, England: John Lennon, Paul McCartney, George Harrison and Ringo Starr	
1/25/64	1 (7)	14	● 1. **I Want To Hold Your Hand/**	
2/2/64	14	8	2. I Saw Her Standing There	Capitol 5112
2/01/64	1 (2)	14	3. **She Loves You**	Swan 4152
2/22/64	3	10	4. **Please Please Me**	Vee-Jay 581
3/07/64	26	2	5. My Bonnie -with Tony Sheridan, lead singer-	MGM 13213
3/21/64	2 (4)	9	6. **Twist And Shout**	Tollie 9001
3/28/64	1 (5)	9	● 7. **Can't Buy Me Love**	Capitol 5150
4/11/64	2 (1)	9	8. **Do You Want To Know A Secret/**	
4/25/64	35	3	9. Thank You Girl	Vee-Jay 587
5/02/64	1 (1)	11	10. **Love Me Do/**	
5/16/64	10	7	11. **P.S. I Love You**	Tollie 9008
7/18/64	1 (2)	12	● 12. **A Hard Day's Night**	Capitol 5222
8/01/64	19	7	13. Ain't She Sweet	Atco 6308
8/08/64	12	7	14. And I Love Her	Capitol 5235
8/15/64	25	5	15. I'll Cry Instead -above 4 tunes are from the film "A Hard Day's Night"-	Capitol 5234

DATE	POS	WKS	ARTIST—Record Title	LABEL & NO.
9/19/64	**17**	5	16. Matchbox/	
9/26/64	**25**	4	17. Slow Down	Capitol 5255
12/05/64	**1** (3)	11	● 18. **I Feel Fine**/	
12/12/64	**4**	8	19. **She's A Woman**	Capitol 5327
2/27/65	**1** (2)	9	● 20. **Eight Days A Week**/	
3/20/65	**39**	1	21. I Don't Want To Spoil The Party	Capitol 5371
5/01/65	**1** (1)	9	22. **Ticket To Ride**	Capitol 5407
8/14/65	**1** (3)	12	● 23. **Help!**	Capitol 5476
			-above 2 tunes from film "Help!"-	
10/02/65	**1** (4)	9	● 24. **Yesterday**	Capitol 5498
12/18/65	**1** (3)	11	● 25. **We Can Work It Out**/	
12/25/65	**5**	8	26. **Day Tripper**	Capitol 5555
3/05/66	**3**	9	● 27. **Nowhere Man**	Capitol 5587
6/11/66	**1** (2)	10	● 28. **Paperback Writer**/	
6/25/66	**23**	5	29. Rain	Capitol 5651
8/27/66	**2** (1)	8	● 30. **Yellow Submarine**/	
9/10/66	**11**	6	31. Eleanor Rigby	Capitol 5715
3/04/67	**1** (1)	9	● 32. **Penny Lane**/	
3/11/67	**8**	7	33. **Strawberry Fields Forever**	Capitol 5810
7/29/67	**1** (1)	9	● 34. **All You Need Is Love**/	
8/12/67	**34**	2	35. Baby You're A Rich Man	Capitol 5964
12/09/67	**1** (3)	10	● 36. **Hello Goodbye**	Capitol 2056
3/23/68	**4**	10	● 37. **Lady Madonna**	Capitol 2138
9/14/68	**1** (9)	19	● 38. **Hey Jude**/	
9/14/68	**12**	11	39. Revolution	Apple 2276
5/10/69	**1** (5)	12	● 40. **Get Back**/	
5/10/69	**35**	3	41. Don't Let Me Down	Apple 2490
			-above two: with Billy Preston-	
6/21/69	**8**	8	● 42. **The Ballad Of John And Yoko**	Apple 2531
10/18/69	**1** (1)	16	● 43. **Come Together**/	
10/18/69	**3**	16	44. **Something**	Apple 2654
3/21/70	**1** (2)	13	● 45. **Let It Be**	Apple 2764
5/23/70	**1** (2)	10	46. **The Long And Winding Road**	Apple 2832
			-above 2 tunes from the film "Let It Be"-	
6/19/76	**7**	11	47. **Got To Get You Into My Life**	Capitol 4274
4/10/82	**12**	8	48. The Beatles' Movie Medley:	Capitol 5107
			Magical Mystery Tour/All You Need Is Love/You've Got To Hide Your Love Away/I Should Have Known Better/ A Hard Day's Night/Ticket To Ride/Get Back	
			BEAU BRUMMELS	
			San Francisco Bay-area quartet	
1/30/65	**15**	8	1. Laugh, Laugh	Autumn 8
5/08/65	**8**	9	2. **Just A Little**	Autumn 10
8/28/65	**38**	1	3. You Tell Me Why	Autumn 16
			BECK, JEFF - see DONOVAN	

DATE	POS	WKS	ARTIST—Record Title	LABEL & NO.
			BECKHAM, BOB	
10/12/59	32	10	1. Just As Much As Ever	Decca 30861
2/29/60	36	1	2. Crazy Arms	Decca 31029
			BEE GEES	
			English trio of brothers: Robin & Maurice (twins), and Barry Gibb	
6/10/67	14	5	1. New York Mining Disaster 1941 Have You Seen My Wife, Mr. Jones	Atco 6487
7/29/67	17	7	2. To Love Somebody	Atco 6503
10/21/67	16	5	3. Holiday	Atco 6521
11/25/67	11	6	4. (The Lights Went Out In) Massachusetts	Atco 6532
2/10/68	15	8	5. Words	Atco 6548
9/07/68	8	10	6. **I've Gotta Get A Message To You**	Atco 6603
1/04/69	6	9	7. **I Started A Joke**	Atco 6639
4/12/69	37	3	8. First Of May	Atco 6657
12/26/70	3	10	● 9. **Lonely Days**	Atco 6795
7/03/71	1 (4)	14	● 10. **How Can You Mend A Broken Heart**	Atco 6824
2/05/72	16	7	11. My World	Atco 6871
8/26/72	16	7	12. Run To Me	Atco 6896
12/02/72	34	4	13. Alive	Atco 6909
6/28/75	1 (2)	12	● 14. **Jive Talkin'**	RSO 510
10/18/75	7	13	15. **Nights On Broadway**	RSO 515
1/17/76	12	12	16. Fanny (Be Tender With My Love)	RSO 519
7/17/76	1 (1)	12	● 17. **You Should Be Dancing**	RSO 853
10/02/76	3	16	● 18. **Love So Right**	RSO 859
1/29/77	12	9	19. Boogie Child	RSO 867
8/13/77	26	5	20. Edge Of The Universe	RSO 880
10/08/77	1 (3)	26	● 21. **How Deep Is Your Love**	RSO 882
12/24/77	1 (4)	22	★ 22. **Stayin' Alive**	RSO 885
2/11/78	1 (8)	18	★ 23. **Night Fever**	RSO 889
			-above 2 tunes from the film: "Saturday Night Fever"-	
11/18/78	1 (2)	17	★ 24. **Too Much Heaven**	RSO 913
2/10/79	1 (2)	13	★ 25. **Tragedy**	RSO 918
4/21/79	1 (1)	13	● 26. **Love You Inside Out**	RSO 925
10/10/81	30	4	27. He's A Liar	RSO 1066
			BEGINNING OF THE END	
6/05/71	15	10	1. Funky Nassau-Part 1	Alston 4595
			BELAFONTE, HARRY	
11/24/56	14	16	1. Jamaica Farewell	RCA 6663
12/29/56	12	3	2. Mary's Boy Child [X]	RCA 6735
1/12/57	5	17	3. **Banana Boat (Day-O)**	RCA 6771
3/23/57	11	10	4. Mama Look At Bubu	RCA 6830
7/08/57	25	3	5. Island In The Sun	RCA 6885
			BELL & JAMES	
			Leroy Bell & Casey James	
3/10/79	15	8	● 1. Livin' It Up (Friday Night)	A&M 2069

The Babys. Realizing that their music alone might not be enough to clinch a deal, the Babys showed record labels a videotape of their stage show produced by one of Britain's top television directors.

Marty Balin left Jefferson Airplane/ Starship more than once during the '70s, but still retains links with Paul Kantner, with whom he founded the band in 1965.

The Bay City Rollers. This Scottish group exported their tartan popularity worldwide, although only one of their ten British top 10 hits ("Money Honey") secured similar chart status in the U.S.

The Beach Boys. Record distributor Herb Newman, musician Joe Saraceno, and producer Hite Morgan were said to have selected the Beach Boys' name for the group's debut single, "Surfin'." Says Mike Love, "We didn't even know we were the Beach Boys until the song came out.

The Beatles. The version of "Love Me Do" that went to No. 1 May, 1964, wasn't the original recording by the Beatles. It took Capitol Records a further 18½ years to get around to releasing that as a 45, featuring session drummer Andy White instead of Ringo.

The Beatles. "Yesterday" was the first of several Beatles U.S. chart-toppers that didn't reach the peak in Britain, largely because it wasn't released there as a single until 1976! The others included "Eight Days A Week" and "The Long And Winding Road."

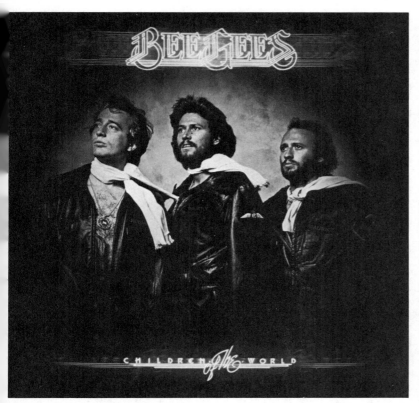

The Bee Gees. Such was Barry and Maurice Gibb's enthusiasm for the talents of brother Robin that in April, 1969, they sued him to stay in the Bee Gees. The case was settled within a couple of months, but Robin left to record solo anyway. You remember "Saved By The Bell" . . .

Pat Benatar. Pat Andrzejewski (a/k/a Benatar) trained as an opera singer but subsequently turned to rock. Her first album was another feather in the cap of producer Mike Chapman, the maestro of powerpop (Sweet, the Knack, Blondie).

George Benson's chart breakthrough came by way of his "Breezin'" album in 1976, produced by Tommy LiPuma. The title track was originally written and recorded by Bobby Womack some years before, and produced by . . . Tommy LiPuma.

Brook Benton's seven-year shut-out from the top 10 ended in 1970 with a song composed by Tony Joe White, "Rainy Night In Georgia." It also inspired an answer, "Cold Night In Georgia," by Dee Dee Warwick.

Chuck Berry. "The only Maybellene I ever knew was the name of a cow," Chuck Berry is once said to have remarked. Rock'n'roll thanks the farmer.

Bobby Bland, onetime valet for B.B. King, never reached the top 10 of Billboard's pop charts, but he collected no less than 23 top hits on the R&B best-sellers chart between 1957 and 1974.

DATE	POS	WKS	ARTIST—Record Title	LABEL & NO.
			BELL NOTES	
			Long Island, New York quintet	
2/09/59	6	11	1. **I've Had It**	Time 1004
			BELL, ARCHIE, & THE DRELLS	
			quartet from Houston, Texas	
4/13/68	1 (2)	13	● 1. **Tighten Up**	Atlantic 2478
8/03/68	9	8	2. **I Can't Stop Dancing**	Atlantic 2534
1/04/69	21	8	3. There's Gonna Be A Showdown	Atlantic 2583
			BELL, BENNY [Paul Wynn, vocal]	
4/19/75	30	4	1. **Shaving Cream** [N]	Vanguard 35183
			-originally released in 1946-	
			BELL, MADELINE	
			lead singer of Blue Mink	
3/09/68	26	5	1. I'm Gonna Make You Love Me	Philips 40517
			BELL, VINCENT	
4/25/70	31	5	1. Airport Love Theme [I]	Decca 32659
			BELL, WILLIAM	
3/12/77	10	9	● 1. **Tryin' To Love Two**	Mercury 73839
			BELLAMY BROTHERS	
			David & Howard Bellamy	
3/06/76	1 (1)	12	1. **Let Your Love Flow**	Warner 8169
7/14/79	39	2	2. If I Said You Have A Beautiful Body Would You Hold It Against Me	Warner 8790
			BELLS	
			Jacki Ralph & Cliff Edwards, lead singers of Canadian quintet	
3/27/71	7	11	● 1. **Stay Awhile**	Polydor 15023
			BELLUS, TONY	
6/29/59	25	11	1. Robbin' The Cradle	NRC 023
			BELMONTS	
			former trio with Dion	
6/19/61	18	6	1. Tell Me Why	Sabrina 500
8/25/62	28	8	2. Come On Little Angel	Sabina 505
			BELVIN, JESSE	
			died in an auto crash 2/6/60 (26)	
4/13/59	31	9	1. Guess Who	RCA 7469
			BENATAR, PAT	
2/09/80	23	10	1. Heartbreaker	Chrysalis 2395
5/17/80	27	6	2. We Live For Love	Chrysalis 2419
10/18/80	9	15	● 3. **Hit Me With Your Best Shot**	Chrysalis 2464
1/31/81	18	10	4. Treat Me Right	Chrysalis 2487
8/01/81	17	9	5. Fire And Ice	Chrysalis 2529
10/31/81	38	2	6. Promises In The Dark	Chrysalis 2555
11/06/82	13	10	7. Shadows Of The Night	Chrysalis 2647
			BENNETT, BOYD, & His Rockets	
7/09/55	5	17	1. **Seventeen**	King 1470
11/12/55	39	1	2. My Boy - Flat Top	King 1494
			-above 2 songs: vocal by Big Moe-	

DATE	POS	WKS	ARTIST—Record Title	LABEL & NO.
			BENNETT, JOE, & THE SPARKLETONES	
9/23/57	17	9	1. Black Slacks	ABC-Para. 9837
			BENNETT, TONY	
5/05/56	16	11	1. Can You Find It In Your Heart	Columbia 40667
8/18/56	11	7	2. From The Candy Store On The Corner To The Chapel On The Hill/	
10/06/56	38	2	3. Happiness Street (Corner Sunshine Square)	Columbia 40726
11/17/56	18	4	4. The Autumn Waltz	Columbia 40770
8/12/57	9	14	5. **In The Middle Of An Island**	Columbia 40965
11/18/57	22	1	6. Ca, C'est L'amour -from the film "Les Girls"-	Columbia 41032
6/30/58	23	1	7. Young And Warm And Wonderful	Columbia 41172
9/22/58	20	8	8. Firefly	Columbia 41237
9/29/62	19	10	9. I Left My Heart In San Francisco	Columbia 42332
2/16/63	14	10	10. I Wanna Be Around	Columbia 42634
6/01/63	18	6	11. The Good Life	Columbia 42779
10/31/64	33	6	12. Who Can I Turn To (When Nobody Needs Me) -from "Roar Of The Greasepaint"-	Columbia 43141
3/20/65	34	4	13. If I Ruled The World -from the musical "Pickwick"-	Columbia 43220
			BENSON, GEORGE	
7/17/76	10	11	1. **This Masquerade**	Warner 8209
9/03/77	24	7	2. The Greatest Love Of All -from the film "The Greatest"-	Arista 0251
4/22/78	7	10	3. **On Broadway**	Warner 8542
3/24/79	18	8	4. Love Ballad	Warner 8759
8/02/80	4	14	5. **Give Me The Night**	Warner 49505
11/21/81	5	16	6. **Turn Your Love Around**	Warner 49846
			BENTON, BROOK	
2/09/59	3	14	1. **It's Just A Matter Of Time**	Mercury 71394
5/04/59	12	9	2. Endlessly/	
6/08/59	38	1	3. So Close	Mercury 71443
8/03/59	16	9	4. Thank You Pretty Baby	Mercury 71478
10/26/59	6	13	5. **So Many Ways**	Mercury 71512
5/09/60	37	1	6. The Ties That Bind	Mercury 71566
8/22/60	7	13	7. **Kiddio/**	
8/29/60	16	10	8. The Same One	Mercury 71652
11/21/60	24	7	9. Fools Rush In	Mercury 71722
2/27/61	11	9	10. Think Twice/	
3/20/61	28	1	11. For My Baby	Mercury 71774
6/05/61	2 (3)	12	12. **The Boll Weevil Song [N]**	Mercury 71820
9/04/61	20	4	13. Frankie And Johnny	Mercury 71859
12/18/61	15	5	14. Revenge	Mercury 71903
1/27/62	19	5	15. Shadrack	Mercury 71912

DATE	POS	WKS	ARTIST—Record Title	LABEL & NO.
9/15/62	13	6	16. Lie To Me	Mercury 72024
12/08/62	3	10	17. **Hotel Happiness**	Mercury 72055
4/06/63	28	4	18. I Got What I Wanted	Mercury 72099
7/13/63	22	4	19. My True Confession	Mercury 72135
10/05/63	32	5	20. Two Tickets To Paradise	Mercury 72177
2/15/64	35	3	21. Going Going Gone	Mercury 72230
1/31/70	4	12	● 22. **Rainy Night In Georgia**	Cotillion 44057
			BENTON, BROOK, & DINAH WASHINGTON	
2/08/60	5	12	1. **Baby (You've Got What It Takes)**	Mercury 71565
6/06/60	7	10	2. **A Rockin' Good Way (To Mess Around And Fall In Love)**	Mercury 71629
			BERNARD, ROD	
3/23/59	20	9	1. This Should Go On Forever	Argo 5327
			BERNSTEIN, ELMER, & Orchestra	
4/07/56	16	9	1. Main Title From "The Man With The Golden Arm" [I]	Decca 29869
			BERRY, CHUCK	
			one of rock music's most influential artists	
8/20/55	5	11	1. **Maybellene**	Chess 1604
6/30/56	29	1	2. Roll Over Beethoven	Chess 1626
4/20/57	3	15	3. **School Day**	Chess 1653
11/11/57	8	13	4. **Rock & Roll Music**	Chess 1671
2/24/58	2 (3)	11	5. **Sweet Little Sixteen**	Chess 1683
5/05/58	8	11	6. **Johnny B. Goode**	Chess 1691
9/15/58	18	5	7. Carol	Chess 1700
4/20/59	32	7	8. Almost Grown	Chess 1722
7/13/59	37	1	9. Back In The U.S.A	Chess 1729
4/04/64	23	5	10. Nadine (Is It You?)	Chess 1883
6/13/64	10	7	11. **No Particular Place To Go**	Chess 1898
8/22/64	14	5	12. You Never Can Tell	Chess 1906
9/09/72	1 (2)	12	● 13. **My Ding-A-Ling [N]**	Chess 2131
1/06/73	27	7	14. Reelin' & Rockin'	Chess 2136
			-live version of tune originally issued as 'B' side of Chess l683-	
			BIG BOPPER	
			J.P. Richardson died with Buddy Holly and Ritchie Valens in a plane crash on 2/3/59 (28)	
8/04/58	6	22	1. **Chantilly Lace [N]**	Mercury 71343
12/22/58	38	1	2. Big Bopper's Wedding [N]	Mercury 71375
			BIG BROTHER & THE HOLDING COMPANY	
			Janis Joplin, lead singer	
9/28/68	12	8	1. Piece Of My Heart	Columbia 44626
			BILK, MR. ACKER [with The Leon Young String Chorale]	
4/07/62	1 (1)	15	● 1. **Stranger On The Shore [I]**	Atco 6217
			BILLY & LILLIE	
			Billy Ford & Lillie Bryant	
1/13/58	9	10	1. **La Dee Dah**	Swan 4002
1/05/59	14	8	2. Lucky Ladybug	Swan 4020

DATE	POS	WKS	ARTIST—Record Title	LABEL & NO.
			BILLY & THE BEATERS	
			Billy Vera	
6/06/81	39	2	1. I Can Take Care Of Myself	Alfa 7002
			BILLY JOE & THE CHECKMATES	
			Billy Joe Hunter	
2/17/62	10	7	1. **Percolator (Twist) [I]**	Dore 620
			BISHOP, ELVIN	
			guitar player with the Paul Butterfield Blues Band	
4/03/76	3	12	● 1. **Fooled Around And Fell In Love**	Capricorn 0252
			BISHOP, STEPHEN	
1/22/77	22	7	1. Save It For A Rainy Day	ABC 12232
7/23/77	11	15	2. On And On	ABC 12260
10/28/78	32	5	3. Everybody Needs Love	ABC 12406
			BLACKBYRDS	
			sextet founded by Donald Byrd	
3/15/75	6	12	1. **Walking In Rhythm**	Fantasy 736
4/17/76	19	6	2. Happy Music	Fantasy 762
			BLACKFOOT	
			Ricky Medlocke, lead singer	
8/04/79	26	6	1. Highway Song	Atco 7104
12/22/79	38	4	2. Train, Train	Atco 7207
			BLACK OAK ARKANSAS	
			Jim 'Dandy' Mangrum lead singer	
1/26/74	25	6	1. Jim Dandy	Atco 6948
			BLACK('S), BILL, Combo	
			Bill, of "Scotty & Bill" on Elvis Presley's Sun recordings, died 10/21/65 (39)	
12/21/59	17	8	1. Smokie - Part 2 [I]	Hi 2018
3/21/60	9	11	2. **White Silver Sands [I]**	Hi 2021
7/04/60	18	8	3. Josephine [I]	Hi 2022
10/03/60	11	9	4. Don't Be Cruel [I]	Hi 2026
12/12/60	16	7	5. Blue Tango [I]	Hi 2027
3/06/61	20	4	6. Hearts Of Stone [I]	Hi 2028
6/26/61	25	4	7. Ole Buttermilk Sky [I]	Hi 2036
1/20/62	26	4	8. Twist-Her [I]	Hi 2042
			BLACK, CILLA	
			from Liverpool, England	
7/25/64	26	4	1. You're My World	Capitol 5196
			BLACK, JEANNE	
5/02/60	4	10	1. **He'll Have To Stay**	Capitol 4368
			BLANCHARD, JACK, & MISTY MORGAN	
3/28/70	23	8	1. Tennessee Bird Walk [N]	Wayside 010
			BLAND, BILLY	
3/28/60	7	13	1. **Let The Little Girl Dance**	Old Town 1076
			BLAND, BOBBY	
1/20/62	28	3	1. Turn On Your Love Light	Duke 344
2/02/63	22	7	2. Call On Me/	Duke 360
2/09/63	33	5	3. That's The Way Love Is	Duke 360

DATE	POS	WKS	ARTIST—Record Title	LABEL & NO.
3/28/64	20	6	4. Ain't Nothing You Can Do	Duke 375
			BLANE, MARCIE	
11/10/62	3	13	1. **Bobby's Girl**	Seville 120
			BLEYER, ARCHIE	
			founder of Cadence Records	
12/04/54	17	6	1. The Naughty Lady Of Shady Lane	Cadence 1254
			BLONDIE	
			Debbie Harry, lead singer	
3/17/79	1 (1)	14	● 1. **Heart Of Glass**	Chrysalis 2295
6/30/79	24	7	2. One Way Or Another	Chrysalis 2336
11/03/79	27	6	3. Dreaming	Chrysalis 2379
3/08/80	1 (6)	19	● 4. **Call Me**	Chrysalis 2414
			-from film "American Gigolo"-	
6/21/80	39	3	5. Atomic	Chrysalis 2410
11/29/80	1 (1)	17	● 6. **The Tide Is High**	Chrysalis 2465
2/14/81	1 (2)	14	● 7. **Rapture**	Chrysalis 2485
6/26/82	37	3	8. Island Of Lost Souls	Chrysalis 2603
			BLOODROCK	
2/27/71	36	2	1. D.O.A	Capitol 3009
			BLOODSTONE	
6/09/73	10	12	● 1. **Natural High**	London 1046
4/06/74	34	4	2. Outside Woman	London 1052
			BLOOD, SWEAT & TEARS	
			David Clayton-Thomas, leader	
3/15/69	2 (3)	11	● 1. **You've Made Me So Very Happy**	Columbia 44776
6/07/69	2 (3)	12	● 2. **Spinning Wheel**	Columbia 44871
10/25/69	2 (1)	12	● 3. **And When I Die**	Columbia 45008
8/15/70	14	6	4. Hi-De-Ho	Columbia 45204
10/10/70	29	6	5. Lucretia Mac Evil	Columbia 45235
8/14/71	32	5	6. Go Down Gamblin'	Columbia 45427
			BLOOM, BOBBY	
			died 2/28/74	
10/17/70	8	11	1. **Montego Bay**	L&R/MGM 157
			BLUE-BELLES	
			group later changed name to Patti LaBelle & The Blue Belles	
5/12/62	15	7	1. I Sold My Heart To The Junkman	Newtown 5000
			BLUE CHEER	
3/23/68	14	10	1. Summertime Blues	Philips 40516
			BLUE HAZE	
12/23/72	27	7	1. Smoke Gets In Your Eyes	A&M 1357
			BLUE JAYS	
9/04/61	31	4	1. Lover's Island	Milestone 2008
			BLUE MAGIC	
6/08/74	8	15	● 1. **Sideshow**	Atco 6961
11/23/74	36	2	2. Three Ring Circus	Atco 7004

DATE	POS	WKS	ARTIST—Record Title	LABEL & NO.
			BLUE OYSTER CULT	
			Donald "Buck Dharma" Roeser, lead guitar & vocals	
9/04/76	12	14	1. (Don't Fear) The Reaper	Columbia 10384
10/03/81	40	3	2. Burnin' For You	Columbia 02415
			BLUE RIDGE RANGERS	
			John Fogerty - one man band	
1/06/73	16	10	1. Jambalaya (On The Bayou)	Fantasy 689
5/19/73	37	2	2. Hearts Of Stone	Fantasy 700
			BLUE STARS	
2/04/56	16	7	1. Lullaby Of Birdland [F]	Mercury 70742
			BLUE SWEDE	
			Swedish	
3/02/74	**1** (1)	14	● 1. **Hooked On A Feeling**	EMI 3627
9/07/74	**7**	8	2. **Never My Love**	EMI 3938
			BLUES BROTHERS	
			John Belushi & Dan Aykroyd	
1/06/79	**14**	9	1. Soul Man	Atlantic 3545
3/31/79	37	3	2. Rubber Biscuit [N]	Atlantic 3564
6/21/80	18	8	3. Gimme Some Lovin'	Atlantic 3666
1/31/81	39	2	4. Who's Making Love	Atlantic 3785
			BLUES IMAGE	
			Mike Pinera, lead singer	
5/23/70	**4**	12	● 1. **Ride Captain Ride**	Atco 6746
			BLUES MAGOOS	
			quintet formed in the Bronx	
1/07/67	**5**	10	1. **(We Ain't Got) Nothin' Yet**	Mercury 72622
			BOB B. SOXX & The Blue Jeans	
			Bob B. Soxx: Bobby Sheen	
12/08/62	**8**	7	1. **Zip-A-Dee Doo-Dah**	Philles 107
3/23/63	38	3	2. Why Do Lovers Break Each Other's Heart?	Philles 110
			BOBBETTES	
8/12/57	**6**	14	1. **Mr. Lee**	Atlantic 1144
			BOND, JOHNNY	
			died 6/12/78 (63)	
8/22/60	26	7	1. Hot Rod Lincoln [S-N]	Republic 2005
			BONDS, GARY "U.S."	
			real name: Gary Anderson	
10/31/60	**6**	11	1. **New Orleans**	Legrand 1003
6/05/61	**1** (2)	12	2. **Quarter To Three**	Legrand 1008
7/31/61	**5**	9	3. **School Is Out**	Legrand 1009
11/06/61	28	2	4. School Is In	Legrand 1012
1/13/62	**9**	11	5. **Dear Lady Twist**	Legrand 1015
4/07/62	**9**	9	6. **Twist, Twist Senora**	Legrand 1018
7/07/62	27	4	7. Seven Day Weekend	Legrand 1019
			-from film "It's Trad-Dad"-	
5/02/81	**11**	13	8. This Little Girl	EMI America 8079
7/10/82	21	9	9. Out Of Work	EMI America 8117
			-above 2 titles produced by Bruce Springsteen-	
			BONEY M	
			German disco quartet	
7/22/78	30	6	1. Rivers Of Babylon	Sire 1027

DATE	POS	WKS	ARTIST—Record Title	LABEL & NO.
			BONNIE SISTERS	
2/25/56	**18**	3	1. Cry Baby	Rainbow 328
			BONOFF, KARLA	
6/05/82	**19**	12	1. Personally	Columbia 02805
			BOOKER T. & THE M.G.'S	
			Booker T. Jones with backing band - formerly the Mar-Keys	
9/01/62	**3**	12	● 1. **Green Onions [I]**	Stax 127
5/20/67	**37**	3	2. Hip Hug-Her [I]	Stax 211
9/02/67	**21**	7	3. Groovin' [I]	Stax 224
8/03/68	**17**	7	4. Soul-Limbo [I]	Stax 0001
12/28/68	**9**	11	5. **Hang 'Em High [I]**	Stax 0013
4/05/69	**6**	10	6. **Time Is Tight [I]**	Stax 0028
			-from soundtrack "Uptight"-	
7/05/69	**37**	3	7. Mrs. Robinson [I]	Stax 0037
			BOONE, DANIEL	
			real name: Peter Lee Stirling	
8/05/72	**15**	11	1. Beautiful Sunday	Mercury 73281
			BOONE, DEBBY	
			Pat Boone's daughter	
9/17/77	**1**(10)	21	★ 1. **You Light Up My Life**	Warner 8455
			BOONE, PAT	
			direct descendant of frontiersman Daniel Boone	
4/02/55	**16**	12	1. Two Hearts	Dot 15338
7/09/55	**1** (2)	20	2. **Ain't That A Shame**	Dot 15377
10/29/55	**7**	10	3. **At My Front Door (Crazy Little Mama)/**	
11/19/55	**26**	5	4. No Other Arms (No Arms Can Ever Hold You)	Dot 15422
12/24/55	**19**	5	5. Gee Whittakers!	Dot 15435
2/04/56	**4**	18	6. **I'll Be Home/**	
2/04/56	**12**	10	7. Tutti' Frutti	Dot 15443
4/28/56	**8**	9	8. **Long Tall Sally**	Dot 15457
6/09/56	**1** (4)	19	9. **I Almost Lost My Mind**	Dot 15472
9/22/56	**5**	17	10. **Friendly Persuasion (Thee I Love)/**	
9/29/56	**20**	8	11. Chains Of Love	Dot 15490
12/22/56	**1** (1)	19	12. **Don't Forbid Me/**	
1/26/57	**37**	2	13. Anastasia	Dot 15521
3/23/57	**5**	13	14. **Why Baby Why/**	
3/23/57	**27**	5	15. I'm Waiting Just For You	Dot 15545
5/13/57	**1** (7)	24	16. **Love Letters In The Sand/**	
5/20/57	**14**	13	17. Bernardine	Dot 15570
			-above 2 tunes from "Bernardine"-	
8/12/57	**6**	14	18. **Remember You're Mine/**	
8/19/57	**20**	8	19. There's A Gold Mine In The Sky	Dot 15602
10/28/57	**1** (6)	19	20. **April Love**	Dot 15660
2/17/58	**4**	15	21. **A Wonderful Time Up There/**	
2/17/58	**11**	12	22. It's Too Soon To Know	Dot 15690
5/12/58	**5**	12	23. **Sugar Moon**	Dot 15750
7/14/58	**7**	10	24. **If Dreams Came True/**	

DATE	POS	WKS	ARTIST—Record Title	LABEL & NO.
8/04/58	39	1	25. That's How Much I Love You	Dot 15785
10/06/58	21	4	26. For My Good Fortune/	
10/06/58	31	2	27. Gee, But It's Lonely	Dot 15825
11/17/58	34	5	28. I'll Remember Tonight -from the film "Mardi Gras"-	Dot 15840
1/26/59	21	8	29. With The Wind And The Rain In Your Hair	Dot 15888
4/06/59	23	7	30. For A Penny	Dot 15914
6/29/59	17	6	31. Twixt Twelve And Twenty	Dot 15955
9/28/59	29	4	32. Fools Hall Of Fame	Dot 15982
3/07/60	18	7	33. (Welcome) New Lovers	Dot 16048
5/22/61	1 (1)	12	34. **Moody River**	Dot 16209
9/04/61	19	5	35. Big Cold Wind	Dot 16244
12/25/61	35	3	36. Johnny Will	Dot 16284
2/24/62	32	3	37. I'll See You In My Dreams	Dot 16312
6/30/62	6	10	38. **Speedy Gonzales [N]**	Dot 16368
			BOSTON quintet from Boston - led by Tom Scholz & Brad Delp	
10/16/76	5	14	1. **More Than A Feeling**	Epic 50266
2/12/77	22	6	2. Long Time	Epic 50329
6/18/77	38	2	3. Peace Of Mind	Epic 50381
8/26/78	4	10	4. **Don't Look Back**	Epic 50590
12/23/78	31	5	5. A Man I'll Never Be	Epic 50638
			BOTKIN, PERRY, JR. - see BARRY DeVORZON	
			BOWEN, JIMMY, with the Rhythm Orchids Buddy Knox was a member of the Rhythm Orchids	
3/09/57	14	12	1. I'm Stickin' With You	Roulette 4001
			BOWIE, DAVID English "glitter rock" star - also see Queen	
2/24/73	15	10	1. Space Oddity	RCA 0876
4/19/75	28	4	2. Young Americans	RCA 10152
8/02/75	1 (2)	14	● 3. **Fame**	RCA 10320
1/10/76	10	16	4. **Golden Years**	RCA 10441
			BOX TOPS Quintet from Memphis area - Alex Chilton, lead singer	
8/26/67	1 (4)	13	1. **The Letter**	Mala 565
12/02/67	24	5	2. Neon Rainbow	Mala 580
3/16/68	2 (2)	12	● 3. **Cry Like A Baby**	Mala 593
6/08/68	26	6	4. Choo Choo Train	Mala 12005
10/12/68	37	1	5. I Met Her In Church	Mala 12017
2/08/69	28	9	6. Sweet Cream Ladies, Forward March	Mala 12035
8/23/69	18	7	7. Soul Deep	Mala 12040
			BOYCE, TOMMY, & BOBBY HART	
8/05/67	39	2	1. Out & About	A&M 858
1/20/68	8	9	2. **I Wonder What She's Doing Tonite**	A&M 893
8/03/68	27	6	3. Alice Long (You're Still My Favorite Girlfriend)	A&M 948

DATE	POS	WKS	ARTIST—Record Title	LABEL & NO.
			BRADLEY, JAN	
2/02/63	**14**	9	1. Mama Didn't Lie	Chess 1845
			BRADLEY, OWEN, QUINTET	
7/29/57	**18**	4	1. White Silver Sands -vocal: Anita Kerr Quartet-	Decca 30363
			BRAM TCHAIKOVSKY	
			Bram's real name: Peter Bramall	
8/18/79	**37**	3	1. Girl Of My Dreams	Polydor 14575
			BRANIGAN, LAURA	
9/04/82	**2** (3)	22	● 1. **Gloria**	Atlantic 4048
			BRASS CONSTRUCTION	
5/08/76	**14**	9	1. Movin' [I]	United Artists 775
			BRASS RING featuring Phil Bodner	
4/16/66	**32**	4	1. The Phoenix Love Theme [I] -from "The Flight Of The Phoenix"	Dunhill 4023
3/04/67	**36**	2	2. The Dis-Advantages Of You [I] -"Benson & Hedges" jingle-	Dunhill 4065
			BRAUN, BOB	
8/18/62	**26**	4	1. Till Death Do Us Part [S]	Decca 31355
			BREAD	
			David Gates, lead singer	
7/11/70	**1** (1)	13	● 1. **Make It With You**	Elektra 45686
10/10/70	**10**	9	2. **It Don't Matter To Me**	Elektra 45701
1/30/71	**28**	4	3. Let Your Love Go	Elektra 45711
4/03/71	**4**	11	4. **If**	Elektra 45720
8/14/71	**37**	2	5. Mother Freedom	Elektra 45740
11/06/71	**3**	10	6. **Baby I'm-A Want You**	Elektra 45751
2/05/72	**5**	11	7. **Everything I Own**	Elektra 45765
5/06/72	**15**	8	8. Diary	Elektra 45784
8/05/72	**11**	9	9. The Guitar Man	Elektra 45803
11/18/72	**15**	8	10. Sweet Surrender	Elektra 45818
2/17/73	**15**	8	11. Aubrey	Elektra 45832
12/04/76	**9**	13	12. **Lost Without Your Love**	Elektra 45365
			BREMERS, BEVERLY	
1/22/72	**15**	10	1. Don't Say You Don't Remember	Scepter 12315
7/22/72	**40**	2	2. We're Free	Scepter 12348
			BRENDA & THE TABULATIONS	
			Brenda Payton	
3/25/67	**20**	6	1. Dry Your Eyes	Dionn 500
5/01/71	**23**	9	2. Right On The Tip Of My Tongue	Top & Bottom 407
			BRENNAN, WALTER	
			Grandpa of TV series "The Real McCoys" - died 9/21/74 (80)	
5/30/60	**30**	3	1. Dutchman's Gold [S] -with Billy Vaughn's Orchestra-	Dot 16066
4/21/62	**5**	9	2. **Old Rivers [S]**	Liberty 55436
12/01/62	**38**	1	3. Mama Sang A Song [S]	Liberty 55508

DATE	POS	WKS	ARTIST—Record Title	LABEL & NO.
			BREWER & SHIPLEY	
			Mike Brewer & Tom Shipley	
3/13/71	10	10	1. **One Toke Over The Line**	Kama Sutra 516
			BREWER, TERESA	
12/18/54	6	12	1. **Let Me Go, Lover!**	Coral 61315
			-with The Lancers-	
3/19/55	17	3	2. Pledging My Love	Coral 61362
6/04/55	20	1	3. Silver Dollar	Coral 61394
7/30/55	15	4	4. The Banjo's Back In Town	Coral 61448
3/03/56	5	17	5. **A Tear Fell/**	
3/10/56	17	10	6. Bo Weevil	Coral 61590
6/16/56	7	16	7. **A Sweet Old Fashioned Girl**	Coral 61636
11/17/56	21	8	8. Mutual Admiration Society	Coral 61737
			-from musical "Happy Hunting"-	
4/27/57	13	9	9. Empty Arms	Coral 61805
11/11/57	8	11	10. **You Send Me**	Coral 61898
10/20/58	38	1	11. The Hula Hoop Song	Coral 62033
4/06/59	40	1	12. Heavenly Lover	Coral 62084
9/12/60	31	6	13. Anymore	Coral 62219
			BRICK	
			Atlanta-based quintet	
11/20/76	3	15	1. **Dazz**	Bang 727
10/01/77	18	10	2. Dusic	Bang 734
			BRIDGES, ALICIA	
9/09/78	5	19	● 1. **I Love The Nightlife (Disco 'Round)**	Polydor 14483
			BRIGGS, LILLIAN	
9/17/55	18	3	1. I Want You To Be My Baby	Epic 9115
			BRIGHTER SIDE OF DARKNESS	
1/06/73	16	8	● 1. Love Jones	20th Century 2002
			BRISTOL, JOHNNY	
7/20/74	8	13	1. **Hang On In There Baby**	MGM 14715
			BROOD, HERMAN	
9/01/79	35	3	1. Saturdaynight	Ariola 7754
			BROOKLYN BRIDGE featuring Johnny Maestro	
1/04/69	3	10	● 1. **Worst That Could Happen**	Buddah 75
			BROOKS, DONNIE	
7/11/60	7	15	1. **Mission Bell**	Era 3018
12/26/60	31	3	2. Doll House	Era 3028
			BROTHERHOOD OF MAN	
5/23/70	13	10	1. United We Stand	Deram 85059
6/19/76	27	4	2. Save Your Kisses For Me	Pye 71066
			BROTHERS FOUR	
			fraternity brothers at the University Of Washington	
3/21/60	2 (4)	15	1. **Greenfields**	Columbia 41571
4/24/61	32	3	2. Frogg [N]	Columbia 41958

Blondie's first hit happened in Britain. The group's update of "Denis" (a 1963 American hit for Randy and the Rainbows) reached number two there in 1978. Debbie Harry and the guys followed it with three more U.K. hits the same year.

The Blues Brothers. Despite their million-selling "Briefcase Full of Blues" album, John Belushi and Dan Aykroyd's revival of "Soul Man" failed to top the chart performance of the Sam & Dave original.

Gary U.S. Bonds. The writers of 1961's "Quarter to Three" took legal action against 1962's "Dancin' Party," claiming that the latter (a hit for Chubby Checker) was creatively too close to the Gary Bonds' chart-topper for comfort.

Karla Bonoff's 1982 success, "Personally," was recorded six years earlier by southern soul singer Jackie ("Precious Precious") Moore. The tune was written by Paul Kelly, whose own "Stealing In The Name of The Lord" was an R&B hit in 1970.

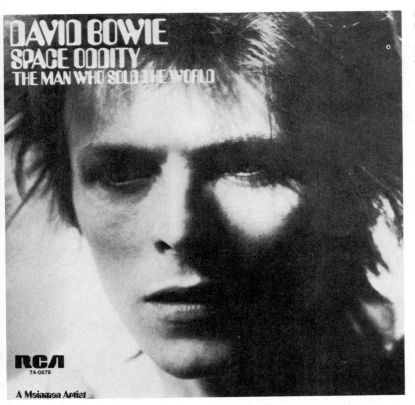

David Bowie. "Space Oddity" became David Bowie's first U.S. top 20 hit in 1973, more than three years after it broke in Britain. Record buyers there even sent the song back to the charts in 1975, when it reached No. 1.

The Brothers Four (they met as fraternity brothers at the University of Washington) hit the top 40 but once. "Green Fields" was co-written by Terry Gilkyson, a chart traveller in his own right with "Marianne."

The Brothers Johnson. As teenage musicians performing in and around their native Los Angeles, George and Louis Johnson backed Bobby Womack, the Supremes, and David Ruffin, among others.

James Brown is among the ten acts of the rock era with the most top 40 hits, yet the Godfather of Soul has never reached No. 1. It's a dubious distinction he shares with Fats Domino.

Jackson Browne. This German-born singer-songwriter has seen his songs recorded by acts as diverse as Nico and the Jackson Five, Johnny Rivers and Joan Baez, and Tom Rush and Joe Cocker.

The Buckinghams came from the city of Chicago and were produced by the man later responsible for the success of the group Chicago, James William Guercio.

DATE	POS	WKS	ARTIST—Record Title	LABEL & NO.
			BROTHERS JOHNSON	
			George & Louis Johnson	
5/22/76	3	12	● 1. **I'll Be Good To You**	A&M 1806
9/18/76	30	6	2. Get The Funk Out Ma Face	A&M 1851
7/30/77	5	13	● 3. **Strawberry Letter 23**	A&M 1949
4/12/80	7	13	4. **Stomp!**	A&M 2216
			BROWN('S), AL, Tunetoppers featuring Cookie Brown	
5/02/60	23	5	1. The Madison	Amy 804
			BROWN, ARTHUR [The Crazy World Of]	
9/21/68	2 (1)	11	● 1. **Fire**	Atlantic 2556
			BROWN, BOOTS, & His Blockbusters	
9/15/58	23	3	1. Cerveza [I]	RCA 7269
			BROWN, BUSTER	
			died 1/31/76 (61)	
3/28/60	38	3	1. Fannie Mae	Fire 1008
			BROWN, CHUCK, & The Soul Searchers	
3/17/79	34	5	● 1. Bustin' Loose, Part 1	Source 40967
			BROWN, JAMES	
			Black music's all-time #1 artist	
5/30/60	33	2	1. Think	Federal 12370
4/03/61	40	2	2. Bewildered	King 5442
5/19/62	35	4	3. Night Train [I]	King 5614
5/18/63	18	7	4. Prisoner Of Love	King 5739
2/15/64	23	7	5. Oh Baby Don't You Weep (Part 1)	King 5842
9/12/64	24	5	6. Out Of Sight	Smash 1919
8/07/65	8	9	7. **Papa's Got A Brand New Bag (Part 1)**	King 5999
11/20/65	3	10	8. **I Got You (I Feel Good)**	King 6015
5/07/66	8	8	9. **It's A Man's Man's Man's World**	King 6035
1/28/67	29	4	10. Bring It Up	King 6071
8/12/67	7	8	11. **Cold Sweat (Part 1)**	King 6110
11/25/67	40	1	12. Get It Together (Part 1)	King 6122
12/30/67	28	5	13. I Can't Stand Myself (When You Touch Me)/	
2/17/68	36	4	14. There Was A Time	King 6144
3/23/68	6	10	15. **I Got The Feelin'**	King 6155
6/01/68	14	7	16. Licking Stick - Licking Stick	King 6166
			-all of above on King labeled as: James Brown & The Famous Flames	
9/14/68	10	10	17. **Say It Loud - I'm Black And I'm Proud**	King 6187
12/07/68	31	2	18. Goodbye My Love	King 6198
2/08/69	15	7	19. Give It Up Or Turnit A Loose	King 6213
4/19/69	20	6	20. I Don't Want Nobody To Give Me Nothing (Open Up The Door, I'll Get It Myself)	King 6224
6/21/69	11	10	21. Mother Popcorn (You Got To Have A Mother For Me) (Part 1)	King 6245
6/28/69	30	5	22. The Popcorn [I]	King 6240
9/27/69	37	2	23. World (Part 1)	King 6258
11/01/69	21	5	24. Let A Man Come In And Do The Popcorn (Part One)	King 6255

DATE	POS	WKS	ARTIST—Record Title	LABEL & NO.
12/13/69	24	8	25. Ain't It Funky Now (Part 1) [I]	King 6280
1/24/70	40	2	26. Let A Man Come In And Do The Popcorn (Part Two)	King 6275
2/28/70	32	6	27. It's A New Day (Part 1 & Part 2)	King 6292
5/23/70	32	2	28. Brother Rapp (Part 1 & Part 2)	King 6310
8/01/70	15	7	29. Get Up I Feel Like Being Like A Sex Machine (Part 1)	King 6318
10/17/70	13	8	30. Super Bad (Part 1 & Part 2)	King 6329
1/16/71	34	5	31. Get Up, Get Into It, Get Involved	King 6347
3/13/71	29	6	32. Soul Power (Part 1)	King 6368
6/26/71	35	3	33. Escape-ism (Part 1) [S]	People 2500
7/17/71	15	9	34. Hot Pants (She Got To Use What She Got, To Get What She Wants) (Part 1)	People 2501
9/11/71	22	6	35. Make It Funky (Part 1)	Polydor 14088
12/04/71	35	3	36. I'm A Greedy Man (Part 1)	Polydor 14100
2/26/72	27	4	37. Talking Loud And Saying Nothing	Polydor 14109
4/01/72	40	2	38. King Heroin [S]	Polydor 14116
9/09/72	18	8	● 39. Get On The Good Foot (Part 1)	Polydor 14139
2/10/73	27	4	40. I Got Ants In My Pants (and I want to dance) (Part 1)	Polydor 14162
4/13/74	26	9	● 41. The Payback (Part 1)	Polydor 14223
8/03/74	29	4	42. My Thang	Polydor 14244
9/21/74	31	3	43. Papa Don't Take No Mess (Part 1)	Polydor 14255
			BROWN, MAXINE	
1/30/61	19	6	1. All In My Mind	Nomar 103
4/24/61	25	5	2. Funny	Nomar 106
12/05/64	24	7	3. Oh No Not My Baby	Wand 162
			BROWN, NAPPY	
4/30/55	25	4	1. Don't Be Angry	Savoy 1155
			BROWN, PETER	
10/08/77	18	8	1. Do Ya Wanna Get Funky With Me	Drive 6258
5/06/78	8	14	2. **Dance With Me** -with Betty Wright-	Drive 6269
			BROWN, POLLY lead singer of Pickettywitch	
2/08/75	16	7	1. Up In A Puff Of Smoke	GTO 1002
			BROWN, ROY died 5/25/81	
7/01/57	29	1	1. Let The Four Winds Blow	Imperial 5439
			BROWN, RUTH	
3/02/57	25	5	1. Lucky Lips	Atlantic 1125
10/13/58	24	2	2. This Little Girl's Gone Rockin' -sax solo by King Curtis-	Atlantic 1197
			BROWN, SHIRLEY	
11/23/74	22	6	1. Woman To Woman	Truth 3206
			BROWNE, JACKSON	
4/08/72	8	9	1. **Doctor My Eyes**	Asylum 11004
2/19/77	23	6	2. Here Come Those Tears Again	Asylum 45379

DATE	POS	WKS	ARTIST—Record Title	LABEL & NO.
3/04/78	11	12	3. Running On Empty	Asylum 45460
7/08/78	20	7	4. Stay/	
		4	5. **The Load-Out**	Asylum 45485
7/26/80	19	10	6. Boulevard	Asylum 47003
10/18/80	22	5	7. That Girl Could Sing	Asylum 47036
8/21/82	7	12	8. **Somebody's Baby** -from the soundtrack "Fast Times At Ridgemont High"-	Asylum 69982
			BROWNS featuring Jim Edward Brown	
8/03/59	1 (4)	14	1. **The Three Bells**	RCA 7555
11/23/59	13	9	2. Scarlet Ribbons (For Her Hair)	RCA 7614
3/28/60	5	12	3. **The Old Lamplighter**	RCA 7700
			BROWNSVILLE STATION Ann Arbor, Michigan foursome	
12/08/73	3	13	● 1. **Smokin' In The Boy's Room**	Big Tree 16011
10/05/74	31	3	2. Kings Of The Party	Big Tree 16001
			BRUBECK, DAVE, Quartet Paul Desmond died 5/30/77 (52)	
9/25/61	25	6	1. Take Five [I]	Columbia 41479
			BRYANT, ANITA	
7/27/59	30	7	1. Till There Was You -from "The Music Man"-	Carlton 512
5/02/60	5	12	2. **Paper Roses**	Carlton 528
8/08/60	10	9	3. **In My Little Corner Of The World**	Carlton 530
12/26/60	18	6	4. Wonderland By Night	Carlton 537
			BRYANT, RAY, Combo	
5/09/60	30	4	● 1. The Madison Time - Part 1 [S-I] -dance calls by Eddie Morrison-	Columbia 41628
			B.T. EXPRESS B.T.: Brothers Trucking	
10/05/74	2 (2)	14	1. **Do It ('Til You're Satisfied)**	Roadshow 12395
2/08/75	4	11	2. **Express [I]**	Roadshow 7001
9/06/75	40	2	3. Give It What You Got/	
11/01/75	31	3	4. Peace Pipe	Roadshow 7003
			BUBBLE PUPPY	
3/15/69	14	7	1. Hot Smoke & Sasafrass	Int'l. Artists 128
			BUCHANAN & GOODMAN Bill Buchanan & Dickie Goodman	
8/11/56	3	10	● 1. **The Flying Saucer (Parts 1 & 2) [N]**	Luniverse 101
7/29/57	18	8	2. Flying Saucer The 2nd [N]	Luniverse 105
12/30/57	32	2	3. Santa & The Satellite (Parts 1 & 2) [X-N]	Luniverse 107
			BUCHANAN BROTHERS Terry Cashman, Gene Pistilli, & Tommy West	
5/31/69	22	7	1. Medicine Man (Part 1)	Event 3302
			BUCKINGHAM, LINDSEY member of Fleetwood Mac	
11/07/81	9	14	1. **Trouble**	Asylum 47223

DATE	POS	WKS	ARTIST—Record Title	LABEL & NO.
			BUCKINGHAMS	
			Chicago quintet	
1/21/67	**1** (2)	10	1. **Kind Of A Drag**	U.S.A. 860
4/08/67	**6**	10	2. **Don't You Care**	Columbia 44053
7/01/67	**5**	10	3. **Mercy, Mercy, Mercy**	Columbia 44182
9/30/67	**12**	7	4. Hey Baby (They're Playing Our Song)	Columbia 44254
12/23/67	**11**	10	5. Susan	Columbia 44378
			BUCKNER & GARCIA	
			Gary Buckner & Jerry Garcia	
1/30/82	**9**	14	● 1. **Pac-Man Fever** [N]	Columbia 02673
			BUFFALO SPRINGFIELD	
			Stephen Stills, Neil Young, Jim Messina, Richie Furay, Dewey Martin and Bruce Palmer	
2/18/67	**7**	11	1. **For What It's Worth (Stop, Hey What's That Sound)**	Atco 6459
			BUFFETT, JIMMY	
6/29/74	**30**	5	1. Come Monday	Dunhill 4385
5/07/77	**8**	15	2. **Margaritaville**	ABC 12254
10/22/77	**37**	3	3. Changes In Latitudes, Changes In Attitudes	ABC 12305
5/27/78	**32**	4	4. Cheeseburger In Paradise [N]	ABC 12358
10/20/79	**35**	3	5. Fins	MCA 41109
			BUGGLES	
			Geoff Downes & Trevor Horne joined "Yes" in 1980	
12/15/79	**40**	1	1. Video Killed The Radio Star	Island 49114
			BULL & THE MATADORS	
11/16/68	**39**	1	1. The Funky Judge	Toddlin' Town 108
			BULLET	
12/25/71	**28**	5	1. White Lies, Blue Eyes	Big Tree 123
			BUOYS	
4/17/71	**17**	8	1. Timothy	Scepter 12275
			BURDON, ERIC, & WAR	
			also see Animals, and War	
7/11/70	**3**	13	● 1. **Spill The Wine**	MGM 14118
			BURKE, SOLOMON	
11/13/61	**24**	7	1. Just Out Of Reach (Of My Two Open Arms)	Atlantic 2114
5/25/63	**37**	2	2. If You Need Me	Atlantic 2185
5/23/64	**33**	4	3. Goodbye Baby (Baby Goodbye)	Atlantic 2226
4/03/65	**22**	5	4. Got To Get You Off My Mind	Atlantic 2276
7/03/65	**28**	5	5. Tonight's The Night	Atlantic 2288
			BURNETTE, DORSEY	
			died 8/19/79 (46)	
2/22/60	**23**	9	1. (There Was A) Tall Oak Tree	Era 3012
			BURNETTE, JOHNNY	
			brother of Dorsey and father of Rocky - drowned on 8/1/64 (30)	
8/15/60	**11**	11	1. Dreamin'	Liberty 55258
11/21/60	**8**	11	2. **You're Sixteen**	Liberty 55285
2/20/61	**17**	6	3. Little Boy Sad	Liberty 55298
11/06/61	**18**	4	4. God, Country And My Baby	Liberty 55379

DATE	POS	WKS	ARTIST—Record Title	LABEL & NO.
			BURNETTE, ROCKY	
			Johnny Burnette's son	
6/07/80	8	12	1. **Tired Of Toein' The Line**	EMI America 8043
			BUSCH, LOU, & His Orchestra	
			died 9/19/79 (69) - also see Joe "Fingers" Carr	
3/24/56	35	2	1. 11th Hour Melody	Capitol 3349
			BUSTERS	
9/28/63	25	5	1. Bust Out [I]	Arlen 735
			BUTLER, JERRY	
6/16/58	11	9	1. For Your Precious Love	Abner/Falcon 1013
			-with The Impressions-	
11/07/60	7	13	2. **He Will Break Your Heart**	Vee-Jay 354
4/03/61	27	4	3. Find Another Girl	Vee-Jay 375
8/07/61	25	4	4. I'm A Telling You	Vee-Jay 390
10/30/61	11	11	5. Moon River	Vee-Jay 405
			-from "Breakfast At Tiffany's"-	
8/18/62	20	4	6. Make It Easy On Yourself	Vee-Jay 451
12/28/63	31	5	7. Need To Belong	Vee-Jay 567
11/25/67	38	2	8. Mr. Dream Merchant	Mercury 72721
6/08/68	20	9	9. Never Give You Up	Mercury 72798
10/05/68	16	8	10. Hey, Western Union Man	Mercury 72850
1/18/69	39	2	11. Are You Happy	Mercury 72876
3/08/69	4	12	● 12. **Only The Strong Survive**	Mercury 72898
6/21/69	24	7	13. Moody Woman	Mercury 72929
9/06/69	20	9	14. What's The Use Of Breaking Up	Mercury 72960
			BUTLER, JERRY, & BRENDA LEE EAGER	
2/05/72	21	10	● 1. Ain't Understanding Mellow	Mercury 73255
			BUTLER, JERRY, & BETTY EVERETT	
9/19/64	5	11	1. **Let It Be Me**	Vee-Jay 613
			BYRD, CHARLIE - see STAN GETZ	
			BYRDS	
			Los Angeles-based group: Roger McGuinn, Gene Clark, Chris Hillman, Mike Clarke, and David Crosby	
6/05/65	1 (1)	10	1. **Mr. Tambourine Man**	Columbia 43271
8/21/65	40	1	2. All I Really Want To Do	Columbia 43332
11/06/65	1 (3)	11	3. **Turn! Turn! Turn!**	Columbia 43424
			-from the Book of Ecclesiastes-	
4/30/66	14	6	4. Eight Miles High	Columbia 43578
10/22/66	36	2	5. Mr. Spaceman	Columbia 43766
2/18/67	29	3	6. So You Want To Be A Rock 'N' Roll Star	Columbia 43987
4/29/67	30	3	7. My Back Pages	Columbia 44054
			BYRNES, EDWARD	
			Kookie of TVs "77 Sunset Strip"	
4/27/59	4	11	1. **Kookie, Kookie (Lend Me Your Comb) [N]**	Warner 5047
			-with Connie Stevens-	
			CADETS	
			also recorded as The Jacks	
7/21/56	15	7	1. Stranded In The Jungle [N]	Modern 994

DATE	POS	WKS	ARTIST—Record Title	LABEL & NO.
			CADILLACS	
			Earl Carroll, lead singer	
2/04/56	17	5	1. Speedo	Josie 785
1/12/59	28	3	2. Peek-A-Boo	Josie 846
			CAIN, TANE	
			wife of Journey's Jonathan Cain	
9/18/82	37	3	1. Holdin' On	RCA 13287
			CAIOLA, AL, & His Orchestra	
1/16/61	35	4	1. The Magnificent Seven [I]	United Artists 261
5/01/61	19	5	2. Bonanza [I]	United Artists 302
			CALDWELL, BOBBY	
2/03/79	9	12	1. **What You Won't Do For Love**	Clouds 11
			CALE, J.J.	
3/11/72	22	8	1. Crazy Mama	Shelter 7314
			CAMPBELL, GLEN	
11/25/67	26	7	1. By The Time I Get To Phoenix	Capitol 2015
5/25/68	36	2	2. I Wanna Live	Capitol 2146
8/03/68	32	3	3. Dreams Of The Everyday Housewife	Capitol 2224
11/02/68	39	1	4. Gentle On My Mind	Capitol 5939
			-originally charted in 1967-	
11/16/68	3	13	● 5. **Wichita Lineman**	Capitol 2302
3/15/69	4	10	● 6. **Galveston**	Capitol 2428
5/17/69	26	5	7. Where's The Playground Susie	Capitol 2494
8/23/69	35	2	8. True Grit	Capitol 2573
11/01/69	23	7	9. Try A Little Kindness	Capitol 2659
1/31/70	19	7	10. Honey Come Back	Capitol 2718
5/09/70	40	2	11. Oh Happy Day	Capitol 2787
9/26/70	10	9	12. **It's Only Make Believe**	Capitol 2905
3/27/71	31	4	13. Dream Baby (How Long Must I Dream)	Capitol 3062
6/21/75	1 (2)	18	● 14. **Rhinestone Cowboy**	Capitol 4095
11/22/75	11	11	15. Country Boy (You Got Your Feet In L.A.)	Capitol 4155
4/17/76	27	5	16. Don't Pull Your Love/Then You Can Tell Me Goodbye	Capitol 4245
3/05/77	1 (1)	15	● 17. **Southern Nights**	Capitol 4376
8/13/77	39	2	18. Sunflower	Capitol 4445
12/09/78	38	2	19. Can You Fool	Capitol 4584
			CAMPBELL, GLEN, & BOBBIE GENTRY	
3/08/69	36	1	1. Let It Be Me	Capitol 2387
3/14/70	27	6	2. All I Have To Do Is Dream	Capitol 2745
			CAMPBELL, JO ANN	
9/08/62	38	3	1. (I'm The Girl On) Wolverton Mountain	Cameo 223
			CANNED HEAT	
			leader, Bob "The Bear" Hite died on 4/6/81 (36)	
9/07/68	16	7	1. On The Road Again	Liberty 56038
12/21/68	11	9	2. Going Up The Country	Liberty 56077
11/07/70	26	6	3. Let's Work Together	Liberty 56151

DATE	POS	WKS	ARTIST—Record Title	LABEL & NO.
			CANNIBAL & THE HEADHUNTERS	
			four Mexican-American youths	
4/17/65	**30**	6	1. Land Of 1000 Dances	Rampart 642
			CANNON, ACE [& his Alto Sax]	
1/27/62	**17**	11	1. Tuff [I]	Hi 2040
5/19/62	**36**	1	2. Blues (Stay Away From Me) [I]	Hi 2051
			CANNON, FREDDY	
5/25/59	**6**	10	1. **Tallahassee Lassie**	Swan 4031
12/07/59	**3**	11	2. **Way Down Yonder In New Orleans**	Swan 4043
3/07/60	**34**	3	3. Chattanooga Shoe Shine Boy	Swan 4050
5/30/60	**28**	4	4. Jump Over	Swan 4053
9/04/61	**35**	1	5. Transistor Sister	Swan 4078
5/26/62	**3**	12	6. **Palisades Park**	Swan 4106
2/15/64	**16**	6	7. Abigail Beecher	Warner 5409
8/28/65	**13**	6	8. Action	Warner 5645
			-from TV's "Where The Action Is"-	
			CAPITOLS	
5/21/66	**7**	11	1. **Cool Jerk**	Karen 1524
			CAPRIS	
1/23/61	**3**	10	1. **There's A Moon Out Tonight**	Old Town 1094
			CAPTAIN & TENNILLE	
			Daryl Dragon & Toni Tennille	
5/24/75	**1** (4)	16	● 1. **Love Will Keep Us Together**	A&M 1672
10/04/75	**4**	14	2. **The Way I Want To Touch You**	A&M 1725
2/07/76	**3**	13	● 3. **Lonely Night (Angel Face)**	A&M 1782
5/08/76	**4**	12	● 4. **Shop Around**	A&M 1817
10/09/76	**4**	15	● 5. **Muskrat Love**	A&M 1870
4/02/77	**13**	8	6. Can't Stop Dancin'	A&M 1912
9/09/78	**10**	14	7. **You Never Done It Like That**	A&M 2063
1/27/79	**40**	1	8. You Need A Woman Tonight	A&M 2106
11/10/79	**1** (1)	22	● 9. **Do That To Me One More Time**	Casablanca 2215
			CARA, IRENE	
7/26/80	**4**	12	1. **Fame**	RSO 1034
9/27/80	**19**	9	2. Out Here On My Own	RSO 1048
			-above 2 tunes from film "Fame"-	
			CARAVELLES	
			English duo: Andrea & Lois	
11/23/63	**3**	10	1. **You Don't Have To Be A Baby To Cry**	Smash 1852
			CAREFREES	
4/11/64	**39**	1	1. We Love You Beatles [N]	London Int'l. 10614
			CARGILL, HENSON	
1/20/68	**25**	7	1. Skip A Rope	Monument 1041
			CARLTON, CARL	
10/12/74	**6**	10	1. **Everlasting Love**	Back Beat 27001
9/26/81	**22**	7	● 2. She's A Bad Mama Jama (She's Built, She's Stacked)	20th Century 2488

DATE	POS	WKS	ARTIST—Record Title	LABEL & NO.
			CARMEN, ERIC	
			lead singer of The Raspberries	
1/17/76	**2** (3)	14	● 1. **All By Myself**	Arista 0165
5/22/76	**11**	10	2. Never Gonna Fall In Love Again	Arista 0184
9/18/76	**34**	3	3. Sunrise	Arista 0200
9/24/77	**23**	8	4. She Did It	Arista 0266
10/28/78	**19**	7	5. Change Of Heart	Arista 0354
			CARNES, KIM	
			also see Gene Cotton and Kenny Rogers	
6/14/80	**10**	15	1. More Love	EMI America 8045
4/11/81	**1** (9)	20	● 2. **Bette Davis Eyes**	EMI America 8077
8/29/81	**28**	6	3. Draw Of The Cards	EMI America 8087
9/11/82	**29**	6	4. Voyeur	EMI America 8127
			CAROSONE, RENATO	
5/12/58	**18**	9	1. Torero [F]	Capitol 71080
			CARPENTERS	
			Karen and brother Richard - Karen died on 2/4/83 (32)	
6/27/70	**1** (4)	15	● 1. **(They Long To Be) Close To You**	A&M 1183
10/03/70	**2** (4)	14	● 2. **We've Only Just Begun**	A&M 1217
2/13/71	**3**	12	● 3. **For All We Know**	A&M 1243
			-from "Lovers & Other Strangers"-	
5/22/71	**2** (2)	11	● 4. **Rainy Days And Mondays**	A&M 1260
9/11/71	**2** (2)	12	● 5. **Superstar**	A&M 1289
1/22/72	**2** (2)	11	● 6. **Hurting Each Other**	A&M 1322
5/13/72	**12**	8	7. It's Going To Take Some Time	A&M 1351
7/22/72	**7**	9	8. **Goodbye To Love**	A&M 1367
3/10/73	**3**	11	● 9. **Sing**	A&M 1413
6/16/73	**2** (1)	12	● 10. **Yesterday Once More**	A&M 1446
10/20/73	**1** (2)	16	● 11. **Top Of The World**	A&M 1468
4/27/74	**11**	9	12. I Won't Last A Day Without You	A&M 1521
12/07/74	**1** (1)	12	● 13. **Please Mr. Postman**	A&M 1646
4/12/75	**4**	9	14. **Only Yesterday**	A&M 1677
8/16/75	**17**	7	15. Solitaire	A&M 1721
3/13/76	**12**	8	16. There's A Kind Of Hush (All Over The World)	A&M 1800
7/04/76	**25**	5	17. I Need To Be In Love	A&M 1828
6/18/77	**35**	3	18. All You Get From Love Is A Love Song	A&M 1940
11/05/77	**32**	4	19. Calling Occupants Of Interplanetary Craft	A&M 1978
7/04/81	**16**	9	20. Touch Me When We're Dancing	A&M 2344
			CARR, CATHY	
4/07/56	**2** (1)	18	1. **Ivory Tower**	Fraternity 734
			CARR, JOE "FINGERS"	
			real name: Lou Busch	
6/16/56	**19**	10	1. Portuguese Washerwomen [I]	Capitol 3418
			CARR, VALERIE	
6/09/58	**19**	2	1. When The Boys Talk About The Girls	Roulette 4066

DATE	POS	WKS	ARTIST—Record Title	LABEL & NO.
			CARR, VIKKI	
9/30/67	3	11	1. **It Must Be Him**	Liberty 55986
1/27/68	34	1	2. The Lesson	Liberty 56012
6/28/69	35	4	3. With Pen In Hand	Liberty 56092
			CARRACK, PAUL	
			formerly with Ace, and Squeeze	
10/30/82	37	2	1. I Need You	Epic 03146
			CARRADINE, KEITH	
			son of actor John Carradine	
6/12/76	17	12	1. I'm Easy	ABC 12117
			-from the soundtrack "Nashville"-	
			CARROLL, DAVID, & His Orchestra	
1/08/55	8	17	1. **Melody Of Love [I]**	Mercury 70516
12/17/55	20	1	2. It's Almost Tomorrow	Mercury 70717
			-vocal: Jack Halloran Singers-	
			CARS	
			Boston-area quintet led by Ric Ocasek	
8/12/78	27	7	1. Just What I Needed	Elektra 45491
12/09/78	35	5	2. My Best Friend's Girl	Elektra 45537
7/28/79	14	9	3. Let's Go	Elektra 46063
10/11/80	37	3	4. Touch And Go	Elektra 47039
12/12/81	4	17	5. **Shake It Up**	Elektra 47250
			CARSON, KIT	
			real name: Liza Morrow	
12/31/55	11	11	1. Band Of Gold	Capitol 3283
			CARSON, MINDY	
8/27/55	13	8	1. Wake The Town And Tell The People	Columbia 40537
1/05/57	34	2	2. Since I Met You Baby	Columbia 40789
			CARTER, CLARENCE	
8/17/68	6	11	● 1. **Slip Away**	Atlantic 2508
11/30/68	13	11	● 2. **Too Weak To Fight**	Atlantic 2569
3/29/69	31	5	3. Snatching It Back	Atlantic 2605
8/01/70	4	12	● 4. **Patches**	Atlantic 2748
			CARTER, MEL	
7/24/65	8	11	1. **Hold Me, Thrill Me, Kiss Me**	Imperial 66113
11/27/65	38	2	2. (All Of A Sudden) My Heart Sings	Imperial 66138
5/21/66	32	2	3. Band Of Gold	Imperial 66165
			CASCADES	
			quintet from San Diego	
1/26/63	3	13	1. **Rhythm Of The Rain**	Valiant 6026
			CASH, ALVIN, & THE CRAWLERS	
1/30/65	14	7	1. Twine Time [I]	Mar-V-Lus 6002
			CASH, JOHNNY	
10/20/56	17	11	1. I Walk The Line	Sun 241
2/10/58	14	13	2. Ballad Of A Teenage Queen	Sun 283
6/09/58	11	13	3. Guess Things Happen That Way	Sun 295
9/01/58	24	6	4. The Ways Of A Woman In Love	Sun 302
11/10/58	38	1	5. All Over Again	Columbia 41251

DATE	POS	WKS	ARTIST—Record Title	LABEL & NO.
2/02/59	32	6	6. Don't Take Your Guns To Town	Columbia 41313
6/22/63	17	10	7. Ring Of Fire	Columbia 42788
3/14/64	35	3	8. Understand Your Man	Columbia 42964
6/29/68	32	6	9. Folsom Prison Blues	Columbia 44513
			-original version released in 1956 on Sun 232-	
8/02/69	2 (3)	11	● 10. A Boy Named Sue [N]	Columbia 44944
4/25/70	19	6	11. What Is Truth	Columbia 45134
5/15/76	29	3	12. One Piece At A Time [N]	Columbia 10321
			CASH, JOHNNY, & JUNE CARTER	
2/21/70	36	2	1. If I Were A Carpenter	Columbia 45064
			CASH, ROSANNE	
			Johnny Cash's daughter	
6/13/81	22	7	1. Seven Year Ache	Columbia 11426
			CASHMAN & WEST	
			Terry Cashman & Tommy West -- also see Buchanan Brothers	
10/21/72	27	7	1. American City Suite:	Dunhill 4324
			-Sweet City Song/All Around The Town/A Friend Is Dying-	
			CASINOS	
1/28/67	6	10	1. **Then You Can Tell Me Goodbye**	Fraternity 977
			CASSIDY, DAVID	
			played Keith and was lead singer for TV's The Partridge Family	
11/13/71	9	11	● 1. **Cherish**	Bell 45150
3/25/72	37	2	2. Could It Be Forever	Bell 45187
6/10/72	25	5	3. How Can I Be Sure	Bell 45220
10/14/72	38	2	4. Rock Me Baby	Bell 45260
			CASSIDY, SHAUN	
			Shaun & David are half-brothers	
6/04/77	1 (1)	12	● 1. **Da Doo Ron Ron**	Warner 8365
8/20/77	3	15	● 2. **That's Rock 'N' Roll**	Warner 8423
11/26/77	7	12	● 3. **Hey Deanie**	Warner 8488
4/22/78	31	5	4. Do You Believe In Magic	Warner 8533
			CASTAWAYS	
			Minneapolis quintet	
9/18/65	12	9	1. Liar, Liar	Soma 1433
			CASTELLS	
7/03/61	20	7	1. Sacred	Era 3048
5/26/62	21	5	2. So This Is Love	Era 3073
			CASTLEMAN, BOOMER	
5/31/75	33	3	1. Judy Mae	Mums 6038
			CASTOR, JIMMY [Bunch]	
2/04/67	31	3	1. Hey, Leroy, Your Mama's Callin' You [I]	Smash 2069
5/27/72	6	10	● 2. **Troglodyte (Cave Man) [N]**	RCA 1029
3/22/75	16	8	3. The Bertha Butt Boogie (Part 1) [N]	Atlantic 3232
			CAT MOTHER & the ALL NIGHT NEWS BOYS	
7/12/69	21	6	1. Good Old Rock 'N Roll (medley)	Polydor 14002
			-Jimi Hendrix, producer-	
			CATE BROTHERS	
			twins Earl & Ernie Cate	
4/17/76	24	8	1. Union Man	Asylum 45294

DATE	POS	WKS	ARTIST—Record Title	LABEL & NO.
			CATES, GEORGE, & His Orchestra	
			also see Steve Allen	
4/21/56	4	19	1. **Moonglow And Theme From "Picnic" [I]**	Coral 61618
			-featuring The Stan Wrightsman Quartet - from film "Picnic"-	
			CATHY JEAN & THE ROOMMATES	
3/06/61	12	10	1. Please Love Me Forever	Valmor 007
			CAVALIERE, FELIX	
			lead singer of The Rascals	
4/12/80	36	3	1. Only A Lonely Heart Sees	Epic 50829
			C COMPANY Featuring TERRY NELSON	
5/01/71	37	3	● 1. Battle Hymn Of Lt. Calley [S]	Plantation 73
			CELEBRATION featuring MIKE LOVE	
			Mike is one of The Beach Boys	
6/03/78	28	4	1. Almost Summer	MCA 40891
			CERRONE	
			French - Jean-Marc Cerrone	
3/26/77	36	3	1. Love In 'C' Minor (Part 1) [I]	Cotillion 44215
			CHAD & JEREMY	
			English - Chad Stuart & Jeremy Clyde	
6/13/64	21	6	1. Yesterday's Gone	World Artists 1021
9/19/64	7	9	2. **A Summer Song**	World Artists 1027
12/12/64	15	8	3. Willow Weep For Me	World Artists 1034
3/13/65	23	5	4. If I Loved You	World Artists 1041
5/29/65	17	6	5. Before And After	Columbia 43277
8/28/65	35	3	6. I Don't Wanna Lose You Baby	Columbia 43339
8/13/66	30	2	7. Distant Shores	Columbia 43682
			CHAIRMEN OF THE BOARD	
			General Johnson, lead singer	
2/07/70	3	12	● 1. **Give Me Just A Little More Time**	Invictus 9074
6/06/70	38	2	2. (You've Got Me) Dangling On A String	Invictus 9078
9/12/70	38	2	3. Everything's Tuesday	Invictus 9079
12/12/70	13	9	4. Pay To The Piper	Invictus 9081
			CHAKACHAS	
2/19/72	8	10	● 1. **Jungle Fever [I]**	Polydor 15030
			CHAMBERLAIN, RICHARD	
			star of TV's "Dr. Kildare"	
6/23/62	10	10	1. **Theme From Dr. Kildare (Three Stars Will Shine Tonight)**	MGM 13075
10/27/62	21	5	2. Love Me Tender	MGM 13097
3/09/63	14	7	3. All I Have To Do Is Dream	MGM 13121
			CHAMBERS BROTHERS	
			four brothers from Mississippi	
9/14/68	11	9	1. Time Has Come Today	Columbia 44414
12/21/68	37	2	2. I Can't Turn You Loose	Columbia 44679
			CHAMPAIGN	
3/28/81	12	13	1. How 'Bout Us	Columbia 11433

DATE	POS	WKS	ARTIST—Record Title	LABEL & NO.
			CHAMPS	
			Seals & Crofts were members - joining group after "Tequila"	
3/03/58	**1** (5)	16	1. **Tequila [I]**	Challenge 1016
6/02/58	**30**	5	2. El Rancho Rock [I]	Challenge 59007
2/08/60	**30**	5	3. Too Much Tequila [I]	Challenge 59063
7/14/62	**40**	1	4. Limbo Rock [I]	Challenge 9131
			CHANDLER, GENE	
1/27/62	**1** (3)	11	1. **Duke Of Earl**	Vee-Jay 416
8/01/64	**19**	7	2. Just Be True	Constellation 130
11/14/64	**39**	1	3. Bless Our Love	Constellation 136
1/16/65	**40**	1	4. What Now	Constellation 141
5/22/65	**18**	6	5. Nothing Can Stop Me	Constellation 149
8/08/70	**12**	11	● 6. Groovy Situation	Mercury 73083
			CHANGE	
7/19/80	**40**	1	1. A Lover's Holiday	RFC 49208
			CHANNEL, BRUCE	
2/10/62	**1** (3)	12	1. **Hey! Baby**	Smash 1731
			CHANSON	
12/16/78	**21**	9	1. Don't Hold Back	Ariola 7717
			CHANTAY'S	
4/06/63	**4**	11	1. **Pipeline [I]**	Dot 16440
			CHANTELS	
1/27/58	**15**	12	1. Maybe	End 1005
4/07/58	**39**	3	2. Every Night (I Pray)	End 1015
9/11/61	**14**	8	3. Look In My Eyes	Carlton 555
12/11/61	**29**	3	4. Well, I Told You	Carlton 564
			CHAPIN, HARRY	
			died in an auto accident on 7/16/81 (38)	
4/22/72	**24**	9	1. Taxi	Elektra 45770
3/16/74	**36**	2	2. W-O-L-D	Elektra 45874
11/02/74	**1** (1)	12	● 3. **Cat's In The Cradle**	Elektra 45203
11/22/80	**23**	6	4. Sequel	Boardwalk 5700
			-sequel to his 1972 hit "Taxi"-	
			CHARLENE	
			Charlene Duncan	
3/27/82	**3**	14	1. **I've Never Been To Me**	Motown 1611
			-originally charted in 1977-	
			CHARLES, JIMMY, & The Revelletts	
9/05/60	**5**	11	1. **A Million To One**	Promo 1002
			CHARLES, RAY	
11/25/57	**34**	1	1. Swanee River Rock (Talkin' 'Bout That River)	Atlantic 1154
7/20/59	**6**	11	2. **What'd I Say (Part 1)**	Atlantic 2031
12/14/59	**40**	1	3. I'm Movin' On	Atlantic 2043
8/08/60	**40**	1	4. Sticks And Stones	ABC-Para. 10118
10/10/60	**1** (1)	10	5. **Georgia On My Mind**	ABC-Para. 10135
12/12/60	**28**	5	6. Ruby	ABC-Para. 10164

DATE	POS	WKS	ARTIST—Record Title	LABEL & NO.
3/27/61	8	9	7. **One Mint Julep [I]**	Impulse 200
9/18/61	1 (2)	11	8. **Hit The Road Jack**	ABC-Para. 10244
12/04/61	9	10	9. **Unchain My Heart**	ABC-Para. 10266
4/21/62	20	4	10. Hide 'Nor Hair	ABC-Para. 10314
5/19/62	1 (5)	14	● 11. **I Can't Stop Loving You**	ABC-Para. 10330
8/04/62	2 (1)	9	12. **You Don't Know Me**	ABC-Para. 10345
12/01/62	7	9	13. **You Are My Sunshine/**	
12/08/62	29	5	14. Your Cheating Heart	ABC-Para. 10375
3/16/63	20	4	15. Don't Set Me Free	ABC-Para. 10405
4/27/63	8	8	16. **Take These Chains From My Heart**	ABC-Para. 10435
7/06/63	21	5	17. No One/	
7/06/63	29	4	18. Without Love (There Is Nothing)	ABC-Para. 10453
9/14/63	4	11	19. **Busted**	ABC-Para. 10481
12/21/63	20	7	20. That Lucky Old Sun	ABC-Para. 10509
3/21/64	38	2	21. My Heart Cries For You/	
3/21/64	39	1	22. Baby, Don't You Cry	ABC-Para. 10530
1/15/66	6	9	23. **Crying Time**	ABC-Para. 10739
4/16/66	19	5	24. Together Again	ABC-Para. 10785
6/25/66	31	4	25. Let's Go Get Stoned	ABC 10808
10/01/66	32	2	26. I Chose To Sing The Blues	ABC 10840
6/10/67	15	9	27. Here We Go Again	ABC/TRC 10938
9/23/67	33	3	28. In The Heat Of The Night	ABC/TRC 10970
12/02/67	25	3	29. Yesterday	ABC/TRC 11009
7/20/68	35	3	30. Eleanor Rigby	ABC/TRC 11090
4/17/71	36	4	31. Don't Change On Me	ABC/TRC 11291
5/15/71	36	2	32. Booty Butt [I]	Tangerine 1015
			CHARLES, RAY, SINGERS	
5/02/64	3	12	1. **Love Me With All Your Heart**	Command 4046
7/25/64	29	4	2. Al-Di-La	Command 4049
12/19/64	32	5	3. One More Time	Command 4057
			CHARMS	
11/27/54	15	15	1. Hearts Of Stone	DeLuxe 6062
1/15/55	26	3	2. Ling, Ting, Tong	DeLuxe 6076
			OTIS WILLIAMS & HIS CHARMS:	
4/14/56	11	15	3. Ivory Tower	DeLuxe 6093
			CHARTBUSTERS	
8/15/64	33	3	1. She's The One	Mutual 502
			CHASE	
			Bill Chase and 3 other members killed in plane crash on 8/9/74	
6/26/71	24	8	1. Get It On	Epic 10738
			CHEAP TRICK	
			Chicago rock quartet	
5/26/79	7	13	● 1. **I Want You To Want Me**	Epic 50680
9/15/79	35	3	2. Ain't That A Shame	Epic 50743
10/27/79	26	5	3. Dream Police	Epic 50774
1/19/80	32	3	4. Voices	Epic 50814

DATE	POS	WKS	ARTIST—Record Title	LABEL & NO.
			CHECKER, CHUBBY	
			real name: Ernest Evans -- also see Bobby Rydell	
6/15/59	38	2	1. The Class [N]	Parkway 804
8/08/60	1 (1)	15	2. **The Twist**	Parkway 811
10/31/60	14	9	3. The Hucklebuck	Parkway 813
1/30/61	1 (3)	14	4. **Pony Time**	Parkway 818
5/01/61	24	4	5. Dance The Mess Around	Parkway 822
7/03/61	8	15	6. **Let's Twist Again**	Parkway 824
10/02/61	7	11	7. **The Fly**	Parkway 830
11/20/61	1 (2)	18	8. **The Twist** -re-entry of 1960 hit-	Parkway 811
3/10/62	3	12	9. **Slow Twistin'** -with Dee Dee Sharp-	Parkway 835
7/07/62	12	7	10. Dancin' Party	Parkway 842
9/29/62	2 (2)	17	11. **Limbo Rock/**	
9/29/62	10	9	12. Popeye The Hitchhiker	Parkway 849
2/23/63	20	8	13. Let's Limbo Some More/	
3/23/63	15	7	14. Twenty Miles	Parkway 862
6/01/63	12	7	15. Birdland	Parkway 873
8/03/63	25	5	16. Twist It Up	Parkway 879
11/23/63	12	9	17. Loddy Lo/	
1/11/64	17	8	18. Hooka Tooka	Parkway 890
4/04/64	23	5	19. Hey, Bobba Needle	Parkway 907
7/11/64	40	1	20. Lazy Elsie Molly	Parkway 920
5/22/65	40	1	21. Let's Do The Freddie	Parkway 949
			CHECKMATES, LTD. featuring SONNY CHARLES	
5/31/69	13	10	1. Black Pearl	A&M 1053
			CHEECH & CHONG	
			Richard Marin & Thomas Chong	
9/29/73	15	7	1. Basketball Jones Featuring Tyrone Shoelaces [N]	Ode 66038
12/29/73	24	5	2. Sister Mary Elephant (Shudd-Up!) [C]	Ode 66041
8/31/74	9	8	3. **Earache My Eye Featuring Alice Bowie [C]**	Ode 66102
			CHEERS	
			actor Bert Convy was a member	
9/24/55	6	11	1. **Black Denim Trousers**	Capitol 3219
			CHER	
			also see Sonny & Cher	
8/07/65	15	6	1. All I Really Want To Do	Imperial 66114
11/06/65	25	3	2. Where Do You Go	Imperial 66136
3/26/66	2 (1)	9	3. **Bang Bang (My Baby Shot Me Down)**	Imperial 66160
8/20/66	32	3	4. Alfie	Imperial 66192
11/18/67	9	9	5. **You Better Sit Down Kids**	Imperial 66261
10/02/71	1 (2)	14	● 6. **Gypsys, Tramps & Thieves**	Kapp 2146
2/12/72	7	10	7. **The Way Of Love**	Kapp 2158
6/03/72	22	6	8. Living In A House Divided	Kapp 2171
9/01/73	1 (2)	14	● 9. **Half-Breed**	MCA 40102
2/02/74	1 (1)	12	● 10. **Dark Lady**	MCA 40161
6/15/74	27	4	11. Train Of Thought	MCA 40245

DATE	POS	WKS	ARTIST—Record Title	LABEL & NO.
3/17/79	8	11	● 12. Take Me Home	Casablanca 965
			CHERI	
			Canadian duo	
6/05/82	39	2	1. Murphy's Law [N]	Venture 149
			CHERRY, DON	
12/10/55	4	18	1. Band Of Gold	Columbia 40597
4/14/56	29	6	2. Wild Cherry	Columbia 40665
8/11/56	22	6	3. Ghost Town	Columbia 40705
			CHI-LITES	
			Eugene Record, leader of 4-man group from Chicago	
5/08/71	26	6	1. (For God's Sake) Give More Power To The People	
				Brunswick 55450
10/30/71	3	13	2. Have You Seen Her	Brunswick 55462
4/15/72	1 (1)	14	3. Oh Girl	Brunswick 55471
3/24/73	33	5	4. A Letter To Myself	Brunswick 55491
9/01/73	30	5	5. Stoned Out Of My Mind	Brunswick 55500
			CHIC	
12/10/77	6	17	● 1. Dance, Dance, Dance (Yowsah, Yowsah, Yowsah)	Atlantic 3435
6/17/78	38	1	2. Everybody Dance	Atlantic 3469
11/18/78	1 (5)	19	★ 3. Le Freak	Atlantic 3519
3/10/79	7	12	● 4. I Want Your Love	Atlantic 3557
7/07/79	1 (1)	14	● 5. Good Times	Atlantic 3584
			CHICAGO	
			original name: Chicago Transit Authority	
4/25/70	9	11	1. Make Me Smile	Columbia 45127
8/01/70	4	11	2. 25 Or 6 To 4	Columbia 45194
11/21/70	7	11	3. Does Anybody Really Know What Time It Is?	
				Columbia 45264
3/06/71	20	6	4. Free	Columbia 45331
5/29/71	35	4	5. Lowdown	Columbia 45370
7/10/71	7	11	6. Beginnings/	
		10	7. Colour My World	Columbia 45417
10/30/71	24	6	8. Questions 67 And 68/	
			-re-entry of 1969 hit-	
		6	9. I'm A Man	Columbia 45467
8/12/72	3	10	● 10. Saturday In The Park	Columbia 45657
11/18/72	24	6	11. Dialogue (Part I & II)	Columbia 45717
7/07/73	10	12	12. Feelin' Stronger Every Day	Columbia 45880
10/20/73	4	14	● 13. Just You 'N' Me	Columbia 45933
4/06/74	9	12	14. (I've Been) Searchin' So Long	Columbia 46020
7/13/74	6	8	15. Call On Me	Columbia 46062
10/26/74	11	10	16. Wishing You Were Here	Columbia 10049
3/08/75	13	7	17. Harry Truman	Columbia 10092
5/10/75	5	7	18. Old Days	Columbia 10131
7/17/76	32	4	19. Another Rainy Day In New York City	Columbia 10360
8/21/76	1 (2)	17	● 20. If You Leave Me Now	Columbia 10390
10/15/77	4	12	21. Baby, What A Big Surprise	Columbia 10620

DATE	POS	WKS	ARTIST—Record Title	LABEL & NO.
10/28/78	14	8	22. Alive Again	Columbia 10845
1/13/79	14	9	23. No Tell Lover	Columbia 10879
6/26/82	1 (2)	18	● 24. **Hard To Say I'm Sorry** -from the film "Summer Lovers"-	Full Moon 29979
10/23/82	22	8	25. Love Me Tomorrow	Full Moon 29911
			CHICAGO LOOP	
11/26/66	37	3	1. (When She Needs Good Lovin') She Comes To Me	DynoVoice 226
			CHIFFONS	
3/09/63	1 (4)	12	1. **He's So Fine**	Laurie 3152
6/08/63	5	9	2. **One Fine Day**	Laurie 3179
10/19/63	40	1	3. A Love So Fine	Laurie 3195
1/04/64	36	2	4. I Have A Boyfriend	Laurie 3212
5/28/66	10	7	5. **Sweet Talkin' Guy**	Laurie 3340
			CHILLIWACK	
			Canadian	
10/31/81	22	11	1. My Girl (Gone, Gone, Gone)	Millennium 11813
2/27/82	33	3	2. I Believe	Millennium 13102
			CHIMES	
1/16/61	11	6	1. Once In Awhile	Tag 444
5/15/61	38	1	2. I'm In The Mood For Love	Tag 445
			CHIPMUNKS with DAVID SEVILLE	
			David (Alvin, Simon & Theodore's creator) died 1/16/72 (52)	
12/08/58	1 (4)	11	1. **The Chipmunk Song [N-X]**	Liberty 55168
2/23/59	3	9	2. **Alvin's Harmonica [N]**	Liberty 55179
7/13/59	16	6	3. Ragtime Cowboy Joe [N]	Liberty 55200
3/07/60	33	2	4. Alvin's Orchestra [N]	Liberty 55233
12/26/60	21	1	5. Rudolph The Red Nosed Reindeer [N-X]	Liberty 55289
1/06/62	39	1	6. The Chipmunk Song [N-X] -re-entry of 1958 hit-	Liberty 55250
3/31/62	40	1	7. The Alvin Twist [N]	Liberty 55424
12/29/62	40	1	8. The Chipmunk Song [N-X] -re-entry of 1958 hit-	Liberty 55250
			CHORDETTES	
			quartet from Sheboygan, Wisconsin	
3/10/56	14	9	1. Eddie My Love	Cadence 1284
6/02/56	5	17	2. **Born To Be With You**	Cadence 1291
10/13/56	16	10	3. Lay Down Your Arms	Cadence 1299
9/16/57	8	8	4. **Just Between You And Me**	Cadence 1330
3/10/58	2 (2)	12	5. **Lollipop**	Cadence 1345
5/26/58	17	7	6. Zorro	Cadence 1349
3/30/59	27	4	7. No Other Arms, No Other Lips	Cadence 1361
7/03/61	13	8	8. Never On Sunday	Cadence 1402
			CHRISTIAN, CHRIS	
11/14/81	37	3	1. I Want You, I Need You	Boardwalk 126

DATE	POS	WKS	ARTIST—Record Title	LABEL & NO.
			CHRISTIE	
			English - Jeff Christie, leader	
10/24/70	23	8	1. Yellow River	Epic 10626
			CHRISTIE, LOU	
2/16/63	24	6	1. The Gypsy Cried	Roulette 4457
4/27/63	6	10	2. Two Faces Have I	Roulette 4481
1/22/66	1 (1)	10	● 3. Lightnin' Strikes	MGM 13412
4/23/66	16	4	4. Rhapsody In The Rain	MGM 13473
9/13/69	10	9	5. I'm Gonna Make You Mine	Buddah 116
			CHURCH, EUGENE, & The Fellows	
2/23/59	36	2	1. Pretty Girls Everywhere	Class 235
			CITY BOY	
9/09/78	27	6	1. 5.7.0.5	Mercury 73999
			C.J. & CO.	
7/09/77	36	2	1. Devil's Gun	Westbound 55400
			CLANTON, JIMMY	
7/21/58	4	15	1. Just A Dream	Ace 546
11/17/58	25	5	2. A Letter To An Angel/	
12/01/58	38	2	3. A Part Of Me	Ace 551
8/17/59	33	6	4. My Own True Love	Ace 567
12/21/59	5	11	5. Go, Jimmy, Go	Ace 575
5/30/60	22	6	6. Another Sleepless Night	Ace 585
9/01/62	7	10	7. Venus In Blue Jeans	Ace 8001
			CLAPTON, ERIC	
			premiere English rock guitarist - also see Cream, and Derek & The Dominos	
11/14/70	18	8	1. After Midnight	Atco 6784
8/03/74	1 (1)	10	● 2. I Shot The Sheriff	RSO 409
11/23/74	26	5	3. Willie And The Hand Jive	RSO 503
11/13/76	24	6	4. Hello Old Friend	RSO 861
2/04/78	3	17	● 5. Lay Down Sally	RSO 886
6/10/78	16	7	6. Wonderful Tonight	RSO 895
			ERIC CLAPTON & HIS BAND:	
11/25/78	9	11	7. Promises/	
3/24/79	40	2	8. Watch Out For Lucy	RSO 910
7/26/80	30	5	9. Tulsa Time/	
		5	10. Cocaine	RSO 1039
3/14/81	10	12	11. I Can't Stand It	RSO 1060
			CLARK, CLAUDINE	
7/21/62	5	10	1. Party Lights	Chancellor 1113
			CLARK, DAVE, Five	
			Mike Smith, lead singer of British quintet	
3/07/64	6	11	1. Glad All Over	Epic 9656
4/11/64	4	10	2. Bits And Pieces	Epic 9671
5/09/64	11	9	3. Do You Love Me	Epic 9678
6/20/64	4	9	4. Can't You See That She's Mine	Epic 9692

DATE	POS	WKS	ARTIST—Record Title	LABEL & NO.
8/08/64	3	9	5. **Because**	Epic 9704
10/17/64	15	6	6. Everybody Knows (I Still Love You)	Epic 9722
12/05/64	14	9	7. Any Way You Want It	Epic 9739
2/27/65	14	6	8. Come Home	Epic 9763
5/08/65	23	5	9. Reelin' And Rockin'	Epic 9786
7/10/65	7	8	10. **I Like It Like That**	Epic 9811
9/04/65	4	9	11. **Catch Us If You Can**	Epic 9833
11/20/65	1 (1)	11	12. **Over And Over**	Epic 9863
2/19/66	18	5	13. At The Scene	Epic 9882
4/23/66	12	5	14. Try Too Hard	Epic 10004
7/02/66	28	4	15. Please Tell Me Why	Epic 10031
4/15/67	7	7	16. **You Got What It Takes**	Epic 10144
7/01/67	35	2	17. You Must Have Been A Beautiful Baby	Epic 10179
			CLARK, DEE	
1/12/59	21	6	1. Nobody But You	Abner 1019
5/25/59	18	9	2. Just Keep It Up	Abner 1026
9/14/59	20	9	3. Hey Little Girl	Abner 1029
1/04/60	33	5	4. How About That	Abner 1032
3/06/61	34	4	5. Your Friends	Vee-Jay 372
5/22/61	2 (1)	12	6. **Raindrops**	Vee-Jay 383
			CLARK, LOUIS - see ROYAL PHILHARMONIC ORCHESTRA	
			CLARK, PETULA	
			English	
1/02/65	1 (2)	13	● 1. **Downtown**	Warner 5494
4/03/65	3	9	2. **I Know A Place**	Warner 5612
7/31/65	22	5	3. You'd Better Come Home	Warner 5643
10/30/65	21	4	4. Round Every Corner	Warner 5661
1/15/66	1 (2)	10	5. **My Love**	Warner 5684
4/02/66	11	7	6. A Sign Of The Times	Warner 5802
7/30/66	9	7	7. **I Couldn't Live Without Your Love**	Warner 5835
10/29/66	21	6	8. Who Am I	Warner 5863
12/31/66	16	7	9. Color My World	Warner 5882
3/18/67	3	9	10. **This Is My Song** -from "A Countess From Hong Kong"	Warner 7002
6/17/67	5	7	11. **Don't Sleep In The Subway**	Warner 7049
9/16/67	26	4	12. The Cat In The Window (The Bird In The Sky)	Warner 7073
12/30/67	31	2	13. The Other Man's Grass Is Always Greener	Warner 7097
3/02/68	15	9	14. Kiss Me Goodbye	Warner 7170
8/24/68	37	1	15. Don't Give Up	Warner 7216
			CLARK, ROY	
7/12/69	19	6	1. Yesterday, When I Was Young	Dot 17246
			CLARK, SANFORD	
			guitar: Al Casey	
8/11/56	7	15	1. **The Fool**	Dot 15481

Glen Campbell's most collectible single, "Guess I'm Dumb," never reached *Billboard*'s Hot 100, let alone the top 40. The 1965 release was written, arranged, and produced by Brian Wilson of the Beach Boys, with whom Glen sometimes performed.

Freddy Cannon. Dick Clark's "American Bandstand" was largely responsible for the popularity of Freddy Cannon, a former truck driver from Boston whose mother co-wrote one of his biggest hits, "Tallahassee Lassie."

The Carpenters. Karen Carpenter had "a heaven-sent voice, like no one before her and no one since" in the words of Burt Bacharach, composer of the Carpenters' breakthrough (and biggest) hit, "Close to You."

The Cars. Boston radio stations helped the Cars get on the road to success. By airing the band's self-recorded material, they attracted A&R men from record companies around the country.

Johnny Cash's best-known pop hit, "A Boy Named Sue," was written by Shel Silverstein, poet, cartoonist (for *Playboy*) and composer of the Dr. Hook smash, "Sylvia's Mother."

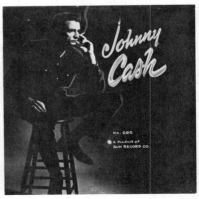

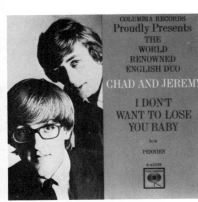

Chad and Jeremy. A folkier version of Peter & Gordon, Chad Stuart and Jeremy Clyde never duplicated U.S. chart achievements in their British homeland.

Ray Charles. The genius of Ray Charles influenced the course of black music and thousands of musicians. Among those in his debt are Nick Ashford and Valerie Simpson, whose first hit came when Ray recorded their song, "Let's Go Get Stoned."

Cheap Trick is the only American rock band (so far!) to secure a career breakthrough on the strength of a live album recorded at Tokyo's Budokan concert hall.

Chubby Checker. "He looks like a little Fats Domino," said Dick Clark's wife about the ex-chicken plucker who was recording material in the Philadelphia studios of Cameo Records. And so Ernest Evans became Chubby Checker.

The Dave Clark 5. Dave Clark was one of the British invasion's shrewdest superstars, managing the group, retaining ownership of all their hits and investing royalties wisely. "We always knew the bubble would burst," he says.

Patsy Cline could "cry on both sides of the microphone," according to Ben Hecht, who wrote the song by which Patsy won the "Arthur Godfrey Talent Scout" show in 1957, "Walking After Midnight."

DATE	POS	WKS	ARTIST—Record Title	LABEL & NO.
			CLARKE, STANLEY/GEORGE DUKE	
6/13/81	19	9	1. Sweet Baby	Epic 01052
			CLARKE, TONY	
5/08/65	31	2	1. The Entertainer	Chess 1924
			CLASH	
			British new wave quartet	
4/26/80	23	7	1. Train In Vain (Stand By Me)	Epic 50851
			CLASSICS	
7/20/63	20	5	1. Till Then	Musicnote 1116
			CLASSICS IV Featuring DENNIS YOST	
1/13/68	3	12	1. Spooky	Imperial 66259
11/16/68	5	12	● 2. Stormy	Imperial 66328
2/22/69	2 (1)	10	3. Traces	Imperial 66352
5/31/69	19	7	4. Everyday With You Girl	Imperial 66378
			DENNIS YOST & THE CLASSICS IV:	
12/09/72	39	3	5. What Am I Crying For?	MGM South 7002
			CLAY, TOM	
7/24/71	8	7	1. **What The World Needs Now Is Love/Abraham, Martin And John [S]** -vocals: The Blackberries-	Mowest 5002
			CLEFTONES	
			quintet from Queens, New York	
6/19/61	18	4	1. Heart And Soul	Gee 1064
			CLIFF, JIMMY	
			Jamaican reggae singer/composer	
12/27/69	25	7	1. Wonderful World, Beautiful People	A&M 1146
			CLIFFORD, BUZZ	
1/30/61	6	10	1. **Baby Sittin' Boogie [N]**	Columbia 41876
			CLIFFORD, MIKE	
10/13/62	12	8	1. Close To Cathy	United Artists 489
			CLIMAX featuring Sonny Geraci	
			Sonny was lead singer of The Outsiders	
1/22/72	3	12	● 1. **Precious And Few**	Carousel 30055
			CLIMAX BLUES BAND	
			English quartet	
3/26/77	3	14	1. **Couldn't Get It Right**	Sire 736
4/04/81	12	17	2. I Love You	Warner 49669
			CLINE, PATSY	
			killed in a plane crash on 3/5/63 (30) with Cowboy Copas and Hawkshaw Hawkins	
3/02/57	12	11	1. Walkin' After Midnight	Decca 30221
7/24/61	12	10	2. I Fall To Pieces	Decca 31205
11/06/61	9	7	3. **Crazy**	Decca 31317
2/24/62	14	8	4. She's Got You	Decca 31354
			CLIQUE	
9/27/69	22	7	1. Sugar On Sunday	White Whale 323

DATE	POS	WKS	ARTIST—Record Title	LABEL & NO.
			CLOONEY, ROSEMARY	
			also see Benny Goodman	
4/13/57	**10**	9	1. **Mangos**	Columbia 40835
			CLOVERS	
			group had 13 consecutive Top 10 R&B hits from '51 thru '54	
7/28/56	**30**	3	1. Love, Love, Love	Atlantic 1094
11/02/59	**23**	5	2. Love Potion No. 9	United Artists 180
			COASTERS	
			Leiber/Stoller wrote and produced nearly all the Coaster's hits	
5/20/57	**3**	22	1. **Searchin'**/	
5/20/57	**8**	11	2. **Young Blood**	Atco 6087
6/09/58	**1** (1)	15	3. **Yakety Yak**	Atco 6116
2/09/59	**2** (3)	12	4. **Charlie Brown** [N]	Atco 6132
6/01/59	**9**	8	5. **Along Came Jones** [N]	Atco 6141
9/07/59	**7**	11	6. **Poison Ivy**/	
9/21/59	**38**	1	7. I'm A Hog For You	Atco 6146
1/25/60	**36**	1	8. Run Red Run	Atco 6153
2/27/61	**37**	2	9. Wait A Minute	Atco 6186
5/29/61	**23**	6	10. Little Egypt (Ying-Yang) [N]	Atco 6192
			COATES, ODIA - see PAUL ANKA	
			COCHRAN, EDDIE	
			died in an auto accident in England on 4/17/60 (21)	
3/30/57	**18**	8	1. Sittin' In The Balcony	Liberty 55056
8/25/58	**8**	12	2. **Summertime Blues**	Liberty 55144
1/05/59	**35**	1	3. C'mon Everybody	Liberty 55166
			COCKBURN, BRUCE	
			Canadian	
5/03/80	**21**	9	1. Wondering Where The Lions Are	Millennium 11786
			COCKER, JOE	
			English	
1/10/70	**30**	7	1. She Came In Through The Bathroom Window	A&M 1147
5/09/70	**7**	9	2. **The Letter**	A&M 1174
			-w/Leon Russell & Shelter People-	
10/24/70	**11**	7	3. Cry Me A River	A&M 1200
6/19/71	**22**	6	4. High Time We Went	A&M 1258
1/29/72	**33**	5	5. Feeling Alright	A&M 1063
			-re-entry of 1969 hit-	
10/07/72	**27**	5	6. Midnight Rider	A&M 1370
			-with The Chris Stainton Band-	
2/15/75	**5**	10	7. **You Are So Beautiful**	A&M 1641
			COCKER, JOE, & JENNIFER WARNES	
10/02/82	**1** (3)	15	1. **Up Where We Belong**	Island 99996
			-love theme from the film "An Officer & A Gentleman"-	
			COFFEY, DENNIS, & The Detroit Guitar Band	
11/13/71	**6**	15	● 1. **Scorpio** [I]	Sussex 226
3/11/72	**18**	8	2. Taurus [I]	Sussex 233

DATE	POS	WKS	ARTIST—Record Title	LABEL & NO.
			COLE, COZY	
			died of cancer 1/29/81 (73)	
9/29/58	3	14	1. **Topsy II/ [I]**	
10/27/58	27	3	2. Topsy I [I]	Love 5004
12/28/58	36	1	3. Turvy II [I]	Love 5014
			COLE, NAT KING	
			formed The King Cole Trio in 1939 - died 2/15/65 (45)	
3/05/55	7	16	1. **Darling Je Vous Aime Beaucoup/**	
3/05/55	23	4	2. The Sand And The Sea	Capitol 3027
5/07/55	2 (1)	20	3. **A Blossom Fell/**	
5/21/55	8	10	4. **If I May**	Capitol 3095
			-with The Four Knights-	
7/16/55	24	2	5. My One Sin	Capitol 3136
10/22/55	13	8	6. Someone You Love/	
11/12/55	21	5	7. Forgive My Heart	Capitol 3234
3/03/56	18	3	8. Ask Me	Capitol 3328
4/21/56	21	6	9. Too Young To Go Steady	Capitol 3390
			-from musical "Strip For Action"-	
7/21/56	16	12	10. That's All There Is To That	Capitol 3456
			-with The Four Knights-	
11/03/56	11	10	11. Night Lights/	
11/10/56	25	2	12. To The Ends Of The Earth	Capitol 3551
2/23/57	18	5	13. Ballerina	Capitol 3619
7/01/57	6	18	14. **Send For Me/**	
8/05/57	21	1	15. My Personal Possession	Capitol 3737
			-with The Four Knights-	
10/21/57	30	4	16. With You On My Mind	Capitol 3782
2/24/58	33	3	17. Angel Smile	Capitol 3860
4/14/58	5	16	18. **Looking Back**	Capitol 3939
7/28/58	38	2	19. Come Closer To Me	Capitol 4004
2/15/60	30	3	20. Time And The River	Capitol 4325
8/18/62	2 (2)	13	21. **Ramblin' Rose**	Capitol 4804
12/01/62	13	8	22. Dear Lonely Hearts	Capitol 4870
5/25/63	6	9	23. **Those Lazy-Hazy-Crazy Days Of Summer**	Capitol 4965
9/28/63	12	9	24. That Sunday, That Summer	Capitol 5027
5/16/64	22	6	25. I Don't Want To Be Hurt Anymore	Capitol 5155
10/24/64	34	4	26. I Don't Want To See Tomorrow	Capitol 5261
			COLE, NATALIE	
			Nat King Cole's daughter	
10/04/75	6	11	1. **This Will Be**	Capitol 4109
2/28/76	32	5	2. Inseparable	Capitol 4193
6/26/76	25	7	3. Sophisticated Lady (She's A Different Lady)	Capitol 4259
2/26/77	5	14	● 4. **I've Got Love On My Mind**	Capitol 4360
2/11/78	10	15	● 5. **Our Love**	Capitol 4509
8/09/80	21	9	6. Someone That I Used To Love	Capitol 4869
			COLLINS, DAVE & ANSIL	
7/03/71	22	8	1. Double Barrel	Big Tree 115

DATE	POS	WKS	ARTIST—Record Title	LABEL & NO.
			COLLINS, DOROTHY	
			star of TV's "Your Hit Parade"	
12/03/55	16	2	1. My Boy - Flat Top	Coral 61510
2/11/56	17	2	2. Seven Days	Coral 61562
			COLLINS, JUDY	
11/23/68	8	9	1. **Both Sides Now**	Elektra 45639
1/09/71	15	11	2. Amazing Grace	Elektra 45709
3/17/73	32	5	3. Cook With Honey	Elektra 45831
7/26/75	36	3	4. Send In The Clowns	Elektra 45253
10/15/77	19	8	5. Send In The Clowns	Elektra 45253
			-re-entry of 1975 hit-	
			COLLINS, PHIL	
			member of Genesis, and Brand X	
4/11/81	19	9	1. I Missed Again	Atlantic 3790
7/11/81	19	8	2. In The Air Tonight	Atlantic 3824
			COLTER, JESSI	
			Waylon Jenning's wife	
4/26/75	4	14	1. **I'm Not Lisa**	Capitol 4009
			COLTRANE, CHI	
9/30/72	17	9	1. Thunder And Lightning	Columbia 45640
			COMMANDER CODY & His Lost Planet Airmen	
			George Frayne is Commander Cody	
4/15/72	9	11	1. **Hot Rod Lincoln [N]**	Paramount 0146
			COMMODORES	
			Lionel Richie, lead singer	
7/06/74	22	6	1. Machine Gun [I]	Motown 1307
6/28/75	19	7	2. Slippery When Wet	Motown 1338
2/14/76	5	14	3. **Sweet Love**	Motown 1381
10/09/76	7	11	4. **Just To Be Close To You**	Motown 1402
2/19/77	39	1	5. Fancy Dancer	Motown 1408
6/25/77	4	13	6. **Easy**	Motown 1418
9/17/77	5	11	7. **Brick House**	Motown 1425
1/14/78	24	7	8. Too Hot Ta Trot	Motown 1432
7/08/78	1 (2)	6	9. **Three Times A Lady**	Motown 1443
11/04/78	38	2	10. Flying High	Motown 1452
8/18/79	4	12	11. **Sail On**	Motown 1466
10/13/79	1 (1)	15	12. **Still**	Motown 1474
1/26/80	25	6	13. Wonderland	Motown 1479
7/12/80	20	11	14. Old-Fashion Love	Motown 1489
7/11/81	8	15	15. **Lady (You Bring Me Up)**	Motown 1514
10/10/81	4	15	16. **Oh No**	Motown 1527
			COMO, PERRY	
			vocalist with Ted Weem's band from 1936 to 1942	
2/05/55	2 (3)	14	1. **Ko Ko Mo (I Love You So)**	RCA 5994
8/13/55	5	14	2. **Tina Marie/**	
8/20/55	20	1	3. Fooled	RCA 6192
11/19/55	11	11	4. All At Once You Love Her	RCA 6294
			-from musical "Pipe Dream"-	

DATE	POS	WKS	ARTIST—Record Title	LABEL & NO.
3/10/56	1 (1)	20	5. **Hot Diggity (Dog Ziggity Boom)/**	
3/10/56	10	10	6. **Juke Box Baby**	RCA 6427
6/16/56	4	14	7. **More/**	
6/23/56	8	12	8. **Glendora**	RCA 6554
8/25/56	18	3	9. Somebody Up There Likes Me	RCA 6590
3/02/57	1 (2)	19	10. **Round And Round**	RCA 6815
5/27/57	13	7	11. The Girl With The Golden Braids	RCA 6904
10/14/57	12	14	12. Just Born (To Be Your Baby)/	
10/21/57	18	8	13. Ivy Rose	RCA 7050
1/13/58	1 (1)	16	● 14. **Catch A Falling Star/**	
1/20/58	4	12	15. **Magic Moments**	RCA 7128
4/21/58	6	11	16. **Kewpie Doll/**	
5/05/58	19	1	17. Dance Only With Me -from musical "Say Darling"-	RCA 7202
8/04/58	28	6	18. Moon Talk	RCA 7274
11/17/58	33	2	19. Love Makes The World Go 'Round	RCA 7353
3/23/59	29	3	20. Tomboy	RCA 7464
2/22/60	22	6	21. Delaware [N]	RCA 7670
4/28/62	23	6	22. Caterina	RCA 8004
7/20/63	39	1	23. (I Love You) Don't You Forget It	RCA 8186
5/01/65	25	6	24. Dream On Little Dreamer	RCA 8533
5/31/69	38	1	25. Seattle -from TV's "Here Come The Brides"-	RCA 9722
12/05/70	10	13	26. **It's Impossible**	RCA 0387
5/19/73	29	8	27. And I Love You So	RCA 0906
			COMO, PERRY, & JAYE P. MORGAN	
6/11/55	12	5	1. Chee Chee-Oo-Chee (Sang The Little Bird)/	
6/25/55	18	1	2. Two Lost Souls -from musical "Damn Yankees"-	RCA 6137
			CON FUNK SHUN	
1/21/78	23	6	1. Ffun	Mercury 73959
2/28/81	40	1	2. Too Tight	Mercury 76089
			CONLEY, ARTHUR	
4/01/67	2 (1)	11	● 1. **Sweet Soul Music**	Atco 6463
7/01/67	31	3	2. Shake, Rattle & Roll	Atco 6494
4/06/68	14	9	3. Funky Street	Atco 6563
			CONNIFF, RAY, & The Singers	
7/09/66	9	9	1. **Somewhere, My Love** -Lara's Theme from "Dr. Zhivago"-	Columbia 43626
			CONNOR, CHRIS	
			with Stan Kenton from '52-'53	
2/16/57	34	3	1. I Miss You So	Atlantic 1105
			CONNORS, NORMAN, Featuring Michael Henderson	
10/02/76	27	10	1. You Are My Starship	Buddah 542
			CONTI, BILL	
5/07/77	1 (1)	13	● 1. **Gonna Fly Now (Theme From "Rocky") [I]**	United Artists 940

DATE	POS	WKS	ARTIST—Record Title	LABEL & NO.
			CONTOURS	
			Detroit sextet	
9/22/62	**3**	11	1. **Do You Love Me**	Gordy 7005
			COOKE, SAM	
			died in a shooting incident 12/11/64 (29)	
10/28/57	**1** (3)	17	1. **You Send Me**	Keen 34013
12/23/57	**18**	10	2. I'll Come Running Back To You	Specialty 619
1/06/58	**17**	7	3. (I Love You) For Sentimental Reasons	Keen 4002
3/24/58	**26**	5	4. Lonely Island/	
3/31/58	**39**	1	5. You Were Made For Me	Keen 4009
9/08/58	**22**	6	6. Win Your Love For Me	Keen 2006
12/15/58	**26**	7	7. Love You Most Of All	Keen 2008
3/30/59	**31**	5	8. Everybody Likes To Cha Cha Cha	Keen 2018
7/06/59	**28**	4	9. Only Sixteen	Keen 2022
5/23/60	**12**	11	10. Wonderful World	Keen 2112
8/29/60	**2** (2)	13	11. **Chain Gang**	RCA 7783
12/19/60	**29**	2	12. Sad Mood	RCA 7816
3/20/61	**31**	4	13. That's It-I Quit-I'm Movin' On	RCA 7853
6/26/61	**17**	9	14. Cupid	RCA 7883
2/17/62	**9**	13	15. **Twistin' The Night Away**	RCA 7983
6/16/62	**17**	9	16. Having A Party/	
8/04/62	**13**	5	17. Bring It On Home To Me	RCA 8036
			-backup vocals by Lou Rawls-	
10/20/62	**12**	8	18. Nothing Can Change This Love	RCA 8088
2/02/63	**13**	8	19. Send Me Some Lovin'	RCA 8129
5/04/63	**10**	9	20. **Another Saturday Night**	RCA 8164
8/17/63	**14**	7	21. Frankie And Johnny	RCA 8215
11/09/63	**11**	8	22. Little Red Rooster	RCA 8247
2/15/64	**11**	7	23. Good News	RCA 8299
6/27/64	**11**	7	24. Good Times/	
7/04/64	**35**	4	25. Tennessee Waltz	RCA 8368
10/24/64	**31**	4	26. Cousin Of Mine	RCA 8426
1/16/65	**7**	9	27. **Shake**/	
2/13/65	**31**	4	28. A Change Is Gonna Come	RCA 8486
8/28/65	**32**	3	29. Sugar Dumpling	RCA 8631
			COOKIES	
			also see Earl-Jean	
12/01/62	**17**	8	1. Chains	Dimension 1002
3/23/63	**7**	9	2. **Don't Say Nothin' Bad (About My Baby)**	Dimension 1008
1/18/64	**33**	4	3. Girls Grow Up Faster Than Boys	Dimension 1020
			COOLEY, EDDIE, & The Dimples	
11/24/56	**20**	8	1. Priscilla	Royal Roost 621
			COOLIDGE, RITA	
6/11/77	**2** (1)	17	● 1. **(Your Love Has Lifted Me) Higher And Higher**	A&M 1922
10/15/77	**7**	13	● 2. **We're All Alone**	A&M 1965
2/04/78	**20**	7	3. The Way You Do The Things You Do	A&M 2004
7/29/78	**25**	6	4. You	A&M 2058

DATE	POS	WKS	ARTIST—Record Title	LABEL & NO.
1/05/80	38	2	5. I'd Rather Leave While I'm In Love	A&M 2199
			COOPER, ALICE	
			real name: Vincent Furnier	
3/20/71	21	8	1. Eighteen	Warner 7449
6/24/72	7	10	2. **School's Out**	Warner 7596
10/21/72	26	6	3. Elected	Warner 7631
3/10/73	35	3	4. Hello Hurray	Warner 7673
5/12/73	25	8	5. No More Mr. Nice Guy	Warner 7691
5/03/75	12	11	6. Only Women	Atlantic 3254
10/30/76	12	14	● 7. I Never Cry	Warner 8228
6/11/77	9	13	8. **You And Me**	Warner 8349
11/11/78	12	11	9. How You Gonna See Me Now	Warner 8695
7/05/80	40	1	10. Clones (We're All)	Warner 49204
			COOPER, LES, & The Soul Rockers	
11/17/62	22	11	1. Wiggle Wobble [I]	Everlast 5019
			COPELAND, KEN	
4/20/57	12	8	1. Pledge Of Love	Imperial 5432
			COREY, JILL	
2/02/57	21	5	1. I Love My Baby (My Baby Loves Me)	Columbia 40794
8/05/57	11	9	2. Love Me To Pieces	Columbia 40955
			CORNELIUS BROTHERS & SISTER ROSE	
			Edward, Carter & Rose Cornelius	
5/15/71	3	13	● 1. **Treat Her Like A Lady**	United Art. 50721
6/17/72	2 (2)	11	● 2. **Too Late To Turn Back Now**	United Art. 50910
9/23/72	23	7	3. Don't Ever Be Lonely (A Poor Little Fool Like Me)	United Art. 50954
2/03/73	37	2	4. I'm Never Gonna Be Alone Anymore	United Art. 50996
			CORNELL, DON	
			vocalist with Sammy Kaye's band	
5/14/55	14	6	1. Most Of All	Coral 61393
9/10/55	7	13	2. **The Bible Tells Me So**/	
11/05/55	26	3	3. Love Is A Many-Splendored Thing	Coral 61467
11/12/55	25	1	4. Young Abe Lincoln	Coral 61521
			CORSAIRS Featuring JAY "BIRD" UZZELL	
1/27/62	12	10	1. Smoky Places	Tuff 1808
			CORTEZ, DAVE 'BABY'	
3/30/59	1 (1)	14	1. **The Happy Organ [I]**	Clock 1009
8/11/62	10	9	2. **Rinky Dink [I]**	Chess 1829
			COSBY, BILL	
9/16/67	4	8	1. **Little Ole Man (Uptight-Everything's Alright) [N]**	Warner 7072
			COSTA, DON, & His Orchestra	
			died on 1/19/83 (57)	
6/27/60	27	4	1. Theme From "The Unforgiven" (The Need For Love) [I]	United Artists 221
8/29/60	19	11	2. Never On Sunday [I]	United Artists 234

DATE	POS	WKS	ARTIST—Record Title	LABEL & NO.
6/05/61	37	3	3. Never On Sunday [I] -re-entry of 1960 hit-	United Artists 234
			COTTON, GENE	
1/22/77	33	3	1. You've Got Me Runnin'	ABC 12227
3/04/78	23	7	2. Before My Heart Finds Out	Ariola 7675
11/11/78	40	2	3. Like A Sunday In Salem (The Amos & Andy Song)	Ariola 7723
			COTTON, GENE, with KIM CARNES	
8/05/78	36	3	1. You're A Part Of Me	Ariola 7704
			COUGAR, JOHN John "Cougar" Mellencamp	
11/10/79	28	7	1. I Need A Lover	Riva 202
11/08/80	27	7	2. This Time	Riva 205
3/14/81	17	12	3. Ain't Even Done With The Night	Riva 207
5/22/82	2 (4)	22	● 4. **Hurts So Good**	Riva 209
8/07/82	1 (4)	17	● 5. **Jack & Diane**	Riva 210
			COUNT FIVE	
9/24/66	5	9	1. **Psychotic Reaction**	Double Shot 104
			COVAY, DON	
8/11/73	29	5	1. I Was Checkin' Out She Was Checkin' In	Mercury 73385
			COVAY, DON, & The Goodtimers	
10/03/64	35	5	1. Mercy, Mercy	Rosemart 801
			COVEN	
10/30/71	26	6	1. One Tin Soldier [The Legend Of Billy Jack]	Warner 7509
			COWBOY CHURCH SUNDAY SCHOOL	
1/01/55	8	21	1. **Open Up Your Heart (And Let The Sunshine In) [N]**	Decca 29367
			COWSILLS Rhode Island family	
10/21/67	2 (2)	12	1. **The Rain, The Park & Other Things**	MGM 13810
2/03/68	21	6	2. We Can Fly	MGM 13886
6/22/68	10	9	3. **Indian Lake**	MGM 13944
3/29/69	2 (2)	13	● 4. **Hair**	MGM 14026
			CRABBY APPLETON Michael Fennelly, lead singer	
6/27/70	36	5	1. Go Back	Elektra 45687
			CRADDOCK, BILLY "CRASH"	
7/27/74	16	9	1. Rub It In	ABC 12013
12/28/74	33	2	2. Ruby, Baby	ABC 12036
			CRAMER, FLOYD played piano on all of Elvis Presley's early RCA recordings	
10/31/60	2 (4)	15	1. **Last Date [I]**	RCA 7775
3/13/61	4	11	2. **On The Rebound [I]**	RCA 7840
6/26/61	8	8	3. **San Antonio Rose [I]**	RCA 7893
2/24/62	36	2	4. Chattanooga Choo Choo [I]	RCA 7978
			CRANE, LES	
10/23/71	8	10	1. Desiderata [S]	Warner 7520

DATE	POS	WKS	ARTIST—Record Title	LABEL & NO.
			CRAWFORD, JOHNNY	
			Mark McCain of TV's "Rifleman"	
6/02/62	8	9	1. **Cindy's Birthday**	Del-Fi 4178
8/25/62	14	6	2. Your Nose Is Gonna Grow	Del-Fi 4181
11/24/62	12	7	3. Rumors	Del-Fi 4188
1/26/63	29	4	4. Proud	Del-Fi 4193
			CRAWFORD, RANDY - see CRUSADERS	
			CRAZY ELEPHANT	
4/05/69	12	8	1. Gimme Gimme Good Lovin'	Bell 763
			CRAZY OTTO	
			real name: Fritz Schulz-Reichel - also see Johnny Maddox	
2/26/55	19	5	1. Glad Rag Doll/ [I]	
2/26/55	21	3	2. Smiles [I]	Decca 29403
			CREAM	
			British: Eric Clapton, Ginger Baker and Jack Bruce	
2/24/68	36	2	1. Sunshine Of Your Love	Atco 6544
7/20/68	5	10	● 2. **Sunshine Of Your Love**	Atco 6544
			-re-entry of earlier 1968 hit-	
10/19/68	6	9	3. **White Room**	Atco 6617
2/08/69	28	6	4. Crossroads	Atco 6646
			CREEDENCE CLEARWATER REVIVAL	
			California quartet led by John Fogerty	
9/28/68	11	9	1. Suzie Q. (Part One)	Fantasy 616
2/08/69	2 (3)	12	● 2. **Proud Mary**	Fantasy 619
5/17/69	2 (1)	12	● 3. **Bad Moon Rising**	Fantasy 622
8/09/69	2 (1)	11	4. **Green River/**	
8/09/69	30	7	5. Commotion	Fantasy 625
11/08/69	3	13	● 6. **Down On The Corner/**	
		13	7. **Fortunate Son**	Fantasy 634
2/07/70	2 (2)	9	● 8. **Travelin' Band/**	
		9	9. **Who'll Stop The Rain**	Fantasy 637
5/02/70	4	10	● 10. **Up Around The Bend**	Fantasy 641
8/15/70	2 (1)	12	● 11. **Lookin' Out My Back Door**	Fantasy 645
2/06/71	8	9	● 12. **Have You Ever Seen The Rain**	Fantasy 655
7/24/71	6	8	13. **Sweet Hitch-Hiker**	Fantasy 665
5/20/72	25	5	14. Someday Never Comes	Fantasy 676
			CRENSHAW, MARSHALL	
8/14/82	36	4	1. Someday, Someway	Warner 29974
			CRESCENDOS	
			also see Dale Ward	
1/20/58	5	14	1. **Oh Julie**	Nasco 6005
			CRESTS	
			New York quartet - Johnny Maestro, lead singer	
12/22/58	2 (2)	14	1. **16 Candles**	Coed 506
4/13/59	28	7	2. Six Nights A Week	Coed 509
9/14/59	22	9	3. The Angels Listened In	Coed 515
4/04/60	14	8	4. Step By Step	Coed 525

DATE	POS	WKS	ARTIST—Record Title	LABEL & NO.
7/18/60	20	8	5. Trouble In Paradise	Coed 531
			CREW-CUTS	
			Canadian quartet	
1/29/55	**3**	13	1. **Earth Angel/**	
1/29/55	**6**	12	2. **Ko Ko Mo (I Love You So)**	Mercury 70529
4/30/55	**14**	8	3. Don't Be Angry	Mercury 70597
6/25/55	**16**	7	4. A Story Untold	Mercury 70634
8/27/55	**10**	8	5. **Gum Drop**	Mercury 70668
12/17/55	**11**	15	6. Angels In The Sky/	
1/07/56	**31**	8	7. Mostly Martha	Mercury 70741
2/18/56	**18**	5	8. Seven Days	Mercury 70782
1/26/57	**17**	3	9. Young Love	Mercury 71022
			CREWE, BOB, Generation	
1/21/67	**15**	7	1. Music To Watch Girls By [I]	DynoVoice 229
			CRICKETS	
			Lubbock, Texas quartet: Buddy Holly, Jerry Allison, Joe Mauldin & Niki Sullivan (left Nov.'57)	
8/19/57	**1** (1)	16	● 1. **That'll Be The Day**	Brunswick 55009
12/02/57	**10**	13	2. **Oh, Boy!**	Brunswick 55035
3/10/58	**17**	8	3. Maybe Baby	Brunswick 55053
8/04/58	**27**	4	4. Think It Over	Brunswick 55072
			CRITTERS	
9/03/66	**17**	8	1. Mr. Dieingly Sad	Kapp 769
8/05/67	**39**	3	2. Don't Let The Rain Fall Down On Me	Kapp 838
			CROCE, JIM	
			killed in a plane crash on 9/20/73 (30)	
7/22/72	**8**	10	1. **You Don't Mess Around With Jim**	ABC 11328
11/04/72	**17**	8	2. Operator (That's Not The Way It Feels)	ABC 11335
3/17/73	**37**	3	3. One Less Set Of Footsteps	ABC 11346
6/02/73	**1** (2)	16	● 4. **Bad, Bad Leroy Brown**	ABC 11359
10/13/73	**10**	13	5. **I Got A Name**	ABC 11389
			-from film "Last American Hero"-	
12/01/73	**1** (2)	12	● 6. **Time In A Bottle**	ABC 11405
3/16/74	**9**	11	7. **I'll Have To Say I Love You In A Song**	ABC 11424
6/29/74	**32**	6	8. Workin' At The Car Wash Blues	ABC 11447
			CROSBY, BING	
			began career with Paul Whiteman in 1926 -- died on 10/14/77 (76)	
12/31/55	**7**	2	1. **White Christmas [X]**	Decca 29342
			-originally charted December, 1942, and re-entered the pop charts for 18 more seasons-	
10/21/57	**25**	1	2. Around The World (In Eighty Days)	Decca 30262
12/23/57	**34**	2	3. White Christmas [X]	Decca 29342
12/19/60	**26**	2	4. White Christmas [X]	Decca 23778
12/18/61	**12**	3	5. White Christmas [X]	Decca 23778
12/29/62	**38**	1	6. White Christmas [X]	Decca 23778
			CROSBY, BING, & GRACE KELLY	
			Grace died in an auto accident on 9/14/82 (52)	
10/06/56	**3**	22	1. **True Love**	Capitol 3507
			-from the film "High Society"-	

Nat 'King' Cole's biggest hit, "Nature Boy," was written by eden ahbez, a Brooklyn spiritualist who believed that only gods should use capital letters in their names.

Phil Collins. As a child actor, Phil Collins appeared in a stage version of Dickens' *Oliver Twist* in the role of the Artful Dodger. As a member of Genesis, he dodged rock critics for years.

Perry Como. The world's most relaxed singer, Perry Como collected his first million-seller with a vocal version of Chopin's *Polonaise In A,* "Till The End of Time."

Sam Cooke. Singing aside, Sam Cooke formed one of the first black-owned record labels, Sar, with such artists as Johnnie Taylor and the Valentinos with Bobby Womack.

Rita Coolidge once sang with the Mad Dogs & Englishmen entourage of Joe Cocker, whose "Delta Lady" hit was written for Rita by Leon Russell.

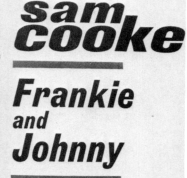

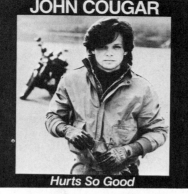

Hurts So Good

Alice Cooper. The spectacle that was Alice Cooper in the '70s began life the previous decade as a British soundalike band, the Earwigs. They mutated into the Spiders and then signed with Frank Zappa's record label.

John Cougar says that the artist who most influenced his style was Detroit's Mitch Ryder. The '80s rocker is already halfway to matching Ryder's four top 20 hits.

The Cowsills were a family affair: the wife, daughter, and four sons of an ex-Navy officer who ran up $100,000 in debts trying to establish the group. "The Rain, The Park And Other Things" finally did the trick.

Creedence Clearwater Revival. What's in a name? The Golliwogs were signed to Fantasy Records for three years without a hit, but when they became Creedence Clearwater Revival—shazam!

Crosby, Stills & Nash. Upon signing Crosby, Stills & Nash to Atlantic Records in 1969, company chairman Ahmet Ertegun predicted that the group would have "the vocal impact of the Everly Brothers." If you say so, Ahmet.

DATE	POS	WKS	ARTIST—Record Title	LABEL & NO.
			CROSBY, DAVID, & GRAHAM NASH	
6/10/72	36	4	1. Immigration Man	Atlantic 2873
			CROSBY, STILLS & NASH	
			David Crosby, Stephen Stills & Graham Nash	
8/02/69	28	6	1. Marrakesh Express	Atlantic 2652
10/25/69	21	9	2. Suite: Judy Blue Eyes	Atlantic 2676
7/02/77	7	12	3. **Just A Song Before I Go**	Atlantic 3401
7/03/82	9	12	4. **Wasted On The Way**	Atlantic 4058
10/09/82	18	9	5. Southern Cross	Atlantic 89969
			CROSBY, STILLS, NASH & YOUNG	
			David Crosby, Stephen Stills, Graham Nash & Neil Young	
4/04/70	11	10	1. Woodstock	Atlantic 2723
6/20/70	16	9	2. Teach Your Children	Atlantic 2735
7/11/70	14	7	3. Ohio	Atlantic 2740
10/10/70	30	6	4. Our House	Atlantic 2760
			CROSS COUNTRY	
			group evolved from The Tokens	
9/22/73	30	4	1. In The Midnight Hour	Atco 6934
			CROSS, CHRISTOPHER	
3/01/80	2 (4)	17	1. **Ride Like The Wind**	Warner 49184
7/05/80	1 (1)	13	2. **Sailing**	Warner 49507
10/25/80	15	12	3. Never Be The Same	Warner 49580
4/25/81	20	7	4. Say You'll Be Mine	Warner 49705
8/29/81	1 (3)	17	● 5. **Arthur's Theme (Best That You Can Do)**	Warner 49787
			CROW	
11/29/69	19	10	1. Evil Woman Don't Play Your Games With Me	Amaret 112
			CROWELL, RODNEY	
			Rosanne Cash's husband	
6/28/80	37	2	1. Ashes By Now	Warner 49224
			CRUSADERS	
10/27/79	36	3	1. Street Life	MCA 41054
			-vocal by Randy Crawford-	
			CRYSTALS	
			Brooklyn female quintet founded by producer Phil Spector	
12/11/61	20	7	1. There's No Other (Like My Baby)	Philles 100
4/28/62	13	8	2. Uptown	Philles 102
10/06/62	1 (2)	12	3. **He's A Rebel**	Philles 106
1/19/63	11	8	4. He's Sure The Boy I Love	Philles 109
5/11/63	3	10	5. **Da Doo Ron Ron (When He Walked Me Home)**	Philles 112
8/31/63	6	9	6. **Then He Kissed Me**	Philles 115
			CUFF LINKS	
10/04/69	9	9	1. **Tracy**	Decca 32533
			CUMMINGS, BURTON	
			lead singer of The Guess Who	
11/06/76	10	15	● 1. **Stand Tall**	Portrait 70001
10/24/81	37	2	2. You Saved My Soul	Alfa 7008

DATE	POS	WKS	ARTIST—Record Title	LABEL & NO.
			CURB, MIKE, Congregation	
2/27/71	34	4	1. Burning Bridges -from the film "Kelly's Heroes"-	MGM 14151
			CYMARRON	
7/17/71	17	7	1. Rings	Entrance 7500
			CYMBAL, JOHNNY	
			also see Derek	
3/16/63	16	8	1. Mr. Bass Man [N]	Kapp 503
			CYRKLE	
			American group handled by The Beatles' manager Brian Epstein	
6/04/66	2 (1)	11	1. **Red Rubber Ball**	Columbia 43589
8/27/66	16	5	2. Turn-Down Day	Columbia 43729
			DADDY DEWDROP	
			Richard Monda	
4/10/71	9	11	1. **Chick-A-Boom (Don't Ya Jes' Love It)**	Sunflower 105
			DADDY-O'S	
6/23/58	39	3	1. Got A Match? [I]	Cabot 122
			DALE & GRACE	
			Dale Houston & Grace Broussard	
10/26/63	1 (2)	12	1. **I'm Leaving It Up To You**	Montel 921
2/08/64	8	7	2. **Stop And Think It Over**	Montel 922
			DALE, ALAN	
4/30/55	14	7	1. Cherry Pink (And Apple Blossom White) -from the film "Under Water!"-	Coral 61373
7/02/55	10	7	2. **Sweet And Gentle**	Coral 61435
			DALTREY, ROGER	
			lead singer of The Who	
10/25/80	20	8	1. Without Your Love	Polydor 2121
			DAMON('S), LIZ, ORIENT EXPRESS	
1/30/71	33	3	1. 1900 Yesterday	White Whale 368
			DAMONE, VIC	
6/02/56	4	16	1. **On The Street Where You Live** -from musical "My Fair Lady"-	Columbia 40654
9/30/57	16	4	2. An Affair To Remember (Our Love Affair)	Columbia 40945
5/22/65	30	4	3. You Were Only Fooling (While I Was Falling In Love)	Warner 5616
			DANA, VIC	
4/25/64	27	5	1. Shangri-La	Dolton 92
3/06/65	10	8	2. **Red Roses For A Blue Lady**	Dolton 304
6/04/66	30	4	3. I Love You Drops	Dolton 319
			DANCER, PRANCER & NERVOUS [The Singing Reindeer]	
12/28/59	34	1	1. The Happy Reindeer [X-N]	Capitol 4300
			DANIELS, CHARLIE, Band	
7/21/73	9	9	1. **Uneasy Rider** [N]	Kama Sutra 576
3/15/75	29	3	2. The South's Gonna Do It	Kama Sutra 598
7/21/79	3	12	● 3. **The Devil Went Down To Georgia**	Epic 50700

DATE	POS	WKS	ARTIST—Record Title	LABEL & NO.
6/28/80	11	8	4. In America	Epic 50888
9/27/80	31	4	5. The Legend Of Wooley Swamp	Epic 50921
4/17/82	22	8	6. Still In Saigon	Epic 02828
			DANLEERS	
6/30/58	7	10	1. **One Summer Night**	Mercury 71322
			DANNY & THE JUNIORS	
			Danny Rapp, lead singer of quartet from Philadelphia	
12/09/57	1 (7)	18	1. **At The Hop**	ABC-Paramount 9871
3/10/58	19	7	2. Rock And Roll Is Here To Stay	ABC-Paramount 9888
7/21/58	39	1	3. Dottie	ABC-Paramount 9926
10/10/60	27	3	4. Twistin' U.S.A.	Swan 4060
			DANTE & The EVERGREENS	
			Dante Drowty	
6/13/60	15	8	1. Alley-Oop [N]	Madison 130
			DARIN, BOBBY	
			died on 12/20/73 (37) - also see Rinky-Dinks	
6/30/58	3	13	1. **Splish Splash**	Atco 6117
10/27/58	9	14	2. **Queen Of The Hop**	Atco 6127
2/23/59	38	2	3. Plain Jane	Atco 6133
5/04/59	2 (1)	13	4. **Dream Lover**	Atco 6140
9/07/59	1 (9)	22	5. **Mack The Knife**	Atco 6147
1/25/60	6	11	6. **Beyond The Sea**	Atco 6158
4/04/60	21	6	7. Clementine	Atco 6161
6/20/60	19	5	8. Won't You Come Home Bill Bailey	Atco 6167
10/17/60	20	8	9. Artificial Flowers -from the musical "Tenderloin"-	Atco 6179
2/20/61	14	7	10. Lazy River	Atco 6188
7/10/61	40	1	11. Nature Boy	Atco 6196
9/11/61	5	9	12. **You Must Have Been A Beautiful Baby**	Atco 6206
1/13/62	15	8	13. Irresistible You/	
1/20/62	30	5	14. Multiplication -from film "Come September"-	Atco 6214
4/14/62	24	5	15. What'd I Say (Part 1)	Atco 6221
7/21/62	3	9	16. **Things**	Atco 6229
10/27/62	32	3	17. If A Man Answers	Capitol 4837
2/02/63	3	12	18. **You're The Reason I'm Living**	Capitol 4897
5/25/63	10	7	19. **18 Yellow Roses**	Capitol 4970
10/08/66	8	9	20. **If I Were A Carpenter**	Atlantic 2350
2/11/67	32	3	21. Lovin' You	Atlantic 2376
			DARREN, JAMES	
11/06/61	3	12	1. **Goodbye Cruel World**	Colpix 609
2/17/62	6	8	2. **Her Royal Majesty**	Colpix 622
5/05/62	11	7	3. Conscience	Colpix 630
8/04/62	39	1	4. Mary's Little Lamb	Colpix 644

DATE	POS	WKS	ARTIST—Record Title	LABEL & NO.
2/18/67	35	2	5. All -from film "Run For Your Wife"-	Warner 5874
			DARTELLS	
4/27/63	11	9	1. Hot Pastrami	Dot 16453
			DAVID & JONATHAN Roger Greenaway & Roger Cook	
1/29/66	18	5	1. Michelle	Capitol 5563
			DAVIS, MAC	
8/05/72	**1** (3)	13	1. **Baby Don't Get Hooked On Me**	Columbia 45618
5/25/74	11	14	2. One Hell Of A Woman	Columbia 46004
9/07/74	9	10	3. **Stop And Smell The Roses**	Columbia 10018
12/21/74	15	8	4. Rock N' Roll (I Gave You The Best Years Of My Life)	Columbia 10070
			DAVIS, PAUL	
12/07/74	23	8	1. Ride 'Em Cowboy	Bang 712
9/11/76	35	3	2. Superstar	Bang 726
10/29/77	7	25	3. **I Go Crazy**	Bang 733
10/07/78	17	12	4. Sweet Life	Bang 738
4/12/80	23	6	5. Do Right	Bang 4808
11/28/81	11	13	6. Cool Night	Arista 0645
3/20/82	6	13	7. **'65 Love Affair**	Arista 0661
8/28/82	40	2	8. Love Or Let Me Be Lonely	Arista 0697
			DAVIS, SAMMY, JR.	
5/28/55	9	12	1. **Something's Gotta Give/** -from film "Daddy Long Legs"-	
6/25/55	20	1	2. Love Me Or Leave Me	Decca 29484
7/02/55	13	6	3. That Old Black Magic	Decca 29541
10/06/62	17	10	4. What Kind Of Fool Am I -from the musical "Stop The World - I Want To Get Off"-	Reprise 20048
2/01/64	17	9	5. The Shelter Of Your Arms	Reprise 20216
6/24/67	37	4	6. Don't Blame The Children [S]	Reprise 0566
1/18/69	11	11	7. I've Gotta Be Me -from musical "Golden Rainbow"-	Reprise 0779
4/15/72	**1** (3)	16	● 8. **The Candy Man** -from the film "Willy Wonka & The Chocolate Factory"-	MGM 14320
			DAVIS, SKEETER	
9/05/60	39	1	1. (I Can't Help You) I'm Falling Too	RCA 7767
1/16/61	26	2	2. My Last Date (With You)	RCA 7825
2/16/63	**2** (1)	13	3. **The End Of The World**	RCA 8098
9/21/63	7	11	4. **I Can't Stay Mad At You**	RCA 8219
			DAVIS, SPENCER, Group British quartet - Steve Winwood, lead singer	
1/28/67	7	9	1. **Gimme Some Lovin'**	United Artists 50108
4/08/67	10	7	2. **I'm A Man**	United Artists 50144
			DAVIS, TYRONE	
1/04/69	5	11	● 1. **Can I Change My Mind**	Dakar 602
4/12/69	34	2	2. Is It Something You've Got	Dakar 605

DATE	POS	WKS	ARTIST—Record Title	LABEL & NO.
4/04/70	3	11	● 3. **Turn Back The Hands Of Time**	Dakar 616
8/25/73	32	3	4. There It Is	Dakar 4523
10/30/76	38	4	5. Give It Up (Turn It Loose)	Columbia 10388
			DAWN	
			Tony Orlando, Joyce Wilson & Telma Hopkins	
8/29/70	3	13	● 1. **Candida**	Bell 903
12/05/70	1 (3)	16	● 2. **Knock Three Times**	Bell 938
4/10/71	25	5	3. I Play And Sing	Bell 970
7/10/71	33	6	4. Summer Sand	Bell 45107
			DAWN FEATURING TONY ORLANDO:	
11/13/71	39	1	5. What Are You Doing Sunday	Bell 45141
3/17/73	1 (4)	17	● 6. **Tie A Yellow Ribbon Round The Ole Oak Tree**	Bell 45318
7/28/73	3	13	● 7. **Say, Has Anybody Seen My Sweet Gypsy Rose**	Bell 45374
			TONY ORLANDO & DAWN:	
12/01/73	27	7	8. Who's In The Strawberry Patch With Sally	Bell 45424
9/07/74	7	9	9. **Steppin' Out (Gonna Boogie Tonight)**	Bell 45601
1/11/75	11	8	10. Look In My Eyes Pretty Woman	Bell 45620
3/29/75	1 (3)	10	● 11. **He Don't Love You (Like I Love You)**	Elektra 45240
7/12/75	14	6	12. Mornin' Beautiful	Elektra 45260
9/20/75	34	3	13. You're All I Need To Get By	Elektra 45275
2/21/76	22	6	14. Cupid	Elektra 45302
			DAY, BOBBY	
			member of The Hollywood Flames	
8/04/58	2 (2)	19	1. **Rock-In Robin**	Class 229
			DAY, DORIS	
			vocalist with Les Brown's band	
7/23/55	13	9	1. I'll Never Stop Loving You -from film "Love Me Or Leave Me"-	Columbia 40505
7/07/56	2 (3)	22	2. **Whatever Will Be, Will Be (Que Sera, Sera)** -from film "The Man Who Knew Too Much"-	Columbia 40704
7/21/58	6	12	3. **Everybody Loves A Lover**	Columbia 41195
			DAZZ BAND	
			8-man ultrafunk band - formerly known as Kinsman Dazz	
5/15/82	5	16	1. **Let It Whip**	Motown 1609
			DEAL, BILL, & THE RHONDELS	
3/15/69	39	1	1. May I	Heritage 803
5/31/69	35	3	2. I've Been Hurt	Heritage 812
9/13/69	23	5	3. What Kind Of Fool Do You Think I Am	Heritage 817
			DEAN & JEAN	
			Welton Young & Brenda Lee Jones	
3/21/64	32	3	1. Hey Jean, Hey Dean	Rust 5075
12/14/68	35	2	2. Tra La La La Suzy	Rust 5067
			DEAN, JIMMY	
1/06/58	32	1	1. Little Sandy Sleighfoot [X-N]	Columbia 41025
10/09/61	1 (5)	13	● 2. **Big Bad John**	Columbia 42175
1/20/62	24	3	3. Dear Ivan [S]	Columbia 42259
2/10/62	22	5	4. The Cajun Queen/ [S]	Columbia 42282
2/10/62	26	5	5. To A Sleeping Beauty [S] -background music: "Memories"-	

DATE	POS	WKS	ARTIST—Record Title	LABEL & NO.
4/14/62	8	9	6. P.T. 109	Columbia 42338
10/06/62	29	5	7. Little Black Book	Columbia 42529
5/22/76	35	2	● 8. I.O.U. [S]	Casino 052
			DE CASTRO SISTERS	
			Peggy, Babette & Cherie	
5/07/55	17	4	1. Boom Boom Boomerang -bass voice: Thurl Ravenscroft-	Abbott 3003
			DEE, JOEY, & The Starliters	
12/04/61	1 (3)	14	1. **Peppermint Twist - Part 1** -inspired by New York's 'Peppermint Lounge'-	Roulette 4401
3/03/62	20	4	2. Hey, Let's Twist	Roulette 4408
3/31/62	6	9	3. **Shout - Part 1**	Roulette 4416
9/15/62	18	6	4. What Kind Of Love Is This -from "Two Tickets To Paris"-	Roulette 4438
6/01/63	36	1	5. Hot Pastrami With Mashed Potatoes - Part I	Roulette 4488
			DEE, JOHNNY	
			John D. Loudermilk	
4/06/57	38	1	1. Sittin' In The Balcony	Colonial 430
			DEE, KIKI	
			also see Elton John	
10/19/74	12	10	1. I've Got The Music In Me	Rocket 40293
			DEE, LENNY	
2/12/55	19	15	1. Plantation Boogie [I]	Decca 29360
			DEE, TOMMY, with Carol Kay & the Teen-Aires	
4/13/59	11	8	1. Three Stars [S] -inspired by the Buddy Holly plane crash-	Crest 1057
			DEEP PURPLE	
			British quintet led by Ritchie Blackmore	
8/24/68	4	9	1. **Hush**	Tetragrammaton 1503
12/07/68	38	3	2. Kentucky Woman	Tetragrammaton 1508
6/16/73	4	12	● 3. **Smoke On The Water**	Warner 7710
			DEES, RICK, & His Cast Of Idiots	
			Memphis disc jockey	
9/04/76	1 (1)	16	★ 1. Disco Duck (Part 1) [N]	'RSO 857
			DeFRANCO FAMILY featuring Tony DeFranco	
9/29/73	3	14	● 1. **Heartbeat - It's A Lovebeat**	20th Century 2030
1/26/74	32	4	2. Abra-Ca-Dabra	20th Century 2070
5/25/74	18	6	3. Save The Last Dance For Me	20th Century 2088
			DE JOHN SISTERS	
			Julie & Dux DeGiovanni	
12/25/54	6	13	1. **(My Baby Don't Love Me) No More**	Epic 9085
			DEKKER, DESMOND, & THE ACES	
6/07/69	9	7	1. **Israelites**	Uni 55129

DATE	POS	WKS	ARTIST—Record Title	LABEL & NO.
			DELANEY & BONNIE & FRIENDS	
			Delaney & Bonnie Bramlett	
6/26/71	13	10	1. Never Ending Song Of Love	Atco 6804
10/09/71	20	7	2. Only You Know And I Know	Atco 6838
			DELEGATES	
11/04/72	8	6	1. **Convention '72 [N]**	Mainstream 5525
			DELFONICS	
			Philadelphia trio	
2/24/68	4	12	1. **La - La - Means I Love You**	Philly Groove 150
10/05/68	35	4	2. Break Your Promise	Philly Groove 152
1/25/69	35	1	3. Ready Or Not Here I Come (Can't Hide From Love)	Philly Groove 154
10/04/69	40	2	4. You Got Yours And I'll Get Mine	Philly Groove 157
2/07/70	10	10	● 5. **Didn't I (Blow Your Mind This Time)**	Philly Groove 161
7/25/70	40	1	6. Trying To Make A Fool Of Me	Philly Groove 162
			DELL-VIKINGS	
3/02/57	4	22	1. **Come Go With Me**	Dot 15538
7/15/57	9	13	2. **Whispering Bells**	Dot 15592
7/15/57	12	1	3. Cool Shake	Mercury 71132
			DELLS	
			Chicago-area quintet	
2/17/68	20	7	1. There Is	Cadet 5590
7/20/68	10	10	2. **Stay In My Corner**	Cadet 5612
			-originally released in 1965-	
11/02/68	18	5	3. Always Together	Cadet 5621
2/08/69	38	2	4. Does Anybody Know I'm Here	Cadet 5631
6/21/69	22	6	5. I Can Sing A Rainbow/Love Is Blue	Cadet 5641
8/23/69	10	10	6. **Oh, What A Night**	Cadet 5649
			-original version made the R&B charts in 1956-	
9/18/71	30	6	7. The Love We Had (Stays On My Mind)	Cadet 5683
6/23/73	34	2	● 8. Give Your Baby A Standing Ovation	Cadet 5696
			DEMENSIONS	
8/08/60	16	9	1. Over The Rainbow	Mohawk 116
			DENNY, MARTIN [The Exotic Sounds of]	
4/27/59	4	13	1. **Quiet Village [I]**	Liberty 55162
11/16/59	28	2	2. The Enchanted Sea [I]	Liberty 55212
			DENVER, JOHN	
6/26/71	2 (1)	14	● 1. **Take Me Home, Country Roads**	RCA 0445
			-with Fat City-	
1/06/73	9	12	2. Rocky Mountain High	RCA 0829
2/16/74	1 (1)	13	● 3. **Sunshine On My Shoulders**	RCA 0213
6/15/74	1 (2)	11	● 4. **Annie's Song**	RCA 0295
10/05/74	5	10	● 5. **Back Home Again**	RCA 10065
1/11/75	13	8	6. Sweet Surrender	RCA 10148
4/05/75	1 (1)	15	● 7. **Thank God I'm A Country Boy**	RCA 10239
8/30/75	1 (1)	13	● 8. **I'm Sorry/**	RCA 10239
		7	9. **Calypso**	RCA 10353
			-inspired by Jacques Cousteau's ship "Calypso"-	

DATE	POS	WKS	ARTIST—Record Title	LABEL & NO.
12/13/75	13	9	10. Fly Away -background vocal: Olivia Newton-John-	RCA 10517
3/20/76	29	4	11. Looking For Space	RCA 10586
10/02/76	36	2	12. Like A Sad Song	RCA 10774
4/30/77	32	3	13. My Sweet Lady -also flip side of RCA 10239-	RCA 10911
9/05/81	36	4	14. Some Days Are Diamonds (Some Days Are Stone)	RCA 12246
4/24/82	31	5	15. Shanghai Breezes	RCA 13071
			DEODATO Eumir Deodato	
2/17/73	**2** (1)	10	1. **Also Sprach Zarathustra (2001) [I]**	CTI 12
			DEREK Derek is actually Johnny Cymbal	
11/23/68	**11**	11	1. Cinnamon	Bang 558
			DEREK & THE DOMINOS Derek is Eric Clapton	
6/17/72	**10**	10	1. **Layla** -re-entry of 1971 hit-	Atco 6809
			DERRINGER, RICK lead singer of The McCoys and member of Johnny and Edgar Winters' bands	
3/02/74	**23**	6	1. Rock And Roll, Hoochie Koo	Blue Sky 2751
			DeSARIO, TERI, with K.C. K.C. of KC & The Sunshine Band	
12/22/79	**2** (2)	16	● 1. **Yes, I'm Ready**	Casablanca 2227
			DeSHANNON, JACKIE	
6/19/65	**7**	9	1. **What The World Needs Now Is Love**	Imperial 66110
7/26/69	**4**	10	● 2. **Put A Little Love In Your Heart**	Imperial 66385
12/06/69	**40**	1	3. Love Will Find A Way	Imperial 66419
			DESMOND, JOHNNY	
3/26/55	**6**	11	1. **Play Me Hearts And Flowers (I Wanna Cry)**	Coral 61379
8/13/55	**3**	16	2. **The Yellow Rose Of Texas**	Coral 61476
12/03/55	**17**	1	3. Sixteen Tons	Coral 61529
			DETERGENTS	
12/19/64	**19**	6	1. Leader Of The Laundromat [N]	Roulette 4590
			DETROIT EMERALDS	
2/19/72	**36**	4	1. You Want It, You Got It	Westbound 192
7/29/72	**24**	7	2. Baby Let Me Take You (In My Arms)	Westbound 203
			DeVAUGHN, WILLIAM	
5/18/74	**4**	10	● 1. **Be Thankful For What You Got**	Roxbury 0236
			DEVO	
10/04/80	**14**	15	● 1. **Whip It**	Warner 49550
			DeVORZON, BARRY, & PERRY BOTKIN, JR. also see Barry & The Tamerlanes	
10/02/76	**8**	16	● 1. **Nadia's Theme (The Young And The Restless) [I]** -previously entitled "Cotton's Dream"-	A&M 1856

Bobby Darin. An unusual battle developed between Bobby Darin and Buddy Holly in 1958 with "Early In The Morning." Bobby co-wrote the song and recorded it under the name of Rinky Dinks, but Buddy's rush-released cover version almost matched the original's chart placing.

Neil Diamond has been a superstar for almost 20 years, but how many know his song "Santa Santa," recorded by a teenage group from the Philippines (the Rocky Fellers) for Christmas 1962?

The Diamonds mined more than one dozen top 40 hits in the '50s, frequently by covering R&B originals by Frankie Lymon and the Teenagers, the Willows, the Gladiolas, the G-Clefs, the Clovers, and the Rays.

Dion wrote many of his own early '60s chart records, among them "Runaround Sue," "Lovers Who Wander," and "Donna The Prima Donna." His sometimes collaborator was Ernie Maresca, whose "Shout! Shout!" was a 1962 top 10 success.

Carl Dobkins' "My Heart Is An Open Book," was one of lyricist Hal David's pre-Burt Bacharach hits. His partner for that ditty was Lee Pockriss, among whose other achievements was "Teeny Weeny Yellow Polka Dot Bikini."

Fats Domino. After a factory accident badly injured Fats Domino's piano-playing hands, doctors thought he would need to have them amputated. They were wrong, however, and rock'n'roll was the beneficiary.

MACK THE KNIFE
WAS THERE A CALL FOR ME

ATCO 6147

BOBBY DARIN

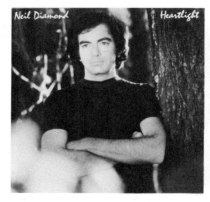

Neil Diamond — Heartlight

HIGH SIGN
DON'T LET ME DOWN
THE DIAMONDS
Mercury 71291

DION
LAURIE 3070
"LONELY TEENAGER"
"LITTLE MISS BLUE"

CARL DOBKINS, Jr.
DECCA RECORDS
LUCKY DEVIL
(There's A Little Song A-Singing)
IN MY HEART
9-31020

I WANT YOU TO KNOW
THE BIG BEAT
Fats Domino Sings
IMPERIAL 5477/45-5477

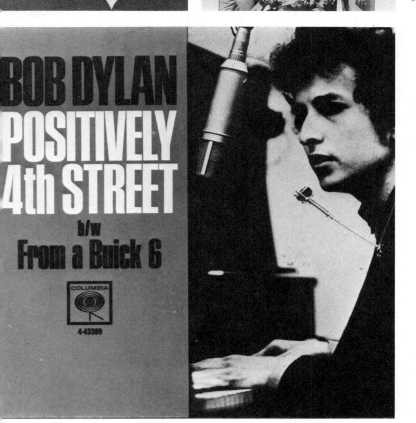

The Doobie Brothers' biggest hit, "What A Fool Believes," won Grammy awards in 1978 as record of the year and song of the year. It was produced by onetime member of Harper's Bizarre, Ted Templeman.

The Doors. An explicit performance of "The End" was said to have caused the Doors to be ejected from the Whiskey A Go-Go in Los Angeles, only the first of many such incidents during the band's career. The song was later used in the soundtrack of "Apocalypse Now."

Joe Dowell. Elvis Presley sang "Wooden Heart" in his movie "G.I. Blues," but when RCA Records didn't release the performance as a single, Nashville producer Shelby Singleton rush-released Joe Dowell's version.

The Drifters. There have been literally dozens of Drifters during the past three decades, and one member from the '50s, Johnny Moore, is still with the group today.

Bob Dylan. Minnesota-born Bob Zimmerman made his first trip East in February, 1961, to visit the Greystone Park Hospital in Greystone Park, New Jersey. The patient he saw was Woody Guthrie.

DATE	POS	WKS	ARTIST—Record Title	LABEL & NO.
			DEVOTIONS	
4/04/64	36	1	1. Rip Van Winkle [N]	Roulette 4541
			DeYOUNG, CLIFF	
2/16/74	17	8	1. My Sweet Lady -from TV soundtrack "Sunshine"-	MCA 40156
			DIAMOND, LEO, with Orchestra	
2/19/55	30	1	1. Melody Of Love [I]	RCA 5973
			DIAMOND, NEIL	
			also see Barbra Streisand	
9/10/66	6	9	1. **Cherry, Cherry**	Bang 528
11/26/66	16	6	2. I Got The Feelin' (Oh No No)	Bang 536
2/11/67	18	5	3. You Got To Me	Bang 540
4/29/67	10	8	4. **Girl, You'll Be A Woman Soon**	Bang 542
8/05/67	13	7	5. I Thank The Lord For The Night Time	Bang 547
10/28/67	22	6	6. Kentucky Woman	Bang 551
3/29/69	22	7	7. Brother Love's Travelling Salvation Show	Uni 55109
7/12/69	4	12	● 8. **Sweet Caroline (Good Times Never Seemed So Good)**	Uni 55136
11/15/69	6	12	● 9. **Holly Holy**	Uni 55175
3/21/70	24	8	10. Shilo	Bang 575
5/16/70	30	4	11. Soolaimon (African Trilogy II)	Uni 55224
8/15/70	21	7	12. Solitary Man -re-entry of Neil's first hit-	Bang 578
8/29/70	1 (1)	14	● 13. **Cracklin' Rosie**	Uni 55250
11/21/70	20	9	14. He Ain't Heavy…He's My Brother	Uni 55264
12/05/70	36	5	15. Do It -also flip side of Bang 519-	Bang 580
4/03/71	4	8	16. **I Am…I Said**	Uni 55278
11/27/71	14	7	17. Stones	Uni 55310
5/13/72	1 (1)	12	● 18. **Song Sung Blue**	Uni 55326
9/02/72	11	7	19. Play Me	Uni 55346
11/25/72	17	8	20. Walk On Water	Uni 55352
4/21/73	31	4	21. "Cherry Cherry" from Hot August Night -live version of 1966 hit-	MCA 40017
11/24/73	34	3	22. Be -from film "Jonathan Livingston Seagull"-	Columbia 45942
10/19/74	5	10	23. **Longfellow Serenade**	Columbia 10043
3/01/75	34	2	24. I've Been This Way Before	Columbia 10084
6/26/76	11	8	25. If You Know What I Mean	Columbia 10366
12/24/77	16	9	26. Desiree	Columbia 10657
2/17/79	20	6	27. Forever In Blue Jeans	Columbia 10897
1/19/80	17	10	28. September Morn'	Columbia 11175
11/01/80	2 (3)	17	29. **Love On The Rocks**	Capitol 4939
1/31/81	6	12	30. **Hello Again**	Capitol 4960
5/02/81	8	13	31. **America** -above 3 from "The Jazz Singer"-	Capitol 4994
11/14/81	11	12	32. Yesterday's Songs	Columbia 02604
3/06/82	27	5	33. On The Way To The Sky	Columbia 02712
6/19/82	35	4	34. Be Mine Tonight	Columbia 02928

DATE	POS	WKS	ARTIST—Record Title	LABEL & NO.
10/02/82	5	11	35. **Heartlight** -inspired by the film "E.T."-	Columbia 03219
			DIAMONDS Dave Somerville, lead singer of Canadian quartet	
3/17/56	12	11	1. Why Do Fools Fall In Love	Mercury 70790
5/12/56	14	11	2. The Church Bells May Ring	Mercury 70835
7/28/56	30	2	3. Love, Love, Love	Mercury 70889
9/29/56	34	1	4. Soft Summer Breeze/	
9/29/56	35	2	5. Ka-Ding-Dong	Mercury 70934
3/16/57	2 (8)	21	6. **Little Darlin'**	Mercury 71060
7/15/57	13	2	7. Words Of Love	Mercury 71128
9/30/57	16	1	8. Zip Zip	Mercury 71165
11/04/57	10	8	9. **Silhouettes**	Mercury 71197
1/06/58	4	14	10. **The Stroll**	Mercury 71242
5/19/58	37	1	11. High Sign	Mercury 71291
7/28/58	16	1	12. Kathy-O	Mercury 71330
11/17/58	29	6	13. Walking Along	Mercury 71366
2/09/59	18	10	14. She Say (Oom Dooby Doom)	Mercury 71404
8/07/61	22	4	15. One Summer Night	Mercury 71831
			DIBANGO, MANU	
7/21/73	35	3	1. Soul Makossa [I]	Atlantic 2971
			DICK & DEEDEE Dick St. John & DeeDee Sperling	
8/28/61	2 (2)	10	1. **The Mountain's High**	Liberty 55350
5/12/62	22	5	2. Tell Me	Liberty 55412
4/06/63	17	6	3. Young And In Love	Warner 5342
12/21/63	27	4	4. Turn Around	Warner 5396
12/12/64	13	10	5. Thou Shalt Not Steal	Warner 5482
			DICKENS, "LITTLE" JIMMY	
11/13/65	15	5	1. May The Bird Of Paradise Fly Up Your Nose [N]	Columbia 43388
			DICKY DOO & THE DON'TS Gerry Granahan, lead singer	
2/17/58	28	6	1. Click-Clack	Swan 4001
5/12/58	40	1	2. Nee Nee Na Na Na Na Nu Nu [I]	Swan 4006
			DIDDLEY, BO real name: Ellas McDaniel	
10/05/59	20	7	1. Say Man [N]	Checker 931
			DIESEL rock quartet from Holland	
10/17/81	25	6	1. Sausalito Summernight	Regency 7339
			DINNING, MARK brother of Dinning Sisters trio	
1/04/60	1 (2)	14	1. **Teen Angel**	MGM 12845
			DINO, DESI & BILLY Jr.'s: Dean Martin & Desi Arnaz - with Billy Hinsche	
7/24/65	17	7	1. I'm A Fool	Reprise 0367
10/16/65	25	5	2. Not The Lovin' Kind	Reprise 0401

DATE	POS	WKS	ARTIST—Record Title	LABEL & NO.
			DINO, KENNY	
12/04/61	24	6	1. Your Ma Said You Cried In Your Sleep Last Night	Musicor 1013
			DINO, PAUL	
4/10/61	38	1	1. Ginnie Bell	Promo 2180
			DION	
			Dion Di Muci	
11/14/60	12	11	1. Lonely Teenager	Laurie 3070
10/02/61	1 (2)	12	2. **Runaround Sue**	Laurie 3110
12/18/61	2 (1)	13	3. **The Wanderer/**	
12/18/61	36	1	4. The Majestic	Laurie 3115
5/05/62	3	9	5. **Lovers Who Wander**	Laurie 3123
7/21/62	8	8	6. **Little Diane**	Laurie 3134
11/24/62	10	9	7. **Love Came To Me**	Laurie 3145
1/26/63	2 (3)	11	8. **Ruby Baby**	Columbia 42662
3/30/63	21	6	9. Sandy	Laurie 3153
5/04/63	21	6	10. This Little Girl	Columbia 42776
7/27/63	31	3	11. Be Careful Of Stones That You Throw	Columbia 42810
9/28/63	6	8	12. **Donna The Prima Donna**	Columbia 42852
11/23/63	6	9	13. **Drip Drop**	Columbia 42917
11/02/68	4	12	● 14. **Abraham, Martin And John**	Laurie 3464
			DION & THE BELMONTS	
			Belmonts: Angelo D'Aleo, Freddie Milano and Carlo Mastrangelo - also see The Belmonts	
5/26/58	22	10	1. I Wonder Why	Laurie 3013
9/15/58	19	8	2. No One Knows	Laurie 3015
1/05/59	40	1	3. Don't Pity Me	Laurie 3021
4/27/59	5	13	4. **A Teenager In Love**	Laurie 3027
1/11/60	3	11	5. **Where Or When**	Laurie 3044
5/16/60	30	2	6. When You Wish Upon A Star	Laurie 3052
8/15/60	38	1	7. In The Still Of The Night	Laurie 3059
			DIRE STRAITS	
2/17/79	4	12	1. **Sultans Of Swing**	Warner 8736
			DIRKSEN, SENATOR EVERETT McKINLEY	
			Senator from Illinois ('50-'69) - died on 9/7/69 (73)	
1/07/67	29	3	1. Gallant Men [S]	Capitol 5805
			DIRT BAND - **see NITTY GRITTY DIRT BAND**	
			DISCO TEX & THE SEX-O-LETTES	
			featuring Sir Monti Rock III	
12/28/74	10	9	1. **Get Dancin'**	Chelsea 3004
5/17/75	23	5	2. I Wanna Dance Wit' Choo (Doo Dat Dance), Part 1	Chelsea 3015
			DIXIEBELLES with Cornbread & Jerry	
10/26/63	9	8	1. **(Down At) Papa Joe's**	Sound Stage 7 2507
2/08/64	15	5	2. Southtown, U.S.A	Sound Stage 7 2517

DATE	POS	WKS	ARTIST—Record Title	LABEL & NO.
			DIXIE CUPS	
			trio from New Orleans	
5/16/64	**1** (3)	11	1. **Chapel Of Love**	Red Bird 001
8/01/64	**12**	7	2. People Say	Red Bird 006
11/21/64	**39**	1	3. You Should Have Seen The Way He Looked At Me	Red Bird 012
5/01/65	**20**	5	4. Iko Iko	Red Bird 024
			DOBKINS, CARL, JR.	
6/01/59	**3**	16	1. **My Heart Is An Open Book**	Decca 30803
1/18/60	**25**	8	2. Lucky Devil	Decca 31020
			DR. BUZZARD'S ORIGINAL "SAVANNAH" BAND	
			Cory Daye, lead singer	
12/11/76	**27**	8	1. Whispering/Cherchez La Femme/Se Si Bon	RCA 10827
			DR. HOOK	
			Ray (eye patch) Sawyer, leader	
5/06/72	**5**	10	1. **Sylvia's Mother**	Columbia 45562
2/03/73	**6**	11	2. **The Cover Of "Rolling Stone"** [N]	Columbia 45732
			-above 2 shown as: Dr. Hook & The Medicine Show-	
2/07/76	**6**	14	3. **Only Sixteen**	Capitol 4171
7/31/76	**11**	14	4. A Little Bit More	Capitol 4280
10/14/78	**6**	16	● 5. **Sharing The Night Together**	Capitol 4621
6/02/79	**6**	16	● 6. **When You're In Love With A Beautiful Woman**	Capitol 4705
11/03/79	**12**	14	7. Better Love Next Time	Capitol 4785
3/15/80	**5**	15	● 8. **Sexy Eyes**	Capitol 4831
11/29/80	**34**	5	9. Girls Can Get It	Casablanca 2314
3/27/82	**25**	6	10. Baby Makes Her Blue Jeans Talk	Casablanca 2347
			DR. JOHN	
			Mac Rebennack	
5/12/73	**9**	13	1. **Right Place Wrong Time**	Atco 6914
			DOGGETT, BILL	
8/25/56	**2** (3)	22	1. **Honky Tonk (Parts 1 & 2)** [I]	King 4950
			-Clifford Scott on sax-	
12/15/56	**26**	5	2. Slow Walk [I]	King 5000
12/02/57	**35**	1	3. Soft [I]	King 5080
			DOMINO, FATS	
			prior to first pop hit, Fats had a string of hits on the R&B charts from 1950-1954	
7/16/55	**10**	13	1. **Ain't That A Shame**	Imperial 5348
4/07/56	**35**	1	2. Bo Weevil	Imperial 5375
5/05/56	**3**	18	3. **I'm In Love Again/**	Imperial 5386
5/19/56	**21**	10	4. My Blue Heaven	
7/28/56	**14**	8	5. When My Dreamboat Comes Home	Imperial 5396
10/13/56	**2** (3)	21	6. **Blueberry Hill**	Imperial 5407
1/12/57	**5**	12	7. **Blue Monday**	Imperial 5417
			-from "The Girl Can't Help It"-	
3/09/57	**4**	14	8. **I'm Walkin'**	Imperial 5428
5/27/57	**6**	13	9. **Valley Of Tears/**	
7/22/57	**22**	4	10. It's You I Love	Imperial 5442

DATE	POS	WKS	ARTIST—Record Title	LABEL & NO.
8/26/57	29	2	11. When I See You	Imperial 5454
10/21/57	23	6	12. Wait And See -from the film "Jamboree"-	Imperial 5467
12/23/57	26	9	13. The Big Beat	Imperial 5477
5/05/58	22	7	14. Sick And Tired	Imperial 5515
12/01/58	6	12	15. **Whole Lotta Loving**	Imperial 5553
5/25/59	16	7	16. I'm Ready	Imperial 5585
8/10/59	8	10	17. **I Want To Walk You Home/**	
8/10/59	17	9	18. I'm Gonna Be A Wheel Some Day	Imperial 5606
11/09/59	8	10	19. **Be My Guest/**	
11/09/59	33	2	20. I've Been Around	Imperial 5629
2/15/60	25	5	21. Country Boy	Imperial 5645
7/04/60	6	11	22. **Walking To New Orleans/**	
7/18/60	21	7	23. Don't Come Knockin'	Imperial 5675
9/12/60	15	9	24. Three Nights A Week	Imperial 5687
11/14/60	14	11	25. My Girl Josephine/	
12/05/60	38	3	26. Natural Born Lover	Imperial 5704
2/06/61	22	6	27. What A Price/	
2/13/61	33	4	28. Ain't That Just Like A Woman	Imperial 5723
4/03/61	32	2	29. Fell In Love On Monday/	
4/17/61	32	2	30. Shu Rah	Imperial 5734
6/19/61	23	5	31. It Keeps Rainin'	Imperial 5753
7/31/61	15	6	32. Let The Four Winds Blow	Imperial 5764
10/23/61	22	4	33. What A Party	Imperial 5779
12/25/61	30	3	34. Jambalaya (On The Bayou)	Imperial 5796
3/17/62	22	5	35. You Win Again	Imperial 5816
10/26/63	35	1	36. Red Sails In The Sunset	ABC-Para. 10484
			DON & JUAN	
			Roland Trone & Claude Johnson	
2/24/62	7	9	1. **What's Your Name**	Big Top 3079
			DONALDSON, BO, & THE HEYWOODS	
			Cincinnati, Ohio septet	
5/11/74	1 (2)	12	● 1. **Billy, Don't Be A Hero**	ABC 11435
8/24/74	15	7	2. Who Do You Think You Are	ABC 12006
12/14/74	39	1	3. The Heartbreak Kid	ABC 12039
			DONEGAN, LONNIE, & His Skiffle Group	
			Scottish	
3/31/56	8	11	1. **Rock Island Line**	London 1650
8/14/61	5	9	2. **Does Your Chewing Gum Lose It's Flavor (On The Bedpost Over Night) [N]**	Dot 15911
			DONNER, RAL	
			Ral was narrator and Elvis's voice in film "This Is Elvis"	
5/01/61	19	8	1. Girl Of My Best Friend -with The Starfires-	Gone 5102
7/24/61	4	9	2. **You Don't Know What You've Got (Until You Lose It)**	Gone 5108
11/13/61	39	1	3. Please Don't Go	Gone 5114
2/03/62	18	4	4. She's Everything (I Wanted You To Be)	Gone 5121

DATE	POS	WKS	ARTIST—Record Title	LABEL & NO.
			DONNIE & THE DREAMERS	
			Donnie is Louis Bugio	
6/12/61	35	3	1. Count Every Star	Whale 500
			DONOVAN	
			Donovan Leitch - Scottish	
6/12/65	23	5	1. Catch The Wind	Hickory 1309
8/13/66	1 (1)	10	2. **Sunshine Superman**	Epic 10045
11/19/66	2 (3)	10	● 3. **Mellow Yellow**	Epic 10098
2/25/67	19	5	4. Epistle To Dippy	Epic 10127
8/26/67	11	6	5. There Is A Mountain	Epic 10212
12/09/67	23	5	6. Wear Your Love Like Heaven	Epic 10253
3/30/68	26	5	7. Jennifer Juniper	Epic 10300
6/29/68	5	10	8. **Hurdy Gurdy Man**	Epic 10345
10/19/68	33	4	9. Lalena	Epic 10393
3/01/69	35	2	10. To Susan On The West Coast Waiting/	
4/26/69	7	10	11. **Atlantis**	Epic 10434
8/30/69	36	2	12. Goo Goo Barabajagal (Love Is Hot)	Epic 10510
			-with The Jeff Beck Group-	
			DOOBIE BROTHERS	
			California group led by Tom Johnston ('71-'78) and Michael McDonald ('76-'81)	
9/23/72	11	10	1. Listen To The Music	Warner 7619
2/17/73	35	2	2. Jesus Is Just Alright	Warner 7661
5/26/73	8	11	3. **Long Train Runnin'**	Warner 7698
9/15/73	15	8	4. China Grove	Warner 7728
6/01/74	32	2	5. Another Park, Another Sunday	Warner 7795
1/11/75	1 (1)	12	● 6. **Black Water**	Warner 8062
			-original flip of Warner 7795-	
5/17/75	11	9	7. Take Me In Your Arms (Rock Me)	Warner 8092
8/30/75	40	1	8. Sweet Maxine	Warner 8126
5/15/76	13	8	9. Takin' It To The Streets	Warner 8196
1/22/77	37	2	10. It Keeps You Runnin'	Warner 8282
2/10/79	1 (1)	14	● 11. **What A Fool Believes**	Warner 8725
5/19/79	14	9	12. Minute By Minute	Warner 8828
9/15/79	25	6	13. Dependin' On You	Warner 49029
9/06/80	5	11	14. **Real Love**	Warner 49503
12/06/80	24	7	15. One Step Closer	Warner 49622
			DOORS	
			Jim Morrison, leader of quartet formed at UCLA, died 7/3/71 (27)	
6/24/67	1 (3)	14	● 1. **Light My Fire**	Elektra 45615
10/07/67	12	7	2. People Are Strange	Elektra 45621
12/30/67	25	4	3. Love Me Two Times	Elektra 45624
5/04/68	39	3	4. The Unknown Soldier	Elektra 45628
7/13/68	1 (2)	11	● 5. **Hello, I Love You**	Elektra 45635
1/04/69	3	12	● 6. **Touch Me**	Elektra 45646
4/24/71	11	9	7. Love Her Madly	Elektra 45726
7/24/71	14	9	8. Riders On The Storm	Elektra 45738

DATE	POS	WKS	ARTIST—Record Title	LABEL & NO.
			DORE, CHARLIE	
			British female vocalist	
3/22/80	**13**	10	1. Pilot Of The Airwaves	Island 49166
			DORMAN, HAROLD	
4/18/60	**21**	9	1. Mountain Of Love	Rita 1003
			DORSEY, JIMMY, Orchestra & Chorus	
4/13/57	**2** (4)	26	1. **So Rare**	Fraternity 755
9/09/57	**21**	2	2. June Night	Fraternity 777
			-featuring Dick Stabile on sax -- recorded 5 days after Jimmy's death on 6/12/57 (53)-	
			DORSEY, LEE	
9/25/61	**7**	10	1. **Ya Ya**	Fury 1053
1/20/62	**27**	5	2. Do-Re-Mi	Fury 1056
7/31/65	**28**	4	3. Ride Your Pony	Amy 927
8/13/66	**8**	9	4. **Working In The Coal Mine**	Amy 958
11/19/66	**23**	5	5. Holy Cow	Amy 965
			DORSEY, TOMMY, Orchestra, starring Warren Covington	
			younger brother of Jimmy Dorsey - died 11/26/56 (51)	
9/15/58	**7**	14	1. **Tea For Two Cha Cha [I]**	Decca 30704
			DOUGLAS, CARL	
			Jamaican	
11/09/74	**1** (2)	12	● 1. Kung Fu Fighting	20th Century 2140
			DOUGLAS, CAROL	
12/21/74	**11**	11	1. Doctor's Orders	Midland Int'l. 10113
			DOUGLAS, MIKE	
			TV talk show host - vocalist with Kay Kyser's band	
1/08/66	**6**	7	1. **The Men In My Little Girl's Life [N]**	Epic 9876
			DOVE, RONNIE	
9/26/64	**40**	1	1. Say You	Diamond 167
11/14/64	**14**	7	2. Right Or Wrong	Diamond 173
4/10/65	**14**	7	3. One Kiss For Old Times' Sake	Diamond 179
6/26/65	**16**	6	4. A Little Bit Of Heaven	Diamond 184
9/18/65	**21**	5	5. I'll Make All Your Dreams Come True	Diamond 188
11/27/65	**25**	4	6. Kiss Away	Diamond 191
2/05/66	**18**	7	7. When Liking Turns To Loving	Diamond 195
5/07/66	**20**	5	8. Let's Start All Over Again	Diamond 198
7/09/66	**27**	4	9. Happy Summer Days	Diamond 205
9/24/66	**22**	5	10. I Really Don't Want To Know	Diamond 208
12/10/66	**18**	6	11. Cry	Diamond 214
			DOVELLS	
			Len Barry, lead singer	
9/18/61	**2** (2)	14	1. **Bristol Stomp**	Parkway 827
3/03/62	**37**	2	2. Do The New Continental	Parkway 833
6/23/62	**27**	5	3. Bristol Twistin' Annie	Parkway 838
9/15/62	**25**	7	4. Hully Gully Baby	Parkway 845
5/11/63	**3**	11	5. **You Can't Sit Down**	Parkway 867

DATE	POS	WKS	ARTIST—Record Title	LABEL & NO.
			DOWELL, JOE	
7/17/61	**1** (1)	12	1. **Wooden Heart**	Smash 1708
7/28/62	**23**	4	2. Little Red Rented Rowboat	Smash 1759
			DOZIER, LAMONT	
			1/3 of songwriting team Holland-Dozier-Holland	
2/16/74	**15**	9	1. Trying To Hold On To My Woman	ABC 11407
7/06/74	**26**	6	2. Fish Ain't Bitin'	ABC 11438
			DRAKE, CHARLIE	
			British	
2/17/62	**21**	6	1. My Boomerang Won't Come Back [N]	United Artists 398
			DRAKE, PETE, & His Talking Steel Guitar	
4/11/64	**25**	5	1. Forever	Smash 1867
			DRAMATICS	
			Detroit quintet	
7/31/71	**9**	11	1. **Whatcha See Is Whatcha Get**	Volt 4058
3/04/72	**5**	11	2. **In The Rain**	Volt 4075
			DRAPER, RUSTY	
8/20/55	**18**	4	1. Seventeen	Mercury 70651
10/01/55	**3**	16	2. **The Shifting, Whispering Sands**	Mercury 70696
12/31/55	**11**	12	3. Are You Satisfied?	Mercury 70757
9/22/56	**20**	8	4. In The Middle Of The House [N]	Mercury 70921
5/27/57	**6**	12	5. **Freight Train**	Mercury 71102
			DREAMLOVERS	
			backup vocal group for Chubby Checker's "The Twist"	
8/28/61	**10**	6	1. **When We Get Married**	Heritage 102
			DREAM WEAVERS Featuring Wade Buff	
11/12/55	**7**	21	1. **It's Almost Tomorrow**	Decca 29683
5/19/56	**33**	1	2. A Little Love Can Go A Long, Long Way	Decca 29905
			-from Goodyear TV show "Joey"-	
			DRIFTERS	
			featured various lead singers, including Ben E. King, Bobby Hendricks, Rudy Lewis, & Johnny Moore	
6/29/59	**2** (1)	14	1. **There Goes My Baby**	Atlantic 2025
11/02/59	**15**	9	2. Dance With Me/	
11/23/59	**33**	5	3. (If You Cry) True Love, True Love	Atlantic 2040
3/14/60	**16**	6	4. This Magic Moment	Atlantic 2050
9/19/60	**1** (3)	14	5. **Save The Last Dance For Me**	Atlantic 2071
12/31/60	**17**	7	6. I Count The Tears	Atlantic 2087
4/10/61	**32**	6	7. Some Kind Of Wonderful	Atlantic 2096
6/26/61	**14**	8	8. Please Stay	Atlantic 2105
9/25/61	**16**	9	9. Sweets For My Sweet	Atlantic 2117
3/24/62	**28**	4	10. When My Little Girl Is Smiling	Atlantic 2134
12/29/62	**5**	11	11. **Up On The Roof**	Atlantic 2162
4/06/63	**9**	8	12. **On Broadway**	Atlantic 2182
10/05/63	**25**	5	13. I'll Take You Home	Atlantic 2201
7/11/64	**4**	12	14. **Under The Boardwalk**	Atlantic 2237
10/10/64	**33**	5	15. I've Got Sand In My Shoes	Atlantic 2253

DATE	POS	WKS	ARTIST—Record Title	LABEL & NO.
11/28/64	18	7	16. Saturday Night At The Movies	Atlantic 2260
			DRUSKY, ROY	
6/26/61	35	1	1. Three Hearts In A Tangle	Decca 31193
			DUALS	
10/02/61	25	6	1. Stick Shift [I]	Sue 745
			DUBS	
11/18/57	23	8	1. Could This Be Magic	Gone 5011
			DUDLEY, DAVE	
7/20/63	32	4	1. Six Days On The Road	Golden Wing 3020
			DUKE, GEORGE - see STANLEY CLARKE	
			DUKE, PATTY	
			star of TV's "Patty Duke Show"	
7/17/65	8	8	1. **Don't Just Stand There**	United Artists 875
10/30/65	22	4	2. Say Something Funny	United Artists 915
			DUNDAS, DAVID	
			English	
11/27/76	17	13	1. Jeans On	Chrysalis 2094
			DUPREE, ROBBIE	
5/03/80	6	15	1. **Steal Away**	Elektra 46621
8/09/80	15	12	2. Hot Rod Hearts	Elektra 47005
			DUPREES featuring Joey Vann	
8/25/62	7	9	1. **You Belong To Me**	Coed 569
11/10/62	13	6	2. My Own True Love	Coed 571
			-Tara's Theme from "Gone With The Wind"-	
9/14/63	37	3	3. Why Don't You Believe Me	Coed 584
11/30/63	18	6	4. Have You Heard	Coed 585
			DYKE & THE BLAZERS	
			Dyke is Lester Christian	
7/05/69	35	3	1. We Got More Soul	Original Sound 86
11/01/69	36	1	2. Let A Woman Be A Woman - Let A Man Be A Man	Original Sound 89
			DYLAN, BOB	
			led the folk/rock movement	
5/15/65	39	1	1. Subterranean Homesick Blues	Columbia 43242
8/14/65	2 (2)	9	2. **Like A Rolling Stone**	Columbia 43346
10/09/65	7	7	3. **Positively 4th Street**	Columbia 43389
4/23/66	2 (1)	9	4. **Rainy Day Women #12 & 35**	Columbia 43592
7/16/66	20	4	5. I Want You	Columbia 43683
10/01/66	33	3	6. Just Like A Woman	Columbia 43792
8/02/69	7	11	7. **Lay Lady Lay**	Columbia 44926
12/25/71	33	4	8. George Jackson	Columbia 45516
9/29/73	12	11	9. Knockin' On Heaven's Door	Columbia 45913
3/29/75	31	3	10. Tangled Up In Blue	Columbia 10106
1/03/76	33	3	11. Hurricane (Part 1)	Columbia 10245
			-dedicated to boxer Rubin Carter-	
10/06/79	24	6	12. Gotta Serve Somebody	Columbia 11072

DATE	POS	WKS	ARTIST—Record Title	LABEL & NO.
			DYSON, RONNIE	
7/25/70	8	9	1. **(If You Let Me Make Love To You Then) Why Can't I Touch You?** -from the musical "Salvation"-	Columbia 45110
4/07/73	28	4	2. One Man Band (Plays All Alone)	Columbia 45776
			EAGER, BRENDA LEE - **see JERRY BUTLER**	
			EAGLES	
			Don Henley, Glenn Frey, Randy Meisner (replaced by Timothy B. Schmit), Don Felder & Joe Walsh	
6/24/72	12	8	1. Take It Easy	Asylum 11005
9/30/72	9	10	2. **Witchy Woman**	Asylum 11008
2/03/73	22	6	3. Peaceful Easy Feeling	Asylum 11013
6/22/74	32	3	4. Already Gone	Asylum 11036
12/28/74	1 (1)	14	5. **Best Of My Love**	Asylum 45218
6/14/75	1 (1)	14	6. **One Of These Nights**	Asylum 45257
9/27/75	2 (2)	11	7. **Lyin' Eyes**	Asylum 45279
1/17/76	4	14	8. **Take It To The Limit**	Asylum 45293
12/25/76	1 (1)	13	● 9. **New Kid In Town**	Asylum 45373
3/12/77	1 (1)	15	● 10. **Hotel California**	Asylum 45386
5/28/77	11	8	11. Life In The Fast Lane	Asylum 45403
12/23/78	18	5	12. Please Come Home For Christmas [X]	Asylum 45555
10/13/79	1 (1)	13	● 13. **Heartache Tonight**	Asylum 46545
12/08/79	8	12	14. **The Long Run**	Asylum 46569
3/01/80	8	12	15. **I Can't Tell You Why**	Asylum 46608
1/10/81	21	7	16. Seven Bridges Road	Asylum 47100
			EARL-JEAN	
			Earl-Jean McCree of The Cookies	
8/08/64	38	1	1. I'm Into Somethin' Good	Colpix 729
			EARLS	
			Bronx quartet	
1/12/63	24	4	1. Remember Then	Old Town 1130
			EARTH, WIND & FIRE	
			Chicago group led by Maurice White	
4/27/74	29	7	1. Mighty Mighty	Columbia 46007
10/12/74	33	2	2. Devotion	Columbia 10026
3/22/75	1 (1)	14	● 3. **Shining Star**	Columbia 10090
7/26/75	12	11	4. That's The Way Of The World	Columbia 10172
12/13/75	5	12	● 5. **Sing A Song**	Columbia 10251
4/24/76	39	2	6. Can't Hide Love	Columbia 10309
8/14/76	12	12	● 7. Getaway	Columbia 10373
12/11/76	21	10	8. Saturday Nite	Columbia 10439
11/26/77	13	13	9. Serpentine Fire	Columbia 10625
4/01/78	32	5	10. Fantasy	Columbia 10688
8/05/78	9	9	● 11. **Got To Get You Into My Life**	Columbia 10796
12/16/78	8	11	● 12. **September**	ARC 10854
7/28/79	2 (2)	13	● 13. **After The Love Has Gone**	ARC 11033
10/31/81	3	16	● 14. **Let's Groove**	ARC 02536

The Eagles. The group's version of "Please Come Home For Christmas" in 1978 was more successful than the rhythm & blues original by Charles Brown 17 years earlier. Listen, this is important stuff.

Earth, Wind & Fire. As a session drummer for Chess Records in the '60s, Earth, Wind & Fire founder Maurice White played on recordings by the Dells, Jackie Ross, Billy Stewart, Chuck Berry, and Etta James.

Duane Eddy's interest in the guitar was said to have been spurred at age 17 by the gift of a Chet Atkins album.

The Electric Light Orchestra's music for the movie "Xanadu" yielded them three top 10 hits, including the title tune performed with Olivia Newton-John. It was her eleventh top 10 success, and eleven was about the number of people who paid to see the movie.

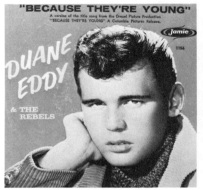

David Essex. A one-hit wonder in America, David Essex has reached the top 10 in his British homeland many times. He's also played Che Guevara in the London production of *Evita*.

The Everly Brothers. When Ike Everly was a barber, one of his regular customers was Boudleaux Bryant. The well-trimmed songwriter was later to pen "Bye Bye Love," "Wake Up Little Susie," and "Bird Dog" for Ike's offspring, Don and Phil.

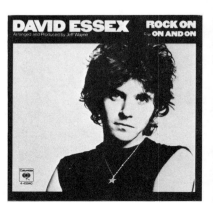

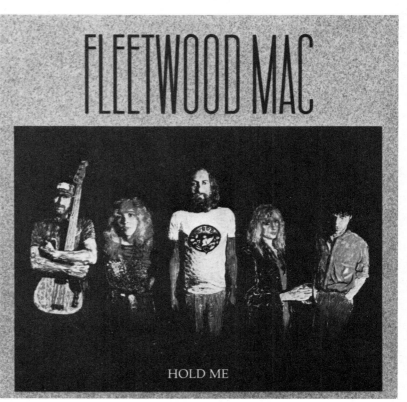

HOLD ME

Eddie Fisher's first wife, Debbie Reynolds collected a million-selling chart-topper ("Tammy") within two years of their marriage. How come he couldn't do the same for Elizabeth Taylor?

Fleetwood Mac. So many players have been part of Fleetwood Mac's past that one music business manager put a group on the road in the early '70s with that name but with none of the original members.

The Fleetwoods. Perhaps the '50s forerunners of the Carpenters, the Fleetwoods called themselves Two Girls and A Guy before seeking something snappier at the suggestion of the Seattle distributor who helped them secure a recording deal.

Foreigner founder Mick Jones says that their name was chosen to suggest "travellers going from one unknown place to another"—a reflection of the bandmembers' experience with acts such as Spooky Tooth, King Crimson, If, Storm, Ian Hunter, and Leslie West.

The Four Lads. Before the Four Lads embarked upon their own prosperous recording career, the Canadian group backed Johnny Ray on his mega-hit, "Cry."

DATE	POS	WKS	ARTIST—Record Title	LABEL & NO.
			EARTH, WIND & FIRE with THE EMOTIONS	
5/26/79	6	12	● 1. **Boogie Wonderland**	ARC 10956
			EASTON, SHEENA	
			Scottish	
2/28/81	**1** (2)	15	● 1. **Morning Train (Nine To Five)**	EMI America 8071
6/06/81	18	9	2. Modern Girl	EMI America 8080
8/22/81	4	14	3. **For Your Eyes Only**	Liberty 1418
12/19/81	15	12	4. You Could Have Been With Me	EMI America 8101
5/08/82	30	6	5. When He Shines	EMI America 8113
			EASYBEATS	
			members George Young & Harry Vanda formed "Flash & The Pan"	
4/22/67	16	8	1. Friday On My Mind	United Artists 50106
			EASY RIDERS - **see TERRY GILKYSON**	
			ECHOES	
			Brooklyn trio	
3/27/61	12	9	1. Baby Blue	Seg-Way 103
			EDDY, DUANE	
			#1 rock & roll instrumentalist	
7/07/58	6	12	1. **Rebel-'Rouser [I]**	Jamie 1104
9/15/58	27	5	2. Ramrod [I]	Jamie 1109
11/17/58	15	9	3. Cannonball [I]	Jamie 1111
2/02/59	23	8	4. The Lonely One [I]	Jamie 1117
4/20/59	30	2	5. "Yep!" [I]	Jamie 1122
6/29/59	9	11	6. **Forty Miles Of Bad Road [I]**	Jamie 1126
10/26/59	37	3	7. Some Kind-A Earthquake [I]	Jamie 1130
1/11/60	26	5	8. Bonnie Came Back [I]	Jamie 1144
6/06/60	4	12	9. **Because They're Young [I]**	Jamie 1156
10/31/60	27	4	10. Peter Gunn [I]	Jamie 1168
1/16/61	18	7	11. "Pepe" [I]	Jamie 1175
4/17/61	39	1	12. Theme From Dixie [I]	Jamie 1183
8/11/62	33	3	13. The Ballad Of Paladin [I] -from "Have Gun-Will Travel"-	RCA 8047
11/03/62	12	10	14. (Dance With The) Guitar Man	RCA 8087
2/23/63	28	5	15. Boss Guitar	RCA 8131
			EDISON LIGHTHOUSE	
			English studio group	
2/28/70	5	12	● 1. **Love Grows (Where My Rosemary Goes)**	Bell 858
			EDMUNDS, DAVE	
			Welsh	
1/16/71	4	9	1. **I Hear You Knocking**	MAM 3601
			EDSELS	
			Ohio quintet	
6/05/61	21	5	1. Rama Lama Ding Dong	Twin 700

DATE	POS	WKS	ARTIST—Record Title	LABEL & NO.
			EDWARD BEAR	
			Canadian trio	
1/27/73	**3**	12	● 1. **Last Song**	Capitol 3452
5/26/73	**37**	2	2. Close Your Eyes	Capitol 3581
			EDWARDS, BOBBY	
10/16/61	**11**	9	1. You're The Reason	Crest 1075
			EDWARDS, JONATHAN	
12/04/71	**4**	12	● 1. **Sunshine**	Capricorn 8021
			EDWARDS, TOMMY	
			died on 10/22/69 (47)	
8/25/58	**1** (6)	19	1. **It's All In The Game** -written by U.S. Vice President Charles Dawes - original version charted in 1951-	MGM 12688
11/17/58	**15**	9	2. Love Is All We Need	MGM 12722
3/02/59	**11**	8	3. Please Mr. Sun/	
3/23/59	**27**	4	4. The Morning Side Of The Mountain -original version charted in '51-	MGM 12757
6/08/59	**26**	4	5. My Melancholy Baby	MGM 12794
6/06/60	**18**	7	6. I Really Don't Want To Know	MGM 12890
			EGAN, WALTER	
7/01/78	**8**	13	● 1. **Magnet And Steel**	Columbia 10719
			8TH DAY	
6/05/71	**11**	10	● 1. She's Not Just Another Woman	Invictus 9087
10/16/71	**28**	6	2. You've Got To Crawl (Before You Walk)	Invictus 9098
			EL CHICANO	
5/02/70	**28**	5	1. Viva Tirado - Part I [I]	Kapp 2085
12/22/73	**40**	1	2. Tell Her She's Lovely	MCA 40104
			EL DORADOS	
			Chicago quintet	
10/15/55	**17**	6	1. At My Front Door	Vee-Jay 147
			ELBERT, DONNIE	
11/20/71	**15**	8	1. Where Did Our Love Go	All Platinum 2330
2/12/72	**22**	6	2. I Can't Help Myself (Sugar Pie, Honey Bunch)	Avco 4587
			ELECTRIC INDIAN	
8/23/69	**16**	8	1. Keem-O-Sabe [I]	United Artists 50563
			ELECTRIC LIGHT ORCHESTRA	
			British band led by Jeff Lynne - also see Olivia Newton-John	
1/25/75	**9**	10	1. **Can't Get It Out Of My Head**	United Artists 573
12/13/75	**10**	12	2. **Evil Woman**	United Artists 729
4/10/76	**14**	9	3. Strange Magic	United Artists 770
11/13/76	**13**	14	4. Livin' Thing	United Artists 888
3/05/77	**24**	6	5. Do Ya -originally charted by The Move (forerunner of ELO) in 1972-	United Artists 939
7/09/77	**7**	16	● 6. **Telephone Line**	United Artists 1000
12/10/77	**13**	10	7. Turn To Stone	Jet 1099
3/11/78	**17**	12	8. Sweet Talkin' Woman	Jet 1145

DATE	POS	WKS	ARTIST—Record Title	LABEL & NO.
7/29/78	35	3	9. Mr. Blue Sky	Jet 5050
6/02/79	8	11	10. **Shine A Little Love**	Jet 5057
8/11/79	4	11	● 11. **Don't Bring Me Down**	Jet 5060
11/17/79	37	2	12. Confusion	Jet 5064
1/26/80	39	2	13. Last Train To London	Jet 5067
6/14/80	16	8	● 14. I'm Alive	MCA 41246
8/16/80	13	9	15. All Over The World	MCA 41289
			-above 2 from film "Xanadu"-	
8/08/81	10	13	16. **Hold On Tight**	Jet 02408
11/28/81	38	2	17. Twilight	Jet 02559
			ELECTRIC PRUNES	
			Seattle quartet	
1/21/67	11	8	1. I Had Too Much To Dream (Last Night)	Reprise 0532
4/22/67	27	5	2. Get Me To The World On Time	Reprise 0564
			ELEGANTS	
			Vito Picone, lead singer	
7/28/58	1 (1)	16	1. **Little Star**	Apt 25005
			ELGART, LARRY, & His Manhattan Swing Orchestra	
			big band leader in the '40's	
7/03/82	31	5	1. Hooked On Swing (medley) [I]	RCA 13219
			ELLEDGE, JIMMY	
12/25/61	22	7	1. Funny How Time Slips Away	RCA 7946
			ELLIMAN, YVONNE	
			Hawaiian - portrayed Mary Magdalene in "Jesus Christ Superstar"	
5/22/71	28	6	1. I Don't Know How To Love Him	Decca 32785
			-from "Jesus Christ Superstar"-	
11/06/76	14	12	2. Love Me	RSO 858
4/16/77	15	9	3. Hello Stranger	RSO 871
2/25/78	1 (1)	16	● 4. **If I Can't Have You**	RSO 884
			-from "Saturday Night Fever"-	
12/01/79	34	3	5. Love Pains	RSO 1007
			ELLIS, SHIRLEY	
12/07/63	8	10	1. **The Nitty Gritty**	Congress 202
1/09/65	3	10	2. **The Name Game**	Congress 230
4/03/65	8	7	3. **The Clapping Song (Clap Pat Clap Slap)**	Congress 234
			EMERSON, LAKE & PALMER	
			English: Keith Emerson, Greg Lake & Carl Palmer	
10/21/72	39	2	1. From The Beginning	Cotillion 44158
			EMOTIONS	
			sister trio from Chicago - also see Earth, Wind & Fire	
7/19/69	39	1	1. So I Can Love You	Volt 4010
7/02/77	1 (5)	17	2. **Best Of My Love**	Columbia 10544
			ENCHANTMENT	
3/05/77	25	5	1. Gloria	United Artists 912
3/11/78	33	4	2. It's You That I Need	Roadshow 1124

DATE	POS	WKS	ARTIST—Record Title	LABEL & NO.
			ENGLAND DAN & JOHN FORD COLEY	
			England Dan is the brother of Jim Seals of Seals & Crofts	
7/10/76	**2** (2)	17	● 1. **I'd Really Love To See You Tonight**	Big Tree 16069
10/30/76	**10**	12	2. **Nights Are Forever Without You**	Big Tree 16079
6/18/77	**21**	8	3. It's Sad To Belong	Big Tree 16088
11/05/77	**23**	6	4. Gone Too Far	Big Tree 16102
3/11/78	**9**	8	5. **We'll Never Have To Say Goodbye Again**	Big Tree 16110
4/07/79	**10**	10	6. **Love Is The Answer**	Big Tree 16131
			ENGLISH CONGREGATION	
2/19/72	**29**	5	1. Softly Whispering I Love You	Atco 6865
			EPPS, PRESTON	
6/01/59	**14**	9	1. Bongo Rock [I]	Original Sound 4
			EQUALS	
9/28/68	**32**	6	1. Baby, Come Back	RCA 9583
			ERNIE [Jim Henson of Sesame Street]	
			also see Kermit	
8/29/70	**16**	7	1. Rubber Duckie [N]	Columbia 45207
			ERUPTION	
			Precious Wilson, lead singer	
6/10/78	**18**	6	1. I Can't Stand The Rain	Ariola 7686
			ESQUIRES	
9/16/67	**11**	10	1. Get On Up	Bunky 7750
12/16/67	**22**	5	2. And Get Away	Bunky 7752
			ESSEX Featuring Anita Humes	
6/22/63	**1** (2)	10	1. **Easier Said Than Done**	Roulette 4494
9/14/63	**12**	6	2. A Walkin' Miracle	Roulette 4515
			ESSEX, DAVID	
			British	
1/12/74	**5**	14	● 1. **Rock On**	Columbia 45940
			EVANS, PAUL	
10/05/59	**9**	11	1. **Seven Little Girls Sitting In The Back Seat**	Guaranteed 200
			-with The Curls-	
2/15/60	**16**	7	2. Midnite Special	Guaranteed 205
5/30/60	**10**	8	3. **Happy-Go-Lucky-Me**	Guaranteed 208
			EVERETT, BETTY	
			also see Jerry Butler	
3/21/64	**6**	10	1. **The Shoop Shoop Song (It's In His Kiss)**	Vee-Jay 585
2/15/69	**26**	6	2. There'll Come A Time	Uni 55100
			EVERLY BROTHERS	
			Don & Phil Everly - the #1 duo of the rock era	
5/27/57	**2** (4)	22	1. **Bye Bye Love**	Cadence 1315
9/30/57	**1** (4)	20	2. **Wake Up Little Susie**	Cadence 1337
2/17/58	**26**	3	3. This Little Girl Of Mine	Cadence 1342
4/28/58	**1** (5)	16	4. **All I Have To Do Is Dream/**	
5/12/58	**30**	2	5. Claudette	Cadence 1348
8/11/58	**1** (1)	15	6. **Bird Dog/**	
8/18/58	**10**	11	7. **Devoted To You**	Cadence 1350

DATE	POS	WKS	ARTIST—Record Title	LABEL & NO.
11/24/58	2 (1)	11	8. **Problems**/	
12/15/58	40	1	9. Love Of My Life	Cadence 1355
4/20/59	16	8	10. Take A Message To Mary/	
4/20/59	22	6	11. Poor Jenny	Cadence 1364
8/24/59	4	13	12. **('Til) I Kissed You**	Cadence 1369
1/25/60	7	11	13. **Let It Be Me**	Cadence 1376
5/02/60	1 (5)	13	14. **Cathy's Clown**	Warner 5151
6/27/60	8	9	15. **When Will I Be Loved**	Cadence 1380
9/12/60	7	10	16. **So Sad (To Watch Good Love Go Bad)**/	
9/12/60	21	7	17. Lucille	Warner 5163
11/28/60	22	4	18. Like Strangers	Cadence 1388
2/13/61	7	10	19. **Walk Right Back**/	
2/13/61	8	9	20. **Ebony Eyes**	Warner 5199
6/12/61	27	3	21. Temptation	Warner 5220
10/09/61	20	6	22. Don't Blame Me	Warner 5501
2/03/62	6	9	23. **Crying In The Rain**	Warner 5250
6/02/62	9	7	24. **That's Old Fashioned (That's The Way Love Should Be)**	Warner 5273
12/05/64	31	2	25. Gone, Gone, Gone	Warner 5478
7/08/67	40	2	26. Bowling Green	Warner 7020
			EVERY MOTHERS' SON	
5/27/67	6	12	1. **Come On Down To My Boat**	MGM 13733
			EXCITERS	
12/15/62	4	10	1. **Tell Him**	United Artists 544
			EXILE	
8/05/78	1 (4)	17	● 1. **Kiss You All Over**	Warner 8589
2/03/79	40	1	2. You Thrill Me	Warner 8711
			EYE TO EYE	
7/17/82	37	3	1. Nice Girls	Warner 50050
			FABARES, SHELLEY	
			Mary Stone of TV's "Donna Reed Show"	
3/17/62	1 (2)	13	1. **Johnny Angel**	Colpix 621
6/30/62	21	6	2. Johnny Loves Me	Colpix 636
			FABIAN	
			Fabian Forte - age 15 at time of first hit	
2/02/59	31	3	1. I'm A Man	Chancellor 1029
4/06/59	9	11	2. **Turn Me Loose**	Chancellor 1033
6/22/59	3	10	3. **Tiger**	Chancellor 1037
9/28/59	29	3	4. Come On And Get Me	Chancellor 1041
11/30/59	9	11	5. **Hound Dog Man**/	
12/07/59	12	9	6. This Friendly World	Chancellor 1044
			-above 2 from "Hound Dog Man"-	
3/14/60	31	3	7. About This Thing Called Love/	
3/14/60	39	2	8. String Along	Chancellor 1047
			FABRIC, BENT, & His Piano	
			Danish	
8/25/62	7	12	1. **Alley Cat [I]**	Atco 6226

DATE	POS	WKS	ARTIST—Record Title	LABEL & NO.
			FACENDA, TOMMY	
11/09/59	28	3	1. High School U.S.A. [N] -Atlantic released 28 different versions of this record, each mentioning the names of high schools in specific cities-	Atlantic 51 TO 78
			FACES	
			Rod Stewart, lead singer of British group descended from The Small Faces	
1/15/72	17	8	1. Stay With Me	Warner 7545
			FACTS OF LIFE	
4/09/77	31	4	1. Sometimes	Kayvette 5128
			FAGEN, DONALD	
			member of Steely Dan	
10/30/82	26	7	1. I.G.Y. (What A Beautiful World) -I.G.Y.: International Geo-physical Year (Jul'57-Dec'58)-	Warner 29900
			FAIRCHILD, BARBARA	
5/12/73	32	5	1. Teddy Bear Song	Columbia 45743
			FAITH, ADAM	
			British	
2/20/65	31	2	1. It's Alright -with The Roulettes-	Amy 913
			FAITH, PERCY, & His Orchestra	
			died 2/9/76 (67)	
1/25/60	1 (9)	17	● 1. The Theme From "A Summer Place" [I]	Columbia 41490
6/27/60	35	1	2. Theme For Young Lovers [I]	Columbia 41655
			FAITHFULL, MARIANNE	
			English	
12/19/64	22	6	1. As Tears Go By	London 9697
3/27/65	26	5	2. Come And Stay With Me	London 9731
6/26/65	32	5	3. This Little Bird	London 9759
9/04/65	24	5	4. Summer Nights	London 9780
			FALCONS	
6/08/59	17	10	1. You're So Fine	Unart 2013
			FAME, GEORGIE	
			English	
2/27/65	21	6	1. Yeh, Yeh -with The Blue Flames-	Imperial 66086
3/02/68	7	12	2. The Ballad Of Bonnie And Clyde	Epic 10283
			FANCY	
8/03/74	14	8	1. Wild Thing	Big Tree 15004
11/16/74	19	4	2. Touch Me	Big Tree 16026
			FANNY	
11/06/71	40	1	1. Charity Ball	Reprise 1033
3/15/75	29	4	2. Butter Boy	Casablanca 814
			FANTASTIC JOHNNY C	
			Johnny Corley	
11/04/67	7	12	1. Boogaloo Down Broadway	Phil-L.A. Soul 305
8/10/68	34	2	2. Hitch It To The Horse	Phil-L.A. Soul 315

DATE	POS	WKS	ARTIST—Record Title	LABEL & NO.
			FARDON, DON	
			British	
9/21/68	**20**	6	1. (The Lament Of The Cherokee) Indian Reservation	GNP Crescendo 405
			FARGO, DONNA	
7/08/72	**11**	9	1. The Happiest Girl In The Whole U.S.A	Dot 17409
11/11/72	**5**	14	● 2. **Funny Face**	Dot 17429
			FELICIANO, JOSE	
8/03/68	**3**	11	1. **Light My Fire**	RCA 9550
10/26/68	**25**	7	2. Hi-Heel Sneakers	RCA 9641
			FENDER, FREDDY	
			real name: Baldermar Huerta	
3/08/75	**1** (1)	15	● 1. **Before The Next Teardrop Falls**	ABC/Dot 17540
7/19/75	**8**	14	● 2. **Wasted Days And Wasted Nights**	ABC/Dot 17558
11/08/75	**20**	6	3. Secret Love	ABC/Dot 17585
3/20/76	**32**	4	4. You'll Lose A Good Thing	ABC/Dot 17607
			FENDERMEN	
			Phil Humphrey & Jim Sundquist	
6/13/60	**5**	13	1. **Mule Skinner Blues**	Soma 1137
			FERGUSON, JAY	
			also see Spirit and Jo Jo Gunne	
1/28/78	**9**	12	1. **Thunder Island**	Asylum 45444
6/09/79	**31**	4	2. Shakedown Cruise	Asylum 46041
			FERGUSON, JOHNNY	
4/18/60	**27**	3	1. Angela Jones	MGM 12855
			FERGUSON, MAYNARD	
			played trumpet for Stan Kenton's Orchestra	
5/28/77	**28**	6	1. Gonna Fly Now (Theme From "Rocky") [I]	Columbia 10468
			FERKO STRING BAND	
6/18/55	**14**	6	1. Alabama Jubilee [I]	Media 1010
			FERRANTE & TEICHER	
			Arthur Ferrante & Louis Teicher	
8/08/60	**10**	18	1. **Theme From The Apartment** [I]	United Artists 231
11/28/60	**2** (1)	18	2. **Exodus** [I]	United Artists 274
4/17/61	**37**	1	3. Love Theme From One Eyed Jacks [I]	United Artists 300
11/13/61	**8**	8	4. **Tonight** [I]	United Artists 373
			-from "West Side Story"-	
11/29/69	**10**	11	5. **Midnight Cowboy** [I]	United Artists 50554
			FIELDS, ERNIE, Orchestra	
10/12/59	**4**	14	1. **In The Mood** [I]	Rendezvous 110
			FIESTAS	
4/27/59	**11**	11	1. So Fine	Old Town 1062
			5TH DIMENSION	
			Marilyn McCoo, Billy Davis Jr., Lamonte McLemore, Florence LaRue, Ron Townson	
2/04/67	**16**	7	1. Go Where You Wanna Go	Soul City 753
6/17/67	**7**	10	2. **Up-Up And Away**	Soul City 756

DATE	POS	WKS	ARTIST—Record Title	LABEL & NO.
12/09/67	34	1	3. Paper Cup	Soul City 760
2/24/68	29	5	4. Carpet Man	Soul City 762
6/22/68	3	12	● 5. **Stoned Soul Picnic**	Soul City 766
10/26/68	13	6	6. Sweet Blindness	Soul City 768
1/11/69	25	6	7. California Soul	Soul City 770
3/15/69	1 (6)	16	8. **Aquarius/Let The Sunshine In** -from the musical "Hair"-	Soul City 772
8/09/69	20	7	9. Workin' On A Groovy Thing	Soul City 776
10/04/69	1 (3)	14	● 10. **Wedding Bell Blues**	Soul City 779
1/24/70	21	6	11. Blowing Away	Soul City 780
5/02/70	24	5	12. Puppet Man	Bell 880
6/27/70	27	5	13. Save The Country	Bell 895
11/21/70	2 (2)	15	● 14. **One Less Bell To Answer**	Bell 940
3/13/71	19	8	15. Love's Lines, Angles And Rhymes	Bell 965
10/02/71	12	9	16. Never My Love	Bell 45134
1/29/72	37	3	17. Together Let's Find Love	Bell 45170
4/22/72	8	13	● 18. **(Last Night) I Didn't Get To Sleep At All**	Bell 45195
9/30/72	10	12	19. **If I Could Reach You**	Bell 45261
2/10/73	32	4	20. Living Together, Growing Together -from the film "Lost Horizon"-	Bell 45310
			FIFTH ESTATE	
6/10/67	11	6	1. Ding Dong! The Witch Is Dead -from "The Wizard Of Oz"-	Jubilee 5573
			FINNEGAN, LARRY	
3/31/62	11	8	1. Dear One	Old Town 1113
			FIREBALLS	
			quartet led by George Tomsco (lead quitar) & Jimmy Gilmer (vocals) -- also see Jimmy Gilmer & Fireballs	
10/26/59	39	2	1. Torquay [I]	Top Rank 2008
2/01/60	24	6	2. Bulldog [I]	Top Rank 2026
8/07/61	27	3	3. Quite A Party [I]	Warwick 644
1/27/68	9	10	4. **Bottle Of Wine**	Atco 6491
			FIREFALL	
			Denver quintet led by Rick Roberts	
9/25/76	9	14	1. **You Are The Woman**	Atlantic 3335
4/30/77	34	3	2. Cinderella	Atlantic 3392
9/17/77	11	12	3. Just Remember I Love You	Atlantic 3420
10/28/78	11	9	4. Strange Way	Atlantic 3518
5/10/80	35	3	5. Headed For A Fall	Atlantic 3657
2/28/81	37	3	6. Staying With It -with Lisa Nemzo-	Atlantic 3791
			FIREFLIES Featuring Ritchie Adams	
9/28/59	21	10	1. You Were Mine	Ribbon 6901
			FIRST CHOICE	
			Philadelphia trio	
4/28/73	28	5	1. Armed And Extremely Dangerous	Philly Groove 175

DATE	POS	WKS	ARTIST—Record Title	LABEL & NO.
			FIRST CLASS	
			English studio group	
8/17/74	4	11	1. **Beach Baby**	UK 49022
			FIRST EDITION - see KENNY ROGERS	
			FISHER, EDDIE	
			1st charted hit was in l950	
3/05/55	16	2	1. A Man Chases A Girl/	
			-from film "There's No Business Like Show Business"-	
4/02/55	20	1	2. (I'm Always Hearing) Wedding Bells	RCA 6015
5/14/55	6	13	3. **Heart**	RCA 6097
			-from musical "Damn Yankees"-	
8/27/55	11	8	4. Song Of The Dreamer	RCA 6196
12/24/55	7	16	5. **Dungaree Doll**/	
12/31/55	20	1	6. Everybody's Got A Home But Me	RCA 6337
			-from Broadway's "Pipe Dream"-	
6/30/56	18	7	7. On The Street Where You Live	RCA 6529
			-from musical "My Fair Lady"-	
10/20/56	10	17	8. **Cindy, Oh Cindy**	RCA 6677
			FISHER, MISS TONI	
11/23/59	3	14	1. **The Big Hurt**	Signet 275
7/14/62	37	1	2. West Of The Wall	Big Top 3097
			FITZGERALD, ELLA	
5/30/60	27	7	1. Mack The Knife	Verve 10209
			-with The Paul Smith Quartet-	
			FIVE AMERICANS	
			Dallas quintet	
2/12/66	26	5	1. I See The Light	HBR 454
3/18/67	5	9	2. **Western Union**	Abnak 118
6/17/67	36	2	3. Sound Of Love	Abnak 120
9/16/67	36	1	4. Zip Code	Abnak 123
			FIVE BLOBS	
			Bernie Nee - one man group	
11/03/58	33	3	1. The Blob	Columbia 41250
			-from film of the same title-	
			FIVE FLIGHTS UP	
10/03/70	37	5	1. Do What You Wanna Do	T-A 202
			FIVE KEYS	
			group led by Rudy West & Maryland Pierce	
12/25/54	28	2	1. Ling, Ting, Tong	Capitol 2945
10/06/56	23	6	2. Out Of Sight, Out Of Mind	Capitol 3502
1/12/57	35	2	3. Wisdom Of A Fool	Capitol 3597
			FIVE MAN ELECTRICAL BAND	
			Canadian - Les Emmerson, lead singer	
7/10/71	3	12	● 1. **Signs**	Lionel 3213
10/30/71	26	6	2. Absolutely Right	Lionel 3220
			FIVE SATINS	
9/29/56	24	6	1. In The Still Of The Nite	Ember 1005
8/12/57	25	8	2. To The Aisle	Ember 1019

DATE	POS	WKS	ARTIST—Record Title	LABEL & NO.
			FIVE STAIRSTEPS	
			Chicago family group	
6/20/70	8	11	● 1. **O-o-h Child**	Buddah 165
			5000 VOLTS	
11/15/75	26	5	1. I'm On Fire	Philips 40801
			FLACK, ROBERTA	
3/25/72	1 (6)	15	1. **The First Time Ever I Saw Your Face**	Atlantic 2864
2/03/73	1 (5)	13	● 2. **Killing Me Softly With His Song**	Atlantic 2940
10/13/73	30	5	3. Jesse	Atlantic 2982
7/06/74	1 (1)	13	● 4. **Feel Like Makin' Love**	Atlantic 3025
6/24/78	24	5	5. If Ever I See You Again	Atlantic 3483
4/17/82	13	11	6. Making Love	Atlantic 4005
			FLACK, ROBERTA, & DONNY HATHAWAY	
			Donny died on 1/13/79 (33)	
7/03/71	29	9	1. You've Got A Friend	Atlantic 2808
6/24/72	5	11	● 2. **Where Is The Love**	Atlantic 2879
3/18/78	2 (2)	14	● 3. **The Closer I Get To You**	Atlantic 3463
			FLAMING EMBER	
			Detroit quartet	
11/15/69	26	6	1. Mind, Body And Soul	Hot Wax 6902
6/20/70	24	10	2. Westbound # 9	Hot Wax 7003
11/28/70	34	6	3. I'm Not My Brothers Keeper	Hot Wax 7006
			FLAMINGOS	
			Chicago quintet led by Nate Nelson and Zeke Carey	
6/08/59	11	11	1. I Only Have Eyes For You	End 1046
5/23/60	30	3	2. Nobody Loves Me Like You	End 1068
			FLARES	
10/09/61	25	9	1. Foot Stomping - Part 1	Felsted 8624
			FLASH	
			English quartet	
7/29/72	29	6	1. Small Beginnings	Capitol 3345
			FLASH CADILLAC & THE CONTINENTAL KIDS	
10/02/76	29	6	1. Did You Boogie (With Your Baby) -with Wolfman Jack-	Private Stock 45079
			FLEETWOOD MAC	
			English-American band: Mick Fleetwood, Christine McVie, John McVie, Stevie Nicks & Lindsey Buckingham	
12/13/75	20	7	1. Over My Head	Reprise 1339
4/10/76	11	11	2. Rhiannon (Will You Ever Win)	Reprise 1345
7/31/76	11	13	3. Say You Love Me	Reprise 1356
1/22/77	10	11	4. **Go Your Own Way**	Warner 8304
4/30/77	1 (1)	13	● 5. **Dreams**	Warner 8371
7/23/77	3	14	6. **Don't Stop**	Warner 8413
10/29/77	9	9	7. **You Make Loving Fun**	Warner 8483
10/13/79	8	10	8. Tusk	Warner 49077
12/22/79	7	11	9. Sara	Warner 49150
3/29/80	20	7	10. Think About Me	Warner 49196

DATE	POS	WKS	ARTIST—Record Title	LABEL & NO.
6/19/82	**4**	15	11. **Hold Me**	Warner 29966
9/25/82	**12**	8	12. Gypsy	Warner 29918
			FLEETWOODS	
			Gary Troxel, Barbara Ellis, & Gretchen Christopher	
3/16/59	**1** (4)	12	1. **Come Softly To Me**	Dolphin 1
6/22/59	**39**	1	2. Graduation's Here	Dolton 3
9/14/59	**1** (1)	12	3. **Mr. Blue**	Dolton 5
2/29/60	**28**	3	4. Outside My Window	Dolton 15
6/27/60	**23**	4	5. Runaround	Dolton 22
5/08/61	**10**	8	6. **Tragedy**	Dolton 40
10/02/61	**30**	4	7. (He's) The Great Impostor	Dolton 45
11/24/62	**36**	2	8. Lovers By Night, Strangers By Day	Dolton 62
7/13/63	**32**	4	9. Goodnight My Love	Dolton 75
			FLINT, SHELBY	
2/06/61	**22**	5	1. Angel On My Shoulder	Valiant 6001
			FLIRTATIONS	
5/24/69	**34**	2	1. Nothing But A Heartache	Deram 85038
			FLOATERS	
7/30/77	**2** (2)	11	● 1. **Float On**	ABC 12284
			FLOCK OF SEAGULLS	
			British techno-pop quartet	
9/04/82	**9**	10	1. **I Ran (So Far Away)**	Jive 102
			FLOOD, DICK	
9/14/59	**23**	4	1. The Three Bells (The Jimmy Brown Story)	Monument 408
			FLOYD, EDDIE	
			member of The Falcons	
11/19/66	**28**	6	1. Knock On Wood	Stax 194
9/07/68	**40**	2	2. I've Never Found A Girl (To Love Me Like You Do)	Stax 0002
11/16/68	**17**	9	3. Bring It On Home To Me	Stax 0012
			FLYING MACHINE	
			English studio group	
10/18/69	**5**	12	● 1. **Smile A Little Smile For Me**	Congress 6000
			FOCUS	
			Dutch	
4/21/73	**9**	11	1. **Hocus Pocus [I]**	Sire 704
			FOGELBERG, DAN	
3/01/75	**31**	3	1. Part Of The Plan	Epic 50055
1/19/80	**2** (2)	13	2. **Longer**	Full Moon 50824
4/19/80	**21**	6	3. Heart Hotels	Full Moon 50862
12/27/80	**9**	13	4. **Same Old Lang Syne**	Full Moon 50961
9/19/81	**7**	10	5. **Hard To Say**	Full Moon 02488
12/19/81	**9**	16	6. **Leader Of The Band**	Full Moon 02647
4/24/82	**18**	8	7. Run For The Roses	Full Moon 02821
11/13/82	**23**	9	8. Missing You	Full Moon 03289
			FOGELBERG, DAN/TIM WEISBERG	
11/04/78	**24**	7	1. The Power Of Gold	Full Moon 50606

DATE	POS	WKS	ARTIST—Record Title	LABEL & NO.
			FOGERTY, JOHN	
			leader of Creedence Clearwater Revival, & the Blue Ridge Rangers	
10/04/75	27	6	1. Rockin' All Over The World	Asylum 45274
			FOGHAT	
			British quartet led by Lonesome Dave Peverett - formerly with Savoy Brown	
1/10/76	20	12	1. Slow Ride	Bearsville 0306
12/25/76	34	4	2. Drivin' Wheel	Bearsville 0313
10/15/77	33	3	3. I Just Want To Make Love To You	Bearsville 0319
			-live version of 1972 hit-	
6/24/78	36	2	4. Stone Blue	Bearsville 0325
12/08/79	23	10	5. Third Time Lucky (First Time I Was A Fool)	Bearsville 49125
			FONTANA, WAYNE - see MINDBENDERS	
			FONTANE SISTERS	
			Marge, Bea & Geri - featuring Billy Vaughn's Orchestra	
12/11/54	1 (3)	20	1. **Hearts Of Stone**	Dot 15265
2/26/55	13	8	2. Rock Love	Dot 15333
6/04/55	13	6	3. Rollin' Stone	Dot 15370
8/20/55	3	15	4. **Seventeen**	Dot 15386
11/26/55	11	11	5. Daddy-O	Dot 15428
12/31/55	36	1	6. Nuttin' For Christmas [N]	Dot 15434
3/17/56	11	11	7. Eddie My Love	Dot 15450
7/14/56	38	1	8. I'm In Love Again	Dot 15462
1/12/57	13	10	9. The Banana Boat Song	Dot 15527
4/28/58	12	9	10. Chanson D'amour (Song of Love)	Dot 15736
			FORBERT, STEVE	
1/05/80	11	12	1. Romeo's Tune	Nemperor 7525
			FORD, FRANKIE	
3/09/59	14	12	1. Sea Cruise	Ace 554
			-with Huey "Piano" Smith-	
			FORD, "TENNESSEE" ERNIE	
3/19/55	5	17	1. **Ballad Of Davy Crockett**	Capitol 3058
11/12/55	1 (8)	19	2. **Sixteen Tons**	Capitol 3262
3/10/56	17	1	3. That's All	Capitol 3343
9/23/57	23	1	4. In The Middle Of An Island	Capitol 3762
			FOREIGNER	
			English-American group led by Mick Jones (guitar), & Lou Gramm (vocals)	
4/23/77	4	13	1. **Feels Like The First Time**	Atlantic 3394
8/13/77	6	15	2. **Cold As Ice**	Atlantic 3410
1/14/78	20	8	3. Long, Long Way From Home	Atlantic 3439
7/08/78	3	14	● 4. **Hot Blooded**	Atlantic 3488
9/30/78	2 (2)	12	● 5. **Double Vision**	Atlantic 3514
1/20/79	15	8	6. Blue Morning, Blue Day	Atlantic 3543
9/22/79	12	9	7. Dirty White Boy	Atlantic 3618
11/24/79	14	9	8. Head Games	Atlantic 3633
7/11/81	4	17	9. **Urgent**	Atlantic 3831
10/17/81	2(10)	19	● 10. **Waiting For A Girl Like You**	Atlantic 3868

DATE	POS	WKS	ARTIST—Record Title	LABEL & NO.
3/06/82	**26**	6	11. Juke Box Hero	Atlantic 4017
6/05/82	**26**	6	12. Break It Up	Atlantic 4044
			FORTUNES	
			British quintet	
9/11/65	**7**	8	1. **You've Got Your Troubles**	Press 9773
11/27/65	**27**	4	2. Here It Comes Again	Press 9798
6/19/71	**15**	9	3. Here Comes That Rainy Day Feeling Again	Capitol 3086
			FOUNDATIONS	
			English - Clem Curtis, leader	
1/13/68	**11**	10	1. Baby, Now That I've Found You	Uni 55038
1/18/69	**3**	13	● 2. **Build Me Up Buttercup**	Uni 55101
			FOUR ACES Featuring Al Alberts	
			Al with Dave Mahoney, Lou Silvestri and Sod Vocarro	
1/15/55	**3**	21	1. **Melody Of Love**	Decca 29395
5/28/55	**13**	6	2. Heart	Decca 29476
			-from musical "Damn Yankees"-	
8/27/55	**1** (6)	21	3. **Love Is A Many-Splendored Thing**	Decca 29625
12/03/55	**14**	12	4. A Woman In Love	Decca 29725
			-from film "Guys And Dolls"-	
8/04/56	**22**	5	5. I Only Know I Love You	Decca 29989
10/20/56	**20**	2	6. You Can't Run Away From It	Decca 30041
			FOUR COINS	
			from Pennsylvania	
1/15/55	**28**	1	1. I Love You Madly	Epic 9082
12/10/55	**22**	8	2. Memories Of You	Epic 9129
			-from "The Benny Goodman Story"-	
6/17/57	**11**	14	3. Shangri-La	Epic 9213
10/14/57	**28**	4	4. My One Sin	Epic 9229
11/17/58	**21**	8	5. The World Outside	Epic 9295
			-theme from "Warsaw Concerto"-	
			FOUR ESQUIRES	
			from Boston, Massachusetts	
12/16/57	**25**	1	1. Love Me Forever	Paris 509
11/03/58	**21**	6	2. Hideaway	Paris 520
			FOUR FRESHMEN	
			formed in Indianapolis at Butler University	
6/09/56	**17**	7	1. Graduation Day	Capitol 3410
			FOUR JACKS AND A JILL	
			South African group	
5/18/68	**18**	7	1. Master Jack	RCA 9473
			FOUR KNIGHTS - see NAT KING COLE	
			FOUR LADS	
			Canadian: Jimmie, Connie, Bernie & Frankie	
9/03/55	**2** (6)	25	1. **Moments To Remember**	Columbia 40539
1/28/56	**2** (4)	19	2. **No, Not Much!**	Columbia 40629
4/28/56	**3**	18	3. **Standing On The Corner/**	
			-from Broadway's "The Most Happy Fella"-	
4/28/56	**24**	6	4. My Little Angel	Columbia 40674
9/15/56	**16**	6	5. The Bus Stop Song (A Paper Of Pins)/	
			-from the film "Bus Stop"-	
9/15/56	**20**	6	6. A House With Love In It	Columbia 40736

DATE	POS	WKS	ARTIST—Record Title	LABEL & NO.
2/02/57	9	15	7. **Who Needs You**	Columbia 40811
5/20/57	17	4	8. I Just Don't Know	Columbia 40914
12/09/57	8	9	9. **Put A Light In The Window**	Columbia 41058
4/07/58	10	7	10. **There's Only One Of You**	Columbia 41136
7/14/58	12	6	11. Enchanted Island	Columbia 41194
11/24/58	32	3	12. The Mocking Bird -new version of 1956 hit-	Columbia 41266
			FOUR PREPS	
			Bruce, Glen, Ed & Marv formed group at Hollywood High School	
1/20/58	2 (3)	14	1. **26 Miles (Santa Catalina)**	Capitol 3845
5/05/58	3	14	2. **Big Man**	Capitol 3960
9/01/58	21	6	3. Lazy Summer Night -from "Andy Hardy Comes Home"-	Capitol 4023
1/11/60	13	11	4. Down By The Station	Capitol 4312
5/16/60	24	3	5. Got A Girl [N]	Capitol 4362
9/11/61	17	4	6. More Money For You And Me (medley) [N]	Capitol 4599
			FOUR SEASONS	
			formed in Newark, New Jersey in 1956 as The Four Lovers, the group's success was mainly due to 'the "sound" of Frankie Valli' - also see The Wonder Who	
9/01/62	1 (5)	12	1. **Sherry**	Vee-Jay 456
10/27/62	1 (5)	14	2. **Big Girls Don't Cry**	Vee-Jay 465
12/22/62	23	2	3. Santa Claus Is Coming To Town [X]	Vee-Jay 478
1/26/63	1 (3)	12	4. **Walk Like A Man**	Vee-Jay 485
5/04/63	22	6	5. Ain't That A Shame!	Vee-Jay 512
7/20/63	3	10	6. **Candy Girl/**	
8/10/63	36	3	7. Marlena	Vee-Jay 539
11/02/63	36	2	8. New Mexican Rose	Vee-Jay 562
2/08/64	3	11	9. **Dawn (Go Away)**	Philips 40166
3/07/64	16	8	10. Stay	Vee-Jay 582
4/18/64	6	8	11. **Ronnie**	Philips 40185
6/27/64	1 (2)	11	● 12. **Rag Doll**	Philips 40211
6/27/64	28	5	13. Alone	Vee-Jay 597
9/05/64	10	6	14. **Save It For Me**	Philips 40225
11/21/64	20	5	15. Big Man In Town	Philips 40238
1/30/65	12	6	16. Bye, Bye, Baby (Baby Goodbye)	Philips 40260
7/10/65	30	3	17. Girl Come Running	Philips 40305
10/30/65	3	12	18. **Let's Hang On!**	Philips 40317
2/12/66	9	6	19. **Working My Way Back To You**	Philips 40350
5/28/66	13	7	20. Opus 17 (Don't You Worry 'Bout Me)	Philips 40370
9/17/66	9	8	21. **I've Got You Under My Skin**	Philips 40393
12/24/66	10	8	22. **Tell It To The Rain**	Philips 40412
3/18/67	16	7	23. Beggin'	Philips 40433
6/17/67	9	8	24. **C'mon Marianne**	Philips 40460
11/18/67	30	4	25. Watch The Flowers Grow	Philips 40490
3/09/68	24	5	26. Will You Love Me Tomorrow	Philips 40523
9/20/75	3	12	27. **Who Loves You**	Warner 8122
1/31/76	1 (3)	15	● 28. **December, 1963 (Oh, What A Night)**	Warner 8168

DATE	POS	WKS	ARTIST—Record Title	LABEL & NO.
7/04/76	38	2	29. Silver Star	Warner 8203
			FOUR TOPS	
			from Detroit: Levi Stubbs, Duke Fakir, Lawrence Payton, & Obie Benson -- also see The Supremes	
8/29/64	11	10	1. Baby I Need Your Loving	Motown 1062
2/20/65	24	6	2. Ask The Lonely	Motown 1073
5/22/65	1 (2)	13	3. **I Can't Help Myself**	Motown 1076
8/07/65	5	8	4. **It's The Same Old Song**	Motown 1081
11/20/65	19	6	5. Something About You	Motown 1084
3/12/66	18	6	6. Shake Me, Wake Me (When It's Over)	Motown 1090
9/17/66	1 (2)	12	7. **Reach Out I'll Be There**	Motown 1098
12/24/66	6	9	8. **Standing In The Shadows Of Love**	Motown 1102
3/18/67	4	8	9. **Bernadette**	Motown 1104
6/03/67	14	6	10. 7 Rooms Of Gloom	Motown 1110
9/30/67	19	5	11. You Keep Running Away	Motown 1113
2/17/68	14	6	12. Walk Away Renee	Motown 1119
5/11/68	20	6	13. If I Were A Carpenter	Motown 1124
5/30/70	24	8	14. It's All In The Game	Motown 1164
9/26/70	11	10	15. Still Water (Love)	Motown 1170
2/27/71	40	2	16. Just Seven Numbers (Can Straighten Out My Life)	Motown 1175
10/02/71	38	3	17. Mac Arthur Park (Part II)	Motown 1189
12/02/72	10	9	18. **Keeper Of The Castle**	Dunhill 4330
2/24/73	4	12	● 19. **Ain't No Woman (Like The One I've Got)**	Dunhill 4339
7/28/73	15	8	20. Are You Man Enough -from film "Shaft In Africa"-	Dunhill 4354
11/17/73	33	3	21. Sweet Understanding Love	Dunhill 4366
9/19/81	11	11	22. When She Was My Girl	Casablanca 2338
			FOUR VOICES	
3/17/56	20	4	1. Lovely One	Columbia 40643
			FOXX, INEZ	
			vocal accompaniment by her brother Charlie Foxx	
8/03/63	7	10	1. **Mockingbird**	Symbol 919
			FOXY	
8/26/78	9	13	1. **Get Off**	Dash 5046
4/28/79	21	9	2. Hot Number	Dash 5050
			FRAMPTON, PETER	
			member of English groups: The Herd, and Humble Pie	
3/13/76	6	14	1. **Show Me The Way**	A&M 1795
7/17/76	12	11	2. Baby, I Love Your Way	A&M 1832
10/09/76	10	10	3. **Do You Feel Like We Do**	A&M 1867
6/11/77	2 (3)	13	4. **I'm In You**	A&M 1941
9/10/77	18	10	5. Signed, Sealed, Delivered (I'm Yours)	A&M 1972
6/09/79	14	9	6. I Can't Stand It No More	A&M 2148
			FRANCIS, CONNIE	
3/03/58	4	15	1. **Who's Sorry Now**	MGM 12588
6/09/58	36	2	2. I'm Sorry I Made You Cry	MGM 12647

DATE	POS	WKS	ARTIST—Record Title	LABEL & NO.
8/04/58	**14**	11	3. Stupid Cupid	MGM 12683
11/17/58	**30**	1	4. Fallin'	MGM 12713
12/15/58	**2** (2)	14	5. **My Happiness**	MGM 12738
3/30/59	**22**	4	6. If I Didn't Care	MGM 12769
6/01/59	**5**	12	7. **Lipstick On Your Collar/**	
6/01/59	**9**	11	8. **Frankie**	MGM 12793
9/21/59	**34**	4	9. You're Gonna Miss Me	MGM 12824
12/07/59	**7**	11	10. **Among My Souvenirs/**	
12/21/59	**36**	2	11. God Bless America	MGM 12841
3/14/60	**8**	9	12. **Mama/**	
3/28/60	**17**	6	13. Teddy	MGM 12878
5/16/60	**1** (2)	16	14. **Everybody's Somebody's Fool/**	
6/06/60	**19**	8	15. Jealous Of You [F]	MGM 12899
8/22/60	**1** (2)	14	16. **My Heart Has A Mind Of Its Own**	MGM 12923
11/21/60	**7**	10	17. **Many Tears Ago**	MGM 12964
1/30/61	**4**	12	18. **Where The Boys Are/**	
2/20/61	**34**	2	19. No One	MGM 12971
4/24/61	**7**	9	20. **Breakin' In A Brand New Broken Heart**	MGM 12995
7/03/61	**6**	9	21. **Together**	MGM 13019
10/09/61	**14**	7	22. (He's My) Dreamboat	MGM 13039
12/04/61	**10**	9	23. **When The Boy In Your Arms (Is The Boy In Your Heart)/**	
1/06/62	**26**	1	24. Baby's First Christmas [X]	MGM 13051
2/24/62	**1** (1)	10	25. **Don't Break The Heart That Loves You**	MGM 13059
5/19/62	**7**	7	26. **Second Hand Love**	MGM 13074
8/11/62	**9**	6	27. **Vacation**	MGM 13087
11/03/62	**24**	4	28. I Was Such A Fool (To Fall In Love With You)	MGM 13096
1/05/63	**18**	6	29. I'm Gonna' Be Warm This Winter	MGM 13116
3/16/63	**17**	7	30. Follow The Boys	MGM 13127
6/08/63	**23**	5	31. If My Pillow Could Talk	MGM 13143
8/31/63	**36**	3	32. Drownin' My Sorrows	MGM 13160
11/09/63	**28**	4	33. Your Other Love	MGM 13176
3/07/64	**24**	6	34. Blue Winter	MGM 13214
5/30/64	**25**	5	35. Be Anything (But Be Mine)	MGM 13237
			FRANKE & THE KNOCKOUTS	
			quintet led by Frankie Previte	
3/21/81	**10**	14	1. **Sweetheart**	Millennium 11801
8/01/81	**27**	5	2. You're My Girl	Millennium 11808
5/08/82	**24**	7	3. Without You (Not Another Lonely Night)	Millennium 13105
			FRANKLIN, ARETHA	
11/20/61	**37**	2	1. Rock-A-Bye Your Baby With A Dixie Melody	Columbia 42157
3/18/67	**9**	9	● 2. **I Never Loved A Man (The Way I Love You)**	Atlantic 2386
5/06/67	**1** (2)	11	● 3. **Respect**	Atlantic 2403
8/05/67	**4**	8	● 4. **Baby I Love You**	Atlantic 2427
10/07/67	**8**	8	5. **A Natural Woman (You Make Me Feel Like)**	Atlantic 2441

DATE	POS	WKS	ARTIST—Record Title	LABEL & NO.
12/16/67	2 (2)	11	● 6. **Chain Of Fools**	Atlantic 2464
3/02/68	5	12	● 7. **(Sweet Sweet Baby) Since You've Been Gone/**	
4/13/68	16	7	8. Ain't No Way	Atlantic 2486
5/25/68	7	9	● 9. **Think**	Atlantic 2518
8/24/68	6	8	10. **The House That Jack Built/**	
8/24/68	10	10	● 11. **I Say A Little Prayer**	Atlantic 2546
11/23/68	14	8	● 12. See Saw/	
12/28/68	31	2	13. My Song	Atlantic 2574
3/01/69	19	6	14. The Weight	Atlantic 2603
4/26/69	28	6	15. I Can't See Myself Leaving You	Atlantic 2619
8/09/69	13	9	16. Share Your Love With Me	Atlantic 2650
11/15/69	17	7	17. Eleanor Rigby	Atlantic 2683
2/28/70	13	9	18. Call Me	Atlantic 2706
6/13/70	23	5	19. Spirit In The Dark	Atlantic 2731
8/22/70	11	8	● 20. Don't Play That Song	Atlantic 2751
12/19/70	37	2	21. Border Song (Holy Moses)	Atlantic 2772
3/06/71	19	7	22. You're All I Need To Get By	Atlantic 2787
4/24/71	6	11	● 23. **Bridge Over Troubled Water**	Atlantic 2796
8/07/71	2 (2)	11	● 24. **Spanish Harlem**	Atlantic 2817
11/06/71	9	8	● 25. **Rock Steady**	Atlantic 2838
3/25/72	5	11	● 26. **Day Dreaming**	Atlantic 2866
6/17/72	26	6	27. All The King's Horses	Atlantic 2883
3/10/73	33	5	28. Master Of Eyes (The Deepness Of Your Eyes)	Atlantic 2941
7/21/73	20	10	29. Angel	Atlantic 2969
12/15/73	3	17	● 30. **Until You Come Back To Me (That's What I'm Gonna Do)**	Atlantic 2995
5/04/74	19	8	31. I'm In Love	Atlantic 2999
7/10/76	28	6	32. Something He Can Feel	Atlantic 3326
9/11/82	24	6	33. Jump To It	Arista 0699
			FREBERG, STAN	
10/22/55	16	2	1. The Yellow Rose Of Texas [C]	Capitol 3249
4/27/57	25	1	2. Banana Boat (Day-O) [C] -interruptions by Peter Leeds-	Capitol 3687
11/18/57	32	3	3. Wun'erful, Wun'erful! (Parts 1 & 2) [C] -with Peggy Taylor & Daws Butler-	Capitol 3815
			FRED, JOHN, & His Playboy Band John Fred Gourrier	
12/16/67	1 (2)	13	● 1. **Judy In Disguise (With Glasses)**	Paula 282
			FREDDIE & THE DREAMERS Freddie Garrity, leader of English quintet	
3/27/65	1 (2)	8	1. **I'm Telling You Now**	Tower 125
4/24/65	36	2	2. I Understand (Just How You Feel)	Mercury 72377
5/15/65	18	5	3. Do The Freddie	Mercury 72428
5/15/65	21	5	4. You Were Made For Me	Tower 127
			FREE British quartet - Paul Rodgers & Simon Kirke formed Bad Company	
9/05/70	4	13	1. **All Right Now**	A&M 1206

DATE	POS	WKS	ARTIST—Record Title	LABEL & NO.
			FREE MOVEMENT	
9/18/71	5	11	1. **I've Found Someone Of My Own**	Decca 32818
			FREEMAN, BOBBY	
5/26/58	5	12	1. **Do You Want To Dance**	Josie 835
8/18/58	37	1	2. Betty Lou Got A New Pair Of Shoes	Josie 841
9/26/60	37	3	3. (I Do The) Shimmy Shimmy	King 5373
7/25/64	5	10	4. **C'mon And Swim**	Autumn 2
			FREEMAN, ERNIE	
			died 5/15/81 (57)	
11/18/57	4	12	1. **Raunchy [I]**	Imperial 5474
			FREHLEY, ACE	
			member of Kiss	
12/02/78	13	12	1. New York Groove	Casablanca 941
			FREY, GLENN	
			member of The Eagles	
7/17/82	31	5	1. I Found Somebody	Asylum 47466
9/11/82	15	11	2. The One You Love	Asylum 69974
			FRIEDMAN, DEAN	
5/21/77	26	10	1. Ariel	Lifesong 45022
			FRIEND AND LOVER	
			James & wife Cathy Post	
6/01/68	10	11	1. **Reach Out Of The Darkness**	Verve Forecast 5069
			FRIENDS OF DISTINCTION	
			Los Angeles-based quartet	
4/26/69	3	13	● 1. **Grazing In The Grass**	RCA 0107
10/11/69	15	12	● 2. Going In Circles	RCA 0204
3/21/70	6	11	3. **Love Or Let Me Be Lonely**	RCA 0319
			FRIJID PINK	
			Michigan quintet	
2/21/70	7	11	● 1. **House Of The Rising Sun**	Parrot 341
			FROST, MAX, & THE TROOPERS	
9/28/68	22	9	1. Shape Of Things To Come -from film "Wild In The Streets"-	Tower 419
			FULLER, BOBBY, Four	
			Bobby died on 7/18/66 (22)	
2/12/66	9	8	1. **I Fought The Law**	Mustang 3014
5/07/66	26	3	2. Love's Made A Fool Of You	Mustang 3016
			FUNKADELIC	
			a George Clinton "Parliafunkadelicment Thang" - also see Parliaments	
11/04/78	28	5	● 1. One Nation Under A Groove (Part 1)	Warner 8618
			FURAY, RICHIE	
			member of Buffalo Springfield, Poco, & Souther, Hillman, Furay Band	
12/15/79	39	2	1. I Still Have Dreams	Asylum 46534
			FUZZ	
4/17/71	21	8	1. I Love You For All Seasons	Calla 174

The Four Seasons were one of the few American groups to retain and increase their popularity throughout the British invasion of the mid '60s, thanks in large part to the vocal talents of Francis Castellucio a/k/a Frankie Valli.

The Four Tops, whose first recording sessions for Motown produced an album of jazz standards before their classic "Baby I Need Your Loving" hit, have been together for 30 years without a membership change.

Connie Francis. It was Connie Francis' father who suggested that she record the oldie "Who's Sorry Now" after the teenage singer's first ten singles for MGM records were somewhat less than spectacular hits.

Aretha Franklin. Several years before her Atlantic hits secured Aretha Franklin the title of "Queen of Soul," both she and sister Erma were contracted to the same record company, CBS. By all accounts, 'Ree did not appreciate the competition.

Glenn Frey. Detroit native Glenn Frey played in the band of another Motor City son, Bob Seger, before helping to form the Eagles in Los Angeles during the early '70s.

Annette Funicello. From The Mouseketeers to peanut butter by way of beach blanket movies, Annette Funicello has retained her charms. Look for her 1965 non-hit with the Beach Boys, "The Monkey's Uncle."

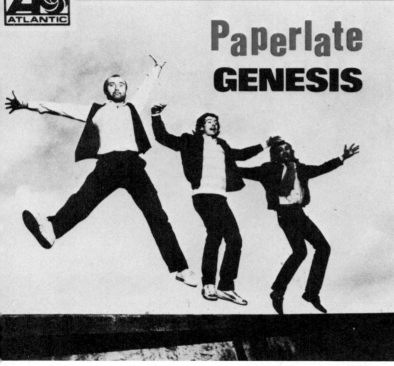

Paperlate · You Might Recall

stereo

ATLANTIC

Paperlate GENESIS

The Gap Band's Ronnie, Charles, and Robert Wilson took their name from the initials of three streets in the heart of their Tulsa hometown's black community: Greenwood, Archer, Pine. Really, they did.

Leif Garrett. When Leif Garrett gravitated from acting to singing, producer Michael Lloyd knew where to go for material: the '60s. Among the artists whose hits Leif resurrected were Dion, the Beach Boys, and Paul Anka.

Marvin Gaye's "I Heard It Through The Grapevine" was actually recorded before Gladys Knight and the Pips' chart-topping version, but gathered dust in the Motown vaults for a couple of years.

Genesis owe their music business break to producer and self-styled pop eccentric Jonathan King, a one-hit wonder in his own right with "Everyone's Gone To The Moon."

Andy Gibb. When Barry Gibb teamed up with Barbra Streisand for "What Kind Of Fool," the result was a top 10 single. When brother Andy got together with Victoria Principal for "All I Have To Do Is Dream" . . .

Bobby Goldsboro wrote most of his own hits—except the biggest, "Honey." That was authored by Bobby Russell, whose other composing credits include "Little Green Apples" and "He Ain't Heavy, He's My Brother."

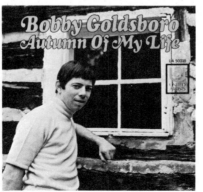

DATE	POS	WKS	ARTIST—Record Title	LABEL & NO.
			GADABOUTS featuring Wild Bill Putnam	
8/04/56	39	1	1. Stranded In The Jungle [N]	Mercury 70898
			GALE, SUNNY	
1/08/55	17	1	1. Let Me Go, Lover!	RCA 5952
			GALLERY	
			Jim Gold, leader of Detroit sextet	
4/29/72	4	13	● 1. **Nice To Be With You**	Sussex 232
10/07/72	22	8	2. I Believe In Music	Sussex 239
2/10/73	23	8	3. Big City Miss Ruth Ann	Sussex 248
			GALLOP, FRANK	
			radio & TV announcer	
5/07/66	34	5	1. The Ballad Of Irving [C]	Kapp 745
			GAP BAND	
			trio of brothers from Tulsa	
7/03/82	24	6	1. Early In The Morning	Total Exp. 8201
9/11/82	31	7	2. You Dropped A Bomb On Me	Total Exp. 8203
			GARDNER, DAVE	
			comedian "Brother" Dave Gardner	
7/22/57	22	4	1. White Silver Sands	OJ 1002
			GARDNER, DON, & DEE DEE FORD	
7/07/62	20	7	1. I Need Your Loving	Fire 508
			GARFUNKEL, ART	
			also see Simon & Garfunkel	
10/06/73	9	10	1. **All I Know**	Columbia 45926
2/09/74	38	1	2. I Shall Sing	Columbia 45983
10/19/74	34	3	3. Second Avenue	Columbia 10020
9/27/75	18	12	4. I Only Have Eyes For You	Columbia 10190
1/31/76	39	2	5. Break Away	Columbia 10273
			GARFUNKEL, ART, with JAMES TAYLOR & PAUL SIMON	
2/11/78	17	7	1. (What A) Wonderful World	Columbia 10676
			GARI, FRANK	
2/13/61	27	5	1. Utopia	Crusade 1020
5/15/61	23	6	2. Lullaby Of Love	Crusade 1021
8/14/61	30	3	3. Princess	Crusade 1022
9/05/64	4	13	1. **We'll Sing In The Sunshine**	RCA 8388
			GARRETT, LEIF	
9/17/77	20	8	1. Surfin' USA	Atlantic 3423
12/03/77	13	9	2. Runaround Sue	Atlantic 3440
12/09/78	10	15	3. **I Was Made For Dancin'**	Scotti Bros. 403
			GATES, DAVID	
			lead singer of Bread	
2/15/75	29	5	1. Never Let Her Go	Elektra 45223
2/18/78	15	12	2. Goodbye Girl	Elektra 45450
10/07/78	30	5	3. Took The Last Train	Elektra 45500

DATE	POS	WKS	ARTIST—Record Title	LABEL & NO.
			GAYE, MARVIN	
3/02/63	30	3	1. Hitch Hike	Tamla 54075
6/15/63	10	10	2. **Pride And Joy**	Tamla 54079
11/23/63	22	10	3. Can I Get A Witness	Tamla 54087
3/28/64	15	7	4. You're A Wonderful One	Tamla 54093
6/27/64	15	8	5. Try It Baby	Tamla 54095
10/10/64	27	6	6. Baby Don't You Do It	Tamla 54101
12/12/64	6	11	7. **How Sweet It Is To Be Loved By You**	Tamla 54107
4/10/65	8	8	8. **I'll Be Doggone**	Tamla 54112
7/24/65	25	5	9. Pretty Little Baby	Tamla 54117
10/23/65	8	9	10. **Ain't That Peculiar**	Tamla 54122
3/12/66	29	4	11. One More Heartache	Tamla 54129
7/22/67	33	3	12. Your Unchanging Love	Tamla 54153
2/03/68	34	3	13. You	Tamla 54160
10/19/68	32	4	14. Chained	Tamla 54170
11/23/68	1 (7)	15	15. **I Heard It Through The Grapevine**	Tamla 54176
5/10/69	4	13	16. **Too Busy Thinking About My Baby**	Tamla 54181
9/13/69	7	9	17. **That's The Way Love Is**	Tamla 54185
7/11/70	40	2	18. The End Of Our Road	Tamla 54195
3/06/71	2 (3)	13	19. **What's Going On**	Tamla 54201
7/17/71	4	10	20. **Mercy Mercy Me (The Ecology)**	Tamla 54207
10/16/71	9	8	21. **Inner City Blues (Make Me Wanna Holler)**	Tamla 54209
12/30/72	7	9	22. **Trouble Man**	Tamla 54228
7/28/73	1 (2)	17	23. **Let's Get It On**	Tamla 54234
11/17/73	21	8	24. Come Get To This	Tamla 54241
10/26/74	28	3	25. Distant Lover	Tamla 54253
5/08/76	15	9	26. I Want You	Tamla 54264
4/23/77	1 (1)	15	27. **Got To Give It Up - Pt. 1**	Tamla 54280
			GAYE, MARVIN, & DIANA ROSS	
10/13/73	12	10	1. You're A Special Part Of Me	Motown 1280
3/30/74	19	10	2. My Mistake (Was To Love You)	Motown 1269
			GAYE, MARVIN, & TAMMI TERRELL	
			Tammi died on 3/16/70 (23)	
6/03/67	19	9	1. Ain't No Mountain High Enough	Tamla 54149
9/30/67	5	10	2. **Your Precious Love**	Tamla 54156
12/16/67	10	9	3. **If I Could Build My Whole World Around You**	Tamla 54161
4/27/68	8	11	4. **Ain't Nothing Like The Real Thing**	Tamla 54163
8/10/68	7	10	5. **You're All I Need To Get By**	Tamla 54169
10/19/68	24	6	6. Keep On Lovin' Me Honey	Tamla 54173
2/15/69	30	4	7. Good Lovin' Ain't Easy To Come By	Tamla 54179
			GAYE, MARVIN, & MARY WELLS	
5/23/64	19	6	1. Once Upon A Time/	
6/13/64	17	6	2. What's The Matter With You Baby	Motown 1057
			GAYE, MARVIN, & KIM WESTON	
2/04/67	14	7	1. It Takes Two	Tamla 54141

DATE	POS	WKS	ARTIST—Record Title	LABEL & NO.
			GAYLE, CRYSTAL	
			younger sister of Loretta Lynn	
9/24/77	**2** (3)	18	● 1. **Don't It Make My Brown Eyes Blue**	United Artists 1016
9/02/78	**18**	11	2. Talking In Your Sleep	United Artists 1214
11/03/79	**15**	10	3. Half The Way	Columbia 11087
			GAYNOR, GLORIA	
12/07/74	**9**	10	1. **Never Can Say Goodbye**	MGM 14748
1/20/79	**1** (3)	17	★ 2. **I Will Survive**	Polydor 14508
			G-CLEFS	
9/15/56	**24**	1	1. Ka-Ding Dong	Pilgrim 715
10/16/61	**9**	11	2. **I Understand (Just How You Feel)**	Terrace 7500
			-Auld Lang Syne-	
			GEDDES, DAVID	
8/23/75	**4**	9	1. **Run Joey Run**	Big Tree 16044
11/22/75	**18**	6	2. The Last Game Of The Season (A Blind Man In The Bleachers)	Big Tree 16052
			GEILS, J., BAND	
			Boston group led by Peter Wolf, Seth Justman, & J. Geils	
1/15/72	**39**	2	1. Looking For A Love	Atlantic 2844
5/26/73	**30**	6	2. Give It To Me	Atlantic 2953
11/23/74	**12**	7	3. Must Of Got Lost	Atlantic 3214
1/20/79	**35**	3	4. One Last Kiss	EMI America 8007
3/08/80	**32**	5	5. Come Back	EMI America 8032
5/24/80	**38**	3	6. Love Stinks	EMI America 8039
11/28/81	**1** (6)	20	● 7. **Centerfold**	EMI America 8102
3/06/82	**4**	12	● 8. **Freeze-Frame**	EMI America 8108
7/03/82	**40**	2	9. Angel In Blue	EMI America 8100
			GENE & DEBBE	
			Gene Thomas & Debbe Nevills	
3/09/68	**17**	12	1. Playboy	TRX 5006
			GENESIS	
			English group formed in 1966 featuring Phil Collins, Peter Gabriel, Mike Rutherford, Tony Banks & Steve Hackett	
6/03/78	**23**	5	1. Follow You Follow Me	Atlantic 3474
6/21/80	**14**	11	2. Misunderstanding	Atlantic 3662
11/07/81	**29**	6	3. No Reply At All	Atlantic 3858
1/23/82	**26**	6	4. Abacab	Atlantic 3891
5/08/82	**40**	2	5. Man On The Corner	Atlantic 4025
7/24/82	**32**	5	6. Paperlate	Atlantic 4053
			GENTRY, BOBBIE	
			also see Glen Campbell	
8/12/67	**1** (4)	12	● 1. **Ode To Billie Joe**	Capitol 5950
1/31/70	**31**	4	2. Fancy	Capitol 2675
			GENTRYS	
			Memphis-based group	
9/25/65	**4**	11	1. **Keep On Dancing**	MGM 13379
			GEORGE, BARBARA	
12/18/61	**3**	11	1. **I Know (You Don't Love Me No More)**	A.F.O. 302

DATE	POS	WKS	ARTIST—Record Title	LABEL & NO.
			GERRY & THE PACEMAKERS	
			quartet from Liverpool, England - led by Gerry Marsden	
6/06/64	4	9	1. **Don't Let The Sun Catch You Crying**	Laurie 3251
8/08/64	9	7	2. **How Do You Do It?**	Laurie 3261
10/17/64	17	6	3. I Like It	Laurie 3271
1/09/65	14	5	4. I'll Be There	Laurie 3279
2/13/65	6	9	5. **Ferry Across The Mersey**	Laurie 3284
4/24/65	23	5	6. It's Gonna Be Alright	Laurie 3293
			-above 2 from film "Ferry Cross The Mersey"-	
10/08/66	28	4	7. Girl On A Swing	Laurie 3354
			GET WET	
5/23/81	39	2	1. Just So Lonely	Boardwalk 02018
			GETZ, STAN / CHARLIE BYRD	
10/27/62	15	10	1. Desafinado [I]	Verve 10260
			GETZ, STAN / ASTRUD GILBERTO	
6/20/64	5	10	1. **The Girl From Ipanema**	Verve 10323
			GIBB, ANDY	
			Bee Gees' younger brother - also see Olivia Newton-John	
5/28/77	1 (4)	23	● 1. **I Just Want To Be Your Everything**	RSO 872
12/10/77	1 (2)	22	● 2. **(Love Is) Thicker Than Water**	RSO 883
4/22/78	1 (7)	19	★ 3. **Shadow Dancing**	RSO 893
7/22/78	5	13	● 4. **An Everlasting Love**	RSO 904
11/04/78	9	13	● 5. **(Our Love) Don't Throw It All Away**	RSO 911
2/02/80	4	12	6. **Desire**	RSO 1019
12/06/80	15	11	7. Time Is Time	RSO 1059
4/11/81	40	1	8. Me (Without You)	RSO 1056
			GIBB, BARRY -	
			see **SAMANTHA SANG / BARBRA STREISAND**	
			GIBB, ROBIN	
			twin brother of Bee Gees' Maurice Gibb	
8/19/78	15	9	1. Oh! Darling	RSO 907
			-from film "Sgt. Pepper's Lonely Hearts Club Band"-	
			GIBBS, GEORGIA	
			real name: Fredda Lipson	
1/29/55	2 (1)	19	1. **Tweedle Dee**	Mercury 70517
3/26/55	1 (3)	20	2. **Dance With Me Henry (Wallflower)**	Mercury 70572
7/09/55	12	4	3. Sweet And Gentle	Mercury 70647
9/17/55	14	4	4. I Want You To Be My Baby	Mercury 70685
4/14/56	36	1	5. Rock Right	Mercury 70811
5/26/56	30	4	6. Kiss Me Another	Mercury 70850
8/25/56	20	8	7. Happiness Street	Mercury 70920
12/22/56	24	1	8. Tra La La	Mercury 70998
10/20/58	32	1	9. The Hula Hoop Song	Roulette 4106
			GIBBS, TERRI	
			Terri was born blind	
2/28/81	13	12	1. Somebody's Knockin'	MCA 41309

DATE	POS	WKS	ARTIST—Record Title	LABEL & NO.
			GIBSON, DON	
3/31/58	7	17	1. **Oh Lonesome Me**	RCA 7133
7/14/58	20	8	2. Blue Blue Day	RCA 7010
3/28/60	29	6	3. Just One Time	RCA 7690
7/10/61	21	8	4. Sea Of Heartbreak	RCA 7890
			GILBERTO, ASTRUD see STAN GETZ	
			GILDER, NICK member of Sweeny Todd	
8/05/78	1 (1)	18	★ 1. **Hot Child In The City**	Chrysalis 2226
			GILKYSON, TERRY, & THE EASY RIDERS Terry, Rich Dehr & Frank Miller - also see Frankie Laine, and Dean Martin	
2/09/57	4	14	1. **Marianne**	Columbia 40817
			GILLEY, MICKEY	
6/28/80	22	9	1. Stand By Me -from soundtrack "Urban Cowboy"-	Full Moon/Asy. 46640
			GILMER, JIMMY, & THE FIREBALLS also see The Fireballs	
9/28/63	1 (5)	13	● 1. **Sugar Shack**	Dot 16487
1/04/64	15	8	2. Daisy Petal Pickin'	Dot 16539
			GILREATH, JAMES	
4/27/63	21	6	1. Little Band Of Gold	Joy 274
			GINO & GINA	
6/09/58	20	1	1. (It's Been A Long Time) Pretty Baby	Mercury 71283
			GLAHE, WILL, & His Orchestra	
11/25/57	16	15	1. Liechtensteiner Polka [F]	London 1755
			GLASS BOTTLE featuring Gary Criss	
9/18/71	36	3	1. I Ain't Got Time Anymore	Avco Embassy 4575
			GLAZER, TOM & The Do-Re-Mi Children's **Chorus**	
6/15/63	14	7	1. On Top Of Spaghetti [N] -"On Top Of Old Smokey" parody-	Kapp 526
			GLENCOVES	
7/27/63	38	2	1. Hootenanny	Select 724
			GLITTER, GARY British - real name: Paul Gadd	
8/05/72	7	9	1. **Rock And Roll Part 2 [I]**	Bell 45237
12/02/72	35	3	2. I Didn't Know I Loved You (Till I Saw You Rock And Roll)	Bell 45276
			GO-GO'S Belinda Carlisle, lead singer of Los Angeles female quintet	
10/24/81	20	13	1. Our Lips Are Sealed	I.R.S. 9901
2/13/82	2 (3)	15	● 2. **We Got The Beat**	I.R.S. 9903
7/17/82	8	9	3. Vacation	I.R.S. 9907

DATE	POS	WKS	ARTIST—Record Title	LABEL & NO.
			GODSPELL [Original Cast]	
6/24/72	13	9	1. Day By Day -vocal by Robin Lamont-	Bell 45210
			GOLD, ANDREW	
			member of Linda Ronstadt's band	
4/16/77	7	13	1. **Lonely Boy**	Asylum 45384
3/04/78	25	9	2. Thank You For Being A Friend	Asylum 45456
			GOLDEN EARRING	
			Dutch rock quartet	
6/22/74	13	10	1. Radar Love	Track 40202
			GOLDSBORO, BOBBY	
			played guitar for Roy Orbison's band from '62-'64	
2/15/64	9	8	1. **See The Funny Little Clown**	United Artists 672
5/23/64	39	2	2. Whenever He Holds You	United Artists 710
2/20/65	13	8	3. Little Things	United Artists 810
6/05/65	27	6	4. Voodoo Woman	United Artists 862
3/12/66	23	5	5. It's Too Late	United Artists 980
1/14/67	35	3	6. Blue Autumn	United Artists 50087
3/30/68	1 (5)	13	● 7. **Honey**	United Artists 50283
7/13/68	19	7	8. Autumn Of My Life	United Artists 50318
11/30/68	36.	2	9. The Straight Life	United Artists 50461
1/09/71	11	11	10. Watching Scotty Grow	United Artists 50727
10/06/73	21	8	11. Summer (The First Time)	United Artists 251
			GOMM, IAN	
10/06/79	18	5	1. Hold On	Stiff/Epic 50747
			GONE ALL STARS	
3/03/58	30	4	1. "7-11" (Mambo No. 5) [I]	Gone 5016
			GONZALEZ	
2/10/79	26	5	1. Haven't Stopped Dancing Yet	Capitol 4674
			GOODMAN, BENNY, Trio, with ROSEMARY CLOONEY	
3/17/56	20	1	1. Memories Of You -from "The Benny Goodman Story"-	Columbia 40616
			GOODMAN, DICKIE	
			also see Buchanan & Goodman	
2/23/74	33	4	1. Energy Crisis '74 [N]	Rainy Wednesday 206
9/13/75	4	7	● 2. **Mr. Jaws [N]**	Cash 451
			GORDON, BARRY	
			7 years old in 1955	
12/17/55	6	4	1. **Nuttin' For Christmas [X-N]**	MGM 12092

DATE	POS	WKS	ARTIST—Record Title	LABEL & NO.
			GORE, LESLEY	
			17 years old in 1963	
5/18/63	**1** (2)	11	1. **It's My Party**	Mercury 72119
7/20/63	**5**	9	2. **Judy's Turn To Cry**	Mercury 72143
10/19/63	**5**	11	3. **She's A Fool**	Mercury 72180
1/11/64	**2** (3)	10	4. **You Don't Own Me**	Mercury 72206
4/04/64	**12**	7	5. That's The Way Boys Are	Mercury 72259
6/20/64	**37**	1	6. I Don't Wanna Be A Loser	Mercury 72270
8/15/64	**14**	6	7. Maybe I Know	Mercury 72309
1/23/65	**27**	5	8. Look Of Love	Mercury 72372
7/17/65	**13**	7	9. Sunshine, Lollipops And Rainbows	Mercury 72433
			-from the film "Ski Party"-	
10/09/65	**32**	3	10. My Town, My Guy And Me	Mercury 72475
3/04/67	**16**	9	11. California Nights	Mercury 72649
			GORME, EYDIE	
			also see Steve & Eydie	
6/16/56	**39**	1	1. Too Close For Comfort	ABC-Paramount 9684
			-from musical "Mr. Wonderful"-	
9/01/56	**34**	3	2. Mama, Teach Me To Dance	ABC-Paramount 9722
12/30/57	**24**	1	3. Love Me Forever	ABC-Paramount 9863
5/26/58	**11**	9	4. You Need Hands	ABC-Paramount 9925
2/09/63	**7**	11	5. **Blame It On The Bossa Nova**	Columbia 42661
			GOULET, ROBERT	
			played Lancelot in Broadway's "Camelot"	
11/28/64	**16**	9	1. My Love, Forgive Me (Amore, Scusami)	Columbia 43131
			GQ	
4/14/79	**12**	11	● 1. Disco Nights (Rock-Freak)	Arista 0388
8/11/79	**20**	8	2. I Do Love You	Arista 0426
			GRACIE, CHARLIE	
2/23/57	**1** (2)	14	1. **Butterfly**	Cameo 105
5/20/57	**16**	6	2. Fabulous	Cameo 107
			GRAHAM CENTRAL STATION	
			Larry Graham, leader - formerly with Sly & The Family Stone	
9/13/75	**38**	2	1. Your Love	Warner 8105
			GRAHAM, LARRY	
8/09/80	**9**	9	● 1. **One In A Million You**	Warner 49221
			GRAMMER, BILLY	
12/08/58	**4**	15	1. Gotta Travel On	Monument 400
			GRANAHAN, GERRY	
			also see Dicky Doo & The Don'ts	
6/16/58	**23**	8	1. No Chemise, Please	Sunbeam 102
			GRANATA, ROCCO, & the International Quintet	
11/23/59	**31**	7	1. Marina [F]	Laurie 3041

DATE	POS	WKS	ARTIST—Record Title	LABEL & NO.
			GRAND FUNK RAILROAD	
			Flint, Michigan quartet: Mark Farner, Don Brewer, Mel Schacher & Craig Frost	
9/05/70	22	8	1. Closer To Home	Capitol 2877
2/05/72	29	5	2. Footstompin' Music	Capitol 3255
11/04/72	29	6	3. Rock 'N Roll Soul	Capitol 3363
8/18/73	1 (1)	13	● 4. **We're An American Band**	Capitol 3660
12/29/73	19	6	5. Walk Like A Man	Capitol 3760
3/30/74	1 (2)	14	● 6. **The Loco-Motion**	Capitol 3840
7/20/74	11	8	7. Shinin' On	Capitol 3917
12/21/74	3	12	8. **Some Kind Of Wonderful**	Capitol 4002
4/19/75	4	12	9. **Bad Time**	Capitol 4046
			-above 6 shown as Grand Funk-	
			GRANT, EARL	
			died 6/10/70 (39)	
9/29/58	7	13	1. **The End**	Decca 30719
			GRANT, GOGI	
			real name: Audrey Brown	
10/01/55	9	10	1. **Suddenly There's A Valley**	Era 1003
5/05/56	1 (8)	22	2. **The Wayward Wind**	Era 1013
			GRANT, JANIE	
5/15/61	29	5	1. Triangle	Caprice 104
			GRASS ROOTS	
			Los Angeles-based quartet: Warren Entner, Rob Grill, Creed Bratton & Rick Coonce	
7/16/66	28	4	1. Where Were You When I Needed You	Dunhill 4029
6/03/67	8	9	2. **Let's Live For Today**	Dunhill 4084
9/02/67	23	4	3. Things I Should Have Said	Dunhill 4094
9/21/68	5	12	● 4. **Midnight Confessions**	Dunhill 4144
1/11/69	28	2	5. Bella Linda	Dunhill 4162
5/17/69	31	5	6. The River Is Wide	Dunhill 4187
8/09/69	15	10	7. I'd Wait A Million Years	Dunhill 4198
11/22/69	24	7	8. Heaven Knows	Dunhill 4217
6/13/70	35	3	9. Baby Hold On	Dunhill 4237
2/13/71	15	11	10. Temptation Eyes	Dunhill 4263
6/19/71	9	9	11. **Sooner Or Later**	Dunhill 4279
10/30/71	16	8	12. Two Divided By Love	Dunhill 4289
3/18/72	34	3	13. Glory Bound	Dunhill 4302
7/22/72	39	2	14. The Runway	Dunhill 4316
			GRAY, DOBIE	
1/23/65	13	7	1. The "In" Crowd	Charger 105
3/31/73	5	15	● 2. **Drift Away**	Decca 33057
2/10/79	37	2	3. You Can Do It	Infinity 50003
			GREAN, CHARLES RANDOLPH, Sounde	
7/05/69	13	8	1. **Quentin's Theme** [I]	Ranwood 840
			-from TV series "Dark Shadows"-	

DATE	POS	WKS	ARTIST—Record Title	LABEL & NO.
			GREAVES, R.B.	
10/25/69	**2** (1)	13	● 1. **Take A Letter Maria**	Atco 6714
2/14/70	27	5	2. Always Something There To Remind Me	Atco 6726
			GRECCO, CYNDI	
6/12/76	**25**	5	1. Making Our Dreams Come True	Private Stock 45086
			-from TV's "LaVerne & Shirley"-	
			GREEN, AL	
8/21/71	**11**	15	● 1. Tired Of Being Alone	Hi 2194
12/11/71	**1** (1)	15	● 2. **Let's Stay Together**	Hi 2202
4/08/72	**4**	11	● 3. **Look What You Done For Me**	Hi 2211
7/15/72	**3**	11	● 4. **I'm Still In Love With You**	Hi 2216
11/04/72	**3**	12	● 5. **You Ought To Be With Me**	Hi 2227
3/03/73	**10**	9	● 6. **Call Me (Come Back Home)**	Hi 2235
7/21/73	**10**	12	● 7. **Here I Am (Come And Take Me)**	Hi 2247
12/22/73	**19**	8	8. Livin' For You	Hi 2257
5/11/74	**32**	3	9. Let's Get Married	Hi 2262
11/02/74	**7**	11	● 10. **Sha-La-La (Make Me Happy)**	Hi 2274
3/22/75	**13**	8	11. L-O-V-E (Love)	Hi 2282
11/29/75	**28**	6	12. Full Of Fire	Hi 2300
12/18/76	**37**	4	13. Keep Me Cryin'	Hi 2319
			GREEN, GARLAND	
10/18/69	**20**	4	1. Jealous Kind Of Fella	Uni 55143
			GREENBAUM, NORMAN	
3/07/70	**3**	14	● 1. **Spirit In The Sky**	Reprise 0885
			GREENE, LORNE	
			Ben Cartwright of "Bonanza"	
11/07/64	**1** (1)	10	1. **Ringo** [S]	RCA 8444
			GREGG, BOBBY, & His Friends	
4/14/62	**29**	5	1. The Jam - Part 1 [I]	Cotton 1003
			GRIFFITH, ANDY	
			Sheriff Andy Taylor of "The Andy Griffith Show"	
4/02/55	**26**	1	1. Make Yourself Comfortable [C]	Capitol 3057
			-vocal by Jean Wilson-	
			GROCE, LARRY	
2/07/76	**9**	9	1. **Junk Food Junkie** [N]	Warner 8165
			-recorded live at McCabe's in Santa Monica-	
			GROSS, HENRY	
			lead guitarist of Sha-Na-Na	
4/03/76	**6**	13	● 1. **Shannon**	Lifesong 45002
8/21/76	**37**	2	2. Springtime Mama	Lifesong 45008
			GUARALDI, VINCE, Trio	
			Vince died on 2/6/76 (43)	
2/09/63	**22**	6	1. Cast Your Fate To The Wind [I]	Fantasy 563
			GUESS WHO	
			Canadian group featuring Burton Cummings, lead singer, and Randy Bachman, lead guitar (left group in '70)	
6/05/65	**22**	7	1. Shakin' All Over	Scepter 1295
			-Chad Allan, lead singer-	
4/26/69	**6**	11	● 2. **These Eyes**	RCA 0102

DATE	POS	WKS	ARTIST—Record Title	LABEL & NO.
7/26/69	**10**	9	● 3. **Laughing/**	
11/08/69	**22**	6	4. Undun	RCA 0195
1/17/70	**5**	10	5. **No Time**	RCA 0300
3/28/70	**1** (3)	14	● 6. **American Woman/**	
		13	7. **No Sugar Tonight**	RCA 0325
8/08/70	**17**	8	8. Hand Me Down World	RCA 0367
11/07/70	**10**	8	9. **Share The Land**	RCA 0388
6/12/71	**29**	4	10. Albert Flasher	RCA 0458
9/04/71	**19**	8	11. Rain Dance	RCA 0522
4/20/74	**39**	1	12. Star Baby	RCA 0217
8/10/74	**6**	11	13. **Clap For The Wolfman** -with Wolfman Jack-	RCA 0324
12/14/74	**28**	4	14. Dancin' Fool	RCA 10075
			GUIDRY, GREG	
3/20/82	**17**	10	1. Goin' Down	Columbia 02691
			GUITAR, BONNIE	
4/27/57	**6**	10	1. **Dark Moon**	Dot 15550
			GUNHILL ROAD	
6/02/73	**40**	1	1. Back When My Hair Was Short	Kama Sutra 569
			GUTHRIE, ARLO	
			Woody Guthrie's son	
9/09/72	**18**	9	1. The City Of New Orleans	Reprise 1103
			HAGGARD, MERLE, & The Strangers	
1/05/74	**28**	3	1. If We Make It Through December	Capitol 3746
			HAIRCUT ONE HUNDRED	
			British sextet led by Nick Heyward	
7/17/82	**37**	4	1. Love Plus One	Arista 0672
			HALEY, BILL, & His Comets	
			Bill died on 2/9/8l (55)	
11/20/54	**11**	15	1. Dim, Dim The Lights (I Want Some Atmosphere)	Decca 29317
3/05/55	**17**	8	2. Mambo Rock/	
3/19/55	**26**	2	3. Birth Of The Boogie	Decca 29418
5/14/55	**1** (8)	24	4. **(We're Gonna) Rock Around The Clock** -in film "The Blackboard Jungle"-	Decca 29124
7/23/55	**15**	4	5. Razzle-Dazzle	Decca 29552
11/19/55	**9**	13	6. **Burn That Candle**	Decca 29713
1/14/56	**6**	15	7. **See You Later, Alligator**	Decca 29791
4/07/56	**16**	5	8. R-O-C-K/ -in film "Rock Around The Clock"-	
4/07/56	**18**	5	9. The Saints Rock 'N Roll	Decca 29870
9/01/56	**25**	4	10. Rip It Up	Decca 30028
11/24/56	**34**	3	11. Rudy's Rock [I] -sax solo: Rudy Pompilli (died 2/5/76 - 47)-	Decca 30085
4/21/58	**22**	6	12. Skinny Minnie	Decca 30592
5/25/74	**39**	1	13. (We're Gonna) Rock Around The Clock -re-entry of l955 hit-	MCA 60025

DATE	POS	WKS	ARTIST—Record Title	LABEL & NO.
			HALL, DARYL, & JOHN OATES	
			met at Philadelphia's Temple University	
4/03/76	4	17	● 1. **Sara Smile**	RCA 10530
8/14/76	7	16	2. **She's Gone**	Atlantic 3332
			-re-entry of 1974 hit-	
12/25/76	39	3	3. Do What You Want, Be What You Are	RCA 10808
2/05/77	1 (2)	14	● 4. **Rich Girl**	RCA 10860
5/28/77	28	4	5. Back Together Again	RCA 10970
9/30/78	20	7	6. It's A Laugh	RCA 11371
12/01/79	18	10	7. Wait For Me	RCA 11747
8/30/80	30	4	8. How Does It Feel To Be Back	RCA 12048
10/11/80	12	14	9. You've Lost That Lovin' Feeling	RCA 12103
2/14/81	1 (3)	17	● 10. **Kiss On My List**	RCA 12142
5/16/81	5	14	11. **You Make My Dreams**	RCA 12217
9/12/81	1 (2)	16	● 12. **Private Eyes**	RCA 12296
11/21/81	1 (1)	17	● 13. **I Can't Go For That (No Can Do)**	RCA 12357
4/03/82	9	11	14. **Did It In A Minute**	RCA 13065
7/24/82	33	5	15. Your Imagination	RCA 13252
11/06/82	1 (4)	17	● 16. **Maneater**	RCA 13354
			HALL, JIMMY	
			former member of Wet Willie	
11/01/80	27	4	1. I'm Happy That Love Has Found You	Epic 50931
			HALL, LARRY	
12/07/59	15	11	1. Sandy	Strand 25007
			HALL, TOM T.	
1/19/74	12	9	1. I Love	Mercury 73436
			HALOS	
8/28/61	25	4	1. "Nag"	7 Arts 709
			HAMILTON, JOE FRANK & REYNOLDS	
			Dan Hamilton, Joe Frank Carollo & Tom Reynolds	
6/12/71	4	11	● 1. **Don't Pull Your Love**	Dunhill 4276
7/19/75	1 (1)	12	● 2. **Fallin' In Love**	Playboy 6024
12/13/75	21	8	3. Winners And Losers	Playboy 6054
			HAMILTON, BOBBY	
8/04/58	40	1	1. Crazy Eyes For You	Apt 25002
			HAMILTON, GEORGE IV	
			also see Paul Anka	
11/17/56	6	14	1. **A Rose And A Baby Ruth**	ABC-Para. 9765
3/09/57	33	4	2. Only One Love	ABC-Para. 9782
12/09/57	10	12	3. **Why Don't They Understand**	ABC-Para. 9862
4/07/58	25	1	4. Now And For Always	ABC-Para. 9898
7/20/63	15	7	5. Abilene	RCA 8181
			HAMILTON, ROY	
			died 7/20/69 (40)	
4/23/55	6	16	1. **Unchained Melody**	Epic 9102
			-from film "Unchained"-	
1/27/58	13	11	2. Don't Let Go	Epic 9257

DATE	POS	WKS	ARTIST—Record Title	LABEL & NO.
2/13/61	12	7	3. You Can Have Her	Epic 9434
			HAMILTON, RUSS	
8/05/57	4	17	1. **Rainbow**	Kapp 184
			HAMLISCH, MARVIN	
4/20/74	3	12	● 1. **The Entertainer [I]** -from film "The Sting"-	MCA 40174
			HAMMOND, ALBERT	
			English	
11/04/72	5	13	● 1. **It Never Rains In Southern California**	Mums 6011
4/13/74	31	4	2. I'm A Train	Mums 6026
			HAPPENINGS	
			New Jersey quartet	
7/30/66	3	11	1. **See You In September**	B.T. Puppy 520
10/22/66	12	5	2. Go Away Little Girl	B.T. Puppy 522
4/29/67	3	9	3. **I Got Rhythm**	B.T. Puppy 527
7/22/67	13	6	4. My Mammy	B.T. Puppy 530
			HARNELL, JOE, & His Orchestra	
1/26/63	14	8	1. Fly Me To The Moon-Bossa Nova [I]	Kapp 497
			HARPERS BIZARRE	
			Santa Cruz, California quintet	
3/18/67	13	7	1. The 59th Street Bridge Song (Feelin' Groovy)	Warner 5890
6/17/67	37	3	2. Come To The Sunshine	Warner 7028
			HARPO, SLIM	
			real name: James Moore -- died 1/31/70 (46)	
7/10/61	34	2	1. Rainin' In My Heart	Excello 2194
3/05/66	16	8	2. Baby Scratch My Back [I]	Excello 2273
			HARRIS, BETTY	
10/26/63	23	6	1. Cry To Me	Jubilee 5456
			HARRIS, EDDIE	
5/29/61	36	3	1. Exodus [I]	Vee-Jay 378
			HARRIS, EMMYLOU	
4/11/81	37	3	1. Mister Sandman	Warner 49684
			HARRIS, MAJOR	
4/19/75	5	14	● 1. **Love Won't Let Me Wait**	Atlantic 3248
			HARRIS, RICHARD	
			British actor	
5/25/68	2 (1)	10	1. **MacArthur Park**	Dunhill 4134
			HARRIS, ROLF	
			Australian	
6/22/63	3	9	1. **Tie Me Kangaroo Down, Sport [N]**	Epic 9596
			HARRIS, THURSTON	
10/28/57	6	13	1. **Little Bitty Pretty One**	Aladdin 3398
			HARRISON, GEORGE	
			The Beatles' lead guitarist	
12/05/70	1 (4)	13	● 1. **My Sweet Lord/**	
		13	2. **Isn't It A Pity**	Apple 2995
3/06/71	10	8	3. **What Is Life**	Apple 1828

DATE	POS	WKS	ARTIST—Record Title	LABEL & NO.
8/28/71	23	5	4. Bangla-Desh	Apple 1836
5/26/73	1 (1)	11	**5. Give Me Love (Give Me Peace On Earth)**	Apple 1862
12/14/74	15	6	6. Dark Horse	Apple 1877
2/01/75	36	2	7. Ding Dong; Ding Dong	Apple 1879
10/11/75	20	6	8. You	Apple 1884
12/11/76	25	7	9. This Song	Dark Horse 8294
2/12/77	19	7	10. Crackerbox Palace	Dark Horse 8313
3/31/79	16	8	11. Blow Away	Dark Horse 8763
5/23/81	2 (3)	11	**12. All Those Years Ago**	Dark Horse 49725
			HARRISON, WILBERT	
4/27/59	1 (2)	12	**1. Kansas City**	Fury 1023
1/24/70	32	4	2. Let's Work Together (Part 1)	Sue 11
			HART, FREDDIE	
9/25/71	17	12	● 1. Easy Loving	Capitol 3115
			HARTMAN, DAN	
			member of Edgar Winter Group	
12/02/78	29	7	● 1. Instant Replay	Blue Sky 2772
			HARVEY & THE MOONGLOWS	
			also see The Moonglows	
10/20/58	22	4	1. Ten Commandments Of Love	Chess 1705
			HATHAWAY, DONNY - see ROBERTA FLACK	
			HAVENS, RICHIE	
4/24/71	16	9	1. Here Comes The Sun	Stormy Forest 656
			HAWKINS, DALE	
7/01/57	27	5	1. Susie-Q	Checker 863
10/13/58	32	3	2. La-Do-Dada	Checker 900
			HAWKINS, EDWIN, Singers	
			also see Melanie	
5/03/69	4	9	● **1. Oh Happy Day**	Pavilion 20001
			-featuring Dorothy Morrison-	
			HAWKINS, RONNIE, & The Hawks	
			also see The Band	
9/21/59	26	7	1. Mary Lou	Roulette 4177
			HAWLEY, DEANE	
7/04/60	29	5	1. Look For A Star	Dore 554
			-from film "Circus Of Horrors"-	
			HAYES, BILL	
			Doug Williams of TV soap "Days Of Our Lives"	
2/26/55	1 (5)	20	**1. The Ballad Of Davy Crockett**	Cadence 1256
2/16/57	33	3	2. Wringle, Wrangle	ABC-Para. 9785
			-from movie "Westward Ho, The Wagons"-	
			HAYES, ISAAC	
9/27/69	37	4	1. By The Time I Get To Phoenix/	
10/18/69	30	5	2. Walk On By	Enterprise 9003
6/12/71	22	5	3. Never Can Say Goodbye	Enterprise 9031
10/23/71	1 (2)	12	**4. Theme From Shaft**	Enterprise 9038
3/25/72	30	5	5. Do Your Thing	Enterprise 9042

DATE	POS	WKS	ARTIST—Record Title	LABEL & NO.
12/02/72	38	2	6. Theme From The Men [I]	Enterprise 9058
1/12/74	30	5	7. Joy - Pt. 1	Enterprise 9085
12/08/79	18	12	8. Don't Let Go	Polydor 2011
			HAYMAN, RICHARD, & JAN AUGUST	
			Jan died on 1/17/76 (71)	
2/11/56	11	11	1. A Theme from "The Three Penny Opera" (Moritat) [I]	Mercury 70781
			HAYWOOD, LEON	
11/01/75	15	8	1. I Want'a Do Something Freaky To You	20th Century 2228
			HAZLEWOOD, LEE - see NANCY SINATRA	
			HEAD, MURRAY, With The Trinidad Singers	
5/08/71	14	8	1. Superstar -re-entry of 1970 hit-	Decca 32603
			HEAD, ROY	
9/18/65	2 (2)	9	1. **Treat Her Right**	Back Beat 546
12/04/65	39	1	2. Just A Little Bit	Scepter 12116
12/18/65	32	2	3. Apple Of My Eye	Back Beat 555
			HEART	
			Canadian - Ann & Nancy Wilson, leaders	
5/29/76	35	2	1. Crazy On You	Mushroom 7021
9/04/76	9	14	2. **Magic Man**	Mushroom 7011
7/02/77	11	12	3. Barracuda	Portrait 70004
5/13/78	24	7	4. Heartless	Mushroom 7031
10/28/78	15	9	5. Straight On	Portrait 70020
3/17/79	34	3	6. Dog & Butterfly	Portrait 70025
3/15/80	33	4	7. Even It Up	Epic 50847
11/29/80	8	11	8. **Tell It Like It Is**	Epic 50950
6/19/82	33	4	9. This Man Is Mine	Epic 02925
			HEATHERTON, JOEY	
			movie/TV actress	
7/15/72	24	7	1. Gone	MGM 14387
			HEATWAVE	
8/27/77	2 (2)	17	★ 1. **Boogie Nights**	Epic 50370
2/04/78	18	11	● 2. Always And Forever	Epic 50490
6/03/78	7	11	● 3. **The Groove Line**	Epic 50524
			HEBB, BOBBY	
7/23/66	2 (2)	11	● 1. **Sunny**	Philips 40365
11/05/66	39	1	2. A Satisfied Mind	Philips 40400
			HEFTI, NEAL	
3/05/66	35	4	1. Batman Theme [I]	RCA 8755
			HELMS, BOBBY	
10/14/57	7	15	1. **My Special Angel**	Decca 30423
10/14/57	36	2	2. Fraulein	Decca 30194
12/23/57	6	4	3. **Jingle Bell Rock** [X]	Decca 30513
12/28/58	35	1	4. Jingle Bell Rock [X]	Decca 30513
12/26/60	36	1	5. Jingle Bell Rock [X]	Decca 30513

Bill Haley and his Comets. Decca Records scheduled three hours of studio time for Bill Haley and his Comets to record "Rock Around The Clock" and one other tune. The group ran 40 minutes over, but then, studio time was cheaper in 1954.

Roy Hamilton saw three of his hits—"Ebb Tide," "Unchained Melody," and "You Can Have Her"—subsequently recorded by the Righteous Brothers, with more than a hint of his blues-styled delivery.

George Harrison's favorite oldie isn't "He's So Fine." Really, it's not. Ask his lawyer.

Herman's Hermits. The most successful single by Herman's Hermits, "Mrs. Brown You've Got A Lovely Daughter," was originally recorded by British actor Tom Courtenay for a television play.

Eddie Hodges. With songs like "(Girls, Girls, Girls) Made To Love," written by the Everly Brothers, teen star Eddie Hodges was only concerned with the simple pleasures. "Ain't Gonna Wash For A Week" he also proclaimed, so that "her" kisses would stay in place.

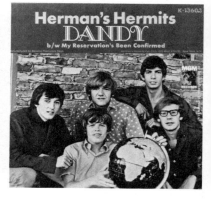

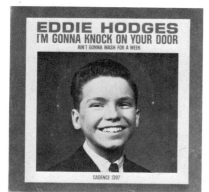

The Hollies can look back at a highly respectable U.S. chart record: seven top 20 entries. But they had three times as many hits in Britain—almost as many as the Beatles.

Buddy Holly. Apart from his musical contributions to the rock era, Buddy Holly is among the handful of stars to merit a full-length movie about his life and legend. The others include Elvis, the Beatles, and ahem, Fabian and Frankie Avalon.

Mary Hopkin. It was '60s supermodel Twiggy who told Paul McCartney about Welsh singer Mary Hopkin, after the latter appeared on a television talent show. "Those Were The Days" was Apple Records' second release.

Johnny Horton's chart-topping "Battle Of New Orleans" was based on an old fiddle tune, "The 8th Of January." Songwriter Jimmie Driftwood also collected royalties from later versions by Harper's Bizarre, the Nitty Gritty Dirt Band, and Buck Owens.

Engelbert Humperdinck's "Release Me" was predated by a top 10 version by "Little Esther" Phillips. The song was the biggest hit of both artists' careers.

DATE	POS	WKS	ARTIST—Record Title	LABEL & NO.
			HENDERSON, JOE	
6/02/62	8	10	1. **Snap Your Fingers**	Todd 1072
			HENDERSON, MICHAEL - see **NORMAN CONNORS**	
			HENDRICKS, BOBBY	
			member of The Drifters & The Swallows in 1958	
9/01/58	25	4	1. Itchy Twitchy Feeling	Sue 706
			HENDRIX, JIMI	
			died 9/18/70 (27)	
9/28/68	20	8	1. All Along The Watchtower	Reprise 0767
			HENHOUSE FIVE PLUS TOO	
			a Ray Stevens creation	
2/05/77	40	1	1. In The Mood [N]	Warner 8301
			HENRY, CLARENCE "Frog Man"	
1/12/57	20	3	1. Ain't Got No Home [N]	Argo 5259
3/20/61	4	11	2. **But I Do**	Argo 5378
			-also titled "I Don't Know Why"-	
5/29/61	12	7	3. You Always Hurt The One You Love	Argo 5388
			HENSON, JIM - see ERNIE / KERMIT	
			HERMAN'S HERMITS	
			English quintet led by Peter Noone	
11/14/64	13	9	1. I'm Into Something Good	MGM 13280
2/20/65	2 (2)	11	2. **Can't You Hear My Heartbeat**	MGM 13310
4/17/65	1 (3)	11	● 3. **Mrs. Brown You've Got A Lovely Daughter**	MGM 13341
4/17/65	5	10	4. **Silhouettes**	MGM 13332
6/05/65	4	8	5. **Wonderful World**	MGM 13354
7/10/65	1 (1)	8	● 6. **I'm Henry VIII, I Am**	MGM 13367
9/25/65	7	8	7. **Just A Little Bit Better**	MGM 13398
1/01/66	8	8	8. **A Must To Avoid**	MGM 13437
			-from the film "Hold On!"-	
2/26/66	3	7	9. **Listen People**	MGM 13462
			-from film "When The Boys Meet The Girls"-	
4/16/66	9	7	10. **Leaning On The Lamp Post**	MGM 13500
			-from the film "Hold On!"-	
7/23/66	12	5	11. This Door Swings Both Ways	MGM 13548
10/15/66	5	8	12. **Dandy**	MGM 13603
12/24/66	27	5	13. East West	MGM 13639
3/04/67	4	9	● 14. **There's A Kind Of Hush/**	
3/18/67	35	4	15. No Milk Today	MGM 13681
7/08/67	18	4	16. Don't Go Out Into The Rain (You're Going To Melt)	MGM 13761
9/16/67	39	2	17. Museum	MGM 13787
2/03/68	22	6	18. I Can Take Or Leave Your Loving	MGM 13885
			HERNANDEZ, PATRICK	
8/04/79	16	11	● 1. Born To Be Alive	Columbia 10986
			HESITATIONS	
2/17/68	38	2	1. Born Free	Kapp 878

DATE	POS	WKS	ARTIST—Record Title	LABEL & NO.
			HEYWOOD, EDDIE	
			also see Hugo Winterhalter	
7/21/56	11	18	1. Soft Summer Breeze [I]	Mercury 70863
			HIBBLER, AL	
			vocalist with Duke Ellington	
4/09/55	3	19	1. **Unchained Melody**	Decca 29441
			-from the film "Unchained"-	
10/15/55	4	22	2. **He**	Decca 29660
2/25/56	21	5	3. 11TH Hour Melody	Decca 29789
7/14/56	22	2	4. Never Turn Back	Decca 29950
8/25/56	10	12	5. **After The Lights Go Down Low**	Decca 29982
			HIGGINS, BERTIE	
1/16/82	8	18	1. **Key Largo**	Kat Family 02524
			HIGH INERGY	
11/19/77	12	11	1. You Can't Turn Me Off (In The Middle Of Turning Me On)	Gordy 7155
			HIGHLIGHTS Featuring Frank Pisani	
11/10/56	19	5	1. City Of Angels	Bally 1016
			HIGHWAYMEN	
			formed at Wesleyan University in Conneticut	
7/31/61	1 (2)	11	1. **Michael**	United Artists 258
12/25/61	13	13	2. Cotton Fields	United Artists 370
			HILL, BUNKER	
10/13/62	33	3	1. Hide & Go Seek, Part 1	Mala 451
			HILL, DAN	
			Canadian	
12/24/77	3	15	● 1. **Sometimes When We Touch**	20th Century 2355
			HILL, JESSIE	
5/09/60	28	4	1. Ooh Poo Pah Doo - Part II [I]	Minit 607
			HILLSIDE SINGERS	
12/11/71	13	10	1. I'd Like To Teach The World To Sing (In Perfect Harmony)	Metromedia 231
			-adapted from "Coca-Cola" jingle-	
			HILLTOPPERS featuring Jimmy Sacca	
			quartet formed at Western Kentucky College in Bowling Green	
7/30/55	20	4	1. The Kentuckian Song	Dot 15375
11/12/55	8	13	2. **Only You (And You Alone)**	Dot 15423
1/21/56	31	1	3. My Treasure	Dot 15437
10/06/56	38	2	4. Ka-Ding-Dong	Dot 15489
			-featuring Chuck Schrouder-	
2/09/57	3	13	5. **Marianne**	Dot 15537
11/25/57	22	4	6. The Joker (That's What They Call Me)	Dot 15662
			HINTON, JOE	
			died 8/13/68	
9/05/64	13	9	1. Funny	Back Beat 541
			HIRT, AL	
			trumpeteer from New Orleans	
1/25/64	4	13	1. **Java [I]**	RCA 8280
5/02/64	15	8	2. Cotton Candy [I]	RCA 8346

DATE	POS	WKS	ARTIST—Record Title	LABEL & NO.
8/01/64	30	4	3. Sugar Lips [I]	RCA 8391
			HODGES, EDDIE	
			14 years old in 1961	
7/24/61	12	8	1. I'm Gonna Knock On Your Door	Cadence 1397
7/07/62	14	8	2. (Girls, Girls, Girls) Made To Love	Cadence 1421
			HOLDEN, RON, with The Thunderbirds	
4/25/60	7	13	1. **Love You So**	Donna 1315
			HOLLAND, AMY	
9/13/80	22	6	1. How Do I Survive	Capitol 4884
			HOLLAND, EDDIE	
			1/3 of 'Holland-Dozier-Holland'	
3/10/62	30	4	1. Jamie	Motown 1021
			HOLLIDAY, JENNIFER	
7/31/82	22	7	1. And I Am Telling You I'm Not Going -from Broadway cast "Dreamgirls"-	Geffen 29983
			HOLLIES	
			English quintet formed by Allan Clarke & Graham Nash	
1/08/66	32	4	1. Look Through Any Window	Imperial 66134
8/20/66	5	9	2. **Bus Stop**	Imperial 66186
11/12/66	7	7	3. **Stop Stop Stop**	Imperial 66214
4/15/67	11	9	4. On A Carousel	Imperial 66231
6/24/67	28	3	5. Pay You Back With Interest	Imperial 66240
7/08/67	9	10	6. **Carrie-Anne**	Epic 10180
5/18/68	40	1	7. Jennifer Eccles	Epic 10298
2/07/70	7	11	8. **He Ain't Heavy, He's My Brother**	Epic 10532
7/08/72	2 (2)	13	● 9. **Long Cool Woman (In A Black Dress)**	Epic 10871
12/02/72	26	5	10. Long Dark Road	Epic 10920
6/08/74	6	11	● 11. **The Air That I Breathe**	Epic 11100
			HOLLOWAY, BRENDA	
5/23/64	13	6	1. Every Little Bit Hurts	Tamla 54094
3/27/65	25	5	2. When I'm Gone	Tamla 54111
11/04/67	39	1	3. You've Made Me So Very Happy	Tamla 54155
			HOLLY, BUDDY	
			killed in a plane crash with the Big Bopper and Ritchie Valens on 2/3/59 (22) -- also see The Crickets	
11/11/57	3	16	1. **Peggy Sue**	Coral 61885
6/09/58	37	2	2. Rave On	Coral 61985
8/11/58	32	4	3. Early In The Morning	Coral 62006
3/09/59	13	9	4. It Doesn't Matter Anymore	Coral 62074
			HOLLYWOOD ARGYLES	
			Gary Paxton of Skip & Flip, member	
6/13/60	1 (1)	11	1. **Alley-Oop [N]**	Lute 5905
			HOLLYWOOD FLAMES	
			formerly Bobby Day's backing group The Satellites	
12/02/57	11	12	1. Buzz-Buzz-Buzz	Ebb 119
			HOLMAN, EDDIE	
1/10/70	2 (1)	12	● 1. **Hey There Lonely Girl**	ABC 11240

DATE	POS	WKS	ARTIST—Record Title	LABEL & NO.
			HOLMES, CLINT	
5/05/73	2 (2)	15	● 1. **Playground In My Mind**	Epic 10891
			-featuring Clint's son, Philip-	
			HOLMES, RUPERT	
			also see Street People	
11/10/79	1 (2)	16	● 1. **Escape (The Pina Colada Song)**	Infinity 50035
2/09/80	6	12	2. **Him**	MCA 41173
6/14/80	32	3	3. Answering Machine	MCA 41235
			HOMBRES	
10/07/67	12	10	1. Let It Out (Let It All Hang Out)	Verve Forecast 5058
			HOMER & JETHRO	
			Henry Haynes & Kenneth Burns - Homer (Henry) died 8/7/71 (54)	
9/14/59	14	7	1. The Battle Of Kookamonga [C]	RCA 7585
			HONDELLS	
10/03/64	9	9	1. **Little Honda**	Mercury 72324
			HONEYCOMBS	
			English quintet	
10/10/64	5	9	1. **Have I The Right?**	Interphon 7707
			HONEY CONE	
5/01/71	1 (1)	13	● 1. **Want Ads**	Hot Wax 7011
8/21/71	11	10	● 2. **Stick-Up**	Hot Wax 7106
12/11/71	15	8	3. One Monkey Don't Stop No Show - Part 1	Hot Wax 7110
3/25/72	23	6	4. The Day I Found Myself	Hot Wax 7113
			HOPKIN, MARY	
			British	
10/12/68	2 (3)	12	● 1. **Those Were The Days**	Apple 1801
5/03/69	13	7	2. Goodbye	Apple 1806
3/28/70	39	2	3. Temma Harbour	Apple 1816
			HORNE, JIMMY "BO"	
6/24/78	38	1	1. Dance Across The Floor	Sunshine Sound 1003
			HORNE, LENA	
7/09/55	19	1	1. Love Me Or Leave Me	RCA 6073
			HORTON, JOHNNY	
			killed in an auto crash on 11/5/60 (33)	
5/04/59	1 (6)	18	● 1. **The Battle Of New Orleans**	Columbia 41339
3/14/60	3	13	2. **Sink The Bismarck**	Columbia 41568
			-inspired by film of same title-	
10/17/60	4	18	3. **North To Alaska**	Columbia 41782
			HOT	
4/02/77	6	19	● 1. **Angel In Your Arms**	Big Tree 16085
			HOT BUTTER	
8/19/72	9	12	1. **Popcorn [I]**	Musicor 1458
			HOT CHOCOLATE	
			Errol Brown lead singer of sextet from the West Indies & England	
3/08/75	8	9	1. **Emma**	Big Tree 16031
7/05/75	28	4	2. Disco Queen	Big Tree 16038

DATE	POS	WKS	ARTIST—Record Title	LABEL & NO.
12/06/75	3	15	● 3. **You Sexy Thing**	Big Tree 16047
8/13/77	31	5	4. So You Win Again	Big Tree 16096
12/02/78	6	13	● 5. **Every 1's A Winner**	Infinity 50002
			HOTLEGS	
			also see 10cc	
9/05/70	22	6	1. Neanderthal Man	Capitol 2886
			HOUSTON, DAVID	
8/27/66	24	8	1. Almost Persuaded	Epic 10025
			HOUSTON, THELMA	
1/29/77	1 (1)	17	1. **Don't Leave Me This Way**	Tamla 54278
5/19/79	34	3	2. Saturday Night, Sunday Morning	Tamla 54297
			HUDSON BROTHERS	
			Bill, Bret & Mark	
10/26/74	21	5	1. So You Are A Star	Casablanca 0108
8/02/75	26	4	2. Rendezvous	Rocket 40417
			HUES CORPORATION	
6/15/74	1 (1)	10	● 1. **Rock The Boat**	RCA 0232
10/26/74	18	5	2. Rockin' Soul	RCA 10066
			HUGHES, FRED	
6/19/65	23	6	1. Oo Wee Baby, I Love You	Vee-Jay 684
			HUGHES, JIMMY	
7/11/64	17	9	1. Steal Away	Fame 6401
			HUGO & LUIGI [Orchestra & Chorus]	
			producers Hugo Peretti & Luigi Creatore	
1/04/60	35	3	1. Just Come Home	RCA 7639
			HUMAN BEINZ	
1/06/68	8	11	1. **Nobody But Me**	Capitol 5990
			HUMAN LEAGUE	
			British 6-member electronic pop band, led by Philip Oakey	
4/10/82	1 (3)	21	● 1. **Don't You Want Me**	A&M 2397
			HUMPERDINCK, ENGELBERT	
			real name: Arnold Dorsey - born in India	
4/29/67	4	10	1. **Release Me (And Let Me Love Again)**	Parrot 40011
7/15/67	20	4	2. There Goes My Everything	Parrot 40015
10/14/67	25	5	3. The Last Waltz	Parrot 40019
1/06/68	18	7	4. Am I That Easy To Forget	Parrot 40023
6/01/68	19	5	5. A Man Without Love	Parrot 40027
11/23/68	31	3	6. Les Bicyclettes De Belsize	Parrot 40032
9/27/69	38	1	7. I'm A Better Man	Parrot 40040
1/03/70	16	8	8. Winter World Of Love	Parrot 40044
11/20/76	8	14	● 9. **After The Lovin'**	Epic 50270
			HUMPHREY, PAUL, & His Cool Aid Chemists	
5/15/71	29	7	1. Cool Aid [I]	Lizard 21006
			HUNTER, IVORY JOE	
			died 11/8/74 (60)	
12/01/56	12	15	1. Since I Met You Baby	Atlantic 1111

DATE	POS	WKS	ARTIST—Record Title	LABEL & NO.
			HUNTER, TAB	
			movie/TV star of the '50's	
1/19/57	**1** (6)	17	1. **Young Love**	Dot 15533
3/30/57	**11**	8	2. Ninety-Nine Ways	Dot 15548
2/23/59	**31**	4	3. (I'll Be With You In) Apple Blossom Time	Warner 5032
			HUSKY, FERLIN	
3/09/57	**4**	19	1. **Gone**	Capitol 3628
12/26/60	**12**	13	2. Wings Of A Dove	Capitol 4406
			HYLAND, BRIAN	
			16 years old during "Itsy..."	
7/11/60	**1** (1)	13	1. **Itsy Bitsy Teenie Weenie Yellow Polkadot Bikini** [N]	Leader 805
9/04/61	**20**	5	2. Let Me Belong To You	ABC-Para. 10236
4/07/62	**21**	6	3. Ginny Come Lately	ABC-Para. 10294
6/30/62	**3**	11	4. **Sealed With A Kiss**	ABC-Para. 10336
10/13/62	**25**	4	5. Warmed Over Kisses (Left Over Love)	ABC-Para. 10359
8/06/66	**20**	8	6. The Joker Went Wild	Philips 40377
11/26/66	**25**	3	7. Run, Run, Look And See	Philips 40405
10/24/70	**3**	13	● 8. **Gypsy Woman**	Uni 55240
			HYMAN, DICK, Trio	
1/28/56	**8**	15	1. **Moritat - A Theme from "The Three Penny Opera"** [I]	MGM 12149
			HYMAN, DICK, & His Electric Eclectics	
7/05/69	**38**	2	1. The Minotaur [I]	Command 4126
			IAN, JANIS	
			16 years old in 1967	
6/17/67	**14**	8	1. Society's Child (Baby I've Been Thinking)	Verve 5027
7/12/75	**3**	14	2. **At Seventeen**	Columbia 10154
			IDES OF MARCH	
			Chicago group led by Jim Peterik of Survivor	
4/11/70	**2** (1)	10	1. **Vehicle**	Warner 7378
			IDOL, BILLY	
			former leader of British punk group 'Generation X'	
8/07/82	**23**	9	1. Hot In The City	Chrysalis 2605
			IFIELD, FRANK	
			British	
9/22/62	**5**	8	1. **I Remember You**	Vee-Jay 457
			IKETTES	
			Ike & Tina Turner's backing vocal group	
2/03/62	**19**	8	1. I'm Blue (The Gong-Gong Song)	Atco 6212
4/10/65	**36**	4	2. Peaches "N" Cream	Modern 1005
			ILLUSION	
8/23/69	**32**	6	1. Did You See Her Eyes	Steed 718
			IMPALAS	
			Brooklyn quartet	
4/13/59	**2** (2)	11	1. **Sorry (I Ran All The Way Home)**	Cub 9022

DATE	POS	WKS	ARTIST—Record Title	LABEL & NO.
			IMPRESSIONS	
			Curtis Mayfield, lead singer '61-'70 - also see Jerry Butler	
11/20/61	20	8	1. Gypsy Woman	ABC-Para. 10241
10/12/63	4	11	2. **It's All Right**	ABC-Para. 10487
1/25/64	12	7	3. Talking About My Baby	ABC-Para. 10511
4/18/64	14	9	4. I'm So Proud	ABC-Para. 10544
6/27/64	10	10	5. **Keep On Pushing**	ABC-Para. 10554
9/19/64	15	8	6. You Must Believe Me	ABC-Para. 10581
12/12/64	7	7	7. **Amen**	ABC-Para. 10602
3/06/65	14	5	8. People Get Ready	ABC-Para. 10622
4/24/65	29	4	9. Woman's Got Soul	ABC-Para. 10647
1/01/66	33	2	10. You've Been Cheatin'	ABC-Para. 10750
2/03/68	14	8	11. We're A Winner	ABC 11022
10/05/68	22	7	12. Fool For You	Curtom 1932
12/28/68	25	6	13. This Is My Country	Curtom 1934
7/12/69	21	9	14. Choice Of Colors	Curtom 1943
6/13/70	28	8	15. Check Out Your Mind	Curtom 1951
6/29/74	17	6	16. Finally Got Myself Together (I'm A Changed Man)	Curtom 1997
			INDEPENDENTS	
4/28/73	21	9	● 1. Leaving Me	Wand 11252
			INGMANN, JORGEN, & His Guitar	
			Danish	
2/20/61	2 (2)	13	1. **Apache [I]**	Atco 6184
			INGRAM, JAMES - see QUINCY JONES	
			INGRAM, LUTHER	
6/24/72	3	13	1. **(If Loving You Is Wrong) I Don't Want To Be Right**	KoKo 2111
1/20/73	40	2	2. I'll Be Your Shelter (In Time Of Storm)	KoKo 2113
			INNOCENCE	
			Pete Anders & Vinnie Poncia - also recorded as Trade Winds	
1/07/67	34	3	1. There's Got To Be A Word!	Kama Sutra 214
			INNOCENTS	
			Kathy Young's backup vocal group	
9/19/60	28	3	1. Honest I Do	Indigo 105
1/09/61	28	3	2. Gee Whiz	Indigo 111
			INSTANT FUNK	
3/31/79	20	8	● 1. I Got My Mind Made Up (You Can Get It Girl)	Salsoul 2078
			INTRIGUES	
10/04/69	31	4	1. In A Moment	Yew 1001
			INTRUDERS	
			Philadelphia quartet	
4/06/68	6	11	● 1. **Cowboys To Girls**	Gamble 214
8/10/68	26	4	2. (Love Is Like A) Baseball Game	Gamble 217
6/30/73	36	6	3. I'll Always Love My Mama (Part 1)	Gamble 2506

DATE	POS	WKS	ARTIST—Record Title	LABEL & NO.
			IRIS, DONNIE	
			leader of The Jaggerz	
2/07/81	29	6	1. Ah! Leah!	MCA 51025
2/13/82	37	2	2. Love Is Like A Rock	MCA 51223
5/01/82	25	6	3. My Girl	MCA 52031
			IRISH ROVERS	
4/06/68	7	9	1. **The Unicorn**	Decca 32254
4/18/81	37	4	2. Wasn't That A Party	Epic 51007
			-shown as The Rovers-	
			IRON BUTTERFLY	
			America's 1st 'heavy metal' rock band	
9/28/68	30	7	1. In-A-Gadda-Da-Vida	Atco 6606
			IRONHORSE	
			Randy Bachman, leader	
4/21/79	36	3	1. Sweet Lui-Louise	Scotti Bros. 406
			IRWIN, BIG DEE	
			also see The Pastels	
7/13/63	38	2	1. Swinging On A Star	Dimension 1010
			-vocal duet with Little Eva-	
			ISLANDERS	
			Randy Starr, leader	
10/19/59	15	8	1. The Enchanted Sea [I]	Mayflower 16
			ISLEY BROTHERS	
			family group from Cincinnati led by Ronald, Rudolph & O'Kelly	
6/30/62	17	11	1. Twist And Shout	Wand 124
3/19/66	12	8	2. This Old Heart Of Mine (Is Weak For You)	Tamla 54128
3/29/69	2 (1)	12	● 3. **It's Your Thing**	T-Neck 901
6/21/69	23	7	4. I Turned You On	T-Neck 902
7/03/71	18	9	5. Love The One You're With	T-Neck 930
8/19/72	24	7	6. Pop That Thang	T-Neck 935
8/18/73	6	15	● 7. **That Lady (Part 1)**	T-Neck 2251
7/12/75	4	13	● 8. **Fight The Power - Part 1**	T-Neck 2256
11/22/75	22	9	9. For The Love Of You (Part 1 & 2)	T-Neck 2259
8/06/77	40	1	10. Livin' In The Life	T-Neck 2264
5/24/80	39	2	11. Don't Say Goodnight (It's Time For Love) (Parts 1 & 2)	T-Neck 2290
			IVES, BURL	
1/06/62	9	11	1. **A Little Bitty Tear**	Decca 31330
4/21/62	10	8	2. **Funny Way Of Laughin'**	Decca 31371
8/11/62	19	4	3. Call Me Mr. In-Between	Decca 31405
12/08/62	39	1	4. Mary Ann Regrets	Decca 31433
			IVY THREE	
8/29/60	8	7	1. **Yogi** [N]	Shell 720
			JACKS, TERRY	
			Terry and wife Susan were The Poppy Family	
2/09/74	1 (3)	15	● 1. **Seasons In The Sun**	Bell 45432

DATE	POS	WKS	ARTIST—Record Title	LABEL & NO.
			JACKSON 5	
			Michael, Marlon, Jackie, Tito & Jermaine - replaced by Randy in '75	
12/06/69	**1** (1)	16	1. **I Want You Back**	Motown 1157
3/21/70	**1** (2)	12	2. **ABC**	Motown 1163
6/06/70	**1** (2)	12	3. **The Love You Save**	Motown 1166
9/19/70	**1** (5)	16	4. **I'll Be There**	Motown 1171
2/06/71	**2** (2)	9	5. **Mama's Pearl**	Motown 1177
4/10/71	**2** (3)	11	6. **Never Can Say Goodbye**	Motown 1179
7/31/71	**20**	6	7. Maybe Tomorrow	Motown 1186
12/25/71	**10**	8	8. **Sugar Daddy**	Motown 1194
4/29/72	**13**	8	9. Little Bitty Pretty One	Motown 1199
7/29/72	**16**	8	10. Lookin' Through The Windows	Motown 1205
11/18/72	**18**	8	11. Corner Of The Sky -from Broadway musical "Pippin"-	Motown 1214
4/14/73	**28**	4	12. Hallelujah Day	Motown 1224
9/22/73	**28**	7	13. Get It Together	Motown 1277
3/30/74	**2** (2)	16	14. **Dancing Machine**	Motown 1286
11/30/74	**38**	2	15. Whatever You Got, I Want	Motown 1308
2/22/75	**15**	7	16. I Am Love (Parts I & II)	Motown 1310
			THE JACKSONS:	
12/11/76	**6**	15	● 17. **Enjoy Yourself**	Epic 50289
5/07/77	**28**	3	18. Show You The Way To Go	Epic 50350
3/31/79	**7**	14	★ 19. **Shake Your Body (Down To The Ground)**	Epic 50656
10/11/80	**12**	9	20. Lovely One	Epic 50938
1/10/81	**22**	8	21. Heartbreak Hotel	Epic 50959
			JACKSON, CHUCK	
3/13/61	**36**	2	1. I Don't Want To Cry	Wand 106
6/02/62	**23**	6	2. Any Day Now (My Wild Beautiful Bird)	Wand 122
			JACKSON, DEON	
2/19/66	**11**	9	1. Love Makes The World Go Round	Carla 2526
			JACKSON, JERMAINE	
			member of The Jackson 5	
1/13/73	**9**	13	1. **Daddy's Home**	Motown 1216
5/03/80	**9**	14	2. **Let's Get Serious**	Motown 1469
8/30/80	**34**	4	3. You're Supposed To Keep Your Love For Me	Motown 1490
8/21/82	**18**	7	4. Let Me Tickle Your Fancy -backing vocals by Devo-	Motown 1628
			JACKSON, J.J.	
11/05/66	**22**	7	1. But It's Alright	Calla 119
			JACKSON, JOE	
7/07/79	**21**	8	1. Is She Really Going Out With Him?	A&M 2132
10/16/82	**6**	15	2. **Steppin' Out**	A&M 2428
			JACKSON, MICHAEL	
			member of The Jacksons	
11/06/71	**4**	13	1. **Got To Be There**	Motown 1191
3/18/72	**2** (2)	11	2. **Rockin' Robin**	Motown 1197
6/10/72	**16**	9	3. I Wanna Be Where You Are	Motown 1202

DATE	POS	WKS	ARTIST—Record Title	LABEL & NO.
9/09/72	**1** (1)	11	4. **Ben**	Motown 1207
7/12/75	23	6	5. Just A Little Bit Of You	Motown 1349
9/01/79	**1** (1)	12	● 6. **Don't Stop 'Til You Get Enough**	Epic 50742
11/24/79	**1** (4)	19	● 7. **Rock With You**	Epic 50797
2/23/80	**10**	11	8. **Off The Wall**	Epic 50838
5/10/80	**10**	11	9. **She's Out Of My Life**	Epic 50871
			JACKSON, MILLIE	
5/13/72	27	6	1. Ask Me What You Want	Spring 123
9/29/73	24	8	2. Hurts So Good -from the film "Cleopatra Jones"	Spring 139
			JACKSON, STONEWALL	
6/08/59	**4**	12	1. **Waterloo**	Columbia 41393
			JACKSON, WANDA	
10/10/60	37	1	1. Let's Have A Party	Capitol 4397
8/14/61	29	3	2. Right Or Wrong	Capitol 4553
11/27/61	27	3	3. In The Middle Of A Heartache	Capitol 4635
			JACOBS, DICK, & His Orchestra	
4/07/56	22	7	1. "Main Title" And "Molly-O" -from film "The Man With The Golden Arm"-	Coral 61606
11/03/56	16	9	2. Petticoats Of Portugal	Coral 61724
9/16/57	17	4	3. Fascination -from film "Love In The Afternoon"	Coral 61864
			JAGGERZ Donnie Iris, leader of Pittsburgh group	
2/14/70	**2** (1)	11	● 1. **The Rapper**	Kama Sutra 502
			JAMES, ETTA	
6/06/60	33	4	1. All I Could Do Was Cry	Argo 5359
11/21/60	34	3	2. My Dearest Darling	Argo 5368
4/03/61	30	4	3. Trust In Me	Argo 5385
9/04/61	39	2	4. Don't Cry, Baby	Argo 5393
3/31/62	37	4	5. Something's Got A Hold On Me	Argo 5409
9/08/62	34	2	6. Stop The Wedding	Argo 5418
5/11/63	25	6	7. Pushover	Argo 5437
12/30/67	23	7	8. Tell Mama	Cadet 5578
4/06/68	35	4	9. Security	Cadet 5594
			JAMES, JONI	
2/19/55	**2** (1)	16	1. **How Important Can It Be?**	MGM 11919
10/22/55	**6**	10	2. **You Are My Love**	MGM 12066
8/11/56	30	2	3. Give Us This Day	MGM 12288
10/20/58	19	8	4. There Goes My Heart	MGM 12706
2/16/59	33	4	5. There Must Be A Way	MGM 12746
1/25/60	35	3	6. Little Things Mean A Lot	MGM 12849
1/23/61	38	1	7. My Last Date (With You)	MGM 12933
			JAMES, RICK	
8/05/78	**13**	10	1. You And I	Gordy 7156
7/18/81	40	2	2. Give It To Me Baby	Gordy 7197

DATE	POS	WKS	ARTIST—Record Title	LABEL & NO.
9/05/81	16	10	3. Super Freak (Part 1)	Gordy 7205
			JAMES, SONNY [The Southern Gentleman]	
1/05/57	1 (1)	17	1. **Young Love**	Capitol 3602
4/20/57	25	1	2. First Date, First Kiss, First Love	Capitol 3674
			JAMES, TOMMY	
6/26/71	4	11	1. **Draggin' The Line**	Roulette 7103
10/23/71	40	1	2. I'm Comin' Home	Roulette 7110
2/23/80	19	9	3. Three Times In Love	Millennium 11785
			JAMES, TOMMY, & THE SHONDELLS	
6/18/66	1 (2)	10	● 1. **Hanky Panky**	Roulette 4686
8/20/66	21	5	2. Say I Am (What I Am)	Roulette 4695
12/10/66	31	4	3. It's Only Love	Roulette 4710
3/11/67	4	12	4. **I Think We're Alone Now**	Roulette 4720
5/06/67	10	8	5. **Mirage**	Roulette 4736
7/15/67	25	5	6. I Like The Way	Roulette 4756
9/02/67	18	6	7. Gettin' Together	Roulette 4762
5/04/68	3	13	8. **Mony Mony**	Roulette 7008
11/23/68	38	2	9. Do Something To Me	Roulette 7024
12/21/68	1 (2)	15	10. **Crimson And Clover**	Roulette 7028
4/05/69	7	8	11. **Sweet Cherry Wine**	Roulette 7039
6/28/69	2 (3)	12	12. **Crystal Blue Persuasion**	Roulette 7050
10/25/69	19	5	13. Ball Of Fire	Roulette 7060
12/20/69	23	7	14. She	Roulette 7066
			JAMIES	
9/15/58	26	4	1. Summertime, Summertime	Epic 9281
8/04/62	38	1	2. Summertime, Summertime -re-entry of 1958 hit-	Epic 9281
			JAN & ARNIE	
			Jan Berry & Arnie Ginsburg	
5/26/58	8	11	1. **Jennie Lee**	Arwin 108
			JAN & DEAN	
			Jan Berry & Dean Torrence - Jan was critically injured in a car accident in April of '66	
8/10/59	10	9	1. **Baby Talk**	Dore 522
7/10/61	25	4	2. Heart And Soul	Challenge 9111
4/20/63	28	5	3. Linda	Liberty 55531
6/22/63	1 (2)	11	4. **Surf City**	Liberty 55580
9/21/63	11	8	5. Honolulu Lulu	Liberty 55613
12/21/63	10	9	6. **Drag City**	Liberty 55641
3/28/64	8	11	7. **Dead Man's Curve/**	
4/04/64	37	4	8. The New Girl In School	Liberty 55672
7/04/64	3	10	9. **The Little Old Lady (From Pasadena)**	Liberty 55704
10/10/64	16	5	10. Ride The Wild Surf	Liberty 55724
11/21/64	25	5	11. Sidewalk Surfin'	Liberty 55727
6/26/65	27	4	12. You Really Know How To Hurt A Guy	Liberty 55792
11/13/65	30	2	13. I Found A Girl	Liberty 55833
6/18/66	21	6	14. Popsicle	Liberty 55886

DATE	POS	WKS	ARTIST—Record Title	LABEL & NO.
			JANKOWSKI, HORST	
6/05/65	12	9	1. A Walk In The Black Forest [I]	Mercury 72425
			JARMELS	
8/28/61	12	6	1. A Little Bit Of Soap	Laurie 3098
			JARREAU, AL	
9/12/81	15	11	1. We're In This Love Together	Warner 49746
			JAY & THE AMERICANS	
			Jay Black, lead singer of Brooklyn group	
4/07/62	5	11	1. **She Cried**	United Artists 415
9/21/63	25	4	2. Only In America	United Artists 626
10/03/64	3	11	3. **Come A Little Bit Closer**	United Artists 759
1/16/65	11	7	4. Let's Lock The Door (And Throw Away The Key)	United Artists 805
6/19/65	4	11	5. **Cara, Mia**	United Artists 881
9/25/65	13	6	6. Some Enchanted Evening	United Artists 919
12/04/65	18	6	7. Sunday And Me	United Artists 948
6/11/66	25	4	8. Crying	United Artists 50016
1/25/69	6	10	● 9. **This Magic Moment**	United Artists 50475
1/17/70	19	7	10. Walkin' In The Rain	United Artists 50605
			JAY & THE TECHNIQUES	
			Jay Proctor, lead singer of Allentown, Pennsylvania group	
8/19/67	6	11	1. **Apples, Peaches, Pumpkin Pie**	Smash 2086
11/11/67	14	9	2. Keep The Ball Rollin'	Smash 2124
2/10/68	39	2	3. Strawberry Shortcake	Smash 2142
			JAYE, JERRY	
5/06/67	29	6	1. My Girl Josephine	Hi 2120
			JAYHAWKS	
			also recorded as The Marathons and The Vibrations	
7/28/56	18	2	1. Stranded In The Jungle [N]	Flash 109
			JAYNETTS	
9/07/63	2 (2)	10	1. **Sally, Go 'Round The Roses**	Tuff 369
			JB's	
			James Brown's backing band	
6/23/73	22	6	● 1. Doing It To Death	People 621
			-Fred Wesley, leader-	
			JEFFERSON	
			English	
1/24/70	23	6	1. Baby Take Me In Your Arms	Janus 106
			JEFFERSON AIRPLANE	
			formed in San Francisco by Marty Balin & Paul Kantner - featuring lead singer Grace Slick	
5/06/67	5	9	1. **Somebody To Love**	RCA 9140
7/01/67	8	9	2. **White Rabbit**	RCA 9248
			JEFFERSON STARSHIP	
9/13/75	3	13	1. **Miracles**	Grunt 10367
8/14/76	12	11	2. With Your Love	Grunt 10746

DATE	POS	WKS	ARTIST—Record Title	LABEL & NO.
3/25/78	8	11	3. **Count On Me**	Grunt 11196
6/24/78	12	8	4. Runaway	Grunt 11274
11/24/79	14	11	5. Jane	Grunt 11750
5/02/81	29	6	6. Find Your Way Back	Grunt 12211
11/13/82	28	6	7. Be My Lady	Grunt 13350
			JEFFREY, JOE, Group	
7/05/69	14	8	1. My Pledge Of Love	Wand 11200
			JELLY BEANS	
7/18/64	9	7	1. **I Wanna Love Him So Bad**	Red Bird 10003
			JENNINGS, WAYLON	
			also see Waylon & Willie	
6/11/77	25	7	1. Luckenbach, Texas (Back To The Basics Of Love)	RCA 10924
11/01/80	21	9	● 2. Theme From The Dukes Of Hazzard (Good Ol' Boys)	RCA 12067
			JENSEN, KRIS	
10/06/62	20	6	1. Torture	Hickory 1173
			JETHRO TULL	
			English group led by Ian Anderson	
11/25/72	11	10	1. Living In The Past	Chrysalis 2006
11/30/74	12	10	2. Bungle In The Jungle	Chrysalis 2101
			JETT, JOAN, & THE BLACKHEARTS	
			former leader of L.A. girl band The Runaways	
2/13/82	1 (7)	16	★ 1. **I Love Rock 'N Roll**	Boardwalk 135
5/15/82	7	10	2. **Crimson And Clover**	Boardwalk 144
8/28/82	20	7	3. Do You Wanna Touch Me (Oh Yeah)	Boardwalk 150
			JIGSAW	
			Australian	
10/11/75	3	14	1. **Sky High** -from movie "The Dragon Flies"-	Chelsea 3022
3/13/76	30	5	2. Love Fire	Chelsea 3037
			JIMENEZ, JOSE	
			Jose is comedian Bill Dana	
9/18/61	19	4	1. The Astronaut (Parts 1 & 2) [C] -interviewed by Don Hinckley-	Kapp 409
			JIVE BOMBERS Featuring Clarence Palmer	
3/16/57	36	1	1. Bad Boy	Savoy 1508
			JIVE FIVE Featuring Eugene Pitt	
8/14/61	3	12	1. **My True Story**	Beltone 1006
9/11/65	36	3	2. I'm A Happy Man	United Artists 853
			JO JO GUNNE	
			Jay Ferguson, leader	
4/15/72	27	6	1. Run Run Run	Asylum 11003
			JO, DAMITA	
			real name: Damita Jo DuBlanc	
11/07/60	22	8	1. I'll Save The Last Dance For You	Mercury 71690
7/17/61	12	7	2. I'll Be There	Mercury 71840

DATE	POS	WKS	ARTIST—Record Title	LABEL & NO.
			JO, SAMI	
3/23/74	21	7	1. Tell Me A Lie	MGM South 7029
			JOEL, BILLY	
			began career with The Hassles from Long Island, New York	
4/06/74	25	4	1. Piano Man	Columbia 45963
12/28/74	34	5	2. The Entertainer	Columbia 10064
12/10/77	3	18	● 3. **Just The Way You Are**	Columbia 10646
4/15/78	17	8	4. Movin' Out (Anthony's Song)	Columbia 10708
6/17/78	24	5	5. Only The Good Die Young	Columbia 10750
9/09/78	17	9	6. She's Always A Woman	Columbia 10788
11/11/78	3	16	● 7. **My Life**	Columbia 10853
3/03/79	14	6	8. Big Shot	Columbia 10913
5/12/79	24	4	9. Honesty	Columbia 10959
3/22/80	7	11	10. **You May Be Right**	Columbia 11231
5/24/80	1 (2)	19	● 11. **It's Still Rock And Roll To Me**	Columbia 11276
8/16/80	19	9	12. Don't Ask Me Why	Columbia 11331
11/01/80	36	3	13. Sometimes A Fantasy	Columbia 11379
9/26/81	17	8	14. Say Goodbye To Hollywood	Columbia 02518
12/12/81	23	9	15. She's Got A Way	Columbia 02628
10/16/82	20	8	16. Pressure	Columbia 03244
			JOHN & ERNEST	
			John Free & Ernest Smith - a Dickie Goodman production	
5/12/73	31	4	1. Super Fly Meets Shaft [N]	Rainy Wed. 201
			JOHN, ELTON	
			English - #1 popular recording artist of the '70's	
12/19/70	8	11	1. **Your Song**	Uni 55265
4/10/71	34	4	2. Friends	Uni 55277
1/01/72	24	7	3. Levon	Uni 55314
5/27/72	6	12	4. **Rocket Man**	Uni 55328
8/26/72	8	7	5. **Honky Cat**	Uni 55343
12/23/72	1 (3)	14	● 6. **Crocodile Rock**	MCA 40000
4/21/73	2 (1)	12	7. **Daniel**	MCA 40046
8/11/73	12	9	8. Saturday Night's Alright For Fighting	MCA 40105
11/03/73	2 (3)	14	● 9. **Goodbye Yellow Brick Road**	MCA 40148
3/02/74	1 (1)	16	● 10. **Bennie And The Jets**	MCA 40198
7/06/74	2 (2)	9	● 11. **Don't Let The Sun Go Down On Me**	MCA 40259
9/21/74	4	9	12. **The Bitch Is Back**	MCA 40297
12/07/74	1 (2)	10	● 13. **Lucy In The Sky With Diamonds**	MCA 40344
			-with the reggae guitars of Dr. Winston O'Boogie (John Lennon)-	
3/15/75	1 (2)	17	● 14. **Philadelphia Freedom**	MCA 40364
7/12/75	4	10	● 15. **Someone Saved My Life Tonight**	MCA 40421
10/18/75	1 (3)	12	● 16. **Island Girl**	MCA 40461
1/31/76	14	5	17. Grow Some Funk Of Your Own/	
		5	18. **I Feel Like A Bullet (In The Gun Of Robert Ford)**	MCA 40505
11/20/76	6	11	● 19. **Sorry Seems To Be The Hardest Word**	MCA/Rocket 40645
2/26/77	28	3	20. Bite Your Lip (Get up and dance!)	MCA/Rocket 40677
4/29/78	34	3	21. Ego	MCA 40892

DATE	POS	WKS	ARTIST—Record Title	LABEL & NO.
11/18/78	22	6	22. Part-Time Love	MCA 40973
6/23/79	9	14	● 23. **Mama Can't Buy You Love**	MCA 41042
10/27/79	31	4	24. Victim Of Love	MCA 41126
5/10/80	3	17	● 25. **Little Jeannie**	MCA 41236
9/20/80	39	2	26. (Sartorial Eloquence) Don't Ya Wanna Play This Game No More?	MCA 41293
5/30/81	21	6	27. Nobody Wins	Geffen 49722
9/05/81	34	3	28. Chloe	Geffen 49788
4/17/82	13	10	29. Empty Garden (Hey Hey Johnny)	Geffen 50049
8/14/82	12	10	30. Blue Eyes	Geffen 29954
			JOHN, ELTON, & KIKI DEE	
7/17/76	1 (4)	15	● 1. **Don't Go Breaking My Heart**	Rocket 40585
			JOHN, LITTLE WILLIE	
			died in prison 5/26/68 (30)	
7/14/56	24	9	1. Fever	King 4935
4/21/58	20	7	2. Talk To Me, Talk To Me	King 5108
7/25/60	38	1	3. Heartbreak (It's Hurtin' Me)	King 5356
10/10/60	13	10	4. Sleep	King 5394
			JOHN, ROBERT	
1/29/72	3	13	● 1. **The Lion Sleeps Tonight**	Atlantic 2846
6/30/79	1 (1)	19	● 2. **Sad Eyes**	EMI America 8015
8/23/80	31	4	3. Hey There Lonely Girl	EMI America 8049
			JOHNNIE & JOE	
			Johnnie Richardson & Joe Rivers	
5/27/57	8	15	1. **Over The Mountain; Across The Sea**	Chess 1654
			JOHNNY & THE HURRICANES	
			Johnny Paris, leader - from Toledo, Ohio	
6/01/59	23	6	1. Crossfire [I]	Warwick 502
8/17/59	5	13	2. **Red River Rock [I]** -"Red River Valley" rock version-	Warwick 509
11/16/59	25	6	3. Reveille Rock [I]	Warwick 513
2/22/60	15	10	4. Beatnik Fly [I] -adaptation of "Blue Tail Fly"-	Warwick 520
			JOHNS, SAMMY	
3/01/75	5	12	● 1. **Chevy Van**	Grc 2046
			JOHNSON, BETTY	
12/15/56	9	18	1. **I Dreamed**	Bally 1020
6/24/57	25	1	2. Little White Lies	Bally 1033
2/24/58	17	11	3. The Little Blue Man [N]	Atlantic 1169
6/30/58	19	1	4. Dream	Atlantic 1186
			JOHNSON, MARV	
4/20/59	30	6	1. Come To Me	United Artists 160
11/16/59	10	16	2. **You Got What It Takes**	United Artists 185
3/21/60	9	10	3. **I Love The Way You Love**	United Artists 208
10/10/60	20	4	4. (You've Got To) Move Two Mountains	United Artists 241

DATE	POS	WKS	ARTIST—Record Title	LABEL & NO.
			JOHNSON, MICHAEL	
5/27/78	12	10	1. Bluer Than Blue	EMI America 8001
9/23/78	32	5	2. Almost Like Being In Love	EMI America 8004
9/29/79	19	9	3. This Night Won't Last Forever	EMI America 8019
			JOHNSTON, TOM	
			former lead singer of The Doobie Brothers	
1/12/80	34	2	1. Savannah Nights	Warner 49096
			JOLI, FRANCE	
9/29/79	15	8	1. Come To Me	Prelude 8001
			JON & ROBIN & The In Crowd	
			Jon & Robin Abnor	
5/27/67	18	6	1. Do It Again A Little Bit Slower	Abnak 119
			JONES GIRLS	
			sisters Shirley, Brenda & Valorie	
8/18/79	38	1	● 1. You Gonna Make Me Love Somebody Else	Phil. Int'l. 3680
			JONES, ETTA	
12/12/60	36	1	1. Don't Go To Strangers	Prestige 180
			JONES, JACK	
			son of actor Allan Jones	
11/30/63	14	10	1. Wives And Lovers	Kapp 551
12/26/64	30	5	2. Dear Heart	Kapp 635
3/20/65	15	7	3. The Race Is On	Kapp 651
7/16/66	35	4	4. The Impossible Dream	Kapp 755
			-from musical "Man Of La Mancha"-	
3/25/67	39	2	5. Lady	Kapp 800
			JONES, JIMMY	
1/18/60	2 (1)	15	1. **Handy Man**	Cub 9049
5/09/60	3	10	2. **Good Timin'**	Cub 9067
			JONES, JOE	
10/10/60	3	9	1. **You Talk Too Much**	Roulette 4304
			JONES, LINDA	
			died 3/24/72 (26)	
7/22/67	21	7	1. Hypnotized	Loma 2070
			JONES, QUINCY	
			top record producer/arranger	
7/22/78	21	7	1. Stuff Like That	A&M 2043
			-vocals: Ashford & Simpson, and Chaka Khan-	
5/09/81	28	4	2. Ai No Corrida	A&M 2309
			-featuring vocals by Dune-	
			JONES, QUINCY, Featuring JAMES INGRAM	
9/19/81	17	10	1. Just Once	A&M 2357
2/13/82	14	11	2. One Hundred Ways	A&M 2387
			JONES, RICKIE LEE	
5/12/79	4	12	1. **Chuck E.'s In Love**	Warner 8825
9/01/79	40	1	2. Young Blood	Warner 49018

The Impressions. One of black music's most influential songwriters, Curtis Mayfield never left any doubt as to the origin of his compositions. "They were church songs. The difference was, I left the word 'God' out."

The Jackson Five. Officially, Motown claimed that Diana Ross discovered the Jackson Five, but the teenage group was in reality brought to the company's attention by one of its lesser-known artists, Bobby ("Does Your Mama Know About Me") Taylor.

Sonny James. Jimmy Loden and Arthur Gelien battled it out in the winter of '57 with different versions of "Young Love." That's Sonny James and Tab Hunter to everyone but their mothers.

Tommy James and the Shondells' first chart entry, "Hanky Panky," was originally waxed by songwriters Jeff Barry and Ellie Greenwich when they were the Raindrops, circa 1963.

Jay & the Americans. There were a couple of Jays (Traynor and Black) fronting the Americans through their chart years in the '60s. Black later made several solo sides, including a version of "Love Is In The Air" that lost out to John Paul Jones.

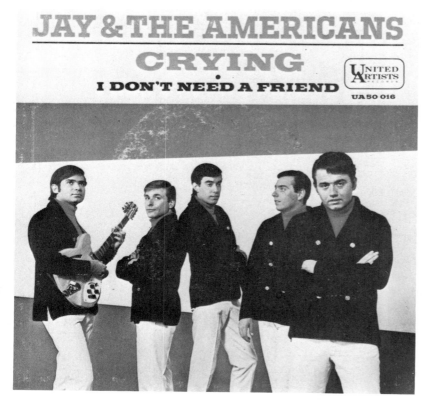

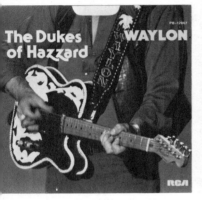

JOAN JETT & the BLACKHEARTS

CRIMSON AND CLOVER

b/w OH WOE IS ME

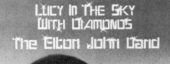

LUCY IN THE SKY WITH DIAMONDS
The Elton John Band

Jefferson Starship. Sly Stone produced Grace Slick when she was a member of the Great Society, before the formation of Jefferson Airplane. And yes, Sly did turn up for the recording session.

Waylon Jennings was Buddy Holly's bass player for a while, and would have been on the fateful flight that killed Holly if he hadn't given up his seat to the Big Bopper.

Joan Jett was originally a member of the Runaways, the girl group assembled by pop's quirkiest producer, Kim Fowley, as a sort of '70s version of the Shangri-Las.

Elton John. Reg Dwight of Pinner, the most popular solo star of the '70s, had to share his biggest hit (four weeks at No. 1) with Pauline Matthews of Bradford. They're better known as Elton John and Kiki Dee.

Johnny and the Hurricanes' first success, "Crossfire," was recorded in an old Detroit movie theater to get the right reverb effect.

Journey. San Francisco's Journey was the first rock group immortalized in a video game, named after their platinum album, "Escape."

153

DATE	POS	WKS	ARTIST—Record Title	LABEL & NO.
			JONES, TOM	
			Welsh	
5/01/65	10	9	1. **It's Not Unusual**	Parrot 9737
7/03/65	3	10	2. **What's New Pussycat?**	Parrot 9765
9/18/65	27	5	3. With These Hands	Parrot 9787
1/01/66	25	6	4. Thunderball	Parrot 9801
1/21/67	11	7	5. Green, Green Grass Of Home	Parrot 40009
4/01/67	27	4	6. Detroit City	Parrot 40012
4/13/68	15	11	7. Delilah	Parrot 40025
10/05/68	35	2	8. Help Yourself	Parrot 40029
6/07/69	13	9	9. Love Me Tonight	Parrot 40038
8/09/69	6	14	● 10. **I'll Never Fall In Love Again**	Parrot 40018
			-re-entry of 1967 hit-	
1/03/70	5	10	● 11. **Without Love (There Is Nothing)**	Parrot 40045
5/09/70	13	7	12. Daughter Of Darkness	Parrot 40048
8/29/70	14	7	13. I (Who Have Nothing)	Parrot 40051
11/28/70	25	7	14. Can't Stop Loving You	Parrot 40056
2/20/71	2 (1)	12	● 15. **She's A Lady**	Parrot 40058
6/12/71	26	6	16. Puppet Man/	
		3	17. **Resurrection Shuffle**	Parrot 40064
2/12/77	15	10	18. Say You'll Stay Until Tomorrow	Epic 50308
			JOPLIN, JANIS	
			"Pearl", lead singer of 'Big Brother & The Holding Company', died 10/3/70 (27)	
2/20/71	1 (2)	12	1. **Me And Bobby McGee**	Columbia 45314
			JOURNEY	
			West Coast Bay-area quintet led by Steve Perry (vocals) & Neal Schon (guitar)	
8/25/79	16	12	1. Lovin', Touchin', Squeezin'	Columbia 11036
3/29/80	23	6	2. Any Way You Want It	Columbia 11213
7/05/80	32	4	3. Walks Like A Lady	Columbia 11275
4/04/81	34	4	4. The Party's Over (Hopelessly In Love)	Columbia 60505
8/01/81	4	14	5. **Who's Crying Now**	Columbia 02241
11/07/81	9	13	6. **Don't Stop Believin'**	Columbia 02567
1/23/82	2 (6)	14	7. **Open Arms**	Columbia 02687
6/12/82	19	9	8. Still They Ride	Columbia 02883
			JUNIOR	
			Junior Giscombe	
4/10/82	30	3	1. Mama Used To Say	Mercury 76132
			JUST US	
5/07/66	34	2	1. I Can't Grow Peaches On A Cherry Tree	Colpix 803
			JUSTIS, BILL, & His Orchestra	
			Bill died on 7/15/82 (55)	
11/18/57	2 (1)	14	1. **Raunchy [I]**	Phillips 3519
			KAEMPFERT, BERT, & His Orchestra	
			German - produced 1st Beatles' recording - died 6/21/80 (56)	
11/21/60	1 (3)	15	1. **Wonderland By Night [I]**	Decca 31141
4/10/61	31	4	2. Tenderly [I]	Decca 31236
2/13/65	11	10	3. Red Roses For A Blue Lady [I]	Decca 31722

DATE	POS	WKS	ARTIST—Record Title	LABEL & NO.
5/29/65	33	3	4. Three O'Clock In The Morning [I]	Decca 31778
			KALIN TWINS	
			Herbie & Hal	
6/30/58	5	13	1. **When**	Decca 30642
10/20/58	12	9	2. Forget Me Not	Decca 30745
			KALLEN, KITTY	
			vocalist with Jimmy Dorsey and Harry James' bands	
11/09/59	34	3	1. If I Give My Heart To You	Columbia 41473
1/12/63	18	6	2. My Coloring Book	RCA 8124
			KALLEN, KITTY, & GEORGIE SHAW	
2/11/56	39	1	1. Go On With The Wedding	Decca 29776
			KANSAS	
			sextet from Topeka led by Steve Walsh & Kerry Livgren	
2/05/77	11	13	1. Carry On Wayward Son	Kirshner 4267
12/17/77	28	6	2. Point Of Know Return	Kirshner 4273
2/18/78	6	15	● 3. **Dust In The Wind**	Kirshner 4274
6/23/79	23	8	4. People Of The South Wind	Kirshner 4284
11/08/80	40	1	5. Hold On	Kirshner 4291
5/29/82	17	9	6. Play The Game Tonight	Kirshner 02903
			KASENETZ-KATZ Singing Orchestral Circus	
			producers Jerry Kasenetz & Jeff Katz	
11/09/68	25	6	1. Quick Joey Small (Run Joey Run)	Buddah 64
			KAYE, SAMMY, & His Orchestra	
5/02/64	36	2	1. Charade [I]	Decca 31589
			KC & THE SUNSHINE BAND	
			KC is Harry Wayne Casey - also see Teri DeSario	
8/02/75	1 (1)	9	1. **Get Down Tonight**	T.K. 1009
11/01/75	1 (2)	13	2. **That's The Way (I Like It)**	T.K. 1015
7/31/76	1 (1)	16	3. **(Shake, Shake, Shake) Shake Your Booty**	T.K. 1019
1/29/77	37	2	4. I Like To Do It	T.K. 1020
4/02/77	1 (1)	16	5. **I'm Your Boogie Man**	T.K. 1022
8/13/77	2 (3)	14	6. **Keep It Comin' Love**	T.K. 1023
3/25/78	35	3	7. Boogie Shoes	T.K. 1025
6/24/78	35	2	8. It's The Same Old Song	T.K. 1028
9/29/79	1 (1)	18	9. **Please Don't Go**	T.K. 1035
			K-DOE, ERNIE	
			real name: Ernest Kador, Jr.	
4/03/61	1 (1)	12	1. **Mother-In-Law**	Minit 623
			-bass vocal: Benny Spellman-	
			KEITH	
			James Barry Keefer	
11/12/66	39	1	1. Ain't Gonna Lie	Mercury 72596
1/07/67	7	9	2. **98.6**	Mercury 72639
4/08/67	37	2	3. Tell Me To My Face	Mercury 72652
			KELLER, JERRY	
7/20/59	14	8	1. Here Comes Summer	Kapp 277
			KELLY, GRACE - see BING CROSBY	

DATE	POS	WKS	ARTIST—Record Title	LABEL & NO.
			KELLY, MONTY, & His Orchestra	
4/04/60	30	3	1. Summer Set [I]	Carlton 527
			KENDRICKS, EDDIE	
			lead singer of The Temptations thru 1971	
9/15/73	1 (2)	16	1. **Keep On Truckin' (Part 1)**	Tamla 54238
1/26/74	2 (2)	13	2. **Boogie Down**	Tamla 54243
6/01/74	28	4	3. Son Of Sagittarius	Tamla 54247
4/05/75	18	10	4. Shoeshine Boy	Tamla 54257
3/20/76	36	3	5. He's A Friend	Tamla 54266
			KENNER, CHRIS	
			died 1/25/76	
7/03/61	2 (3)	10	1. **I Like It Like That, Part 1**	Instant 3229
			KENTON, STAN	
			died 8/25/79 (67)	
11/17/62	32	4	1. Mama Sang A Song [S]	Capitol 4847
			KERMIT [Jim Henson]	
			also see Ernie	
10/20/79	25	7	1. Rainbow Connection -from "The Muppet Movie"-	Atlantic 3610
			KERR, ANITA - see LITTLE DIPPERS	
			KHAN, CHAKA	
			lead singer of Rufus	
11/18/78	21	8	1. I'm Every Woman	Warner 8683
			KIHN, GREG, Band	
7/11/81	15	13	1. The Breakup Song (They Don't Write 'Em)	Beserkley 47149
			KILGORE, THEOLA	
5/11/63	21	8	1. The Love Of My Man	Serock 2004
			KIM, ANDY	
6/01/68	21	8	1. How'd We Ever Get This Way	Steed 707
10/19/68	31	3	2. Shoot'em Up, Baby	Steed 710
6/21/69	9	12	● 3. **Baby, I Love You**	Steed 716
11/08/69	36	1	4. So Good Together	Steed 720
11/28/70	17	8	5. Be My Baby	Steed 729
7/20/74	1 (1)	13	● 6. **Rock Me Gently**	Capitol 3895
11/23/74	28	4	7. Fire, Baby I'm On Fire	Capitol 3962
			KIMBERLY, ADRIAN	
7/10/61	34	1	1. The Graduation Song…Pomp And Circumstance [I]	Calliope 6501
			KING CURTIS	
			saxophonist Curtis Ousley -- died 8/14/71 (37)	
4/07/62	17	8	1. Soul Twist [I] -with The Noble Knights-	Enjoy 1000
9/23/67	33	4	2. Memphis Soul Stew [I]	Atco 6511
10/07/67	28	4	3. Ode To Billie Joe [I] -shown only as The Kingpins-	Atco 6516
			KING FLOYD	
12/12/70	6	13	● 1. **Groove Me**	Chimneyville 435
4/03/71	29	7	2. Baby Let Me Kiss You	Chimneyville 437

DATE	POS	WKS	ARTIST—Record Title	LABEL & NO.
			KING HARVEST	
1/06/73	13	11	1. Dancing In The Moonlight	Perception 515
			KING, B.B.	
			Riley B. ("Blues Boy") King	
6/13/64	34	3	1. Rock Me Baby	Kent 393
5/25/68	39	1	2. Paying The Cost To Be The Boss	BluesWay 61015
1/31/70	15	8	3. The Thrill Is Gone	BluesWay 61032
4/03/71	40	1	4. Ask Me No Questions	ABC 11290
9/22/73	38	2	5. To Know You Is To Love You	ABC 11373
2/09/74	28	6	6. I Like To Live The Love	ABC 11406
			KING, BEN E.	
			lead singer of The Drifters ('59-'60)	
1/30/61	10	10	1. **Spanish Harlem**	Atco 6185
5/22/61	4	11	2. **Stand By Me**	Atco 6194
8/21/61	18	5	3. Amor	Atco 6203
5/19/62	11	7	4. Don't Play That Song (You Lied)	Atco 6222
8/03/63	29	6	5. I (Who Have Nothing)	Atco 6267
3/08/75	5	9	6. **Supernatural Thing - Part 1**	Atlantic 3241
			KING, CAROLE	
9/22/62	22	4	1. It Might As Well Rain Until September	Dimension 2000
5/22/71	1 (5)	15	● 2. **It's Too Late/**	
		12	3. **I Feel The Earth Move**	Ode 66015
9/04/71	14	9	4. So Far Away	Ode 66019
2/05/72	9	8	5. **Sweet Seasons**	Ode 66022
12/09/72	24	7	6. Been To Canaan	Ode 66031
8/11/73	28	5	7. Believe In Humanity	Ode 66035
12/08/73	37	2	8. Corazon [I]	Ode 66039
9/14/74	2 (1)	12	9. **Jazzman**	Ode 66101
1/18/75	9	8	10. **Nightingale**	Ode 66106
3/06/76	28	6	11. Only Love Is Real	Ode 66119
8/20/77	30	5	12. Hard Rock Cafe	Capitol 4455
6/14/80	12	10	13. One Fine Day	Capitol 4864
			KING, CLAUDE	
6/16/62	6	11	1. **Wolverton Mountain**	Columbia 42352
			KING, EVELYN	
			nicknamed "Champagne"	
7/22/78	9	10	● 1. **Shame**	RCA 11122
3/03/79	23	8	● 2. I Don't Know If It's Right	RCA 11386
9/12/81	40	2	3. I'm In Love	RCA 12243
10/02/82	17	8	4. Love Come Down	RCA 13273
			KING, FREDDY	
			died on 12/27/76 (42)	
4/03/61	29	4	1. Hide Away [I]	Federal 12401
			KING, JONATHAN	
10/23/65	17	7	1. Everyone's Gone To The Moon	Parrot 9774

DATE	POS	WKS	ARTIST—Record Title	LABEL & NO.
			KING, PEGGY	
2/05/55	30	1	1. Make Yourself Comfortable	Columbia 40363
			KING, TEDDI	
			died on 11/18/77 (48)	
3/03/56	18	2	1. Mr. Wonderful	RCA 6392
			KINGSMEN	
			Bill Haley's Comets, without Haley	
9/22/58	35	2	1. Week End [I]	East West 115
			KINGSMEN	
			Portland quintet led by Lynn Easton	
11/30/63	2 (6)	13	1. **Louie Louie**	Wand 143
4/04/64	16	8	2. Money	Wand 150
1/30/65	4	9	3. **The Jolly Green Giant**	Wand 172
			KINGSTON TRIO	
			Bob Shane, Nick Reynolds, Dave Guard - replaced by John Stewart in '61	
10/06/58	1 (1)	18	● 1. **Tom Dooley**	Capitol 4049
3/30/59	12	9	2. The Tijuana Jail	Capitol 4167
6/29/59	15	6	3. M.T.A. [N]	Capitol 4221
9/21/59	20	8	4. A Worried Man	Capitol 4271
3/14/60	32	5	5. El Matador	Capitol 4338
8/08/60	37	2	6. Bad Man Blunder [N]	Capitol 4379
3/03/62	21	7	7. Where Have All The Flowers Gone	Capitol 4671
2/23/63	21	5	8. Greenback Dollar	Capitol 4898
4/20/63	8	8	9. **Reverend Mr. Black**	Capitol 4951
8/31/63	33	4	10. Desert Pete	Capitol 5005
			KINKS	
			English group led by brothers Ray & Dave Davies	
10/24/64	7	10	1. **You Really Got Me**	Reprise 0306
1/16/65	7	10	2. **All Day And All Of The Night**	Reprise 0334
3/27/65	6	8	3. **Tired Of Waiting For You**	Reprise 0347
7/10/65	23	4	4. Set Me Free	Reprise 0379
9/04/65	34	3	5. Who'll Be The Next In Line	Reprise 0366
1/08/66	13	9	6. A Well Respected Man	Reprise 0420
6/18/66	36	1	7. Dedicated Follower Of Fashion	Reprise 0471
8/27/66	14	7	8. Sunny Afternoon	Reprise 0497
9/12/70	9	12	9. **Lola**	Reprise 0930
8/19/78	30	5	10. A Rock 'N' Roll Fantasy	Arista 0342
			KISS	
			Gene Simmons, Ace Frehley, Paul Stanley & Peter Criss	
11/29/75	12	10	1. Rock And Roll All Nite -live version-	Casablanca 850
4/17/76	31	4	2. Shout It Out Loud	Casablanca 854
9/25/76	7	13	● 3. **Beth**	Casablanca 863
1/15/77	15	8	4. Hard Luck Woman	Casablanca 873
4/09/77	16	8	5. Calling Dr. Love	Casablanca 880
7/30/77	25	7	6. Christine Sixteen	Casablanca 889
4/15/78	39	2	7. Rocket Ride	Casablanca 915
6/16/79	11	11	● 8. I Was Made For Lovin' You	Casablanca 983

DATE	POS	WKS	ARTIST—Record Title	LABEL & NO.
			KISSOON, MAC & KATIE	
9/04/71	**20**	9	1. Chirpy Chirpy Cheep Cheep	ABC 11306
			KNACK	
			quartet led by Doug Fieger	
7/21/79	**1** (6)	16	● 1. **My Sharona**	Capitol 4731
9/22/79	**11**	11	2. Good Girls Don't	Capitol 4771
3/08/80	**38**	2	3. Baby Talks Dirty	Capitol 4822
			KNICKERBOCKERS	
			New Jersey quartet	
1/01/66	**20**	9	1. Lies	Challenge 59321
			KNIGHT, FREDERICK	
5/27/72	**27**	9	1. I've Been Lonely For So Long	Stax 0117
			KNIGHT, GLADYS, & THE PIPS	
			The Pips: Gladys' brother Merald and cousins William Guest & Edward Patten	
6/05/61	**6**	10	1. **Every Beat Of My Heart** -shown only as the Pips-	Vee-Jay 386
1/20/62	**19**	6	2. Letter Full Of Tears	Fury 1054
7/04/64	**38**	1	3. Giving Up	Maxx 326
8/19/67	**39**	2	4. Everybody Needs Love	Soul 35034
11/04/67	**2** (3)	14	5. **I Heard It Through The Grapevine**	Soul 35039
2/17/68	**15**	8	6. The End Of Our Road	Soul 35042
7/06/68	**40**	1	7. It Should Have Been Me	Soul 35045
8/09/69	**19**	8	8. The Nitty Gritty	Soul 35063
11/15/69	**17**	10	9. Friendship Train	Soul 35068
4/04/70	**25**	5	10. You Need Love Like I Do (Don't You)	Soul 35071
12/19/70	**9**	12	11. **If I Were Your Woman**	Soul 35078
6/19/71	**17**	9	12. I Don't Want To Do Wrong	Soul 35083
1/08/72	**27**	5	13. Make Me The Woman That You Go Home To	Soul 35091
4/08/72	**33**	6	14. Help Me Make It Through The Night	Soul 35094
2/17/73	**2** (2)	12	15. **Neither One Of Us (Wants To Be The First To Say Goodbye)**	Soul 35098
6/02/73	**19**	8	16. Daddy Could Swear, I Declare	Soul 35105
7/07/73	**28**	7	17. Where Peaceful Waters Flow	Buddah 363
9/15/73	**1** (2)	16	● 18. **Midnight Train To Georgia**	Buddah 383
12/08/73	**4**	13	● 19. **I've Got To Use My Imagination**	Buddah 393
3/09/74	**3**	13	● 20. **Best Thing That Ever Happened To Me**	Buddah 403
6/01/74	**5**	11	● 21. **On And On** -from the film "Claudine"-	Buddah 423
11/16/74	**21**	9	22. I Feel A Song (In My Heart)	Buddah 433
5/24/75	**11**	12	23. The Way We Were/Try To Remember	Buddah 463
11/29/75	**22**	7	24. Part Time Love	Buddah 513
			KNIGHT, JEAN	
6/19/71	**2** (2)	13	1. **Mr. Big Stuff**	Stax 0088
			KNIGHT, ROBERT	
10/28/67	**13**	8	1. Everlasting Love	Rising Sons 705
			KNIGHT, SONNY	
11/24/56	**17**	9	1. Confidential	Dot 15507

Carole King. Brooklyn-born neighbors Carole King and Neil Sedaka traded vinyl tributes in the late '50s: Neil waxed "Oh! Carol" and watched it soar into the top 10, while Carole cut "Oh! Neil" and observed it plummeting into oblivion.

The Kingston Trio waxed their biggest seller, "Tom Dooley," as part of their very first LP for Capitol Records. They made 30 more albums, but never again a No. 1 single.

The Kinks. Hard to believe that the man responsible for hits by the Bachelors also produced the Kink's "You Really Got Me" and the Who's "I Can't Explain." But then Shel Talmy went to school with Phil Spector, so that probably explains it.

The Knack. Producer Mike Chapman recently explained the Knack's failure to follow "My Sharona": "I went into the studio under the wrong circumstances, chose the wrong songs, they gave me the wrong songs, and I was stupid enough to record them." Hey, Mike, honesty *is* the best policy.

Gladys Knight and the Pip's "Midnight Train To Georgia" was originally intended by songwriter Jim Weatherly to be a country ballad, "Midnight Plane To Houston." But a change in the lyrics yielded a pop and r&b smash, and Gladys and the group's biggest hit to date.

Produced by John Lennon. Yoko Ono and Jack Douglas
From the Geffen Records album.
John Lennon/Yoko Ono—Double Fantasy (GHS 2001)
© 1981 and ℗ 1980 The David Geffen Company
All rights reserved. Unauthorized duplication is a violation of applicable laws.
Made in U.S.A. GEF 49644

Photo: Jack Mitchell

Cheryl Ladd. Since Cheryl Ladd obviously felt the need to gift the world with her vocal abilities, she at least had the good taste to record songs by Barry Mann, Cynthia Weil, and Phil Spector for her debut album.

Nicolette Larson. After years of session-singer credentials in California, Nicolette Larson stepped into the limelight herself with a song from the pen of Neil Young, "Lotta Love."

John Lennon. In 1963, Britain's *New Musical Express* reported John Lennon's professional ambition as "to be rich and famous." Somehow, he managed it.

The Lettermen. Aside from middle-of-the-road melodies like "When I Fall In Love" and "Theme From *A Summer Place*," the Lettermen also recorded the most appalling lyric written by Barry Mann, "Come Back Silly Girl."

Gary Lewis and the Playboys. One of the authors of Gary Lewis and the Playboys' "This Diamond Ring" was Al Kooper, later involved with the Blues Project and Blood, Sweat & Tears. He finally got around to recording "Ring" himself in 1976.

DATE	POS	WKS	ARTIST—Record Title	LABEL & NO.
			KNOBLOCK, FRED	
7/26/80	**18**	7	1. Why Not Me	Scotti Bros. 518
			KNOBLOCK, FRED, & SUSAN ANTON	
12/27/80	**28**	9	1. Killin' Time	Scotti Bros. 609
			KNOX, BUDDY	
			also see Jimmy Bowen	
3/02/57	**1** (1)	15	1. **Party Doll**	Roulette 4002
6/03/57	**17**	7	2. Rock Your Little Baby To Sleep	Roulette 4009
9/09/57	**9**	15	3. **Hula Love**	Roulette 4018
8/04/58	**22**	11	4. Somebody Touched Me	Roulette 4082
			-above hits with The Rhythm Orchids-	
1/09/61	**25**	4	5. Lovey Dovey	Liberty 55290
			KOFFMAN, MOE, Quartette	
			Canadian	
2/10/58	**23**	5	1. The Swingin' Shepherd Blues [I]	Jubilee 5311
			KOKOMO	
			real name: Jimmy Wisner	
3/06/61	**8**	11	1. **Asia Minor [I]**	Felsted 8612
			KOOL & THE GANG	
			Jersey City group led by Robert "Kool" Bell	
10/06/73	**29**	6	1. Funky Stuff	De-Lite 557
1/05/74	**4**	16	● 2. **Jungle Boogie**	De-Lite 559
5/18/74	**6**	11	● 3. **Hollywood Swinging**	De-Lite 561
10/12/74	**37**	2	4. Higher Plane	De-Lite 1562
6/28/75	**35**	3	5. Spirit Of The Boogie	De-Lite 1567
11/10/79	**8**	14	● 6. **Ladies Night**	De-Lite 801
2/09/80	**5**	13	7. **Too Hot**	De-Lite 802
11/22/80	**1** (2)	21	★ 8. **Celebration**	De-Lite 807
6/27/81	**39**	2	9. Jones Vs. Jones	De-Lite 813
11/07/81	**17**	12	10. Take My Heart (You Can Have It If You Want It)	De-Lite 815
4/03/82	**10**	9	11. **Get Down On It**	De-Lite 818
9/11/82	**21**	7	12. Big Fun	De-Lite 822
			KORGIS	
			British trio	
11/08/80	**18**	11	1. Everybody's Got To Learn Sometime	Asylum 47055
			KRAFTWERK	
			German duo	
4/12/75	**25**	5	1. Autobahn [I]	Vertigo 203
			KRAMER, BILLY J., with The Dakotas	
			English quintet	
5/02/64	**7**	12	1. **Little Children/**	
6/13/64	**9**	8	2. **Bad To Me**	Imperial 66027
8/15/64	**30**	3	3. I'll Keep You Satisfied	Imperial 66048
9/19/64	**23**	5	4. From A Window	Imperial 66051

DATE	POS	WKS	ARTIST—Record Title	LABEL & NO.
			KRISTOFFERSON, KRIS	
10/02/71	26	7	1. Loving Her Was Easier (Than Anything I'll Ever Do Again)	Monument 8525
7/07/73	16	19	● 2. Why Me	Monument 8571
			KUBAN, BOB, & The In-Men	
2/19/66	12	7	1. The Cheater -Walter Scott, lead singer-	Musicland 20001
			LABELLE Patti LaBelle, leader	
2/01/75	1 (1)	13	● 1. **Lady Marmalade**	Epic 50048
			LaBELLE, PATTI, & THE BLUE BELLES also see Blue-Belles	
11/02/63	37	3	1. Down The Aisle (Wedding Song)	Newtown 5777
2/08/64	34	1	2. You'll Never Walk Alone	Parkway 896
			LADD, CHERYL Kris Monroe of TV's "Charlie's Angels"	
8/26/78	34	3	1. Think It Over	Capitol 4599
			LADY FLASH Barry Manilow's back-up singers	
8/14/76	27	6	1. Street Singin'	RSO 852
			LAI, FRANCIS, & His Orchestra	
2/27/71	31	4	1. Theme From Love Story [I] -Georges Pludermacher on piano-	Paramount 0064
			LAINE, FRANKIE	
9/03/55	17	3	1. Humming Bird	Columbia 40526
12/17/55	19	10	2. A Woman In Love -from the film "Guys And Dolls"-	Columbia 40583
12/08/56	3	18	3. **Moonlight Gambler**	Columbia 40780
4/20/57	10	8	4. **Love Is A Golden Ring** -with The Easy Riders-	Columbia 40856
3/04/67	39	2	5. I'll Take Care Of Your Cares	ABC 10891
5/06/67	35	3	6. Making Memories	ABC 10924
3/01/69	24	7	7. You Gave Me A Mountain	ABC 11174
			LANCE, MAJOR	
8/10/63	8	10	1. **The Monkey Time**	Okeh 7175
11/02/63	13	8	2. Hey Little Girl	Okeh 7181
1/11/64	5	10	3. **Um, Um, Um, Um, Um, Um**	Okeh 7187
4/11/64	20	6	4. The Matador	Okeh 7191
9/19/64	24	5	5. Rhythm	Okeh 7203
4/03/65	40	1	6. Come See	Okeh 7216
			LANE, MICKEY LEE	
11/28/64	38	1	1. Shaggy Dog	Swan 4183
			LANSON, SNOOKY star of 'Your Hit Parade'	
12/03/55	20	6	1. It's Almost Tomorrow	Dot 15424
			LARKS	
11/28/64	7	11	1. **The Jerk**	Money 106

DATE	POS	WKS	ARTIST—Record Title	LABEL & NO.
			LaROSA, JULIUS	
7/23/55	13	7	1. Domani (Tomorrow)	Cadence 1265
10/08/55	20	5	2. Suddenly There's A Valley	Cadence 1270
2/18/56	15	7	3. Lipstick And Candy And Rubbersole Shoes	RCA 6416
6/16/58	21	1	4. Torero	RCA 7227
			LARSEN-FEITEN BAND	
			Neil Larsen & Buzz Feiten	
9/13/80	29	6	1. Who'll Be The Fool Tonight	Warner 49282
			LARSON, NICOLETTE	
12/23/78	8	14	1. **Lotta Love**	Warner 8664
2/16/80	35	3	2. Let Me Go, Love	Warner 49130
			-duet with Michael McDonald-	
			LaSALLE, DENISE	
9/25/71	13	9	● 1. Trapped By A Thing Called Love	Westbound 182
			LASLEY, DAVID	
4/24/82	36	4	1. If I Had My Wish Tonight	EMI America 8111
			LAST, JAMES	
4/26/80	28	6	1. The Seduction (Love Theme From "American Gigolo") [I]	Polydor 2071
			LATIMORE	
			Benny Latimore	
11/23/74	31	3	1. Let's Straighten It Out	Glades 1722
3/26/77	37	2	2. Somethin' 'Bout 'Cha	Glades 1739
			LATTISAW, STACY	
			13 years old in 1980	
10/04/80	21	10	1. Let Me Be Your Angel	Cotillion 46001
8/01/81	26	7	2. Love On A Two Way Street	Cotillion 46015
			LAUREN, ROD	
1/11/60	31	5	1. If I Had A Girl	RCA 7645
			LAURIE SISTERS	
4/16/55	30	1	1. Dixie Danny	Mercury 70548
			LAWRENCE, EDDIE	
9/01/56	34	1	1. The Old Philosopher [C]	Coral 61671
			LAWRENCE, STEVE	
			also see Steve & Eydie	
1/19/57	18	8	1. The Banana Boat Song	Coral 61761
3/09/57	5	12	2. **Party Doll**	Coral 61792
12/14/59	9	13	3. **Pretty Blue Eyes**	ABC-Paramount 10058
3/28/60	7	9	4. **Footsteps**	ABC-Paramount 10085
4/03/61	9	10	5. **Portrait Of My Love**	United Artists 291
12/08/62	1 (2)	12	6. **Go Away Little Girl**	Columbia 42601
3/30/63	26	6	7. Don't Be Afraid, Little Darlin'	Columbia 42699
6/15/63	27	3	8. Poor Little Rich Girl	Columbia 42795
11/09/63	26	4	9. Walking Proud	Columbia 42865

DATE	POS	WKS	ARTIST—Record Title	LABEL & NO.
			LAWRENCE, VICKI	
			actress on "Carol Burnett Show"	
3/17/73	1 (2)	14	● 1. **The Night The Lights Went Out In Georgia**	Bell 45303
			LAYNE, JOY	
2/16/57	20	5	1. Your Wild Heart	Mercury 71038
			LE ROUX	
3/20/82	18	6	1. Nobody Said It Was Easy (Lookin' For The Lights)	RCA 13059
			LEAPY LEE	
11/09/68	16	8	1. Little Arrows	Decca 32380
			LEAVES	
6/18/66	31	4	1. Hey Joe	Mira 222
			LeBLANC & CARR	
			Lenny LeBlanc & Pete Carr	
2/04/78	13	10	1. Falling	Big Tree 16100
			LED ZEPPELIN	
			Robert Plant, lead singer; Jimmy Page, John Paul Jones, & John Bonham (Bonham died 9/25/80-33)	
12/06/69	4	13	● 1. **Whole Lotta Love**	Atlantic 2690
12/12/70	16	10	2. Immigrant Song	Atlantic 2777
1/15/72	15	8	3. Black Dog	Atlantic 2849
11/24/73	20	8	4. D'yer Mak'er	Atlantic 2986
5/17/75	38	2	5. Trampled Under Foot	Swan Song 70102
1/12/80	21	8	6. Fool In The Rain	Swan Song 71003
			-the classic "Stairway To Heaven" was released only as an album cut on "Led Zeppelin IV" in Nov. '71-	
			LEE, BRENDA	
			Brenda's 1st charted hit was at the age of 12 in 1957	
2/15/60	4	15	1. **Sweet Nothin's**	Decca 30967
6/06/60	1 (3)	18	2. **I'm Sorry/**	
6/20/60	6	9	3. **That's All You Gotta Do**	Decca 31093
9/19/60	1 (1)	13	4. **I Want To Be Wanted/**	
10/31/60	40	1	5. Just A Little	Decca 31149
12/19/60	14	3	6. Rockin' Around The Christmas Tree [X]	Decca 30776
			-recorded in 1958-	
1/16/61	7	9	7. **Emotions/**	
2/06/61	33	2	8. I'm Learning About Love	Decca 31195
4/03/61	6	10	9. **You Can Depend On Me**	Decca 31231
6/26/61	4	10	10. **Dum Dum**	Decca 31272
10/09/61	3	12	11. **Fool #1/**	
10/16/61	31	3	12. Anybody But Me	Decca 31309
1/20/62	4	12	13. **Break It To Me Gently**	Decca 31348
4/28/62	6	8	14. **Everybody Loves Me But You**	Decca 31379
7/21/62	15	7	15. Heart In Hand/	
7/21/62	29	4	16. It Started All Over Again	Decca 31407
10/06/62	3	12	17. **All Alone Am I**	Decca 31424
2/16/63	32	3	18. Your Used To Be	Decca 31454
4/20/63	6	10	19. **Losing You**	Decca 31478

DATE	POS	WKS	ARTIST—Record Title	LABEL & NO.
7/27/63	24	6	20. My Whole World Is Falling Down/	
7/27/63	25	5	21. I Wonder	Decca 31510
10/12/63	17	5	22. The Grass Is Greener	Decca 31539
12/28/63	12	8	23. As Usual	Decca 31570
3/28/64	25	5	24. Think	Decca 31599
10/31/64	17	7	25. Is It True	Decca 31690
6/26/65	13	8	26. Too Many Rivers	Decca 31792
11/13/65	33	3	27. Rusty Bells	Decca 31849
10/29/66	11	8	28. Coming On Strong	Decca 32018
2/11/67	37	2	29. Ride, Ride, Ride	Decca 32079
			LEE, CURTIS	
7/17/61	7	8	1. **Pretty Little Angel Eyes**	Dunes 2007
			LEE, DICKEY	
9/08/62	6	11	1. **Patches**	Smash 1758
12/29/62	14	8	2. I Saw Linda Yesterday	Smash 1791
6/19/65	14	7	3. Laurie (Strange Things Happen)	TCF Hall 102
			LEE, JACKIE	
12/18/65	14	9	1. The Duck	Mirwood 5502
			LEE, JOHNNY	
8/02/80	5	13	● 1. **Lookin' For Love**	Full Moon/Asy. 47004
			-from the movie "Urban Cowboy"-	
			LEE, LAURA	
10/16/71	36	4	1. Women's Love Rights	Hot Wax 7105
			LEE, PEGGY	
			vocalist with Benny Goodman	
3/24/56	14	10	1. Mr. Wonderful	Decca 29834
7/21/58	8	13	2. **Fever**	Capitol 3998
10/11/69	11	8	3. Is That All There Is	Capitol 2602
			LEFEVRE, RAYMOND, & His Orchestra	
11/03/58	30	5	1. The Day The Rains Came [I]	Kapp 231
4/06/68	37	5	2. Ame Caline (Soul Coaxing) [I]	Four Corners 147
			LEFT BANKE	
			New York quintet	
9/24/66	5	10	1. **Walk Away Renee**	Smash 2041
2/04/67	15	6	2. Pretty Ballerina	Smash 2074
			LEMON PIPERS	
			Ivan Browne, lead singer	
12/23/67	1 (1)	12	● 1. **Green Tambourine**	Buddah 23
			LENNON SISTERS	
			Dianne, Peggy, Kathy, & Janet	
9/29/56	15	10	1. Tonight You Belong To Me	Coral 61701
			-with Lawrence Welk's Orchestra-	
			LENNON, JOHN	
			John Lennon and wife Yoko Ono, with backing musicians PLASTIC ONO BAND, released records under various combinations of their names -- John was murdered 12/8/80 (40)	
8/09/69	14	6	1. Give Peace A Chance	Apple 1809
12/13/69	30	7	2. Cold Turkey	Apple 1813

DATE	POS	WKS	ARTIST—Record Title	LABEL & NO.
3/07/70	3	12	● 3. **Instant Karma (We All Shine On)**	Apple 1818
4/10/71	11	8	4. Power To The People	Apple 1830
10/23/71	3	9	5. **Imagine**	Apple 1840
12/01/73	18	8	6. Mind Games	Apple 1868
10/05/74	1 (1)	11	7. **Whatever Gets You Thru The Night** -backing vocals by Elton John-	Apple 1874
1/11/75	9	8	8. **#9 Dream**	Apple 1878
4/05/75	20	5	9. Stand By Me	Apple 1881
11/01/80	1 (5)	19	● 10. **(Just Like) Starting Over**	Geffen 49604
1/17/81	2 (3)	17	● 11. **Woman**	Geffen 49644
4/11/81	10	10	12. **Watching The Wheels**	Geffen 49695
			LEONETTI, TOMMY	
			died 9/15/79 (50)	
7/07/56	23	2	1. Free	Capitol 3442
			LESTER, KETTY	
3/10/62	5	11	1. **Love Letters**	Era 3068
			LETTERMEN	
			original trio: Tony Butala, Jim Pike, and Bob Engemann	
9/25/61	13	9	1. The Way You Look Tonight	Capitol 4586
12/04/61	7	11	2. **When I Fall In Love**	Capitol 4658
3/10/62	17	7	3. Come Back Silly Girl	Capitol 4699
7/17/65	16	5	4. Theme From "A Summer Place"	Capitol 5437
1/06/68	7	11	5. **Goin' Out Of My Head/Can't Take My Eyes Off You**	Capitol 2054
8/16/69	12	10	6. Hurt So Bad	Capitol 2482
			LEWIS, BARBARA	
5/25/63	3	10	1. **Hello Stranger**	Atlantic 2184
3/14/64	38	1	2. Puppy Love	Atlantic 2214
7/17/65	11	9	3. Baby, I'm Yours	Atlantic 2283
10/09/65	11	8	4. Make Me Your Baby	Atlantic 2300
8/13/66	28	4	5. Make Me Belong To You	Atlantic 2346
			LEWIS, BOBBY	
5/29/61	1 (7)	17	1. **Tossin' And Turnin'**	Beltone 1002
9/11/61	9	7	2. **One Track Mind**	Beltone 1012
			LEWIS, GARY, & THE PLAYBOYS	
			eldest son of Jerry Lewis	
1/23/65	1 (2)	11	● 1. **This Diamond Ring**	Liberty 55756
4/17/65	2 (2)	9	2. **Count Me In**	Liberty 55778
7/17/65	2 (1)	9	3. **Save Your Heart For Me**	Liberty 55809
10/09/65	4	8	4. **Everybody Loves A Clown**	Liberty 55818
12/18/65	3	11	5. **She's Just My Style**	Liberty 55846
3/19/66	9	7	6. **Sure Gonna Miss Her**	Liberty 55865
5/21/66	8	7	7. **Green Grass**	Liberty 55880
8/13/66	13	5	8. My Heart's Symphony	Liberty 55898
10/22/66	15	6	9. (You Don't Have To) Paint Me A Picture	Liberty 55914
1/07/67	21	6	10. Where Will The Words Come From	Liberty 55933
6/10/67	39	2	11. Girls In Love	Liberty 55971
7/27/68	19	9	12. Sealed With A Kiss	Liberty 56037

DATE	POS	WKS	ARTIST—Record Title	LABEL & NO.
			LEWIS, HUEY, & THE NEWS	
			San Francisco 6-man rock band	
2/20/82	7	13	1. **Do You Believe In Love**	Chrysalis 2589
6/12/82	36	4	2. Hope You Love Me Like You Say You Do	Chrysalis 2604
			LEWIS, JERRY	
			popular comedian/actor	
11/24/56	10	15	1. **Rock-A-Bye Your Baby With A Dixie Melody**	Decca 30124
			LEWIS, JERRY LEE	
			"The Killer" with 'His Pumping Piano' was one of early rock 'n roll's most dynamic performers	
7/15/57	3	20	1. **Whole Lot Of Shakin' Going On**	Sun 267
12/02/57	2 (4)	13	2. **Great Balls Of Fire**	Sun 281
3/10/58	7	9	3. **Breathless**	Sun 288
6/02/58	21	8	4. High School Confidential	Sun 296
4/24/61	30	4	5. What'd I Say	Sun 356
1/15/72	40	1	6. Me And Bobby McGee	Mercury 73248
			LEWIS, RAMSEY	
8/21/65	5	12	1. **The "In" Crowd** [I]	Argo 5506
11/27/65	11	6	2. Hang On Sloopy [I]	Cadet 5522
2/05/66	29	4	3. A Hard Day's Night [I]	Cadet 5525
			-all of above: Ramsey Lewis Trio-	
8/20/66	19	6	4. Wade In The Water [I]	Cadet 5541
			LIGHTFOOT, GORDON	
			Canadian	
1/23/71	5	11	1. **If You Could Read My Mind**	Reprise 0974
5/11/74	1 (1)	11	● 2. **Sundown**	Reprise 1194
10/05/74	10	7	3. **Carefree Highway**	Reprise 1309
5/03/75	26	4	4. Rainy Day People	Reprise 1328
9/25/76	2 (2)	13	5. **Wreck Of The Edmund Fitzgerald**	Reprise 1369
3/25/78	33	3	6. The Circle Is Small (I Can See It In Your Eyes)	Warner 8518
			LIGHTHOUSE	
			Canadian rock band	
10/09/71	24	8	1. One Fine Morning	Evolution 1048
11/25/72	34	5	2. Sunny Days	Evolution 1069
			LIND, BOB	
2/12/66	5	9	1. **Elusive Butterfly**	World Pacific 77808
			LINDEN, KATHY	
3/31/58	7	11	1. **Billy**	Felsted 8510
4/27/59	11	10	2. Goodbye Jimmy, Goodbye	Felsted 8571
			LINDISFARNE	
11/25/78	33	4	1. Run For Home	Atco 7093
			LINDSAY, MARK	
			lead singer of Paul Revere & The Raiders	
1/10/70	10	11	● 1. **Arizona**	Columbia 45037
7/11/70	25	5	2. Silver Bird	Columbia 45180
			LIPPS, INC.	
			Steve Greenberg production - features singer Cynthia Johnson	
4/19/80	1 (4)	15	★ 1. **Funkytown**	Casablanca 2233

DATE	POS	WKS	ARTIST—Record Title	LABEL & NO.
			LITTLE ANTHONY & THE IMPERIALS	
			Anthony Gourdine, lead singer of Brooklyn quartet	
8/18/58	4	14	1. **Tears On My Pillow**	End 1027
1/18/60	24	7	2. Shimmy, Shimmy, Ko-Ko-Bop	End 1060
9/05/64	15	8	3. I'm On The Outside (Looking In)	DCP 1104
11/21/64	6	12	4. **Goin' Out Of My Head**	DCP 1119
2/13/65	10	8	5. **Hurt So Bad**	DCP 1128
7/17/65	16	7	6. Take Me Back	DCP 1136
11/06/65	34	1	7. I Miss You So	DCP 1149
			LITTLE CAESAR & THE ROMANS	
			Little Caesar is Carl Burnett	
5/29/61	9	9	1. **Those Oldies But Goodies (Remind Me Of You)**	Del-Fi 4158
			LITTLE DIPPERS	
			Anita Kerr Singers	
2/08/60	9	10	1. **Forever**	University 210
			LITTLE EVA	
			Eva Boyd -- also see Big Dee Irwin	
7/21/62	1 (1)	12	1. **The Loco-Motion**	Dimension 1000
11/24/62	12	8	2. Keep Your Hands Off My Baby	Dimension 1003
2/23/63	20	6	3. Let's Turkey Trot	Dimension 1006
			LITTLE JOE & THE THRILLERS	
			Joe Cook	
10/07/57	22	9	1. Peanuts	Okeh 7088
			LITTLE JOEY & THE FLIPS	
			Joey Hall	
7/14/62	33	3	1. Bongo Stomp	Joy 262
			LITTLE MILTON	
			Milton Campbell	
4/24/65	25	7	1. We're Gonna Make It	Checker 1105
			LITTLE RICHARD	
			Richard Penniman - billed often as 'The King Of Rock 'N Roll'	
1/28/56	17	5	1. Tutti-Frutti	Specialty 561
4/07/56	6	12	2. **Long Tall Sally/**	
6/30/56	33	1	3. Slippin' And Slidin' (Peepin' And Hidin')	Specialty 572
7/14/56	17	7	4. Rip It Up	Specialty 579
4/06/57	21	7	5. Lucille	Specialty 598
6/24/57	10	13	6. **Jenny, Jenny**	Specialty 606
10/07/57	8	12	7. **Keep A Knockin'**	Specialty 611
			-from film "Mr. Rock 'n' Roll"-	
2/24/58	10	10	8. **Good Golly, Miss Molly**	Specialty 624
6/23/58	31	3	9. Ooh! My Soul	Specialty 633
			LITTLE RIVER BAND	
			Australian - Glenn Shorrock, lead singer	
11/06/76	28	6	1. It's A Long Way There	Harvest 4318
9/24/77	14	11	2. Help Is On Its Way	Harvest 4428
1/21/78	16	9	3. Happy Anniversary	Harvest 4524
8/12/78	3	14	4. **Reminiscing**	Harvest 4605
1/27/79	10	14	5. **Lady**	Harvest 4667
8/04/79	6	14	6. **Lonesome Loser**	Capitol 4748

DATE	POS	WKS	ARTIST—Record Title	LABEL & NO.
11/10/79	**10**	13	7. **Cool Change**	Capitol 4789
9/05/81	**6**	14	8. **The Night Owls**	Capitol 5033
12/26/81	**10**	15	9. **Take It Easy On Me**	Capitol 5057
4/24/82	**14**	9	10. Man On Your Mind	Capitol 5061
			LITTLE SISTER	
			Vanetta Stewart, sister of Sly Stone	
3/28/70	**22**	6	1. You're The One - Part I	Stone Flower 9000
1/30/71	**32**	3	2. Somebody's Watching You	Stone Flower 9001
			LOBO	
			Kent Lavoie	
4/24/71	**5**	10	1. **Me And You And A Dog Named Boo**	Big Tree 112
10/14/72	**2** (2)	10	● 2. **I'd Love You To Want Me**	Big Tree 147
1/13/73	**8**	10	3. **Don't Expect Me To Be Your Friend**	Big Tree 158
5/05/73	**27**	5	4. It Sure Took A Long, Long Time	Big Tree 16001
7/21/73	**22**	8	5. How Can I Tell Her	Big Tree 16004
5/11/74	**37**	2	6. Standing At The End Of The Line	Big Tree 15001
4/26/75	**27**	4	7. Don't Tell Me Goodnight	Big Tree 16033
9/08/79	**23**	8	8. Where Were You When I Was Falling In Love	MCA 41065
			LOCKLIN, HANK	
6/13/60	**8**	15	1. **Please Help Me, I'm Falling**	RCA 7692
			LOGGINS & MESSINA	
			Kenny Loggins & Jim Messina	
12/02/72	**4**	13	● 1. **Your Mama Don't Dance**	Columbia 45719
4/28/73	**18**	8	2. Thinking Of You	Columbia 45815
11/24/73	**16**	8	3. My Music	Columbia 45952
			LOGGINS, DAVE	
7/13/74	**5**	10	1. **Please Come To Boston**	Epic 11115
			LOGGINS, KENNY	
8/19/78	**5**	15	1. **Whenever I Call You "Friend"**	Columbia 10794
			-harmony vocal by Stevie Nicks-	
11/24/79	**11**	16	2. This Is It	Columbia 11109
4/05/80	**36**	2	3. Keep The Fire	Columbia 11215
8/23/80	**7**	12	4. **I'm Alright**	Columbia 11317
			-theme from film "Caddyshack"-	
			LOGGINS, KENNY, with STEVE PERRY	
			Steve is lead singer of Journey	
9/25/82	**17**	6	1. Don't Fight It	Columbia 03192
			LOLITA	
			Lolita Ditta - German	
11/14/60	**5**	14	1. **Sailor (Your Home Is The Sea) [F]**	Kapp 349
			LONDON SYMPHONY ORCHESTRA - see JOHN WILLIAMS	
			LONDON, JULIE	
			Dixie McCall of TV's "Emergency"	
12/03/55	**9**	13	1. **Cry Me A River**	Liberty 55006

DATE	POS	WKS	ARTIST—Record Title	LABEL & NO.
			LONDON, LAURIE	
			English lad - 13 years old	
3/24/58	**1** (4)	14	● 1. **He's Got The Whole World (In His Hands)**	Capitol 3891
			LONG, SHORTY	
			drowned on 6/29/69	
6/15/68	**8**	8	1. **Here Comes The Judge** [N]	Soul 35044
			LOOKING GLASS	
			New Jersey quartet	
7/01/72	**1** (1)	14	● 1. **Brandy (You're A Fine Girl)**	Epic 10874
9/29/73	**33**	3	2. Jimmy Loves Mary-Anne	Epic 11001
			LOPEZ, TRINI	
8/10/63	**3**	11	1. **If I Had A Hammer**	Reprise 20198
12/14/63	**23**	6	2. Kansas City	Reprise 20236
2/06/65	**20**	5	3. Lemon Tree	Reprise 0336
5/07/66	**39**	3	4. I'm Comin' Home, Cindy	Reprise 0455
			LOS BRAVOS	
			Mike Kennedy, lead singer	
9/10/66	**4**	8	1. **Black Is Black**	Press 60002
			LOS INDIOS TABAJARAS	
			Brazilian	
10/12/63	**6**	10	1. **Maria Elena** [I]	RCA 8216
			LOST GENERATION	
8/01/70	**30**	5	1. The Sly, Slick, And The Wicked	Brunswick 55436
			LOU, BONNIE	
11/26/55	**14**	3	1. Daddy-O	King 4835
			LOUDERMILK, JOHN D.	
			also see Johnny Dee	
12/04/61	**32**	3	1. Language Of Love	RCA 7938
			LOVE	
			Los Angeles quintet	
9/10/66	**33**	3	1. 7 And 7 Is	Elektra 45605
			LOVE & KISSES	
6/24/78	**22**	6	1. Thank God It's Friday	Casablanca 925
			LOVE UNLIMITED	
			Glodean & Linda James (sisters), Diane Taylor - produced by Barry White (husband of Glodean)	
5/06/72	**14**	9	● 1. **Walkin' In The Rain With The One I Love**	Uni 55319
1/04/75	**27**	7	2. I Belong To You	20th Century 2141
			LOVE UNLIMITED ORCHESTRA	
			Barry White, conductor	
12/22/73	**1** (1)	16	● 1. **Love's Theme** [I]	20th Century 2069
3/15/75	**22**	5	2. Satin Soul [I]	20th Century 2162
			LOVE, DARLENE	
5/11/63	**39**	1	1. (Today I Met) The Boy I'm Gonna Marry	Philles 111
8/24/63	**26**	4	2. Wait Til' My Bobby Gets Home	Philles 114

Huey Lewis and the News. "Do You Believe In Love?" asked California's Huey Lewis and the News in 1982, extending the Lovin' Spoonful's 1965 question, "Do You Believe In Magic?" More importantly, asked the Fabulous Thunderbirds, "How Do You Spell Love?" M-o-n-e-y.

Jerry Lee Lewis. What made Jerry Lee Lewis infamous is what very nearly made a loser out of the piano-pumping rocker, too: marriage to his 14-year-old cousin in 1958. It was in all the papers.

Little Anthony and the Imperials. Little Anthony and Teddy Randazzo both got started in Brooklyn groups in the mid '50s, the Duponts and the Three Chuckles respectively. Nine years later, they teamed up and "Goin' Out Of My Head" was one of the results. Teddy produced it.

Little Richard was going nowhere with Peacock Records of Houston when California's Specialty label offered to buy out his contract. It was probably the best $600 Art Rupe ever spent.

Lovin' Spoonful founder John Sebastian recalls the important role of his father, a classical harmonica player, in his musical education: "You hear a cat practicing in the next room six hours a day, and you gotta pick up something."

Henry Mancini is widely credited as the first jazz musician to write extensively for television via work for the "Peter Gunn" series. This yielded a chart-topping album for him in 1959, and a hit for Duane Eddy, too, the following year.

Manfred Mann. For a couple of years, the Manfreds prospered by updating American r&b originals, including the Exciters' "Do Wah Diddy Diddy," the Shirelles' "Sha-La-La," and Marie Knight's "Come Tomorrow." Then they turned to Dylan.

Steve Martin's Egyptian excursion, "King Tut," charted exactly 20 years after the biggest hit ("Yakety Yak") by the group whose style he borrowed for the record, the Coasters.

Paul McCartney. As well as chart achievements that make him the most successful of the ex-Beatles, Paul McCartney own hundreds of classic song copyrights from the past several decades, including many of Buddy Holly's hits. Tomorrow, the world.

Michael McDonald. One of the many musicians who recorded with Steely Dan in the mid '70s, Michael McDonald left that aggregation (with Jeff Baxter) to become a creative force with the Doobie Brothers. His "What A Fool Believes" was the Grammy-winning record of the year in 1979.

Melanie. Many major recording artists have formed their own record labels; few have prospered with them. Thanks to the chart-topping "Brand New Key," Melanie's Neighborhood Records was one of the exceptions.

DATE	POS	WKS	ARTIST—Record Title	LABEL & NO.
			LOVERBOY	
			Canadian quintet - Paul Dean, leader	
3/21/81	35	6	1. Turn Me Loose	Columbia 11421
1/09/82	29	8	2. Working For The Weekend	Columbia 02589
5/15/82	26	6	3. When It's Over	Columbia 02814
			-backing vocals by Nancy Nash-	
			LOVIN' SPOONFUL	
			John Sebastian, lead singer and co-founder with Zal Yanovsky, Steve Boone, & Joe Butler	
9/18/65	9	8	1. **Do You Believe In Magic**	Kama Sutra 201
12/11/65	10	9	2. **You Didn't Have To Be So Nice**	Kama Sutra 205
3/12/66	2 (2)	10	3. **Daydream**	Kama Sutra 208
5/14/66	2 (2)	9	4. **Did You Ever Have To Make Up Your Mind?**	Kama Sutra 209
7/23/66	1 (3)	10	● 5. **Summer In The City**	Kama Sutra 211
10/22/66	10	8	6. **Rain On The Roof**	Kama Sutra 216
12/31/66	8	8	7. **Nashville Cats**	Kama Sutra 219
2/25/67	15	5	8. Darling Be Home Soon	Kama Sutra 220
			-from "You're A Big Boy Now"-	
5/20/67	18	5	9. Six O'Clock	Kama Sutra 225
11/11/67	27	3	10. She Is Still A Mystery	Kama Sutra 239
			LOWE, JIM	
9/29/56	1 (3)	22	1. **The Green Door**	Dot 15486
5/13/57	15	6	2. Four Walls/	
5/13/57	20	5	3. Talkin' To The Blues	Dot 15569
			LOWE, NICK	
			member of Brinsley Schwarz	
8/18/79	12	10	1. Cruel To Be Kind	Columbia 11018
			L.T.D.	
			also see Jeffrey Osborne	
11/06/76	20	8	1. Love Ballad	A&M 1847
11/12/77	4	12	● 2. **(Every Time I Turn Around) Back In Love Again**	A&M 1974
1/31/81	40	1	3. Shine On	A&M 2283
			LUKE, ROBIN	
8/18/58	5	15	1. **Susie Darlin'**	Dot 15781
			LULU	
9/23/67	1 (5)	15	● 1. **To Sir With Love**	Epic 10187
1/06/68	32	3	2. Best Of Both Worlds	Epic 10260
2/07/70	22	8	3. Oh Me Oh My (I'm A Fool For You Baby)	Atco 6722
8/22/81	18	10	4. I Could Never Miss You (More Than I Do)	Alfa 7006
			LUMAN, BOB	
			died 12/27/78 (40)	
9/26/60	7	9	1. **Let's Think About Living** [N]	Warner 5172
			LUNDBERG, VICTOR	
11/25/67	10	4	1. **An Open Letter To My Teenage Son** [S]	Liberty 55996
			LYMAN, ARTHUR, Group	
6/12/61	4	10	1. **Yellow Bird** [I]	Hi Fi 5024

DATE	POS	WKS	ARTIST—Record Title	LABEL & NO.
			LYMON, FRANKIE, & The Teenagers	
			rock's 1st teenage star at age 13 - died 2/28/68 (25)	
2/18/56	6	16	1. **Why Do Fools Fall In Love**	Gee 1002
5/12/56	13	11	2. I Want You To Be My Girl	Gee 1012
8/26/57	20	7	3. Goody Goody	Gee 1039
			LYNN, BARBARA	
7/14/62	8	8	1. **You'll Lose A Good Thing**	Jamie 1220
			LYNN, CHERYL	
1/06/79	12	12	● 1. Got To Be Real	Columbia 10808
			LYNNE, GLORIA	
2/29/64	28	4	1. I Wish You Love	Everest 2036
			LYNYRD SKYNYRD	
			leader Ronnie Van Zant died in a plane crash 10/20/77 (28)	
8/24/74	8	11	1. **Sweet Home Alabama**	MCA 40258
1/04/75	19	5	2. Free Bird	MCA 40328
7/19/75	27	3	3. Saturday Night Special	MCA 40416
1/08/77	38	2	4. Free Bird	MCA 40665
			-live version of '74 studio hit-	
1/07/78	13	11	5. What's Your Name	MCA 40819
			M	
			M is Robin Scott	
8/25/79	1 (1)	20	● 1. **Pop Muzik**	Sire 49033
			MABLEY, MOMS	
			died on 5/23/75	
7/19/69	35	2	1. Abraham, Martin And John	Mercury 72935
			MacGREGOR, BYRON	
1/12/74	4	9	● 1. **Americans [S]**	Westbound 222
			MacGREGOR, MARY	
12/25/76	1 (2)	16	● 1. **Torn Between Two Lovers**	Ariola America 7638
10/06/79	39	2	2. Good Friend	RSO 938
			-from the movie "Meatballs"-	
			MACK, LONNIE	
6/22/63	5	10	1. **Memphis [I]**	Fraternity 906
9/21/63	24	4	2. Wham! [I]	Fraternity 912
			MacKENZIE, GISELE	
			star of TV's "Your Hit Parade"	
6/04/55	4	19	1. **Hard To Get**	X 0137
			MacRAE, GORDON	
10/06/58	18	6	1. The Secret	Capitol 4033
			MADDOX, JOHNNY, & The Rhythm Masters	
2/05/55	2 (7)	20	1. **The Crazy Otto (Medley) [I]**	Dot 15325
			-inspired by the honky tonk piano player Crazy Otto-	
			MADIGAN, BETTY	
9/08/58	31	3	1. Dance Everyone Dance	Coral 62007

DATE	POS	WKS	ARTIST—Record Title	LABEL & NO.
			MAESTRO, JOHNNY	
			lead singer of The Crests and Brooklyn Bridge	
3/20/61	20	5	1. Model Girl	Coed 545
5/22/61	33	4	2. What A Surprise	Coed 549
			MAGGARD, CLEDUS, & The Citizen's Band	
1/24/76	19	9	1. The White Knight [N]	Mercury 73751
			MAGIC LANTERNS	
11/30/68	29	5	1. Shame, Shame	Atlantic 2560
			MAHARIS, GEORGE	
			Buzz Murdock of TV's "Route 66"	
5/26/62	25	5	1. Teach Me Tonight	Epic 9504
			MAIN INGREDIENT	
			original lead singer, Don McPherson, died 7/4/71 (29)	
9/02/72	3	10	● 1. **Everybody Plays The Fool**	RCA 0731
3/16/74	10	14	● 2. **Just Don't Want To Be Lonely**	RCA 0205
8/10/74	35	2	3. Happiness Is Just Around The Bend	RCA 0305
			MAJORS	
9/08/62	22	5	1. A Wonderful Dream	Imperial 5855
			MAKEBA, MIRIAM	
			married to Hugh Masekela	
10/28/67	12	8	1. Pata Pata [F]	Reprise 0606
			MALO	
			Jorge Santana (brother of Carlos), lead singer	
4/01/72	18	8	1. Suavecito	Warner 7559
			MALTBY, RICHARD	
3/31/56	14	8	1. Themes From "The Man With The Golden Arm" [I]	Vik 0196
			MAMA CASS	
			Cass Elliot of The Mamas & The Papas - died on 7/29/74 (30)	
7/27/68	12	8	1. Dream A Little Dream Of Me	Dunhill 4145
			-with The Mamas & The Papas-	
8/02/69	30	7	2. It's Getting Better	Dunhill 4195
11/15/69	36	3	3. Make Your Own Kind Of Music	Dunhill 4214
			MAMAS & THE PAPAS	
			Cass Elliot, Michelle Gilliam, John Phillips, & Denny Doherty	
2/05/66	4	13	● 1. **California Dreamin'**	Dunhill 4020
4/16/66	1 (3)	10	● 2. **Monday, Monday**	Dunhill 4026
7/09/66	5	8	3. **I Saw Her Again**	Dunhill 4031
11/05/66	24	4	4. Look Through My Window	Dunhill 4050
12/17/66	5	9	5. **Words Of Love**	Dunhill 4057
3/04/67	2 (3)	9	6. **Dedicated To The One I Love**	Dunhill 4077
5/13/67	5	7	7. **Creeque Alley**	Dunhill 4083
9/02/67	20	5	8. Twelve Thirty (Young Girls Are Coming To The Canyon)	Dunhill 4099
11/04/67	26	5	9. Glad To Be Unhappy	Dunhill 4107
			MANCHESTER, MELISSA	
6/14/75	6	11	1. **Midnight Blue**	Arista 0116
10/18/75	30	5	2. Just Too Many People	Arista 0146

DATE	POS	WKS	ARTIST—Record Title	LABEL & NO.
2/28/76	27	4	3. Just You And I	Arista 0168
1/06/79	10	14	4. **Don't Cry Out Loud**	Arista 0373
11/24/79	39	2	5. Pretty Girls	Arista 0456
4/05/80	32	5	6. Fire In The Morning	Arista 0485
7/10/82	5	15	7. **You Should Hear How She Talks About You**	Arista 0676
			MANCINI, HENRY [Orchestra & Chorus]	
			Henry is the all-time leading Grammy winner with 20 awards	
4/18/60	21	8	1. Mr. Lucky [I]	RCA 7705
11/13/61	11	16	2. Moon River	RCA 7916
			-from "Breakfast At Tiffany's"-	
3/02/63	33	10	3. Days Of Wine And Roses	RCA 8120
1/25/64	36	4	4. Charade	RCA 8256
5/09/64	31	2	5. The Pink Panther Theme [I]	RCA 8286
5/24/69	● 1 (2)	12	6. **Love Theme From Romeo & Juliet [I]**	RCA 0131
2/06/71	13	8	7. Theme From Love Story [I]	RCA 9927
			MANDRELL, BARBARA	
5/12/79	31	5	1. (If Loving You Is Wrong) I Don't Want To Be Right	ABC 12451
			MANFRED MANN	
			British band led by Manfred	
9/12/64	1 (2)	12	1. **Do Wah Diddy Diddy**	Ascot 2157
11/28/64	12	9	2. Sha La La	Ascot 2165
7/23/66	29	5	3. Pretty Flamingo	United Artists 50040
3/09/68	10	10	4. **Mighty Quinn (Quinn The Eskimo)**	Mercury 72770
			MANFRED MANN'S EARTH BAND	
12/18/76	● 1 (1)	15	1. **Blinded By The Light**	Warner 8252
6/04/77	40	1	2. Spirit In The Night	Warner 8355
			-re-entry of 1976 hit-	
			MANGIONE, CHUCK	
3/18/78	4	16	1. **Feels So Good [I]**	A&M 2001
2/16/80	18	9	2. Give It All You Got [I]	A&M 2211
			-featured song by ABC Sports for the 1980 Winter Olympics-	
			MANHATTAN TRANSFER	
			New York quartet	
11/01/75	22	5	1. Operator	Atlantic 3292
5/31/80	30	4	2. Twilight Zone/Twilight Tone	Atlantic 3649
6/13/81	7	13	3. **Boy From New York City**	Atlantic 3816
			MANHATTANS	
			original lead singer, George Smith, died in 1970	
2/15/75	37	2	1. Don't Take Your Love	Columbia 10045
5/29/76	★ 1 (2)	17	2. **Kiss And Say Goodbye**	Columbia 10310
5/31/80	● 5	14	3. **Shining Star**	Columbia 11222
			MANILOW, BARRY	
			Barry gained prominence as a writer of commercial jingles	
12/07/74	● 1 (1)	12	1. **Mandy**	Bell 45613
3/29/75	12	8	2. It's A Miracle	Arista 0108
7/26/75	6	12	3. **Could It Be Magic**	Arista 0126

DATE	POS	WKS	ARTIST—Record Title	LABEL & NO.
11/22/75	1 (1)	16	● 4. **I Write The Songs**	Arista 0157
4/10/76	10	10	5. **Tryin' To Get The Feeling Again**	Arista 0172
10/09/76	29	5	6. This One's For You	Arista 0206
12/25/76	10	13	7. **Weekend In New England**	Arista 0212
5/28/77	1 (1)	13	● 8. **Looks Like We Made It**	Arista 0244
10/22/77	23	5	9. Daybreak	Arista 0273
2/18/78	3	16	● 10. **Can't Smile Without You**	Arista 0305
6/10/78	19	4	11. Even Now	Arista 0330
7/08/78	8	9	● 12. **Copacabana (At The Copa)**	Arista 0339
10/07/78	11	10	13. Ready To Take A Chance Again -from the movie "Foul Play"-	Arista 0357
1/06/79	9	10	14. **Somewhere In The Night**	Arista 0382
10/20/79	9	10	15. **Ships**	Arista 0464
2/02/80	20	7	16. When I Wanted You	Arista 0481
5/17/80	36	4	17. I Don't Want To Walk Without You	Arista 0501
12/06/80	10	11	18. **I Made It Through The Rain**	Arista 0566
10/17/81	15	10	19. The Old Songs	Arista 0633
1/23/82	21	7	20. Somewhere Down The Road	Arista 0658
4/24/82	32	4	21. Let's Hang On	Arista 0675
9/18/82	38	2	22. Oh Julie	Arista 0698
			MANN, BARRY	
8/21/61	7	9	1. **Who Put The Bomp (In The Bomp, Bomp, Bomp) [N]**	ABC-Para. 10237
			MANN, CARL	
7/27/59	25	6	1. Mona Lisa	Phillips 3539
			MANN, GLORIA	
2/12/55	18	2	1. Earth Angel (Will You Be Mine)	Sound 109
12/24/55	19	8	2. Teen Age Prayer	Sound 126
			MANN, HERBIE	
4/26/75	14	6	1. Hijack	Atlantic 3246
3/17/79	26	6	2. Superman	Atlantic 3547
			MANTOVANI & His Orchestra	
			English - Annunzio Paola Mantovani - died 3/29/80 (74)	
7/22/57	12	14	1. Around The World (In Eighty Days) [I] -trumpet solo: Stan Newsome-	London 1746
1/23/61	31	2	2. Main Theme From Exodus [I]	London 1953
			MARATHONS	
			also recorded as The Jayhawks and The Vibrations	
5/22/61	20	7	1. Peanut Butter	Arvee 5027
			MARCELS	
			Cornelius Harp, lead singer; Fred Johnson, bass singer	
3/20/61	1 (3)	11	1. **Blue Moon**	Colpix 186
10/30/61	7	9	2. **Heartaches**	Colpix 612
			MARCH, LITTLE PEGGY	
4/06/63	1 (3)	11	1. **I Will Follow Him**	RCA 8139
6/29/63	32	3	2. I Wish I Were A Princess	RCA 8189
9/28/63	26	4	3. Hello Heartache, Goodbye Love	RCA 8221

DATE	POS	WKS	ARTIST—Record Title	LABEL & NO.
			MARCHAN, BOBBY	
			member of Huey Smith's Clowns	
7/11/60	31	4	1. There's Something On Your Mind, Part 2 [N]	Fire 1022
			MARDONES, BENNY	
7/12/80	11	12	1. Into The Night	Polydor 2091
			MARESCA, ERNIE	
4/21/62	6	9	1. **Shout! Shout! (Knock Yourself Out)**	Seville 117
			MARIE, TEENA	
1/17/81	37	3	1. I Need Your Lovin'	Gordy 7189
			MARK IV	
2/09/59	24	7	1. I Got A Wife [N]	Mercury 71403
			MARKETTS	
2/17/62	31	3	1. Surfer's Stomp [I]	Liberty 55401
12/28/63	3	11	2. **Out Of Limits [I]**	Warner 5391
2/26/66	17	5	3. Batman Theme [I]	Warner 5696
			MAR-KEYS	
			Steve Cropper and Duck Dunn, members	
7/17/61	3	12	1. **Last Night [I]**	Satellite 107
			MARKHAM, PIGMEAT	
			died on 12/13/81	
7/06/68	19	4	1. Here Comes The Judge [N]	Chess 2049
			MARLOWE, MARION	
7/16/55	14	2	1. The Man In The Raincoat	Cadence 1266
			MARMALADE	
4/04/70	10	11	1. **Reflections Of My Life**	London 20058
			MARSHALL TUCKER BAND	
			Doug Gray, lead singer; Toy Caldwell, lead guitar	
12/20/75	38	2	1. Fire On The Mountain	Capricorn 0244
4/16/77	14	13	2. Heard It In A Love Song	Capricorn 0270
			MARTERIE, RALPH, & His Orchestra	
			died on 10/8/78 (63)	
3/30/57	25	3	1. Tricky [I]	Mercury 71050
5/13/57	10	6	2. **Shish-Kebab [I]**	Mercury 71092
			MARTHA & THE VANDELLAS	
5/18/63	29	8	1. Come And Get These Memories	Gordy 7014
8/17/63	4	11	2. **Heat Wave**	Gordy 7022
12/07/63	8	9	3. **Quicksand**	Gordy 7025
9/05/64	2 (2)	11	4. **Dancing In The Street**	Gordy 7033
12/26/64	34	4	5. Wild One	Gordy 7036
3/13/65	8	8	6. **Nowhere To Run**	Gordy 7039
9/11/65	36	2	7. You've Been In Love Too Long	Gordy 7045
2/19/66	22	7	8. My Baby Loves Me	Gordy 7048
11/12/66	9	7	9. **I'm Ready For Love**	Gordy 7056
3/18/67	10	10	10. **Jimmy Mack**	Gordy 7058

DATE	POS	WKS	ARTIST—Record Title	LABEL & NO.
9/09/67	**25**	6	11. Love Bug Leave My Heart Alone MARTHA REEVES & THE VANDELLAS:	Gordy 7062
12/02/67	**11**	9	12. Honey Chile	Gordy 7067
			MARTIN, BOBBI	
1/02/65	**19**	7	1. Don't Forget I Still Love You	Coral 62426
4/11/70	**13**	10	2. For The Love Of Him	United Artists 50602
			MARTIN, DEAN	
12/03/55	**1** (6)	19	1. **Memories Are Made Of This** -with The Easy Riders-	Capitol 3295
4/07/56	**27**	4	2. Innamorata -from film "Artists & Models"-	Capitol 3352
5/26/56	**22**	6	3. Standing On The Corner -from musical "Most Happy Fella"-	Capitol 3414
4/07/58	**4**	18	4. **Return To Me**	Capitol 3894
8/04/58	**30**	3	5. Angel Baby	Capitol 3988
8/11/58	**12**	10	6. Volare (Nel Blu Dipinto Di Blu)	Capitol 4028
7/11/64	**1** (1)	13	● 7. **Everybody Loves Somebody**	Reprise 0281
10/17/64	**6**	8	8. **The Door Is Still Open To My Heart**	Reprise 0307
1/09/65	**25**	5	9. You're Nobody Till Somebody Loves You	Reprise 0333
3/13/65	**22**	5	10. Send Me The Pillow You Dream On	Reprise 0344
6/12/65	**32**	3	11. (Remember Me) I'm The One Who Loves You	Reprise 0369
8/21/65	**21**	7	12. Houston	Reprise 0393
11/13/65	**10**	8	13. **I Will**	Reprise 0415
3/05/66	**32**	4	14. Somewhere There's A Someone	Reprise 0443
6/11/66	**35**	1	15. Come Running Back	Reprise 0466
7/22/67	**25**	4	16. In The Chapel In The Moonlight	Reprise 0601
9/09/67	**38**	2	17. Little Ole Wine Drinker, Me	Reprise 0608
			MARTIN, MOON	
9/22/79	**30**	4	1. Rolene	Capitol 4765
			MARTIN, STEVE	
7/08/78	**17**	7	● 1. King Tut [N] -with The Toot Uncommons-	Warner 8577
			MARTIN, TONY	
5/26/56	**10**	11	1. **Walk Hand In Hand**	RCA 6493
			MARTIN, TRADE	
11/17/62	**28**	4	1. That Stranger Used To Be My Girl	Coed 570
			MARTIN, VINCE, with The Tarriers also see Tarriers	
10/13/56	**9**	15	1. **Cindy, Oh Cindy**	Glory 247
			MARTINDALE, WINK TV game show host	
9/28/59	**7**	12	1. **Deck Of Cards [S]**	Dot 15968
			MARTINO, AL	
5/04/63	**3**	11	1. **I Love You Because**	Capitol 4930
8/17/63	**15**	8	2. Painted, Tainted Rose	Capitol 5000
11/16/63	**22**	6	3. Living A Lie	Capitol 5060

DATE	POS	WKS	ARTIST—Record Title	LABEL & NO.
2/15/64	9	8	4. **I Love You More And More Every Day**	Capitol 5108
5/30/64	20	6	5. Tears And Roses	Capitol 5183
9/12/64	33	4	6. Always Together	Capitol 5239
12/18/65	15	9	7. Spanish Eyes	Capitol 5542
4/02/66	30	4	8. Think I'll Go Somewhere And Cry Myself To Sleep	
6/17/67	27	5	9. Mary In The Morning	Capitol 5598
2/08/75	17	8	10. To The Door Of The Sun (Alle Porte Del Sole)	Capitol 5904
12/06/75	33	4	11. Volare	Capitol 3987
				Capitol 4134
			MARVELETTES	
			Gladys Horton, lead singer	
10/16/61	1 (1)	15	1. **Please Mr. Postman**	Tamla 54046
3/03/62	34	1	2. Twistin' Postman	Tamla 54054
5/26/62	7	11	3. **Playboy**	Tamla 54060
9/01/62	17	7	4. Beechwood 4-5789	Tamla 54065
12/05/64	25	8	5. Too Many Fish In The Sea	Tamla 54105
7/03/65	34	1	6. I'll Keep Holding On	Tamla 54116
1/29/66	7	8	7. **Don't Mess With Bill**	Tamla 54126
2/18/67	13	7	8. The Hunter Gets Captured By The Game	Tamla 54143
5/20/67	23	5	9. When You're Young And In Love	Tamla 54150
1/06/68	17	8	10. My Baby Must Be A Magician	Tamla 54158
			MARVELOWS	
7/03/65	37	1	1. I Do	ABC-Para. 10629
			MASEKELA, HUGH	
6/22/68	1 (2)	10	● 1. **Grazing In The Grass [I]**	Uni 55066
			MASHMAKHAN	
11/07/70	31	4	1. As The Years Go By	Epic 10634
			MASON, BARBARA	
6/12/65	5	10	1. **Yes, I'm Ready**	Arctic 105
9/04/65	27	5	2. Sad, Sad Girl	Arctic 108
2/24/73	31	5	3. Give Me Your Love	Buddah 331
12/28/74	28	4	4. From His Woman To You	Buddah 441
			MASON, DAVE	
10/08/77	12	10	1. We Just Disagree	Columbia 10575
7/08/78	39	2	2. Will You Still Love Me Tomorrow	Columbia 10749
			MATHEWS, TOBIN, & Co.	
11/14/60	30	4	1. Ruby Duby Du [I] -from the movie "Key Witness"-	Chief 7022
			MATHIS, JOHNNY	
5/06/57	14	20	1. Wonderful! Wonderful!	Columbia 40784
5/20/57	5	23	2. **It's Not For Me To Say** -from the movie "Lizzie"-	Columbia 40851
9/16/57	1 (1)	22	3. **Chances Are/**	
10/14/57	9	14	4. **The Twelfth Of Never**	Columbia 40993
12/16/57	22	7	5. Wild Is The Wind/	
1/06/58	21	1	6. No Love (But Your Love)	Columbia 41060

DATE	POS	WKS	ARTIST—Record Title	LABEL & NO.
2/10/58	22	1	7. Come To Me	Columbia 41082
5/05/58	21	7	8. All The Time/ -from musical "Oh Captain!"-	
5/19/58	21	2	9. Teacher, Teacher	Columbia 41152
7/14/58	14	11	10. A Certain Smile	Columbia 41193
10/20/58	21	8	11. Call Me	Columbia 41253
5/04/59	35	3	12. Someone	Columbia 41355
7/20/59	20	8	13. Small World -from Broadway musical "Gypsy"-	Columbia 41410
10/19/59	12	12	14. Misty	Columbia 41483
3/28/60	25	5	15. Starbright	Columbia 41583
10/13/62	6	9	16. **Gina**	Columbia 42582
2/09/63	9	10	17. **What Will Mary Say**	Columbia 42666
6/08/63	30	4	18. Every Step Of The Way	Columbia 42799
			MATHIS, JOHNNY, & DIONNE WARWICK	
5/29/82	38	3	1. Friends In Love	Arista 0673
			MATHIS, JOHNNY, & DENIECE WILLIAMS	
4/22/78	1 (1)	11	● 1. **Too Much, Too Little, Too Late**	Columbia 10693
			MATTHEWS' SOUTHERN COMFORT	
			Ian Matthews, lead singer	
4/24/71	23	9	1. Woodstock	Decca 32774
			MATTHEWS, IAN	
12/16/78	13	12	1. Shake It	Mushroom 7039
			MAURIAT, PAUL, & His Orchestra	
1/27/68	1 (5)	15	● 1. **Love Is Blue [I]**	Philips 40495
			MAXWELL, ROBERT [His Harp & Orchestra]	
4/18/64	15	7	1. Shangri-La [I]	Decca 25622
			MAYER, NATHANIEL, & The Fabulous Twilights	
5/26/62	22	6	1. Village Of Love	Fortune 449
			MAYFIELD, CURTIS	
			lead singer of The Impressions from 1961-1970	
1/02/71	29	4	1. (Don't Worry) If There's A Hell Below We're All Going To Go	
9/23/72	4	11	● 2. **Freddie's Dead** -Theme from "Superfly"-	Curtom 1955 Curtom 1975
11/25/72	8	13	● 3. **Superfly**	Curtom 1978
8/25/73	39	2	4. Future Shock	Curtom 1987
8/03/74	40	1	5. Kung Fu	Curtom 1999
			McANALLY, MAC	
8/13/77	37	2	1. It's A Crazy World	Ariola America 7665
			McCALL, C.W.	
			real name: Bill Fries	
3/22/75	40	1	1. Wolf Creek Pass [N]	MGM 14764
12/13/75	1 (1)	11	● 2. **Convoy [N]**	MGM 14839

DATE	POS	WKS	ARTIST—Record Title	LABEL & NO.
			McCANN, PETER	
5/21/77	5	16	● 1. **Do You Wanna Make Love**	20th Century 2335
			McCARTNEY, PAUL	
			Paul McCartney and wife Linda, with their band WINGS, released records under various combinations of these names	
3/13/71	5	11	1. **Another Day**	Apple 1829
8/21/71	1 (1)	12	● 2. **Uncle Albert/Admiral Halsey**	Apple 1837
3/25/72	21	6	3. Give Ireland Back To The Irish	Apple 1847
7/08/72	28	3	4. Mary Had A Little Lamb	Apple 1851
12/30/72	10	9	5. **Hi, Hi, Hi**	Apple 1857
4/28/73	1 (4)	15	● 6. **My Love**	Apple 1861
7/21/73	2 (3)	12	● 7. **Live And Let Die**	Apple 1863
12/08/73	10	10	8. Helen Wheels	Apple 1869
2/23/74	7	10	9. Jet	Apple 1871
5/04/74	1 (1)	13	● 10. **Band On The Run**	Apple 1873
11/23/74	3	10	11. **Junior's Farm/**	
2/22/75	39	1	12. Sally G	Apple 1875
6/07/75	1 (1)	11	● 13. **Listen To What The Man Said**	Capitol 4091
10/25/75	39	2	14. Letting Go	Capitol 4145
11/15/75	12	6	15. Venus And Mars Rock Show	Capitol 4175
4/17/76	1 (5)	15	● 16. **Silly Love Songs**	Capitol 4256
7/17/76	3	11	● 17. **Let 'Em In**	Capitol 4293
2/19/77	10	11	18. **Maybe I'm Amazed**	Capitol 4385
12/24/77	33	4	19. Girls' School	Capitol 4504
4/08/78	1 (2)	12	20. **With A Little Luck**	Capitol 4559
7/15/78	25	5	21. I've Had Enough	Capitol 4594
10/14/78	39	2	22. London Town	Capitol 4625
3/31/79	5	13	● 23. **Goodnight Tonight**	Columbia 10939
6/30/79	20	6	24. Getting Closer	Columbia 11020
9/22/79	29	4	25. Arrow Through Me	Columbia 11070
5/10/80	1 (3)	16	● 26. **Coming Up (Live at Glasgow)**	Columbia 11263
7/17/82	10	11	27. **Take It Away**	Columbia 03018
			McCARTNEY, PAUL, & STEVIE WONDER	
4/10/82	1 (7)	15	● 1. **Ebony And Ivory**	Columbia 02860
			McCLAIN, ALTON, & DESTINY	
5/19/79	32	4	1. It Must Be Love	Polydor 14532
			McCLINTON, DELBERT	
			leader of the Ron-Dels	
12/20/80	8	14	1. **Giving It Up For Your Love**	Capitol 4948
			McCLURE, BOBBY - see FONTELLA BASS	
			McCOO, MARILYN, & BILLY DAVIS, JR.	
			Marilyn & husband Billy were members of The 5th Dimension	
10/23/76	1 (1)	18	● 1. **You Don't Have To Be A Star (To Be In My Show)**	ABC 12208
4/02/77	15	8	2. Your Love	ABC 12262
			McCOY, VAN	
			died on 7/6/79 (35)	
5/31/75	1 (1)	12	● 1. **The Hustle [I]** -with The Soul City Symphony-	Avco 4653

DATE	POS	WKS	ARTIST—Record Title	LABEL & NO.
			McCOYS	
			Rick Derringer, lead singer	
9/04/65	**1** (1)	11	1. **Hang On Sloopy**	Bang 506
11/27/65	**7**	8	2. **Fever**	Bang 511
5/14/66	**22**	6	3. Come On Let's Go	Bang 522
			McCRACKLIN, JIMMY	
3/03/58	**7**	10	1. **The Walk**	Checker 885
			McCRAE, GEORGE	
6/15/74	**1** (2)	10	1. **Rock Your Baby**	T.K. 1004
3/01/75	**37**	2	2. I Get Lifted	T.K. 1007
			McCRAE, GWEN	
			George McCrae's wife	
6/21/75	**9**	8	1. **Rockin' Chair**	Cat 1996
			McDANIELS, GENE	
4/03/61	**3**	12	1. **A Hundred Pounds Of Clay**	Liberty 55308
8/07/61	**31**	2	2. A Tear	Liberty 55344
10/16/61	**5**	10	3. **Tower Of Strength**	Liberty 55371
2/10/62	**10**	7	4. **Chip Chip**	Liberty 55405
9/01/62	**21**	5	5. Point Of No Return	Liberty 55480
12/15/62	**31**	2	6. Spanish Lace	Liberty 55510
			McDEVITT, CHAS., Skiffle Group	
6/10/57	**40**	1	1. Freight Train -vocal by Nancy Wiskey-	Chic 1008
			McDONALD, MICHAEL	
			former lead singer of The Doobie Brothers	
8/28/82	**4**	13	1. **I Keep Forgettin' (Every Time You're Near)**	Warner 29933
			McDOWELL, RONNIE	
9/17/77	**13**	9	● 1. The King Is Gone -Elvis Presley tribute-	Scorpion 135
			McFADDEN & WHITEHEAD	
			Gene McFadden & John Whitehead	
6/02/79	**13**	11	★ 1. Ain't No Stoppin' Us Now	Phil. Int'l. 3681
			McFADDEN, BOB, & DOR	
			Bob is actually Rod McKuen	
9/14/59	**39**	1	1. The Mummy [N]	Brunswick 55140
			McGOVERN, MAUREEN	
7/14/73	**1** (2)	11	● 1. **The Morning After** -from "The Poseidon Adventure"-	20th Century 2010
8/11/79	**18**	9	2. Different Worlds -theme from TV series "Angie"-	Warner 8835
			McGRIFF, JIMMY	
10/27/62	**20**	7	1. I've Got A Woman, Part I [I]	Sue 770
			McGUINN, CLARK & HILLMAN	
			Roger McGuinn, Gene Clark & Chris Hillman of The Byrds	
4/28/79	**33**	4	1. Don't You Write Her Off	Capitol 4693

DATE	POS	WKS	ARTIST—Record Title	LABEL & NO.
			McGUIRE SISTERS	
			Phyllis, Dorothy & Christine	
1/08/55	**1**(10)	21	1. **Sincerely/**	
1/29/55	**17**	6	2. No More	Coral 61323
3/26/55	**11**	7	3. It May Sound Silly	Coral 61369
6/04/55	**5**	14	4. **Something's Gotta Give**	Coral 61423
			-from the film "Daddy Long Legs"-	
10/29/55	**10**	13	5. **He**	Coral 61501
5/19/56	**13**	12	6. Picnic/	
6/02/56	**37**	1	7. Delilah Jones	Coral 61627
			-from "Man With The Golden Arm"-	
8/11/56	**32**	3	8. Weary Blues	Coral 61670
10/27/56	**37**	3	9. Ev'ry Day Of My Life	Coral 61703
12/22/56	**32**	3	10. Goodnight My Love, Pleasant Dreams	Coral 61748
1/06/58	**1** (4)	19	11. **Sugartime**	Coral 61924
6/09/58	**25**	1	12. Ding Dong	Coral 61991
1/19/59	**11**	12	13. May You Always	Coral 62059
4/17/61	**20**	7	14. Just For Old Time's Sake	Coral 62249
			McGUIRE, BARRY	
			member of New Christy Minstrels	
8/28/65	**1** (1)	10	1. **Eve Of Destruction**	Dunhill 4009
			McKENZIE, BOB & DOUG	
			Rick Moranis & Dave Thomas of 'SCTV', with Geddy Lee of Rush	
2/20/82	**16**	9	1. Take Off [N]	Mercury 76134
			McKENZIE, SCOTT	
6/10/67	**4**	10	1. **San Francisco (Be Sure To Wear Flowers In Your Hair)**	Ode 103
11/11/67	**24**	3	2. Like An Old Time Movie	Ode 105
			McLAIN, TOMMY	
7/23/66	**15**	7	1. Sweet Dreams	MSL 197
			McLEAN, DON	
12/04/71	**1** (4)	17	● 1. **American Pie - Parts I & II**	United Artists 50856
4/01/72	**12**	10	2. Vincent/	
			-a tribute to artist Van Gogh-	
		7	3. **Castles In The Air**	United Artists 50887
1/20/73	**21**	8	4. Dreidel	United Artists 51100
1/24/81	**5**	15	5. **Crying**	Millennium 11799
5/02/81	**23**	6	6. Since I Don't Have You	Millennium 11804
12/12/81	**36**	5	7. Castles In The Air	Millennium 11819
			-new version of 1972 hit-	
			McLEAN, PHIL	
12/18/61	**21**	6	1. Small Sad Sam [S-N]	Versatile 107
			-parody of "Big Bad John"-	
			McNAMARA, ROBIN	
7/18/70	**11**	8	1. Lay A Little Lovin' On Me	Steed 724

DATE	POS	WKS	ARTIST—Record Title	LABEL & NO.
			McPHATTER, CLYDE	
			former lead singer of The Dominoes and The Drifters - died on 6/13/72 (38)	
6/09/56	16	12	1. Treasure Of Love	Atlantic 1092
2/23/57	19	2	2. Without Love (There Is Nothing)	Atlantic 1117
7/08/57	26	3	3. Just To Hold My Hand	Atlantic 1133
10/20/58	6	20	4. **A Lover's Question**	Atlantic 1199
8/03/59	38	2	5. Since You've Been Gone	Atlantic 2028
8/22/60	23	5	6. Ta Ta	Mercury 71660
3/24/62	7	10	7. **Lover Please**	Mercury 71941
6/30/62	25	5	8. Little Bitty Pretty One	Mercury 71987
			MEAD, SISTER JANET	
3/09/74	4	11	● 1. **The Lord's Prayer**	A&M 1491
			MEAT LOAF	
			Marvin Lee Aday	
4/29/78	11	13	● 1. Two Out Of Three Ain't Bad	Epic 50513
9/16/78	39	2	2. Paradise By The Dashboard Light [N]	Epic 50588
			-female vocal: Ellen Foley; baseball announcer: Phil Rizzuto-	
1/20/79	39	1	3. You Took The Words Right Out Of My Mouth	Epic 50634
			MECO	
			Meco Monardo	
8/27/77	1 (2)	13	★ 1. **Star Wars Theme/Cantina Band [I]**	Millennium 604
1/21/78	25	6	2. Theme From Close Encounters [I]	Millennium 608
10/21/78	35	3	3. Themes From The Wizard Of Oz [N]	Millennium 620
7/05/80	18	8	4. Empire Strikes Back (Medley) [I]	RSO 1038
4/03/82	35	3	5. Pop Goes The Movies, Part 1 [I]	Arista 0660
			MEISNER, RANDY	
			member of Poco, and The Eagles	
11/08/80	22	7	1. Deep Inside My Heart	Epic 50939
2/07/81	19	9	2. Hearts On Fire	Epic 50964
8/28/82	28	6	3. Never Been In Love	Epic 03032
			MEL & TIM	
			Mel Harden & Tim McPherson	
11/08/69	10	11	● 1. **Backfield In Motion**	Bamboo 107
9/16/72	19	9	2. Starting All Over Again	Stax 0127
			MELANIE	
			Melanie Safka	
5/16/70	6	14	1. **Lay Down (Candles In The Rain)**	Buddah 167
			-with The Edwin Hawkins Singers-	
9/05/70	32	4	2. Peace Will Come (According To Plan)	Buddah 186
11/27/71	1 (3)	14	● 3. **Brand New Key**	Neighbor. 4201
2/19/72	31	5	4. Ring The Living Bell	Neighbor. 4202
2/26/72	35	3	5. The Nickel Song	Buddah 268
4/07/73	36	2	6. Bitter Bad	Neighbor. 4210
			MELLO-TONES	
5/13/57	24	1	1. Rosie Lee	Gee 1037

DATE	POS	WKS	ARTIST—Record Title	LABEL & NO.
			MELVIN, HAROLD, & THE BLUENOTES	
			Teddy Pendergrass, lead singer	
10/28/72	3	11	● 1. **If You Don't Know Me By Now**	Phil. Int'l. 3520
10/20/73	7	12	● 2. **The Love I Lost (Part 1)**	Phil. Int'l. 3533
5/03/75	15	10	3. Bad Luck (Part 1)	Phil. Int'l. 3562
12/20/75	12	12	4. Wake Up Everybody (Part 1)	Phil. Int'l. 3579
			MEN AT WORK	
			Australian quintet, led by Colin Hay	
8/07/82	1 (1)	17	1. **Who Can It Be Now?**	Columbia 02888
			MENDES, SERGIO, & BRASIL '66	
			Lani Hall and Karen Phillipp, lead vocalists	
6/01/68	4	11	1. **The Look Of Love** -from the film "Casino Royale"-	A&M 924
8/24/68	6	10	2. **The Fool On The Hill**	A&M 961
12/07/68	16	6	3. Scarborough Fair	A&M 986
			MERCY	
5/03/69	2 (2)	10	● 1. **Love (Can Make You Happy)**	Sundi 6811
			MESSINA, JIM see LOGGINS & MESSINA	
			METERS	
3/22/69	34	1	1. Sophisticated Cissy [I]	Josie 1001
5/24/69	23	3	2. Cissy Strut [I]	Josie 1005
			MFSB	
3/16/74	1 (2)	14	● 1. **TSOP (The Sound Of Philadelphia) [I]** -featuring The Three Degrees-	Phil. Int'l. 3540
			MICHAELS, LEE	
9/04/71	6	12	1. **Do You Know What I Mean**	A&M 1262
12/25/71	39	1	2. Can I Get A Witness	A&M 1303
			MICKEY & SYLVIA	
			Mickey Baker & Sylvia Robinson - also see Sylvia	
1/12/57	11	14	1. Love Is Strange	Groove 0175
			MIDLER, BETTE	
1/20/73	17	11	1. Do You Want To Dance?	Atlantic 2928
6/09/73	8	11	2. **Boogie Woogie Bugle Boy**	Atlantic 2964
11/10/73	40	1	3. Friends	Atlantic 2980
7/07/79	40	2	4. Married Men	Atlantic 3582
3/01/80	35	3	5. When A Man Loves A Woman	Atlantic 3643
4/26/80	3	16	● 6. **The Rose** -above 2 from film "The Rose"-	Atlantic 3656
1/17/81	39	2	7. My Mother's Eyes -from the film "Divine Madness"-	Atlantic 3771
			MILES, GARRY	
			real name: Buzz Cason - also see Garry Mills (different artist with different version of same song)	
7/18/60	16	6	1. Look For A Star -from film "Circus Of Horrors"-	Liberty 55261
			MILES, JOHN	
5/14/77	34	5	1. Slowdown	London 20092

DATE	POS	WKS	ARTIST—Record Title	LABEL & NO.
			MILLER, CHUCK	
6/18/55	9	14	1. **The House Of Blue Lights**	Mercury 70627
			MILLER, JODY	
5/15/65	12	5	1. Queen Of The House	Capitol 5402
9/25/65	25	5	2. Home Of The Brave	Capitol 5483
			MILLER, MITCH [Orchestra & Chorus]	
8/06/55	1 (6)	19	1. **The Yellow Rose Of Texas**	Columbia 40540
2/18/56	19	3	2. Lisbon Antigua [I]	Columbia 40635
8/11/56	8	12	3. **Song For A Summer Night (Parts 1 & 2)** -Part 1: Instrumental; 2: vocal-	Columbia 40730
1/27/58	20	11	4. March From The River Kwai And Colonel Bogey [I] -from "Bridge On The River Kwai"-	Columbia 41066
1/26/59	16	10	5. The Children's Marching Song [N] -from "Inn Of The 6th Happiness"-	Columbia 41317
			MILLER, NED	
1/26/63	6	8	1. **From A Jack To A King**	Fabor 114
			MILLER, ROGER	
7/04/64	7	8	1. **Dang Me [N]**	Smash 1881
10/03/64	9	8	2. **Chug-A-Lug [N]**	Smash 1926
1/02/65	31	3	3. Do-Wacka-Do [N]	Smash 1947
2/06/65	4	12	● 4. **King Of The Road**	Smash 1965
5/22/65	7	7	5. **Engine Engine #9**	Smash 1983
8/07/65	34	2	6. One Dyin' And A Buryin'	Smash 1994
10/02/65	31	3	7. Kansas City Star [N]	Smash 1998
11/27/65	8	8	8. **England Swings**	Smash 2010
3/05/66	26	5	9. Husbands And Wives [N]	Smash 2024
7/23/66	40	1	10. You Can't Roller Skate In A Buffalo Herd [N]	Smash 2043
5/06/67	37	1	11. Walkin' In The Sunshine	Smash 2081
3/16/68	39	6	12. Little Green Apples	Smash 2148
			MILLER, STEVE, BAND rock group from the West Coast	
11/17/73	1 (1)	16	● 1. **The Joker**	Capitol 3732
6/05/76	11	9	2. Take The Money And Run	Capitol 4260
9/04/76	1 (1)	14	3. **Rock'n Me**	Capitol 4323
1/08/77	2 (2)	15	● 4. **Fly Like An Eagle**	Capitol 4372
5/14/77	8	13	5. **Jet Airliner**	Capitol 4424
9/03/77	23	7	6. Jungle Love	Capitol 4466
11/12/77	17	9	7. Swingtown	Capitol 4496
11/14/81	24	9	8. Heart Like A Wheel	Capitol 5068
6/19/82	1 (2)	19	● 9. **Abracadabra**	Capitol 5126
			MILLS BROTHERS Harry, Herbert & Donald -- Harry died on 6/28/82 (68)	
6/17/57	39	1	1. Queen Of The Senior Prom	Decca 30299
3/03/58	21	2	2. Get A Job	Dot 15695
3/02/68	23	10	3. Cab Driver	Dot 17041

DATE	POS	WKS	ARTIST—Record Title	LABEL & NO.
			MILLS, FRANK	
3/03/79	3	12	● 1. **Music Box Dancer** [I]	Polydor 14517
			MILLS, GARRY	
			also see Garry Miles	
7/04/60	26	5	1. Look For A Star - Part I	Imperial 5674
			-from film "Circus Of Horrors"-	
			MILLS, HAYLEY	
			15 year-old English actress	
9/18/61	8	11	1. **Let's Get Together**	Vista 385
			-from film "The Parent Trap"-	
4/14/62	21	6	2. Johnny Jingo	Vista 395
			MILLS, STEPHANIE	
			star of Broadway show "The Wiz"	
9/01/79	22	6	1. What Cha Gonna Do With My Lovin'	20th Century 2403
8/30/80	6	16	● 2. **Never Knew Love Like This Before**	20th Century 2460
			MILLS, STEPHANIE, & TEDDY PENDERGRASS	
7/04/81	40	2	1. Two Hearts	20th Century 2492
			MILSAP, RONNIE	
			Ronnie was born blind	
8/27/77	16	10	1. It Was Almost Like A Song	RCA 10976
1/24/81	24	9	2. Smoky Mountain Rain	RCA 12084
7/11/81	5	15	3. **(There's) No Gettin' Over Me**	RCA 12264
11/28/81	20	11	4. I Wouldn't Have Missed It For The World	RCA 12342
5/29/82	14	9	5. Any Day Now	RCA 13216
			MIMMS, GARNET	
5/07/66	30	3	1. I'll Take Good Care Of You	United Artists 995
			MIMMS, GARNET, & The Enchanters	
9/07/63	4	11	1. **Cry Baby**	United Artists 629
12/07/63	26	5	2. For Your Precious Love/	
12/07/63	30	4	3. Baby Don't You Weep	United Artists 658
			MINDBENDERS	
			English - lead singer Wayne Fontana left group late in '65	
3/27/65	1 (1)	10	1. **Game Of Love**	Fontana 1509
			-Wayne Fontana & The Mindbenders-	
4/30/66	2 (2)	10	2. **A Groovy Kind Of Love**	Fontana 1541
			MINEO, SAL	
			died 2/12/76 (37)	
5/20/57	9	13	1. **Start Movin' (In My Direction)**	Epic 9216
9/23/57	27	3	2. Lasting Love	Epic 9227
			MIRACLES	
			led by singer/songwriter/producer Smokey Robinson, The Miracles were Motown's first successful recording group	
12/31/60	2 (1)	13	1. **Shop Around**	Tamla 54034
2/17/62	35	2	2. What's So Good About Good-By	Tamla 54053
6/30/62	39	1	3. I'll Try Something New	Tamla 54059
1/12/63	8	10	4. **You've Really Got A Hold On Me**	Tamla 54073
5/04/63	31	3	5. A Love She Can Count On	Tamla 54078
8/31/63	8	9	6. **Mickey's Monkey**	Tamla 54083

DATE	POS	WKS	ARTIST—Record Title	LABEL & NO.
1/04/64	35	3	7. I Gotta Dance To Keep From Crying	Tamla 54089
7/25/64	27	4	8. I Like It Like That	Tamla 54098
10/10/64	35	1	9. That's What Love Is Made Of	Tamla 54102
4/17/65	16	7	10. Ooo Baby Baby	Tamla 54113
8/07/65	16	8	11. The Tracks Of My Tears	Tamla 54118
11/06/65	14	6	12. My Girl Has Gone	Tamla 54123
1/22/66	11	7	13. Going To A Go-Go	Tamla 54127
11/26/66	17	6	14. (Come 'Round Here) I'm The One You Need	Tamla 54140
			SMOKEY ROBINSON & THE MIRACLES: (Tamla 54l45 thru 54205)	
3/11/67	20	7	15. The Love I Saw In You Was Just A Mirage	Tamla 54145
7/08/67	23	8	16. More Love	Tamla 54152
11/25/67	4	12	17. **I Second That Emotion**	Tamla 54159
3/09/68	11	10	18. If You Can Want	Tamla 54162
6/29/68	31	3	19. Yester Love	Tamla 54167
8/31/68	26	6	20. Special Occasion	Tamla 54172
1/25/69	8	11	21. **Baby, Baby Don't Cry**	Tamla 54178
7/19/69	33	2	22. Abraham, Martin And John	Tamla 54184
7/26/69	32	4	23. Doggone Right/	
10/04/69	37	3	24. Here I Go Again	Tamla 54183
12/27/69	37	4	25. Point It Out	Tamla 54189
10/31/70	1 (2)	14	26. **The Tears Of A Clown**	Tamla 54199
4/17/71	18	8	27. I Don't Blame You At All	Tamla 54205
9/14/74	13	9	28. Do It Baby	Tamla 54248
12/13/75	1 (1)	19	29. **Love Machine (Part 1)**	Tamla 54262
			MITCHELL, GUY	
2/25/56	23	4	1. Ninety Nine Years (Dead Or Alive)	Columbia 40631
11/03/56	1(10)	22	2. **Singing The Blues**	Columbia 40769
2/02/57	16	8	3. Knee Deep In The Blues	Columbia 40820
4/13/57	10	12	4. **Rock-A-Billy**	Columbia 40877
10/19/59	1 (2)	16	5. **Heartaches By The Number**	Columbia 41476
			MITCHELL, JONI	
			also see James Taylor	
12/30/72	25	8	1. You Turn Me On, I'm A Radio	Asylum 11010
4/20/74	7	11	2. **Help Me**	Asylum 11034
8/24/74	22	7	3. Free Man In Paris	Asylum 11041
1/25/75	24	4	4. Big Yellow Taxi	Asylum 45221
			-live version of '70 studio hit-	
			MITCHELL, WILLIE	
			president of Hi Records	
10/03/64	31	5	1. 20-75 [I]	Hi 2075
4/13/68	23	10	2. Soul Serenade [I]	Hi 2140
			MOCEDADES	
2/16/74	9	11	1. **Eres Tu (Touch The Wind) [F]**	Tara 100
			MODUGNO, DOMENICO	
8/04/58	1 (5)	13	1. **Nel Blu Dipinto Di Blu (Volare) [F]**	Decca 30677
			MOJO MEN	
3/18/67	36	3	1. Sit Down, I Think I Love You	Reprise 0539

DATE	POS	WKS	ARTIST—Record Title	LABEL & NO.
			MOMENTS	
			also see Ray, Goodman & Brown	
4/18/70	3	14	● 1. **Love On A Two-Way Street**	Stang 5012
2/02/74	17	9	2. Sexy Mama	Stang 5052
8/02/75	39	3	3. Look At Me (I'm In Love)	Stang 5060
			MONEY, EDDIE	
4/08/78	11	11	1. Baby Hold On	Columbia 10663
7/29/78	22	8	2. Two Tickets To Paradise	Columbia 10765
2/24/79	22	8	3. Maybe I'm A Fool	Columbia 10900
7/24/82	16	12	4. Think I'm In Love	Columbia 02964
			MONKEES	
			Davy Jones, Michael Nesmith, Mickey Dolenz, & Peter Tork	
9/24/66	1 (1)	12	● 1. **Last Train To Clarksville**	Colgems 1001
12/17/66	1 (7)	13	● 2. **I'm A Believer/**	
12/31/66	20	6	3. (I'm Not Your) Steppin' Stone	Colgems 1002
3/25/67	2 (1)	10	● 4. **A Little Bit Me, A Little Bit You/**	
4/15/67	39	1	5. The Girl I Knew Somewhere	Colgems 1004
7/29/67	3	9	● 6. **Pleasant Valley Sunday/**	
8/05/67	11	7	7. Words	Colgems 1007
11/18/67	1 (4)	12	● 8. **Daydream Believer**	Colgems 1012
3/09/68	3	7	● 9. **Valleri/**	
3/30/68	34	1	10. Tapioca Tundra	Colgems 1019
6/22/68	19	6	11. D. W. Washburn	Colgems 1023
			MONOTONES	
4/07/58	5	12	1. **Book Of Love**	Argo 5290
			MONRO, MATT	
6/26/61	18	9	1. My Kind Of Girl	Warwick 636
12/26/64	23	5	2. Walk Away	Liberty 55745
			MONROE, VAUGHN	
			died on 5/21/73 (61)	
11/12/55	38	1	1. Black Denim Trousers And Motorcycle Boots	RCA 6260
2/18/56	38	1	2. Don't Go To Strangers	RCA 6358
9/08/56	11	8	3. In The Middle Of The House [N]	RCA 6619
			MONTE, LOU	
3/17/58	12	11	1. Lazy Mary (Luna Mezzo Mare) [F]	RCA 7160
12/15/62	5	9	2. **Pepino The Italian Mouse [N]**	Reprise 20106
			MONTENEGRO, HUGO [His Orchestra & Chorus]	
			Hugo died on 2/6/81 (55)	
4/06/68	2 (1)	14	1. **The Good, The Bad And The Ugly [I]**	RCA 9423
			MONTEZ, CHRIS	
9/08/62	4	9	1. **Let's Dance**	Monogram 505
2/12/66	22	5	2. Call Me	A&M 780
5/28/66	16	7	3. The More I See You	A&M 796
9/10/66	33	2	4. There Will Never Be Another You	A&M 810
12/03/66	36	2	5. Time After Time	A&M 822

DATE	POS	WKS	ARTIST—Record Title	LABEL & NO.
			MONTGOMERY, MELBA	
6/08/74	39	1	1. No Charge [N]	Elektra 45883
			MOODY BLUES	
			English: Justin Hayward, John Lodge, Graeme Edge, Mike Pinder & Ray Thomas	
3/27/65	10	8	1. **Go Now!**	London 9726
8/24/68	24	6	2. Tuesday Afternoon (Forever Afternoon)	Deram 85028
5/30/70	21	8	3. Question	Threshold 67004
9/04/71	23	7	4. The Story In Your Eyes	Threshold 67006
5/13/72	29	7	5. Isn't Life Strange	Threshold 67009
9/02/72	2 (2)	14	● 6. **Nights In White Satin**	Deram 85023
2/17/73	12	8	7. I'm Just A Singer (In A Rock And Roll Band)	Threshold 67012
9/02/78	39	2	8. Steppin' In A Slide Zone	London 270
6/13/81	12	9	9. Gemini Dream	Threshold 601
8/15/81	15	11	10. The Voice	Threshold 602
			MOONEY, ART, & His Orchestra	
4/23/55	6	17	1. **Honey-Babe** -from the film "Battle Cry"-	MGM 11900
			MOONGLOWS	
			Harvey Fuqua, lead singer - also see Harvey & The Moonglows	
3/26/55	20	1	1. Sincerely	Chess 1581
10/13/56	25	1	2. See Saw	Chess 1629
			MOORE, BOB, & His Orchestra	
9/11/61	7	10	1. **Mexico [I]**	Monument 446
			MOORE, BOBBY & The Rhythm Aces	
7/30/66	27	4	1. Searching For My Love	Checker 1129
			MOORE, DOROTHY	
4/10/76	3	16	1. **Misty Blue**	Malaco 1029
9/10/77	27	7	2. I Believe You	Malaco 1042
			MOORE, JACKIE	
1/23/71	30	7	● 1. Precious, Precious	Atlantic 2681
			MORGAN, JANE	
9/09/57	7	21	1. **Fascination** -with The Troubadors -- from the film "Love In The Afternoon"-	Kapp 191
10/13/58	21	10	2. The Day The Rains Came	Kapp 235
8/31/59	39	1	3. With Open Arms	Kapp 284
			MORGAN, JAYE P.	
			also see Perry Como	
11/27/54	3	21	1. **That's All I Want From You**	RCA 5896
3/12/55	12	8	2. Danger! Heartbreak Ahead	RCA 6016
8/20/55	6	14	3. **The Longest Walk**	RCA 6182
11/12/55	12	8	4. Pepper-Hot Baby/	
12/10/55	40	1	5. If You Don't Want My Love	RCA 6282
			MORGAN, RUSS, & His Orchestra	
			Russ died on 8/8/69 (65)	
11/12/55	30	4	1. Dogface Soldier -from movie "From Hell And Back"-	Decca 29703
3/17/56	19	3	2. The Poor People Of Paris [I]	Decca 29835

DATE	POS	WKS	ARTIST—Record Title	LABEL & NO.
			MORMON TABERNACLE CHOIR	
			Richard P. Condie, directs the 375-voice choir	
9/21/59	13	11	1. Battle Hymn Of The Republic	Columbia 41459
			-with The Philadelphia Orchestra, Eugene Ormandy, conductor-	
			MORODER, GIORGIO	
3/10/79	33	4	1. Chase [I]	Casablanca 956
			-from film "Midnight Express"-	
			MORRISON, VAN	
			lead singer of Irish group Them	
8/19/67	10	10	1. **Brown Eyed Girl**	Bang 545
4/25/70	39	2	2. Come Running	Warner 7383
12/05/70	9	9	3. **Domino**	Warner 7434
3/06/71	23	8	4. Blue Money	Warner 7462
11/20/71	28	4	5. Wild Night	Warner 7518
			MOTELS	
			Martha Davis, lead singer of quintet from Los Angeles	
5/29/82	9	15	1. **Only The Lonely**	Capitol 5114
			MOTHERLODE	
9/13/69	18	7	1. When I Die	Buddah 131
			MOTT THE HOOPLE	
			Ian Hunter, leader	
11/04/72	37	3	1. All The Young Dudes	Columbia 45673
			MOUNTAIN	
			Leslie West, leader	
6/13/70	21	9	1. Mississippi Queen	Windfall 532
			MOUTH & MacNEAL	
			Willem Duyn & Maggie MacNeal	
6/17/72	8	12	● 1. **How Do You Do?**	Philips 40715
			MOZART, MICKEY, Quintet	
6/08/59	30	6	1. Little Dipper [I]	Roulette 4148
			MULDAUR, MARIA	
4/13/74	6	14	1. **Midnight At The Oasis**	Reprise 1183
1/25/75	12	8	2. I'm A Woman	Reprise 1319
			MUNGO JERRY	
			Ray Dorset, lead singer	
7/25/70	3	11	● 1. **In The Summertime**	Janus 125
			MURMAIDS	
12/07/63	3	11	1. **Popsicles And Icicles**	Chattahoochee 628
			MURPHEY, MICHAEL	
10/07/72	37	2	1. Geronimo's Cadillac	A&M 1368
5/03/75	3	13	● 2. **Wildfire**	Epic 50084
9/13/75	21	7	3. Carolina In The Pines	Epic 50131
2/21/76	39	2	4. Renegade	Epic 50184
8/28/82	19	11	5. What's Forever For	Liberty 1466
			MURPHY, WALTER, Band	
7/04/76	1 (1)	22	● 1. **A Fifth Of Beethoven [I]**	Private Stock 45073
			-based on Beethoven's Fifth Symphony-	

DATE	POS	WKS	ARTIST—Record Title	LABEL & NO.
			MURRAY, ANNE	
			Canadian	
8/22/70	8	11	● 1. **Snowbird**	Capitol 2738
2/10/73	7	13	2. **Danny's Song**	Capitol 3481
1/19/74	12	10	3. Love Song	Capitol 3776
5/25/74	8	10	4. **You Won't See Me**	Capitol 3867
8/19/78	1 (1)	17	● 5. **You Needed Me**	Capitol 4574
2/10/79	12	12	6. I Just Fall In Love Again	Capitol 4675
6/23/79	25	7	7. Shadows In The Moonlight	Capitol 4716
10/20/79	12	10	8. Broken Hearted Me	Capitol 4773
1/19/80	12	12	9. Daydream Believer	Capitol 4813
10/18/80	33	4	10. Could I Have This Dance	Capitol 4920
5/02/81	34	4	11. Blessed Are The Believers	Capitol 4987
			MUSIC EXPLOSION	
5/27/67	2 (2)	13	● 1. **Little Bit O'soul**	Laurie 3380
			MUSIC MACHINE	
12/10/66	15	8	1. Talk Talk	Original Sound 61
			MYLES, BILLY	
11/25/57	25	6	1. The Joker (That's What They Call Me)	Ember 1026
			MYSTICS	
6/15/59	20	9	1. Hushabye	Laurie 3028
			NAPOLEON XIV	
			Napoleon is Jerry Samuels	
7/30/66	3	5	1. **They're Coming To Take Me Away, Ha-Haaa! [N]**	Warner 5831
			NASH, GRAHAM	
			member of The Hollies, and Crosby, Stills & Nash -- also see David Crosby	
7/10/71	35	4	1. Chicago	Atlantic 2804
			NASH, JOHNNY	
			also see Paul Anka	
2/03/58	23	1	1. A Very Special Love	ABC-Para. 9874
10/05/68	5	12	2. **Hold Me Tight**	JAD 207
1/24/70	39	1	3. Cupid	JAD 220
10/07/72	1 (4)	14	● 4. **I Can See Clearly Now**	Epic 10902
3/03/73	12	10	5. Stir It Up	Epic 10949
			NASHVILLE TEENS	
10/10/64	14	6	1. Tobacco Road	London 9689
			NATURAL FOUR	
2/09/74	31	4	1. Can This Be Real	Curtom 1990
			NAUGHTON, DAVID	
			star of TV's "Makin' It"	
5/12/79	5	16	● 1. **Makin' It** -from the film "Meatballs"-	RSO 916
			NAZARETH	
			Dan McCafferty, lead singer	
1/03/76	8	14	● 1. **Love Hurts**	A&M 1671

DATE	POS	WKS	ARTIST—Record Title	LABEL & NO.
			NEELY, SAM	
10/07/72	29	6	1. Loving You Just Crossed My Mind	Capitol 3381
11/09/74	34	2	2. You Can Have Her	A&M 1612
			NEIGHBORHOOD	
8/08/70	29	4	1. Big Yellow Taxi	Big Tree 102
			NELSON, RICKY	
			Ricky starred with his family on radio & TV in "The Adventures of Ozzie & Harriet" from '49-'66	
5/06/57	17	9	1. I'm Walking/	
5/27/57	2 (1)	15	2. **A Teenager's Romance**	Verve 10047
9/16/57	14	7	3. You're My One And Only Love	Verve 10070
10/07/57	3	18	4. **Be-Bop Baby**/	
10/28/57	29	3	5. Have I Told You Lately That I Love You	Imperial 5463
12/30/57	2 (3)	14	6. **Stood Up**/	
12/30/57	18	9	7. Waitin' In School	Imperial 5483
4/07/58	4	10	8. **Believe What You Say**/	
4/07/58	18	8	9. My Bucket's Got A Hole In It	Imperial 5503
7/07/58	1 (2)	15	10. **Poor Little Fool**	Imperial 5528
10/20/58	7	16	11. **Lonesome Town**/	
10/20/58	10	13	12. **I Got A Feeling**	Imperial 5545
3/09/59	6	12	13. **Never Be Anyone Else But You**/	
3/16/59	9	10	14. **It's Late**	Imperial 5565
7/13/59	9	9	15. **Just A Little Too Much**/	
7/13/59	9	8	16. **Sweeter Than You**	Imperial 5595
12/07/59	20	8	17. I Wanna Be Loved/	
12/21/59	38	1	18. Mighty Good	Imperial 5614
5/09/60	12	9	19. Young Emotions	Imperial 5663
9/19/60	27	4	20. I'm Not Afraid/	
9/26/60	34	2	21. Yes Sir, That's My Baby	Imperial 5685
1/09/61	25	4	22. You Are The Only One	Imperial 5707
5/01/61	1 (2)	15	● 23. **Travelin' Man**/	
5/08/61	9	13	24. **Hello Mary Lou**	Imperial 5741
10/09/61	11	9	25. A Wonder Like You/	
10/09/61	16	8	26. **Everlovin'**	Imperial 5770
3/17/62	5	10	27. **Young World**	Imperial 5805
8/25/62	5	9	28. **Teen Age Idol**	Imperial 5864
12/29/62	6	9	29. **It's Up To You**	Imperial 5901
6/15/63	25	5	30. String Along	Decca 31495
10/05/63	12	9	31. Fools Rush In	Decca 31533
1/11/64	6	9	32. **For You**	Decca 31574
5/09/64	26	5	33. The Very Thought Of You	Decca 31612
1/03/70	33	6	34. She Belongs To Me	Decca 32550
9/16/72	6	12	● 35. **Garden Party**	Decca 32980
			NELSON, SANDY	
9/14/59	4	12	1. **Teen Beat [I]**	Original Sound 5
11/20/61	7	12	2. **Let There Be Drums [I]**	Imperial 5775
3/03/62	29	4	3. Drums Are My Beat [I]	Imperial 5809

DATE	POS	WKS	ARTIST—Record Title	LABEL & NO.
			NELSON, WILLIE	
			also see Waylon & Willie	
10/11/75	**21**	9	1. Blue Eyes Crying In The Rain	Columbia 10176
9/27/80	**20**	10	2. On The Road Again	Columbia 11351
			-from film "Honeysuckle Rose"-	
4/10/82	**5**	15	3. **Always On My Mind**	Columbia 02741
9/18/82	**40**	3	4. Let It Be Me	Columbia 03073
			NEON PHILHARMONIC	
5/10/69	**17**	7	1. Morning Girl	Warner 7261
			NERO, PETER	
11/20/71	**21**	8	1. Theme From "Summer Of '42" [I]	Columbia 45399
			NERVOUS NORVUS	
			real name: Jimmy Drake	
6/09/56	**8**	9	1. **Transfusion [N]**	Dot 15470
8/11/56	**24**	4	2. Ape Call [N]	Dot 15485
			-ape calls: Red Blanchard-	
			NESMITH, MICHAEL, & The First National Band	
			member of The Monkees	
9/05/70	**21**	7	1. Joanne	RCA 0368
			NEVILLE, AARON	
12/17/66	**2** (1)	11	1. **Tell It Like It Is**	Par-Lo 101
			NEWBEATS	
			Larry Henley, lead singer, with Dean & Marc Mathis	
8/22/64	**2** (2)	11	1. **Bread And Butter**	Hickory 1269
11/07/64	**16**	7	2. Everything's Alright	Hickory 1282
2/20/65	**40**	1	3. Break Away (From That Boy)	Hickory 1290
10/30/65	**12**	9	4. Run, Baby Run (Back Into My Arms)	Hickory 1332
			NEW BIRTH	
5/05/73	**35**	4	1. I Can Understand It	RCA 0912
8/23/75	**36**	2	2. Dream Merchant	Buddah 470
			NEW CHRISTY MINSTRELS	
			Randy Sparks, founder -- Kenny Rogers & Barry McGuire were members	
7/27/63	**14**	7	1. Green, Green	Columbia 42805
11/16/63	**29**	3	2. Saturday Night	Columbia 42887
5/16/64	**17**	9	3. Today	Columbia 43000
			-from film "Advance To The Rear"-	
			NEW COLONY SIX	
5/11/68	**22**	6	1. I Will Always Think About You	Mercury 72775
2/15/69	**16**	9	2. Things I'd Like To Say	Mercury 72858
			NEW ENGLAND	
6/16/79	**40**	1	1. Don't Ever Wanna Lose Ya	Infinity 50013
			NEW SEEKERS	
			group formed by Keith Potger as a spin-off of The Seekers	
9/19/70	**14**	9	1. Look What They've Done To My Song Ma	Elektra 45699
12/18/71	**7**	9	● 2. **I'd Like To Teach The World To Sing (In Perfect Harmony)**	Elektra 45762

DATE	POS	WKS	ARTIST—Record Title	LABEL & NO.
4/14/73	29	4	3. Pinball Wizard/See Me, Feel Me -from the rock opera "Tommy"-	Verve 10709
			NEW VAUDEVILLE BAND English - Geoff Stevens, leader	
11/05/66	1 (3)	13	● 1. **Winchester Cathedral**	Fontana 1562
			NEW YORK CITY	
4/28/73	17	12	1. I'm Doin' Fine Now	Chelsea 0113
			NEWBURY, MICKEY	
12/04/71	26	7	1. An American Trilogy	Elektra 45750
			NEWMAN, JIMMY	
7/22/57	23	1	1. A Fallen Star	Dot 15574
			NEWMAN, RANDY nephew of composers Alfred, Emil, & Lionel Newman	
12/10/77	2 (3)	13	● 1. **Short People [N]**	Warner 8492
			NEWTON, JUICE	
3/07/81	4	16	● 1. **Angel Of The Morning**	Capitol 4976
6/20/81	2 (2)	19	● 2. **Queen Of Hearts**	Capitol 4997
11/07/81	7	18	3. **The Sweetest Thing (I've Ever Known)**	Capitol 5046
5/22/82	7	13	4. **Love's Been A Little Bit Hard On Me**	Capitol 5120
9/11/82	11	10	5. Break It To Me Gently	Capitol 5148
			NEWTON, WAYNE Las Vegas's #1 entertainer	
8/03/63	13	8	1. Danke Schoen	Capitol 4989
3/27/65	23	5	2. Red Roses For A Blue Lady	Capitol 5366
6/10/72	4	13	● 3. **Daddy Don't You Walk So Fast**	Chelsea 0100
3/22/80	35	3	4. Years	Aries II 108
			NEWTON-JOHN, OLIVIA English/Australian -- also see John Denver	
7/17/71	25	10	1. If Not For You	Uni 55281
12/15/73	6	14	● 2. **Let Me Be There**	MCA 40101
5/11/74	5	12	● 3. **If You Love Me (Let Me Know)**	MCA 40209
8/24/74	1 (2)	10	● 4. **I Honestly Love You**	MCA 40280
2/08/75	1 (1)	11	● 5. **Have You Never Been Mellow**	MCA 40349
6/21/75	3	12	● 6. **Please Mr. Please**	MCA 40418
10/11/75	13	7	7. Something Better To Do	MCA 40459
1/03/76	30	4	8. Let It Shine	MCA 40495
4/17/76	23	6	9. Come On Over	MCA 40525
9/04/76	33	4	10. Don't Stop Believin'	MCA 40600
2/19/77	20	9	11. Sam	MCA 40670
7/22/78	3	15	● 12. **Hopelessly Devoted To You** -from the film "Grease"-	RSO 903
12/09/78	3	17	● 13. **A Little More Love**	MCA 40975
5/05/79	11	8	14. Deeper Than The Night	MCA 41009
6/14/80	1 (4)	16	● 15. **Magic** -from the film "Xanadu"-	MCA 41247
10/17/81	1(10)	21	★ 16. **Physical**	MCA 51182
2/27/82	5	10	17. Make A Move On Me	MCA 52000

DATE	POS	WKS	ARTIST—Record Title	LABEL & NO.
9/25/82	3	13	18. Heart Attack	MCA 52100
			NEWTON-JOHN, OLIVIA/ELECTRIC LIGHT ORCHESTRA	
8/30/80	8	10	1. Xanadu	MCA 41285
			NEWTON-JOHN, OLIVIA, & ANDY GIBB	
4/19/80	12	8	1. I Can't Help It	RSO 1026
			NEWTON-JOHN, OLIVIA, & CLIFF RICHARD	
11/22/80	20	11	1. Suddenly -from the film "Xanadu"-	MCA 51007
			NEWTON-JOHN, OLIVIA, & JOHN TRAVOLTA	
4/08/78	1 (1)	16	★ 1. You're The One That I Want	RSO 891
8/19/78	5	12	● 2. Summer Nights -above titles from film "Grease"-	RSO 906
			NICHOLAS, PAUL	
			English	
9/17/77	6	15	● 1. Heaven On The 7th Floor	RSO 878
			NICKS, STEVIE	
			lead singer of Fleetwood Mac	
8/01/81	3	15	1. Stop Draggin' My Heart Around -with Tom Petty & Heartbreakers-	Modern Rec. 7336
11/07/81	6	15	2. Leather And Lace -with Don Henley of The Eagles-	Modern Rec. 7341
3/06/82	11	11	3. Edge Of Seventeen (Just Like The White Winged Dove)	Modern Rec. 7401
6/12/82	32	4	4. After The Glitter Fades	Modern Rec. 7405
			NIELSEN/PEARSON	
			Reid Nielsen/Mark Pearson	
11/15/80	38	2	1. If You Should Sail	Capitol 4910
			NIGHT	
			Stevie Lange & Chris Thompson lead singers -- also see Chris Thompson	
8/04/79	18	8	1. Hot Summer Nights	Planet 45903
			NIGHTINGALE, MAXINE	
			English	
3/13/76	2 (2)	15	● 1. Right Back Where We Started From	United Artists 752
7/07/79	5	14	● 2. Lead Me On	Windsong 11530
			NILSSON	
			Harry Nilsson	
9/06/69	6	9	1. Everybody's Talkin' -from the film "Midnight Cowboy"-	RCA 0161
11/29/69	34	2	2. I Guess The Lord Must Be In New York City	RCA 0261
5/08/71	34	4	3. Me And My Arrow	RCA 0443
1/15/72	1 (4)	14	● 4. Without You	RCA 0604
4/08/72	27	6	5. Jump Into The Fire	RCA 0673
7/08/72	8	10	6. Coconut	RCA 0718
10/14/72	23	6	7. Spaceman	RCA 0788
5/25/74	39	2	8. Daybreak -from the film "Son Of Dracula"-	RCA 0246

DATE	POS	WKS	ARTIST—Record Title	LABEL & NO.
			1910 FRUITGUM CO.	
			studio group produced by Jerry Kasenetz and Jeff Katz	
2/10/68	4	11	● 1. **Simon Says**	Buddah 24
8/10/68	5	11	● 2. **1, 2, 3, Red Light**	Buddah 54
12/07/68	37	3	3. Goody Goody Gumdrops	Buddah 71
2/08/69	5	11	● 4. **Indian Giver**	Buddah 91
6/14/69	38	2	5. Special Delivery	Buddah 114
			NITE-LITERS	
9/11/71	39	1	1. K-Jee [I]	RCA 0461
			NITEFLYTE	
11/24/79	37	2	1. If You Want It	Ariola 7747
			NITTY GRITTY DIRT BAND	
			Jeff Hanna, lead singer	
1/02/71	9	13	1. **Mr. Bojangles** -prologue: Uncle Charlie & his dog Teddy-DIRT BAND:	Liberty 56197
1/12/80	13	11	2. An American Dream -harmony vocal: Linda Ronstadt-	United Artists 1330
7/12/80	25	9	3. Make A Little Magic	United Artists 1356
			NITZSCHE, JACK	
9/07/63	39	2	1. The Lonely Surfer [I]	Reprise 20202
			NOBLE, NICK	
8/20/55	22	3	1. The Bible Tells Me So	Wing 90003
3/24/56	27	6	2. To You, My Love	Mercury 70821
7/15/57	20	1	3. A Fallen Star	Mercury 71124
9/30/57	37	1	4. Moonlight Swim	Mercury 71169
			NOBLES, CLIFF, & Co.	
6/08/68	2 (3)	12	● 1. **The Horse [I]**	Phil-L.A. Soul 313
			NOGUEZ, JACKY, & His Orchestra	
			French	
7/27/59	24	5	1. Ciao, Ciao Bambina [I]	Jamie 1127
			NOLAN, KENNY	
12/11/76	3	20	● 1. **I Like Dreamin'**	20th Century 2287
5/07/77	20	11	2. Love's Grown Deep	20th Century 2331
			NORMAN, CHRIS - see SUZI QUATRO	
			NORTH, FREDDIE	
11/27/71	39	1	1. She's All I Got	Mankind 12004
			NOVA, ALDO	
			from Montreal, Canada	
5/01/82	23	7	1. Fantasy	Portrait 02799
			NU TORNADOS	
12/15/58	26	6	1. Philadelphia U.S.A	Carlton 492
			NUGENT, TED	
			leader of The Amboy Dukes	
9/10/77	30	6	1. Cat Scratch Fever	Epic 50425
			NUMAN, GARY	
			British	
3/29/80	9	17	1. **Cars**	Atco 7211

Bette Midler. Two versions of "You're Movin' Out Today" missed *Billboard's* Top 40 in 1977, both by co-writers of the song, Midler and Carole Bayer Sager. In Britain, however, the latter took the tune into the top 10.

Roger Miller is among a small group of acts who have won five Grammy awards in a single year. That was in 1965, and he was "King Of The Road."

The Miracles' first recording was an answer disc to the Silhouettes' No. 1, "Get A Job." The recording was leased to End Records, which paid out $3.19 in royalties, so Berry Gordy decided to start his own record company.

Guy Mitchell. Among Guy Mitchell's hits was a song "The Roving Kind" that started life as an old British sea shanty, "The Pirate Ship." Publisher Howie Richmond came across the original lyrics while reading Sinclair Lewis' novel, *Arrowsmith.*

The Monkees. More than $100,000 was spent to launch the Monkees in 1966, twice the amount expended on behalf of the Beatles in America a couple of years before.

Jane Morgan's sole chart-topper, "Fascination," was based on a turn-of-the-century tune, "Valse Tzigane" by F. D. Marchetti. She subsequently married music business biggie Jerry Weintraub, manager of John Denver, Frank Sinatra, and the Moody Blues.

Rick Nelson was one of a handful of solo stars who specialized in double-sided hits during rock's first decade. He placed both sides of 11 records in the top 40, second only to Elvis, who placed both sides of 25 records.

Juice Newton's first top 10 entry, "Angel Of The Morning," was previously the sole hit of Merrilee Rush's recording career, in 1968. The sensitive song was written by Chip Taylor, also author of "Wild Thing." Chip cut "Angel" himself in 1972.

Olivia Newton-John. In her pre-top 40 days, Olivia Newton-John briefly belonged to Toomorrow (*sic*), the carefully-manufactured creation of entrepreneur Don Kirschner (the Monkees, the Archies). Both Donny and Livvy would undoubtedly prefer to forget the experience.

Roy Orbison's early recordings were made in the New Mexico studio of Buddy Holly's producer, Norman Petty, years before his first successful song ("Claudette," waxed by the Everly Brothers) and first top 40 hit ("Only The Lonely").

The Orlons. Remember the Orlons? Short song titles—no time to waste: "Wah-Watusi," "South Street," "Not Me," "Crossfire!" "Bon-Doo-Wah," "Knock, Knock," and "Shimmy Shimmy."

Buck Owens. Millions of record buyers worldwide had never heard of Buck Owens when they put a version of one of his best-known hits ("Act Naturally") into their collections. The Beatles cut it as the flip of "Yesterday."

DATE	POS	WKS	ARTIST—Record Title	LABEL & NO.
			NUTTY SQUIRRELS	
			creators: Don Elliot & Sascha Burland	
11/30/59	14	7	1. Uh! Oh! Part 2 [N]	Hanover 4540
			OAK	
7/12/80	36	3	1. King Of The Hill	Mercury 76049
			-shown as Rick Pinette & Oak-	
			OAK RIDGE BOYS	
6/06/81	5	14	★ 1. **Elvira**	MCA 51084
2/13/82	12	9	2. Bobbie Sue	MCA 51231
			O'BANION, JOHN	
4/18/81	24	7	1. Love You Like I Never Loved Before	Elektra 47125
			OCEAN	
			Canadian	
3/27/71	2 (1)	12	● 1. **Put Your Hand In The Hand**	Kama Sutra 519
			OCEAN, BILLY	
5/01/76	22	6	1. Love Really Hurts Without You	Ariola 7621
			O'DAY, ALAN	
5/07/77	1 (1)	17	● 1. **Undercover Angel**	Pacific 001
			O'DELL, KENNY	
12/16/67	38	2	1. Beautiful People	Vegas 718
			ODYSSEY	
12/17/77	21	12	1. Native New Yorker	RCA 11129
			OHIO EXPRESS	
			studio group formed by producers Jerry Kasenetz and Jeff Katz	
11/18/67	29	5	1. Beg, Borrow And Steal	Cameo 483
5/18/68	4	11	● 2. **Yummy Yummy Yummy**	Buddah 38
8/31/68	33	5	3. Down At Lulu's	Buddah 56
11/02/68	15	10	● 4. **Chewy Chewy**	Buddah 70
4/26/69	30	4	5. Mercy	Buddah 102
			OHIO PLAYERS	
			originally known as the Ohio Untouchables	
4/14/73	15	9	● 1. Funky Worm [N]	Westbound 214
9/22/73	31	6	2. Ecstasy	Westbound 216
9/14/74	13	7	● 3. Skin Tight	Mercury 73609
12/28/74	1 (1)	12	● 4. **Fire**	Mercury 73643
10/11/75	33	3	5. Sweet Sticky Thing	Mercury 73713
11/22/75	1 (1)	14	● 6. **Love Rollercoaster**	Mercury 73734
3/27/76	30	5	7. Fopp	Mercury 73775
7/31/76	18	10	8. Who'd She Coo?	Mercury 73814
			O'JAYS	
			Eddie Levert, Walt Williams, William Powell (died 5/26/77) - replaced by Sam Strain	
8/12/72	3	12	● 1. **Back Stabbers**	Phil. Int'l. 3517
1/27/73	1 (1)	13	● 2. **Love Train**	Phil. Int'l. 3524
6/30/73	33	2	3. Time To Get Down	Phil. Int'l. 3531
1/12/74	10	11	4. **Put Your Hands Together**	Phil. Int'l. 3535
5/04/74	9	10	● 5. **For The Love Of Money**	Phil. Int'l. 3544

DATE	POS	WKS	ARTIST—Record Title	LABEL & NO.
11/15/75	5	14	● 6. **I Love Music (Part 1)**	Phil. Int'l. 3577
3/27/76	20	6	7. Livin' For The Weekend	Phil. Int'l. 3587
6/03/78	4	11	● 8. **Use Ta Be My Girl**	Phil. Int'l. 3642
1/05/80	28	5	9. Forever Mine	Phil. Int'l. 3727
			O'KAYSIONS	
			Donny Weaver, lead singer	
9/07/68	5	11	● 1. **Girl Watcher**	ABC 11094
			O'KEEFE, DANNY	
9/23/72	9	10	1. **Good Time Charlie's Got The Blues**	Signpost 70006
			OLDFIELD, MIKE	
			English	
3/30/74	7	10	1. **Tubular Bells [I]** -theme from film "The Exorcist"-	Virgin 55100
			OLIVER	
			William Oliver Swofford	
6/07/69	3	11	1. **Good Morning Starshine** -from Broadway musical "Hair"-	Jubilee 5659
8/30/69	2 (2)	12	● 2. **Jean** -from "The Prime Of Miss Jean Brodie"-	Crewe 334
12/20/69	35	2	3. Sunday Mornin'	Crewe 337
			OLSSON, NIGEL	
			Elton John's drummer '71-'76	
1/27/79	18	9	1. Dancin' Shoes	Bang 740
5/19/79	34	4	2. Little Bit Of Soap	Bang 4800
			OLYMPICS	
			Walter Ward, founder & leader	
8/04/58	8	11	1. **Western Movies [N]**	Demon 1508
6/08/63	40	2	2. The Bounce	Tri Disc 106
			100 PROOF Aged In Soul	
10/03/70	8	10	● 1. **Somebody's Been Sleeping**	Hot Wax 7004
			ORBISON, ROY	
6/20/60	2 (1)	15	1. **Only The Lonely (Know How I Feel)**	Monument 421
10/17/60	9	8	2. **Blue Angel**	Monument 425
12/31/60	27	3	3. I'm Hurtin'	Monument 433
4/24/61	1 (1)	15	4. **Running Scared**	Monument 438
8/28/61	2 (1)	14	5. **Crying**/	
10/09/61	25	5	6. Candy Man	Monument 447
3/03/62	4	9	7. **Dream Baby (How Long Must I Dream)**	Monument 456
6/23/62	26	6	8. The Crowd	Monument 461
10/27/62	25	5	9. Leah/	
10/27/62	33	4	10. Workin' For The Man	Monument 467
2/23/63	7	10	11. **In Dreams**	Monument 806
6/22/63	22	5	12. Falling	Monument 815
9/28/63	5	10	13. **Mean Woman Blues**/	
10/12/63	29	5	14. Blue Bayou	Monument 824
12/21/63	15	5	15. Pretty Paper [X]	Monument 830
4/25/64	9	9	16. **It's Over**	Monument 837

DATE	POS	WKS	ARTIST—Record Title	LABEL & NO.
9/05/64	**1** (3)	14	● 17. **Oh, Pretty Woman** -with The Candymen-	Monument 851
2/20/65	**21**	6	18. Goodnight	Monument 873
8/07/65	**39**	2	19. (Say) You're My Girl	Monument 891
9/18/65	**25**	5	20. Ride Away	MGM 13386
2/12/66	**31**	4	21. Breakin' Up Is Breakin' My Heart	MGM 13446
5/21/66	**39**	2	22. Twinkle Toes	MGM 13498
			ORIGINAL CASTE	
2/07/70	**34**	2	1. One Tin Soldier -from film "Billy Jack"-	T-A 186
			ORIGINALS	
10/18/69	**14**	13	1. Baby, I'm For Real	Soul 35066
3/07/70	**12**	9	2. The Bells	Soul 35069
			ORLANDO, TONY also see Dawn, and Wind	
5/29/61	**39**	2	1. Halfway To Paradise	Epic 9441
9/04/61	**15**	7	2. Bless You	Epic 9452
			ORLEANS John Hall, founder	
8/30/75	**6**	11	1. **Dance With Me**	Asylum 45261
8/14/76	**5**	12	2. **Still The One**	Asylum 45336
4/07/79	**11**	9	3. Love Takes Time	Infinity 50006
			ORLONS Philadelphia quartet - Shirley Brickley, lead singer	
6/23/62	**2** (2)	11	1. **The Wah Watusi**	Cameo 218
11/03/62	**4**	11	2. **Don't Hang Up**	Cameo 231
3/02/63	**3**	10	3. **South Street**	Cameo 243
7/06/63	**12**	7	4. Not Me	Cameo 257
10/19/63	**19**	5	5. Cross Fire!	Cameo 273
			OSBORNE, JEFFREY lead singer of L.T.D.	
8/14/82	**39**	2	1. I Really Don't Need No Light	A&M 2410
11/20/82	**29**	6	2. On The Wings Of Love	A&M 2434
			OSMOND, DONNY first charted hit was at age 13	
5/01/71	**7**	11	● 1. **Sweet And Innocent**	MGM 14227
8/21/71	**1** (3)	13	● 2. **Go Away Little Girl**	MGM 14285
12/04/71	**9**	9	● 3. **Hey Girl**	MGM 14322
3/04/72	**3**	10	● 4. **Puppy Love**	MGM 14367
6/17/72	**13**	8	5. Too Young	MGM 14407
9/16/72	**13**	9	6. Why/	
		9	7. **Lonely Boy**	MGM 14424
3/24/73	**8**	9	● 8. **The Twelfth Of Never**	MGM 14503
8/04/73	**23**	7	9. A Million To One/	
		7	10. **Young Love**	MGM 14583
12/15/73	**14**	8	11. Are You Lonesome Tonight	MGM 14677
7/24/76	**38**	3	12. C'mon Marianne	Polydor 14320

DATE	POS	WKS	ARTIST—Record Title	LABEL & NO.
			OSMOND, DONNY & MARIE	
7/27/74	4	10	● 1. **I'm Leaving It (All) Up To You**	MGM 14735
12/14/74	8	10	2. **Morning Side Of The Mountain**	MGM 14765
1/24/76	14	13	3. Deep Purple	MGM 14840
12/25/76	21	8	4. Ain't Nothing Like The Real Thing	Polydor 14363
1/07/78	38	3	5. (You're My) Soul And Inspiration	Polydor 14439
11/18/78	38	2	6. On The Shelf	Polydor 14510
			OSMOND, LITTLE JIMMY	
6/03/72	38	3	1. Long Haired Lover From Liverpool	MGM 14376
			OSMOND, MARIE	
10/06/73	5	12	● 1. **Paper Roses**	MGM 14609
4/05/75	40	2	2. Who's Sorry Now	MGM 14786
6/04/77	39	1	3. This Is The Way That I Feel	Polydor 14385
			OSMONDS	
			Alan, Donny, Jay, Merrill and Wayne	
1/23/71	1 (5)	12	● 1. **One Bad Apple**	MGM 14193
5/29/71	14	7	2. Double Lovin'	MGM 14259
9/18/71	3	12	● 3. **Yo-Yo**	MGM 14295
1/29/72	4	12	● 4. **Down By The Lazy River**	MGM 14324
7/08/72	14	6	5. Hold Her Tight	MGM 14405
11/11/72	14	8	6. Crazy Horses	MGM 14450
7/07/73	36	2	7. Goin' Home	MGM 14562
10/06/73	36	3	8. Let Me In	MGM 14617
9/21/74	10	7	9. **Love Me For A Reason**	MGM 14746
8/23/75	22	6	10. The Proud One	MGM 14791
			O'SULLIVAN, GILBERT	
			Irish	
7/01/72	1 (6)	15	● 1. **Alone Again (Naturally)**	MAM 3619
11/11/72	2 (2)	14	● 2. **Clair**	MAM 3626
4/07/73	17	8	3. Out Of The Question	MAM 3628
7/14/73	7	11	● 4. **Get Down**	MAM 3629
11/10/73	25	4	5. Ooh Baby	MAM 3633
			OTIS & CARLA	
			Otis Redding & Carla Thomas	
6/03/67	26	4	1. Tramp	Stax 216
9/23/67	30	2	2. Knock On Wood	Stax 228
			OTIS, JOHNNY, Show	
			Johnny's R&B Caravan featured the top R&B artists of the '50's	
6/30/58	9	15	1. **Willie And The Hand Jive**	Capitol 3966
			OUTLAWS	
			Florida country-rock band - Henry Paul, member	
10/11/75	34	3	1. There Goes Another Love Song	Arista 0150
2/14/81	31	4	2. (Ghost) Riders In The Sky	Arista 0582
			OUTSIDERS	
			Cleveland quintet - Sonny Geraci, lead singer	
3/26/66	5	10	1. **Time Won't Let Me**	Capitol 5573
6/04/66	21	5	2. Girl In Love	Capitol 5646

DATE	POS	WKS	ARTIST—Record Title	LABEL & NO.
8/20/66	15	6	3. Respectable	Capitol 5701
12/10/66	37	2	4. Help Me Girl	Capitol 5759
			OWEN, REG, & His Orchestra	
12/22/58	10	13	1. **Manhattan Spiritual [I]**	Palette 5005
			OWENS, BUCK, & His Buckaroos	
			from 1963-1972, Buck had 25 consecutive Top 10 hits on the Country charts	
2/13/65	25	5	1. I've Got A Tiger By The Tail	Capitol 5336
			OWENS, DONNIE	
11/03/58	25	8	1. Need You	Guyden 2001
			OZARK MOUNTAIN DAREDEVILS	
			country-rock group from Springfield, Missouri	
6/08/74	25	5	1. If You Wanna Get To Heaven	A&M 1515
3/22/75	3	12	2. **Jackie Blue**	A&M 1654
			PABLO CRUISE	
			rock quartet from San Francisco	
6/11/77	6	14	1. **Whatcha Gonna Do?**	A&M 1920
7/01/78	6	12	2. **Love Will Find A Way**	A&M 2048
10/21/78	21	8	3. Don't Want To Live Without It	A&M 2076
11/10/79	19	10	4. I Want You Tonight	A&M 2195
7/25/81	13	11	5. Cool Love	A&M 2349
			PACIFIC GAS & ELECTRIC	
			West Coast quintet	
6/20/70	14	9	1. Are You Ready?	Columbia 45158
			PAGE, PATTI	
12/18/54	8	7	1. **Let Me Go, Lover!**	Mercury 70511
11/12/55	16	8	2. Croce Di Oro (Cross Of Gold)	Mercury 70713
1/14/56	11	8	3. Go On With The Wedding	Mercury 70766
6/16/56	2 (1)	22	4. **Allegheny Moon**	Mercury 70878
11/03/56	11	12	5. Mama From The Train	Mercury 70971
3/23/57	14	6	6. A Poor Man's Roses (Or A Rich Man's Gold)	Mercury 71059
6/03/57	3	17	7. **Old Cape Cod/**	
6/03/57	12	5	8. Wondering	Mercury 71101
11/11/57	23	3	9. I'll Remember Today	Mercury 71189
2/10/58	13	8	10. Belonging To Someone	Mercury 71247
5/05/58	20	1	11. Another Time, Another Place	Mercury 71294
6/30/58	9	10	12. **Left Right Out Of Your Heart**	Mercury 71331
10/20/58	39	1	13. Fibbin'	Mercury 71355
7/04/60	31	5	14. One Of Us (Will Weep Tonight)	Mercury 71639
5/12/62	27	4	15. Most People Get Married	Mercury 71950
5/22/65	8	9	16. **Hush, Hush, Sweet Charlotte**	Columbia 43251
			PALMER, ROBERT	
			British	
5/06/78	16	9	1. Every Kinda People	Island 100
8/11/79	14	10	2. Bad Case Of Loving You (Doctor, Doctor)	Island 49016

DATE	POS	WKS	ARTIST—Record Title	LABEL & NO.
			PAPER LACE	
			English quintet	
7/13/74	**1** (1)	11	● 1. **The Night Chicago Died**	Mercury 73492
			PARADE	
5/06/67	**20**	5	1. Sunshine Girl	A&M 841
			PARADONS	
9/26/60	**18**	7	1. Diamonds And Pearls	Milestone 2003
			PARIS SISTERS	
			Albeth, Priscilla & Sherrell	
10/02/61	**5**	11	1. **I Love How You Love Me**	Gregmark 6
3/03/62	**34**	3	2. He Knows I Love Him Too Much	Gregmark 10
			PARKER, FESS	
			starred in movie "Davy Crockett" and TV's "Daniel Boone"	
3/12/55	**5**	17	1. **Ballad Of Davy Crockett**	Columbia 40449
2/09/57	**12**	6	2. Wringle Wrangle	Disneyland 43
			-from "Westward Ho, The Wagons"-	
			PARKER, RAY, JR.	
			leader of Raydio	
4/10/82	**4**	14	1. **The Other Woman**	Arista 0669
8/21/82	**38**	3	2. Let Me Go	Arista 0695
			PARKER, RAY, JR., & RAYDIO	
2/11/78	**8**	16	● 1. **Jack And Jill**	Arista 0283
6/09/79	**9**	14	2. **You Can't Change That**	Arista 0399
			-above 2 shown only as Raydio-	
6/07/80	**30**	5	3. Two Places At The Same Time	Arista 0494
4/25/81	**4**	15	4. **A Woman Needs Love (Just Like You Do)**	Arista 0592
8/08/81	**21**	6	5. That Old Song	Arista 0616
			PARKER, ROBERT	
5/21/66	**7**	9	1. **Barefootin'**	Nola 721
			PARKS, MICHAEL	
			star of TV series "Then Came Bronson"	
3/28/70	**20**	8	1. Long Lonesome Highway	MGM 14104
			PARLIAMENT	
6/12/76	**15**	10	● 1. Tear The Roof Off The Sucker (Give Up The Funk)	Casablanca 856
2/25/78	**16**	12	● 2. Flash Light	Casablanca 909
			PARLIAMENTS	
			George Clinton's original group - later evolved into Parliament and Funkadelic	
8/05/67	**20**	7	1. (I Wanna) Testify	Revilot 207
			PARSONS, ALAN, Project	
			studio group headed by Parsons & Eric Woolfson	
9/11/76	**37**	2	1. (The System Of) Doctor Tarr And Professor Fether	20th Century 2297
9/24/77	**36**	3	2. I Wouldn't Want To Be Like You	Arista 0260
11/17/79	**27**	8	3. Damned If I Do	Arista 0454
1/24/81	**16**	10	4. Games People Play	Arista 0573
6/06/81	**15**	12	5. Time	Arista 0598
7/31/82	**3**	17	6. **Eye In The Sky**	Arista 0696

DATE	POS	WKS	ARTIST—Record Title	LABEL & NO.
			PARSONS, BILL	
12/28/58	2 (1)	13	1. **The All American Boy** [N] -Bobby Bare is the real vocalist on this song (label error listed Parsons as the artist)-	Fraternity 835
			PARTON, DOLLY	
11/12/77	3	13	● 1. **Here You Come Again**	RCA 11123
4/08/78	19	8	2. Two Doors Down	RCA 11240
9/23/78	37	4	3. Heartbreaker	RCA 11296
1/13/79	25	7	4. Baby I'm Burnin'	RCA 11420
5/03/80	36	3	5. Starting Over Again	RCA 11926
12/20/80	1 (2)	18	● 6. **9 To 5**	RCA 12133
			PARTRIDGE FAMILY	
			David Cassidy, lead singer; with stepmother Shirley Jones	
10/31/70	1 (3)	16	● 1. **I Think I Love You**	Bell 910
·2/20/71	6	11	● 2. **Doesn't Somebody Want To Be Wanted**	Bell 963
5/15/71	9	8	3. **I'll Meet You Halfway**	Bell 996
8/21/71	13	10	4. I Woke Up In Love This Morning	Bell 45130
1/01/72	20	6	5. It's One Of Those Nights (Yes Love)	Bell 45160
7/29/72	28	4	6. Breaking Up Is Hard To Do	Bell 45235
1/27/73	39	2	7. Looking Through The Eyes Of Love	Bell 45301
			PASTEL SIX	
1/19/63	25	5	1. The Cinnamon Cinder (It's A Very Nice Dance)	Zen 102
			PASTELS	
			Big Dee Irwin, lead singer	
3/03/58	24	3	1. Been So Long	Argo 5287
			PATIENCE & PRUDENCE	
			McIntyre sisters - ages 11 & 14	
8/25/56	4	17	1. **Tonight You Belong To Me**	Liberty 55022
12/01/56	11	12	2. Gonna Get Along Without Ya Now	Liberty 55040
			PATTON, ROBBIE	
8/01/81	26	6	1. Don't Give It Up	Liberty 1420
			PATTY & THE EMBLEMS	
8/15/64	37	3	1. Mixed-Up, Shook-Up, Girl	Herald 590
			PAUL & PAULA	
			Ray Hildebrand & Jill Jackson	
1/12/63	1 (3)	12	● 1. **Hey Paula**	Philips 40084
3/23/63	6	8	2. **Young Lovers**	Philips 40096
6/22/63	27	4	3. First Quarrel	Philips 40114
			PAUL, BILLY	
11/18/72	1 (3)	14	● 1. **Me And Mrs. Jones**	Phil. Int'l. 3521
4/20/74	37	3	2. Thanks For Saving My Life	Phil. Int'l. 3538
			PAUL, LES, & MARY FORD	
			husband & wife (separated May, 1963)- Mary died on 9/30/77 (53)	
7/09/55	7	13	1. **Hummingbird**	Capitol 3165
11/12/55	38	2	2. Amukiriki (The Lord Willing)	Capitol 3248
2/23/57	35	2	3. Cinco Robles	Capitol 3612
9/08/58	32	4	4. Put A Ring On My Finger	Columbia 41222

DATE	POS	WKS	ARTIST—Record Title	LABEL & NO.
7/03/61	37	1	5. Jura (I Swear I Love You)	Columbia 41994
			PAVONE, RITA	
7/04/64	26	4	1. Remember Me	RCA 8365
			PAYNE, FREDA	
5/30/70	3	15	● 1. **Band Of Gold**	Invictus 9075
10/10/70	24	8	2. Deeper & Deeper	Invictus 9080
6/26/71	12	10	● 3. Bring The Boys Home	Invictus 9092
			PEACHES & HERB	
			Francine Barker (replaced by Linda Greene in '79) & Herb Fame	
2/25/67	21	6	1. Let's Fall In Love	Date 1523
4/15/67	8	9	2. **Close Your Eyes**	Date 1549
7/08/67	20	5	3. For Your Love	Date 1563
10/14/67	13	7	4. Love Is Strange	Date 1574
1/13/68	31	3	5. Two Little Kids	Date 1586
1/27/79	5	13	● 6. **Shake Your Groove Thing**	Polydor 14514
3/31/79	1 (4)	15	★ 7. **Reunited**	Polydor 14547
3/15/80	19	8	8. I Pledge My Love	Polydor 2053
			PEARL, LESLIE	
7/10/82	28	7	1. If The Love Fits Wear It	RCA 13235
			PEEBLES, ANN	
12/22/73	38	1	1. I Can't Stand The Rain	Hi 2248
			PENDERGRASS, TEDDY	
			lead singer of Harold Melvin & The Blue Notes -- also see Stephanie Mills	
8/12/78	25	6	● 1. Close The Door	Phil. Int'l. 3648
			PENGUINS	
			Los Angeles quartet	
12/25/54	8	15	1. **Earth Angel (Will You Be Mine)**	DooTone 348
			PEOPLE	
5/25/68	14	10	1. I Love You	Capitol 2078
			PEOPLE'S CHOICE	
9/04/71	38	2	1. I Likes To Do It [I]	Phil-L.A. Soul 349
9/13/75	11	11	● 2. Do It Any Way You Wanna [I]	TSOP 4769
			PEPPERMINT RAINBOW	
4/12/69	32	5	1. Will You Be Staying After Sunday	Decca 32410
			PERICOLI, EMILIO	
6/09/62	6	10	1. **Al Di La' [F]** -from film "Rome Adventure"-	Warner 5259
			PERKINS, CARL	
3/10/56	2 (4)	17	1. **Blue Suede Shoes**	Sun 234
			PERKINS, TONY	
			movie actor	
10/07/57	24	1	1. Moon-Light Swim	RCA 7020
			PERRY, STEVE - see KENNY LOGGINS	

DATE	POS	WKS	ARTIST—Record Title	LABEL & NO.
			PERSUADERS	
9/18/71	**15**	9	● 1. Thin Line Between Love & Hate	Atco 6822
12/08/73	**39**	3	2. Some Guys Have All The Luck	Atco 6943
			PETER & GORDON	
			English: Peter Asher & Gordon Waller	
5/16/64	**1** (1)	11	1. **A World Without Love**	Capitol 5175
7/11/64	**12**	6	2. Nobody I Know	Capitol 5211
10/24/64	**16**	6	3. I Don't Want To See You Again	Capitol 5272
1/23/65	**9**	9	4. **I Go To Pieces**	Capitol 5335
5/08/65	**14**	8	5. True Love Ways	Capitol 5406
7/24/65	**24**	5	6. To Know You Is To Love You	Capitol 5461
3/12/66	**14**	8	7. Woman	Capitol 5579
11/05/66	**6**	10	8. **Lady Godiva**	Capitol 5740
1/14/67	**15**	5	9. Knight In Rusty Armour	Capitol 5808
4/15/67	**31**	3	10. Sunday For Tea	Capitol 5864
			PETER, PAUL & MARY	
			Peter Yarrow, Paul Stookey, & Mary Travers	
6/09/62	**35**	2	1. Lemon Tree	Warner 5274
9/08/62	**10**	8	2. **If I Had A Hammer**	Warner 5296
3/30/63	**2** (1)	11	3. **Puff The Magic Dragon**	Warner 5348
7/13/63	**2** (1)	12	4. **Blowin' In The Wind**	Warner 5368
9/28/63	**9**	8	5. **Don't Think Twice, It's All Right**	Warner 5385
12/28/63	**35**	2	6. Stewball	Warner 5399
4/04/64	**33**	3	7. Tell It On The Mountain	Warner 5418
2/13/65	**30**	4	8. For Lovin' Me	Warner 5496
9/02/67	**9**	8	9. **I Dig Rock And Roll Music**	Warner 7067
12/23/67	**35**	2	10. Too Much Of Nothing	Warner 7092
5/17/69	**21**	7	11. Day Is Done	Warner 7279
11/08/69	**1** (1)	15	● 12. **Leaving On A Jet Plane**	Warner 7340
			PETERS, BERNADETTE	
			film comedienne	
5/10/80	**31**	5	1. Gee Whiz	MCA 41210
			PETERSEN, PAUL	
			Jeff Stone of TV's "Donna Reed Show"	
3/31/62	**19**	7	1. She Can't Find Her Keys	Colpix 620
12/15/62	**6**	10	2. **My Dad**	Colpix 663
			PETERSON, RAY	
6/15/59	**25**	7	1. The Wonder Of You	RCA 7513
6/27/60	**7**	11	2. **Tell Laura I Love Her**	RCA 7745
12/19/60	**9**	9	3. **Corinna, Corinna**	Dunes 2002
9/25/61	**29**	3	4. Missing You	Dunes 2006
			PETS	
6/09/58	**34**	1	1. Cha-Hua-Hua [I]	Arwin 109
			PETTY, TOM, & The HEARTBREAKERS	
			also see Stevie Nicks	
2/18/78	**40**	1	1. Breakdown	Shelter 62008
12/08/79	**10**	13	2. **Don't Do Me Like That**	Backstreet 41138

DATE	POS	WKS	ARTIST—Record Title	LABEL & NO.
2/09/80	**15**	10	3. Refugee	Backstreet 41169
5/16/81	**19**	7	4. The Waiting	Backstreet 51100
			PHILLIPS, JOHN	
			member of The Mamas & The Papas	
6/20/70	**32**	7	1. Mississippi	Dunhill 4236
			PHILLIPS, "LITTLE ESTHER"	
11/17/62	**8**	10	1. **Release Me**	Lenox 5555
9/20/75	**20**	9	2. What A Diff'rence A Day Makes	Kudu 925
			PHILLIPS, PHIL, with The Twilights	
7/20/59	**2** (2)	14	1. **Sea Of Love**	Mercury 71465
			PHOTOGLO, JIM	
5/31/80	**31**	4	1. We Were Meant To Be Lovers	20th Century 2446
			-shown only as Photoglo-	
5/30/81	**25**	7	2. Fool In Love With You	20th Century 2487
			PICKETT, BOBBY "BORIS", & The Crypt-Kickers	
9/15/62	**1** (2)	12	● 1. **Monster Mash [N]**	Garpax 44167
12/22/62	**30**	4	2. Monsters' Holiday [X-N]	Garpax 44171
6/30/73	**10**	12	3. **Monster Mash [N]**	Parrot 348
			-re-entry of 1962 hit-	
			PICKETT, WILSON	
8/14/65	**21**	6	1. In The Midnight Hour	Atlantic 2289
3/05/66	**13**	8	2. 634-5789 (Soulsville, U.S.A.)	Atlantic 2320
8/13/66	**6**	8	3. **Land Of 1000 Dances**	Atlantic 2348
12/10/66	**23**	6	4. Mustang Sally	Atlantic 2365
2/25/67	**29**	3	5. Everybody Needs Somebody To Love	Atlantic 2381
4/22/67	**32**	2	6. I Found A Love - Part 1	Atlantic 2394
8/26/67	**8**	9	7. **Funky Broadway**	Atlantic 2430
11/11/67	**22**	5	8. Stag-O-Lee	Atlantic 2448
5/11/68	**15**	6	9. She's Lookin' Good	Atlantic 2504
7/06/68	**24**	4	10. I'm A Midnight Mover	Atlantic 2528
1/04/69	**23**	6	11. Hey Jude	Atlantic 2591
5/23/70	**25**	9	12. Sugar Sugar	Atlantic 2722
10/24/70	**14**	9	13. Engine Number 9	Atlantic 2765
2/06/71	**17**	8	● 14. Don't Let The Green Grass Fool You	Atlantic 2781
5/15/71	**13**	9	● 15. Don't Knock My Love - Pt. 1	Atlantic 2797
1/15/72	**24**	8	16. Fire And Water	Atlantic 2852
			PIERCE, WEBB	
			Webb's first 20 releases hit the Top 10 on the Country charts	
8/31/59	**24**	7	1. I Ain't Never	Decca 30923
			PILOT	
			Scottish quartet	
5/10/75	**5**	12	● 1. **Magic**	EMI 3992
			PINK FLOYD	
			English: Dave Gilmour, Rick Wright, Roger Waters, and Nick Mason	
6/23/73	**13**	9	1. Money	Harvest 3609
2/09/80	**1** (4)	19	● 2. **Another Brick In The Wall (Part II)**	Columbia 11187

Peaches & Herb. During several of the 10 years that separated Peaches & Herb from the top 40, Herb worked as a policeman in Washington, D.C. "It was cool for a while," he remembers, "But I guess the novelty wore off."

Peter and Gordon. Peter Asher probably enjoyed his three years of hits as one-half of Peter and Gordon, but to play safe for his retirement, he's been managing and producing James Taylor and Linda Ronstadt.

Peter, Paul & Mary popularized the songs of Bob Dylan before his own public recognition, and for a time were managed by Albert Grossman, who also handled Dylan.

Gene Pitney. Though known for his own many hits, Gene Pitney also wrote successful songs for Roy Orbison ("Today's Teardrops"), Bobby Vee ("Rubber Ball"), Ricky Nelson ("Hello Mary Lou"), and the Crystals ("He's a Rebel").

The Platters. The impresario who guided the Platters' career, Buck Ram, was also involved in writing several of their biggest hits: "Only You," "The Great Pretender," and "Twilight Time".

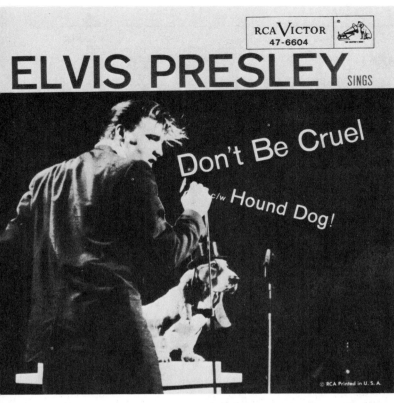

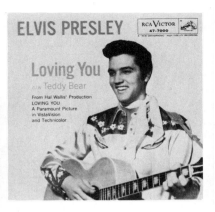

Elvis Presley, "I've got a young man and he's different," Sam Phillips told musician Scotty Moore after the Sun Records chief first heard the boy from Tupelo. "He's nervous and timid and extremely polite. Work with him and see what you can do."

Elvis Presley. Before "crossover" became fashionable in the music business, Elvis virtually defined the description with three records: "Don't Be Cruel," "Teddy Bear," and "Jailhouse Rock," all of which went to No. 1 on *Billboard's* pop, country, and r&b charts.

Elvis Presley. For Elvis Presley's 107 singles that made the top 40 a further 42 fell short — although they did place on *Billboard's* Hot 100. At least a dozen more also failed to reach the Hot 100, spending time instead between positions 101 and 121.

Johnny Preston's summit-seizing "Running Bear" was written and produced by the Big Bopper, J.P. Richardson, although it was released only after the latter's death in 1959. J.P. himself provided the graphic Indian imitations heard on the record.

Gary Puckett and the Union Gap. San Diego's Outcasts gave birth to the Union Gap, who sent vocalist Gary Puckett's name to the front after their first hit, "Woman Woman." Jerry Fuller, author of Ricky Nelson's "Travelin' Man" and "Young World" years before, was the group's producer.

DATE	POS	WKS	ARTIST—Record Title	LABEL & NO.
			PINK LADY	
			Japanese - Mie & Kei	
7/21/79	37	3	1. Kiss In The Dark	Elektra 46040
			PIPKINS	
			British - Tony Burrows, leader	
6/06/70	9	10	1. **Gimme Dat Ding [N]**	Capitol 2819
			PIPS - see GLADYS KNIGHT	
			PITNEY, GENE	
2/27/61	39	1	1. (I Wanna) Love My Life Away	Musicor 1002
12/18/61	13	10	2. Town Without Pity	Musicor 1009
5/19/62	4	8	3. **(The Man Who Shot) Liberty Valance**	Musicor 1020
9/29/62	2 (1)	11	4. **Only Love Can Break A Heart**	Musicor 1022
1/05/63	12	8	5. Half Heaven - Half Heartache	Musicor 1026
4/13/63	12	7	6. Mecca	Musicor 1028
8/03/63	21	6	7. True Love Never Runs Smooth	Musicor 1032
11/16/63	17	6	8. Twenty Four Hours From Tulsa	Musicor 1034
8/29/64	7	10	9. **It Hurts To Be In Love**	Musicor 1040
11/07/64	9	9	10. **I'm Gonna Be Strong**	Musicor 1045
3/20/65	31	4	11. I Must Be Seeing Things	Musicor 1070
5/22/65	13	7	12. Last Chance To Turn Around	Musicor 1093
8/21/65	28	4	13. Looking Through The Eyes Of Love	Musicor 1103
12/18/65	37	2	14. Princess In Rags	Musicor 1130
5/14/66	25	5	15. Backstage	Musicor 1171
6/15/68	16	8	16. She's A Heartbreaker	Musicor 1306
			PIXIES THREE	
10/05/63	40	1	1. Birthday Party	Mercury 72130
			PLASTIC ONO BAND - see JOHN LENNON	
			PLATT, EDDIE, & His Orchestra	
3/10/58	20	4	1. Tequila [I]	ABC-Para. 9899
			PLATTERS	
			Tony Williams, lead singer through 1961 - replaced by Sonny Turner	
10/01/55	5	20	1. **Only You (And You Alone)**	Mercury 70633
12/24/55	1 (2)	19	2. **The Great Pretender**	Mercury 70753
3/31/56	4	16	3. **(You've Got) The Magic Touch**	Mercury 70819
7/07/56	1 (5)	20	4. **My Prayer/**	
8/11/56	39	1	5. Heaven On Earth	Mercury 70893
10/06/56	11	12	6. You'll Never Never Know/	
10/13/56	23	9	7. It Isn't Right	Mercury 70948
1/12/57	20	6	8. On My Word Of Honor/	
1/26/57	31	2	9. One In A Million	Mercury 71011
3/23/57	11	11	10. I'm Sorry/	
4/06/57	23	9	11. He's Mine	Mercury 71032
6/10/57	24	7	12. My Dream	Mercury 71093
4/07/58	1 (1)	14	13. **Twilight Time**	Mercury 71289
12/01/58	1 (3)	16	14. **Smoke Gets In Your Eyes**	Mercury 71383
4/06/59	12	11	15. Enchanted	Mercury 71427

DATE	POS	WKS	ARTIST—Record Title	LABEL & NO.
2/15/60	8	11	16. **Harbor Lights**	Mercury 71563
8/22/60	36	1	17. Red Sails In The Sunset	Mercury 71656
10/24/60	21	8	18. To Each His Own	Mercury 71697
1/30/61	30	2	19. If I Didn't Care	Mercury 71749
8/21/61	25	4	20. I'll Never Smile Again	Mercury 71847
6/04/66	31	5	21. I Love You 1000 Times	Musicor 1166
3/25/67	14	7	22. With This Ring	Musicor 1229
			PLAYER	
			quintet from Los Angeles	
11/19/77	1 (3)	16	● 1. **Baby Come Back**	RSO 879
4/01/78	10	12	2. **This Time I'm In It For Love**	RSO 890
10/21/78	27	3	3. Prisoner Of Your Love	RSO 908
			PLAYMATES	
			Donny Conn, Morey Carr & Chic Hetti	
1/27/58	19	7	1. Jo-Ann	Roulette 4037
6/09/58	22	2	2. Don't Go Home	Roulette 4072
11/10/58	4	12	3. **Beep Beep [N]**	Roulette 4115
7/27/59	15	9	4. What Is Love?	Roulette 4160
11/21/60	37	2	5. Wait For Me	Roulette 4276
			POCO	
			group formed by Richie Furay and Jim Messina, both from Buffalo Springfield	
2/10/79	17	9	1. Crazy Love	ABC 12439
6/16/79	20	7	2. Heart Of The Night	MCA 41023
			POINT BLANK	
			6-man rock band from Texas	
8/29/81	39	2	1. Nicole	MCA 51132
			POINTER SISTERS	
			Bonnie, Anita, Ruth & June - Bonnie left group in 1978	
9/08/73	11	12	1. Yes We Can Can	Blue Thumb 229
11/09/74	13	8	2. Fairytale	Blue Thumb 254
8/23/75	20	8	3. How Long (Betcha' Got A Chick On The Side)	Blue Thumb 265
12/16/78	2 (2)	16	● 4. **Fire**	Planet 45901
4/14/79	30	4	5. Happiness	Planet 45902
8/30/80	3	17	● 6. **He's So Shy**	Planet 47916
6/27/81	2 (3)	16	● 7. **Slow Hand**	Planet 47929
2/13/82	13	10	8. Should I Do It	Planet 47960
7/24/82	16	8	9. American Music	Planet 13254
10/30/82	30	6	10. I'm So Excited	Planet 13327
			POINTER, BONNIE	
7/28/79	11	15	1. Heaven Must Have Sent You	Motown 1459
2/16/80	40	2	2. I Can't Help Myself (Sugar Pie, Honey Bunch)	Motown 1478
			POLICE	
			British: Sting (Gordon Sumner), lead singer; Andy Summers, & Stewart Copeland (from U.S.)	
4/07/79	32	5	1. Roxanne	A&M 2096
11/22/80	10	13	2. **De Do Do Do, De Da Da Da**	A&M 2275
2/21/81	10	13	3. **Don't Stand So Close To Me**	A&M 2301
10/10/81	3	15	4. **Every Little Thing She Does Is Magic**	A&M 2371

DATE	POS	WKS	ARTIST—Record Title	LABEL & NO.
1/30/82	11	10	5. Spirits In The Material World	A&M 2390
			PONI-TAILS	
			Cleveland trio	
7/28/58	7	12	1. **Born Too Late**	ABC-Para. 9934
			POPPY FAMILY featuring Susan Jacks	
			Canadian -- also see Terry Jacks	
4/25/70	2 (2)	13	● 1. **Which Way You Goin' Billy?**	London 129
9/19/70	29	6	2. That's Where I Went Wrong	London 139
			POSEY, SANDY	
8/06/66	12	12	1. Born A Woman	MGM 13501
12/10/66	12	8	2. Single Girl	MGM 13612
4/08/67	31	2	3. What A Woman In Love Won't Do	MGM 13702
7/01/67	12	8	4. I Take It Back	MGM 13744
			POST, MIKE	
6/21/75	10	10	1. **The Rockford Files [I]**	MGM 14772
10/03/81	10	10	2. **The Theme From Hill Street Blues [I]**	Elektra 47186
			-featuring Larry Carlton-	
4/03/82	25	7	3. Theme From Magnum P.I. [I]	Elektra 47400
			POURCEL('S), FRANCK, French Fiddles	
4/27/59	9	11	1. **Only You [I]**	Capitol 4165
			POWELL, JANE	
			movie actress	
10/06/56	15	9	1. True Love	Verve 2018
			POWERS, JOEY	
12/07/63	10	9	1. **Midnight Mary**	Amy 892
			POZO-SECO SINGERS	
			Don Williams, lead singer	
10/08/66	32	6	1. I Can Make It With You	Columbia 43784
1/14/67	32	4	2. Look What You've Done	Columbia 43927
			PRADO, PEREZ, & His Orchestra	
3/05/55	1(10)	26	1. **Cherry Pink And Apple Blossom White [I]**	RCA 5965
			-trumpet solo: Billy Regis -- from the film "Under Water!"-	
6/23/58	1 (1)	17	● 2. **Patricia [I]**	RCA 7245
			PRATT & McCLAIN	
			Truett Pratt & Jerry McClain	
4/24/76	5	10	1. **Happy Days**	Reprise 1351
			-with Brother Love-	
			PRELUDE	
			British trio	
11/02/74	22	5	1. After The Goldrush	Island 002
			PREMIERS	
7/04/64	19	6	1. Farmer John	Warner 5443
			PRESIDENTS	
11/14/70	11	9	1. 5-10-15-20 (25-30 Years Of Love)	Sussex 207

DATE	POS	WKS	ARTIST—Record Title	LABEL & NO.
			PRESLEY, ELVIS	
			Elvis - the #1 artist of the rock era, was born in Tupelo, Mississippi on 1/8/35, and died in Memphis, Tennessee on 8/16/77 at the age of 42	
3/10/56	**1** (8)	22	1. **Heartbreak Hotel**/	
3/17/56	**19**	10	2. I Was The One	RCA 47-6420
4/28/56	**20**	5	3. Blue Suede Shoes	RCA EPA-747
			-from E.P. "Elvis Presley"-	
6/02/56	**1** (1)	19	4. **I Want You, I Need You, I Love You**/	
6/09/56	**31**	3	5. My Baby Left Me	RCA 47-6540
8/04/56	**1**(11)	24	6. **Don't Be Cruel**/	
8/04/56	**1**	23	7. **Hound Dog**	RCA 47-6604
10/20/56	**1** (5)	19	8. **Love Me Tender**/	
			-from Elvis's first movie -- tune adapted from "Aura Lee"-	
11/10/56	**20**	4	9. Anyway You Want Me (That's How I Will Be)	RCA 47-6643
11/24/56	**2** (2)	14	10. **Love Me**/	
12/29/56	**19**	4	11. When My Blue Moon Turns To Gold Again	RCA EPA-992
			-above 2 from E.P. "Elvis"-	
1/05/57	**24**	3	12. Poor Boy	RCA EPA-4006
			-from film/E.P. "Love Me Tender"-	
1/26/57	**1** (3)	14	13. **Too Much**/	
2/09/57	**21**	4	14. Playing For Keeps	RCA 47-6800
4/06/57	**1** (9)	22	15. **All Shook Up**	RCA 47-6870
4/29/57	**25**	1	16. (There'll Be) Peace In The Valley (For Me)	RCA EPA-4054
			-from E.P. "Peace In The Valley"-	
6/24/57	**1** (7)	18	17. **(Let Me Be Your) Teddy Bear**/	
7/08/57	**20**	13	18. Loving You	RCA 47-7000
			-above 2 from film "Loving You"-	
10/14/57	**1** (7)	19	19. **Jailhouse Rock**/	
10/21/57	**18**	6	20. Treat Me Nice	RCA 47-7035
			-above 2 from the film "Jailhouse Rock"-	
1/27/58	**1** (5)	16	21. **Don't**/	
2/03/58	**8**	7	22. **I Beg Of You**	RCA 47-7150
4/21/58	**2** (4)	13	23. **Wear My Ring Around Your Neck**/	
5/05/58	**15**	2	24. Doncha' Think It's Time	RCA 47-7240
6/30/58	**1** (2)	14	● 25. **Hard Headed Woman**/	
7/14/58	**25**	4	26. Don't Ask Me Why	RCA 47-7280
			-above 2 from film "King Creole"-	
11/10/58	**4**	14	27. **One Night**/	
11/10/58	**8**	12	28. **I Got Stung**	RCA 47-7410
3/30/59	**2** (1)	11	29. **(Now and Then There's) A Fool Such As I**/	
3/30/59	**4**	10	30. I Need Your Love Tonight	RCA 47-7506
7/13/59	**1** (2)	10	31. **A Big Hunk O' Love**/	
7/13/59	**12**	10	32. My Wish Came True	RCA 47-7600
4/11/60	**1** (4)	13	33. **Stuck On You**/	
4/25/60	**17**	7	34. Fame And Fortune	RCA 47-7740
7/25/60	**1** (5)	16	35. **It's Now Or Never**/	
			-adapted from "O Sole Mio"-	
8/01/60	**32**	2	36. A Mess Of Blues	RCA 47-7777
11/14/60	**1** (6)	14	37. **Are You Lonesome To-night?**/	
			-written in 1926-	
11/28/60	**20**	8	38. I Gotta Know	RCA 47-7810

DATE	POS	WKS	ARTIST—Record Title	LABEL & NO.
2/20/61	1 (2)	11	39. **Surrender/** -adapted from "Come Back To Sorrento"-	
3/13/61	32	2	40. Lonely Man -from film "Wild In The Country"-	RCA 47-7850
4/24/61	14	5	41. Flaming Star -from E.P. "Elvis By Request"-	RCA LPC-128
5/22/61	5	7	42. **I Feel So Bad/**	
6/19/61	26	2	43. Wild In The Country	RCA 47-7880
8/28/61	5	10	44. **Little Sister/**	
9/04/61	4	7	45. **(Marie's the Name) His Latest Flame**	RCA 47-7908
12/18/61	2 (1)	12	● 46. **Can't Help Falling In Love/**	
12/18/61	23	5	47. Rock-A-Hula Baby -above 2 from film "Blue Hawaii"-	RCA 47-7968
3/24/62	1 (2)	11	48. **Good Luck Charm/**	
4/07/62	31	5	49. Anything That's Part Of You	RCA 47-7992
5/19/62	15	7	50. Follow That Dream -from film/E.P. of same title-	RCA EPA-4368
8/11/62	5	9	51. **She's Not You**	RCA 47-8041
10/06/62	30	4	52. King Of The Whole Wide World -from the film/E.P."Kid Galahad"-	RCA EPA-4371
10/27/62	2 (5)	14	53. **Return To Sender** -from film "Girls! Girls! Girls!"-	RCA 47-8100
2/23/63	11	7	54. One Broken Heart For Sale -from film "It Happened At The World's Fair"-	RCA 47-8134
7/13/63	3	8	55. **(You're the) Devil In Disguise**	RCA 47-8188
11/02/63	8	7	56. **Bossa Nova Baby/** -from the film "Fun In Acapulco"-	
11/09/63	32	3	57. Witchcraft	RCA 47-8243
3/07/64	12	7	58. Kissin' Cousins/	
3/14/64	29	4	59. It Hurts Me	RCA 47-8307
5/23/64	34	2	60. Kiss Me Quick -recorded June 25, 1961-	RCA 447-0639
5/30/64	21	5	61. What'd I Say/	
5/30/64	29	4	62. Viva Las Vegas -above 2 from the film "Viva Las Vegas"-	RCA 47-8360
8/08/64	16	6	63. Such A Night -recorded April 4, 1960-	RCA 47-8400
10/24/64	12	8	64. Ask Me/	
10/24/64	16	8	65. Ain't That Loving You Baby -recorded June 10, 1958-	RCA 47-8440
3/13/65	21	6	66. Do The Clam -from the film "Girl Happy"-	RCA 47-8500
5/08/65	3	11	67. **Crying In The Chapel** -recorded October 31, 1960-	RCA 447-0643
7/03/65	11	6	68. (Such An) Easy Question -recorded March 18, 1962 -- from the film "Tickle Me"-	RCA 47-8585
9/18/65	11	7	69. I'm Yours -recorded June 26, 1961-	RCA 47-8657
12/04/65	14	6	70. Puppet On A String -from the film "Girl Happy"-	RCA 447-0650
1/22/66	33	3	71. Tell Me Why -recorded January 12, 1957-	RCA 47-8740
4/09/66	25	5	72. Frankie And Johnny	RCA 47-8780
7/09/66	19	5	73. Love Letters	RCA 47-8870
11/05/66	40	2	74. Spinout	RCA 47-8941

DATE	POS	WKS	ARTIST—Record Title	LABEL & NO.
2/18/67	33	4	75. Indescribably Blue	RCA 47-9056
11/04/67	38	2	76. Big Boss Man	RCA 47-9341
4/20/68	28	4	77. U.S. Male	RCA 47-9465
12/14/68	12	11	78. If I Can Dream	RCA 47-9670
4/12/69	35	2	79. Memories -from the TV special "Elvis"-	RCA 47-9731
5/17/69	3	11	● 80. **In The Ghetto**	RCA 47-9741
8/02/69	35	4	81. Clean Up Your Own Back Yard -from the film "The Trouble With Girls"-	RCA 47-9747
9/20/69	1 (1)	13	● 82. **Suspicious Minds**	RCA 47-9764
12/13/69	6	11	● 83. **Don't Cry Daddy**	RCA 47-9768
2/21/70	16	8	84. Kentucky Rain	RCA 47-9791
5/23/70	9	11	● 85. **The Wonder Of You** -recorded live at Las Vegas-	RCA 47-9835
8/22/70	32	3	86. I've Lost You/	
		3	87. **The Next Step Is Love**	RCA 47-9873
11/07/70	11	8	88. You Don't Have To Say You Love Me	RCA 47-9916
1/02/71	21	8	89. I Really Don't Want To Know/	
		8	90. **There Goes My Everything**	RCA 47-9960
3/27/71	33	4	91. Where Did They Go, Lord/	
		4	92. **Rags To Riches**	RCA 47-9980
8/14/71	36	2	93. I'm Leavin'	RCA 47-9998
3/11/72	40	1	94. Until It's Time For You To Go	RCA 74-0619
9/09/72	2 (1)	12	● 95. **Burning Love**	RCA 74-0769
12/23/72	20	8	96. Separate Ways -featured in film "Elvis On Tour"-	RCA 74-0815
5/05/73	17	7	97. Steamroller Blues -recorded live in Hawaii-	RCA 74-0910
3/23/74	39	2	98. I've Got A Thing About You Baby	RCA APBO-0196
6/29/74	17	7	99. If You Talk In Your Sleep	RCA APBO-0280
11/09/74	14	9	100. Promised Land	RCA PB-10074
2/15/75	20	6	101. My Boy	RCA PB-10191
6/07/75	35	3	102. T-R-O-U-B-L-E	RCA PB-10278
5/01/76	28	5	103. Hurt	RCA PB-10601
2/05/77	31	5	104. Moody Blue	RCA PB-10857
7/16/77	18	12	●105. Way Down	RCA PB-10998
12/03/77	22	7	●106. My Way -recorded live from Elvis's tour-	RCA PB-11165
2/28/81	28	5	107. Guitar Man -re-entry/re-mix of 1968 hit-	RCA PB-12158
			PRESTON, BILLY also see Beatles' "Get Back"	
5/13/72	2 (1)	14	● 1. **Outa-Space [I]**	A&M 1320
5/19/73	1 (2)	14	● 2. **Will It Go Round In Circles**	A&M 1411
10/13/73	4	13	● 3. **Space Race [I]**	A&M 1463
8/03/74	1 (1)	14	● 4. **Nothing From Nothing**	A&M 1544
1/04/75	22	6	5. Struttin' [I]	A&M 1644
			PRESTON, BILLY, & SYREETA Syreeta Wright - formerly married to Stevie Wonder	
3/01/80	4	15	1. **With You I'm Born Again**	Motown 1477

DATE	POS	WKS	ARTIST—Record Title	LABEL & NO.
			PRESTON, JOHNNY	
			protege of the Big Bopper	
12/21/59	1 (3)	14	1. **Running Bear**	Mercury 71474
4/04/60	7	12	2. **Cradle Of Love**	Mercury 71598
7/25/60	14	7	3. Feel So Fine	Mercury 71651
			PRETENDERS	
			British quartet led by Chrissie Hynde from Akron, Ohio	
4/12/80	14	12	1. Brass In Pocket (I'm Special)	Sire 49181
			PRICE, LLOYD	
4/06/57	29	6	1. Just Because	ABC-Para. 9792
1/05/59	1 (4)	15	2. **Stagger Lee**	ABC-Para. 9972
3/30/59	23	4	3. Where Were You (On Our Wedding Day)?	ABC-Para. 9997
5/11/59	2 (3)	14	4. **Personality**	ABC-Para. 10018
8/17/59	3	12	5. **I'm Gonna Get Married**	ABC-Para. 10032
11/23/59	20	9	6. Come Into My Heart	ABC-Para. 10062
2/15/60	14	8	7. Lady Luck	ABC-Para. 10075
5/30/60	40	1	8. No If's - No And's	ABC-Para. 10102
7/18/60	19	7	9. Question	ABC-Para. 10123
10/26/63	21	6	10. Misty	Double-L 722
			PRICE, RAY	
11/07/70	11	14	1. For The Good Times	Columbia 45178
			PRIDE, CHARLEY	
			Charley's had 27 #1 hits on the Country charts ('69-'82)	
12/18/71	21	11	● 1. Kiss An Angel Good Mornin'	RCA 0550
			PRIMA, LOUIS	
			died 8/24/78 (67)	
12/12/60	15	9	1. Wonderland By Night [I]	Dot 16151
			PRIMA, LOUIS, & KEELY SMITH	
			husband & wife (divorced in '62) - back-up band: Sam Butera & The Witnesses	
11/24/58	18	7	1. That Old Black Magic -from the film "Senior Prom"-	Capitol 4063
			PRINCE	
12/08/79	11	12	● 1. I Wanna Be Your Lover	Warner 49050
			PRISM	
3/13/82	39	2	1. Don't Let Him Know	Capitol 5082
			PROBY, P.J.	
			real name: James Marcus Smith	
2/25/67	23	5	1. Niki Hoeky	Liberty 55936
			PROCOL HARUM	
			English quintet formed by Gary Brooker	
7/01/67	5	10	1. **A Whiter Shade Of Pale**	Deram 7507
11/11/67	34	2	2. Homburg	A&M 885
6/24/72	16	8	3. Conquistador	A&M 1347
			PRUETT, JEANNE	
6/23/73	28	5	1. Satin Sheets	MCA 40015

DATE	POS	WKS	ARTIST—Record Title	LABEL & NO.
			PUCKETT, GARY, & THE UNION GAP	
12/02/67	4	15	● 1. **Woman, Woman**	Columbia 44297
3/16/68	2 (3)	13	● 2. **Young Girl**	Columbia 44450
6/22/68	2 (2)	11	● 3. **Lady Willpower**	Columbia 44547
9/28/68	7	10	● 4. **Over You**	Columbia 44644
3/22/69	15	8	5. Don't Give In To Him	Columbia 44788
9/06/69	9	9	6. **This Girl Is A Woman Now**	Columbia 44967
			PURE PRAIRIE LEAGUE	
4/12/75	27	3	1. Amie	RCA 10184
5/24/80	10	11	2. **Let Me Love You Tonight**	Casablanca 2266
10/04/80	34	4	3. I'm Almost Ready	Casablanca 2294
5/23/81	28	6	4. Still Right Here In My Heart	Casablanca 2332
			PURIFY, JAMES & BOBBY	
			James Purify & Bobby Dickey	
10/22/66	6	10	1. **I'm Your Puppet**	Bell 648
2/25/67	38	1	2. Wish You Didn't Have To Go	Bell 660
5/13/67	25	5	3. Shake A Tail Feather	Bell 669
10/07/67	23	5	4. Let Love Come Between Us	Bell 685
			PURSELL, BILL	
2/16/63	9	10	1. **Our Winter Love [I]**	Columbia 42619
			PYRAMIDS	
2/22/64	18	6	1. Penetration [I]	Best 13002
			Q	
4/09/77	23	7	1. Dancin' Man	Epic 50335
			QUAKER CITY BOYS	
1/26/59	39	1	1. Teasin'	Swan 4023
			QUARTERFLASH	
			group from Portland-area originally known as Seafood Mama	
11/07/81	3	19	1. **Harden My Heart**	Geffen 49824
3/13/82	16	7	2. Find Another Fool	Geffen 50006
			QUATRO, SUZI, & CHRIS NORMAN	
			Chris is lead singer of Smokie	
2/24/79	4	15	● 1. **Stumblin' In**	RSO 917
			QUEEN	
			British: Freddie Mercury, lead singer; Brian May, John Deacon and Roger Taylor	
3/29/75	12	11	1. Killer Queen	Elektra 45226
2/07/76	9	17	● 2. **Bohemian Rhapsody**	Elektra 45297
6/12/76	16	11	3. You're My Best Friend	Elektra 45318
12/04/76	13	12	4. Somebody To Love	Elektra 45362
11/26/77	4	17	★ 5. **We Are The Champions**/	
		10	6. **We Will Rock You**	Elektra 45441
12/09/78	24	6	7. Bicycle Race/	
		6	8. **Fat Bottomed Girls**	Elektra 45541
1/12/80	1 (4)	17	● 9. **Crazy Little Thing Called Love**	Elektra 46579
8/30/80	1 (3)	21	★ 10. **Another One Bites The Dust**	Elektra 47031

DATE	POS	WKS	ARTIST—Record Title	LABEL & NO.
5/15/82	**11**	8	11. Body Language	Elektra 47452
			QUEEN & DAVID BOWIE	
12/05/81	**29**	8	1. Under Pressure	Elektra 47235
			? (QUESTION MARK) & THE MYSTERIANS	
			Rudy Martinez (?), lead singer	
9/17/66	**1** (1)	12	● 1. **96 Tears**	Cameo 428
12/10/66	**22**	6	2. I Need Somebody	Cameo 441
			QUIN-TONES	
9/08/58	**18**	6	1. Down The Aisle Of Love	Hunt 321
			RABBITT, EDDIE	
3/03/79	**30**	4	1. Every Which Way But Loose	Elektra 45554
7/14/79	**13**	10	2. Suspicions	Elektra 46053
7/26/80	**5**	15	● 3. **Drivin' My Life Away**	Elektra 46656
12/06/80	**1** (2)	18	● 4. **I Love A Rainy Night**	Elektra 47066
8/08/81	**5**	15	5. **Step By Step**	Elektra 47174
12/05/81	**15**	10	6. Someone Could Lose A Heart Tonight	Elektra 47239
5/22/82	**35**	4	7. I Don't Know Where To Start	Elektra 47435
			RAFFERTY, GERRY	
			co-leader of Stealers Wheel	
5/13/78	**2** (6)	15	● 1. **Baker Street**	United Artists 1192
			-sax solo by Raphael Ravenscroft-	
8/26/78	**12**	11	2. Right Down The Line	United Artists 1233
1/06/79	**28**	6	3. Home And Dry	United Artists 1266
6/16/79	**17**	7	4. Days Gone Down (Still Got The Light In Your Eyes)	United Artists 1298
9/08/79	**21**	8	5. Get It Right Next Time	United Artists 1316
			RAIDERS - see PAUL REVERE...	
			RAINBOW	
			Ritchie (Deep Purple) Blackmore, leader	
6/19/82	**40**	1	1. Stone Cold	Mercury 76146
			RAINDROPS	
			Jeff Barry & Ellie Greenwich	
8/31/63	**17**	7	1. The Kind Of Boy You Can't Forget	Jubilee 5455
			RAINWATER, MARVIN	
6/10/57	**18**	12	1. Gonna Find Me A Bluebird	MGM 12412
			RAM JAM	
7/23/77	**18**	8	1. Black Betty	Epic 50357
			RAMBEAU, EDDIE	
6/05/65	**35**	2	1. Concrete And Clay	DynoVoice 204
			RAMRODS	
2/20/61	**30**	1	1. (Ghost) Riders In The Sky [I]	Amy 813
			RAN-DELLS	
8/31/63	**16**	8	1. Martian Hop	Chairman 4403
			RANDOLPH, BOOTS	
3/30/63	**35**	3	1. Yakety Sax [I]	Monument 804

DATE	POS	WKS	ARTIST—Record Title	LABEL & NO.
			RANDY & THE RAINBOWS	
			Randy Safuto, lead singer	
7/27/63	**10**	10	1. **Denise**	Rust 5059
			RARE EARTH	
			Detroit rock group	
4/04/70	**4**	17	1. **Get Ready**	Rare Earth 5012
8/22/70	**7**	11	2. **(I Know) I'm Losing You**	Rare Earth 5017
1/02/71	**17**	8	3. Born To Wander	Rare Earth 5021
8/07/71	**7**	10	4. **I Just Want To Celebrate**	Rare Earth 5031
12/18/71	**19**	7	5. Hey Big Brother	Rare Earth 5038
6/17/78	**39**	2	6. Warm Ride	Prodigal 0640
			RASCALS	
			Felix Cavaliere, lead singer; Eddie Brigati, Gene Cornish & Dino Danelli	
3/26/66	**1** (1)	12	1. **Good Lovin'**	Atlantic 2321
7/09/66	**20**	4	2. You Better Run	Atlantic 2338
2/25/67	**16**	9	3. I've Been Lonely Too Long	Atlantic 2377
5/06/67	**1** (4)	11	● 4. **Groovin'**	Atlantic 2401
7/22/67	**10**	8	5. **A Girl Like You**	Atlantic 2424
9/23/67	**4**	9	6. **How Can I Be Sure**	Atlantic 2438
12/23/67	**20**	5	7. It's Wonderful -all titles above shown as by The Young Rascals-	Atlantic 2463
4/20/68	**3**	11	● 8. **A Beautiful Morning**	Atlantic 2493
7/27/68	**1** (5)	13	● 9. **People Got To Be Free**	Atlantic 2537
12/14/68	**24**	6	10. A Ray Of Hope	Atlantic 2584
3/01/69	**39**	2	11. Heaven	Atlantic 2599
6/07/69	**27**	5	12. See	Atlantic 2634
9/20/69	**26**	6	13. Carry Me Back	Atlantic 2664
			RASPBERRIES	
			Eric Carmen, lead singer	
8/19/72	**5**	11	● 1. **Go All The Way**	Capitol 3348
12/09/72	**16**	9	2. I Wanna Be With You	Capitol 3473
5/12/73	**35**	7	3. Let's Pretend	Capitol 3546
10/12/74	**18**	6	4. Overnight Sensation (Hit Record)	Capitol 3946
			RAWLS, LOU	
			member of gospel group The Pilgrim Travelers ('55-'59)	
10/15/66	**13**	8	1. Love Is A Hurtin' Thing	Capitol 5709
5/06/67	**29**	4	2. Dead End Street	Capitol 5869
8/30/69	**18**	8	3. Your Good Thing (Is About To End)	Capitol 2550
10/16/71	**17**	11	4. A Natural Man	MGM 14262
7/10/76	**2** (2)	13	● 5. **You'll Never Find Another Love Like Mine**	Phil. Int'l. 3592
2/25/78	**24**	8	6. Lady Love	Phil. Int'l. 3634
			RAY, DIANE	
9/07/63	**31**	3	1. Please Don't Talk To The Lifeguard	Mercury 72117
			RAY, GOODMAN & BROWN	
			Harry Ray, Al Goodman & William Brown - formerly known as The Moments	
2/16/80	**5**	14	● 1. **Special Lady**	Polydor 2033

DATE	POS	WKS	ARTIST—Record Title	LABEL & NO.
			RAY, JAMES	
12/25/61	**22**	7	1. If You Gotta Make A Fool Of Somebody	Caprice 110
			RAY, JOHNNIE	
9/08/56	**2** (1)	23	1. **Just Walking In The Rain**	Columbia 40729
1/19/57	**10**	10	2. **You Don't Owe Me A Thing/**	
2/02/57	**36**	2	3. Look Homeward, Angel	Columbia 40803
5/06/57	**12**	5	4. Yes Tonight, Josephine	Columbia 40893
			RAYBURN, MARGIE	
11/11/57	**9**	13	1. **I'm Available**	Liberty 55102
			RAYDIO - see RAY PARKER, JR.	
			RAYS	
			Hal Miller, lead singer of New York quartet	
10/21/57	**3**	17	1. **Silhouettes**	Cameo 117
			REA, CHRIS	
7/29/78	**12**	10	1. Fool (If You Think It's Over)	United Artists 1198
			REBELS	
1/26/63	**8**	12	1. **Wild Weekend [I]**	Swan 4125
			REDBONE	
			"swamp rock" group led by brothers Pat & Lolly Vegas	
1/08/72	**21**	7	1. The Witch Queen Of New Orleans	Epic 10749
2/09/74	**5**	18	● 2. **Come And Get Your Love**	Epic 11035
			REDDING, GENE	
7/06/74	**24**	5	1. This Heart	Haven 7000
			REDDING, OTIS	
			killed in a plane crash on 12/10/67 (26) -- also see Otis & Carla	
6/19/65	**21**	6	1. I've Been Loving You Too Long (To Stop Now)	Volt 126
10/23/65	**35**	3	2. Respect	Volt 128
4/02/66	**31**	3	3. Satisfaction	Volt 132
10/29/66	**29**	4	4. Fa-Fa-Fa-Fa-Fa (Sad Song)	Volt 138
12/31/66	**25**	6	5. Try A Little Tenderness	Volt 141
2/10/68	**1** (4)	14	● 6. **(Sittin' On) The Dock Of The Bay**	Volt 157
5/11/68	**25**	5	7. The Happy Song (Dum-Dum)	Volt 163
7/27/68	**36**	1	8. Amen	Atco 6592
12/14/68	**21**	5	9. Papa's Got A Brand New Bag	Atco 6636
			REDDY, HELEN	
5/08/71	**13**	9	1. I Don't Know How To Love Him -from "Jesus Christ Superstar"-	Capitol 3027
10/14/72	**1** (1)	14	● 2. **I Am Woman**	Capitol 3350
3/10/73	**12**	10	3. Peaceful	Capitol 3527
7/28/73	**1** (1)	14	● 4. **Delta Dawn**	Capitol 3645
11/17/73	**3**	13	● 5. **Leave Me Alone (Ruby Red Dress)**	Capitol 3768
3/30/74	**15**	9	6. Keep On Singing	Capitol 3845
7/20/74	**9**	12	7. **You And Me Against The World**	Capitol 3897
11/02/74	**1** (1)	13	● 8. **Angie Baby**	Capitol 3972
3/01/75	**22**	5	9. Emotion	Capitol 4021

DATE	POS	WKS	ARTIST—Record Title	LABEL & NO.
7/26/75	35	2	10. Bluebird	Capitol 4108
8/30/75	8	9	11. **Ain't No Way To Treat A Lady**	Capitol 4128
12/27/75	19	9	12. Somewhere In The Night	Capitol 4192
8/21/76	29	5	13. I Can't Hear You No More	Capitol 4312
6/11/77	18	12	14. You're My World	Capitol 4418
			REDEYE	
12/26/70	27	7	1. Games	Pentagram 204
			REED, JERRY	
1/09/71	8	14	● 1. **Amos Moses** [N]	RCA 9904
5/29/71	9	9	2. **When You're Hot, You're Hot** [N]	RCA 9976
			REED, JIMMY	
			died 8/29/76 (50)	
11/04/57	32	3	1. Honest I Do	Vee-Jay 253
2/29/60	37	2	2. Baby What You Want Me To Do	Vee-Jay 333
			REED, LOU	
			leader of Velvet Underground	
3/31/73	16	8	1. Walk On The Wild Side	RCA 0887
			REESE, DELLA	
			gospel singer with Mahalia Jackson's troupe in her teens	
9/09/57	12	13	1. And That Reminds Me	Jubilee 5292
10/05/59	2 (1)	15	2. **Don't You Know**	RCA 7591
12/28/59	16	8	3. Not One Minute More	RCA 7644
			REEVES, JIM	
			killed in a plane crash on 7/31/64 (39)	
5/06/57	11	14	1. Four Walls	RCA 6874
1/11/60	2 (3)	20	2. **He'll Have To Go**	RCA 7643
7/11/60	37	1	3. I'm Gettin' Better	RCA 7756
11/28/60	31	4	4. Am I Losing You	RCA 7800
			REEVES, MARTHA - **see MARTHA & THE VANDELLAS**	
			REFLECTIONS	
			Detroit quartet	
5/02/64	6	9	1. **(Just Like) Romeo & Juliet**	Golden World 9
			REGENTS	
			Bronx quintet	
5/22/61	13	7	1. Barbara-Ann	Gee 1065
7/31/61	28	4	2. Runaround	Gee 1071
			REID, CLARENCE	
9/13/69	40	2	1. Nobody But You Babe	Alston 4574
			RENAY, DIANE	
2/15/64	6	8	1. **Navy Blue**	20th Century 456
4/25/64	29	4	2. Kiss Me Sailor	20th Century 477
			RENE & RENE	
12/14/68	14	9	1. Lo Mucho Que Te Quiero (The More I Love You)	White Whale 287

DATE	POS	WKS	ARTIST—Record Title	LABEL & NO.
			REO SPEEDWAGON	
			Champaign, Illinois quintet featuring Kevin Kronin (vocals) & Gary Richrath (guitar)	
12/27/80	**1** (1)	20	● 1. **Keep On Loving You**	Epic 50953
3/28/81	**5**	15	2. **Take It On The Run**	Epic 01054
7/04/81	**24**	6	3. Don't Let Him Go	Epic 02127
8/29/81	**20**	7	4. In Your Letter	Epic 02457
6/19/82	**7**	13	5. **Keep The Fire Burnin'**	Epic 02967
10/02/82	**26**	6	6. Sweet Time	Epic 03175
			REUNION	
			Joey (Ohio Express) Levine, lead singer	
9/28/74	**8**	10	1. **Life Is A Rock (But The Radio Rolled Me)** [N]	RCA 10056
			REVELS	
11/23/59	**35**	2	1. Midnight Stroll	Norgolde 103
			REVERE, PAUL, & THE RAIDERS	
			Mark Lindsay, lead singer	
4/17/61	**38**	1	1. Like, Long Hair [I]	Gardena 116
12/25/65	**11**	11	2. Just Like Me	Columbia 43461
3/26/66	**4**	12	3. **Kicks**	Columbia 43556
7/09/66	**6**	7	4. **Hungry**	Columbia 43678
10/15/66	**20**	5	5. The Great Airplane Strike	Columbia 43810
12/17/66	**4**	10	6. **Good Thing**	Columbia 43907
3/04/67	**22**	6	7. Ups And Downs	Columbia 44018
5/06/67	**5**	8	8. **Him Or Me - What's It Gonna Be?**	Columbia 44094
9/02/67	**17**	5	9. I Had A Dream	Columbia 44227
2/24/68	**19**	6	10. Too Much Talk	Columbia 44444
7/13/68	**27**	6	11. Don't Take It So Hard	Columbia 44553
3/08/69	**18**	9	12. Mr. Sun, Mr. Moon	Columbia 44744
6/14/69	**20**	8	13. Let Me	Columbia 44854
			RAIDERS:	
5/29/71	**1** (1)	15	● 14. **Indian Reservation (The Lament Of The Cherokee Reservation Indian)**	Columbia 45332
10/02/71	**23**	6	15. Birds Of A Feather	Columbia 45453
			REYNOLDS, DEBBIE	
			movie actress	
7/22/57	**1** (5)	23	1. **Tammy** -from "Tammy & The Bachelor"-	Coral 61851
1/20/58	**20**	1	2. A Very Special Love	Coral 61897
2/22/60	**25**	8	3. Am I That Easy To Forget	Dot 15985
			REYNOLDS, JODY	
5/26/58	**5**	14	1. **Endless Sleep**	Demon 1507
			REYNOLDS, LAWRENCE	
10/11/69	**28**	6	1. Jesus Is A Soul Man	Warner 7322
			RHYTHM HERITAGE	
1/10/76	**1** (1)	12	● 1. **Theme From S.W.A.T.** [I]	ABC 12135
5/08/76	**20**	8	2. Barretta's Theme ("Keep Your Eye On The Sparrow")	ABC 12177

DATE	POS	WKS	ARTIST—Record Title	LABEL & NO.
			RICH, CHARLIE	
5/02/60	22	9	1. Lonely Weekends	Phillips 3552
9/25/65	21	7	2. Mohair Sam	Smash 1993
6/09/73	15	12	● 3. Behind Closed Doors	Epic 10950
10/27/73	1 (2)	17	● 4. **The Most Beautiful Girl**	Epic 11040
2/23/74	18	8	5. There Won't Be Anymore	RCA 0195
3/09/74	11	9	6. A Very Special Love Song	Epic 11091
8/24/74	24	7	7. I Love My Friend	Epic 20006
6/28/75	19	6	8. Every Time You Touch Me (I Get High)	Epic 50103
			RICHARD, CLIFF	
			except for Elvis Presley, Cliff is Britain's all-time most successful charted artist - also see Olivia Newton-John	
11/02/59	30	4	1. Living Doll -with The Drifters-	ABC-Para. 10042
1/18/64	25	7	2. It's All In The Game	Epic 9633
8/14/76	6	12	● 3. **Devil Woman**	Rocket 40574
11/17/79	7	14	4. **We Don't Talk Anymore**	EMI America 8025
4/05/80	34	3	5. Carrie	EMI America 8035
9/27/80	10	13	6. **Dreaming**	EMI America 8057
1/24/81	17	11	7. A Little In Love	EMI America 8068
2/06/82	23	8	8. Daddy's Home	EMI America 8103
			RICHIE, LIONEL	
			leader of The Commodores -- also see Diana Ross	
10/23/82	1 (2)	13	● 1. **Truly**	Motown 1644
			RIDDLE, NELSON, & His Orchestra	
			arranger-conductor for Frank Sinatra & many other top artists	
12/31/55	1 (4)	24	1. **Lisbon Antigua [I]**	Capitol 3287
3/31/56	20	4	2. Port Au Prince [I]	Capitol 3374
8/04/56	39	2	3. Theme From "The Proud Ones" [I]	Capitol 3472
8/04/62	30	3	4. Route 66 Theme [I]	Capitol 4741
			RIGHTEOUS BROTHERS	
			Bill Medley & Bobby Hatfield	
12/26/64	1 (2)	13	1. **You've Lost That Lovin' Feelin'**	Philles 124
4/17/65	9	10	2. **Just Once In My Life**	Philles 127
7/31/65	4	11	3. **Unchained Melody**	Philles 129
12/11/65	5	8	4. **Ebb Tide**	Philles 130
3/19/66	1 (3)	11	● 5. **(You're My) Soul And Inspiration**	Verve 10383
6/18/66	18	5	6. He	Verve 10406
8/27/66	30	3	7. Go Ahead And Cry	Verve 10430
6/15/74	3	10	8. **Rock And Roll Heaven**	Haven 7002
10/05/74	20	4	9. Give It To The People	Haven 7004
12/07/74	32	3	10. Dream On	Haven 7006
			RILEY, JEANNIE C.	
8/31/68	1 (1)	12	● 1. **Harper Valley P.T.A**	Plantation 3
			RINKY-DINKS	
			group is actually Bobby Darin	
8/11/58	24	5	1. Early In The Morning	Atco 6121

DATE	POS	WKS	ARTIST—Record Title	LABEL & NO.
			RIOS, MIGUEL	
6/20/70	**14**	8	1. A Song Of Joy -based on the last movement of Beethoven's 9th Symphony - Waldo De Los Rios, conductor-	A&M 1193
			RIP CHORDS	
			Southern California quintet	
1/04/64	**4**	11	1. **Hey Little Cobra**	Columbia 42921
5/23/64	**28**	5	2. Three Window Coupe	Columbia 43035
			RIPERTON, MINNIE	
			lead singer of Rotary Connection - Minnie died on 7/12/79 (30)	
2/15/75	**1** (1)	13	● 1. **Lovin' You**	Epic 50057
			RITCHIE FAMILY	
			assemblage of studio musicians by Ritchie Rome	
9/06/75	**11**	12	1. Brazil [I]	20th Century 2218
10/02/76	**17**	11	2. The Best Disco In Town	Marlin 3306
			RITENOUR, LEE	
5/23/81	**15**	9	1. Is It You -vocal: Eric Tagg-	Elektra 47124
			RITTER, TEX	
			father of TV star John Ritter - Tex died on 1/2/74 (67)	
7/07/56	**28**	6	1. The Wayward Wind	Capitol 3430
8/14/61	**20**	4	2. I Dreamed Of A Hill-Billy Heaven [S]	Capitol 4567
			RIVERS, JOHNNY	
			early hits recorded live at L.A.'s "Whisky A Go Go"	
6/13/64	**2** (2)	10	1. **Memphis**	Imperial 66032
8/22/64	**12**	7	2. Maybelline	Imperial 66056
11/14/64	**9**	9	3. **Mountain Of Love**	Imperial 66075
2/27/65	**20**	4	4. Midnight Special	Imperial 66087
6/19/65	**7**	8	5. **Seventh Son**	Imperial 66112
10/30/65	**26**	4	6. Where Have All The Flowers Gone	Imperial 66133
1/15/66	**35**	3	7. Under Your Spell Again	Imperial 66144
3/26/66	**3**	10	8. **Secret Agent Man**	Imperial 66159
6/25/66	**19**	6	9. (I Washed My Hands In) Muddy Water	Imperial 66175
10/08/66	**1** (1)	12	10. **Poor Side Of Town**	Imperial 66205
2/18/67	**3**	8	11. **Baby I Need Your Lovin'**	Imperial 66227
6/17/67	**10**	6	12. **The Tracks Of My Tears**	Imperial 66244
12/02/67	**14**	8	13. Summer Rain	Imperial 66267
11/11/72	**6**	14	● 14. **Rockin' Pneumonia - Boogie Woogie Flu**	United Artists 50960
5/05/73	**38**	2	15. Blue Suede Shoes	United Artists 198
8/09/75	**22**	5	16. Help Me Rhonda	Epic 50121
7/30/77	**10**	15	● 17. **Swayin' To The Music (Slow Dancin')**	Big Tree 16094
			RIVIERAS	
2/01/64	**5**	9	1. **California Sun**	Riviera 1401
			ROAD APPLES	
12/27/75	**35**	4	1. Let's Live Together	Polydor 14285

DATE	POS	WKS	ARTIST—Record Title	LABEL & NO.
			ROBBINS, MARTY	
			died 12/8/82 (57)	
11/24/56	17	7	1. Singing The Blues	Columbia 21545
4/27/57	2 (1)	21	2. **A White Sport Coat (And A Pink Carnation)**	Columbia 40864
12/09/57	15	9	3. The Story Of My Life	Columbia 41013
5/05/58	26	5	4. Just Married	Columbia 41143
8/25/58	27	5	5. She Was Only Seventeen (He Was One Year More)	Columbia 41208
3/16/59	38	3	6. The Hanging Tree	Columbia 41325
11/30/59	1 (2)	16	7. **El Paso**	Columbia 41511
4/11/60	26	4	8. Big Iron	Columbia 41589
8/01/60	31	3	9. Is There Any Chance	Columbia 41686
12/05/60	34	5	10. Ballad Of The Alamo	Columbia 41809
2/13/61	3	12	11. **Don't Worry**	Columbia 41922
8/18/62	16	7	12. Devil Woman	Columbia 42486
12/08/62	18	5	13. Ruby Ann	Columbia 42614
			ROBERT & JOHNNY	
			Robert Carr & Johnny Mitchell	
3/03/58	32	6	1. We Belong Together	Old Town 1047
			ROBERTS, AUSTIN	
11/11/72	12	10	1. Something's Wrong With Me	Chelsea 0101
8/30/75	9	9	2. **Rocky**	Private Stock 45020
			ROBERTSON, DON	
5/05/56	6	14	1. **The Happy Whistler [I]**	Capitol 3391
			ROBIC, IVO	
			Yugoslavian	
8/31/59	13	11	1. Morgen [F]	Laurie 3033
			ROBINSON, FLOYD	
8/03/59	20	12	1. Makin' Love	RCA 7529
			ROBINSON, SMOKEY	
			leader of The Miracles	
1/19/74	27	6	1. Baby Come Close	Tamla 54239
5/31/75	26	6	2. Baby That's Backatcha	Tamla 54258
10/18/75	36	3	3. The Agony And The Ecstasy	Tamla 54261
11/17/79	4	17	4. **Cruisin'**	Tamla 54306
5/03/80	31	4	5. Let Me Be The Clock	Tamla 54311
3/21/81	2 (3)	16	● 6. **Being With You**	Tamla 54321
2/27/82	33	5	7. Tell Me Tomorrow - Part 1	Tamla 1601
			ROBINSON, VICKI SUE	
6/19/76	10	13	1. **Turn The Beat Around**	RCA 10562
			ROCHELL & THE CANDLES with Johnny Wyatt	
			Rochell Henderson	
3/27/61	26	4	1. Once Upon A Time	Swingin' 623
			ROCK-A-TEENS	
10/12/59	16	9	1. Woo-Hoo [I]	Roulette 4192
			ROCKETS	
8/11/79	30	6	1. Oh Well	RSO 935

Eddie Rabbitt. Brooklyn-born Eddie Rabbitt spent several years on *Billboard's* country charts before crossing to pop, not to mention several years as a trucker, fruit picker, and soda jerk.

Gerry Rafferty. The stars of "Baker Street" (six weeks at number 2, thanks to Andy Gibb) were Gerry Rafferty and Raphael Ravenscroft. The latter provided the record's distinctive saxophone work.

Rainbow. The longevity of heavy metal as a popular art form is underscored by Rainbow, founded by Ritchie Blackmore of Deep Purple. He's changed the band's line-up more than once, of course, but not the music.

Paul Revere and the Raiders revived Richard Berry's "Louie Louie" the same year as the Kingsmen—everyone recognizes a good melody—but the latter group grabbed the hit.

The Righteous Brothers. Rock'n'roll radio seldom played anything longer than three minutes in 1964, so producer Phil Spector printed the running time of the Righteous Brothers' "You've Lost That Loving Feelin' " as 3:05. By the time deejays realized the record was closer to four minutes, it was already on the air.

Jimmie Rodgers' lowest-charting top 40 record, "It's Over," was subsequently remade in blistering soul style by Detroit's Terry Lindsey. Listen, you want trivia, you got it.

PAINT IT, BLACK
THE ROLLING STONES

LONDON 45-901

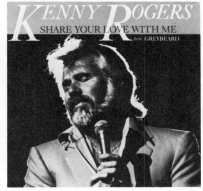

WALKING IN THE RAIN
HOW DOES IT FEEL
THE RONETTES

LINDA RONSTADT

Back in the USA

YOUNG WINGS CAN FLY
♥♥ DAY DREAMING ♥♥
RUBY AND THE ROMANTICS
KAPP K-557

R U S H
TOM SAWYER

Kenny Rogers labored long and hard before he became a solo superstar, including improbable experience as bass player with the Bobby Doyle Trio, a jazz combo, and a spell touring with the Kirby Stone Four.

The Rolling Stones. "They sit before you at a press conference like five unfolding switch blades, their faces set into rehearsed snarls . . ." wrote journalist Pete Hamill about the Rolling Stones in 1966, ". . . their hair studiously unkempt and matted, their clothes part of some private conceit, and the way they talk and songs they sing all become part of some long, mean reach for the jugular."

The Ronettes were resident dancers at New York's Peppermint Lounge and appeared in "Twist Around The Clock" (proclaimed the ads: "The first full-length movie about the twist") before Phil Spector lent them his Midas touch.

Linda Ronstadt. With one exception, Linda Ronstadt's top 10 hits have been revivals of earlier rock'n'roll and r&b successes. And with one exception, they have topped the chart peaks of the original versions.

Ruby & the Romantics' songbook has proved remarkably durable, generating successful revivals for Frankie Valli ("Our Day Will Come"), Eddie Holman and Stacy Lattisaw ("Hey There Lonely Girl/Boy"), and the Marvelettes ("When You're Young And In Love.")

Rush. A debut album on their own enterprise, Moon Records, helped Rush secure the interest of America's Mercury label. Once signed, the group toured with Kiss and Aerosmith—count the decibels—and then became bill-toppers in their own right.

DATE	POS	WKS	ARTIST—Record Title	LABEL & NO.
			ROCKY FELLERS	
			father and his four sons	
4/27/63	16	8	1. Killer Joe	Scepter 1246
			RODGERS, EILEEN	
9/08/56	18	10	1. Miracle Of Love	Columbia 40708
9/29/58	26	4	2. Treasure Of Your Love	Columbia 41214
			RODGERS, JIMMIE	
			nearly died as the result of a mysterious scull fracture 12/2/67	
8/19/57	1 (4)	23	1. **Honeycomb**	Roulette 4015
11/18/57	3	14	2. **Kisses Sweeter Than Wine**	Roulette 4031
2/24/58	7	9	3. **Oh-Oh, I'm Falling In Love Again**	Roulette 4045
5/19/58	3	15	4. Secretly/	
5/26/58	16	1	5. Make Me A Miracle	Roulette 4070
8/11/58	10	10	6. **Are You Really Mine**	Roulette 4090
12/01/58	11	10	7. Bimbombey	Roulette 4116
3/30/59	36	3	8. I'm Never Gonna Tell	Roulette 4129
6/15/59	32	4	9. Ring-A-Ling-A-Lario/	
7/06/59	40	1	10. Wonderful You	Roulette 4158
10/12/59	32	3	11. Tucumcari	Roulette 4191
2/01/60	24	5	12. Tender Love And Care (T.L.C.)	Roulette 4218
6/18/66	37	2	13. It's Over	Dot 16861
10/14/67	31	4	14. Child Of Clay	A&M 871
			ROE, TOMMY	
8/11/62	1 (2)	11	● 1. **Sheila**	ABC-Para. 10329
11/03/62	35	2	2. Susie Darlin'	ABC-Para. 10362
10/26/63	3	11	3. **Everybody**	ABC-Para. 10478
2/08/64	36	4	4. Come On	ABC-Para. 10515
7/02/66	8	10	● 5. **Sweet Pea**	ABC-Para. 10762
10/01/66	6	11	6. **Hooray For Hazel**	ABC 10852
1/28/67	23	5	7. It's Now Winters Day	ABC 10888
2/15/69	1 (4)	13	● 8. **Dizzy**	ABC 11164
5/17/69	29	3	9. Heather Honey	ABC 11211
12/06/69	8	11	● 10. **Jam Up Jelly Tight**	ABC 11247
9/25/71	25	7	11. Stagger Lee	ABC 11307
			ROGERS, JULIE	
12/05/64	10	9	1. **The Wedding**	Mercury 72332
			ROGERS, KENNY	
4/23/77	5	13	● 1. **Lucille**	United Artists 929
9/10/77	28	4	2. Daytime Friends	United Artists 1027
7/15/78	32	3	3. Love Or Something Like It	United Artists 1210
12/23/78	16	13	4. The Gambler	United Artists 1250
5/12/79	5	13	● 5. **She Believes In Me**	United Artists 1273
9/22/79	7	12	6. **You Decorated My Life**	United Artists 1315
12/01/79	3	15	● 7. **Coward Of The County**	United Artists 1327
6/28/80	14	8	8. Love The World Away	United Artists 1359
			-from the film "Urban Cowboy"-	

DATE	POS	WKS	ARTIST—Record Title	LABEL & NO.
10/04/80	**1** (6)	19	● 9. **Lady**	Liberty 1380
6/13/81	**3**	14	● 10. **I Don't Need You**	Liberty 1415
9/12/81	**14**	10	11. Share Your Love With Me	Liberty 1430
1/16/82	**13**	11	12. Through The Years	Liberty 1444
7/24/82	**13**	10	13. Love Will Turn You Around -from the film "Six Pack"-	Liberty 1471
			ROGERS, KENNY, & KIM CARNES	
4/12/80	**4**	14	1. **Don't Fall In Love With A Dreamer**	United Artists 1345
			ROGERS, KENNY, & THE FIRST EDITION	
			Kenny plus 3 other members were originally with The New Christy Minstrels	
2/24/68	**5**	8	1. **Just Dropped In (To See What Condition My Condition Was In)**	Reprise 0655
2/08/69	**19**	8	2. But You Know I Love You -above 2: The First Edition-	Reprise 0799
7/05/69	**6**	9	3. **Ruby, Don't Take Your Love To Town**	Reprise 0829
10/25/69	**26**	6	4. Ruben James	Reprise 0854
3/14/70	**11**	12	5. **Something's Burning**	Reprise 0888
7/25/70	**17**	8	6. Tell It All Brother	Reprise 0923
11/14/70	**33**	5	7. Heed The Call	Reprise 0953
			ROGERS, TIMMIE "Oh Yeah!"	
11/04/57	**36**	4	1. Back To School Again	Cameo 116
			ROLLING STONES	
			British: Mick Jagger-lead singer, Keith Richards-lead guitar, Bill Wyman-bass, Charlie Watts-drums, Brian Jones-guitar (died 7/3/69-27), replaced by Mick Taylor, who was replaced in 1975 by Ron Wood	
8/01/64	**24**	5	1. Tell Me (You're Coming Back)	London 9682
8/22/64	**26**	6	2. It's All Over Now	London 9687
11/07/64	**6**	9	3. **Time Is On My Side**	London 9708
1/30/65	**19**	5	4. Heart Of Stone	London 9725
4/10/65	**9**	8	5. **The Last Time**	London 9741
6/19/65	**1** (4)	12	● 6. **(I Can't Get No) Satisfaction**	London 9766
10/16/65	**1** (2)	11	7. **Get Off Of My Cloud**	London 9792
1/08/66	**6**	6	8. **As Tears Go By**	London 9808
3/05/66	**2** (3)	9	9. **19th Nervous Breakdown**	London 9823
5/21/66	**1** (2)	10	10. **Paint It, Black**	London 901
7/16/66	**8**	8	11. **Mothers Little Helper/**	
8/06/66	**24**	4	12. Lady Jane	London 902
10/08/66	**9**	6	13. **Have You Seen Your Mother, Baby, Standing In The Shadow?**	London 903
2/04/67	**1** (1)	9	● 14. **Ruby Tuesday**	London 904
9/23/67	**14**	6	15. Dandelion	London 905
1/13/68	**25**	4	16. She's A Rainbow	London 906
6/15/68	**3**	11	17. **Jumpin' Jack Flash**	London 908
7/26/69	**1** (4)	14	● 18. **Honky Tonk Women**	London 910
5/01/71	**1** (2)	12	19. **Brown Sugar**	Roll. Stones 19100
7/03/71	**28**	5	20. Wild Horses	Roll. Stones 19101
5/06/72	**7**	9	21. **Tumbling Dice**	Roll. Stones 19103
7/29/72	**22**	4	22. Happy	Roll. Stones 19104

DATE	POS	WKS	ARTIST—Record Title	LABEL & NO.
9/22/73	1 (1)	13	● 23. **Angie**	Roll. Stones 19105
2/02/74	15	6	24. Doo Doo Doo Doo Doo (Heartbreaker)	Roll. Stones 19109
8/17/74	16	7	25. It's Only Rock 'N Roll (But I Like It)	Roll. Stones 19301
11/16/74	17	7	26. Ain't Too Proud To Beg	Roll. Stones 19302
5/08/76	10	7	27. **Fool To Cry**	Roll. Stones 19304
6/10/78	1 (1)	16	● 28. **Miss You**	Roll. Stones 19307
9/23/78	8	9	29. **Beast Of Burden**	Roll. Stones 19309
1/13/79	31	4	30. Shattered	Roll. Stones 19310
7/05/80	3	14	31. **Emotional Rescue**	Roll. Stones 20001
10/18/80	26	5	32. She's So Cold	Roll. Stones 21001
8/29/81	2 (3)	18	33. **Start Me Up**	Roll. Stones 21003
12/12/81	13	12	34. Waiting On A Friend	Roll. Stones 21004
4/10/82	20	6	35. Hang Fire	Roll. Stones 21300
7/03/82	25	5	36. Going To A Go-Go	Roll. Stones 21301
			RONALD & RUBY	
3/24/58	20	3	1. Lollipop	RCA 7174
			RONDO, DON	
11/03/56	11	12	1. Two Different Worlds	Jubilee 5256
7/29/57	7	15	2. **White Silver Sands**	Jubilee 5288
			RONETTES	
			New York trio: Ronnie Spector, Estelle Bennett & Nedra Talley	
9/14/63	2 (3)	10	1. **Be My Baby**	Philles 116
1/11/64	24·	6	2. Baby, I Love You	Philles 118
5/16/64	39	1	3. (The Best Part Of) Breakin' Up	Philles 120
7/18/64	34	4	4. Do I Love You?	Philles 121
11/21/64	23	7	5. Walking In The Rain	Philles 123
			RONNIE & THE HI-LITES	
			Ronnie Goodson died on 11/4/80 (33)	
4/21/62	16	8	1. I Wish That We Were Married	Joy 260
			RONNY & THE DAYTONAS	
			Ronny is Bucky Wilkin	
8/22/64	4	10	1. **G.T.O**	Mala 481
1/08/66	27	5	2. Sandy	Mala 513
			RONSTADT, LINDA	
			also see Nitty Gritty Dirt Band	
12/09/67	13	13	1. Different Drum	Capitol 2004
			-shown as Linda Ronstadt & The Stone Poneys-	
9/12/70	25	7	2. Long Long Time	Capitol 2846
1/04/75	1 (1)	10	3. **You're No Good**	Capitol 3990
4/26/75	2 (2)	13	4. **When Will I Be Loved**	Capitol 4050
10/04/75	5	10	5. **Heat Wave/**	
		8	6. **Love Is A Rose**	Asylum 45282
1/24/76	25	6	7. Tracks Of My Tears	Asylum 45295
9/04/76	11	11	8. That'll Be The Day	Asylum 45340
10/08/77	3	16	● 9. **Blue Bayou**	Asylum 45431
10/29/77	5	12	10. **It's So Easy**	Asylum 45438
2/25/78	31	3	11. Poor Poor Pitiful Me	Asylum 45462

DATE	POS	WKS	ARTIST—Record Title	LABEL & NO.
5/20/78	32	3	12. Tumbling Dice	Asylum 45479
9/09/78	16	8	13. Back In The U.S.A	Asylum 45519
11/18/78	7	13	14. **Ooh Baby Baby**	Asylum 45546
2/09/80	10	12	15. **How Do I Make You**	Asylum 46602
4/19/80	8	11	16. **Hurt So Bad**	Asylum 46624
7/19/80	31	4	17. I Can't Let Go	Asylum 46654
10/23/82	29	5	18. Get Closer	Asylum 69948
			ROOFTOP SINGERS	
			Erik Darling, leader (founder of The Tarriers)	
1/12/63	1 (2)	11	1. **Walk Right In**	Vanguard 35017
4/20/63	20	5	2. Tom Cat	Vanguard 35019
			ROSE GARDEN	
12/09/67	17	7	1. Next Plane To London	Atco 6510
			ROSE ROYCE	
			Rose is Gwen Dickey	
12/11/76	1 (1)	14	★ 1. **Car Wash**	MCA 40615
3/19/77	10	10	2. **I Wanna Get Next To You**	MCA 40662
			-above 2 from film "Car Wash"-	
10/22/77	39	2	3. Do Your Dance - Part 1	Whitfield 8440
1/13/79	32	4	4. Love Don't Live Here Anymore	Whitfield 8712
			ROSE, DAVID, & His Orchestra	
6/02/62	1 (1)	13	1. **The Stripper [I]**	MGM 13064
			ROSIE & The Originals	
			Rosie Hamlin	
12/12/60	5	12	1. **Angel Baby**	Highland 1011
			ROSS, DIANA	
			Diana was lead singer of The Supremes from 1962-1969 - also see Marvin Gaye	
5/02/70	20	8	1. Reach Out And Touch (Somebody's Hand)	Motown 1165
8/15/70	1 (3)	13	2. **Ain't No Mountain High Enough**	Motown 1169
1/09/71	16	8	3. Remember Me	Motown 1176
5/15/71	29	5	4. Reach Out I'll Be There	Motown 1184
9/11/71	38	3	5. Surrender	Motown 1188
3/03/73	34	4	6. Good Morning Heartache	Motown 1211
			-from "Lady Sings The Blues"-	
7/07/73	1 (1)	16	7. **Touch Me In The Morning**	Motown 1239
1/26/74	14	8	8. Last Time I Saw Him	Motown 1278
11/22/75	1 (1)	13	9. **Theme From Mahogany (Do You Know Where You're Going To)**	Motown 1377
4/24/76	1 (2)	13	10. **Love Hangover**	Motown 1392
8/21/76	25	8	11. One Love In My Lifetime	Motown 1398
12/03/77	27	7	12. Gettin' Ready For Love	Motown 1427
8/18/79	19	9	13. The Boss	Motown 1462
8/09/80	1 (4)	17	● 14. **Upside Down**	Motown 1494
10/04/80	5	13	15. **I'm Coming Out**	Motown 1491
11/15/80	9	15	16. **It's My Turn**	Motown 1496
10/24/81	7	14	17. **Why Do Fools Fall In Love**	RCA 12349
1/30/82	8	10	18. **Mirror, Mirror**	RCA 13021

DATE	POS	WKS	ARTIST—Record Title	LABEL & NO.
10/16/82	**10**	10	19. **Muscles**	RCA 13348
			ROSS, DIANA, & LIONEL RICHIE	
7/18/81	**1** (9)	19	★ 1. **Endless Love**	Motown 1519
			ROSS, JACK	
			died 12/16/82 (66)	
4/07/62	**16**	6	1. Cinderella [C]	Dot 16333
			ROSS, JACKIE	
8/15/64	**11**	8	1. Selfish One	Chess 1903
			ROSS, SPENCER	
1/18/60	**13**	10	1. Tracy's Theme [I]	Columbia 41532
			-from the TV production "Philadelphia Story"-	
			ROUTERS	
			quintet led by Joe Saraceno	
11/24/62	**19**	7	1. Let's Go (pony) [I]	Warner 5283
			ROVER BOYS featuring Billy Albert	
			Canadian	
5/19/56	**16**	7	1. Graduation Day	ABC-Paramount 9700
			ROVERS - see IRISH ROVERS	
			ROXY MUSIC	
			English quintet featuring Bryan Ferry	
2/21/76	**30**	5	1. Love Is The Drug	Atco 7042
			ROYAL GUARDSMEN	
			Florida sextet	
12/17/66	**2** (4)	11	● 1. **Snoopy Vs. The Red Baron** [N]	Laurie 3366
3/11/67	**15**	5	2. The Return Of The Red Baron [N]	Laurie 3379
1/04/69	**35**	5	3. Baby Let's Wait	Laurie 3461
			ROYAL PHILHARMONIC ORCHESTRA	
			Louis Clark, conductor	
11/28/81	**10**	12	1. **Hooked On Classics** [I]	RCA 12304
			ROYAL SCOTS DRAGOON GUARDS	
			The Pipes and Drums and the Military Band	
5/27/72	**11**	8	1. Amazing Grace [I]	RCA 0709
			ROYAL TEENS	
			member Bob Gaudio was an original Four Seasons member	
2/03/58	**3**	12	1. **Short Shorts**	ABC-Para. 9882
11/16/59	**26**	6	2. Believe Me	Capitol 4261
			ROYALTONES	
			Detroit quartet	
11/10/58	**17**	10	1. Poor Boy [I]	Jubilee 5338
			ROYAL, BILLY JOE	
7/31/65	**9**	8	1. **Down In The Boondocks**	Columbia 43305
10/09/65	**14**	8	2. I Knew You When	Columbia 43390
1/15/66	**38**	1	3. I've Got To Be Somebody	Columbia 43465
11/01/69	**15**	10	4. Cherry Hill Park	Columbia 44902

DATE	POS	WKS	ARTIST—Record Title	LABEL & NO.
			RUBETTES	
8/31/74	37	2	1. Sugar Baby Love	Polydor 15089
			RUBICON	
			Jerry Martini, leader (member of Sly & The Family Stone '66-'76)	
4/08/78	28	3	1. I'm Gonna Take Care Of Everything	20th Century 2362
			RUBY & THE ROMANTICS	
			Akron, Ohio quintet featuring Ruby Nash	
2/23/63	1 (1)	10	1. **Our Day Will Come**	Kapp 501
6/15/63	16	6	2. My Summer Love	Kapp 525
8/31/63	27	5	3. Hey There Lonely Boy	Kapp 544
			RUFFIN, DAVID	
			lead singer of The Temptations from 1964-1968	
2/22/69	9	9	1. **My Whole World Ended (The Moment You Left Me)**	Motown 1140
11/29/75	9	11	2. **Walk Away From Love**	Motown 1376
			RUFFIN, JIMMY	
			brother of David Ruffin	
9/10/66	7	14	1. **What Becomes Of The Brokenhearted**	Soul 35022
12/24/66	17	8	2. I've Passed This Way Before	Soul 35027
4/08/67	29	3	3. Gonna Give Her All The Love I've Got	Soul 35032
3/22/80	10	9	4. **Hold On To My Love**	RSO 1021
			RUFUS Featuring CHAKA KHAN	
			also see American Breed	
7/13/74	3	12	● 1. **Tell Me Something Good** -shown only as Rufus-	ABC 11427
11/02/74	11	11	2. You Got The Love	ABC 12032
3/08/75	10	7	3. **Once You Get Started**	ABC 12066
2/14/76	5	12	● 4. **Sweet Thing**	ABC 12149
6/12/76	39	1	5. Dance Wit Me	ABC 12179
3/12/77	30	6	6. At Midnight (My Love Will Lift You Up)	ABC 12239
6/04/77	32	3	7. Hollywood	ABC 12269
5/27/78	38	3	8. Stay	ABC 12349
1/19/80	30	4	9. Do You Love What You Feel	MCA 41131
			RUGBYS	
9/20/69	24	7	1. You, I	Amazon 1
			RUNDGREN, TODD	
			leader of Nazz from '68-'70 - also see Utopia	
12/26/70	20	9	1. We Gotta Get You A Woman -shown as Runt-	Ampex 31001
5/06/72	16	9	2. I Saw The Light	Bearsville 0003
11/10/73	5	12	3. **Hello It's Me** -original version by Nazz in '69-	Bearsville 0009
6/26/76	34	3	4. Good Vibrations	Bearsville 0309
7/08/78	29	5	5. Can We Still Be Friends	Bearsville 0324
			RUSH	
			Canadian trio: Geddy Lee, Alex Lifeson & Neil Peart -- also see Bob & Doug McKenzie	
10/09/82	21	6	1. New World Man	Mercury 76179

DATE	POS	WKS	ARTIST—Record Title	LABEL & NO.
			RUSH, MERRILEE, & The Turnabouts	
6/01/68	7	12	1. **Angel Of The Morning**	Bell 705
			RUSHEN, PATRICE	
6/05/82	23	7	1. Forget Me Nots	Elektra 47427
			RUSSELL, BOBBY	
			married to Vicki Lawrence	
11/23/68	36	2	1. 1432 Franklin Pike Circle Hero	Elf 90020
8/28/71	28	7	2. Saturday Morning Confusion [N]	United Artists 50788
			RUSSELL, BRENDA	
10/13/79	30	6	1. So Good, So Right	Horizon 123
			RUSSELL, LEON	
			also recorded as Hank Wilson -- also see Joe Cocker	
9/23/72	11	7	1. Tight Rope	Shelter 7325
9/13/75	14	10	2. Lady Blue	Shelter 40378
			RYAN, CHARLIE, & The Timberline Riders	
8/08/60	33	4	1. Hot Rod Lincoln [S-N]	4 Star 7047
			RYDELL, BOBBY	
			discovered at the age of 9 by Paul Whiteman	
8/10/59	11	9	1. Kissin' Time	Cameo 167
10/26/59	6	14	2. **We Got Love**	Cameo 169
2/08/60	2 (1)	13	3. **Wild One/**	
2/22/60	19	10	4. Little Bitty Girl	Cameo 171
5/16/60	5	8	5. **Swingin' School/** -from "Because They're Young"-	
5/16/60	18	8	6. Ding-A-Ling	Cameo 175
8/01/60	4	11	7. **Volare**	Cameo 179
11/14/60	14	10	8. Sway	Cameo 182
2/06/61	11	8	9. Good Time Baby	Cameo 186
5/08/61	21	5	10. That Old Black Magic	Cameo 190
7/10/61	25	5	11. The Fish	Cameo 192
11/06/61	21	6	12. I Wanna Thank You	Cameo 201
3/10/62	18	7	13. I've Got Bonnie	Cameo 209
6/23/62	14	7	14. I'll Never Dance Again	Cameo 217
10/27/62	10	8	15. **The Cha-Cha-Cha**	Cameo 228
2/23/63	23	6	16. Butterfly Baby	Cameo 242
6/01/63	17	5	17. Wildwood Days	Cameo 252
12/07/63	4	12	18. **Forget Him**	Cameo 280
			RYDELL, BOBBY, & CHUBBY CHECKER	
12/25/61	21	3	1. Jingle Bell Rock [X]	Cameo 205
			RYDER, MITCH	
9/30/67	30	4	1. What Now My Love	DynoVoice 901
			RYDER, MITCH, & The Detroit Wheels	
1/08/66	10	8	1. **Jenny Take A Ride!**	New Voice 806
3/26/66	17	6	2. Little Latin Lupe Lu	New Voice 808
10/22/66	4	14	3. **Devil With A Blue Dress On & Good Golly Miss Molly (medley)**	New Voice 817

DATE	POS	WKS	ARTIST—Record Title	LABEL & NO.
2/18/67	6	9	4. **Sock It To Me-Baby!**	New Voice 820
5/13/67	24	4	5. Too Many Fish In The Sea & Three Little Fishes (medley)	New Voice 822
			SADLER, BARRY, SSgt SSgt (Staff Sergeant) U.S. Army Special Forces	
2/19/66	1 (5)	11	● 1. **The Ballad Of The Green Berets**	RCA 8739
5/14/66	28	4	2. The "A" Team	RCA 8804
			SAFARIS with The Phantom's Band	
7/11/60	6	11	1. **Image Of A Girl**	Eldo 101
			SAGER, CAROLE BAYER	
6/13/81	30	7	1. Stronger Than Before	Boardwalk 02054
			SAILCAT	
7/15/72	12	10	1. Motorcycle Mama	Elektra 45782
			SAINTE-MARIE, BUFFY	
4/29/72	38	2	1. Mister Can't You See	Vanguard 35151
			ST. PETERS, CRISPIAN	
7/09/66	4	8	1. **The Pied Piper**	Jamie 1320
7/22/67	36	2	2. You Were On My Mind	Jamie 1310
			SAKAMOTO, KYU Japanese	
5/25/63	1 (3)	12	1. **Sukiyaki [F]**	Capitol 4945
			SALSOUL ORCHESTRA a Vincent Montana production	
2/14/76	18	9	1. Tangerine [I]	Salsoul 2004
10/30/76	30	5	2. Nice 'N' Naasty	Salsoul 2011
			SALVO, SAMMY	
3/03/58	23	1	1. Oh Julie	RCA 7097
			SAM & DAVE Sam Moore & Dave Prater	
6/04/66	21	7	1. Hold On! I'm A Comin'	Stax 189
9/30/67	2 (3)	11	● 2. **Soul Man**	Stax 231
2/17/68	9	9	3. **I Thank You**	Stax 242
			SAM THE SHAM & The Pharaohs Sam is Domingo Samudio	
5/01/65	2 (2)	14	● 1. **Wooly Bully**	MGM 13322
8/21/65	26	4	2. Ju Ju Hand	MGM 13364
11/13/65	33	3	3. Ring Dang Doo	MGM 13397
7/02/66	2 (2)	11	● 4. **Lil' Red Riding Hood**	MGM 13506
10/15/66	22	5	5. The Hair On My Chinny Chin Chin	MGM 13581
1/21/67	27	4	6. How Do You Catch A Girl	MGM 13649
			SAN REMO GOLDEN STRINGS	
10/09/65	27	5	1. Hungry For Love [I]	Ric-Tic 104
			SANDERS, FELICIA died on 2/7/75	
5/28/55	29	3	1. Blue Star -the "Medic" theme-	Columbia 40508

Sam the Sham & the Pharaohs. It wasn't for "Wooly Bully" that Sam (The Sham) Samudio collected his one and only Grammy. It was for best sleeve notes on the "Sam, Hard And Heavy" album in 1971. Way to go, Sam.

Tommy Sands' ticket to the top 40 came through his appearance in "The Singing Idol," a television play. Tommy's role was supposed to have been taken by Elvis Presley, but pressure of work apparently prevented the King's participation.

John Schneider. When in doubt, record an Elvis oldie. That's what John Schneider did, looking to extend his television popularity (as Bo Duke in "Dukes Of Hazzard") to vinyl.

Neil Sedaka's remarkable '70s comeback had its roots in Britain, where "That's When The Music Takes Me" was a top 20 hit in 1973—two years before "Laughter In The Rain" returned Neil to the U.S. top 40.

The Seekers. Australia gifted the charts with several groups (by way of Britain) in 1967, and the Seekers were among them. Both their top 10 hits were written by Tom Springfield, onetime member of a similar folkie aggregation, the Springfields.

Bob Seger. It's hard to believe that the early recordings of Detroit rocker Bob Seger were made for the Philadelphia label whose earlier artists sang about the Twist, the Bird, the Bristol Stomp, the Mashed Potato, the Gravy, the Freddie, the Wah-Watusi, the Fly, the Pony, the Limbo Rock, the Hitchhiker. . . .

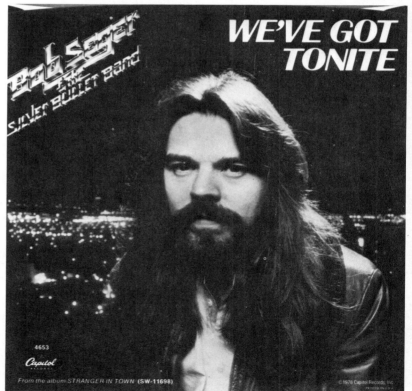

DO THE BIRD

Dee Dee Sharp

bobby sherman
"JULIE, DO YA LOVE ME"

FOOLISH LITTLE GIRL

SCEPTER RECORDS 1248

the SHIRELLES

Dee Dee Sharp was working as a background singer for Cameo Records when label chief Bernie Lowe suggested she augment Chubby Checker's vocal on "Slow Twistin'." The result was a hit, and the springboard to Dee Dee's own solo success.

Bobby Sherman. Through his singing at parties, Bobby Sherman was discovered by Natalie Wood and Sal Mineo, which led to appearances on television's "Shindig" and, later, "Here Come The Brides." Then came the hit records.

The Shirelle's first release, "I Met Him On A Sunday," didn't reach the top 40, but its sales encouraged entrepreneur Florence Greenberg to form her own label, Scepter Records. It went on to become one of the most successful independents of the '60s, with the Shirelles, Chuck Jackson, Dionne Warwick, the Kingsmen, and B.J. Thomas.

Carly Simon. If this were a top 73 book, you would find that Carly Simon first charted as one-half of the Simon Sisters, whose "Winkin', Blinkin' And Nod" climbed to, yes, number 73 on *Billboard's* charts in the spring of '64.

Paul Simon. Simon & Garfunkel once performed together in a school production of "Alice In Wonderland," Paul as the White Rabbit, Art as the Cheshire Cat.

Nancy Sinatra is one half of the only father and daughter combination to top *Billboard's* charts, with a song that took Nancy 35 minutes to record on the eve of a trip to entertain troops in Vietnam. The singers weren't even in the studio together; in fact, Nancy's vocal was originally intended only as a background to her father's performance. It was producer Lee Hazlewood who put it together as a duet.

Carly Simon — Jesse b/w Stardust

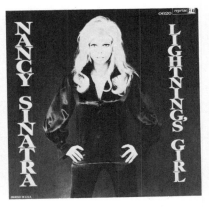

PAUL SIMON · AMERICAN TUNE

NANCY SINATRA — LIGHTNING'S GIRL

DATE	POS	WKS	ARTIST—Record Title	LABEL & NO.
			SANDPEBBLES	
1/06/68	22	6	1. Love Power	Calla 141
			SANDPIPERS	
			Los Angeles-based trio	
8/13/66	9	9	1. **Guantanamera** [F]	A&M 806
11/12/66	30	4	2. Louie, Louie [F]	A&M 819
5/02/70	17	8	3. Come Saturday Morning	A&M 1134
			-from film "The Sterile Cuckoo"-	
			SANDS, JODIE	
6/10/57	15	9	1. With All My Heart	Chancellor 1003
			SANDS, TOMMY	
2/23/57	2 (2)	12	1. **Teen-Age Crush**	Capitol 3639
5/27/57	16	8	2. Goin' Steady	Capitol 3723
2/24/58	24	2	3. Sing Boy Sing	Capitol 3867
			SANFORD/TOWNSEND BAND	
			Ed Sanford/John Townsend	
7/16/77	9	12	1. **Smoke From A Distant Fire**	Warner 8370
			SANG, SAMANTHA	
			Australian	
1/07/78	3	17	★ 1. **Emotion**	Private Stock 45178
			-backing vocal: Barry Gibb-	
			SANTA ESMERALDA featuring Leroy Gomez	
12/10/77	15	12	1. Don't Let Me Be Misunderstood	Casablanca 902
			SANTAMARIA, MONGO	
4/13/63	10	6	1. **Watermelon Man** [I]	Battle 45909
3/08/69	32	2	2. Cloud Nine [I]	Columbia 44740
			SANTANA	
			San Francisco group led by Devadip Carlos Santana	
2/07/70	9	11	1. **Evil Ways**	Columbia 45069
11/21/70	4	12	2. **Black Magic Woman**	Columbia 45270
3/06/71	13	8	3. Oye Como Va [F]	Columbia 45330
10/30/71	12	8	4. Everybody's Everything	Columbia 45472
3/11/72	36	4	5. No One To Depend On	Columbia 45552
11/19/77	27	5	6. She's Not There	Columbia 10616
2/17/79	32	3	7. Stormy	Columbia 10873
1/19/80	35	3	8. You Know That I Love You	Columbia 11144
5/16/81	17	11	9. Winning	Columbia 01050
8/28/82	15	10	10. Hold On	Columbia 03160
			SANTO & JOHNNY	
			Brooklyn brother duo (Farina)	
8/17/59	1 (2)	13	1. **Sleep Walk** [I]	Can. Amer. 103
12/14/59	23	7	2. Tear Drop [I]	Can. Amer. 107
			SANTOS, LARRY	
4/03/76	36	2	1. We Can't Hide It Anymore	Casablanca 844
			SAPPHIRES	
			Philadelphia quartet	
2/22/64	25	5	1. Who Do You Love	Swan 4162

DATE	POS	WKS	ARTIST—Record Title	LABEL & NO.
			SAYER, LEO	
			English	
3/22/75	9	9	1. **Long Tall Glasses (I Can Dance)**	Warner 8043
11/06/76	1 (1)	17	● 2. **You Make Me Feel Like Dancing**	Warner 8283
3/26/77	1 (1)	14	● 3. **When I Need You**	Warner 8332
7/23/77	17	10	4. How Much Love	Warner 8319
11/05/77	38	2	5. Thunder In My Heart	Warner 8465
1/28/78	36	2	6. Easy To Love	Warner 8502
10/18/80	2 (4)	15	● 7. **More Than I Can Say**	Warner 49565
2/14/81	23	6	8. Living In A Fantasy	Warner 49657
			SCAGGS, BOZ	
			original member of The Steve Miller Band	
5/22/76	38	3	1. It's Over	Columbia 10319
8/07/76	3	15	● 2. **Lowdown**	Columbia 10367
3/19/77	11	12	3. Lido Shuffle	Columbia 10491
4/19/80	15	9	4. Breakdown Dead Ahead	Columbia 11241
7/12/80	17	9	5. JoJo	Columbia 11281
9/06/80	14	10	6. Look What You've Done To Me	Columbia 11349
12/27/80	14	9	7. Miss Sun	Columbia 11406
			-backup vocal: Lisa Dal Bello-	
			SCARBURY, JOEY	
6/13/81	2 (2)	18	● 1. **Theme From "Greatest American Hero"** **(Believe It Or Not)**	Elektra 47147
			SCHNEIDER, JOHN	
			Bo Duke of TV's "The Dukes Of Hazzard"	
6/27/81	14	11	1. It's Now Or Never	Scotti Bros. 02105
			SCHUMANN, WALTER [The Voices Of]	
4/09/55	14	6	1. The Ballad Of Davy Crockett	RCA 6041
			SCHWARTZ, EDDIE	
			Canadian	
1/16/82	28	7	1. All Our Tomorrows	Atco 7342
			SCOTT, BOBBY	
1/21/56	13	10	1. Chain Gang	ABC-Para. 9658
			SCOTT, FREDDIE	
8/10/63	10	9	1. **Hey, Girl**	Colpix 692
2/18/67	39	2	2. Are You Lonely For Me	Shout 207
			SCOTT, JACK	
			Canadian-born Jack Scafone, Jr. - featuring the Chantones on the Carlton label	
6/16/58	25	7	1. Leroy/	
7/07/58	3	15	2. **My True Love**	Carlton 462
10/20/58	28	4	3. With Your Love	Carlton 483
12/28/58	8	13	4. **Goodbye Baby**	Carlton 493
8/03/59	35	4	5. The Way I Walk	Carlton 514
1/18/60	5	12	6. **What In The World's Come Over You**	Top Rank 2028
5/09/60	3	12	7. **Burning Bridges/**	
5/30/60	34	2	8. Oh, Little One	Top Rank 2041
9/05/60	38	2	9. It Only Happened Yesterday	Top Rank 2055

DATE	POS	WKS	ARTIST—Record Title	LABEL & NO.
			SCOTT, LINDA	
			real name: Linda Joy Sampson	
4/03/61	3	10	1. **I've Told Every Little Star**	Can. Amer. 123
7/24/61	9	10	2. **Don't Bet Money Honey**	Can. Amer. 127
11/27/61	12	8	3. I Don't Know Why	Can. Amer. 129
			SCOTT, PEGGY, & JO JO BENSON	
7/06/68	31	7	1. Lover's Holiday	SSS Int'l. 736
11/30/68	27	4	2. Pickin' Wild Mountain Berries	SSS Int'l. 748
2/15/69	37	3	3. Soul Shake	SSS Int'l. 761
			SEA, JOHNNY	
6/25/66	35	2	1. Day For Decision [S]	Warner 5820
			SEALS & CROFTS	
			Jim Seals & Dash Crofts from Texas	
10/21/72	6	11	1. **Summer Breeze**	Warner 7606
2/17/73	20	9	2. Hummingbird	Warner 7671
6/16/73	6	12	3. **Diamond Girl**	Warner 7708
10/13/73	21	8	4. We May Never Pass This Way (Again)	Warner 7740
5/17/75	18	8	5. I'll Play For You	Warner 8075
6/05/76	6	15	6. **Get Closer** -featuring Carolyn Willis-	Warner 8190
10/22/77	28	5	7. My Fair Share -Love Theme from "One On One"-	Warner 8405
5/27/78	18	7	8. You're The Love	Warner 8551
			SEARCHERS	
			quartet from Liverpool, England	
3/21/64	13	8	1. Needles And Pins	Kapp 577
6/20/64	16	8	2. Don't Throw Your Love Away	Kapp 593
9/12/64	34	3	3. Some Day We're Gonna Love Again	Kapp 609
11/14/64	35	2	4. When You Walk In The Room	Kapp 618
12/19/64	3	11	5. **Love Potion Number Nine**	Kapp 27
2/20/65	29	3	6. What Have They Done To The Rain	Kapp 644
4/10/65	21	4	7. Bumble Bee	Kapp 49
			SEBASTIAN, JOHN	
			lead singer of Lovin' Spoonful	
4/10/76	1 (1)	11	● 1. **Welcome Back** -from TV's "Welcome Back Kotter"-	Reprise 1349
			SECRETS	
			Cleveland quartet	
12/07/63	18	6	1. The Boy Next Door	Philips 40146
			SEDAKA, NEIL	
12/28/58	14	9	1. The Diary	RCA 7408
10/26/59	9	13	2. **Oh! Carol**	RCA 7595
4/18/60	9	9	3. **Stairway To Heaven**	RCA 7709
8/29/60	17	9	4. You Mean Everything To Me/	
10/03/60	28	3	5. Run Samson Run	RCA 7781
12/31/60	4	12	6. **Calendar Girl**	RCA 7829
5/08/61	11	7	7. Little Devil	RCA 7874
11/27/61	6	11	8. **Happy Birthday, Sweet Sixteen**	RCA 7957

DATE	POS	WKS	ARTIST—Record Title	LABEL & NO.
7/07/62	**1** (2)	12	9. **Breaking Up Is Hard To Do**	RCA 8046
10/20/62	**5**	9	10. **Next Door To An Angel**	RCA 8086
2/16/63	**17**	7	11. Alice In Wonderland	RCA 8137
5/18/63	**26**	5	12. Let's Go Steady Again	RCA 8169
12/07/63	**33**	4	13. Bad Girl	RCA 8254
11/16/74	**1** (1)	15	14. **Laughter In The Rain**	Rocket 40313
4/26/75	**22**	5	15. The Immigrant	Rocket 40370
8/02/75	**27**	4	16. That's When The Music Takes Me	Rocket 40426
9/20/75	**1** (3)	12	● 17. **Bad Blood**	Rocket 40460
			-background vocals: Elton John-	
12/27/75	**8**	11	18. **Breaking Up Is Hard To Do**	Rocket 40500
			-slow version of the 1962 hit-	
5/01/76	**16**	7	19. Love In The Shadows	Rocket 40543
7/24/76	**36**	2	20. Steppin' Out	Rocket 40582
			SEDAKA, NEIL & DARA	
			father and daughter	
5/10/80	**19**	10	1. Should've Never Let You Go	Elektra 46615
			SEEDS	
			Los Angeles psychedelic rock quartet	
2/11/67	**36**	3	1. Pushin' Too Hard	GNP Crescendo 372
			SEEKERS	
			Australian quartet: Judy Durham, lead singer -- also see New Seekers	
4/10/65	**4**	10	1. **I'll Never Find Another You**	Capitol 5383
6/26/65	**19**	7	2. A World Of Our Own	Capitol 5430
12/31/66	**2** (2)	12	● 3. **Georgy Girl**	Capitol 5756
			SEGER, BOB	
			from Detroit - featuring backing band: The Silver Bullet Band	
1/25/69	**17**	9	1. Ramblin' Gamblin' Man	Capitol 2297
1/15/77	**4**	13	2. **Night Moves**	Capitol 4369
5/14/77	**24**	4	3. Mainstreet	Capitol 4422
6/03/78	**4**	11	4. **Still The Same**	Capitol 4581
8/19/78	**12**	10	5. Hollywood Nights	Capitol 4618
11/25/78	**13**	11	6. We've Got Tonite	Capitol 4653
5/05/79	**28**	5	7. Old Time Rock & Roll	Capitol 4702
3/01/80	**6**	12	8. **Fire Lake**	Capitol 4836
5/10/80	**5**	11	9. **Against The Wind**	Capitol 4863
8/16/80	**14**	9	10. You'll Accomp'ny Me	Capitol 4904
9/26/81	**5**	12	11. **Tryin' To Live My Life Without You**	Capitol 5042
			SELLARS, MARILYN	
9/28/74	**37**	2	1. One Day At A Time	Mega 1205
			SENATOR BOBBY	
			Senator Bobby is Bill Minkin	
1/21/67	**20**	4	1. Wild Thing [C]	Parkway 127
			SENSATIONS	
			Yvonne Baker, lead singer	
2/10/62	**4**	12	1. **Let Me In**	Argo 5405

DATE	POS	WKS	ARTIST—Record Title	LABEL & NO.
			SERENDIPITY SINGERS	
			organized at Univ. of Colorado	
3/21/64	6	11	1. **Don't Let The Rain Come Down (Crooked Little Man)**	Philips 40175
6/13/64	30	5	2. Beans In My Ears [N]	Philips 40198
			SEVILLE, DAVID [The Music Of]	
			real name: Ross Bagdasarian - died 1/16/72 (52) -- also see Chipmunks	
4/14/58	1 (3)	18	1. **Witch Doctor** [N]	Liberty 55132
7/14/58	34	2	2. The Bird On My Head [N]	Liberty 55140
			SEYMOUR, PHIL	
			member of Dwight Twilley Band	
2/21/81	22	7	1. Precious To Me	Boardwalk 5703
			SHADES OF BLUE	
5/28/66	12	8	1. Oh How Happy	Impact 1007
			SHADOWS OF KNIGHT	
			Chicago-area rock quintet	
4/16/66	10	8	1. **Gloria**	Dunwich 116
7/02/66	39	1	2. Oh Yeah	Dunwich 122
			SHALAMAR	
4/16/77	25	8	1. Uptown Festival (Motown Medley) [N]	Soul Train 10885
2/02/80	8	13	● 2. **The Second Time Around**	Solar 11709
			SHANGRI-LAS	
			New York quartet (2 pairs of sisters)	
9/05/64	5	9	1. **Remember (Walkin' In The Sand)**	Red Bird 008
10/24/64	1 (1)	10	2. **Leader Of The Pack** [N]	Red Bird 014
1/16/65	18	5	3. Give Him A Great Big Kiss	Red Bird 018
6/19/65	29	4	4. Give Us Your Blessings	Red Bird 030
11/20/65	6	8	5. **I Can Never Go Home Anymore**	Red Bird 043
2/26/66	33	2	6. Long Live Our Love	Red Bird 048
			SHANNON, DEL	
			real name: Charles Westover	
3/27/61	1 (4)	12	1. **Runaway**	Big Top 3067
6/19/61	5	11	2. **Hats Off To Larry**	Big Top 3075
10/09/61	28	5	3. So Long Baby	Big Top 3083
1/06/62	38	2	4. Hey! Little Girl	Big Top 3091
1/26/63	12	7	5. Little Town Flirt	Big Top 3131
7/25/64	22	7	6. Handy Man	Amy 905
12/19/64	9	10	7. **Keep Searchin' (We'll Follow The Sun)**	Amy 915
3/13/65	30	4	8. Stranger In Town	Amy 919
1/23/82	33	4	9. Sea Of Love	Network 47951
			SHARP, DEE DEE	
			also see Chubby Checker	
3/17/62	2 (2)	15	1. **Mashed Potato Time**	Cameo 212
6/23/62	9	9	2. **Gravy (For My Mashed Potatoes)**	Cameo 219
11/10/62	5	9	3. **Ride!**	Cameo 230
3/09/63	10	9	4. **Do The Bird**	Cameo 244
11/02/63	33	5	5. Wild!	Cameo 274

DATE	POS	WKS	ARTIST—Record Title	LABEL & NO.
			SHAW, GEORGIE	
			also see Kitty Kallen	
11/12/55	23	6	1. No Arms Can Ever Hold You (Like These Arms Of Mine	Decca 29679
			SHELLS	
			Brooklyn quintet	
12/31/60	21	5	1. Baby Oh Baby	Johnson 104
			SHEP & THE LIMELITES	
			James (Shep) Sheppard died on 1/24/70	
4/10/61	2 (1)	11	1. **Daddy's Home**	Hull 740
			SHEPHERD SISTERS	
11/04/57	18	7	1. Alone (Why Must I Be Alone)	Lance 125
			SHEPPARD, T.G.	
5/16/81	37	2	1. I Loved 'Em Every One	Warner 49690
			SHERMAN, ALLAN	
			died on 11/21/73 (48)	
8/10/63	2 (3)	8	1. **Hello Mudduh, Hello Fadduh! (A Letter From Camp) [C]** -adaptation of Ponchielli's "Dance Of The Hours"-	Warner 5378
5/08/65	40	1	2. Crazy Downtown [C] -adapted from "Downtown"-	Warner 5614
			SHERMAN, BOBBY	
			regular on TV's "Shindig"	
9/06/69	3	11	● 1. **Little Woman**	Metromedia 121
12/06/69	9	9	● 2. **La La La (If I Had You)**	Metromedia 150
2/28/70	9	11	● 3. **Easy Come, Easy Go**	Metromedia 177
6/06/70	24	5	4. Hey, Mister Sun	Metromedia 188
8/15/70	5	13	● 5. **Julie, Do Ya Love Me**	Metromedia 194
2/27/71	16	7	6. Cried Like A Baby	Metromedia 206
5/15/71	29	5	7. The Drum	Metromedia 217
			SHERRYS	
			Philadelphia quartet	
11/10/62	35	2	1. Pop Pop Pop-Pie	Guyden 2068
			SHIELDS	
9/15/58	12	9	1. You Cheated	Dot 15805
			SHIRELLES	
			Passaic, New Jersey quartet: Shirley Alston, Beverly Lee, Doris Kenner & Micki Harris (died on 6/10/82 (42)	
10/17/60	39	3	1. Tonights The Night	Scepter 1208
12/12/60	1 (2)	15	2. **Will You Love Me Tomorrow**	Scepter 1211
2/06/61	3	14	3. **Dedicated To The One I Love** -re-entry of 1959 hit-	Scepter 1203
5/01/61	4	8	4. **Mama Said**	Scepter 1217
10/23/61	21	5	5. Big John	Scepter 1223
1/06/62	8	11	6. **Baby It's You**	Scepter 1227
3/31/62	1 (3)	13	7. **Soldier Boy**	Scepter 1228
7/07/62	22	6	8. Welcome Home Baby	Scepter 1234
10/06/62	36	3	9. Stop The Music	Scepter 1237
12/15/62	19	9	10. Everybody Loves A Lover	Scepter 1243

DATE	POS	WKS	ARTIST—Record Title	LABEL & NO.
4/20/63	**4**	9	11. **Foolish Little Girl**	Scepter 1248
7/13/63	**26**	4	12. Don't Say Goodnight And Mean Goodbye	Scepter 1255
			SHIRLEY (AND COMPANY)	
			Shirley Goodman of Shirley & Lee	
2/22/75	**12**	8	1. Shame, Shame, Shame	Vibration 532
			SHIRLEY & LEE	
			Shirley Goodman & Leonard Lee	
9/08/56	**20**	9	1. Let The Good Times Roll	Aladdin 3325
1/05/57	**38**	1	2. I Feel Good	Aladdin 3338
			SHIRLEY, DON, Trio	
10/09/61	**40**	1	1. Water Boy [I]	Cadence 1392
			SHOCKING BLUE	
			Dutch quartet	
12/20/69	**1** (1)	13	● 1. **Venus**	Colossus 108
			SHONDELL, TROY	
9/25/61	**6**	12	1. **This Time**	Liberty 55353
			SHORE, DINAH	
			#1 female vocalist of the '40's	
5/21/55	**12**	2	1. Whatever Lola Wants	RCA 6077
			-from Broadway's "Damn Yankees"-	
12/10/55	**20**	1	2. Love And Marriage	RCA 6266
2/23/57	**19**	10	3. Chantez-Chantez	RCA 6792
9/09/57	**15**	7	4. Fascination	RCA 6980
			-from "Love In The Afternoon"-	
12/02/57	**24**	1	5. I'll Never Say "Never Again" Again	RCA 7056
			SIGLER, BUNNY	
7/22/67	**22**	7	1. Let The Good Times Roll & Feel So Good	Parkway 153
			SILHOUETTES	
			Philadelphia quartet	
1/20/58	**1** (2)	13	1. **Get A Job**	Ember 1029
			SILKIE	
			English	
11/06/65	**10**	7	1. **You've Got To Hide Your Love Away**	Fontana 1525
			SILVER	
8/07/76	**16**	12	1. Wham Bam (Shang-A-Lang)	Arista 0189
			SILVER CONDOR	
8/29/81	**32**	4	1. You Could Take My Heart Away	Columbia 02268
			SILVER CONVENTION	
			female trio from Germany	
10/25/75	**1** (3)	13	● 1. **Fly, Robin, Fly [I]**	Mid. Int'l. 10339
4/17/76	**2** (3)	15	● 2. **Get Up And Boogie (That's Right)**	Mid. Int'l. 10571
			SILVETTI	
			Bebu Silvetti	
3/19/77	**39**	3	1. Spring Rain [I]	Salsoul 2014
			SIMEONE, HARRY, Chorale	
12/28/58	**13**	6	1. The Little Drummer Boy [X]	20th Fox 121
12/28/59	**15**	3	2. The Little Drummer Boy [X]	20th Fox 121

DATE	POS	WKS	ARTIST—Record Title	LABEL & NO.
12/19/60	24	3	3. The Little Drummer Boy [X]	20th Fox 121
12/25/61	22	2	4. The Little Drummer Boy [X]	20th Fox 121
12/15/62	28	3	5. The Little Drummer Boy [X]	20th Fox 121
			SIMMONS, JUMPIN' GENE	
8/29/64	11	8	1. Haunted House	Hi 2076
			SIMON & GARFUNKEL	
			Paul Simon & Art Garfunkel	
12/04/65	1 (2)	12	● 1. **The Sounds Of Silence**	Columbia 43396
2/26/66	5	10	2. **Homeward Bound**	Columbia 43511
5/14/66	3	10	3. **I Am A Rock**	Columbia 43617
8/27/66	25	4	4. The Dangling Conversation	Columbia 43728
11/19/66	13	6	5. A Hazy Shade Of Winter	Columbia 43873
4/01/67	16	7	6. At The Zoo	Columbia 44046
8/12/67	23	5	7. Fakin' It	Columbia 44232
3/16/68	11	9	8. Scarborough Fair/Canticle	Columbia 44465
5/04/68	1 (3)	12	● 9. **Mrs. Robinson** -above 2 from "The Graduate"-	Columbia 44511
4/19/69	7	9	10. **The Boxer**	Columbia 44785
2/14/70	1 (6)	13	● 11. **Bridge Over Troubled Water**	Columbia 45079
4/18/70	4	12	● 12. **Cecilia**	Columbia 45133
9/26/70	18	8	13. El Condor Pasa	Columbia 45237
11/01/75	9	9	14. **My Little Town**	Columbia 10230
5/01/82	27	6	15. Wake Up Little Susie	Warner 50053
			SIMON, CARLY	
6/05/71	10	10	1. **That's The Way I've Always Heard It Should Be**	Elektra 45724
1/01/72	13	10	2. **Anticipation**	Elektra 45759
12/16/72	1 (3)	14	● 3. **You're So Vain**	Elektra 45824
4/21/73	17	9	4. The Right Thing To Do	Elektra 45843
6/01/74	14	6	5. Haven't Got Time For The Pain	Elektra 45887
5/24/75	21	5	6. Attitude Dancing	Elektra 45246
8/27/77	2 (3)	15	● 7. **Nobody Does It Better** -from "The Spy Who Loved Me"-	Elektra 45413
5/06/78	6	11	8. **You Belong To Me**	Elektra 45477
8/23/80	11	13	● 9. Jesse	Warner 49518
			SIMON, CARLY, & JAMES TAYLOR	
			husband & wife	
2/16/74	5	13	● 1. **Mockingbird**	Elektra 45880
9/23/78	36	3	2. Devoted To You	Elektra 45506
			SIMON, JOE	
6/08/68	25	7	1. (You Keep Me) Hangin' On	Sound Stage 7 2608
3/29/69	13	11	● 2. The Chokin' Kind	Sound Stage 7 2628
2/06/71	40	3	3. Your Time To Cry	Spring 108
12/11/71	11	11	● 4. Drowning In The Sea Of Love	Spring 120
8/19/72	11	8	● 5. Power Of Love	Spring 128
4/14/73	37	2	6. Step By Step	Spring 133

DATE	POS	WKS	ARTIST—Record Title	LABEL & NO.
8/25/73	**18**	8	7. Theme From Cleopatra Jones -featuring The Mainstreeters-	Spring 138
5/10/75	**8**	11	8. **Get Down, Get Down (Get On The Floor)**	Spring 156
			SIMON, PAUL	
			also see Art Garfunkel	
2/19/72	**4**	11	1. **Mother And Child Reunion**	Columbia 45547
4/22/72	**22**	8	2. Me And Julio Down By The Schoolyard	Columbia 45585
6/02/73	**2** (2)	11	3. **Kodachrome**	Columbia 45859
8/18/73	**2** (1)	14	● 4. **Loves Me Like A Rock** -with The Dixie Hummingbirds-	Columbia 45907
1/05/74	**35**	3	5. American Tune	Columbia 45900
1/03/76	**1** (3)	13	● 6. **50 Ways To Leave Your Lover**	Columbia 10270
5/29/76	**40**	2	7. Still Crazy After All These Years	Columbia 10332
11/05/77	**5**	14	8. **Slip Slidin' Away**	Columbia 10630
8/16/80	**6**	12	9. **Late In The Evening**	Warner 49511
11/22/80	**40**	2	10. One-Trick Pony	Warner 49601
			SIMON, PAUL/PHOEBE SNOW	
9/06/75	**23**	6	1. Gone At Last -with The Jessy Dixon Singers-	Columbia 10197
			SIMONE, NINA	
8/24/59	**18**	11	1. I Loves You, Porgy -from "Porgy & Bess"-	Bethlehem 11021
			SINATRA, FRANK	
			Francis Albert Sinatra was born on 12/12/15 in Hoboken, New Jersey - vocalist with Harry James' Band ('39) and Tommy Dorsey's Band ('40-'42) - also see Nancy & Frank Sinatra	
5/07/55	**1** (2)	21	1. **Learnin' The Blues**	Capitol 3102
9/24/55	**13**	5	2. Same Old Saturday Night	Capitol 3218
11/05/55	**5**	15	3. **Love And Marriage** -from TV production "Our Town"-	Capitol 3260
12/17/55	**7**	9	4. **(Love Is) The Tender Trap**	Capitol 3290
3/24/56	**21**	3	5. Flowers Mean Forgiveness	Capitol 3350
6/02/56	**13**	6	6. (How Little It Matters) How Little We Know	Capitol 3423
11/03/56	**3**	17	7. **Hey! Jealous Lover**	Capitol 3552
2/09/57	**15**	6	8. Can I Steal A Little Love -from film "Rock Pretty Baby"-	Capitol 3608
7/22/57	**25**	1	9. You're Cheatin' Yourself (If You're Cheatin' On Me)	Capitol 3744
10/28/57	**2** (1)	17	10. **All The Way** -from film "The Joker Is Wild"-	Capitol 3793
1/20/58	**6**	14	11. **Witchcraft**	Capitol 3859
9/07/59	**30**	1	12. High Hopes -from film "A Hole In The Head"-	Capitol 4214
11/16/59	**38**	3	13. Talk To Me	Capitol 4284
11/28/60	**25**	2	14. Ol' Mac Donald	Capitol 4466
1/20/62	**34**	3	15. Pocketful Of Miracles	Reprise 20040
10/10/64	**27**	6	16. Softly, As I Leave You	Reprise 0301
1/30/65	**32**	3	17. Somewhere In Your Heart	Reprise 0332
1/15/66	**28**	4	18. It Was A Very Good Year	Reprise 0429
5/28/66	**1** (1)	11	19. **Strangers In The Night** -from "A Man Could Get Killed"-	Reprise 0470

DATE	POS	WKS	ARTIST—Record Title	LABEL & NO.
9/17/66	25	5	20. Summer Wind	Reprise 0509
12/03/66	4	9	21. **That's Life**	Reprise 0531
8/26/67	30	4	22. The World We Knew (Over And Over)	Reprise 0610
11/16/68	23	5	23. Cycles	Reprise 0764
4/12/69	27	6	24. My Way	Reprise 0817
5/31/80	32	6	25. Theme From New York, New York	Reprise 49233
			SINATRA, FRANK, & RAY ANTHONY	
1/22/55	19	4	1. Melody Of Love	Capitol 3018
			SINATRA, FRANK, & KEELY SMITH	
5/12/58	22	1	1. How Are Ya' Fixed For Love?	Capitol 3952
			SINATRA, NANCY	
			daughter of Frank Sinatra	
2/05/66	1 (1)	12	● 1. **These Boots Are Made For Walkin'**	Reprise 0432
4/30/66	7	7	2. **How Does That Grab You, Darlin'?**	Reprise 0461
7/30/66	36	2	3. Friday's Child	Reprise 0491
12/10/66	5	9	● 4. **Sugar Town**	Reprise 0527
4/08/67	15	5	5. Love Eyes	Reprise 0559
10/07/67	24	4	6. Lightning's Girl	Reprise 0620
			SINATRA, NANCY & FRANK	
3/25/67	1 (4)	11	● 1. **Somethin' Stupid**	Reprise 0561
			SINATRA, NANCY, & LEE HAZLEWOOD	
7/08/67	14	7	1. Jackson	Reprise 0595
11/04/67	20	4	2. Lady Bird	Reprise 0629
1/27/68	26	5	3. Some Velvet Morning	Reprise 0651
			SINCLAIR, GORDON	
1/26/74	24	4	1. The Americans (A Canadian's Opinion) -originally broadcast on 6/5/73 on CFRB Radio in Toronto-	Avco 4628
			SINGING DOGS [Don Charles Presents]	
12/17/55	22	2	1. Oh! Susanna [N] -featuring the barking of 5 dogs-	RCA 6344
			SINGING NUN (Soeur Sourire)	
			Belgian	
11/16/63	1 (4)	12	1. **Dominique [F]**	Philips 40152
			SIR DOUGLAS QUINTET	
			Sir Douglas is Doug Sahm	
4/17/65	13	9	1. She's About A Mover	Tribe 8308
3/05/66	31	5	2. The Rains Came	Tribe 8314
3/15/69	27	6	3. Mendocino	Smash 2191
			SISTER SLEDGE	
			Kathie, Debbie, Kim & Joni	
3/10/79	9	13	1. **He's The Greatest Dancer**	Cotillion 44245
5/12/79	2 (2)	11	● 2. **We Are Family**	Cotillion 44251
3/06/82	23	6	3. My Guy	Cotillion 47000
			SIX TEENS Featuring TRUDY WILLIAMS	
9/01/56	25	1	1. A Casual Look	Flip 315

DATE	POS	WKS	ARTIST—Record Title	LABEL & NO.
			SKIP & FLIP	
			Clyde Battin & Garry Paxton	
7/27/59	11	9	1. It Was I	Brent 7002
4/25/60	11	10	2. Cherry Pie	Brent 7010
			SKYLARK	
			Canadian - Donny Gerrard, lead singer	
3/31/73	9	14	1. **Wildflower**	Capitol 3511
			SKYLINERS	
3/23/59	12	10	1. Since I Don't Have You	Calico 103
6/15/59	26	7	2. This I Swear	Calico 106
6/20/60	24	6	3. Pennies From Heaven	Calico 117
			SKYY	
			8-member soul group	
2/20/82	26	4	1. Call Me	Salsoul 2152
			SLAVE	
			12-man funk/rock organization	
7/23/77	32	6	1. Slide [I]	Cotillion 44218
			SLEDGE, PERCY	
4/30/66	**1** (2)	10	● 1. **When A Man Loves A Woman**	Atlantic 2326
8/06/66	17	6	2. Warm And Tender Love	Atlantic 2342
11/19/66	20	7	3. It Tears Me Up	Atlantic 2358
7/22/67	40	1	4. Love Me Tender	Atlantic 2414
4/06/68	11	11	5. Take Time To Know Her	Atlantic 2490
			SLY & THE FAMILY STONE	
			formed in San Francisco: Sly (Sylvester Stewart), sister Rose, brother Freddie & cousin Larry Graham	
3/02/68	8	12	1. **Dance To The Music**	Epic 10256
1/04/69	**1** (4)	14	● 2. **Everyday People**	Epic 10407
4/26/69	22	6	3. Stand!	Epic 10450
8/30/69	**2** (2)	13	4. **Hot Fun In The Summertime**	Epic 10497
1/10/70	**1** (2)	12	● 5. **Thank You (Falettinme Be Mice Elf Agin)**/	
		12	6. **Everybody Is A Star**	Epic 10555
6/20/70	38	3	7. I Want To Take You Higher	Epic 10450
			-re-entry of 1969 hit-	
11/13/71	**1** (3)	13	● 8. **Family Affair**	Epic 10805
2/26/72	23	6	9. Runnin' Away	Epic 10829
7/14/73	12	13	● 10. If You Want Me To Stay	Epic 11017
8/17/74	32	3	11. Time For Livin'	Epic 11140
			SMALL FACES	
			Steve Marriott, founder of British group that evolved into Faces	
1/13/68	16	8	1. Itchycoo Park	Immediate 501
			SMALL, MILLIE	
			Jamaican	
6/06/64	**2** (1)	9	1. **My Boy Lollipop**	Smash 1893
9/05/64	40	2	2. Sweet William	Smash 1920
			SMITH	
			Gayle McCormick, lead singer	
10/04/69	5	11	1. **Baby It's You**	Dunhill 4206

DATE	POS	WKS	ARTIST—Record Title	LABEL & NO.
			SMITH, FRANKIE	WMOT 5356
7/11/81	30	7	● 1. Double Dutch Bus -refers to a jump rope game-	
			SMITH, HUEY (PIANO), & The Clowns	Ace 545
			also see Frankie Ford	
3/31/58	9	9	1. **Don't You Just Know It**	
			SMITH, HURRICANE	Capitol 3383
			name inspired by film "Hurricane Smith"	
12/23/72	3	12	1. **Oh, Babe, What Would You Say?**	
			SMITH, JIMMY	Verve 10255
			jazz organist	
6/09/62	21	7	1. Walk On The Wild Side - Part 1 [I]	
			SMITH, KEELY - see **LOUIS PRIMA / FRANK SINATRA**	
			SMITH, O.C.	
4/20/68	40	2	1. The Son Of Hickory Holler's Tramp	Columbia 44425
9/21/68	2 (1)	12	● 2. **Little Green Apples**	Columbia 44616
9/20/69	34	2	3. Daddy's Little Man	Columbia 44948
			SMITH, PATTI, Group	Arista 0318
5/13/78	13	9	1. Because The Night	
			SMITH, RAY	Judd 1016
			died 11/29/79 (41)	
2/01/60	22	8	1. Rockin' Little Angel	
			SMITH, REX	Columbia 10908
5/12/79	10	10	● 1. **You Take My Breath Away** -from TV film "Sooner Or Later"-	
			SMITH, REX / RACHEL SWEET	Columbia 02169
8/08/81	32	4	1. Everlasting Love	
			SMITH, SAMMI	Mega 0015
2/20/71	8	11	● 1. **Help Me Make It Through The Night**	
			SMITH, SOMETHIN', & THE REDHEADS	
			trio formed at UCLA	
4/02/55	7	23	1. **It's A Sin To Tell A Lie**	Epic 9093
7/14/56	27	3	2. In A Shanty In Old Shanty Town	Epic 9168
			SMITH, VERDELLE	Capitol 5632
8/13/66	38	2	1. Tar And Cement	
			SMITH, WHISTLING JACK	Deram 85005
5/13/67	20	5	1. I Was Kaiser Bill's Batman [I]	
			SMOKIE	RSO 860
			Chris Norman, lead singer - also see Suzi Quatro	
1/22/77	25	8	1. Living Next Door To Alice	
			SNEAKER	Handshake 02557
			L.A.-based sextet	
12/19/81	34	6	1. More Than Just The Two Of Us	
			SNIFF 'N' THE TEARS	Atlantic 3604
8/18/79	15	9	1. Driver's Seat	

O.C. Smith. Bobby Russell wrote it, Roger Miller first recorded it, but O.C. Smith had the smash with "Little Green Apples." That's some distance from singing with Count Basie, which O.C. did as the replacement for Joe Williams.

Rex Smith. Rex 'n' Rachel (Smith 'n' Sweet) took "Everlasting Love" to the top 40 for the third time, but their 1981 version couldn't eclipse Robert Knight's 1967 original or Carl Carlton's 1974 remake.

Sonny and Cher. "The Don & Bonnie Jo Show"? It might have been, because Salvatore Bono recorded as Don Christy in 1959, and Cherilyn Sarkasian LaPier waxed as Bonnie Jo Mason ("Ringo I Love You") in 1964.

Dusty Springfield was recognized as Britain's most soulful solo singer in the '60s, and even dubbed "the white negress" by Cliff Richard.

Rick Springfield. Television's "General Hospital" was responsible for the resurrection of Rick Springfield (eight years separated his first and second top 40 hits) and Patti Austin's "Baby Come To Me." Rick appeared on the soap and Patti's song was played on it.

Bruce Springsteen. Top 40 hits by Bruce Springsteen, "the Future of rock'n'roll," have been relatively few, although Manfred Mann took his song, "Blinded By The Light," to No. 1 in 1977. Bruce also helped Gary U.S. Bonds collect a comeback hit in 1981 with "This Little Girl."

Ringo Starr. "I've got to make it on my own talent now, not the memory of who I used to be," said Ringo Starr not too long ago. Richard, seven top 10 hits *is* making it on your own.

Cat Stevens. Steven Georgiou, son of a Greek restaurant owner, became Cat Stevens, one of the most successful singer-songwriters of the '70s. He later shunned the spotlight and sought personal privacy as a devout Muslim under the name of Usef Islam.

Ray Stevens' first top 10 hit featured a camel named Clyde, so called in honor (?) of fellow Mercury recording artist Clyde McPhatter, who was present during the recording session.

Rod Stewart. Legend would have us believe that Rod Stewart's earliest encounter with the charts was his harmonica playing on Millie Small's 1964 hit, "My Boy Lollipop."

Stray Cats. Two years after reaching the British top 10, America's Stray Cats (Long Island breed) were accepted in their native land with "Rock This Town."

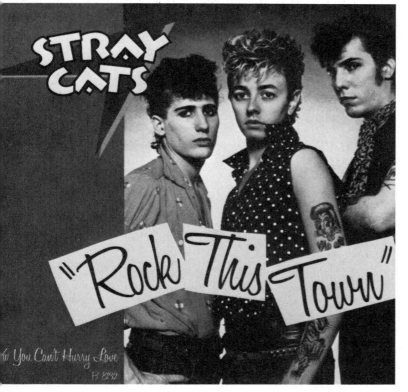

DATE	POS	WKS	ARTIST—Record Title	LABEL & NO.
			SNOW, PHOEBE	
			also see Paul Simon	
2/08/75	5	11	1. **Poetry Man**	Shelter 40353
			SOFT CELL	
			British duo: Marc Almond & David Ball	
5/22/82	8	15	1. **Tainted Love**	Sire 49855
			SOMMERS, JOANIE	
6/16/62	7	11	1. **Johnny Get Angry**	Warner 5275
			SONNY	
			Sonny Bono of Sonny & Cher	
9/04/65	10	8	1. **Laugh At Me**	Atco 6369
			SONNY & CHER	
			Sonny & Cher Bono (divorced in 1974) - also see Cher	
7/31/65	1 (3)	10	● 1. **I Got You Babe**	Atco 6359
9/11/65	8	9	2. **Baby Don't Go**	Reprise 0309
9/25/65	20	4	3. Just You	Atco 6345
10/23/65	15	6	4. But You're Mine	Atco 6381
2/12/66	14	6	5. What Now My Love	Atco 6395
10/15/66	21	4	6. Little Man	Atco 6440
1/28/67	6	8	7. **The Beat Goes On**	Atco 6461
11/13/71	7	11	8. **All I Ever Need Is You**	Kapp 2151
3/11/72	8	11	9. **A Cowboys Work Is Never Done**	Kapp 2163
8/05/72	32	5	10. When You Say Love	Kapp 2176
			-adapted from the "Budweiser" commercial-	
			SOPWITH "CAMEL"	
1/28/67	26	4	1. Hello Hello	Kama Sutra 217
			S.O.S. BAND	
			Atlanta funk/pop band - Mary Davis, lead singer	
6/28/80	3	14	★ 1. **Take Your Time (Do It Right) Part 1**	Tabu 5522
			SOUL CHILDREN	
3/23/74	36	2	1. I'll Be The Other Woman	Stax 0182
			SOUL SURVIVORS	
9/23/67	4	12	1. **Expressway To Your Heart**	Crimson 1010
1/20/68	33	3	2. Explosion In My Soul	Crimson 1012
			SOUL, DAVID	
			Ken of TV's "Starsky & Hutch"	
2/19/77	1 (1)	13	● 1. **Don't Give Up On Us**	Private Stock 45129
			SOUL, JIMMY	
5/05/62	22	8	1. Twistin' Matilda	S.P.Q.R. 3300
4/20/63	1 (2)	11	2. **If You Wanna Be Happy**	S.P.Q.R. 3305
			SOUNDS OF SUNSHINE	
7/24/71	39	2	1. Love Means (You Never Have To Say You're Sorry)	Ranwood 896
			SOUNDS ORCHESTRAL	
			English - Johnny Pearson on piano	
4/10/65	10	11	1. **Cast Your Fate To The Wind [I]**	Parkway 942

DATE	POS	WKS	ARTIST—Record Title	LABEL & NO.
			SOUTH, JOE	
2/01/69	12	9	1. Games People Play	Capitol 2248
1/17/70	12	9	2. Walk A Mile In My Shoes	Capitol 2704
			SOUTHER, HILLMAN, FURAY BAND	
			J.D. Souther, Chris Hillman, Richie Furay	
9/21/74	27	4	1. Fallin' In Love	Asylum 45201
			SOUTHER, J.D.	
			also see James Taylor	
10/20/79	7	13	1. **You're Only Lonely**	Columbia 11079
			SOVINE, RED	
			died 4/4/80 (61)	
8/28/76	40	1	● 1. Teddy Bear [S]	Starday 142
			SPANKY & OUR GANG	
			Spanky McFarlane, lead singer	
6/03/67	9	5	1. **Sunday Will Never Be The Same**	Mercury 72679
9/16/67	31	2	2. Making Every Minute Count	Mercury 72714
10/28/67	14	9	3. Lazy Day	Mercury 72732
2/03/68	30	4	4. Sunday Mornin'	Mercury 72765
5/18/68	17	7	5. Like To Get To Know You	Mercury 72795
			SPIDER	
			Amanda Blue, lead singer of New York-based group	
6/07/80	39	2	1. New Romance (It's A Mystery)	Dreamland 100
			SPINNERS	
			Detroit quintet - also see Dionne Warwick	
7/17/61	27	5	1. That's What Girls Are Made For	Tri-Phi 1001
8/14/65	35	2	2. I'll Always Love You	Motown 1078
8/22/70	14	10	3. It's A Shame	V.I.P. 25057
10/07/72	3	11	● 4. **I'll Be Around**	Atlantic 2904
1/20/73	4	12	● 5. **Could It Be I'm Falling In Love**	Atlantic 2927
5/19/73	11	11	● 6. One Of A Kind (Love Affair)	Atlantic 2962
9/08/73	29	3	7. Ghetto Child	Atlantic 2973
2/23/74	20	8	8. Mighty Love - Pt. 1	Atlantic 3006
6/08/74	18	6	9. I'm Coming Home	Atlantic 3027
10/26/74	15	5	10. Love Don't Love Nobody - Pt. I	Atlantic 3206
4/05/75	37	2	11. Living A Little, Laughing A Little	Atlantic 3252
8/30/75	5	13	● 12. **They Just Can't Stop It the (Games People Play)**	Atlantic 3284
1/24/76	36	3	13. Love Or Leave	Atlantic 3309
10/02/76	2 (3)	17	● 14. **The Rubberband Man**	Atlantic 3355
1/26/80	2 (2)	16	● 15. **Working My Way Back To You/Forgive Me, Girl**	Atlantic 3637
5/24/80	4	14	16. **Cupid/I've Loved You For A Long Time**	Atlantic 3664
			SPIRAL STARECASE Featuring Pat Upton	
5/03/69	12	11	1. More Today Than Yesterday	Columbia 44741
			SPIRIT	
			Jay Ferguson, lead singer, left group in '70 to form Jo Jo Gunne	
3/08/69	25	5	1. I Got A Line On You	Ode 115

DATE	POS	WKS	ARTIST—Record Title	LABEL & NO.
			SPOKESMEN	
10/09/65	36	3	1. The Dawn Of Correction -answer to "Eve Of Destruction"-	Decca 31844
			SPRINGFIELD, DUSTY	
			English - member of The Springfields	
2/15/64	12	7	1. I Only Want To Be With You	Philips 40162
5/02/64	38	2	2. Stay Awhile	Philips 40180
7/11/64	6	10	3. **Wishin' And Hopin'**	Philips 40207
6/04/66	4	10	4. **You Don't Have To Say You Love Me**	Philips 40371
10/01/66	20	5	5. All I See Is You	Philips 40396
4/22/67	40	2	6. I'll Try Anything	Philips 40439
10/14/67	22	5	7. The Look Of Love -from the film "Casino Royale"-	Philips 40465
12/14/68	10	10	8. **Son-Of-A Preacher Man**	Atlantic 2580
5/24/69	31	4	9. The Windmills Of Your Mind	Atlantic 2623
11/29/69	24	9	10. A Brand New Me	Atlantic 2685
			SPRINGFIELD, RICK	
			Australian - plays Noah Drake on TV's "General Hospital"	
9/02/72	14	9	1. Speak To The Sky	Capitol 3340
5/09/81	1 (2)	22	● 2. **Jessie's Girl**	RCA 12201
9/12/81	8	12	3. **I've Done Everything For You**	RCA 12166
12/26/81	20	10	4. Love Is Alright Tonite	RCA 13008
3/13/82	2 (4)	16	5. **Don't Talk To Strangers**	RCA 13070
6/19/82	21	9	6. What Kind Of Fool Am I	RCA 13245
10/09/82	32	5	7. I Get Excited	RCA 13303
			SPRINGFIELDS	
			Dusty Springfield, member	
9/01/62	20	6	1. Silver Threads And Golden Needles	Philips 40038
			SPRINGSTEEN, BRUCE	
			backing group: E-Street Band	
10/11/75	23	5	1. Born To Run	Columbia 10209
7/15/78	33	2	2. Prove It All Night	Columbia 10763
11/08/80	5	14	3. **Hungry Heart**	Columbia 11391
2/21/81	20	6	4. Fade Away	Columbia 11431
			SPYRO GYRA	
			Jay Beckenstein, leader	
7/28/79	24	8	1. Morning Dance [I]	Infinity 50011
			SQUIER, BILLY	
			Boston-bred rocker	
6/20/81	17	11	1. The Stroke	Capitol 5005
10/17/81	35	3	2. In The Dark	Capitol 5040
11/27/82	32	5	3. Everybody Wants You	Capitol 5163
			STAFFORD, JIM	
7/14/73	39	1	1. Swamp Witch [N]	MGM 14496
12/29/73	3	15	● 2. **Spiders & Snakes**	MGM 14648
5/04/74	12	9	3. My Girl Bill [N]	MGM 14718
7/20/74	7	11	4. **Wildwood Weed** [N]	MGM 14737
1/18/75	24	5	5. Your Bulldog Drinks Champagne [N]	MGM 14775

DATE	POS	WKS	ARTIST—Record Title	LABEL & NO.
9/27/75	37	2	6. I Got Stoned And I Missed It [N]	MGM 14819
			STAFFORD, JO	
			member of Tommy Dorsey's vocal group The Pied Pipers	
10/15/55	13	7	1. Suddenly There's A Valley	Columbia 40559
12/03/55	14	14	2. It's Almost Tomorrow	Columbia 40595
12/22/56	38	1	3. On London Bridge	Columbia 40782
			STAFFORD, TERRY	
3/21/64	3	10	1. **Suspicion**	Crusader 101
6/06/64	25	6	2. I'll Touch A Star	Crusader 105
			STALLION	
4/23/77	37	2	1. Old Fashioned Boy (You're The One)	Casablanca 877
			STAMPEDERS	
			Canadian	
9/11/71	8	10	1. **Sweet City Woman**	Bell 45120
4/03/76	40	2	2. Hit The Road Jack	Quality 501
			-with Wolfman Jack-	
			STAMPLEY, JOE	
			lead singer of The Uniques	
3/03/73	37	3	1. Soul Song	Dot 17442
			STANDELLS	
			Los Angeles-area quartet	
6/11/66	11	9	1. Dirty Water	Tower 185
			STANLEY, MICHAEL, Band	
			sextet from Ohio	
1/10/81	33	5	1. He Can't Love You	EMI America 8063
			STAPLE SINGERS	
			"Pops" Staples, and daughters Mavis, Cleo & Yvonne	
3/20/71	27	5	1. Heavy Makes You Happy (Sha-Na-Boom Boom)	Stax 0083
11/13/71	12	10	2. Respect Yourself	Stax 0104
4/15/72	1 (1)	14	3. **I'll Take You There**	Stax 0125
8/26/72	38	3	4. This World	Stax 0137
4/14/73	33	3	5. Oh La De Da	Stax 0156
11/10/73	9	11	● 6. **If You're Ready (Come Go With Me)**	Stax 0179
3/23/74	23	7	7. Touch A Hand, Make A Friend	Stax 0196
11/01/75	1 (1)	12	● 8. **Let's Do It Again**	Curtom 0109
			STAPLETON, CYRIL, & His Orchestra	
9/29/56	25	2	1. The Italian Theme [I]	London 1672
1/19/59	13	10	2. The Children's Marching Song [N]	London 1851
			-featuring the children from film "The Inn Of The Sixth Happiness"-	
			STARBUCK	
			Atlanta septet - Bruce Blackman, lead singer	
5/29/76	3	14	1. **Moonlight Feels Right**	Private Stock 45039
5/21/77	38	2	2. Everybody Be Dancin'	Private Stock 45144
			STARCHER, BUDDY	
5/14/66	39	1	1. History Repeats Itself [S]	Boone 1038
			STARGARD	
3/04/78	21	7	1. Theme Song From "Which Way Is Up"	MCA 40825

DATE	POS	WKS	ARTIST—Record Title	LABEL & NO.
			STARLAND VOCAL BAND	
6/05/76	**1** (2)	14	● 1. **Afternoon Delight**	Windsong 10588
			STARLETS	
6/12/61	**38**	2	1. Better Tell Him No	Pam 1003
			STARR, EDWIN	
9/04/65	**21**	6	1. Agent Double-O-Soul	Ric-Tic 103
3/22/69	**6**	9	2. **Twenty-Five Miles**	Gordy 7083
7/25/70	**1** (3)	13	3. **War**	Gordy 7101
1/02/71	**26**	4	4. Stop The War Now	Gordy 7104
			STARR, KAY	
8/06/55	**17**	1	1. Good And Lonesome	RCA 6146
1/07/56	**1** (6)	20	2. **Rock And Roll Waltz**	RCA 6359
6/30/56	**40**	1	3. Second Fiddle	RCA 6541
9/16/57	**9**	10	4. **My Heart Reminds Me**	RCA 6981
			STARR, RANDY	
			leader of The Islanders	
5/06/57	**32**	2	1. After School	Dale 100
			STARR, RINGO	
			Ringo replaced Pete Best as The Beatles drummer in August of '62	
5/08/71	**4**	11	● 1. **It Don't Come Easy**	Apple 1831
4/15/72	**9**	7	2. **Back Off Boogaloo**	Apple 1849
10/20/73	**1** (1)	12	● 3. **Photograph**	Apple 1865
12/29/73	**1** (1)	12	● 4. **You're Sixteen**	Apple 1870
3/23/74	**5**	11	5. **Oh My My**	Apple 1872
11/30/74	**6**	10	6. **Only You**	Apple 1876
2/22/75	**3**	10	7. **No No Song**	Apple 1880
7/05/75	**31**	3	8. It's All Down To Goodnight Vienna	Apple 1882
10/16/76	**26**	6	9. A Dose Of Rock 'N' Roll	Atlantic 3361
12/05/81	**38**	2	10. Wrack My Brain	Boardwalk 130
			STARS ON 45	
			session musicians from Holland	
5/02/81	**1** (1)	14	● 1. **Stars On 45 [Medley]** -primarily a Beatles' medley-	Radio 3810
4/17/82	**28**	5	2. Stars On 45 III -a tribute to Stevie Wonder-	Radio 4019
			STARZ	
			New York-based quintet	
4/30/77	**33**	2	1. Cherry Baby	Capitol 4399
			STATLER BROTHERS	
			Virginia quartet	
12/11/65	**4**	9	1. **Flowers On The Wall**	Columbia 43315
			STATON, CANDI	
			formerly married to Clarence Carter	
10/03/70	**24**	9	1. Stand By Your Man	Fame 1472
6/26/76	**20**	11	2. Young Hearts Run Free	Warner 8181
			STATUS QUO	
			English	
6/29/68	**12**	11	1. Pictures Of Matchstick Men	Cadet Conc. 7001

DATE	POS	WKS	ARTIST—Record Title	LABEL & NO.
			STEALERS WHEEL	
			British: Gerry Rafferty & Joe Egan	
3/31/73	6	13	1. **Stuck In The Middle With You**	A&M 1416
3/09/74	29	3	2. Star	A&M 1483
			STEAM	
11/08/69	1 (2)	13	● 1. **Na Na Hey Hey Kiss Him Goodbye**	Fontana 1667
			STEEL BREEZE	
			Ric Jacobs, lead singer of 6-man pop band from California	
9/18/82	16	11	1. You Don't Want Me Anymore	RCA 13283
			STEELY DAN	
			Donald Fagen & Walter Becker	
12/30/72	6	11	1. **Do It Again**	ABC 11338
4/07/73	11	11	2. Reeling In The Years	ABC 11352
6/08/74	4	11	3. **Rikki Don't Lose That Number**	ABC 11439
6/21/75	37	2	4. Black Friday	ABC 12101
1/07/78	11	11	5. Peg	ABC 12320
5/06/78	19	8	6. Deacon Blues	ABC 12355
7/01/78	22	5	7. FM (No Static At All) -from the film "FM"-	MCA 40894
9/23/78	26	5	8. Josie	ABC 12404
12/13/80	10	13	9. **Hey Nineteen**	MCA 51036
3/28/81	22	7	10. Time Out Of Mind	MCA 51082
			STEIN, LOU	
3/30/57	31	3	1. Almost Paradise [I]	RKO Unique 385
			STEINMAN, JIM	
			writer & arranger for Meat Loaf	
7/18/81	32	6	1. Rock And Roll Dreams Come Through	Epic/Clev. Int. 0211
			STEPPENWOLF	
			rock quintet led by John Kay	
7/20/68	2 (3)	12	● 1. **Born To Be Wild**	Dunhill 4138
10/26/68	3	13	● 2. **Magic Carpet Ride**	Dunhill 4161
3/15/69	10	8	3. **Rock Me**	Dunhill 4182
9/06/69	31	5	4. Move Over	Dunhill 4205
2/07/70	39	1	5. Monster	Dunhill 4221
5/09/70	35	3	6. Hey Lawdy Mama	Dunhill 4234
10/05/74	29	3	7. Straight Shootin' Woman	Mums 6031
			STEREOS	
10/16/61	29	3	1. I Really Love You	Cub 9095
			STEVE & EYDIE	
			Steve Lawrence & Eydie Gorme	
8/24/63	28	5	1. I Want To Stay Here	Columbia 42815
1/25/64	35	3	2. I Can't Stop Talking About You	Columbia 42932
			STEVENS, CAT	
			English - real name: Stephen Georgiou	
3/06/71	11	10	1. Wild World	A&M 1231
7/10/71	30	7	2. Moon Shadow	A&M 1265
10/09/71	7	10	3. **Peace Train**	A&M 1291
4/22/72	6	11	4. **Morning Has Broken**	A&M 1335

DATE	POS	WKS	ARTIST—Record Title	LABEL & NO.
12/02/72	16	9	5. Sitting	A&M 1396
8/04/73	31	5	6. The Hurt	A&M 1418
4/20/74	10	11	7. **Oh Very Young**	A&M 1503
8/24/74	6	9	8. **Another Saturday Night**	A&M 1602
1/11/75	26	4	9. Ready	A&M 1645
8/16/75	33	4	10. Two Fine People	A&M 1700
7/23/77	33	3	11. (Remember The Days Of The) Old Schoolyard	A&M 1948
			STEVENS, CONNIE	
			Cricket Blake of TV's "Hawaiian Eye" -- also see Edward Byrnes	
3/14/60	3	17	1. **Sixteen Reasons**	Warner 5137
			STEVENS, DODIE	
			age 13 in 1959	
3/09/59	3	14	1. **Pink Shoe Laces**	Crystalette 724
			STEVENS, RAY	
			also see Henhouse Five Plus Too	
9/18/61	35	1	1. Jeremiah Peabody's Poly Unsaturated Quick Dissolving Fast Acting Pleasant Tasting Green & Purple Pills [N]	Mercury 71843
7/14/62	5	9	2. **Ahab, The Arab [N]**	Mercury 71966
6/29/63	17	6	3. Harry The Hairy Ape [N]	Mercury 72125
8/31/68	28	3	4. Mr. Businessman	Monument 1083
4/26/69	8	10	● 5. **Gitarzan [N]**	Monument 1131
7/26/69	27	4	6. Along Came Jones [N]	Monument 1150
4/18/70	1 (2)	13	● 7. **Everything Is Beautiful**	Barnaby 2011
4/27/74	1 (3)	12	● 8. **The Streak [N]**	Barnaby 600
5/24/75	14	10	9. Misty	Barnaby 614
			STEVENSON, B.W	
8/25/73	9	12	1. **My Maria**	RCA 0030
			STEWART, AL	
			Scottish	
1/22/77	8	10	1. **Year Of The Cat**	Janus 266
10/21/78	7	13	2. **Time Passages**	Arista 0362
2/17/79	29	4	3. Song On The Radio	Arista 0389
9/27/80	24	6	4. Midnight Rocks	Arista 0552
			STEWART, AMII	
2/24/79	1 (1)	14	★ 1. **Knock On Wood**	Ariola 7736
			STEWART, BILLY	
			killed in an auto crash on 1/17/70 (32)	
5/01/65	26	4	1. I Do Love You	Chess 1922
7/10/65	24	5	2. Sitting In The Park	Chess 1932
8/06/66	10	7	3. **Summertime**	Chess 1966
11/05/66	29	5	4. Secret Love	Chess 1978

DATE	POS	WKS	ARTIST—Record Title	LABEL & NO.
			STEWART, JOHN	
			member of Kingston Trio '61-'67	
6/02/79	5	13	1. **Gold**	RSO 931
9/29/79	28	5	2. Midnight Wind	RSO 1000
			-above 2 with Stevie Nicks & Lindsey Buckingham-	
1/26/80	34	4	3. Lost Her In The Sun	RSO 1016
			STEWART, ROD	
			English - lead singer with The Jeff Beck Group ('68-'69), and with Faces ('69-'75)	
8/28/71	1 (5)	15	● 1. **Maggie May**	Mercury 73224
11/27/71	24	6	2. (I Know) I'm Losing You	Mercury 73244
			-with Faces-	
9/16/72	13	7	3. You Wear It Well	Mercury 73330
12/16/72	40	1	4. Angel	Mercury 73344
10/23/76	1 (7)	17	● 5. **Tonight's The Night (Gonna Be Alright)**	Warner 8262
2/26/77	21	9	6. The First Cut Is The Deepest	Warner 8321
7/02/77	30	4	7. The Killing Of Georgie (Part 1 & 2)	Warner 8396
11/26/77	4	15	● 8. **You're In My Heart (The Final Acclaim)**	Warner 8475
3/11/78	28	4	9. Hot Legs	Warner 8535
5/27/78	22	6	10. I Was Only Joking	Warner 8568
12/23/78	1 (4)	18	★ 11. **Da Ya Think I'm Sexy?**	Warner 8724
5/12/79	22	6	12. Ain't Love A Bitch	Warner 8810
11/29/80	5	17	13. **Passion**	Warner 49617
10/31/81	5	15	14. **Young Turks**	Warner 49843
2/13/82	20	8	15. Tonight I'm Yours (Don't Hurt Me)	Warner 49886
			STEWART, SANDY	
1/12/63	20	6	1. My Coloring Book	Colpix 669
			STILLS, STEPHEN	
			formed Buffalo Springfield - also see Crosby, Stills & Nash	
12/19/70	14	10	1. Love The One You're With	Atlantic 2778
3/27/71	37	2	2. Sit Yourself Down	Atlantic 2790
			STITES, GARY	
5/18/59	24	5	1. Lonely For You	Carlton 508
			STOLOFF, MORRIS [Columbia Pictures Orchestra]	
			Morris died on 4/16/80 (84)	
4/21/56	1 (3)	22	1. **Moonglow And Theme From "Picnic" [I]**	Decca 29888
			STONE PONEYS - see LINDA RONSTADT	
			STONE, CLIFFIE, & His Orchestra	
8/13/55	14	4	1. The Popcorn Song [N]	Capitol 3131
			STONE, KIRBY, Four	
7/28/58	25	1	1. Baubles, Bangles And Beads	Columbia 41183
			-from Broadway's "Kismet"-	
			STONEBOLT	
9/30/78	29	5	1. I Will Still Love You	Parachute 512
			STOOKEY, PAUL	
			Paul of Peter, Paul & Mary	
9/04/71	24	9	1. Wedding Song (There Is Love)	Warner 7511

DATE	POS	WKS	ARTIST—Record Title	LABEL & NO.
			STORIES	
			Ian Lloyd, lead singer	
7/14/73	1 (2)	15	● 1. **Brother Louie**	Kama Sutra 577
			STORM, BILLY	
			lead singer of The Valiants	
5/18/59	28	6	1. I've Come Of Age	Columbia 41356
			STORM, GALE	
			Margie Albright of TV's "My Little Margie"	
10/22/55	2 (3)	17	1. **I Hear You Knocking**	Dot 15412
12/24/55	6	12	2. **Teen Age Prayer/**	
12/31/55	5	9	3. **Memories Are Made Of This**	Dot 15436
3/03/56	9	14	4. **Why Do Fools Fall In Love**	Dot 15448
5/05/56	6	14	5. **Ivory Tower**	Dot 15458
4/29/57	4	18	6. **Dark Moon**	Dot 15558
			STRANGELOVES	
7/10/65	11	8	1. **I Want Candy**	Bang 501
10/23/65	39	1	2. Cara-Lin	Bang 508
2/05/66	30	4	3. Night Time	Bang 514
			STRAWBERRY ALARM CLOCK	
			west coast 'psychedelic' rock sextet	
10/14/67	1 (1)	14	● 1. **Incense And Peppermints**	Uni 55018
1/27/68	23	6	2. Tomorrow	Uni 55046
			STRAY CATS	
			rockabilly trio from Long Island, New York	
10/23/82	9	13	1. **Rock This Town**	EMI America 8132
			STREET PEOPLE	
			studio group - Rupert Holmes, member	
2/21/70	36	5	1. Jennifer Tomkins	Musicor 1365
			STREISAND, BARBRA	
			America's premier female vocalist	
5/23/64	5	12	1. **People**	Columbia 42965
			-from Broadway's "Funny Girl"-	
1/22/66	32	3	2. Second Hand Rose	Columbia 43469
12/12/70	6	12	3. **Stoney End**	Columbia 45236
8/28/71	40	1	4. Where You Lead	Columbia 45414
8/12/72	37	4	5. Sweet Inspiration/Where You Lead	Columbia 45626
12/22/73	1 (3)	17	● 6. **The Way We Were**	Columbia 45944
1/08/77	1 (3)	18	● 7. **Evergreen**	Columbia 10450
			-Love Theme from "A Star Is Born"-	
5/28/77	4	14	8. **My Heart Belongs To Me**	Columbia 10555
7/01/78	25	5	9. Songbird	Columbia 10756
8/26/78	21	6	10. Love Theme From "Eyes Of Laura Mars"	
			(Prisoner)	Columbia 10777
7/07/79	3	13	● 11. **The Main Event/Fight**	Columbia 11008
2/23/80	37	3	12. Kiss Me In The Rain	Columbia 11179
9/13/80	1 (3)	19	● 13. **Woman In Love**	Columbia 11364
11/28/81	11	11	14. Comin' In And Out Of Your Life	Columbia 02621
			STREISAND, BARBRA, & NEIL DIAMOND	
11/04/78	1 (2)	15	● 1. **You Don't Bring Me Flowers**	Columbia 10840

DATE	POS	WKS	ARTIST—Record Title	LABEL & NO.
			STREISAND, BARBRA, & BARRY GIBB	
			Barry is the eldest brother of The Bee Gees	
11/15/80	3	15	● 1. **Guilty**	Columbia 11390
2/14/81	10	10	2. **What Kind Of Fool**	Columbia 11430
			STREISAND, BARBRA, & DONNNA SUMMER	
10/27/79	1 (2)	13	● 1. **No More Tears (Enough Is Enough)**	Columbia 11125
			STRING-A-LONGS	
1/23/61	3	13	1. **Wheels [I]**	Warwick 603
4/17/61	35	2	2. Brass Buttons [I]	Warwick 625
			STRONG, BARRETT	
3/21/60	23	8	1. Money (That's What I Want)	Anna 1111
			STRUNK, JUD	
			killed in a plane crash on 10/15/81 (45)	
3/24/73	14	10	1. Daisy A Day	MGM 14463
			STYLISTICS	
			Philadelphia quintet - Russell Thompkins, Jr., lead singer	
7/17/71	39	1	1. Stop, Look, Listen (To Your Heart)	Avco Emb. 4572
11/27/71	9	13	● 2. **You Are Everything**	Avco 4581
3/11/72	3	14	● 3. **Betcha By Golly, Wow**	Avco 4591
7/01/72	25	6	4. People Make The World Go Round	Avco 4595
11/11/72	10	8	● 5. **I'm Stone In Love With You**	Avco 4603
3/03/73	5	9	● 6. **Break Up To Make Up**	Avco 4611
6/09/73	23	5	7. You'll Never Get To Heaven (If You Break My Heart)	Avco 4618
11/17/73	14	11	8. Rockin' Roll Baby	Avco 4625
4/13/74	2 (2)	14	● 9. **You Make Me Feel Brand New**	Avco 4634
8/17/74	18	7	10. Let's Put It All Together	Avco 4640
			STYX	
			Chicago-based quintet: Dennis DeYoung, Tommy Shaw, James Young, & John & Chuck Panozzo (brothers)	
1/18/75	6	11	1. **Lady**	Wood. Nickel 10102
3/27/76	27	5	2. Lorelei	A&M 1786
12/18/76	36	2	3. Mademoiselle	A&M 1877
10/29/77	8	15	4. **Come Sail Away**	A&M 1977
4/01/78	29	4	5. Fooling Yourself (The Angry Young Man)	A&M 2007
10/21/78	21	7	6. Blue Collar Man (Long Nights)	A&M 2087
4/07/79	16	13	7. Renegade	A&M 2110
10/20/79	1 (2)	14	● 8. **Babe**	A&M 2188
1/19/80	26	5	9. Why Me	A&M 2206
1/24/81	3	15	10. **The Best Of Times**	A&M 2300
3/28/81	9	13	11. **Too Much Time On My Hands**	A&M 2323
			SUGARHILL GANG	
			rap trio	
1/05/80	36	2	1. Rapper's Delight	Sugar Hill 542

DATE	POS	WKS	ARTIST—Record Title	LABEL & NO.
			SUGARLOAF	
			Jerry Corbetta, lead singer	
9/19/70	**3**	12	1. **Green-Eyed Lady**	Liberty 56183
2/01/75	**9**	11	2. **Don't Call Us, We'll Call You**	Claridge 402
			SUMMER, DONNA	
			America's #1 disco star - also see Barbra Streisand	
12/20/75	**2** (2)	14	● 1. **Love To Love You Baby**	Oasis 401
9/03/77	**6**	14	● 2. **I Feel Love**	Casablanca 884
1/28/78	**37**	3	3. I Love You	Casablanca 907
6/03/78	**3**	14	● 4. **Last Dance**	Casablanca 926
			-from "Thank God It's Friday"-	
9/30/78	**1** (3)	15	● 5. **Mac Arthur Park**	Casablanca 939
1/20/79	**4**	14	● 6. **Heaven Knows**	Casablanca 959
			-with Brooklyn Dreams-	
4/28/79	**1** (3)	17	★ 7. **Hot Stuff**	Casablanca 978
6/09/79	**1** (5)	15	★ 8. **Bad Girls**	Casablanca 988
9/15/79	**2** (2)	14	● 9. **Dim All The Lights**	Casablanca 2201
1/26/80	**5**	12	● 10. **On The Radio**	Casablanca 2236
9/27/80	**3**	13	● 11. **The Wanderer**	Geffen 49563
10/11/80	**36**	3	12. Walk Away	Casablanca 2300
1/10/81	**33**	3	13. Cold Love	Geffen 49634
3/28/81	**40**	2	14. Who Do You Think You're Foolin'	Geffen 49664
7/17/82	**10**	11	15. **Love Is In Control (Finger On The Trigger)**	Geffen 29982
			SUNNY & The Sunglows	
			Sunny Ozuna, lead singer	
9/28/63	**11**	9	1. Talk To Me	Tear Drop 3014
			SUNNYSIDERS	
5/21/55	**12**	10	1. Hey, Mr. Banjo	Kapp 113
			SUNSHINE COMPANY	
11/18/67	**36**	3	1. Back On The Street Again	Imperial 66260
			SUPERTRAMP	
			British quintet: Rick Davies, Roger Hodgson, John Helliwell, Dougie Thomson, & Bob Benberg	
5/17/75	**35**	2	1. Bloody Well Right	A&M 1660
7/02/77	**15**	11	2. Give A Little Bit	A&M 1938
4/28/79	**6**	13	3. **The Logical Song**	A&M 2128
8/04/79	**15**	8	4. Goodbye Stranger	A&M 2162
11/03/79	**10**	11	5. **Take The Long Way Home**	A&M 2193
10/04/80	**15**	8	6. Dreamer	A&M 2269
10/30/82	**11**	11	7. It's Raining Again	A&M 2502
			SUPREMES	
			Diana Ross, lead singer; Mary Wilson, & Florence Ballard (Flo died 2/21/76-32) - Cindy Birdsong replaced Flo in 1967, and Jean Terrell replaced Diana in 1970	
12/28/63	**23**	7	1. When The Lovelight Starts Shining Through His Eyes	Motown 1051
7/18/64	**1** (2)	13	2. **Where Did Our Love Go**	Motown 1060
10/10/64	**1** (4)	12	3. **Baby Love**	Motown 1066
11/21/64	**1** (2)	13	4. **Come See About Me**	Motown 1068

DATE	POS	WKS	ARTIST—Record Title	LABEL & NO.
3/06/65	1 (2)	10	5. **Stop! In The Name Of Love**	Motown 1074
5/08/65	1 (1)	10	6. **Back In My Arms Again**	Motown 1075
8/14/65	11	7	7. Nothing But Heartaches	Motown 1080
10/30/65	1 (2)	10	8. **I Hear A Symphony**	Motown 1083
1/29/66	5	8	9. **My World Is Empty Without You**	Motown 1089
5/07/66	9	7	10. **Love Is Like An Itching In My Heart**	Motown 1094
8/20/66	1 (2)	11	11. **You Can't Hurry Love**	Motown 1097
11/05/66	1 (2)	10	12. **You Keep Me Hangin' On**	Motown 1101
2/04/67	1 (1)	10	13. **Love Is Here And Now You're Gone**	Motown 1103
4/15/67	1 (1)	10	14. **The Happening**	Motown 1107
			DIANA ROSS & THE SUPREMES:	
8/19/67	2 (2)	10	15. **Reflections**	Motown 1111
11/25/67	9	6	16. **In And Out Of Love**	Motown 1116
4/06/68	28	5	17. Forever Came Today	Motown 1122
7/06/68	30	3	18. Some Things You Never Get Used To	Motown 1126
10/26/68	1 (2)	15	19. **Love Child**	Motown 1135
2/01/69	10	7	20. **I'm Livin' In Shame**	Motown 1139
4/26/69	27	5	21. The Composer	Motown 1146
6/14/69	31	4	22. No Matter What Sign You Are	Motown 1148
11/15/69	1 (1)	15	23. **Someday We'll Be Together**	Motown 1156
			SUPREMES:	
3/14/70	10	10	24. **Up The Ladder To The Roof**	Motown 1162
8/01/70	21	8	25. Everybody's Got The Right To Love	Motown 1167
11/21/70	7	12	26. **Stoned Love**	Motown 1172
5/22/71	16	8	27. Nathan Jones	Motown 1182
1/29/72	16	9	28. Floy Joy	Motown 1195
6/03/72	37	3	29. Automatically Sunshine	Motown 1200
8/07/76	40	1	30. I'm Gonna Let My Heart Do The Walking	Motown 1391
			SUPREMES & FOUR TOPS	
12/12/70	14	8	1. River Deep - Mountain High	Motown 1173
			SUPREMES & TEMPTATIONS	
			America's top 2 vocal groups of the rock era	
12/14/68	2 (2)	12	1. **I'm Gonna Make You Love Me**	Motown 1137
3/22/69	25	6	2. I'll Try Something New	Motown 1142
			SURFARIS	
			quintet from Glendora, CA	
7/06/63	2 (1)	10	1. **Wipe Out [I]**	Dot 16479
8/27/66	16	10	2. Wipe Out [I]	Dot 144
			-re-entry of l963 hit-	
			SURVIVOR	
			midwest quintet featuring Dave Bickler & Jim (Ides of March) Peterik	
11/21/81	33	4	1. Poor Man's Son	Scotti Bros. 02560
6/26/82	1 (6)	18	★ 2. **Eye Of The Tiger**	Scotti Bros. 02912
			-from the film "Rocky III"-	
10/16/82	17	7	3. American Heartbeat	Scotti Bros. 03213
			SWAN, BILLY	
10/26/74	1 (2)	12	● 1. **I Can Help**	Monument 8621

DATE	POS	WKS	ARTIST—Record Title	LABEL & NO.
			SWANN, BETTYE	
7/01/67	21	7	1. Make Me Yours	Money 126
4/19/69	38	2	2. Don't Touch Me	Capitol 2382
			SWEATHOG	
12/11/71	33	4	1. Hallelujah	Columbia 45492
			SWEET	
			English foursome - Brian Connolly, lead singer	
3/17/73	3	15	● 1. **Little Willy**	Bell 45251
8/02/75	5	14	2. **Ballroom Blitz**	Capitol 4055
11/22/75	5	11	● 3. **Fox On The Run**	Capitol 4157
3/06/76	20	7	4. Action	Capitol 4220
4/15/78	8	14	5. **Love Is Like Oxygen**	Capitol 4549
			SWEET INSPIRATIONS	
			studio vocal group led by Cissy Houston	
3/30/68	18	10	1. Sweet Inspiration	Atlantic 2476
			SWEET SENSATION	
			8-man British soul band	
2/15/75	14	8	1. Sad Sweet Dreamer	Pye 71002
			SWEET, RACHEL - see REX SMITH	
			SWINGING BLUE JEANS	
			English quartet	
3/28/64	24	5	1. Hippy Hippy Shake	Imperial 66021
			SWINGIN' MEDALLIONS	
6/04/66	17	6	1. Double Shot (Of My Baby's Love)	Smash 2033
			SWITCH	
12/02/78	36	3	1. There'll Never Be	Gordy 7159
			SYLVERS	
			Memphis family of 7	
3/13/76	1 (1)	15	● 1. **Boogie Fever**	Capitol 4179
11/13/76	5	17	● 2. **Hot Line**	Capitol 4336
5/21/77	17	10	3. High School Dance	Capitol 4405
			SYLVERS, FOSTER	
			member of The Sylvers - age 11	
6/30/73	22	8	1. Misdemeanor	MGM 14580
			SYLVESTER	
			Sylvester James	
9/30/78	19	10	1. Dance (Disco Heat)	Fantasy 827
2/17/79	36	3	2. You Make Me Feel (Mighty Real)	Fantasy 846
5/05/79	40	2	3. I (Who Have Nothing)	Fantasy 855
			SYLVIA	
			Sylvia Kirby Allen from Kokomo, Indiana	
10/09/82	15	9	● 1. Nobody	RCA 13223
			SYLVIA	
			Sylvia Robinson of Mickey & Sylvia	
4/21/73	3	13	● 1. **Pillow Talk**	Vibration 521

DATE	POS	WKS	ARTIST—Record Title	LABEL & NO.
			SYMS, SYLVIA	
6/16/56	20	2	1. I Could Have Danced All Night -from musical "My Fair Lady"-	Decca 29903
9/01/56	21	3	2. English Muffins And Irish Stew	Decca 29969
			SYNDICATE OF SOUND rock quintet from San Jose	
6/25/66	8	6	1. **Little Girl**	Bell 640
			SYREETA - see BILLY PRESTON	
			TALKING HEADS New York quartet led by David Byrne	
12/23/78	26	9	1. Take Me To The River	Sire 1032
			TAMS Atlanta quintet	
1/18/64	9	9	1. **What Kind Of Fool (Do You Think I Am)**	ABC-Paramount 10502
			TANEGA, NORMA	
3/19/66	22	6	1. Walkin' My Cat Named Dog	New Voice 807
			TARRIERS movie actor Alan Arkin was an original member - also see Vince Martin	
12/22/56	4	16	1. **The Banana Boat Song**	Glory 249
			TASTE OF HONEY Hazel Payne & Janice Johnson	
7/22/78	1 (3)	17	★ 1. **Boogie Oogie Oogie**	Capitol 4565
4/11/81	3	16	● 2. **Sukiyaki**	Capitol 4953
			TAVARES 5 Tavares brothers	
11/03/73	35	3	1. Check It Out	Capitol 3674
5/17/75	25	5	2. Remember What I Told You To Forget	Capitol 4010
8/23/75	10	13	3. **It Only Takes A Minute**	Capitol 4111
7/10/76	15	12	● 4. Heaven Must Be Missing An Angel	Capitol 4270
12/11/76	34	2	5. Don't Take Away The Music	Capitol 4348
4/23/77	22	7	6. Whodunit	Capitol 4398
4/15/78	32	4	7. More Than A Woman -from "Saturday Night Fever"-	Capitol 4500
11/20/82	33	9	8. A Penny For Your Thoughts	RCA 13292
			TAYLOR, BOBBY, & THE VANCOUVERS Thomas Chong (of Cheech & Chong) was lead guitarist	
5/18/68	29	5	1. Does Your Mama Know About Me	Gordy 7069
			TAYLOR, JAMES brother of artists Livingston, Kate & Alex Taylor - also see Carly Simon & Art Garfunkel	
9/26/70	3	14	1. **Fire And Rain**	Warner 7423
3/20/71	37	1	2. Country Road	Warner 7460
6/19/71	1 (1)	12	● 3. **You've Got A Friend**	Warner 7498
10/16/71	31	5	4. Long Ago And Far Away -backing vocals on above 2: Joni Mitchell-	Warner 7521
12/16/72	14	9	5. Don't Let Me Be Lonely Tonight	Warner 7655
7/19/75	5	10	6. **How Sweet It Is (To Be Loved By You)**	Warner 8109

DATE	POS	WKS	ARTIST—Record Title	LABEL & NO.
8/07/76	22	8	7. Shower The People	Warner 8222
7/09/77	4	13	8. **Handy Man**	Columbia 10557
11/05/77	20	8	9. Your Smiling Face	Columbia 10602
6/30/79	28	5	10. Up On The Roof	Columbia 11005
			TAYLOR, JAMES, & J.D. SOUTHER	
3/14/81	11	10	1. Her Town Too	Columbia 60514
			TAYLOR, JOHNNIE	
			replaced Sam Cooke as lead singer of The Soul Stirrers	
11/02/68	5	13	● 1. **Who's Making Love**	Stax 0009
1/25/69	20	8	2. Take Care Of Your Homework	Stax 0023
5/31/69	36	5	3. Testify (I Wonna)	Stax 0033
7/18/70	37	2	4. Steal Away	Stax 0068
11/14/70	39	2	5. I Am Somebody, Part II	Stax 0078
2/13/71	28	5	6. Jody's Got Your Girl And Gone	Stax 0085
7/14/73	11	12	● 7. I Believe In You (You Believe In Me)	Stax 0161
10/27/73	15	8	8. Cheaper To Keep Her	Stax 0176
3/16/74	34	2	9. We're Getting Careless With Our Love	Stax 0193
3/06/76	1 (4)	13	★ 10. **Disco Lady**	Columbia 10281
6/26/76	33	3	11. Somebody's Gettin' It	Columbia 10334
			TAYLOR, LITTLE JOHNNY	
9/14/63	19	8	1. Part Time Love	Galaxy 722
			TAYLOR, LIVINGSTON	
			James Taylor's brother	
12/16/78	30	5	1. I Will Be In Love With You	Epic 50604
9/13/80	38	2	2. First Time Love	Epic 50894
			TAYLOR, R. DEAN	
9/19/70	5	13	1. **Indiana Wants Me**	Rare Earth 5013
			T-BONES	
			a Joe Saraceno production	
12/25/65	3	11	1. **No Matter What Shape (Your Stomach's In) [I]** -from "Alka Seltzer" jingle-	Liberty 55836
			TECHNIQUES	
11/25/57	29	2	1. Hey! Little Girl	Roulette 4030
			TEDDY BEARS	
			Los Angeles trio featuring producer Phil Spector	
10/13/58	1 (3)	18	1. **To Know Him, Is To Love Him**	Dore 503
			TEE SET	
			Dutch quartet	
2/07/70	5	10	1. **Ma Belle Amie**	Colossus 107
			TEEGARDEN & VAN WINKLE	
			David Teegarden & Skip Knape	
10/17/70	22	5	1. God, Love And Rock & Roll	Westbound 170
			TEEN QUEENS	
			sisters Betty & Rosie Collins	
3/10/56	14	8	1. Eddie My Love	RPM 453

DATE	POS	WKS	ARTIST—Record Title	LABEL & NO.
			TEMPO, NINO, & APRIL STEVENS	
			brother & sister	
10/05/63	1 (1)	12	1. **Deep Purple**	Atco 6273
12/28/63	11	7	2. Whispering	Atco 6281
3/14/64	32	3	3. Stardust	Atco 6286
10/01/66	26	5	4. All Strung Out	White Whale 236
			TEMPOS	
			Pittsburgh quartet	
8/10/59	23	6	1. See You In September	Climax 102
			TEMPTATIONS	
			white group	
5/09/60	29	3	1. Barbara	Goldisc 3001
			TEMPTATIONS	
			original group: David Ruffin, Eddie Kendricks, Otis Williams, Mel Franklin & Paul Williams (died 8/17/73 - 34) - David left in '68 & Eddie in '71 -- also see The Supremes	
3/21/64	11	8	1. The Way You Do The Things You Do	Gordy 7028
7/04/64	33	4	2. I'll Be In Trouble	Gordy 7032
9/26/64	26	6	3. Girl (Why You Wanna Make Me Blue)	Gordy 7035
1/30/65	1 (1)	11	4. **My Girl**	Gordy 7038
4/17/65	18	7	5. It's Growing	Gordy 7040
8/07/65	17	7	6. Since I Lost My Baby	Gordy 7043
11/06/65	13	6	7. My Baby	Gordy 7047
3/26/66	29	3	8. Get Ready	Gordy 7049
6/11/66	13	10	9. Ain't Too Proud To Beg	Gordy 7054
9/03/66	3	9	10. **Beauty Is Only Skin Deep**	Gordy 7055
12/03/66	8	8	11. **(I Know) I'm Losing You**	Gordy 7057
5/13/67	8	8	12. **All I Need**	Gordy 7061
8/12/67	6	9	13. **You're My Everything**	Gordy 7063
10/21/67	14	8	14. (Loneliness Made Me Realize) It's You That I Need	Gordy 7065
1/27/68	4	11	15. **I Wish It Would Rain**	Gordy 7068
5/18/68	13	8	16. I Could Never Love Another (After Loving You)	Gordy 7072
8/17/68	26	5	17. Please Return Your Love To Me	Gordy 7074
11/23/68	6	11	18. **Cloud Nine**	Gordy 7081
2/22/69	6	11	19. **Run Away Child, Running Wild**	Gordy 7084
5/31/69	20	6	20. Don't Let The Joneses Get You Down	Gordy 7086
8/30/69	1 (2)	15	21. **I Can't Get Next To You**	Gordy 7093
1/24/70	7	10	22. **Psychedelic Shack**	Gordy 7096
6/06/70	3	13	23. **Ball Of Confusion (That's What The World Is Today)**	Gordy 7099
10/17/70	33	4	24. Ungena Za Ulimwengu (Unite The World)	Gordy 7102
2/20/71	1 (2)	13	25. **Just My Imagination (Running Away With Me)**	Gordy 7105
11/20/71	18	8	26. Superstar (Remember How You Got Where You Are)	Gordy 7111
3/18/72	30	4	27. Take A Look Around	Gordy 7115
10/28/72	1 (1)	12	28. **Papa Was A Rollin' Stone**	Gordy 7121
3/10/73	7	11	29. **Masterpiece**	Gordy 7126

DATE	POS	WKS	ARTIST—Record Title	LABEL & NO.
7/07/73	40	2	30. The Plastic Man	Gordy 7129
9/08/73	35	4	31. Hey Girl (I Like Your Style)	Gordy 7131
1/12/74	27	4	32. Let Your Hair Down	Gordy 7133
2/01/75	40	1	33. Happy People	Gordy 7138
4/19/75	26	9	34. Shakey Ground	Gordy 7142
8/23/75	37	2	35. Glasshouse	Gordy 7144
			10cc	
			English quartet which evolved from Hotlegs	
6/14/75	2 (3)	11	1. **I'm Not In Love**	Mercury 73678
1/29/77	5	14	● 2. **The Things We Do For Love**	Mercury 73875
6/25/77	40	1	3. People In Love	Mercury 73917
			TEN YEARS AFTER	
			British quartet led by guitarist Alvin Lee	
11/20/71	40	2	1. I'd Love To Change The World	Columbia 45457
			TEX, JOE	
			died 8/13/82 (49)	
1/02/65	5	8	1. **Hold What You've Got**	Dial 4001
10/16/65	23	5	2. I Want To (Do Everything For You)	Dial 4016
1/01/66	29	4	3. A Sweet Woman Like You	Dial 4022
6/18/66	39	1	4. S.Y.S.L.J.F.M. (The Letter Song)	Dial 4028
4/08/67	35	3	5. Show Me	Dial 4055
11/25/67	10	10	● 6. **Skinny Legs And All**	Dial 4063
3/02/68	33	3	7. Men Are Gettin' Scarce	Dial 4069
2/26/72	2 (2)	16	● 8. **I Gotcha**	Dial 1010
4/23/77	12	10	● 9. Ain't Gonna Bump No More (With No Big Fat Woman)	Epic 50313
			THEM	
			Irish quartet led by Van Morrison	
6/26/65	24	6	1. Here Comes The Night	Parrot 9749
12/04/65	33	2	2. Mystic Eyes [I]	Parrot 9796
			THIN LIZZY	
			Irish quartet led by Phil Lynott	
6/05/76	12	9	1. The Boys Are Back In Town	Mercury 73786
			THINK featuring Lou Stallman	
1/01/72	23	5	1. Once You Understand [N]	Laurie 3583
			38 SPECIAL	
			Donnie Van Zant, leader - younger brother of Lynyrd Skynyrd's Ronnie Van Zant	
4/18/81	27	6	1. Hold On Loosely	A&M 2316
5/22/82	10	12	2. **Caught Up In You**	A&M 2412
10/02/82	38	2	3. You Keep Runnin' Away	A&M 2431
			THOMAS, B.J.	
			B.J. = Billy Joe	
3/12/66	8	10	1. **I'm So Lonesome I Could Cry** -with The Triumphs-	Scepter 12129
6/04/66	22	5	2. Mama	Scepter 12139
7/23/66	34	4	3. Billy And Sue -with The Triumphs-	Hickory 1395
8/03/68	28	7	4. The Eyes Of A New York Woman	Scepter 12219

DATE	POS	WKS	ARTIST—Record Title	LABEL & NO.
12/14/68	5	12	● 5. **Hooked On A Feeling**	Scepter 12230
11/22/69	1 (4)	19	● 6. **Raindrops Keep Fallin' On My Head** -from film "Butch Cassidy & The Sundance Kid"-	Scepter 12265
4/11/70	26	6	7. Everybody's Out Of Town	Scepter 12277
7/11/70	9	10	8. **I Just Can't Help Believing**	Scepter 12283
1/09/71	38	3	9. Most Of All	Scepter 12299
3/13/71	16	9	10. No Love At All	Scepter 12307
8/14/71	34	3	11. Mighty Clouds Of Joy	Scepter 12320
2/26/72	15	9	12. Rock And Roll Lullaby -featuring Duane Eddy on guitar-	Scepter 12344
3/01/75	1 (1)	14	● 13. **(Hey Won't You Play) Another Somebody Done Somebody Wrong Song**	ABC 12054
8/06/77	17	10	14. Don't Worry Baby	MCA 40735
			THOMAS, CARLA daughter of Rufus Thomas - also see Otis & Carla	
2/20/61	10	10	1. **Gee Whiz (Look At His Eyes)**	Atlantic 2086
9/24/66	14	10	2. B-A-B-Y	Stax 195
			THOMAS, IAN Canadian	
12/29/73	34	3	1. Painted Ladies	Janus 224
			THOMAS, IRMA	
4/25/64	17	7	1. Wish Someone Would Care	Imperial 66013
			THOMAS, RUFUS father of Carla Thomas	
11/02/63	10	9	1. **Walking The Dog**	Stax 140
2/28/70	28	8	2. Do The Funky Chicken	Stax 0059
1/23/71	25	8	3. (Do The) Push And Pull, Part I	Stax 0079
9/18/71	31	4	4. The Breakdown (Part I)	Stax 0098
			THOMAS, TIMMY	
12/23/72	3	11	1. **Why Can't We Live Together**	Glades 1703
			THOMPSON, CHRIS, & Night also see Night	
10/20/79	17	8	1. If You Remember Me	Planet 45909
			THOMPSON, KAY	
3/17/56	39	2	1. Eloise [N]	Cadence 3
			THOMPSON, SUE	
9/25/61	5	11	1. **Sad Movies (Make Me Cry)**	Hickory 1153
1/13/62	3	11	2. **Norman**	Hickory 1159
7/21/62	31	5	3. Have A Good Time	Hickory 1174
10/20/62	17	6	4. James (Hold The Ladder Steady)	Hickory 1183
2/06/65	23	4	5. Paper Tiger	Hickory 1284
			THOMSON, ALI Scottish - younger brother of Supertramp member Dougie Thomson	
7/12/80	15	9	1. Take A Little Rhythm	A&M 2243
			THREE DEGREES also see MFSB	
7/25/70	29	4	1. Maybe	Roulette 7079
10/19/74	2 (1)	13	● 2. **When Will I See You Again**	Phil. Int'l. 3550

Barbra Streisand. Her work on the show albums of Harold Rome's "I Can Get It For You Wholesale" and his "Needles and Pins" revue helped Barbra Streisand secure her Columbia recording contract in 1962. That's right, 1962.

Styx. Dennis de Young and twin brothers Chuck and John Panozzo first began making music together in Chicago in 1963, but toiled for 16 years before Styx snagged their first chart-topper, "Babe."

Donna Summer. Even before "Love To Love You Baby," Donna Summer was into drama. "The Hostage," her first record, was the graphic saga of a kidnapping, complete with screeching tire effects and tragic ending.

Supertramp. Said to have been sponsored by a publicity-shy millionaire, Supertramp recorded and released their first album in 1970. It all seemed too much for the group's drummer, however, who suffered a nervous breakdown and left.

The Supremes. Mary Wilson complained that "Where Did Our Love Go" was lyrically too juvenile when songwriters Brian and Eddie Holland and Lamont Dozier played it for the Supremes.

A Taste of Honey. After its first chart run for Kyu Sakamoto in 1963, "Sukiyaki" seemed an improbable candidate for an update. Not so to A Taste of Honey. "It's a romantic song with a great arrangement," said Janice Marie Johnson, and they promptly took it into the top ten for a second time.

Three Dog Night. The popularity of Three Dog Night helped a number of now-famous songwriters to secure that fame, including Randy Newman ("Mama Told Me Not To Come"), Laura Nyro ("Eli's Comin' "), Nilsson ("One") and Paul Williams ("An Old Fashioned Love Song," "The Family of Man").

Johnny Tillotson. It was rare in the early '60's for an American artist to cover a British hit, but Johnny Tillotson did with "You Can Never Stop Me Loving You," first recorded by Kenny Lynch. We know, we know: Kenny who?

The Tokens. After a couple of their own hits, the Tokens prospered as producers of other artists through the '60s, including the Chiffons and the Happenings. And Token Hank Medress teamed up with Dave Appell to mastermind the hits of Dawn.

John Travolta shares with the Gibb brothers the distinction of being associated with the record industry's two all-time biggest-selling albums, "Saturday Night Fever" and "Grease."

DATE	POS	WKS	ARTIST—Record Title	LABEL & NO.
			THREE DOG NIGHT	
			Danny Hutton, Chuck Negron & Cory Wells	
3/29/69	29	4	1. Try A Little Tenderness	Dunhill 4177
5/31/69	5	12	● 2. **One**	Dunhill 4191
8/16/69	4	12	3. **Easy To Be Hard**	Dunhill 4203
11/08/69	10	12	4. **Eli's Coming**	Dunhill 4215
3/07/70	15	8	5. Celebrate	Dunhill 4229
6/06/70	1 (2)	13	● 6. **Mama Told Me (Not To Come)**	Dunhill 4239
9/12/70	15	8	7. Out In The Country	Dunhill 4250
12/05/70	19	9	8. One Man Band	Dunhill 4262
3/27/71	1 (6)	15	● 9. **Joy To The World**	Dunhill 4272
7/17/71	7	11	10. **Liar**	Dunhill 4282
11/20/71	4	10	● 11. **An Old Fashioned Love Song**	Dunhill 4294
1/08/72	5	10	12. **Never Been To Spain**	Dunhill 4299
4/01/72	12	8	13. The Family Of Man	Dunhill 4306
8/26/72	1 (1)	9	● 14. **Black & White**	Dunhill 4317
12/09/72	19	9	15. Pieces Of April	Dunhill 4331
6/02/73	3	13	● 16. **Shambala**	Dunhill 4352
11/17/73	17	6	17. Let Me Serenade You	Dunhill 4370
4/13/74	4	12	● 18. **The Show Must Go On**	Dunhill 4382
7/13/74	16	8	19. Sure As I'm Sittin' Here	Dunhill 15001
11/02/74	33	3	20. Play Something Sweet (Brickyard Blues)	Dunhill 15013
8/09/75	32	3	21. Til The World Ends	ABC 12114
			THUNDER, JOHNNY	
1/05/63	4	9	1. **Loop De Loop**	Diamond 129
			THUNDERCLAP NEWMAN	
			British group fraturing Jimmy (Wings) McCulloch	
10/25/69	37	2	1. Something In The Air -from film "The Magic Christian"-	Track 2656
			TIERRA	
			Los Angeles septet - 3 members were formerly with El Chicano	
12/13/80	18	15	1. Together	Boardwalk 5702
			TIJUANA BRASS - see HERB ALPERT	
			TILLOTSON, JOHNNY	
10/24/60	2 (1)	12	1. **Poetry In Motion**	Cadence 1384
2/06/61	25	5	2. Jimmy's Girl	Cadence 1391
8/28/61	7	8	3. **Without You**	Cadence 1404
1/20/62	35	1	4. Dreamy Eyes -re-entry of 1958 hit-	Cadence 1409
5/19/62	3	12	5. **It Keeps Right On A-Hurtin'**	Cadence 1418
8/25/62	17	6	6. Send Me The Pillow You Dream On	Cadence 1424
11/17/62	24	5	7. I Can't Help It (If I'm Still In Love With You)	Cadence 1432
3/23/63	24	6	8. Out Of My Mind	Cadence 1434
8/24/63	18	7	9. You Can Never Stop Me Loving You	Cadence 1437
11/30/63	7	10	10. **Talk Back Trembling Lips**	MGM 13181
3/14/64	37	2	11. Worried Guy	MGM 13193
6/06/64	36	2	12. I Rise, I Fall	MGM 13232

DATE	POS	WKS	ARTIST—Record Title	LABEL & NO.
11/28/64	31	6	13. She Understands Me	MGM 13284
10/02/65	35	2	14. Heartaches By The Number	MGM 13376
			TIN TIN	
			Australian	
5/08/71	20	6	1. Toast And Marmalade For Tea	Atco 6794
			TINY TIM	
			real name: Herbert Khaury	
6/08/68	17	6	1. Tip-Toe Thru' The Tulips With Me [N]	Reprise 0679
			TOBY BEAU	
7/01/78	13	12	1. My Angel Baby	RCA 11250
			TODD, ART & DOTTY	
4/21/58	6	11	1. **Chanson D'Amour (Song Of Love)**	Era 1064
			TODD, NICK	
			Pat Boone's younger brother	
2/10/58	21	2	1. At The Hop	Dot 15675
			TOKENS	
			Brooklyn quartet	
4/24/61	15	6	1. Tonight I Fell In Love	Warwick 615
11/27/61	1 (3)	13	● 2. **The Lion Sleeps Tonight**	RCA 7954
4/09/66	30	5	3. I Hear Trumpets Blow	B.T. Puppy 518
5/20/67	36	2	4. Portrait Of My Love	Warner 5900
			TOM TOM CLUB	
			group formed by Chris Frantz & Tina Weymouth of Talking Heads	
4/10/82	31	4	1. Genius Of Love	Sire 49882
			TOMMY TUTONE	
			San Francisco band led by Tommy Heath	
6/21/80	38	2	1. Angel Say No	Columbia 11278
3/13/82	4	16	2. **867-5309/Jenny**	Columbia 02646
			TONEY, OSCAR, JR.	
6/17/67	23	5	1. For Your Precious Love	Bell 672
			TONY & JOE	
			Tony Savonne & Joe Saraceno	
8/04/58	33	1	1. The Freeze	Era 1075
			TORME, MEL	
12/15/62	36	3	1. Comin' Home Baby	Atlantic 2165
			TORNADOES	
			English quintet	
11/17/62	1 (3)	13	1. **Telstar [I]**	London 9561
			TOROK, MITCHELL	
4/29/57	25	3	1. Pledge Of Love	Decca 30230
8/31/59	27	6	2. Caribbean	Guyden 2018
			TOTO	
			Bobby Kimball, lead singer of Los Angeles sextet	
11/11/78	5	14	● 1. **Hold The Line**	Columbia 10830
2/09/80	26	8	2. 99	Columbia 11173
5/08/82	2 (5)	18	3. **Rosanna**	Columbia 02811
9/11/82	30	5	4. Make Believe	Columbia 03143

DATE	POS	WKS	ARTIST—Record Title	LABEL & NO.
			TOWER OF POWER	
			Oakland-area 'funk' band	
8/26/72	29	5	1. You're Still A Young Man	Warner 7612
6/16/73	17	11	2. So Very Hard To Go	Warner 7687
8/24/74	26	4	3. Don't Change Horses (In The Middle Of A Stream)	Warner 7828
			TOWNSEND, ED	
4/28/58	13	13	1. For Your Love	Capitol 3926
			TOWNSHEND, PETE	
			English - lead guitarist for The Who	
7/05/80	9	12	1. **Let My Love Open The Door**	Atco 7217
			TOYS	
			New York trio	
10/02/65	2 (3)	11	● 1. **A Lover's Concerto** -adapted from Bach: Minuet In G-	DynoVoice 209
1/01/66	18	6	2. Attack	DynoVoice 214
			TRADE WINDS	
			also see Innocence	
2/27/65	32	4	1. New York's A Lonely Town	Red Bird 020
			TRAMMPS	
2/21/76	35	4	1. Hold Back The Night	Buddah 507
6/05/76	27	5	2. That's Where The Happy People Go	Atlantic 3306
3/25/78	11	13	3. Disco Inferno -in film "Saturday Night Fever"-	Atlantic 3389
			TRASHMEN	
			Minneapolis quartet	
12/28/63	4	10	1. **Surfin' Bird**	Garrett 4002
2/29/64	30	4	2. Bird Dance Beat	Garrett 4003
			TRAVIS & BOB	
			Travis Pritchett & Bob Weaver	
4/06/59	8	9	1. **Tell Him No**	Sandy 1017
			TRAVOLTA, JOHN	
			Vinnie Barbarino of TV's "Welcome Back Kotter" - also see Olivia Newton-John	
6/12/76	10	10	1. **Let Her In**	Midland Int'l. 10623
11/27/76	38	2	2. Whenever I'm Away From You	Midland Int'l. 10780
3/19/77	34	3	3. All Strung Out On You	Midland Int'l. 10907
			TREMELOES	
			British	
5/06/67	13	8	1. Here Comes My Baby	Epic 10139
7/15/67	11	10	2. Silence Is Golden	Epic 10184
10/21/67	36	4	3. Even The Bad Times Are Good	Epic 10233
			T. REX	
			British group: Marc Bolan, leader - died on 9/16/77 (28)	
1/29/72	10	11	1. **Bang A Gong (Get It On)**	Reprise 1032

DATE	POS	WKS	ARTIST—Record Title	LABEL & NO.
			TRIUMPH	
			Gil Moore, Rik Emmett, & Mike Levine - from Toronto, Canada	
8/25/79	38	3	1. Hold On	RCA 11569
			TROGGS	
			British foursome - Reg Presley, lead singer	
7/09/66	1 (2)	9	1. **Wild Thing**	Fontana 1548
9/03/66	29	2	2. With A Girl Like You	Fontana 1552
			-above 2 also on Atco 6415-	
3/23/68	7	12	3. **Love Is All Around**	Fontana 1607
			TROY, DORIS	
7/06/63	10	8	1. **Just One Look**	Atlantic 2188
			TRUE, ANDREA, Connection	
4/24/76	4	16	● 1. **More, More, More (Pt. 1)**	Buddah 515
3/26/77	27	5	2. N.Y., You Got Me Dancing	Buddah 564
			TUBES	
			San Francisco rock revue	
8/01/81	35	3	1. Don't Want To Wait Anymore	Capitol 5007
			TUCKER, TANYA	
6/07/75	37	2	1. Lizzie And The Rainman	MCA 40402
			TUCKER, TOMMY	
			died of poisoning 1/17/82 (48)	
2/29/64	11	8	1. Hi-Heel Sneakers	Checker 1067
			TUNE WEAVERS	
			Boston quintet - Margo Sylvia lead singer	
9/23/57	5	14	1. **Happy, Happy Birthday Baby**	Checker 872
			TURBANS	
			Philadelphia quartet - Al Banks lead singer	
1/14/56	33	1	1. When You Dance	Herald 458
			TURNER, IKE & TINA	
			husband & wife revue (separated in '76) with backup trio The Ikettes	
10/03/60	27	6	1. A Fool In Love	Sue 730
9/04/61	14	5	2. It's Gonna Work Out Fine	Sue 749
1/13/62	38	2	3. Poor Fool	Sue 753
8/08/70	34	6	4. I Want To Take You Higher	Liberty 56177
2/13/71	4	11	● 5. **Proud Mary**	Liberty 56216
10/27/73	22	7	6. Nutbush City Limits	United Artists 298
			TURNER, JESSE LEE	
1/26/59	20	6	1. The Little Space Girl [N]	Carlton 496
			TURNER, SAMMY	
7/06/59	3	14	1. **Lavender-Blue**	Big Top 3016
11/16/59	19	7	2. Always	Big Top 3029
			TURNER, SPYDER	
1/14/67	12	8	1. Stand By Me [N]	MGM 13617
			-vocal impressions of Jackie Wilson, David Ruffin, Billy Stewart, Smokey Robinson, and Chuck Jackson-	

DATE	POS	WKS	ARTIST—Record Title	LABEL & NO.
			TURTLES	
			Los Angeles group featuring Howard Kaylan & Marc Volman	
8/21/65	8	8	1. **It Ain't Me Babe**	White Whale 222
11/20/65	29	4	2. Let Me Be	White Whale 224
2/19/66	20	9	3. You Baby	White Whale 227
3/04/67	1 (3)	12	● 4. **Happy Together**	White Whale 244
5/27/67	3	8	5. **She'd Rather Be With Me**	White Whale 249
8/26/67	12	7	6. You Know What I Mean	White Whale 254
12/02/67	14	7	7. She's My Girl	White Whale 260
10/12/68	6	9	8. **Elenore**	White Whale 276
1/25/69	6	9	9. **You Showed Me**	White Whale 292
			TUXEDO JUNCTION	
7/01/78	32	2	1. Chattanooga Choo Choo	Butterfly 1205
			TWILLEY, DWIGHT, Band	
			also see Phil Seymour	
6/21/75	16	8	1. I'm On Fire	Shelter 40380
			TWITTY, CONWAY	
			real name: Harold Jenkins	
9/29/58	1 (2)	17	1. **It's Only Make Believe**	MGM 12677
2/16/59	28	7	2. The Story Of My Love	MGM 12748
8/24/59	29	3	3. Mona Lisa	MGM 12804
10/12/59	10	13	4. **Danny Boy**	MGM 12826
1/18/60	6	10	5. **Lonely Blue Boy**	MGM 12857
4/25/60	26	5	6. What Am I Living For	MGM 12886
7/11/60	35	5	7. Is A Blue Bird Blue	MGM 12911
1/16/61	22	5	8. C'est Si Bon (It's So Good)	MGM 12969
9/15/73	22	7	9. You've Never Been This Far Before	MCA 40094
			TYCOON	
4/28/79	26	5	1. Such A Woman	Arista 0398
			TYLER, BONNIE	
4/22/78	3	15	● 1. **It's A Heartache**	RCA 11249
			TYMES	
			Philadelphia quintet	
6/22/63	1 (1)	12	1. **So Much In Love**	Parkway 871
8/31/63	7	8	2. **Wonderful! Wonderful!**	Parkway 884
1/04/64	19	6	3. Somewhere	Parkway 891
12/28/68	39	1	4. People -from the film "Funny Girl"-	Columbia 44630
9/07/74	12	8	5. You Little Trustmaker	RCA 10022
			UNDERGROUND SUNSHINE	
8/23/69	26	5	1. Birthday	Intrepid 75002
			UNDISPUTED TRUTH	
7/31/71	3	13	1. **Smiling Faces Sometimes**	Gordy 7108
			UNIFICS	
10/19/68	25	5	1. Court Of Love	Kapp 935
1/18/69	36	4	2. The Beginning Of My End	Kapp 957

DATE	POS	WKS	ARTIST—Record Title	LABEL & NO.
			UNION GAP - see GARY PUCKETT	
			UNIT FOUR plus TWO	
			English sextet	
5/29/65	28	4	1. Concrete And Clay	London 9751
			UPCHURCH, PHILIP, Combo	
6/26/61	29	3	1. You Can't Sit Down, Part 2 [I]	Boyd 3398
			URIAH HEEP	
			British quintet featuring David Byron	
9/16/72	39	3	1. Easy Livin	Mercury 73307
			UTOPIA	
			Todd Rundgren, leader	
3/29/80	27	5	1. Set Me Free	Bearsville 49180
			VALE, JERRY	
3/24/56	30	5	1. Innamorata (Sweetheart)	Columbia 40634
			-from film "Artists & Models"-	
7/28/56	14	17	2. You Don't Know Me	Columbia 40710
1/23/65	24	4	3. Have You Looked Into Your Heart	Columbia 43181
			VALENS, RITCHIE	
			died in plane crash with Buddy Holly & the Big Bopper on 2/3/59 (17)	
12/15/58	2 (2)	18	1. **Donna**/	
1/19/59	22	8	2. La Bamba [F]	Del-Fi 4110
			VALENTE, CATERINA	
4/09/55	8	14	1. **The Breeze And I**	Decca 29467
			VALENTI, JOHN	
10/30/76	37	2	1. Anything You Want	Ariola Amer. 7625
			VALENTINO, MARK	
12/08/62	27	3	1. The Push And Kick	Swan 4121
			VALINO, JOE	
10/27/56	12	14	1. Garden Of Eden	Vik 0226
			VALJEAN	
			Valjean Johns	
6/16/62	28	4	1. Theme From Ben Casey [I]	Carlton 573
			VALLI, FRANKIE	
			lead singer of The Four Seasons	
2/12/66	39	1	1. (You're Gonna) Hurt Yourself	Smash 2015
6/03/67	2 (1)	14	● 2. **Can't Take My Eyes Off You**	Philips 40446
9/16/67	18	5	3. I Make A Fool Of Myself	Philips 40484
1/20/68	29	4	4. To Give (The Reason I Live)	Philips 40510
1/18/75	1 (1)	14	● 5. **My Eyes Adored You**	Private Stock 45003
6/14/75	6	9	6. **Swearin' To God**	Private Stock 45021
11/08/75	11	8	7. Our Day Will Come	Private Stock 45043
5/08/76	36	2	8. Fallen Angel	Private Stock 45074
6/17/78	1 (2)	15	★ 9. **Grease**	RSO 897

DATE	POS	WKS	ARTIST—Record Title	LABEL & NO.
			VALLI, JUNE	
5/14/55	29	1	1. Unchained Melody -from the film "Unchained"-	RCA 6078
4/18/60	29	4	2. Apple Green	Mercury 71588
			VAN DYKE, LEROY	
12/08/56	19	7	1. Auctioneer [N]	Dot 15503
11/20/61	5	12	2. **Walk On By**	Mercury 71834
3/31/62	35	2	3. If A Woman Answers (Hang Up The Phone)	Mercury 71926
			VAN HALEN	
			southern California quartet: David Lee Roth, lead singer; Edward & Alex Van Halen (brothers from Holland) & Michael Anthony	
3/11/78	36	3	1. You Really Got Me	Warner 8515
5/26/79	15	9	2. Dance The Night Away	Warner 8823
3/13/82	12	10	3. (Oh) Pretty Woman	Warner 50003
6/26/82	38	3	4. Dancing In The Street	Warner 29986
			VANDROSS, LUTHER	
11/14/81	33	4	1. Never Too Much	Epic 02409
			VANGELIS	
			Greek keyboardist - real name: Evangelos Papathanassiou	
2/20/82	1 (1)	15	1. **Chariots Of Fire - Titles [I]**	Polydor 2189
			VANILLA FUDGE	
			New York foursome featuring Tim Bogert & Carmine Appice	
8/03/68	6	8	1. **You Keep Me Hangin' On** -re-entry of 1967 hit-	Atco 6590
10/26/68	38	4	2. Take Me For A Little While	Atco 6616
			VANITY FARE	
			British quintet	
12/20/69	12	9	1. Early In The Morning	Page One 21027
5/16/70	5	14	● 2. **Hitchin' A Ride**	Page One 21029
			VANNELLI, GINO	
			Canadian	
10/26/74	22	5	1. People Gotta Move	A&M 1614
10/14/78	4	13	2. **I Just Wanna Stop**	A&M 2072
4/04/81	6	14	3. **Living Inside Myself**	Arista 0588
			VANWARMER, RANDY	
4/21/79	4	14	● 1. **Just When I Needed You Most**	Bearsville 0334
			VAPORS	
			British - David Fenton, leader	
11/15/80	36	3	1. Turning Japanese	Liberty 1364
			VAUGHAN, FRANKIE	
			English	
7/28/58	22	1	1. Judy	Epic 9273
			VAUGHAN, SARAH	
11/27/54	6	15	1. **Make Yourself Comfortable**	Mercury 70469
2/26/55	12	9	2. How Important Can It Be?	Mercury 70534
4/23/55	6	11	3. **Whatever Lola Wants** -from Broadway's "Damn Yankees"-	Mercury 70595
7/16/55	14	1	4. Experience Unnecessary	Mercury 70646

DATE	POS	WKS	ARTIST—Record Title	LABEL & NO.
12/03/55	11	7	5. C'est La Vie	Mercury 70727
3/03/56	13	7	6. Mr. Wonderful	Mercury 70777
7/21/56	19	6	7. Fabulous Character	Mercury 70885
1/12/57	19	5	8. The Banana Boat Song	Mercury 71020
8/17/59	7	11	9. **Broken-Hearted Melody**	Mercury 71477
			VAUGHN, BILLY, & His Orchestra	
			Dot Records musical director -- also see Walter Brennan and the Fontane Sisters	
12/11/54	**2** (1)	27	1. **Melody Of Love [I]**	Dot 15247
9/24/55	5	15	2. **The Shifting Whispering Sands (Parts 1 & 2) [S]** -naration by Ken Nordine-	Dot 15409
2/25/56	37	2	3. A Theme From "The Three Penny Opera" (Moritat) [I]	Dot 15444
9/08/56	18	6	4. When The White Lilacs Bloom Again [I]	Dot 15491
12/16/57	10	7	5. **Raunchy/ [I]**	
1/13/58	5	18	6. **Sail Along Silvery Moon [I]**	Dot 15661
4/14/58	30	4	7. Tumbling Tumbleweeds [I]	Dot 15710
8/25/58	20	8	8. La Paloma [I]	Dot 15795
2/02/59	37	1	9. Blue Hawaii [I]	Dot 15879
7/18/60	19	7	10. Look For A Star [I] -from film "Circus Of Horrors"-	Dot 16106
3/06/61	28	3	11. Wheels [I]	Dot 16174
8/11/62	13	8	12. A Swingin' Safari [I]	Dot 16374
			VEE, BOBBY	
			at age 15, Bobby & his group the Shadows, performed as a fill-in act for Buddy Holly after his tragic plane crash	
9/05/60	6	13	1. **Devil Or Angel**	Liberty 55270
12/12/60	6	11	2. **Rubber Ball**	Liberty 55287
2/27/61	33	3	3. Stayin' In	Liberty 55296
8/21/61	**1** (3)	11	4. **Take Good Care Of My Baby**	Liberty 55354
11/20/61	**2** (1)	13	5. **Run To Him**	Liberty 55388
3/17/62	15	6	6. Please Don't Ask About Barbara	Liberty 55419
6/09/62	15	6	7. Sharing You	Liberty 55451
9/15/62	20	6	8. Punish Her	Liberty 55479
12/22/62	3	11	9. **The Night Has A Thousand Eyes**	Liberty 55521
4/13/63	13	7	10. Charms	Liberty 55530
7/20/63	34	2	11. Be True To Yourself	Liberty 55581
8/12/67	3	13	● 12. **Come Back When You Grow Up**	Liberty 55964
12/16/67	37	2	13. Beautiful People -above 2 with The Strangers-	Liberty 56009
5/18/68	35	4	14. My Girl/My Guy (medley)	Liberty 56033
			VELVETS featuring Virgil Johnson	
6/26/61	26	4	1. Tonight (Could Be The Night)	Monument 441
			VENTURES	
			instrumental quartet from Tacoma, Washington: Don Wilson, Nokie Edwards, Bob Bogle & Mel Taylor	
7/25/60	**2** (1)	14	1. **Walk--Don't Run [I]**	Dolton 25
11/14/60	15	10	2. Perfidia [I]	Dolton 28
2/13/61	29	5	3. Ram-Bunk-Shush [I]	Dolton 32

DATE	POS	WKS	ARTIST—Record Title	LABEL & NO.
8/01/64	8	7	4. **Walk-Don't Run '64 [I]** -new version of 1960 hit-	Dolton 96
11/21/64	35	3	5. Slaughter On Tenth Avenue [I]	Dolton 300
4/12/69	4	9	6. **Hawaii Five-O [I]**	Liberty 56068
			VENUS, VIK	
7/26/69	38	3	1. Moonflight [N]	Buddah 118
			VERA, BILLY, & JUDY CLAY also see Billy & The Beaters	
3/23/68	36	1	1. Country Girl - City Man	Atlantic 2480
			VERNE, LARRY	
9/05/60	**1** (1)	10	1. **Mr. Custer [N]**	Era 3024
			VIBRATIONS also recorded as The Jayhawks and The Marathons	
3/13/61	25	4	1. The Watusi	Checker 969
4/25/64	26	5	2. My Girl Sloopy	Atlantic 2221
			VILLAGE PEOPLE New York disco act	
7/29/78	25	6	● 1. Macho Man	Casablanca 922
11/11/78	**2** (3)	20	★ 2. **Y.M.C.A**	Casablanca 945
3/31/79	3	13	● 3. **In The Navy**	Casablanca 973
			VILLAGE STOMPERS	
10/05/63	**2** (1)	12	1. **Washington Square [I]**	Epic 9617
			VINCENT, GENE, & His Blue Caps Gene died on 10/12/71 (36)	
6/23/56	7	15	1. **Be-Bop-A-Lula**	Capitol 3450
9/16/57	13	12	2. **Lotta Lovin'**	Capitol 3763
1/13/58	23	1	3. Dance To The Bop	Capitol 3839
			VINTON, BOBBY	
6/16/62	**1** (4)	13	● 1. **Roses Are Red (My Love)**	Epic 9509
9/15/62	12	7	2. Rain Rain Go Away	Epic 9532
9/22/62	38	2	3. I Love You The Way You Are	Diamond 121
1/05/63	33	3	4. Trouble Is My Middle Name/	
1/12/63	38	2	5. Let's Kiss And Make Up	Epic 9561
3/30/63	21	6	6. Over The Mountain (Across The Sea)	Epic 9577
6/01/63	3	10	7. **Blue On Blue**	Epic 9593
8/24/63	**1** (3)	12	8. **Blue Velvet**	Epic 9614
12/07/63	**1** (4)	12	9. **There! I've Said It Again**	Epic 9638
3/07/64	9	8	10. **My Heart Belongs To Only You**	Epic 9662
5/30/64	13	6	11. Tell Me Why	Epic 9687
8/22/64	17	6	12. Clinging Vine	Epic 9705
11/07/64	**1** (1)	14	13. **Mr. Lonely**	Epic 9730
3/20/65	17	5	14. Long Lonely Nights	Epic 9768
5/22/65	22	6	15. L-O-N-E-L-Y	Epic 9791
10/16/65	38	1	16. What Color (Is A Man)	Epic 9846
12/25/65	23	6	17. Satin Pillows	Epic 9869
5/28/66	40	1	18. Dum-De-Da -aka "She Understands Me"-	Epic 10014

DATE	POS	WKS	ARTIST—Record Title	LABEL & NO.
12/17/66	11	8	19. Coming Home Soldier	Epic 10090
10/14/67	6	11	20. **Please Love Me Forever**	Epic 10228
1/27/68	24	4	21. Just As Much As Ever	Epic 10266
4/13/68	33	6	22. Take Good Care Of My Baby	Epic 10305
8/03/68	23	5	23. Halfway To Paradise	Epic 10350
11/16/68	9	12	● 24. **I Love How You Love Me**	Epic 10397
5/03/69	34	2	25. To Know You Is To Love You	Epic 10461
7/12/69	34	2	26. The Days Of Sand And Shovels	Epic 10485
3/18/72	24	8	27. Every Day Of My Life	Epic 10822
7/08/72	19	10	28. Sealed With A Kiss	Epic 10861
10/12/74	3	11	● 29. **My Melody Of Love**	ABC 12022
4/19/75	33	2	30. Beer Barrel Polka	ABC 12056
			VIRTUES	
			Frank Virtue, lead guitarist	
3/23/59	5	12	1. **Guitar Boogie Shuffle [I]**	Hunt 324
			VISCOUNTS	
1/01/66	39	1	1. Harlem Nocturne [I] -re-release of l959 hit-	Amy 940
			VOGUES	
			quartet from Turtle Creek, PA - Bill Burkette, lead singer	
10/09/65	4	9	1. **You're The One**	Co & Ce 229
12/11/65	4	12	2. **Five O'Clock World**	Co & Ce 232
3/19/66	21	6	3. Magic Town	Co & Ce 234
6/25/66	29	4	4. The Land Of Milk And Honey	Co & Ce 238
7/13/68	7	11	● 5. **Turn Around, Look At Me**	Reprise 0686
9/21/68	7	8	6. **My Special Angel**	Reprise 0766
12/07/68	27	4	7. Till	Reprise 0788
3/29/69	34	2	8. No, Not Much	Reprise 0803
			VOLUME'S	
6/02/62	22	6	1. I Love You	Chex 1002
			VOUDOURIS, ROGER	
4/28/79	21	10	1. Get Used To It	Warner 8762
			VOXPOPPERS	
5/05/58	18	1	1. Wishing For Your Love	Mercury 71282
			WADE, ADAM	
3/27/61	7	10	1. **Take Good Care Of Her**	Coed 546
5/29/61	5	9	2. **The Writing On The Wall**	Coed 550
8/07/61	10	7	3. **As If I Didn't Know**	Coed 553
			WADSWORTH MANSION	
2/13/71	7	7	1. **Sweet Mary**	Sussex 209
			WAIKIKIS	
1/09/65	33	3	1. Hawaii Tattoo [I]	Kapp 30
			WAILERS	
6/01/59	36	2	1. Tall Cool One [I]	Golden Crest 518
5/30/64	38	1	2. Tall Cool One [I] -re-entry of l959 hit-	Golden Crest 518

Triumph. Heavy metal has universal appeal, undoubtedly the reason why Canada saw fit to donate Triumph to the world. Their answer to Britain's Judas Priest, perhaps?

The Turtles. When the Turtles disbanded in 1970, Marc Volman and Howard Kaylan joined Frank Zappa's Mothers of Invention, and began calling themselves the Phlorescent Leech & Eddie. But then, what's in a name?

Conway Twitty. As if the name Conway Twitty isn't enough, Harold Lloyd Jenkins (for it is he) also carries the honorary title of Hatako-Chtokchito-a-Yakni-Toloa, given to him by the Choctaw Indians. That's Great Man of Country Music, for those of you who don't speak Choctaw.

Ritchie Valens. Richard Valenzuela's sole success was twin-sided, and the Mexican rocker (who also recorded under the name Arvee Allens) wrote both "Donna" and "La Bamba."

Van Halen. Three of Van Halen's hits—"You Really Got Me," "Oh Pretty Woman" and "Dancing In The Street"— were originally chart entries in 1964. We're waiting for their version of "Ringo." "Hello Dolly" perhaps. "Everybody Loves Somebody"?

The Ventures. Seattle bricklayer Don Wilson and his building trade boss Bob Bogle formed the Ventures after realizing that they shared a passion for the guitar.

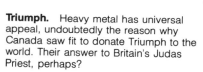

The Ventures International Fan Club, 1215 N. Highland Ave., Los Angeles 28, Calif. • The Ventures play only the Mosrite guitar.

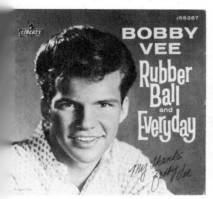

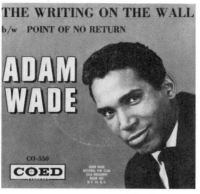

THE WRITING ON THE WALL

b/w POINT OF NO RETURN

Bobby Vee's guitar-playing brothers used to let him sit in on practice sessions providing he stayed silent (listen, this was Fargo, North Dakota). Then the group substituted for Buddy Holly at a Mason City, Iowa concert when the star's plane crashed, and Bobby opened his mouth to sing.

Adam Wade. Balladeer Adam Wade was a cross between Sam Cooke and Johnny Mathis, without the distinctive qualities of either. Nothing personal, Adam.

The Walker Brothers. The two U.S. hits of the Walker Brothers gave no hint of their enormous popularity on the other side of the Atlantic. Why, thousands of British maidens worshipped at the American trio's feet (especially those of lean and moody Scott) and they grabbed nine top 40 chart entries there in two years.

Junior Walker. The wicked saxmanship of Autry DeWalt, alias Junior Walker, was one of the assets acquired by Berry Gordy when his brother-in-law, Harvey Fuqua, merged his Harvey and Tri-Phi record labels with Motown.

Mary Wells hoped to catch Berry Gordy's ear with a tune she wrote with Jackie Wilson in mind. But when the Motown chief heard the 17-year-old perform "Bye Bye Baby," he signed her up to her own recording contract.

Jackie Wilson's patronage of Berry Gordy, who composed the singer's first top 40 hit ("To Be Loved") and his first top 10 entry ("Lonely Teardrops"), encouraged the hustling songwriter to stay in the music business—with well-known results.

DATE	POS	WKS	ARTIST—Record Title	LABEL & NO.
			WAINWRIGHT, LOUDON III	
2/24/73	16	9	1. Dead Skunk [N]	Columbia 45726
			WAKELIN, JOHNNY, & The Kinshasa Band	
			British	
8/16/75	21	6	1. Black Superman - "Muhammad Ali" [N]	Pye 71012
			WALKER BROS.	
			Scott Engel, Gary Leeds & John Maus - from Los Angeles	
11/13/65	16	6	1. Make It Easy On Yourself	Smash 2009
4/30/66	13	7	2. The Sun Ain't Gonna Shine (Anymore)	Smash 2032
			WALKER, JR., & THE ALL STARS	
			real name: Autry DeWalt, Jr.	
3/06/65	4	10	1. **Shotgun**	Soul 35008
7/03/65	36	2	2. Do The Boomerang	Soul 35012
8/21/65	29	5	3. Shake And Fingerpop	Soul 35013
5/21/66	20	6	4. (I'm A) Road Runner	Soul 35015
9/03/66	18	5	5. How Sweet It Is (To Be Loved By You)	Soul 35024
3/11/67	31	4	6. Pucker Up Buttercup	Soul 35030
12/23/67	24	6	7. Come See About Me	Soul 35041
9/14/68	31	6	8. Hip City - Pt. 2	Soul 35048
6/21/69	4	11	9. **What Does It Take (To Win Your Love)**	Soul 35062
11/22/69	16	9	10. These Eyes	Soul 35067
2/28/70	21	9	11. Gotta Hold On To This Feeling	Soul 35070
8/01/70	32	4	12. Do You See My Love (For You Growing)	Soul 35073
			WALLACE, JERRY	
9/15/58	11	9	1. How The Time Flies	Challenge 59013
9/07/59	8	15	2. **Primrose Lane**	Challenge 59047
			-with The Jewels-	
2/01/60	36	2	3. Little Coco Palm	Challenge 59060
1/09/61	26	4	4. There She Goes	Challenge 59098
12/22/62	24	7	5. Shutters And Boards	Challenge 9171
8/22/64	19	7	6. In The Misty Moonlight	Challenge 59246
9/30/72	38	2	7. If You Leave Me Tonight I'll Cry	Decca 32989
			-from TV's 'Night Gallery': "The Tune In Dan's Cafe"-	
			WALSH, JOE	
			member of The James Gang, and The Eagles	
9/22/73	23	7	1. Rocky Mountain Way	Dunhill 4361
7/01/78	12	9	2. Life's Been Good	Asylum 45493
6/14/80	19	8	3. All Night Long	Full Moon/Asy. 46639
			-from the film "Urban Cowboy"-	
6/27/81	34	4	4. A Life Of Illusion	Asylum 47144
			WAMMACK, TRAVIS	
8/09/75	38	2	1. (Shu-Doo-Pa-Poo-Poop) Love Being Your Fool	Capricorn 0239
			WANDERLEY, WALTER	
10/01/66	26	4	1. Summer Samba (So Nice) [I]	Verve 10421

DATE	POS	WKS	ARTIST—Record Title	LABEL & NO.
			WAR	
			also see Eric Burdon	
9/25/71	35	2	1. All Day Music	United Artists 50815
4/01/72	16	10	● 2. Slippin' Into Darkness	United Artists 50867
12/30/72	7	9	● 3. **The World Is A Ghetto**	United Artists 50975
3/24/73	2 (2)	12	● 4. **The Cisco Kid**	United Artists 163
8/04/73	8	10	5. **Gypsy Man**	United Artists 281
12/08/73	15	10	6. Me And Baby Brother	United Artists 350
7/13/74	33	2	7. Ballero [I]	United Artists 432
6/14/75	6	13	● 8. **Why Can't We Be Friends?**	United Artists 629
10/11/75	7	11	9. **Low Rider**	United Artists 706
7/31/76	7	12	● 10. **Summer**	United Artists 834
2/11/78	39	2	11. Galaxy	MCA 40820
			WARD, ANITA	
5/26/79	1 (2)	15	1. **Ring My Bell**	Juana 3422
			WARD, BILLY, & His Dominoes	
			New York quintet - originally The Dominoes with Clyde McPhatter, lead singer	
9/15/56	13	6	1. St. Therese Of The Roses	Decca 29933
			-Jackie Wilson, lead singer-	
7/15/57	12	17	2. Star Dust	Liberty 55071
10/07/57	20	8	3. Deep Purple	Liberty 55099
			WARD, DALE	
			lead singer of The Crescendos	
2/01/64	25	5	1. Letter From Sherry	Dot 16520
			WARD, JOE	
12/24/55	20	3	1. Nuttin For Xmas [N-X]	King 4854
			WARD, ROBIN	
11/16/63	14	7	1. Wonderful Summer	Dot 16530
			WARNES, JENNIFER	
			also see Joe Cocker	
2/26/77	6	14	1. **Right Time Of The Night**	Arista 0223
9/22/79	19	8	2. I Know A Heartache When I See One	Arista 0430
			WARWICK, DIONNE	
			Burt Bacharach & Hal David wrote & produced majority of her hits - also see Johnny Mathis	
1/05/63	21	7	1. Don't Make Me Over	Scepter 1239
1/04/64	8	9	2. **Anyone Who Had A Heart**	Scepter 1262
5/09/64	6	11	3. **Walk On By**	Scepter 1274
9/19/64	34	3	4. You'll Never Get To Heaven (If You Break My Heart)	Scepter 1282
11/07/64	20	6	5. Reach Out For Me	Scepter 1285
1/22/66	39	1	6. Are You There (With Another Girl)	Scepter 12122
4/23/66	8	8	7. **Message To Michael**	Scepter 12133
7/16/66	22	5	8. Trains And Boats And Planes	Scepter 12153

DATE	POS	WKS	ARTIST—Record Title	LABEL & NO.
10/22/66	26	5	9. I Just Don't Know What To Do With Myself	Scepter 12167
5/27/67	15	9	10. Alfie	Scepter 12187
8/26/67	32	3	11. The Windows Of The World	Scepter 12196
11/04/67	4	10	● 12. **I Say A Little Prayer/**	Scepter 12203
2/03/68	2 (4)	11	13. **(Theme From) Valley Of The Dolls**	
4/27/68	10	9	14. **Do You Know The Way To San Jose**	Scepter 12216
9/21/68	33	4	15. Who Is Gonna Love Me?	Scepter 12226
11/23/68	19	6	16. Promises, Promises	Scepter 12231
2/08/69	7	11	17. **This Girl's In Love With You**	Scepter 12241
6/07/69	37	3	18. The April Fools	Scepter 12249
10/11/69	16	7	19. You've Lost That Lovin' Feeling	Scepter 12262
1/03/70	6	10	20. **I'll Never Fall In Love Again** -from "Promises, Promises"-	Scepter 12273
5/09/70	32	3	21. Let Me Go To Him	Scepter 12276
10/31/70	37	2	22. Make It Easy On Yourself	Scepter 12294
7/28/79	5	17	● 23. **I'll Never Love This Way Again**	Arista 0419
12/15/79	15	11	24. Deja Vu	Arista 0459
9/06/80	23	6	25. No Night So Long	Arista 0527
			WARWICK, DIONNE, & SPINNERS	
8/03/74	1 (1)	15	● 1. **Then Came You**	Atlantic 3202
			WASHINGTON, BABY	
			lead singer of The Hearts	
6/01/63	40	1	1. That's How Heartaches Are Made	Sue 783
			WASHINGTON, DINAH	
			vocalist with Lionel Hampton's Band '43-'45 -- died on 12/14/63 (39) -- also see Brook Benton	
6/22/59	8	14	1. **What A Diff'rence A Day Makes**	Mercury 71435
10/26/59	17	8	2. Unforgettable	Mercury 71508
7/18/60	24	6	3. This Bitter Earth	Mercury 71635
11/07/60	30	2	4. Love Walked In	Mercury 71696
11/06/61	23	6	5. September In The Rain	Mercury 71876
6/23/62	36	3	6. Where Are You	Roulette 4424
			WASHINGTON, GROVER, JR.	
3/07/81	2 (3)	16	1. **Just The Two Of Us** -vocal by Bill Withers-	Elektra 47103
			WATTS 103RD STREET RHYTHM BAND - see CHARLES WRIGHT	
			WAYLON & WILLIE	
			Waylon Jennings & Willie Nelson	
3/06/76	25	5	1. Good Hearted Woman	RCA 10529
			WAYNE, THOMAS, With The DeLons	
			died in a car crash on 8/15/71 (29)	
2/16/59	5	13	1. **Tragedy**	Fernwood 109
			WE FIVE	
8/07/65	3	13	1. **You Were On My Mind**	A&M 770
12/25/65	31	2	2. Let's Get Together	A&M 784

DATE	POS	WKS	ARTIST—Record Title	LABEL & NO.
			WEBER, JOAN	
			died 5/13/81 (45)	
12/04/54	**1** (4)	16	1. **Let Me Go Lover**	Columbia 40366
			-from "Studio One" TV production-	
			WEDNESDAY	
2/16/74	34	4	1. Last Kiss	Sussex 507
			WEISBERG, TIM - see DAN FOGELBERG	
			WEISSBERG, ERIC, & STEVE MANDELL	
2/03/73	**2** (4)	11	● 1. **Dueling Banjos [I]**	Warner 7659
			-from the film "Deliverance"-	
			WELCH, BOB	
			member of Fleetwood Mac '71-'74	
11/19/77	**8**	12	1. **Sentimental Lady**	Capitol 4479
2/25/78	**14**	10	2. Ebony Eyes	Capitol 4543
7/01/78	**31**	3	3. Hot Love, Cold World	Capitol 4588
3/17/79	**19**	8	4. Precious Love	Capitol 4685
			WELCH, LENNY	
11/23/63	**4**	12	1. **Since I Fell For You**	Cadence 1439
4/11/64	**25**	5	2. Ebb Tide	Cadence 1422
			-from film "Sweet Bird Of Youth"-	
2/14/70	**34**	4	3. Breaking Up Is Hard To Do	Common. United 3004
			WELK, LAWRENCE, & His Orchestra	
			Lawrence, with his "champagne music", began his TV show in 1955	
3/03/56	**17**	2	1. Moritat (A Theme From "The Threepenny Opera") [I]	Coral 61574
4/07/56	**17**	2	2. The Poor People Of Paris [I]	Coral 61592
12/05/60	**21**	3	3. Last Date [I]	Dot 16145
12/31/60	**1** (2)	13	● 4. Calcutta [I]	Dot 16161
			WELLS, MARY	
			Motown's first successful solo artist -- also see Marvin Gaye	
8/21/61	**33**	3	1. I Don't Want To Take A Chance	Motown 1011
5/05/62	**8**	10	2. **The One Who Really Loves You**	Motown 1024
8/25/62	**9**	9	3. **You Beat Me To The Punch**	Motown 1032
12/15/62	**7**	10	4. **Two Lovers**	Motown 1035
3/09/63	**15**	6	5. Laughing Boy	Motown 1039
7/06/63	**40**	1	6. Your Old Stand By	Motown 1042
10/12/63	**22**	7	7. You Lost The Sweetest Boy/	
1/25/64	**29**	6	8. What's Easy For Two Is So Hard For One	Motown 1048
4/11/64	**1** (2)	13	9. **My Guy**	Motown 1056
1/30/65	**34**	2	10. Use Your Head	20th Century 555
			WESLEY, FRED - see JB's	
			WEST, DOTTIE	
4/25/81	**14**	12	1. What Are We Doin' In Love	Liberty 1404
			-with Kenny Rogers-	
			WESTON, KIM - see MARVIN GAYE	

DATE	POS	WKS	ARTIST—Record Title	LABEL & NO.
			WET WILLIE	
			Jimmy Hall, lead singer	
7/06/74	**10**	11	1. **Keep On Smilin'**	Capricorn 0043
1/28/78	**30**	4	2. Street Corner Serenade	Epic 50478
6/30/79	**29**	5	3. Weekend	Epic 50714
			WHISPERS	
3/15/80	**19**	8	● 1. And The Beat Goes On	Solar 11894
5/24/80	**28**	4	2. Lady	Solar 11928
3/28/81	**28**	5	3. It's A Love Thing	Solar 12154
			WHITCOMB, IAN, & Bluesville	
			English	
6/19/65	**8**	8	1. **You Turn Me On (Turn On Song)**	Tower 134
			WHITE PLAINS	
5/23/70	**13**	10	1. My Baby Loves Lovin'	Deram 85058
			WHITE, BARRY	
			also see Love Unlimited and Love Unlimited Orchestra	
5/05/73	**3**	12	● 1. **I'm Gonna Love You Just A Little More Baby**	20th Century 2018
9/01/73	**32**	6	2. I've Got So Much To Give	20th Century 2042
11/17/73	**7**	15	● 3. **Never, Never Gonna Give Ya Up**	20th Century 2058
8/10/74	**1** (1)	9	● 4. **Can't Get Enough Of Your Love, Babe**	20th Century 2120
11/16/74	**2** (2)	12	● 5. **You're The First, The Last, My Everything**	20th Century 2133
3/22/75	**8**	7	6. **What Am I Gonna Do With You**	20th Century 2177
6/21/75	**40**	2	7. I'll Do For You Anything You Want Me To	20th Century 2208
1/24/76	**32**	4	8. Let The Music Play	20th Century 2265
10/01/77	**4**	12	● 9. **It's Ecstasy When You Lay Down Next To Me**	20th Century 2350
5/27/78	**24**	5	10. Oh What A Night For Dancing	20th Century 2365
			WHITE, TONY JOE	
7/26/69	**8**	8	1. **Polk Salad Annie**	Monument 1104
			WHITING, MARGARET	
12/08/56	**20**	5	1. The Money Tree	Capitol 3586
11/19/66	**26**	5	2. The Wheel Of Hurt	London 101
			WHITTAKER, ROGER	
			English	
5/10/75	**19**	9	1. The Last Farewell	RCA 50030
			WHO	
			English: Roger Daltrey-lead singer, Pete Townshend-guitar, John Entwistle-bass, Keith Moon-drums (Keith died 9/7/78 - 32) - replaced by Kenny Jones	
5/20/67	**24**	4	1. Happy Jack	Decca 32114
10/28/67	**9**	9	2. **I Can See For Miles**	Decca 32206
5/04/68	**40**	2	3. Call Me Lightning	Decca 32288
8/31/68	**25**	6	4. Magic Bus	Decca 32362
5/03/69	**19**	5	5. Pinball Wizard	Decca 32465
8/23/69	**37**	2	6. I'm Free	Decca 32519
8/01/70	**27**	6	7. Summertime Blues	Decca 32708

DATE	POS	WKS	ARTIST—Record Title	LABEL & NO.
10/17/70	12	9	8. See Me, Feel Me -from the film "Tommy"-	Decca 32729
8/07/71	15	10	9. Won't Get Fooled Again -from film "Lifehouse"-	Decca 32846
12/04/71	34	5	10. Behind Blue Eyes	Decca 32888
8/05/72	17	8	11. Join Together	Decca 32983
1/13/73	39	2	12. The Relay	Track 33041
1/03/76	16	10	13. Squeeze Box	MCA 40475
9/16/78	14	9	14. Who Are You	MCA 40948
4/04/81	18	10	15. You Better You Bet	Warner 49698
10/09/82	28	6	16. Athena	Warner 29905
			WILCOX, HARLOW, & the Oakies	
11/22/69	30	6	1. Groovy Grubworm [I]	Plantation 28
			WILD CHERRY	
			Bob Parissi, lead singer	
7/31/76	1 (3)	18	★ 1. **Play That Funky Music**	Epic 50225
			WILDE, KIM	
			Kim's dad, Marty Wilde, made the "Hot 100" in 1960 with "Bad Boy"	
7/17/82	25	8	1. Kids In America	EMI America 8110
			WILLIAMS, ANDY	
			host of his own TV variety show from '57-'71	
8/18/56	7	17	1. **Canadian Sunset**	Cadence 1297
12/22/56	33	3	2. Baby Doll	Cadence 1303
3/02/57	1 (3)	14	3. **Butterfly**	Cadence 1308
6/03/57	8	14	4. **I Like Your Kind Of Love** -with Peggy Powers-	Cadence 1323
10/14/57	17	3	5. Lips Of Wine	Cadence 1336
2/24/58	3	14	6. **Are You Sincere**	Cadence 1340
9/22/58	17	6	7. Promise Me, Love	Cadence 1351
1/12/59	11	15	8. The Hawaiian Wedding Song	Cadence 1358
9/28/59	5	11	9. **Lonely Street**	Cadence 1370
12/28/59	7	9	10. **The Village Of St. Bernadette**	Cadence 1374
6/05/61	37	2	11. The Bilbao Song	Cadence 1398
7/14/62	38	1	12. Stranger On The Shore	Columbia 42451
11/03/62	39	1	13. Don't You Believe It	Columbia 42523
3/23/63	2 (4)	12	14. **Can't Get Used To Losing You/**	
4/13/63	26	7	15. Days Of Wine And Roses	Columbia 42674
7/06/63	13	8	16. Hopeless	Columbia 42784
1/25/64	13	8	17. A Fool Never Learns	Columbia 42950
5/16/64	34	4	18. Wrong For Each Other	Columbia 43015
10/03/64	28	5	19. On The Street Where You Live -from musical "My Fair Lady"-	Columbia 43128
12/19/64	24	7	20. Dear Heart	Columbia 43180
4/24/65	36	3	21. And Roses And Roses	Columbia 43257
10/16/65	40	1	22. Ain't It True	Columbia 43358
4/22/67	34	3	23. Music To Watch Girls By	Columbia 44065
11/30/68	33	4	24. Battle Hymn Of The Republic -with St. Charles Borromeo Choir-	Columbia 44650
5/03/69	22	7	25. Happy Heart	Columbia 44818

DATE	POS	WKS	ARTIST—Record Title	LABEL & NO.
2/27/71	9	10	26. **(Where Do I Begin) Love Story** -from the film "Love Story"-	Columbia 45317
5/20/72	34	4	27. Love Theme From "The Godfather" (Speak Softly Love)	Columbia 45579
			WILLIAMS, BILLY	
			died 10/17/72 (55)	
6/17/57	3	18	1. **I'm Gonna Sit Right Down And Write Myself A Letter**	Coral 61830
2/16/59	39	3	2. Nola	Coral 62069
			WILLIAMS, DANNY	
4/04/64	9	10	1. **White On White**	United Artists 685
			WILLIAMS, DENIECE	
			member of Stevie Wonder's backup vocal group Wonderlove - also see Johnny Mathis	
3/05/77	25	7	1. Free	Columbia 10429
5/01/82	10	9	2. **It's Gonna Take A Miracle**	ARC 02812
			WILLIAMS, DON	
			leader of the Pozo Seco Singers	
11/15/80	24	9	1. I Believe In You	MCA 41304
			WILLIAMS, JOHN [Conductor]	
9/13/75	32	4	1. Theme From "Jaws" (Main Title) [I]	MCA 40439
8/13/77	10	7	2. **Star Wars (Main Title) [I]** -performed by the London Symphony Orchestra-	20th Century 2345
1/21/78	13	8	3. Theme From "Close Encounters Of The Third Kind" [I]	Arista 0300
			WILLIAMS, LARRY	
			died 1/7/80 (44)	
7/08/57	5	17	1. **Short Fat Fannie**	Specialty 608
11/11/57	14	14	2. Bony Moronie	Specialty 615
			WILLIAMS, MASON	
7/13/68	2 (2)	11	1. **Classical Gas [I]**	Warner 7190
			WILLIAMS, MAURICE, & The Zodiacs	
			formerly The Gladiolas	
10/10/60	1 (1)	14	1. **Stay**	Herald 552
			WILLIAMS, OTIS - see CHARMS	
			WILLIAMS, ROGER	
8/20/55	1 (4)	26	1. **Autumn Leaves [I]**	Kapp 116
1/14/56	38	1	2. Wanting You [I]	Kapp 127
3/24/56	37	1	3. La Mer (Beyond The Sea) [I]	Kapp 138
3/16/57	15	10	4. Almost Paradise [I]	Kapp 175
11/11/57	22	7	5. Till	Kapp 197
9/08/58	10	11	6. **Near You [I]**	Kapp 233
10/15/66	7	14	7. **Born Free**	Kapp 767
			WILLIS, CHUCK	
			died 4/10/58 (30)	
5/13/57	12	8	1. C. C. Rider	Atlantic 1130
3/10/58	33	3	2. Betty And Dupree	Atlantic 1168

DATE	POS	WKS	ARTIST—Record Title	LABEL & NO.
5/12/58	9	17	3. **What Am I Living For/**	Atlantic 1179
5/26/58	24	2	4. Hang Up My Rock And Roll Shoes	
			WILSON, AL	
			member of The Rollers	Soul City 767
9/21/68	27	5	1. The Snake	Rocky Road 30073
11/24/73	1 (1)	16	● 2. **Show And Tell**	Rocky Road 30200
11/09/74	30	3	3. La La Peace Song	
5/01/76	29	4	4. I've Got A Feeling (We'll Be Seeing Each Other Again)	Playboy 6062
			WILSON, BRIAN	
			leader of The Beach Boys	
4/23/66	32	3	1. Caroline, No	Capitol 5610
			WILSON, J. FRANK, & The Cavaliers	
9/26/64	2 (1)	12	1. **Last Kiss**	Josie 923
			WILSON, JACKIE	
			Jackie suffered a paralyzing heart attack on 9/25/75 - also see Billy Ward	
4/21/58	22	10	1. To Be Loved	Brunswick 55052
12/08/58	7	16	2. **Lonely Teardrops**	Brunswick 55105
4/13/59	13	9	3. That's Why (I Love You So)	Brunswick 55121
7/06/59	20	6	4. I'll Be Satisfied	Brunswick 55136
10/12/59	37	1	5. You Better Know It	Brunswick 55149
			-from the film "Go Johnny Go"-	
1/04/60	34	3	6. Talk That Talk	Brunswick 55165
4/11/60	4	12	7. **Night/**	
4/25/60	15	9	8. Doggin' Around	Brunswick 55166
8/01/60	12	9	9. (You Were Made For) All My Love/	
8/01/60	15	8	10. A Woman, A Lover, A Friend	Brunswick 55167
10/24/60	8	12	11. **Alone At Last/**	
11/28/60	32	2	12. Am I The Man	Brunswick 55170
1/16/61	9	6	13. **My Empty Arms**	Brunswick 55201
3/27/61	20	5	14. Please Tell Me Why/	
3/27/61	40	1	15. Your One And Only Love	Brunswick 55208
6/26/61	19	5	16. I'm Comin' On Back To You	Brunswick 55216
9/11/61	37	2	17. Years From Now	Brunswick 55219
2/03/62	34	4	18. The Greatest Hurt	Brunswick 55221
3/23/63	5	9	19. **Baby Workout**	Brunswick 55239
8/10/63	33	1	20. Shake! Shake! Shake!	Brunswick 55246
11/19/66	11	8	21. Whispers (Gettin' Louder)	Brunswick 55300
9/02/67	6	9	22. **(Your Love Keeps Lifting Me) Higher And Higher**	Brunswick 55336
12/16/67	32	2	23. Since You Showed Me How To Be Happy	Brunswick 55354
8/31/68	34	2	24. I Get The Sweetest Feeling	Brunswick 55381
			WILSON, MERI	
7/02/77	18	10	● 1. Telephone Man [N]	GRT 127
			WILSON, NANCY	
7/18/64	11	7	1. (You Don't Know) How Glad I Am	Capitol 5198
6/15/68	29	9	2. Face It Girl, It's Over	Capitol 2136

DATE	POS	WKS	ARTIST—Record Title	LABEL & NO.
			WILTON PLACE STREET BAND	
3/12/77	24	7	1. Disco Lucy (I Love Lucy Theme) [I]	Island 078
			WINCHESTER, JESSE	
5/30/81	32	5	1. Say What	Bearsville 49711
			WIND	
			studio group featuring Tony Orlando as lead singer	
10/04/69	28	4	1. Make Believe	Life 200
			WINDING, KAI, & Orchestra	
7/27/63	8	9	1. **More [I]**	Verve 10295
			-Theme from film "Mondo Cane"-	
			WING & A PRAYER FIFE & DRUM CORPS	
12/20/75	14	12	1. Baby Face	Wing & A Prayer 103
			WINGFIELD, PETE	
10/25/75	15	8	1. Eighteen With A Bullet	Island 026
			-hit #18 with a bullet on the 11/22/75 "Hot 100"-	
			WINGS - see PAUL McCARTNEY	
			WINSTONS	
6/14/69	7	10	● 1. **Color Him Father**	Metromedia 117
			WINTER, EDGAR, Group	
			group features Rick Derringer, Ronnie Montrose & Dan Hartman	
4/21/73	1 (1)	14	● 1. **Frankenstein [I]**	Epic 10967
9/08/73	14	9	2. Free Ride	Epic 11024
8/10/74	33	2	3. River's Risin'	Epic 11143
			WINTERHALTER, HUGO [Orchestra & Chorus]	
			Hugo died on 9/17/73 (64)	
7/28/56	2 (2)	23	1. **Canadian Sunset [I]**	RCA 6537
			-piano solo by Eddie Heywood-	
			WINWOOD, STEVE	
			lead singer of The Spencer Davis Group, Blind Faith, and Traffic	
2/28/81	7	12	1. **While You See A Chance**	Island 49656
			WITHERS, BILL	
			also see Grover Washington, Jr.	
8/14/71	3	12	● 1. **Ain't No Sunshine**	Sussex 219
5/27/72	1 (3)	14	● 2. **Lean On Me**	Sussex 235
9/09/72	2 (2)	10	● 3. **Use Me**	Sussex 241
3/03/73	31	5	4. Kissing My Love	Sussex 250
1/21/78	30	4	5. Lovely Day	Columbia 10627
			WOLFMAN JACK - see GUESS WHO / STAMPEDERS	
			WOMACK, BOBBY	
			member of The Valentinos	
1/08/72	27	7	1. That's The Way I Feel About Cha	United Art. 50847
1/13/73	31	6	● 2. Harry Hippie	United Art. 50946
8/11/73	29	6	3. Nobody Wants You When You're Down And Out	United Artists 255
3/09/74	10	11	● 4. **Lookin' For A Love**	United Artists 375

DATE	POS	WKS	ARTIST—Record Title	LABEL & NO.
			WONDER WHO?	
			group is actually The 4 Seasons	
11/27/65	12	8	1. Don't Think Twice	Philips 40324
			WONDER, STEVIE	
			first charted hit at age 13 - also see Paul McCartney	
7/06/63	1 (3)	12	1. **Fingertips - Pt 2**	Tamla 54080
10/19/63	33	4	2. Workout Stevie, Workout	Tamla 54086
			-above 2 shown as Little Stevie Wonder-	
7/11/64	29	4	3. Hey Harmonica Man	Tamla 54096
1/22/66	3	9	4. **Uptight (Everything's Alright)**	Tamla 54124
5/07/66	20	4	5. Nothing's Too Good For My Baby	Tamla 54130
7/30/66	9	8	6. **Blowin In The Wind**	Tamla 54136
11/26/66	9	8	7. **A Place In The Sun**	Tamla 54139
4/01/67	32	3	8. Travlin' Man	Tamla 54147
6/24/67	2 (2)	12	9. **I Was Made To Love Her**	Tamla 54151
10/21/67	12	5	10. I'm Wondering	Tamla 54157
4/27/68	9	9	11. **Shoo-Be-Doo-Be-Doo-Da-Day**	Tamla 54165
8/17/68	35	3	12. You Met Your Match	Tamla 54168
11/09/68	2 (2)	13	13. **For Once In My Life**	Tamla 54174
3/22/69	39	1	14. I Don't Know Why/	
6/21/69	4	11	15. **My Cherie Amour**	Tamla 54180
11/01/69	7	12	16. Yester-Me, Yester-You, Yesterday	Tamla 54188
2/21/70	26	5	17. Never Had A Dream Come True	Tamla 1191
7/04/70	3	13	18. **Signed, Sealed, Delivered I'm Yours**	Tamla 54196
10/31/70	9	8	19. **Heaven Help Us All**	Tamla 54200
3/27/71	13	9	20. We Can Work It Out	Tamla 54202
9/04/71	8	11	21. **If You Really Love Me**	Tamla 54208
6/24/72	33	5	22. Superwoman (Where Were You When I Needed You)	Tamla 54216
12/09/72	1 (1)	13	23. **Superstition**	Tamla 54226
3/31/73	1 (1)	13	24. **You Are The Sunshine Of My Life**	Tamla 54232
9/01/73	4	12	25. **Higher Ground**	Tamla 54235
11/24/73	8	14	26. **Living For The City**	Tamla 54242
4/27/74	16	9	27. Don't You Worry 'Bout A Thing	Tamla 54245
8/17/74	1 (1)	14	28. **You Haven't Done Nothin**	Tamla 54252
			-background vocals: Jackson 5-	
11/30/74	3	14	29. **Boogie On Reggae Woman**	Tamla 54254
12/04/76	1 (1)	15	30. **I Wish**	Tamla 54274
4/16/77	1 (3)	13	31. **Sir Duke**	Tamla 54281
			-a tribute to Duke Ellington-	
9/17/77	32	4	32. Another Star	Tamla 54286
12/03/77	36	5	33. As	Tamla 54291
11/10/79	4	14	34. **Send One Your Love**	Tamla 54303
10/04/80	5	16	35. **Master Blaster (Jammin')**	Tamla 54317
1/17/81	11	11	36. I Ain't Gonna Stand For It	Tamla 54320
1/30/82	4	13	37. **That Girl**	Tamla 1602
6/19/82	13	9	38. Do I Do	Tamla 1612

Gino Vanelli. At the suggestion of a family friend, Gino Vanelli sought the patronage of Trini Lopez to establish his recording career. But it was Herb Alpert who produced the Canadian's first album, and for whose label he enjoyed his biggest hit.

Andy Williams. "Anthony September" was the composer credit on Andy's most successful single, "Butterfly." It was the pseudonym for Tony Mammarella, producer of Dick Clark's "American Bandstand" TV show — although the song was actually written by Philadelphia's Kal Mann and Bernie Lowe.

Stevie Wonder. When "Fingertips" became his first hit in 1963, Little Stevie Wonder was a fifth grade pupil at Detroit's Fitzgerald School who carried a "B" average and liked mathematics and typing best.

The Yardbirds gained not a little publicity by taking over the residency of the Rolling Stones at the Crawdaddy blues club, outside London. They also gained chart recognition by later placing three consecutive singles in the British top 10. Two of them, "For Your Love" and "Heart Full of Soul," were successfully sent Stateside.

Kathy Young. The Rivileers' "A Thousand Stars" was profitably revived by Kathy Young and her Innocents in 1959 for Indigo Records, to which Young signed at the suggestion of Wink Martindale. She later married John Maus of the Walker Brothers.

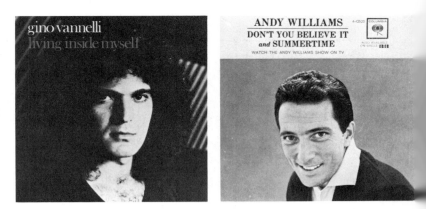

Neil Young — Comes A Time

47-9015

THE YOUNGBLOODS
GRIZZLY BEAR / TEARS ARE FALLING

RCA VICTOR

WS9-02972

Frank & Moon Zappa
Valley Girl

Neil Young. The way slick Rick James tells it, Neil Young and he once shared an apartment and a band, the Mynah Birds. They even recorded for Motown, he says, although nothing was released.

The Youngbloods started out as a mid '60s house band at New York's Cafe A Go-Go, comprising a couple of folkies (Jesse Colin Young and Jerry Corbitt) and a bluegrass musician (Banana Lowell Levinger). One hit was to be their fate.

Frank Zappa. Although the Mothers of Invention first began charting with albums in 1967, Frank Zappa himself had to wait until 1982 for his first top 40 single. Even then, he had to share the glory with daughter Moon Unit.

The Zombies and Laurence Olivier once appeared in the same movie, Otto Preminger's *Bunny Lake Is Missing.* Watch for it on television. Late.

THE ZOMBIES
SHE'S COMING HOME

A MARQUIS ENTERPRISE LTD. PRODUCTION
DIRECTED BY KEN JONES

DATE	POS	WKS	ARTIST—Record Title	LABEL & NO.
			WOOD, BRENTON	
6/24/67	34	1	1. The Oogum Boogum Song	Double Shot 111
9/09/67	9	9	2. **Gimme Little Sign**	Double Shot 116
12/16/67	34	3	3. Baby You Got It	Double Shot 121
			WOOD, LAUREN	
10/27/79	24	6	1. Please Don't Leave -harmony vocal: Michael McDonald-	Warner 49043
			WOODS, STEVIE	
11/14/81	25	10	1. Steal The Night	Cotillion 46016
3/20/82	38	3	2. Just Can't Win 'Em All	Cotillion 46030
			WOOLEY, SHEB	
6/02/58	1 (6)	14	1. **The Purple People Eater [N]**	MGM 12651
			WRAY, LINK, & His Ray Men	
5/12/58	16	10	1. Rumble [I]	Cadence 1347
3/16/59	23	3	2. Raw-Hide [I]	Epic 9300
			WRIGHT, BETTY	
			also see Peter Brown	
9/07/68	33	2	1. Girls Can't Do What The Guys Do	Alston 4569
12/11/71	6	12	● 2. **Clean Up Woman**	Alston 4601
			WRIGHT, CHARLES, & THE WATTS 103rd STREET RHYTHM BAND	
			Charles was a member of The Shields	
3/22/69	11	10	1. Do Your Thing	Warner 7250
5/30/70	16	10	2. Love Land	Warner 7365
9/12/70	12	10	3. Express Yourself	Warner 7417
			WRIGHT, DALE	
2/24/58	38	2	1. She's Neat -with the Rock-Its-	Fraternity 792
			WRIGHT, GARY	
			co-leader of Spooky Tooth	
1/31/76	2 (3)	14	● 1. **Dream Weaver**	Warner 8167
5/15/76	2 (2)	18	2. **Love Is Alive**	Warner 8143
8/01/81	16	10	3. Really Wanna Know You	Warner 49769
			WRIGHT, PRISCILLA	
6/25/55	16	9	1. The Man In The Raincoat -with Don Wright & The Septette-	Unique 303
			WYNETTE, TAMMY	
12/28/68	19	9	1. Stand By Your Man	Epic 10398
			YARBROUGH & PEOPLES	
			Cavin Yarbrough & Alisa Peoples	
3/14/81	19	7	● 1. Don't Stop The Music	Mercury 76085
			YARBROUGH, GLENN	
			member of The Limeliters	
4/17/65	12	9	1. Baby The Rain Must Fall	RCA 8498

DATE	POS	WKS	ARTIST—Record Title	LABEL & NO.
			YARDBIRDS	
			British superstar quintet featuring Eric Clapton, Jeff Beck, and all four Led Zeppelin members - original lead singer, Keith Relf, died on 5/14/76 (33)	
6/05/65	6	9	1. **For Your Love**	Epic 9790
8/21/65	9	8	2. **Heart Full Of Soul**	Epic 9823
11/20/65	17	7	3. I'm A Man	Epic 9857
4/09/66	11	8	4. Shapes Of Things	Epic 10006
7/16/66	13	7	5. Over Under Sideways Down	Epic 10035
12/24/66	30	4	6. Happenings Ten Years Time Ago	Epic 10094
			YELLOW BALLOON	
4/29/67	25	5	1. Yellow Balloon	Canterbury 508
			YES	
			English quintet featuring Jon Anderson, Rick Wakeman, Steve Howe, Peter Banks & Bill Bruford	
12/04/71	40	2	1. Your Move	Atlantic 2819
3/04/72	13	10	2. Roundabout	Atlantic 2854
			YOST, DENNIS - see CLASSICS IV	
			YOUNGBLOODS	
			Jesse Colin Young, lead singer	
8/02/69	5	12	● 1. **Get Together** -re-release of 1967 hit-	RCA 9752
			YOUNG-HOLT UNLIMITED	
			Eldee Young & Isaac Red Holt - 2/3 of the Ramsey Lewis Trio	
1/21/67	40	2	1. Wack Wack [I] -shown as Young Holt Trio-	Brunswick 55305
12/07/68	3	12	● 2. **Soulful Strut** [I]	Brunswick 55391
			YOUNG RASCALS - see RASCALS	
			YOUNG, BARRY	
12/04/65	13	7	1. One Has My Name (The Other Has My Heart)	Dot 16756
			YOUNG, FARON	
5/01/61	12	11	1. Hello Walls	Capitol 4533
			YOUNG, JOHN PAUL	
			Australian	
8/05/78	7	15	1. **Love Is In The Air**	Scotti Bros. 402
			YOUNG, KATHY, with The Innocents	
			also see Innocents	
10/31/60	3	15	1. **A Thousand Stars**	Indigo 108
3/06/61	30	6	2. Happy Birthday Blues	Indigo 115
			YOUNG, NEIL	
			also see Crosby, Stills, Nash & Young, and Buffalo Springfield	
12/05/70	33	3	1. Only Love Can Break Your Heart	Reprise 0958
2/12/72	1 (1)	13	● 2. **Heart Of Gold**	Reprise 1065
5/20/72	31	4	3. Old Man	Reprise 1084
			YOUNG, VICTOR, & His Orchestra	
			Victor died on 11/11/56 (56)	
7/08/57	13	9	1. Around The World In 80 Days [I] -flip side is Bing Crosby's vocal version-	Decca 30262

DATE	POS	WKS	ARTIST—Record Title	LABEL & NO.
			YURO, TIMI	
7/31/61	4	10	1. **Hurt**	Liberty 55343
8/11/62	12	6	2. What's A Matter Baby (Is It Hurting You)	Liberty 55469
8/10/63	24	7	3. Make The World Go Away	Liberty 55587
			ZACHARIAS, HELMUT, & His Magic Violins	
			German	
9/08/56	12	7	1. When The White Lilacs Bloom Again [I]	Decca 30039
			ZACHERLE, JOHN ["The Cool Ghoul"]	
3/10/58	6	7	1. **Dinner With Drac - Part 1 [N]**	Cameo 130
			ZAGER & EVANS	
			Denny Zager & Rick Evans	
6/28/69	1 (6)	12	● 1. **In The Year 2525 (Exordium & Terminus)**	RCA 0174
			ZAGER, MICHAEL, Band	
			member of Ten Wheel Drive	
4/29/78	36	4	1. Let's All Chant [I]	Private Stock 45184
			ZAHND, RICKY, & The Blue Jeaners	
12/24/55	21	2	1. (I'm Gettin') Nuttin' For Christmas [N-X]	Columbia 40576
			ZAPPA, FRANK	
			leader of Mothers Of Invention	
9/04/82	32	3	1. Valley Girl [N] -featuring Frank's daughter: Moon Unit Zappa-	Barking Pumpkin 0297
			ZEVON, WARREN	
4/22/78	21	6	1. Werewolves Of London	Asylum 45472
			ZOMBIES	
			British quintet featuring Rod Argent & Colin Blunstone	
11/07/64	2 (1)	12	1. **She's Not There**	Parrot 9695
1/30/65	6	8	2. **Tell Her No**	Parrot 9723
2/22/69	3	11	● 3. **Time Of The Season**	Date 1628
			ZZ TOP	
			Billy Gibbons, Dusty Hill, and Frank Beard from El Paso, Texas	
8/16/75	20	4	1. Tush	London 220
3/01/80	34	3	2. I Thank You	Warner 49163

THE SONGS

THE SONGS

This section lists, alphabetically, all titles from the artist section. The artist's name is listed below each title, along with the highest position attained (POS) and year of peak popularity (YR). Some titles show the letter F as a position, indicating the title was listed as a flip side and did not chart on its own.

A song with more than one charted version is listed once, with the artist's names listed below in chronological order. Many songs that have the same title, but are different tunes, are listed separately, with the most popular title listed first. This will make it easy to determine if songs are indeed the same, the amount of charted versions of a particular song, and the most popular version.

Cross references have been used throughout to aid in finding a title. If you have trouble, please keep in mind the following: Titles in which an apostrophe is used within a word will come before a title using the complete spelling (Lovin' comes before Loving). A title with dashes between words will follow titles of similar wording (Mother-In-Law follows Mother Popcorn). Titles such as I.O.U., D.O.A., and SOS will be found at the beginning of each letter.

POS/YR	RECORD TITLE/ARTIST

A

POS/YR	RECORD TITLE/ARTIST
	"A" Team
28/66	Ssgt Barry Sadler
	ABC
1/70	Jackson 5
	Abacab
26/82	Genesis
	Abigail Beecher
16/64	Freddy Cannon
	Abilene
15/63	George Hamilton IV
	About This Thing Called Love
31/60	Fabian
	Abra-Ca-Dabra
32/74	Defranco Family featuring Tony Defranco
	Abracadabra
1/82	Steve Miller Band
	Abraham, Martin And John
4/68	Dion
33/69	Miracles
35/69	Moms Mabley
8/71	Tom Clay
	Absolutely Right
26/71	Five Man Electrical Band
	Action
13/65	Freddy Cannon
	Action
20/76	Sweet
	Admiral Halsey..see: Uncle Albert
	Affair To Remember (Our Love Affair)
16/57	Vic Damone
	After Midnight
18/70	Eric Clapton
	After School
32/57	Randy Starr
	After The Glitter Fades
32/82	Stevie Nicks
	After The Goldrush
22/74	Prelude
	After The Lights Go Down Low
10/56	Al Hibbler

POS/YR	RECORD TITLE/ARTIST
	After The Love Has Gone
2/79	Earth Wind & Fire
	After The Lovin'
8/77	Engelbert Humperdinck
	Afternoon Delight
1/76	Starland Vocal Band
	Against The Wind
5/80	Bob Seger
	Agent Double-O-Soul
21/65	Edwin Starr
	Agony And The Ecstasy
36/75	Smokey Robinson
	Ah! Leah!
29/81	Donnie Iris
	Ahab, The Arab
5/62	Ray Stevens
	Ai No Corrida
28/81	Quincy Jones
	Ain't Even Done With The Night
17/81	John Cougar
	Ain't Gonna Bump No More (With No Big Fat Woman)
12/77	Joe Tex
	Ain't Gonna Lie
39/66	Keith
	Ain't Got No Home
20/57	Clarence "Frog Man" Henry
	Ain't It Funky Now (Part 1)
24/69	James Brown
	Ain't It True
40/65	Andy Williams
	Ain't Love A Bitch
22/79	Rod Stewart
	Ain't No Mountain High Enough
19/67	Marvin Gaye & Tammi Terrell
1/70	Diana Ross
	Ain't No Stoppin' Us Now
13/79	McFadden & Whitehead
	Ain't No Sunshine
3/71	Bill Withers
	Ain't No Way
16/68	Aretha Franklin
	Ain't No Way To Treat A Lady
8/75	Helen Reddy

POS/YR	RECORD TITLE/ARTIST
	Ain't No Woman (Like The One I've Got)
4/73	Four Tops
	Ain't Nothing Like The Real Thing
8/68	Marvin Gaye & Tammi Terrell
21/77	Donny & Marie Osmond
	Ain't Nothing You Can Do
20/64	Bobby Bland
	Ain't She Sweet
19/64	Beatles
	Ain't That A Shame
1/55	Pat Boone
10/55	Fats Domino
22/63	Four Seasons
35/79	Cheap Trick
	Ain't That Just Like A Woman
33/61	Fats Domino
	Ain't That Loving You Baby
16/64	Elvis Presley
	Ain't That Peculiar
8/65	Marvin Gaye
	Ain't Too Proud To Beg
13/66	Temptations
17/74	Rolling Stones
	Ain't Understanding Mellow
21/72	Jerry Butler & Brenda Lee Eager
	Air That I Breathe
6/74	Hollies
	Airport Love Theme
31/70	Vincent Bell
	Al Di La'
6/62	Emilio Pericoli
29/64	Ray Charles Singers
	Alabama Jubilee
14/55	Ferko String Band
	Alamo..see: Ballad Of
	Albert Flasher
29/71	Guess Who
	Alfie
32/66	Cher
15/67	Dionne Warwick
	Alice In Wonderland
17/63	Neil Sedaka
	Alice Long (You're Still My Favorite Girlfriend)
27/68	Tommy Boyce & Bobby Hart

POS/YR	RECORD TITLE/ARTIST
	Alien
29/81	Atlanta Rhythm Section
	Alive
34/72	Bee Gees
	Alive Again
14/78	Chicago
	All
35/67	James Darren
	All Alone Am I
3/62	Brenda Lee
	All Along The Watchtower
20/68	Jimi Hendrix
	All American Boy
2/59	Bill Parsons
	All At Once You Love Her
11/55	Perry Como
	All By Myself
2/76	Eric Carmen
	All Day And All Of The Night
7/65	Kinks
	All Day Music
35/71	War
	All I Could Do Was Cry
33/60	Etta James
	All I Ever Need Is You
7/71	Sonny & Cher
	All I Have To Do Is Dream
1/58	Everly Brothers
14/63	Richard Chamberlain
27/70	Glen Campbell & Bobbie Gentry
	All I Know
9/73	Art Garfunkel
	All I Need
8/67	Temptations
	All I Really Want To Do
15/65	Cher
40/65	Byrds
	All I See Is You
20/66	Dusty Springfield
	All In My Mind
19/61	Maxine Brown
	All My Love..see: (You Were Made For)
	All Night Long
19/80	Joe Walsh

POS/YR	RECORD TITLE/ARTIST
	(All Of A Sudden) My Heart Sings
15/59	Paul Anka
38/65	Mel Carter
	All Our Tomorrows
28/82	Eddie Schwartz
	All Out Of Love
2/80	Air Supply
	All Over Again
38/58	Johnny Cash
	All Over The World
13/80	Electric Light Orchestra
	All Right Now
4/70	Free
	All Shook Up
1/57	Elvis Presley
	All Strung Out
26/66	Nino Tempo & April Stevens
34/77	John Travolta
	All The King's Horses
26/72	Aretha Franklin
	All The Time
21/58	Johnny Mathis
	All The Way
2/57	Frank Sinatra
	All The Young Dudes
37/72	Mott The Hoople
	All Those Years Ago
2/81	George Harrison
	All You Get From Love Is A Love Song
35/77	Carpenters
	All You Need Is Love
1/67	Beatles
	Allegheny Moon
2/56	Patti Page
	Alley Cat
7/62	Bent Fabric & His Piano
	Alley-Oop
1/60	Hollywood Argyles
15/60	Dante & The Evergreens
	Almost Grown
32/59	Chuck Berry
	Almost Like Being In Love
32/78	Michael Johnson

POS/YR	RECORD TITLE/ARTIST
	Almost Paradise
15/57	Roger Williams
31/57	Lou Stein
	Almost Persuaded
24/66	David Houston
	Almost Summer
28/78	Celebration featuring Mike Love
	Alone Again (Naturally)
1/72	Gilbert O'Sullivan
	Alone At Last
8/60	Jackie Wilson
	Alone (Why Must I Be Alone)
18/57	Shepherd Sisters
28/64	Four Seasons
	Along Came Jones
9/59	Coasters
27/69	Ray Stevens
	Along Comes Mary
7/66	Association
	Already Gone
32/74	Eagles
	Also Sprach Zarathustra (2001)
2/73	Deodato
	Alvin Twist
40/62	Chipmunks
	Alvin's Harmonica
3/59	Chipmunks
	Alvin's Orchestra
33/60	Chipmunks
	Always
19/59	Sammy Turner
	Always And Forever
18/78	Heatwave
	Always On My Mind
5/82	Willie Nelson
	Always Something There To Remind Me
27/70	R.B. Greaves
	Always Together
18/68	Dells
	Always Together
33/64	Al Martino
	Am I Losing You
31/60	Jim Reeves

POS/YR	RECORD TITLE/ARTIST
	Am I That Easy To Forget
25/60	Debbie Reynolds
18/68	Engelbert Humperdinck
	Am I The Man
32/60	Jackie Wilson
	Amazing Grace
15/71	Judy Collins
11/72	Royal Scots Dragoon Guards
	Ame Caline (Soul Coaxing)
37/68	Raymond Lefevre & His Orchestra
	Amen
7/64	Impressions
36/68	Otis Redding
	America
8/81	Neil Diamond
	American City Suite
27/72	Cashman & West
	American Dream
13/80	Nitty Gritty Dirt Band
	American Heartbeat
17/82	Survivor
	American Music
16/82	Pointer Sisters
	American Pie - Parts I & II
1/72	Don McLean
	American Trilogy
26/71	Mickey Newbury
	American Tune
35/73	Paul Simon
	American Woman
1/70	Guess Who
	Americans
4/74	Byron MacGregor
24/74	Gordon Sinclair
	Amie
27/75	Pure Prairie League
	Among My Souvenirs
7/60	Connie Francis
	Amor
18/61	Ben E. King
	(Amos & Andy Song)..see: Like A Sunday In Salem
	Amos Moses
8/71	Jerry Reed

POS/YR	RECORD TITLE/ARTIST
	Amukiriki (The Lord Willing)
38/55	Les Paul & Mary Ford
	Anastasia
37/57	Pat Boone
	And Get Away
22/67	Esquires
	And I Am Telling You I'm Not Going
22/82	Jennifer Holliday
	And I Love Her
12/64	Beatles
	And I Love You So
29/73	Perry Como
	And Roses And Roses
36/65	Andy Williams
	And That Reminds Me
9/57	Kay Starr
12/57	Della Reese
	And The Beat Goes On
19/80	Whispers
	And When I Die
2/69	Blood Sweat & Tears
	Angel
20/73	Aretha Franklin
	Angel
40/72	Rod Stewart
	Angel Baby
5/61	Rosie & The Originals
	Angel Baby
30/58	Dean Martin
	Angel In Blue
40/82	J. Geils Band
	Angel In Your Arms
6/77	Hot
	Angel Of The Morning
7/68	Merrilee Rush & The Turnabouts
4/81	Juice Newton
	Angel On My Shoulder
22/61	Shelby Flint
	Angel Say No
38/80	Tommy Tutone
	Angel Smile
33/58	Nat King Cole
	Angela Jones
27/60	Johnny Ferguson

POS/YR	RECORD TITLE/ARTIST
11/56	**Angels In The Sky** Crew-Cuts
22/59	**Angels Listened In** Crests
1/73	**Angie** Rolling Stones
	Angie ..see: Different Worlds
1/74	**Angie Baby** Helen Reddy
	(Angry Young Man)..see: Fooling Yourself
1/74	**Annie's Song** John Denver
1/80	**Another Brick In The Wall (Part II)** Pink Floyd
5/71	**Another Day** Paul McCartney
1/80	**Another One Bites The Dust** Queen
32/74	**Another Park, Another Sunday** Doobie Brothers
32/76	**Another Rainy Day In New York City** Chicago
10/63 6/74	**Another Saturday Night** Sam Cooke Cat Stevens
22/60	**Another Sleepless Night** Jimmy Clanton
	Another Somebody Done Somebody Wrong Song..see: (Hey Won't You Play)
32/77	**Another Star** Stevie Wonder
20/58	**Another Time, Another Place** Patti Page
32/80	**Answering Machine** Rupert Holmes
	(Anthony's Song)..see: Movin' Out
13/72	**Anticipation** Carly Simon
23/62 14/82	**Any Day Now** Chuck Jackson Ronnie Milsap
14/64	**Any Way You Want It** Dave Clark Five

POS/YR	RECORD TITLE/ARTIST
23/80	**Any Way You Want It** Journey
31/61	**Anybody But Me** Brenda Lee
31/60	**Anymore** Teresa Brewer
8/64	**Anyone Who Had A Heart** Dionne Warwick
31/62	**Anything That's Part Of You** Elvis Presley
37/76	**Anything You Want** John Valenti
33/76	**Anytime (I'll Be There)** Paul Anka
20/56	**Anyway You Want Me (That's How I Will Be)** Elvis Presley
2/61	**Apache** Jorgen Ingmann & His Guitar
	Apartment..see: Theme From The
24/56	**Ape Call** Nervous Norvus
	Apple Blossom Time..see: I'll Be With You In
29/60	**Apple Green** June Valli
32/65	**Apple Of My Eye** Roy Head
6/67	**Apples, Peaches, Pumpkin Pie** Jay & The Techniques
37/69	**April Fools** Dionne Warwick
28/56	**April In Paris** Count Basie
1/57	**April Love** Pat Boone
1/69	**Aquarius** 5th Dimension
39/69	**Are You Happy** Jerry Butler
39/67	**Are You Lonely For Me** Freddie Scott

POS/YR	RECORD TITLE/ARTIST
	Are You Lonesome Tonight?
1/60	Elvis Presley
14/74	Donny Osmond
	Are You Man Enough
15/73	Four Tops
	Are You Ready?
14/70	Pacific Gas & Electric
	Are You Really Mine
10/58	Jimmie Rodgers
	Are You Satisfied?
11/56	Rusty Draper
	Are You Sincere
3/58	Andy Williams
	Are You There (With Another Girl)
39/66	Dionne Warwick
	Ariel
26/77	Dean Friedman
	Arizona
10/70	Mark Lindsay
	Armed And Extremely Dangerous
28/73	First Choice
	Around The World In 80 Days
12/57	Mantovani & His Orchestra
13/57	Victor Young & His Orchestra
25/57	Bing Crosby
	Arrow Through Me
29/79	Paul McCartney
	Arthur's Theme (Best That You Can Do)
1/81	Christopher Cross
	Artificial Flowers
20/60	Bobby Darin
	As
36/78	Stevie Wonder
	As If I Didn't Know
10/61	Adam Wade
	As Tears Go By
22/65	Marianne Faithfull
6/66	Rolling Stones
	As The Years Go By
31/70	Mashmakhan
	As Usual
12/64	Brenda Lee
	Ashes By Now
37/80	Rodney Crowell

POS/YR	RECORD TITLE/ARTIST
	Asia Minor
8/61	Kokomo
	Ask Me
12/64	Elvis Presley
	Ask Me
18/56	Nat King Cole
	Ask Me No Questions
40/71	B.B. King
	Ask Me What You Want
27/72	Millie Jackson
	Ask The Lonely
24/65	Four Tops
	Astronaut (Parts 1 & 2)
19/61	Jose Jimenez
	At Midnight (My Love Will Lift You Up)
30/77	Rufus Featuring Chaka Khan
	At My Front Door
7/55	Pat Boone
17/55	El Dorados
	At Seventeen
3/75	Janis Ian
	(At The Copa)..see: Copacabana
	At The Hop
1/58	Danny & The Juniors
21/58	Nick Todd
	At The Scene
18/66	Dave Clark Five
	At The Zoo
16/67	Simon & Garfunkel
	Athena
28/82	Who
	Atlanta Lady (Something About Your Love)
27/81	Marty Balin
	Atlantis
7/69	Donovan
	Atomic
39/80	Blondie
	Attack
18/66	Toys
	Attitude Dancing
21/75	Carly Simon
	Aubrey
15/73	Bread

POS/YR	RECORD TITLE/ARTIST
19/56	**Auctioneer** Leroy Van Dyke
25/75	**Autobahn** Kraftwerk
37/72	**Automatically Sunshine** Supremes
1/55 35/55	**Autumn Leaves** Roger Williams Steve Allen
19/68	**Autumn Of My Life** Bobby Goldsboro
18/56	**Autumn Waltz** Tony Bennett

B

POS/YR	RECORD TITLE/ARTIST
14/66	**B-A-B-Y** Carla Thomas
1/79	**Babe** Styx
8/69	**Baby, Baby Don't Cry** Miracles
12/61	**Baby Blue** Echoes
14/72	**Baby Blue** Badfinger
32/68	**Baby, Come Back** Equals
1/78	**Baby Come Back** Player
27/74	**Baby Come Close** Smokey Robinson
33/56	**Baby Doll** Andy Williams
1/72	**Baby Don't Get Hooked On Me** Mac Davis
8/65	**Baby Don't Go** Sonny & Cher
39/64	**Baby, Don't You Cry** Ray Charles
27/64	**Baby Don't You Do It** Marvin Gaye

POS/YR	RECORD TITLE/ARTIST
30/63	**Baby Don't You Weep** Garnet Mimms & The Enchanters
14/76	**Baby Face** Wing & A Prayer Fife & Drum Corps.
11/78	**Baby Hold On** Eddie Money
35/70	**Baby Hold On** Grass Roots
4/67	**Baby I Love You** Aretha Franklin
24/64 9/69	**Baby, I Love You** Ronettes Andy Kim
12/76	**Baby, I Love Your Way** Peter Frampton
11/64 3/67	**Baby I Need Your Loving** Four Tops Johnny Rivers
25/79	**Baby I'm Burnin'** Dolly Parton
14/69	**Baby, I'm For Real** Originals
11/65	**Baby, I'm Yours** Barbara Lewis
3/71	**Baby I'm-A Want You** Bread
8/62 5/69	**Baby It's You** Shirelles Smith
29/71	**Baby Let Me Kiss You** King Floyd
24/72	**Baby Let Me Take You (In My Arms)** Detroit Emeralds
35/69	**Baby Let's Wait** Royal Guardsmen
1/64.	**Baby Love** Supremes
25/82	**Baby Makes Her Blue Jeans Talk** Dr. Hook
11/68	**Baby, Now That I've Found You** Foundations
21/61	**Baby Oh Baby** Shells
16/66	**Baby Scratch My Back** Slim Harpo

POS/YR	RECORD TITLE/ARTIST
6/61	**Baby Sittin' Boogie** Buzz Clifford
23/70	**Baby Take Me In Your Arms** Jefferson
10/59	**Baby Talk** Jan & Dean
38/80	**Baby Talks Dirty** Knack
26/75	**Baby That's Backatcha** Smokey Robinson
12/65	**Baby The Rain Must Fall** Glenn Yarbrough
4/77	**Baby, What A Big Surprise** Chicago
37/60	**Baby What You Want Me To Do** Jimmy Reed
5/63	**Baby Workout** Jackie Wilson
34/67	**Baby You Got It** Brenton Wood
34/67	**Baby You're A Rich Man** Beatles
5/60	**Baby (You've Got What It Takes)** Brook Benton & Dinah Washington
26/61	**Baby's First Christmas** Connie Francis
5/74	**Back Home Again** John Denver
37/81	**Back In Black** AC/DC
	Back In Love Again..see: (Every Time I Turn Around)
1/65	**Back In My Arms Again** Supremes
38/77	**Back In The Saddle** Aerosmith
37/59 16/78	**Back In The U.S.A.** Chuck Berry Linda Ronstadt
9/72	**Back Off Boogaloo** Ringo Starr
33/80	**Back On My Feet Again** Babys

POS/YR	RECORD TITLE/ARTIST
36/67	**Back On The Street Again** Sunshine Company
3/72	**Back Stabbers** O'Jays
36/57	**Back To School Again** Timmie "Oh Yeah!" Rogers
28/77	**Back Together Again** Daryl Hall & John Oates
40/73	**Back When My Hair Was Short** Gunhill Road
10/69	**Backfield In Motion** Mel & Tim
25/66	**Backstage** Gene Pitney
1/73	**Bad, Bad Leroy Brown** Jim Croce
1/75	**Bad Blood** Neil Sedaka
36/57	**Bad Boy** Jive Bombers Featuring Clarence Palmer
14/79	**Bad Case Of Loving You (Doctor, Doctor)** Robert Palmer
33/63	**Bad Girl** Neil Sedaka
1/79	**Bad Girls** Donna Summer
15/75	**Bad Luck (Part 1)** Harold Melvin & The Bluenotes
37/60	**Bad Man Blunder** Kingston Trio
2/69	**Bad Moon Rising** Creedence Clearwater Revival
4/75	**Bad Time** Grand Funk Railroad
9/64	**Bad To Me** Billy J. Kramer
2/78	**Baker Street** Gerry Rafferty
3/70	**Ball Of Confusion (That's What The World Is Today)** Temptations

POS/YR	RECORD TITLE/ARTIST
	Ball Of Fire
19/69	Tommy James & The Shondells
	Ballad Of A Teenage Queen
14/58	Johnny Cash
	Ballad Of Bonnie And Clyde
7/68	Georgie Fame
	Ballad Of Davy Crockett
1/55	Bill Hayes
5/55	"Tennessee" Ernie Ford
5/55	Fess Parker
14/55	Walter Schumann
	Ballad Of Irving
34/66	Frank Gallop
	Ballad Of John And Yoko
8/69	Beatles
	Ballad Of Paladin
33/62	Duane Eddy
	Ballad Of The Alamo
34/60	Marty Robbins
	Ballad Of The Green Berets
1/66	Ssgt Barry Sadler
	Ballerina
18/57	Nat King Cole
	Ballero
33/74	War
	Ballroom Blitz
5/75	Sweet
	Banana Boat (Day-O)
5/57	Harry Belafonte
25/57	Stan Freberg
	Banana Boat Song
4/57	Tarriers
13/57	Fontane Sisters
18/57	Steve Lawrence
19/57	Sarah Vaughan
	Band Of Gold
4/56	Don Cherry
11/56	Kit Carson
32/66	Mel Carter
	Band Of Gold
3/70	Freda Payne
	Band On The Run
1/74	Paul McCartney
	Banda, A
35/67	Herb Alpert & The Tijuana Brass

POS/YR	RECORD TITLE/ARTIST
	Bandit (O'Cangaceiro)
18/55	Eddie Barclay
	Bang A Gong (Get It On)
10/72	T. Rex
	Bang Bang (My Baby Shot Me Down)
2/66	Cher
	Bang-Shang-A-Lang
22/68	Archies
	Bangla-Desh
23/71	George Harrison
	Banjo's Back In Town
15/55	Teresa Brewer
	Barbara
29/60	Temptations
	Barbara Ann
13/61	Regents
2/66	Beach Boys
	Barefootin'
7/66	Robert Parker
	Barracuda
11/77	Heart
	Barretta's Theme ("Keep Your Eye On The Sparrow")
20/76	Rhythm Heritage
	Baseball Game..see: (Love Is Like A)
	Basketball Jones Featuring Tyrone Shoelaces
15/73	Cheech & Chong
	Batman Theme
17/66	Marketts
35/66	Neal Hefti
	Battle Hymn Of Lt. Calley
37/71	C Company Featuring Terry Nelson
	Battle Hymn Of The Republic
13/59	Mormon Tabernacle Choir
33/68	Andy Williams
	Battle Of Kookamonga
14/59	Homer & Jethro
	Battle Of New Orleans
1/59	Johnny Horton
	Baubles, Bangles And Beads
25/58	Kirby Stone Four
	Be
34/73	Neil Diamond

POS/YR	RECORD TITLE/ARTIST
25/64	**Be Anything (But Be Mine)** Connie Francis
31/63	**Be Careful Of Stones That You Throw** Dion
35/82	**Be Mine Tonight** Neil Diamond
2/63 17/70	**Be My Baby** Ronettes Andy Kim
8/59	**Be My Guest** Fats Domino
28/82	**Be My Lady** Jefferson Starship
4/74	**Be Thankful For What You Got** William DeVaughn
6/63	**Be True To Your School** Beach Boys
34/63	**Be True To Yourself** Bobby Vee
3/57	**Be-Bop Baby** Ricky Nelson
7/56	**Be-Bop-A-Lula** Gene Vincent & His Blue Caps
4/74	**Beach Baby** First Class
12/81	**Beach Boys Medley** Beach Boys
30/64	**Beans In My Ears** Serendipity Singers
8/78	**Beast Of Burden** Rolling Stones
6/67	**Beat Goes On** Sonny & Cher
12/82	**Beatles' Movie Medley:** Beatles
15/60	**Beatnik Fly** Johnny & The Hurricanes
3/68	**Beautiful Morning** Rascals
37/67 38/67	**Beautiful People** Bobby Vee Kenny O'Dell
15/72	**Beautiful Sunday** Daniel Boone

POS/YR	RECORD TITLE/ARTIST
3/66	**Beauty Is Only Skin Deep** Temptations
3/64	**Because** Dave Clark Five
13/78	**Because The Night** Patti Smith Group
4/60	**Because They're Young** Duane Eddy
17/62	**Beechwood 4-5789** Marvelettes
24/58	**Been So Long** Pastels
24/72	**Been To Canaan** Carole King
4/58	**Beep Beep** Playmates
33/75	**Beer Barrel Polka** Bobby Vinton
17/65	**Before And After** Chad & Jeremy
23/78	**Before My Heart Finds Out** Gene Cotton
1/75	**Before The Next Teardrop Falls** Freddy Fender
29/67	**Beg, Borrow And Steal** Ohio Express
16/67	**Beggin'** Four Seasons
36/69	**Beginning Of My End** Unifics
7/71	**Beginnings** Chicago
34/71	**Behind Blue Eyes** Who
15/73	**Behind Closed Doors** Charlie Rich
2/81	**Being With You** Smokey Robinson
28/73	**Believe In Humanity** Carole King
26/59	**Believe Me** Royal Teens
4/58	**Believe What You Say** Ricky Nelson

POS/YR	RECORD TITLE/ARTIST
28/69	**Bella Linda** Grass Roots
12/70	**Bells** Originals
13/58	**Belonging To Someone** Patti Page
1/72	**Ben** Michael Jackson
	Ben Casey..see: Theme From
5/68	**Bend Me, Shape Me** American Breed
1/74	**Bennie And The Jets** Elton John
4/67	**Bernadette** Four Tops
14/57	**Bernardine** Pat Boone
16/75	**Bertha Butt Boogie (Part 1)** Jimmy Castor [Bunch]
17/76	**Best Disco In Town** Ritchie Family
32/68	**Best Of Both Worlds** Lulu
1/77	**Best Of My Love** Emotions
1/75	**Best Of My Love** Eagles
3/81	**Best Of Times** Styx
39/64	**(Best Part Of) Breakin' Up** Ronettes
3/74	**Best Thing That Ever Happened To Me** Gladys Knight & The Pips
3/72	**Betcha By Golly, Wow** Stylistics
	(Betcha Got A Chick On The Side)..see: **How Long**
7/76	**Beth** Kiss
1/81	**Bette Davis Eyes** Kim Carnes
12/80	**Better Love Next Time** Dr. Hook

POS/YR	RECORD TITLE/ARTIST
38/61	**Better Tell Him No** Starlets
33/58	**Betty And Dupree** Chuck Willis
37/58	**Betty Lou Got A New Pair Of Shoes** Bobby Freeman
40/61	**Bewildered** James Brown
37/56 6/60	**Beyond The Sea** Roger Williams Bobby Darin
7/55 22/55	**Bible Tells Me So** Don Cornell Nick Noble
24/78	**Bicycle Race** Queen
1/61	**Big Bad John** Jimmy Dean
26/57	**Big Beat** Fats Domino
38/58	**Big Bopper's Wedding** Big Bopper
38/67	**Big Boss Man** Elvis Presley
23/73	**Big City Miss Ruth Ann** Gallery
19/61	**Big Cold Wind** Pat Boone
21/82	**Big Fun** Kool & The Gang
1/62	**Big Girls Don't Cry** Four Seasons
1/59	**Big Hunk O' Love** Elvis Presley
3/60	**Big Hurt** Miss Toni Fisher
26/60	**Big Iron** Marty Robbins
21/61	**Big John** Shirelles
3/58	**Big Man** Four Preps
20/64	**Big Man In Town** Four Seasons

POS/YR	RECORD TITLE/ARTIST
14/79	**Big Shot** Billy Joel
29/70 24/75	**Big Yellow Taxi** Neighborhood Joni Mitchell
3/80	**Biggest Part Of Me** Ambrosia
37/61	**Bilbao Song** Andy Williams
	Bill Bailey..see: Won't You Come Home
7/58	**Billy** Kathy Linden
34/66	**Billy And Sue** B.J. Thomas
1/74	**Billy, Don't Be A Hero** Bo Donaldson & The Heywoods
	Billy Jack..see: One Tin Soldier
11/58	**Bimbombey** Jimmie Rodgers
	Bird ..see: (Do The)
30/64	**Bird Dance Beat** Trashmen
1/58	**Bird Dog** Everly Brothers
34/58	**Bird On My Head** David Seville
12/63	**Birdland** Chubby Checker
3/65	**Birds And The Bees** Jewel Akens
23/71	**Birds Of A Feather** Paul Revere & The Raiders
26/55	**Birth Of The Boogie** Bill Haley & His Comets
26/69	**Birthday** Underground Sunshine
40/63	**Birthday Party** Pixies Three
4/74	**Bitch Is Back** Elton John
28/77	**Bite Your Lip (Get up and dance!)** Elton John

POS/YR	RECORD TITLE/ARTIST
4/64	**Bits And Pieces** Dave Clark Five
36/73	**Bitter Bad** Melanie
1/72	**Black & White** Three Dog Night
18/77	**Black Betty** Ram Jam
6/55 38/55	**Black Denim Trousers** Cheers Vaughn Monroe
15/72	**Black Dog** Led Zeppelin
37/75	**Black Friday** Steely Dan
4/66	**Black Is Black** Los Bravos
4/70	**Black Magic Woman** Santana
13/69	**Black Pearl** Checkmates Ltd. featuring Sonny Charles
17/57	**Black Slacks** Joe Bennett & The Sparkletones
21/75	**Black Superman - "Muhammad Ali"** Johnny Wakelin & The Kinshasa Band
1/75	**Black Water** Doobie Brothers
7/63	**Blame It On The Bossa Nova** Eydie Gorme
39/64	**Bless Our Love** Gene Chandler
15/61	**Bless You** Tony Orlando
34/81	**Blessed Are The Believers** Anne Murray
	Blind Man In The Bleachers..see: Last Game Of The Season
1/77	**Blinded By The Light** Manfred Mann's Earth Band
33/58	**Blob** Five Blobs
35/75	**Bloody Well Right** Supertramp

POS/YR	RECORD TITLE/ARTIST
2/55	**Blossom Fell** Nat King Cole
16/79	**Blow Away** George Harrison
2/63 9/66	**Blowin' In The Wind** Peter Paul & Mary Stevie Wonder
21/70	**Blowing Away** 5th Dimension
9/60	**Blue Angel** Roy Orbison
35/67	**Blue Autumn** Bobby Goldsboro
29/63 3/77	**Blue Bayou** Roy Orbison Linda Ronstadt
20/58	**Blue Blue Day** Don Gibson
21/78	**Blue Collar Man (Long Nights)** Styx
12/82	**Blue Eyes** Elton John
21/75	**Blue Eyes Crying In The Rain** Willie Nelson
37/59	**Blue Hawaii** Billy Vaughn & His Orchestra
5/57	**Blue Monday** Fats Domino
23/71	**Blue Money** Van Morrison
1/61	**Blue Moon** Marcels
15/79	**Blue Morning, Blue Day** Foreigner
3/63	**Blue On Blue** Bobby Vinton
29/55	**Blue Star** Felicia Sanders
2/56 20/56 38/73	**Blue Suede Shoes** Carl Perkins Elvis Presley Johnny Rivers
16/60	**Blue Tango** Bill Black's Combo

POS/YR	RECORD TITLE/ARTIST
1/63	**Blue Velvet** Bobby Vinton
24/64	**Blue Winter** Connie Francis
2/56 29/56	**Blueberry Hill** Fats Domino Louis Armstrong
35/75	**Bluebird** Helen Reddy
12/78	**Bluer Than Blue** Michael Johnson
36/62	**Blues (Stay Away From Me)** Ace Cannon
37/67	**Blue's Theme** Davie Allan & The Arrows
17/56 35/56	**Bo Weevil** Teresa Brewer Fats Domino
12/82	**Bobbie Sue** Oak Ridge Boys
8/59	**Bobby Sox To Stockings** Frankie Avalon
3/62	**Bobby's Girl** Marcie Blane
11/82	**Body Language** Queen
9/76	**Bohemian Rhapsody** Queen
2/61	**Boll Weevil Song** Brook Benton
19/61	**Bonanza** Al Caiola & His Orchestra
14/59	**Bongo Rock** Preston Epps
33/62	**Bongo Stomp** Little Joey & The Flips
	Bonnie And Clyde..see: Ballad
26/60	**Bonnie Came Back** Duane Eddy
14/57	**Bony Moronie** Larry Williams
7/67	**Boogaloo Down Broadway** Fantastic Johnny C

POS/YR	RECORD TITLE/ARTIST
12/77	**Boogie Child** Bee Gees
2/74	**Boogie Down** Eddie Kendricks
1/76	**Boogie Fever** Sylvers
2/77	**Boogie Nights** Heatwave
3/75	**Boogie On Reggae Woman** Stevie Wonder
1/78	**Boogie Oogie Oogie** Taste Of Honey
35/78	**Boogie Shoes** KC & The Sunshine Band
6/79	**Boogie Wonderland** Earth Wind & Fire with The Emotions
8/73	**Boogie Woogie Bugle Boy** Bette Midler
5/58	**Book Of Love** Monotones
17/55	**Boom Boom Boomerang** De Castro Sisters
	Boomerang..see: Do The
36/71	**Booty Butt** Ray Charles
37/70	**Border Song (Holy Moses)** Aretha Franklin
12/66	**Born A Woman** Sandy Posey
7/66 38/68	**Born Free** Roger Williams Hesitations
16/79	**Born To Be Alive** Patrick Hernandez
2/68	**Born To Be Wild** Steppenwolf
5/56	**Born To Be With You** Chordettes
23/75	**Born To Run** Bruce Springsteen
17/71	**Born To Wander** Rare Earth
7/58	**Born Too Late** Poni-Tails

POS/YR	RECORD TITLE/ARTIST
19/79	**Boss** Diana Ross
28/63	**Boss Guitar** Duane Eddy
8/63	**Bossa Nova Baby** Elvis Presley
8/68	**Both Sides Now** Judy Collins
9/68	**Bottle Of Wine** Fireballs
19/80	**Boulevard** Jackson Browne
40/63	**Bounce** Olympics
40/67	**Bowling Green** Everly Brothers
7/69	**Boxer** Simon & Garfunkel
8/65 7/81	**Boy From New York City** Ad Libs Manhattan Transfer
	Boy I'm Gonna Marry..see: (Today I Met)
2/69	**Boy Named Sue** Johnny Cash
18/63	**Boy Next Door** Secrets
10/59	**Boy Without A Girl** Frankie Avalon
12/76	**Boys Are Back In Town** Thin Lizzy
1/71	**Brand New Key** Melanie
24/69	**Brand New Me** Dusty Springfield
1/72	**Brandy (You're A Fine Girl)** Looking Glass
35/61	**Brass Buttons** String-A-Longs
14/80	**Brass In Pocket (I'm Special)** Pretenders
11/75	**Brazil** Ritchie Family

POS/YR	RECORD TITLE/ARTIST
2/64	**Bread And Butter** Newbeats
39/76	**Break Away** Art Garfunkel
40/65	**Break Away (From That Boy)** Newbeats
4/62 11/82	**Break It To Me Gently** Brenda Lee Juice Newton
26/82	**Break It Up** Foreigner
5/73	**Break Up To Make Up** Stylistics
35/68	**Break Your Promise** Delfonics
31/71	**Breakdown** Rufus Thomas
40/78	**Breakdown** Tom Petty & The Heartbreakers
15/80	**Breakdown Dead Ahead** Boz Scaggs
7/61	**Breakin' In A Brand New Broken Heart** Connie Francis
	Breakin' Up ..see: (Best Part Of)
31/66	**Breakin' Up Is Breakin' My Heart** Roy Orbison
22/81	**Breaking Away** Balance
1/62 34/70 28/72 8/76	**Breaking Up Is Hard To Do** Neil Sedaka Lenny Welch Partridge Family Neil Sedaka
15/81	**Breakup Song (They Don't Write 'Em)** Greg Kihn Band
7/58	**Breathless** Jerry Lee Lewis
8/55	**Breeze And I** Caterina Valente
5/77	**Brick House** Commodores
1/70 6/71	**Bridge Over Troubled Water** Simon & Garfunkel Aretha Franklin

POS/YR	RECORD TITLE/ARTIST
13/62 32/65 17/68	**Bring It On Home To Me** Sam Cooke Animals Eddie Floyd
29/67	**Bring It Up** James Brown
12/71	**Bring The Boys Home** Freda Payne
2/61	**Bristol Stomp** Dovells
27/62	**Bristol Twistin' Annie** Dovells
12/79	**Broken Hearted Me** Anne Murray
7/59	**Broken-Hearted Melody** Sarah Vaughan
1/73	**Brother Louie** Stories
22/69	**Brother Love's Travelling Salvation Show** Neil Diamond
32/70	**Brother Rapp (Part 1 & Part 2)** James Brown
10/67	**Brown Eyed Girl** Van Morrison
1/71	**Brown Sugar** Rolling Stones
3/69	**Build Me Up Buttercup** Foundations
24/60	**Bulldog** Fireballs
21/65	**Bumble Bee** Searchers
21/61	**Bumble Boogie** B. Bumble & The Stingers
12/74	**Bungle In The Jungle** Jethro Tull
9/55	**Burn That Candle** Bill Haley & His Comets
40/81	**Burnin' For You** Blue Oyster Cult
3/60	**Burning Bridges** Jack Scott
34/71	**Burning Bridges** Mike Curb Congregation

POS/YR	RECORD TITLE/ARTIST

POS/YR	RECORD TITLE/ARTIST

Burning Love
2/72 · Elvis Presley

Bus Stop
5/66 · Hollies

Bus Stop Song (A Paper Of Pins)
16/56 · Four Lads

Bust Out
25/63 · Busters

Busted
4/63 · Ray Charles

Bustin' Loose, Part 1
34/79 · Chuck Brown & The Soul Searchers

But I Do
4/61 · Clarence "Frog Man" Henry

But It's Alright
22/66 · J.J. Jackson

But You Know I Love You
19/69 · Kenny Rogers & The First Edition

But You're Mine
15/65 · Sonny & Cher

Butter Boy
29/75 · Fanny

Butterfly
1/57 · Charlie Gracie
1/57 · Andy Williams

Butterfly Baby
23/63 · Bobby Rydell

Buzz-Buzz-Buzz
11/57 · Hollywood Flames

By The Time I Get To Phoenix
26/67 · Glen Campbell
37/69 · Isaac Hayes

Bye, Bye, Baby (Baby Goodbye)
12/65 · Four Seasons

Bye Bye Love
2/57 · Everly Brothers

C

C.C. Rider
12/57 · Chuck Willis
34/63 · Lavern Baker
10/66 · Animals

C'est La Vie
11/55 · Sarah Vaughan

C'est Si Bon (It's So Good)
22/61 · Conway Twitty

C'mon And Swim
5/64 · Bobby Freeman

C'mon Everybody
35/58 · Eddie Cochran

C'mon Marianne
9/67 · Four Seasons
38/76 · Donny Osmond

Ca, C'est L'amour
22/57 · Tony Bennett

Cab Driver
23/68 · Mills Brothers

Cajun Queen
22/62 · Jimmy Dean

Calcutta
1/61 · Lawrence Welk & His Orchestra

Calendar Girl
4/61 · Neil Sedaka

California Dreamin'
4/66 · Mamas & The Papas

California Girls
3/65 · Beach Boys

California Nights
16/67 · Lesley Gore

California Soul
25/69 · 5th Dimension

California Sun
5/64 · Rivieras

Call Me
1/80 · Blondie

Call Me
13/70 · Aretha Franklin

Call Me
21/58 · Johnny Mathis

Call Me
22/66 · Chris Montez

Call Me
26/82 · Skyy

Call Me (Come Back Home)
10/73 · Al Green

America got their start in Britain, where "A Horse With No Name" sold better than anything by the group's most obvious influence, Crosby, Nash & Young.

Asia. The biggest-selling group of 1982 featured British musicians with experience in many '60s and '70s bands, including Tomorrow, Family, the Crazy World of Arthur Brown, Atomic Rooster, King Crimson, Uriah Heep, Yes, the Buggles, and Emerson, Lake & Palmer.

Toni Basil. When first offered Toni Basil's "Mickey," every major record company turned it down. It was, they said variously, too disco, too punk, too European, or too pop.

The Beach Boys' revival of "Barbara Ann" (originally a hit for the Regents) was waxed as part of the group's "party" album, and who should happen to drop in to share lead vocals? Why, Dean Torrence of Jan & Dean.

The Beatles. German orchestra leader Bert Kaempfert topped the American charts with "Wonderland By Night" and signed the Beatles (then known as the Beat Boys) to Germany's Polydor Records in the same year, 1961.

The Beatles. Everyone remembers the week in April '64 when the Fab Four occupied the top five of the top 40, including Terry Stafford, Betty Everett, Louis Armstrong, and Bobby Vinton, Yanks whom they graciously allowed into the top 10.

Teresa Brewer. More than 23 years after her original version of "Music Music Music" went to No. 1, Toledo's Teresa Brewer re-recorded the song. It went to number 109.

The Byrds flew "Eight Miles High" in 1966, but radio programmers preferred them closer to the ground. Some stations banned the record because of suspected drug connotations.

Edward Byrnes. The popularity of his character in television's "77 Sunset Strip" was only sufficient to produce one hit for Ed "Kookie" Byrnes, a former ambulance driver. For that, the world can probably be grateful.

Kim Carnes. "Bette Davis Eyes" languished for years on an obscure Jackie DeShannon album before Kim Carnes turned it into one of 1981's biggest hits.

POS/YR	RECORD TITLE/ARTIST
40/68	**Call Me Lightning** Who
19/62	**Call Me Mr. In-Between** Burl Ives
6/74	**Call On Me** Chicago
22/63	**Call On Me** Bobby Bland
16/77	**Calling Dr. Love** Kiss
32/77	**Calling Occupants Of Interplanetary Craft** Carpenters
F/75	**Calypso** John Denver
5/69	**Can I Change My Mind** Tyrone Davis
22/63 39/71	**Can I Get A Witness** Marvin Gaye Lee Michaels
15/57	**Can I Steal A Little Love** Frank Sinatra
31/74	**Can This Be Real** Natural Four
29/78	**Can We Still Be Friends** Todd Rundgren
16/56	**Can You Find It In Your Heart** Tony Bennett
38/78	**Can You Fool** Glen Campbell
1/64	**Can't Buy Me Love** Beatles
5/74	**Can't Get Enough** Bad Company
1/74	**Can't Get Enough Of Your Love, Babe** Barry White
9/75	**Can't Get It Out Of My Head** Electric Light Orchestra
2/63	**Can't Get Used To Losing You** Andy Williams
2/62	**Can't Help Falling In Love** Elvis Presley
39/76	**Can't Hide Love** Earth Wind & Fire

POS/YR	RECORD TITLE/ARTIST
3/78	**Can't Smile Without You** Barry Manilow
13/77	**Can't Stop Dancin'** Captain & Tennille
25/70	**Can't Stop Loving You** Tom Jones
2/67 7/68	**Can't Take My Eyes Off You** Frankie Valli Lettermen
2/65	**Can't You Hear My Heartbeat** Herman's Hermits
4/64	**Can't You See That She's Mine** Dave Clark Five
2/56 7/56	**Canadian Sunset** Hugo Winterhalter Andy Williams
3/70	**Candida** Dawn
	(Candles In The Rain)..see: Lay Down
3/63	**Candy Girl** Four Seasons
25/61	**Candy Man** Roy Orbison
1/72	**Candy Man** Sammy Davis Jr.
15/58	**Cannonball** Duane Eddy
1/77	**Car Wash** Rose Royce
4/65	**Cara, Mia** Jay & The Americans
39/65	**Cara-Lin** Strangeloves
10/74	**Carefree Highway** Gordon Lightfoot
27/59	**Caribbean** Mitchell Torok
18/58	**Carol** Chuck Berry
21/75	**Carolina In The Pines** Michael Murphey
32/66	**Caroline, No** Brian Wilson

POS/YR	RECORD TITLE/ARTIST
29/68	**Carpet Man** 5th Dimension
34/80	**Carrie** Cliff Richard
9/67	**Carrie-Anne** Hollies
26/69	**Carry Me Back** Rascals
11/77	**Carry On Wayward Son** Kansas
9/80	**Cars** Gary Numan
27/67	**Casino Royale** Herb Alpert & The Tijuana Brass
22/63 10/65	**Cast Your Fate To The Wind** Vince Guaraldi Trio Sounds Orchestral
F/72 36/81	**Castles In The Air** Don McLean Don McLean
25/56	**Casual Look** Six Teens Featuring Trudy Williams
26/67	**Cat In The Window (The Bird In The Sky)** Petula Clark
30/77	**Cat Scratch Fever** Ted Nugent
1/74	**Cat's In The Cradle** Harry Chapin
1/58	**Catch A Falling Star** Perry Como
23/65	**Catch The Wind** Donovan
4/65	**Catch Us If You Can** Dave Clark Five
23/62	**Caterina** Perry Como
1/60	**Cathy's Clown** Everly Brothers
10/82	**Caught Up In You** 38 Special
	(Cave Man)..see: Troglodyte
4/70	**Cecilia** Simon & Garfunkel

POS/YR	RECORD TITLE/ARTIST
15/70	**Celebrate** Three Dog Night
1/81	**Celebration** Kool & The Gang
1/82	**Centerfold** J. Geils Band
14/58	**Certain Smile** Johnny Mathis
23/58	**Cerveza** Boots Brown & His Blockbusters
10/62	**Cha-Cha-Cha** Bobby Rydell
34/58	**Cha-Hua-Hua** Pets
2/60	**Chain Gang** Sam Cooke
13/56	**Chain Gang** Bobby Scott
2/68	**Chain Of Fools** Aretha Franklin
32/68	**Chained** Marvin Gaye
17/62	**Chains** Cookies
20/56	**Chains Of Love** Pat Boone
1/57	**Chances Are** Johnny Mathis
31/65	**Change Is Gonna Come** Sam Cooke
19/78	**Change Of Heart** Eric Carmen
37/77	**Changes In Latitudes, Changes In Attitudes** Jimmy Buffett
6/58 12/58	**Chanson D'Amour (Song Of Love)** Art & Dotty Todd Fontane Sisters
19/57	**Chantez-Chantez** Dinah Shore
6/58	**Chantilly Lace** Big Bopper
32/65 25/67	**Chapel In The Moonlight** Bachelors Dean Martin

POS/YR	RECORD TITLE/ARTIST
1/64	**Chapel Of Love** Dixie Cups
36/64 36/64	**Charade** Sammy Kaye & His Orchestra Henry Mancini
1/82	**Chariots Of Fire - Titles** Vangelis
40/71	**Charity Ball** Fanny
2/59	**Charlie Brown** Coasters
13/63	**Charms** Bobby Vee
33/79	**Chase** Giorgio Moroder
36/62 32/78	**Chattanooga Choo Choo** Floyd Cramer Tuxedo Junction
34/60	**Chattanooga Shoe Shine Boy** Freddy Cannon
15/73	**Cheaper To Keep Her** Johnnie Taylor
12/66	**Cheater** Bob Kuban & The In-Men
35/73	**Check It Out** Tavares
28/70	**Check Out Your Mind** Impressions
12/55	**Chee Chee-Oo-Chee (Sang The Little Bird)** Perry Como & Jaye P. Morgan
32/78	**Cheeseburger In Paradise** Jimmy Buffett
1/66 9/71	**Cherish** Association David Cassidy
33/77	**Cherry Baby** Starz
6/66 31/73	**Cherry, Cherry** Neil Diamond Neil Diamond
15/69	**Cherry Hill Park** Billy Joe Royal
11/60	**Cherry Pie** Skip & Flip

POS/YR	RECORD TITLE/ARTIST
1/55 14/55	**Cherry Pink And Apple Blossom White** Perez Prado & His Orchestra Alan Dale
5/75	**Chevy Van** Sammy Johns
15/68	**Chewy Chewy** Ohio Express
35/71	**Chicago** Graham Nash
9/71	**Chick-A-Boom (Don't Ya Jes' Love It)** Daddy Dewdrop
31/67	**Child Of Clay** Jimmie Rodgers
13/59 16/59	**Children's Marching Song** Cyril Stapleton & His Orchestra Mitch Miller
38/60	**China Doll** Ames Brothers
15/73	**China Grove** Doobie Brothers
10/62	**Chip Chip** Gene McDaniels
1/58 39/61 40/62	**Chipmunk Song** Chipmunks Chipmunks Chipmunks
29/79	**Chiquitita** Abba
20/71	**Chirpy Chirpy Cheep Cheep** Mac & Katie Kissoon
34/81	**Chloe** Elton John
21/69	**Choice Of Colors** Impressions
13/69	**Chokin' Kind** Joe Simon
26/68	**Choo Choo Train** Box Tops
25/77	**Christine Sixteen** Kiss
4/79	**Chuck E.'s In Love** Rickie Lee Jones
9/64	**Chug-A-Lug** Roger Miller

POS/YR	RECORD TITLE/ARTIST
14/56	**Church Bells May Ring** Diamonds
24/59	**Ciao, Ciao Bambina** Jacky Noguez & His Orchestra
	Cinco Robles (Five Oaks)
22/57	Russell Arms
35/57	Les Paul & Mary Ford
16/62	**Cinderella** Jack Ross
34/77	**Cinderella** Firefall
	Cindy, Oh Cindy
9/56	Vince Martin with The Tarriers
10/56	Eddie Fisher
8/62	**Cindy's Birthday** Johnny Crawford
11/68	**Cinnamon** Derek
25/63	**Cinnamon Cinder (It's A Very Nice Dance)** Pastel Six
33/78	**Circle Is Small (I Can See It In Your Eyes)** Gordon Lightfoot
38/82	**Circles** Atlantic Starr
2/73	**Cisco Kid** War
23/69	**Cissy Strut** Meters
19/56	**City Of Angels** Highlights Featuring Frank Pisani
18/72	**City Of New Orleans** Arlo Guthrie
2/72	**Clair** Gilbert O'Sullivan
	Clam..see: Do The
6/74	**Clap For The Wolfman** Guess Who
8/65	**Clapping Song (Clap Pat Clap Slap)** Shirley Ellis
38/59	**Class** Chubby Checker
2/68	**Classical Gas** Mason Williams

POS/YR	RECORD TITLE/ARTIST
30/58	**Claudette** Everly Brothers
6/72	**Clean Up Woman** Betty Wright
35/69	**Clean Up Your Own Back Yard** Elvis Presley
21/60	**Clementine** Bobby Darin
	Cleopatra Jones..see: Theme From
28/58	**Click-Clack** Dicky Doo & The Don'ts
17/64	**Clinging Vine** Bobby Vinton
40/80	**Clones (We're All)** Alice Cooper
	Close Encounters..see: Theme From
25/78	**Close The Door** Teddy Pendergrass
12/62	**Close To Cathy** Mike Clifford
	Close To You..see: (They Long To Be)
8/67	**Close Your Eyes** Peaches & Herb
37/73	**Close Your Eyes** Edward Bear
2/78	**Closer I Get To You** Roberta Flack & Donny Hathaway
22/70	**Closer To Home** Grand Funk Railroad
	Cloud Nine
6/68	Temptations
32/69	Mongo Santamaria
F/80	**Cocaine** Eric Clapton
8/72	**Coconut** Nilsson
6/77	**Cold As Ice** Foreigner
33/81	**Cold Love** Donna Summer
7/67	**Cold Sweat (Part 1)** James Brown

POS/YR	RECORD TITLE/ARTIST
30/69	**Cold Turkey** John Lennon
	Colonel Bogey..see: March From The River Kwai
7/69	**Color Him Father** Winstons
16/67	**Color My World** Petula Clark
F/71	**Colour My World** Chicago
17/66	**(Come 'Round Here) I'm The One You Need** Miracles
3/64	**Come A Little Bit Closer** Jay & The Americans
7/70	**Come And Get It** Badfinger
29/63	**Come And Get These Memories** Martha & The Vandellas
5/74	**Come And Get Your Love** Redbone
26/65	**Come And Stay With Me** Marianne Faithfull
32/80	**Come Back** J. Geils Band
17/62	**Come Back Silly Girl** Lettermen
3/67	**Come Back When You Grow Up** Bobby Vee
38/58	**Come Closer To Me** Nat King Cole
21/73	**Come Get To This** Marvin Gaye
4/57 18/82	**Come Go With Me** Dell-Vikings Beach Boys
14/65	**Come Home** Dave Clark Five
20/59	**Come Into My Heart** Lloyd Price
30/74	**Come Monday** Jimmy Buffett
36/64	**Come On** Tommy Roe

POS/YR	RECORD TITLE/ARTIST
	Come On ..also see: C'mon
29/59	**Come On And Get Me** Fabian
6/67	**Come On Down To My Boat** Every Mothers' Son
22/66	**Come On Let's Go** McCoys
28/62	**Come On Little Angel** Belmonts
23/76	**Come On Over** Olivia Newton-John
39/70	**Come Running** Van Morrison
35/66	**Come Running Back** Dean Martin
8/78	**Come Sail Away** Styx
17/70	**Come Saturday Morning** Sandpipers
40/65	**Come See** Major Lance
1/64 24/68	**Come See About Me** Supremes Jr. Walker & The All Stars
1/59	**Come Softly To Me** Fleetwoods
15/79	**Come To Me** France Joli
22/58	**Come To Me** Johnny Mathis
30/59	**Come To Me** Marv Johnson
37/67	**Come To The Sunshine** Harpers Bizarre
1/69 23/78	**Come Together** Beatles Aerosmith
36/62	**Comin' Home Baby** Mel Torme
11/82	**Comin' In And Out Of Your Life** Barbra Streisand
11/67	**Coming Home Soldier** Bobby Vinton

POS/YR	RECORD TITLE/ARTIST
11/66	**Coming On Strong** Brenda Lee
1/80	**Coming Up (Live at Glasgow)** Paul McCartney
30/69	**Commotion** Creedence Clearwater Revival
27/69	**Composer** Supremes
28/65 35/65	**Concrete And Clay** Unit Four plus Two Eddie Rambeau
17/56	**Confidential** Sonny Knight
37/79	**Confusion** Electric Light Orchestra
16/72	**Conquistador** Procol Harum
11/62	**Conscience** James Darren
33/61	**Continental Walk** Hank Ballard & The Midnighters
	Continental Walk..also see: Do The
8/72	**Convention '72** Delegates
1/76	**Convoy** C.W. McCall
32/73	**Cook With Honey** Judy Collins
29/71	**Cool Aid** Paul Humphrey & His Cool Aid Chemists
10/80	**Cool Change** Little River Band
7/66	**Cool Jerk** Capitols
13/81	**Cool Love** Pablo Cruise
11/82	**Cool Night** Paul Davis
12/57	**Cool Shake** Dell-Vikings
8/78	**Copacabana (At The Copa)** Barry Manilow

POS/YR	RECORD TITLE/ARTIST
37/73	**Corazon** Carole King
9/61	**Corinna, Corinna** Ray Peterson
18/72	**Corner Of The Sky** Jackson 5
15/64	**Cotton Candy** Al Hirt
13/62	**Cotton Fields** Highwaymen
33/80	**Could I Have This Dance** Anne Murray
37/72	**Could It Be Forever** David Cassidy
4/73	**Could It Be I'm Falling In Love** Spinners
6/75	**Could It Be Magic** Barry Manilow
23/57	**Could This Be Magic** Dubs
3/77	**Couldn't Get It Right** Climax Blues Band
35/61	**Count Every Star** Donnie & The Dreamers
2/65	**Count Me In** Gary Lewis & The Playboys
8/78	**Count On Me** Jefferson Starship
25/60	**Country Boy** Fats Domino
11/76	**Country Boy (You Got Your Feet In L.A.)** Glen Campbell
36/68	**Country Girl - City Man** Billy Vera & Judy Clay
37/71	**Country Road** James Taylor
25/68	**Court Of Love** Unifics
31/64	**Cousin Of Mine** Sam Cooke
6/73	**Cover Of "Rolling Stone"** Dr. Hook

POS/YR	RECORD TITLE/ARTIST
3/80	**Coward Of The County** Kenny Rogers
6/68	**Cowboys To Girls** Intruders
8/72	**Cowboys Work Is Never Done** Sonny & Cher
19/77	**Crackerbox Palace** George Harrison
1/70	**Cracklin' Rosie** Neil Diamond
7/60	**Cradle Of Love** Johnny Preston
9/61	**Crazy** Patsy Cline
36/60	**Crazy Arms** Bob Beckham
40/65	**Crazy Downtown** Allan Sherman
40/58	**Crazy Eyes For You** Bobby Hamilton
14/72	**Crazy Horses** Osmonds
	Crazy Little Mama..See: At My Front Door
1/80	**Crazy Little Thing Called Love** Queen
15/58	**Crazy Love** Paul Anka
17/79	**Crazy Love** Poco
29/79	**Crazy Love** Allman Brothers Band
22/72	**Crazy Mama** J.J. Cale
35/76	**Crazy On You** Heart
2/55	**Crazy Otto (Medley)** Johnny Maddox & The Rhythm Masters
5/67	**Creeque Alley** Mamas & The Papas
16/71	**Cried Like A Baby** Bobby Sherman

POS/YR	RECORD TITLE/ARTIST
1/69 7/82	**Crimson And Clover** Tommy James & The Shondells Joan Jett & The Blackhearts
16/55	**Croce Di Oro (Cross Of Gold)** Patti Page
1/73	**Crocodile Rock** Elton John
	Crooked Little Man..see: Don't Let The Rain Come Down
19/63	**Cross Fire!** Orlons
	Cross Of Gold..see: Croce Di Oro
23/59	**Crossfire** Johnny & The Hurricanes
28/69	**Crossroads** Cream
26/62	**Crowd** Roy Orbison
12/79	**Cruel To Be Kind** Nick Lowe
4/80	**Cruisin'** Smokey Robinson
18/66	**Cry** Ronnie Dove
4/63	**Cry Baby** Garnet Mimms & The Enchanters
18/56	**Cry Baby** Bonnie Sisters
38/62	**Cry Baby Cry** Angels
2/68	**Cry Like A Baby** Box Tops
9/55 11/70	**Cry Me A River** Julie London Joe Cocker
23/63	**Cry To Me** Betty Harris
2/61 25/66 5/81	**Crying** Roy Orbison Jay & The Americans Don McLean
3/65	**Crying In The Chapel** Elvis Presley
6/62	**Crying In The Rain** Everly Brothers

POS/YR	RECORD TITLE/ARTIST

Crying Time
6/66 — Ray Charles

Crystal Blue Persuasion
2/69 — Tommy James & The Shondells

Cupid
17/61 — Sam Cooke
39/69 — Johnny Nash
22/76 — Dawn
4/80 — Spinners

Cut The Cake
10/75 — Average White Band

Cycles
23/68 — Frank Sinatra

D

D'yer Mak'er
20/73 — Led Zeppelin

D.O.A.
36/71 — Bloodrock

D.W. Washburn
19/68 — Monkees

Da Doo Ron Ron
3/63 — Crystals
1/77 — Shaun Cassidy

Da Ya Think I'm Sexy?
1/79 — Rod Stewart

Daddy Could Swear, I Declare
19/73 — Gladys Knight & The Pips

Daddy Don't You Walk So Fast
4/72 — Wayne Newton

Daddy's Home
2/61 — Shep & The Limelites
9/73 — Jermaine Jackson
23/82 — Cliff Richard

Daddy's Little Man
34/69 — O.C. Smith

Daddy-O
11/55 — Fontane Sisters
14/55 — Bonnie Lou

Daisy A Day
14/73 — Jud Strunk

Daisy Jane
20/75 — America

POS/YR	RECORD TITLE/ARTIST

Daisy Petal Pickin'
15/64 — Jimmy Gilmer & The Fireballs

Damned If I Do
27/79 — Alan Parsons Project

Dance Across The Floor
38/78 — Jimmy "Bo" Horne

Dance, Dance, Dance
8/64 — Beach Boys

Dance, Dance, Dance (Yowsah, Yowsah, Yowsah)
6/78 — Chic

Dance (Disco Heat)
19/78 — Sylvester

Dance Everyone Dance
31/58 — Betty Madigan

Dance On Little Girl
10/61 — Paul Anka

Dance Only With Me
19/58 — Perry Como

Dance The Mess Around
24/61 — Chubby Checker

Dance The Night Away
15/79 — Van Halen

Dance To The Bop
23/57 — Gene Vincent & His Blue Caps

Dance To The Music
8/68 — Sly & The Family Stone

Dance Wit Me
39/76 — Rufus Featuring Chaka Khan

Dance With Me
6/75 — Orleans

Dance With Me
8/78 — Peter Brown

Dance With Me
15/59 — Drifters

Dance With Me Henry (Wallflower)
1/55 — Georgia Gibbs

(Dance With The) Guitar Man
12/62 — Duane Eddy

Dancin' Fool
28/74 — Guess Who

Dancin' Man
23/77 — Q

POS/YR	RECORD TITLE/ARTIST
12/62	**Dancin' Party** Chubby Checker
18/79	**Dancin' Shoes** Nigel Olsson
13/73	**Dancing In The Moonlight** King Harvest
2/64 38/82	**Dancing In The Street** Martha & The Vandellas Van Halen
2/74	**Dancing Machine** Jackson 5
1/77	**Dancing Queen** Abba
14/67	**Dandelion** Rolling Stones
5/66	**Dandy** Herman's Hermits
7/64	**Dang Me** Roger Miller
12/55	**Danger! Heartbreak Ahead** Jaye P. Morgan
25/66	**Dangling Conversation** Simon & Garfunkel
	Dangling On A String..see: (You've Got Me)
2/73	**Daniel** Elton John
13/63	**Danke Schoen** Wayne Newton
10/59	**Danny Boy** Conway Twitty
7/73	**Danny's Song** Anne Murray
15/74	**Dark Horse** George Harrison
1/74	**Dark Lady** Cher
4/57 6/57	**Dark Moon** Gale Storm Bonnie Guitar
19/68	**Darlin'** Beach Boys
15/67	**Darling Be Home Soon** Lovin' Spoonful

POS/YR	RECORD TITLE/ARTIST
7/55	**Darling Je Vous Aime Beaucoup** Nat King Cole
13/70	**Daughter Of Darkness** Tom Jones
	Davy Crockett..see: Ballad Of
3/64	**Dawn (Go Away)** Four Seasons
36/65	**Dawn Of Correction** Spokesmen
4/72	**Day After Day** Badfinger
13/72	**Day By Day** Godspell
5/72	**Day Dreaming** Aretha Franklin
35/66	**Day For Decision** Johnny Sea
23/72	**Day I Found Myself** Honey Cone
21/69	**Day Is Done** Peter Paul & Mary
21/58 30/58	**Day The Rains Came** Jane Morgan Raymond Lefevre & His Orchestra
5/66	**Day Tripper** Beatles
	Day-O..see: Banana Boat
23/77	**Daybreak** Barry Manilow
39/74	**Daybreak** Nilsson
2/66	**Daydream** Lovin' Spoonful
1/67 12/80	**Daydream Believer** Monkees Anne Murray
17/79	**Days Gone Down (Still Got The Light In Your Eyes)** Gerry Rafferty
34/69	**Days Of Sand And Shovels** Bobby Vinton
26/63 33/63	**Days Of Wine And Roses** Andy Williams Henry Mancini

POS/YR	RECORD TITLE/ARTIST
28/77	**Daytime Friends** Kenny Rogers
3/77	**Dazz** Brick
10/81	**De Do Do Do, De Da Da Da** Police
19/78	**Deacon Blues** Steely Dan
29/67	**Dead End Street** Lou Rawls
8/64	**Dead Man's Curve** Jan & Dean
16/73	**Dead Skunk** Loudon Wainwright III
24/64 30/64	**Dear Heart** Andy Williams Jack Jones
24/62	**Dear Ivan** Jimmy Dean
9/62	**Dear Lady Twist** Gary "U.S." Bonds
13/62	**Dear Lonely Hearts** Nat King Cole
11/62	**Dear One** Larry Finnegan
1/76	**December, 1963 (Oh, What A Night)** Four Seasons
7/59	**Deck Of Cards** Wink Martindale
7/58	**Dede Dinah** Frankie Avalon
36/66	**Dedicated Follower Of Fashion** Kinks
3/61 2/67	**Dedicated To The One I Love** Shirelles Mamas & The Papas
22/80	**Deep Inside My Heart** Randy Meisner
20/57 1/63 14/76	**Deep Purple** Billy Ward & His Dominoes Nino Tempo & April Stevens Donny & Marie Osmond
24/70	**Deeper & Deeper** Freda Payne

POS/YR	RECORD TITLE/ARTIST
11/79	**Deeper Than The Night** Olivia Newton-John
15/80	**Deja Vu** Dionne Warwick
22/60	**Delaware** Perry Como
40/58	**Delicious!** Jim Backus & Friend
15/68	**Delilah** Tom Jones
	Delilah Jones..see: Man With The Golden Arm
1/73	**Delta Dawn** Helen Reddy
10/63	**Denise** Randy & The Rainbows
25/79	**Dependin' On You** Doobie Brothers
15/62	**Desafinado** Stan Getz / Charlie Byrd
33/63	**Desert Pete** Kingston Trio
8/71	**Desiderata** Les Crane
4/80	**Desire** Andy Gibb
16/78	**Desiree** Neil Diamond
16/63 27/67	**Detroit City** Bobby Bare Tom Jones
	Devil In Disguise..see: (You're The)
6/60	**Devil Or Angel** Bobby Vee
3/79	**Devil Went Down To Georgia** Charlie Daniels Band
4/66	**Devil With A Blue Dress On** Mitch Ryder & The Detroit Wheels
6/76	**Devil Woman** Cliff Richard
16/62	**Devil Woman** Marty Robbins
36/77	**Devil's Gun** C.J. & Co.

POS/YR	RECORD TITLE/ARTIST
10/58	**Devoted To You**
36/78	Everly Brothers
	Carly Simon & James Taylor
33/74	**Devotion**
	Earth Wind & Fire
24/72	**Dialogue (Part I & II)**
	Chicago
6/73	**Diamond Girl**
	Seals & Crofts
18/60	**Diamonds And Pearls**
	Paradons
35/75	**Diamonds And Rust**
	Joan Baez
1/57	**Diana**
	Paul Anka
10/64	**Diane**
	Bachelors
14/59	**Diary**
	Neil Sedaka
15/72	**Diary**
	Bread
9/82	**Did It In A Minute**
	Daryl Hall & John Oates
29/76	**Did You Boogie (With Your Baby)**
	Flash Cadillac & The Continental Kids
2/66	**Did You Ever Have To Make Up Your Mind?**
	Lovin' Spoonful
32/69	**Did You See Her Eyes**
	Illusion
10/70	**Didn't I (Blow Your Mind This Time)**
	Delfonics
13/68	**Different Drum**
	Linda Ronstadt
18/79	**Different Worlds**
	Maureen McGovern
2/79	**Dim All The Lights**
	Donna Summer
11/55	**Dim, Dim The Lights (I Want Some Atmosphere)**
	Bill Haley & His Comets
25/58	**Ding Dong**
	McGuire Sisters
36/75	**Ding Dong; Ding Dong**
	George Harrison

POS/YR	RECORD TITLE/ARTIST
11/67	**Ding Dong! The Witch Is Dead**
	Fifth Estate
18/60	**Ding-A-Ling**
	Bobby Rydell
6/58	**Dinner With Drac - Part 1**
	John Zacherle
11/66	**Dirty Water**
	Standells
12/79	**Dirty White Boy**
	Foreigner
36/67	**Dis-Advantages Of You**
	Brass Ring featuring Phil Bodner
1/76	**Disco Duck (Part 1)**
	Rick Dees & His Cast Of Idiots
11/78	**Disco Inferno**
	Trammps
1/76	**Disco Lady**
	Johnnie Taylor
24/77	**Disco Lucy (I Love Lucy Theme)**
	Wilton Place Street Band
12/79	**Disco Nights (Rock-Freak)**
	GQ
28/75	**Disco Queen**
	Hot Chocolate
	(Disco Round)..see: I Love The Nightlife
28/74	**Distant Lover**
	Marvin Gaye
30/66	**Distant Shores**
	Chad & Jeremy
	Dixie ..see: Theme From
30/55	**Dixie Danny**
	Laurie Sisters
1/69	**Dizzy**
	Tommy Roe
13/82	**Do I Do**
	Stevie Wonder
34/64	**Do I Love You?**
	Ronettes
36/70	**Do It**
	Neil Diamond
2/74	**Do It ('Til You're Satisfied)**
	B.T. Express

POS/YR	RECORD TITLE/ARTIST
6/73	**Do It Again** Steely Dan
20/68	**Do It Again** Beach Boys
18/67	**Do It Again A Little Bit Slower** Jon & Robin & The In Crowd
11/75	**Do It Any Way You Wanna** People's Choice
13/74	**Do It Baby** Miracles
19/79	**Do It Or Die** Atlanta Rhythm Section
23/80	**Do Right** Paul Davis
38/68	**Do Something To Me** Tommy James & The Shondells
1/80	**Do That To Me One More Time** Captain & Tennille
10/63	**Do The Bird** Dee Dee Sharp
36/65	**Do The Boomerang** Jr. Walker & The All Stars
21/65	**Do The Clam** Elvis Presley
18/65	**Do The Freddie** Freddie & The Dreamers
28/70	**Do The Funky Chicken** Rufus Thomas
37/62	**Do The New Continental** Dovells
25/71	**(Do The) Push And Pull, Part I** Rufus Thomas
1/64	**Do Wah Diddy Diddy** Manfred Mann
37/70	**Do What You Wanna Do** Five Flights Up
39/76	**Do What You Want, Be What You Are** Daryl Hall & John Oates
24/77	**Do Ya** Electric Light Orchestra
	Do Ya Think I'm Sexy?..see: Da Ya
18/77	**Do Ya Wanna Get Funky With Me** Peter Brown

POS/YR	RECORD TITLE/ARTIST
7/82	**Do You Believe In Love** Huey Lewis & The News
9/65 31/78	**Do You Believe In Magic** Lovin' Spoonful Shaun Cassidy
10/76	**Do You Feel Like We Do** Peter Frampton
10/68	**Do You Know The Way To San Jose** Dionne Warwick
6/71	**Do You Know What I Mean** Lee Michaels
	Do You Know Where You're Going To..see: Theme From Mahogony
3/62 11/64	**Do You Love Me** Contours Dave Clark Five
30/80	**Do You Love What You Feel** Rufus Featuring Chaka Khan
32/70	**Do You See My Love (For You Growing)** Jr. Walker & The All Stars
5/77	**Do You Wanna Make Love** Peter McCann
20/82	**Do You Wanna Touch Me (Oh Yeah)** Joan Jett & The Blackhearts
5/58 12/65 17/73	**Do You Want To Dance** Bobby Freeman Beach Boys Bette Midler
2/64	**Do You Want To Know A Secret** Beatles
39/77	**Do Your Dance - Part 1** Rose Royce
11/69	**Do Your Thing** Charles Wright & The Watts 103rd Street Rhythm Band
30/72	**Do Your Thing** Isaac Hayes
27/62	**Do-Re-Mi** Lee Dorsey
31/64	**Do-Wacka-Do** Roger Miller
	Dock Of The Bay..see: (Sittin' On)
	Doctor ..also see: Dr.

POS/YR	RECORD TITLE/ARTIST
	(Doctor, Doctor)..see: Bad Case Of Loving You
8/72	**Doctor My Eyes** Jackson Browne
	Doctor Tarr..see: (System Of)
11/75	**Doctor's Orders** Carol Douglas
38/69	**Does Anybody Know I'm Here** Dells
7/70	**Does Anybody Really Know What Time It Is?** Chicago
5/61	**Does Your Chewing Gum Lose It's Flavor (On The Bedpost Over Night)** Lonnie Donegan & His Skiffle Group
29/68	**Does Your Mama Know About Me** Bobby Taylor & The Vancouvers
19/79	**Does Your Mother Know** Abba
6/71	**Doesn't Somebody Want To Be Wanted** Partridge Family
34/79	**Dog & Butterfly** Heart
30/55	**Dogface Soldier** Russ Morgan & His Orchestra
15/60	**Doggin' Around** Jackie Wilson
32/69	**Doggone Right** Miracles
22/73	**Doing It To Death** JB's
31/60	**Doll House** Donnie Brooks
13/55	**Domani (Tomorrow)** Julius LaRosa
1/63	**Dominique** Singing Nun
9/70	**Domino** Van Morrison
1/58	**Don't** Elvis Presley
19/80	**Don't Ask Me Why** Billy Joel

POS/YR	RECORD TITLE/ARTIST
25/58	**Don't Ask Me Why** Elvis Presley
26/63	**Don't Be Afraid, Little Darlin'** Steve Lawrence
14/55 25/55	**Don't Be Angry** Crew-Cuts Nappy Brown
1/56 11/60	**Don't Be Cruel** Elvis Presley Bill Black's Combo
9/61	**Don't Bet Money Honey** Linda Scott
20/61	**Don't Blame Me** Everly Brothers
37/67	**Don't Blame The Children** Sammy Davis Jr.
1/62	**Don't Break The Heart That Loves You** Connie Francis
4/79	**Don't Bring Me Down** Electric Light Orchestra
12/66	**Don't Bring Me Down** Animals
9/75	**Don't Call Us, We'll Call You** Sugarloaf
26/74	**Don't Change Horses (In The Middle Of A Stream)** Tower Of Power
36/71	**Don't Change On Me** Ray Charles
21/60	**Don't Come Knockin'** Fats Domino
35/73	**Don't Cross The River** America
39/61	**Don't Cry, Baby** Etta James
6/70	**Don't Cry Daddy** Elvis Presley
10/79	**Don't Cry Out Loud** Melissa Manchester
34/72	**Don't Do It** The Band
10/80	**Don't Do Me Like That** Tom Petty & The Heartbreakers

POS/YR	RECORD TITLE/ARTIST
23/72	**Don't Ever Be Lonely (A Poor Little Fool Like Me)** Cornelius Brothers & Sister Rose
40/79	**Don't Ever Wanna Lose Ya** New England
8/73	**Don't Expect Me To Be Your Friend** Lobo
4/80	**Don't Fall In Love With A Dreamer** Kenny Rogers & Kim Carnes
12/76	**(Don't Fear) The Reaper** Blue Oyster Cult
17/82	**Don't Fight It** Kenny Loggins with Steve Perry
1/57	**Don't Forbid Me** Pat Boone
19/65	**Don't Forget I Still Love You** Bobbi Martin
15/69	**Don't Give In To Him** Gary Puckett & The Union Gap
26/81	**Don't Give It Up** Robbie Patton
37/68	**Don't Give Up** Petula Clark
1/77	**Don't Give Up On Us** David Soul
1/76	**Don't Go Breaking My Heart** Elton John & Kiki Dee
22/58	**Don't Go Home** Playmates
17/62	**Don't Go Near The Indians** Rex Allen
18/67	**Don't Go Out Into The Rain (You're Going To Melt)** Herman's Hermits
38/56 36/60	**Don't Go To Strangers** Vaughn Monroe Etta Jones
4/62	**Don't Hang Up** Orlons
21/79	**Don't Hold Back** Chanson
2/77	**Don't It Make My Brown Eyes Blue** Crystal Gayle
8/65	**Don't Just Stand There** Patty Duke

POS/YR	RECORD TITLE/ARTIST
13/71	**Don't Knock My Love - Pt. 1** Wilson Pickett
1/77	**Don't Leave Me This Way** Thelma Houston
13/58 18/80	**Don't Let Go** Roy Hamilton Isaac Hayes
24/81	**Don't Let Him Go** REO Speedwagon
39/82	**Don't Let Him Know** Prism
14/73	**Don't Let Me Be Lonely Tonight** James Taylor
15/65 15/78	**Don't Let Me Be Misunderstood** Animals Santa Esmeralda featuring Leroy Gomez
35/69	**Don't Let Me Down** Beatles
17/71	**Don't Let The Green Grass Fool You** Wilson Pickett
20/69	**Don't Let The Joneses Get You Down** Temptations
6/64	**Don't Let The Rain Come Down (Crooked Little Man)** Serendipity Singers
39/67	**Don't Let The Rain Fall Down On Me** Critters
4/64	**Don't Let The Sun Catch You Crying** Gerry & The Pacemakers
2/74	**Don't Let The Sun Go Down On Me** Elton John
4/78	**Don't Look Back** Boston
21/63	**Don't Make Me Over** Dionne Warwick
33/65	**Don't Mess Up A Good Thing** Fontella Bass & Bobby McClure
7/66	**Don't Mess With Bill** Marvelettes
40/59	**Don't Pity Me** Dion & The Belmonts
11/62 11/70	**Don't Play That Song** Ben E. King Aretha Franklin

POS/YR	RECORD TITLE/ARTIST
4/71 27/76	**Don't Pull Your Love** Hamilton Joe Frank & Reynolds Glen Campbell
26/63	**Don't Say Goodnight And Mean Goodbye** Shirelles
39/80	**Don't Say Goodnight (It's Time For Love)** Isley Brothers
7/63	**Don't Say Nothin' Bad (About My Baby)** Cookies
15/72	**Don't Say You Don't Remember** Beverly Bremers
20/63	**Don't Set Me Free** Ray Charles
5/67	**Don't Sleep In The Subway** Petula Clark
10/81	**Don't Stand So Close To Me** Police
3/77	**Don't Stop** Fleetwood Mac
1/79	**Don't Stop 'Til You Get Enough** Michael Jackson
9/81	**Don't Stop Believin'** Journey
33/76	**Don't Stop Believin'** Olivia Newton-John
19/81	**Don't Stop The Music** Yarbrough & Peoples
34/76	**Don't Take Away The Music** Tavares
27/68	**Don't Take It So Hard** Paul Revere & The Raiders
32/59	**Don't Take Your Guns To Town** Johnny Cash
37/75	**Don't Take Your Love** Manhattans
2/82	**Don't Talk To Strangers** Rick Springfield
27/75	**Don't Tell Me Goodnight** Lobo
9/63 12/65	**Don't Think Twice, It's All Right** Peter Paul & Mary Wonder Who?

POS/YR	RECORD TITLE/ARTIST
22/60	**Don't Throw Away All Those Teardrops** Frankie Avalon
	Don't Throw It All Away..see: (Our Love)
16/64	**Don't Throw Your Love Away** Searchers
38/69	**Don't Touch Me** Bettye Swann
21/78	**Don't Want To Live Without It** Pablo Cruise
35/81	**Don't Want To Wait Anymore** Tubes
3/61	**Don't Worry** Marty Robbins
24/64 17/77	**Don't Worry Baby** Beach Boys B.J. Thomas
29/70	**(Don't Worry) If There's A Hell Below We're All Going To Go** Curtis Mayfield
	Don't Ya Wanna Play This Game No More..see: (Sartorial Eloquence)
39/62	**Don't You Believe It** Andy Williams
6/67	**Don't You Care** Buckinghams
	Don't You Forget It..see: (I Love You)
9/58	**Don't You Just Know It** Huey (Piano) Smith & The Clowns
2/59	**Don't You Know** Della Reese
1/82	**Don't You Want Me** Human League
16/74	**Don't You Worry 'Bout A Thing** Stevie Wonder
	Don't You Worry 'Bout Me..see: Opus 17
33/79	**Don't You Write Her Off** McGuinn Clark & Hillman
15/58	**Doncha' Think It's Time** Elvis Presley
2/59	**Donna** Ritchie Valens
6/63	**Donna The Prima Donna** Dion

POS/YR	RECORD TITLE/ARTIST
15/74	**Doo Doo Doo Doo Doo (Heartbreaker)** Rolling Stones
6/64	**Door Is Still Open To My Heart** Dean Martin
35/74	**Doraville** Atlanta Rhythm Section
26/76	**Dose Of Rock 'N' Roll** Ringo Starr
39/58	**Dottie** Danny & The Juniors
22/71	**Double Barrel** Dave Collins & Ansil
30/81	**Double Dutch Bus** Frankie Smith
14/71	**Double Lovin'** Osmonds
17/66	**Double Shot (Of My Baby's Love)** Swingin' Medallions
2/78	**Double Vision** Foreigner
33/68	**Down At Lulu's** Ohio Express
9/63	**(Down At) Papa Joe's** Dixiebelles with Cornbread & Jerry
4/72	**Down By The Lazy River** Osmonds
13/60	**Down By The Station** Four Preps
9/65	**Down In The Boondocks** Billy Joe Royal
3/69	**Down On The Corner** Creedence Clearwater Revival
37/63	**Down The Aisle (Wedding Song)** Patti LaBelle & The Blue Belles
18/58	**Down The Aisle Of Love** Quin-Tones
1/65	**Downtown** Petula Clark
	Downtown..also see: Crazy Downtown
	Dr. ..see: Doctor
	Dr. Kildare..see: Theme From
	Dr. Zhivago..see: Somewhere My Love

POS/YR	RECORD TITLE/ARTIST
10/64	**Drag City** Jan & Dean
4/71	**Draggin' The Line** Tommy James
28/81	**Draw Of The Cards** Kim Carnes
19/58	**Dream** Betty Johnson
12/68	**Dream A Little Dream Of Me** Mama Cass
4/62 31/71	**Dream Baby (How Long Must I Dream)** Roy Orbison Glen Campbell
	Dream Dream Dream..see: All I Have To Do Is Dream
2/59	**Dream Lover** Bobby Darin
38/67 36/75	**Dream Merchant** Jerry Butler New Birth
6/76	**Dream On** Aerosmith
32/74	**Dream On** Righteous Brothers
25/65	**Dream On Little Dreamer** Perry Como
26/79	**Dream Police** Cheap Trick
2/76	**Dream Weaver** Gary Wright
	Dreamboat..see: (He's My)
15/80	**Dreamer** Supertramp
11/60	**Dreamin'** Johnny Burnette
10/80	**Dreaming** Cliff Richard
27/79	**Dreaming** Blondie
1/77	**Dreams** Fleetwood Mac
32/68	**Dreams Of The Everyday Housewife** Glen Campbell

POS/YR	RECORD TITLE/ARTIST
35/62	**Dreamy Eyes** Johnny Tillotson
21/73	**Dreidel** Don McLean
5/73	**Drift Away** Dobie Gray
6/63	**Drip Drop** Dion
15/79	**Driver's Seat** Sniff 'n' The Tears
5/80	**Drivin' My Life Away** Eddie Rabbitt
34/76	**Drivin' Wheel** Foghat
36/63	**Drownin' My Sorrows** Connie Francis
11/72	**Drowning In The Sea Of Love** Joe Simon
29/71	**Drum** Bobby Sherman
29/62	**Drums Are My Beat** Sandy Nelson
20/67	**Dry Your Eyes** Brenda & The Tabulations
14/66	**Duck** Jackie Lee
2/73	**Dueling Banjos** Eric Weissberg & Steve Mandell
1/62	**Duke Of Earl** Gene Chandler
	Dukes Of Hazzard..see: Theme From The
4/61	**Dum Dum** Brenda Lee
	(Dum, Dum)..see: Happy Song
	Dum-De-Da..see: She Understands Me
7/56	**Dungaree Doll** Eddie Fisher
18/77	**Dusic** Brick
6/78	**Dust In The Wind** Kansas

POS/YR	RECORD TITLE/ARTIST
30/60	**Dutchman's Gold** Walter Brennan
10/75	**Dynomite - Part 1** Bazuka

E

9/74	**Earache My Eye Featuring Alice Bowie** Cheech & Chong
12/70	**Early In The Morning** Vanity Fare
24/58 32/58	**Early In The Morning** Rinky-Dinks Buddy Holly
24/82	**Early In The Morning** Gap Band
3/55 8/55 18/55	**Earth Angel** Crew-Cuts Penguins Gloria Mann
1/63	**Easier Said Than Done** Essex Featuring Anita Humes
27/66	**East West** Herman's Hermits
4/77	**Easy** Commodores
9/70	**Easy Come, Easy Go** Bobby Sherman
39/72	**Easy Livin** Uriah Heep
17/71	**Easy Loving** Freddie Hart
	Easy Question..see: (Such An)
4/69	**Easy To Be Hard** Three Dog Night
36/78	**Easy To Love** Leo Sayer
25/64 5/66	**Ebb Tide** Lenny Welch Righteous Brothers
1/82	**Ebony And Ivory** Paul McCartney & Stevie Wonder

POS/YR	RECORD TITLE/ARTIST
8/61	**Ebony Eyes** Everly Brothers
14/78	**Ebony Eyes** Bob Welch
40/69	**Echo Park** Keith Barbour
31/73	**Ecstasy** Ohio Players
11/56 14/56 14/56	**Eddie My Love** Fontane Sisters Chordettes Teen Queens
11/82	**Edge Of Seventeen (Just Like The White Winged Dove)** Stevie Nicks
26/77	**Edge Of The Universe** Bee Gees
34/78	**Ego** Elton John
1/65	**Eight Days A Week** Beatles
14/66	**Eight Miles High** Byrds
4/82	**867-5309/Jenny** Tommy Tutone
21/71	**Eighteen** Alice Cooper
15/75	**Eighteen With A Bullet** Pete Wingfield
10/63	**18 Yellow Roses** Bobby Darin
18/70	**El Condor Pasa** Simon & Garfunkel
32/60	**El Matador** Kingston Trio
1/60	**El Paso** Marty Robbins
30/58	**El Rancho Rock** Champs
17/63	**El Watusi** Ray Barretto
11/66 35/68 17/69	**Eleanor Rigby** Beatles Ray Charles Aretha Franklin

POS/YR	RECORD TITLE/ARTIST
26/72	**Elected** Alice Cooper
6/68	**Elenore** Turtles
21/56 35/56	**11th Hour Melody** Al Hibbler Lou Busch & His Orchestra
10/69	**Eli's Coming** Three Dog Night
39/56	**Eloise** Kay Thompson
5/66	**Elusive Butterfly** Bob Lind
5/81	**Elvira** Oak Ridge Boys
8/75	**Emma** Hot Chocolate
3/78	**Emotion** Samantha Sang
22/75	**Emotion** Helen Reddy
3/80	**Emotional Rescue** Rolling Stones
7/61	**Emotions** Brenda Lee
18/80	**Empire Strikes Back (Medley)** Meco
13/57	**Empty Arms** Teresa Brewer
13/82	**Empty Garden (Hey Hey Johnny)** Elton John
12/59	**Enchanted** Platters
12/58	**Enchanted Island** Four Lads
15/59 28/59	**Enchanted Sea** Islanders Martin Denny
7/58	**End** Earl Grant
15/68 40/70	**End Of Our Road** Gladys Knight & The Pips Marvin Gaye
2/63	**End Of The World** Skeeter Davis

POS/YR	RECORD TITLE/ARTIST
1/81	**Endless Love** Diana Ross & Lionel Richie
5/58	**Endless Sleep** Jody Reynolds
12/59	**Endlessly** Brook Benton
33/74	**Energy Crisis '74** Dickie Goodman
7/65	**Engine Engine #9** Roger Miller
14/70	**Engine Number 9** Wilson Pickett
8/65	**England Swings** Roger Miller
21/56	**English Muffins And Irish Stew** Sylvia Syms
6/77	**Enjoy Yourself** Jackson 5
	Enough Is Enough..see: No More Tears
3/74	**Entertainer** Marvin Hamlisch
31/65	**Entertainer** Tony Clarke
34/75	**Entertainer** Billy Joel
19/67	**Epistle To Dippy** Donovan
9/74	**Eres Tu (Touch The Wind)** Mocedades
1/79	**Escape (The Pina Colada Song)** Rupert Holmes
35/71	**Escape-ism (Part 1)** James Brown
19/62	**Eso Beso (That Kiss!)** Paul Anka
1/65	**Eve Of Destruction** Barry McGuire
33/80	**Even It Up** Heart
19/78	**Even Now** Barry Manilow
36/67	**Even The Bad Times Are Good** Tremeloes

POS/YR	RECORD TITLE/ARTIST
5/82	**Even The Nights Are Better** Air Supply
1/77	**Evergreen** Barbra Streisand
13/67 6/74 32/81	**Everlasting Love** Robert Knight Carl Carlton Rex Smith / Rachel Sweet
5/78	**Everlasting Love** Andy Gibb
16/61	**Everlovin'** Ricky Nelson
6/61	**Every Beat Of My Heart** Gladys Knight & The Pips
37/56 24/72	**Every Day Of My Life** McGuire Sisters Bobby Vinton
16/78	**Every Kinda People** Robert Palmer
13/64	**Every Little Bit Hurts** Brenda Holloway
3/81	**Every Little Thing She Does Is Magic** Police
39/58	**Every Night (I Pray)** Chantels
30/63	**Every Step Of The Way** Johnny Mathis
13/79	**Every Time I Think Of You** Babys
4/77	**(Every Time I Turn Around) Back In Love Again** L.T.D.
19/75	**Every Time You Touch Me (I Get High)** Charlie Rich
30/79	**Every Which Way But Loose** Eddie Rabbitt
5/81	**Every Woman In The World** Air Supply
3/63	**Everybody** Tommy Roe
38/77	**Everybody Be Dancin'** Starbuck
38/78	**Everybody Dance** Chic

POS/YR	RECORD TITLE/ARTIST
F/70	**Everybody Is A Star** Sly & The Family Stone
15/64	**Everybody Knows (I Still Love You)** Dave Clark Five
31/59	**Everybody Likes To Cha Cha Cha** Sam Cooke
4/65	**Everybody Loves A Clown** Gary Lewis & The Playboys
6/58 19/63	**Everybody Loves A Lover** Doris Day Shirelles
6/62	**Everybody Loves Me But You** Brenda Lee
1/64	**Everybody Loves Somebody** Dean Martin
32/78	**Everybody Needs Love** Stephen Bishop
39/67	**Everybody Needs Love** Gladys Knight & The Pips
29/67	**Everybody Needs Somebody To Love** Wilson Pickett
3/72	**Everybody Plays The Fool** Main Ingredient
32/82	**Everybody Wants You** Billy Squier
12/71	**Everybody's Everything** Santana
20/56	**Everybody's Got A Home But Me** Eddie Fisher
21/70	**Everybody's Got The Right To Love** Supremes
18/80	**Everybody's Got To Learn Sometime** Korgis
26/70	**Everybody's Out Of Town** B.J. Thomas
1/60	**Everybody's Somebody's Fool** Connie Francis
6/69	**Everybody's Talkin'** Nilsson
1/69	**Everyday People** Sly & The Family Stone
19/69	**Everyday With You Girl** Classics IV Featuring Dennis Yost

POS/YR	RECORD TITLE/ARTIST
6/79	**Everyone's A Winner** Hot Chocolate
17/65	**Everyone's Gone To The Moon** Jonathan King
5/72	**Everything I Own** Bread
1/70	**Everything Is Beautiful** Ray Stevens
10/68	**Everything That Touches You** Association
16/64	**Everything's Alright** Newbeats
38/70	**Everything's Tuesday** Chairmen Of The Board
9/70	**Evil Ways** Santana
10/76	**Evil Woman** Electric Light Orchestra
19/69	**Evil Woman Don't Play Your Games With Me** Crow
2/61 31/61 36/61	**Exodus** Ferrante & Teicher Mantovani & His Orchestra Eddie Harris
	Exorcist, Theme From..see: Tubular Bells
14/55	**Experience Unnecessary** Sarah Vaughan
33/68	**Explosion In My Soul** Soul Survivors
4/75	**Express** B.T. Express
12/70	**Express Yourself** Charles Wright & The Watts 103rd Street Rhythm Band
4/67	**Expressway To Your Heart** Soul Survivors
3/82	**Eye In The Sky** Alan Parsons Project
1/82	**Eye Of The Tiger** Survivor
28/68	**Eyes Of A New York Woman** B.J. Thomas

POS/YR	RECORD TITLE/ARTIST

F

POS/YR	RECORD TITLE/ARTIST
22/78	**FM (No Static At All)** Steely Dan
29/66	**Fa-Fa-Fa-Fa-Fa (Sad Song)** Otis Redding
16/57	**Fabulous** Charlie Gracie
19/56	**Fabulous Character** Sarah Vaughan
29/68	**Face It Girl, It's Over** Nancy Wilson
20/81	**Fade Away** Bruce Springsteen
13/74	**Fairytale** Pointer Sisters
23/67	**Fakin' It** Simon & Garfunkel
36/76	**Fallen Angel** Frankie Valli
20/57 23/57	**Fallen Star** Nick Noble Jimmy Newman
30/58	**Fallin'** Connie Francis
1/75	**Fallin' In Love** Hamilton Joe Frank & Reynolds
27/74	**Fallin' In Love** Souther Hillman Furay Band
13/78	**Falling** LeBlanc & Carr
22/63	**Falling** Roy Orbison
1/75	**Fame** David Bowie
4/80	**Fame** Irene Cara
17/60	**Fame And Fortune** Elvis Presley
1/71	**Family Affair** Sly & The Family Stone

POS/YR	RECORD TITLE/ARTIST
12/72	**Family Of Man** Three Dog Night
31/70	**Fancy** Bobbie Gentry
39/77	**Fancy Dancer** Commodores
38/60	**Fannie Mae** Buster Brown
12/76	**Fanny (Be Tender With My Love)** Bee Gees
23/82	**Fantasy** Aldo Nova
32/78	**Fantasy** Earth Wind & Fire
19/64	**Farmer John** Premiers
7/57 15/57 17/57	**Fascination** Jane Morgan Dinah Shore Dick Jacobs & His Orchestra
F/78	**Fat Bottomed Girls** Queen
1/74	**Feel Like Makin' Love** Roberta Flack
10/75	**Feel Like Makin' Love** Bad Company
14/60 22/67	**Feel So Fine** Johnny Preston Bunny Sigler
	Feelin' Groovy..see: 59th Street Bridge
10/73	**Feelin' Stronger Every Day** Chicago
33/72	**Feeling Alright** Joe Cocker
6/75	**Feelings** Morris Albert
4/77	**Feels Like The First Time** Foreigner
4/78	**Feels So Good** Chuck Mangione
20/81	**Feels So Right** Alabama
32/61	**Fell In Love On Monday** Fats Domino

POS/YR	RECORD TITLE/ARTIST
13/76	**Fernando** Abba
6/65	**Ferry Across The Mersey** Gerry & The Pacemakers
24/56 8/58 7/65	**Fever** Little Willie John Peggy Lee McCoys
23/78	**Ffun** Con Funk Shun
39/58	**Fibbin'** Patti Page
1/76	**Fifth Of Beethoven** Walter Murphy Band
1/76	**50 Ways To Leave Your Lover** Paul Simon
13/67	**59th Street Bridge Song (Feelin' Groovy)** Harpers Bizarre
3/79	**Fight (Medley)** Barbra Streisand
4/75	**Fight The Power - Part 1** Isley Brothers
	(Final Acclaim)..see: You're In My Heart
17/74	**Finally Got Myself Together (I'm A Changed Man)** Impressions
16/82	**Find Another Fool** Quarterflash
27/61	**Find Another Girl** Jerry Butler
29/81	**Find Your Way Back** Jefferson Starship
7/60	**Finger Poppin' Time** Hank Ballard & The Midnighters
1/63	**Fingertips - Pt 2** Stevie Wonder
35/79	**Fins** Jimmy Buffett
1/75	**Fire** Ohio Players
2/68	**Fire** Arthur Brown
2/79	**Fire** Pointer Sisters

POS/YR	RECORD TITLE/ARTIST
17/81	**Fire And Ice** Pat Benatar
3/70	**Fire And Rain** James Taylor
24/72	**Fire And Water** Wilson Pickett
28/74	**Fire, Baby I'm On Fire** Andy Kim
32/80	**Fire In The Morning** Melissa Manchester
6/80	**Fire Lake** Bob Seger
38/75	**Fire On The Mountain** Marshall Tucker Band
20/58	**Firefly** Tony Bennett
21/77	**First Cut Is The Deepest** Rod Stewart
25/57	**First Date, First Kiss, First Love** Sonny James
20/60	**First Name Initial** Annette
37/69	**First Of May** Bee Gees
27/63	**First Quarrel** Paul & Paula
1/72	**First Time Ever I Saw Your Face** Roberta Flack
	(First Time I Was A Fool)..see: Third Time Lucky
38/80	**First Time Love** Livingston Taylor
25/61	**Fish** Bobby Rydell
26/74	**Fish Ain't Bitin'** Lamont Dozier
10/63	**500 Hundred Miles Away From Home** Bobby Bare
4/66	**Five O'Clock World** Vogues
	Five Oaks..see: Cinco Robles
27/78	**5.7.0.5.** City Boy

POS/YR	RECORD TITLE/ARTIST
11/70	**5-10-15-20 (25-30 Years Of Love)** Presidents
14/61	**Flaming Star** Elvis Presley
28/66	**Flamingo** Herb Alpert & The Tijuana Brass
16/78	**Flash Light** Parliament
2/77	**Float On** Floaters
21/56	**Flowers Mean Forgiveness** Frank Sinatra
4/66	**Flowers On The Wall** Statler Brothers
16/72	**Floy Joy** Supremes
7/61	**Fly** Chubby Checker
13/76	**Fly Away** John Denver
2/77	**Fly Like An Eagle** Steve Miller Band
14/63	**Fly Me To The Moon-Bossa Nova** Joe Harnell & His Orchestra
1/75	**Fly, Robin, Fly** Silver Convention
38/78	**Flying High** Commodores
3/56	**Flying Saucer (Parts 1 & 2)** Buchanan & Goodman
18/57	**Flying Saucer The 2nd** Buchanan & Goodman
15/62	**Follow That Dream** Elvis Presley
17/63	**Follow The Boys** Connie Francis
23/78	**Follow You Follow Me** Genesis
32/68	**Folsom Prison Blues** Johnny Cash
7/56	**Fool** Sanford Clark
22/68	**Fool For You** Impressions

POS/YR	RECORD TITLE/ARTIST
12/78	**Fool (If You Think It's Over)** Chris Rea
27/60	**Fool In Love** Ike & Tina Turner
25/81	**Fool In Love With You** Jim Photoglo
21/80	**Fool In The Rain** Led Zeppelin
13/64	**Fool Never Learns** Andy Williams
3/61	**Fool Number 1** Brenda Lee
6/68	**Fool On The Hill** Sergio Mendes & Brasil '66
	Fool Such As I..see: (Now And Then There's)
10/76	**Fool To Cry** Rolling Stones
20/55	**Fooled** Perry Como
3/76	**Fooled Around And Fell In Love** Elvin Bishop
29/78	**Fooling Yourself (The Angry Young Man)** Styx
4/63	**Foolish Little Girl** Shirelles
29/59	**Fools Hall Of Fame** Pat Boone
24/60 12/63	**Fools Rush In** Brook Benton Ricky Nelson
25/61	**Foot Stomping - Part 1** Flares
7/60	**Footsteps** Steve Lawrence
29/72	**Footstompin' Music** Grand Funk Railroad
30/76	**Fopp** Ohio Players
23/59	**For A Penny** Pat Boone
3/71	**For All We Know** Carpenters

POS/YR	RECORD TITLE/ARTIST
26/71	**(For God's Sake) Give More Power To The People** Chi-Lites
30/65	**For Lovin' Me** Peter Paul & Mary
28/61	**For My Baby** Brook Benton
21/58	**For My Good Fortune** Pat Boone
2/68	**For Once In My Life** Stevie Wonder
	For Sentimental Reasons..see: (I Love You)
11/70	**For The Good Times** Ray Price
13/70	**For The Love Of Him** Bobbi Martin
9/74	**For The Love Of Money** O'Jays
22/75	**For The Love Of You (Part 1 & 2)** Isley Brothers
7/67	**For What It's Worth (Stop, Hey What's That Sound)** Buffalo Springfield
6/64	**For You** Ricky Nelson
4/81	**For Your Eyes Only** Sheena Easton
6/65	**For Your Love** Yardbirds
13/58 20/67	**For Your Love** Ed Townsend Peaches & Herb
11/58 26/63 23/67	**For Your Precious Love** Jerry Butler Garnet Mimms & The Enchanters Oscar Toney Jr.
9/60 25/64	**Forever** Little Dippers Pete Drake
28/68	**Forever Came Today** Supremes
35/56	**Forever Darling** Ames Brothers
20/79	**Forever In Blue Jeans** Neil Diamond

POS/YR	RECORD TITLE/ARTIST
28/80	**Forever Mine** O'Jays
4/64	**Forget Him** Bobby Rydell
12/58	**Forget Me Not** Kalin Twins
23/82	**Forget Me Nots** Patrice Rushen
2/80	**Forgive Me, Girl (medley)** Spinners
21/55	**Forgive My Heart** Nat King Cole
F/69	**Fortunate Son** Creedence Clearwater Revival
9/59	**Forty Miles Of Bad Road** Duane Eddy
36/79	**Found A Cure** Ashford & Simpson
11/57 15/57	**Four Walls** Jim Reeves Jim Lowe
36/68	**1432 Franklin Pike Circle Hero** Bobby Russell
5/76	**Fox On The Run** Sweet
1/73	**Frankenstein** Edgar Winter Group
9/59	**Frankie** Connie Francis
20/61 14/63 25/66	**Frankie And Johnny** Brook Benton Sam Cooke Elvis Presley
36/57	**Fraulein** Bobby Helms
	Freddie ..see: Do The & Let's Do The
4/72	**Freddie's Dead** Curtis Mayfield
20/71	**Free** Chicago
23/56	**Free** Tommy Leonetti
25/77	**Free** Deniece Williams

POS/YR	RECORD TITLE/ARTIST
	Free Bird
19/75	Lynyrd Skynyrd
38/76	Lynyrd Skynyrd
	Free Man In Paris
22/74	Joni Mitchell
	Free Ride
14/73	Edgar Winter Group
	Freeze
33/58	Tony & Joe
	Freeze-Frame
4/82	J. Geils Band
	Freight Train
6/57	Rusty Draper
40/57	Chas. McDevitt Skiffle Group
	(Friday Night)..see: Livin' It Up
	Friday On My Mind
16/67	Easybeats
	Friday's Child
36/66	Nancy Sinatra
	Friendly Persuasion (Thee I Love)
5/56	Pat Boone
	Friends
34/71	Elton John
	Friends
40/73	Bette Midler
	Friends In Love
38/82	Johnny Mathis & Dionne Warwick
	Friendship Train
17/69	Gladys Knight & The Pips
	Frogg
32/61	Brothers Four
	From A Jack To A King
6/63	Ned Miller
	From A Window
23/64	Billy J. Kramer
	From His Woman To You
28/75	Barbara Mason
	From The Beginning
39/72	Lake Emerson & Palmer
	From The Candy Store On The Corner To The Chapel On The Hill
11/56	Tony Bennett
	Full Of Fire
28/75	Al Green

POS/YR	RECORD TITLE/ARTIST
	Fun ..also see: Ffun
	Fun, Fun, Fun
5/64	Beach Boys
	Funky Broadway
8/67	Wilson Pickett
	Funky Judge
39/68	Bull & The Matadors
	Funky Nassau-Part 1
15/71	Beginning Of The End
	Funky Street
14/68	Arthur Conley
	Funky Stuff
29/73	Kool & The Gang
	Funky Worm
15/73	Ohio Players
	Funkytown
1/80	Lipps Inc.
	Funny
25/61	Maxine Brown
	Funny Face
5/72	Donna Fargo
	Funny How Time Slips Away
22/61	Jimmy Elledge
13/64	Joe Hinton
	Funny Way Of Laughin'
10/62	Burl Ives
	Future Shock
39/73	Curtis Mayfield

G

POS/YR	RECORD TITLE/ARTIST
	G.T.O.
4/64	Ronny & The Daytonas
	Galaxy
39/78	War
	Gallant Men
29/67	Senator Everett Mckinley Dirksen
	Galveston
4/69	Glen Campbell
	Gambler
16/79	Kenny Rogers

POS/YR	RECORD TITLE/ARTIST
1/65	**Game Of Love** Mindbenders
27/71	**Games** Redeye
12/69	**Games People Play** Joe South
16/81	**Games People Play** Alan Parsons Project
	(Games People Play)..see: They Just Can't Stop It
12/56	**Garden Of Eden** Joe Valino
6/72	**Garden Party** Ricky Nelson
31/58	**Gee, But It's Lonely** Pat Boone
19/56	**Gee Whittakers!** Pat Boone
28/61	**Gee Whiz** Innocents
10/61 31/80	**Gee Whiz (Look At His Eyes)** Carla Thomas Bernadette Peters
12/81	**Gemini Dream** Moody Blues
33/81	**General Hospi-Tale** Afternoon Delights
31/82	**Genius Of Love** Tom Tom Club
39/68	**Gentle On My Mind** Glen Campbell
33/71	**George Jackson** Bob Dylan
1/60	**Georgia On My Mind** Ray Charles
2/67	**Georgy Girl** Seekers
37/72	**Geronimo's Cadillac** Michael Murphey
1/58 21/58	**Get A Job** Silhouettes Mills Brothers
1/69	**Get Back** Beatles

POS/YR	RECORD TITLE/ARTIST
6/76	**Get Closer** Seals & Crofts
29/82	**Get Closer** Linda Ronstadt
10/75	**Get Dancin'** Disco Tex & The Sex-O-Lettes
7/73	**Get Down** Gilbert O'Sullivan
8/75	**Get Down, Get Down (Get On The Floor)** Joe Simon
10/82	**Get Down On It** Kool & The Gang
1/75	**Get Down Tonight** KC & The Sunshine Band
24/71	**Get It On** Chase
	(Get It On)..see: Bang A Gong
21/79	**Get It Right Next Time** Gerry Rafferty
28/73	**Get It Together** Jackson 5
40/67	**Get It Together (Part 1)** James Brown
27/67	**Get Me To The World On Time** Electric Prunes
9/78	**Get Off** Foxy
1/65	**Get Off Of My Cloud** Rolling Stones
18/72	**Get On The Good Foot (Part 1)** James Brown
11/67	**Get On Up** Esquires
29/66 4/70	**Get Ready** Temptations Rare Earth
30/76	**Get The Funk Out Ma Face** Brothers Johnson
31/65 5/69	**Get Together** We Five Youngbloods
2/76	**Get Up And Boogie (That's Right)** Silver Convention

Bing Crosby. The Yuletide standard of the past 40 years, "White Christmas," was recorded by Bing Crosby in sunny California during the month of May.

James Darren recorded probably some of the worst songs written by Carole King and Gerry Goffin ("Her Royal Majesty," "They Should Have Given You The Oscar") and Barry Mann and Cynthia Weil ("Conscience").

Doris Day's contribution to the top 40 was modest, but her son, Terry Melcher, produced hits for the Rip Chords, the Byrds, and Paul Revere and the Raiders.

Duane Eddy, rock 'n' roll's premier instrumentalist, also has the distinction of being responsible for the theme songs to two of the most popular television shows of the early 1960s: "Peter Gunn" and "The Ballad of Paladin."

Sheena Easton. Scotland's Sheena Easton got her showbiz break via a British television documentary, which showed her undergoing the "star packaging" treatment. The viewers loved it, and her first record went to the top 10.

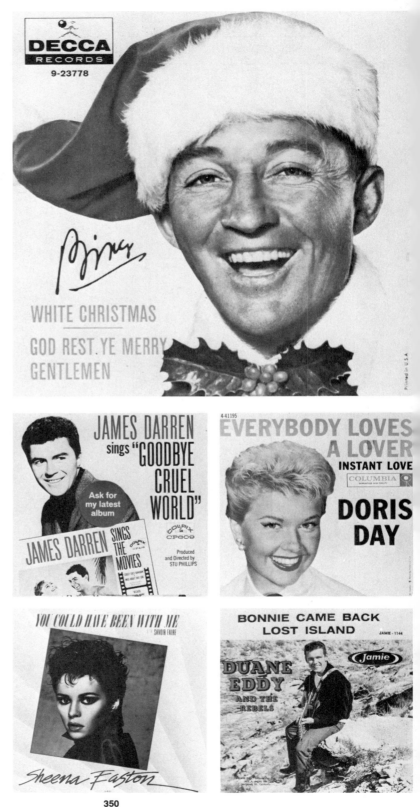

Shirley Ellis' million-selling "The Clapping Song" was updated in 1982 by Pia Zadora, with the aid of the man responsible for arranging the original, Charlie Calello. He has an ear for a tune, that Charlie.

Shelley Fabares' contribution to rock culture may have been "Johnny Angel," but she had the good sense to marry Lou Adler, the man responsible for work by Sam Cooke, Jan & Dean, Johnny Rivers, the Mamas and the Papas, and Carole King.

Fabian. It may be worth noting that an obscure Fabian flipside from 1960, "String Along," became the A-side hit for Rick Nelson three years later. Then again, it may not.

The Four Seasons. A constant component throughout the group's career was the talent of Bob Gaudio, who wrote their first No. 1 ("Sherry"), their last ("December 1963") and many in between.

Gallery's only top 10 success was the product of session musicians and singer Jim Gold, in a recording date put together by Detroit veterans Dennis Coffey and Mike Theodore.

The Grass Roots were originally a studio creation of songwriters Steve Barri and Phil (later P. F.) Sloan. After "Where Were You When I Needed You" became a chart entry, they assembled a "real" group of musicians.

POS/YR	RECORD TITLE/ARTIST
	(Get Up And Dance)..see: Bite Your Lip
34/71	**Get Up, Get Into It, Get Involved** James Brown
15/70	**Get Up I Feel Like Being Like A Sex Machine (Part 1)** James Brown
21/79	**Get Used To It** Roger Voudouris
12/76	**Getaway** Earth Wind & Fire
27/77	**Gettin' Ready For Love** Diana Ross
18/67	**Gettin' Together** Tommy James & The Shondells
20/79	**Getting Closer** Paul McCartney
29/73	**Ghetto Child** Spinners
30/61 31/81	**(Ghost) Riders In The Sky** Ramrods Outlaws
22/56	**Ghost Town** Don Cherry
9/70	**Gimme Dat Ding** Pipkins
12/69	**Gimme Gimme Good Lovin'** Crazy Elephant
9/67	**Gimme Little Sign** Brenton Wood
7/67 18/80	**Gimme Some Lovin'** Spencer Davis Group Blues Brothers
6/62	**Gina** Johnny Mathis
9/58	**Ginger Bread** Frankie Avalon
38/61	**Ginnie Bell** Paul Dino
21/62	**Ginny Come Lately** Brian Hyland
30/65	**Girl Come Running** Four Seasons
5/64	**Girl From Ipanema** Stan Getz / Astrud Gilberto

POS/YR	RECORD TITLE/ARTIST
39/67	**Girl I Knew Somewhere** Monkees
21/66	**Girl In Love** Outsiders
10/67	**Girl Like You** Rascals
19/61	**Girl Of My Best Friend** Ral Donner
37/79	**Girl Of My Dreams** Bram Tchaikovsky
28/66	**Girl On A Swing** Gerry & The Pacemakers
5/68	**Girl Watcher** O'Kaysions
26/64	**Girl (Why You Wanna Make Me Blue)** Temptations
13/57	**Girl With The Golden Braids** Perry Como
10/67	**Girl, You'll Be A Woman Soon** Neil Diamond
34/80	**Girls Can Get It** Dr. Hook
33/68	**Girls Can't Do What The Guys Do** Betty Wright
14/62	**(Girls, Girls, Girls) Made To Love** Eddie Hodges
33/64	**Girls Grow Up Faster Than Boys** Cookies
39/67	**Girls In Love** Gary Lewis & The Playboys
33/78	**Girls' School** Paul McCartney
8/69	**Gitarzan** Ray Stevens
15/77	**Give A Little Bit** Supertramp
18/65	**Give Him A Great Big Kiss** Shangri-Las
21/72	**Give Ireland Back To The Irish** Paul McCartney
18/80	**Give It All You Got** Chuck Mangione
30/73	**Give It To Me** J. Geils Band

POS/YR	RECORD TITLE/ARTIST
40/81	**Give It To Me Baby** Rick James
20/74	**Give It To The People** Righteous Brothers
15/69	**Give It Up Or Turnit A Loose** James Brown
38/76	**Give It Up (Turn It Loose)** Tyrone Davis
40/75	**Give It What You Got** B.T. Express
	Give Me ..also see: Gimme
3/70	**Give Me Just A Little More Time** Chairmen Of The Board
1/73	**Give Me Love (Give Me Peace On Earth)** George Harrison
4/80	**Give Me The Night** George Benson
31/73	**Give Me Your Love** Barbara Mason
	Give More Power To The People..see: **(For God's Sake)**
14/69	**Give Peace A Chance** John Lennon
30/56	**Give Us This Day** Joni James
29/65	**Give Us Your Blessings** Shangri-Las
34/73	**Give Your Baby A Standing Ovation** Dells
8/81	**Giving It Up For Your Love** Delbert McClinton
38/64	**Giving Up** Gladys Knight & The Pips
6/64	**Glad All Over** Dave Clark Five
19/55	**Glad Rag Doll** Crazy Otto
26/67	**Glad To Be Unhappy** Mamas & The Papas
37/75	**Glasshouse** Temptations
8/56	**Glendora** Perry Como

POS/YR	RECORD TITLE/ARTIST
2/82	**Gloria** Laura Branigan
10/66	**Gloria** Shadows Of Knight
25/77	**Gloria** Enchantment
34/72	**Glory Bound** Grass Roots
30/66	**Go Ahead And Cry** Righteous Brothers
5/72	**Go All The Way** Raspberries
1/63 12/66 1/71	**Go Away Little Girl** Steve Lawrence Happenings Donny Osmond
36/70	**Go Back** Crabby Appleton
32/71	**Go Down Gamblin'** Blood Sweat & Tears
5/60	**Go, Jimmy, Go** Jimmy Clanton
10/65	**Go Now!** Moody Blues
11/56 39/56	**Go On With The Wedding** Patti Page Kitty Kallen & Georgie Shaw
16/67	**Go Where You Wanna Go** 5th Dimension
10/77	**Go Your Own Way** Fleetwood Mac
36/60	**God Bless America** Connie Francis
18/61	**God, Country And My Baby** Johnny Burnette
22/70	**God, Love And Rock & Roll** Teegarden & Van Winkle
39/66	**God Only Knows** Beach Boys
	Godfather..see: Love Theme From
17/82	**Goin' Down** Greg Guidry
36/73	**Goin' Home** Osmonds

POS/YR	RECORD TITLE/ARTIST
6/64	**Goin' Out Of My Head** Little Anthony & The Imperials
7/68	Lettermen
16/57	**Goin' Steady** Tommy Sands
35/64	**Going Going Gone** Brook Benton
15/69	**Going In Circles** Friends Of Distinction
	Going To ..also see: Gonna
11/66	**Going To A Go-Go** Miracles
25/82	Rolling Stones
11/69	**Going Up The Country** Canned Heat
5/79	**Gold** John Stewart
10/76	**Golden Years** David Bowie
8/65	**Goldfinger** Shirley Bassey
4/57	**Gone** Ferlin Husky
24/72	Joey Heatherton
23/75	**Gone At Last** Paul Simon/Phoebe Snow
31/64	**Gone, Gone, Gone** Everly Brothers
23/77	**Gone Too Far** England Dan & John Ford Coley
18/57	**Gonna Find Me A Bluebird** Marvin Rainwater
1/77	**Gonna Fly Now (Theme From "Rocky")** Bill Conti
28/77	Maynard Ferguson
11/56	**Gonna Get Along Without Ya Now** Patience & Prudence
29/67	**Gonna Give Her All The Love I've Got** Jimmy Ruffin
36/69	**Goo Goo Barabajagal (Love Is Hot)** Donovan
17/55	**Good And Lonesome** Kay Starr
	Good Foot..see: Get On The

POS/YR	RECORD TITLE/ARTIST
39/79	**Good Friend** Mary MacGregor
11/79	**Good Girls Don't** Knack
10/58	**Good Golly Miss Molly** Little Richard
4/66	Mitch Ryder & The Detroit Wheels
25/76	**Good Hearted Woman** Waylon & Willie
18/63	**Good Life** Tony Bennett
1/66	**Good Lovin'** Rascals
30/69	**Good Lovin' Ain't Easy To Come By** Marvin Gaye & Tammi Terrell
36/75	**Good Lovin' Gone Bad** Bad Company
1/62	**Good Luck Charm** Elvis Presley
34/73	**Good Morning Heartache** Diana Ross
3/69	**Good Morning Starshine** Oliver
11/64	**Good News** Sam Cooke
21/69	**Good Old Rock 'N Roll (medley)** Cat Mother & the All Night News Boys
2/68	**Good, The Bad And The Ugly** Hugo Montenegro
4/67	**Good Thing** Paul Revere & The Raiders
11/61	**Good Time Baby** Bobby Rydell
9/72	**Good Time Charlie's Got The Blues** Danny O'Keefe
1/79	**Good Times** Chic
11/64	**Good Times** Sam Cooke
3/60	**Good Timin'** Jimmy Jones
40/79	**Good Timin'** Beach Boys

POS/YR	RECORD TITLE/ARTIST
	Good Vibrations
1/66	Beach Boys
34/76	Todd Rundgren
	Goodbye
13/69	Mary Hopkin
	Goodbye Baby
8/59	Jack Scott
	Goodbye Baby (Baby Goodbye)
33/64	Solomon Burke
	Goodbye Cruel World
3/61	James Darren
	Goodbye Girl
15/78	David Gates
	Goodbye Jimmy, Goodbye
11/59	Kathy Linden
	Goodbye My Love
31/68	James Brown
	Goodbye Stranger
15/79	Supertramp
	Goodbye To Love
7/72	Carpenters
	Goodbye Yellow Brick Road
2/73	Elton John
	Goodnight
21/65	Roy Orbison
	Goodnight My Love
32/56	McGuire Sisters
32/63	Fleetwoods
27/69	Paul Anka
	Goodnight Tonight
5/79	Paul McCartney
	Goody Goody
20/57	Frankie Lymon & The Teenagers
	Goody Goody Gumdrops
37/68	1910 Fruitgum Co.
	Got A Girl
24/60	Four Preps
	Got A Match?
39/58	Daddy-O's
	Got To Be Real
12/79	Cheryl Lynn
	Got To Be There
4/71	Michael Jackson

POS/YR	RECORD TITLE/ARTIST
	Got To Get You Into My Life
7/76	Beatles
9/78	Earth Wind & Fire
	Got To Get You Off My Mind
22/65	Solomon Burke
	Got To Give It Up - Pt. 1
1/77	Marvin Gaye
	Gotta Hold On To This Feeling
21/70	Jr. Walker & The All Stars
	Gotta Serve Somebody
24/79	Bob Dylan
	Gotta Travel On
4/59	Billy Grammer
	Graduation Day
16/56	Rover Boys featuring Billy Albert
17/56	Four Freshmen
	Graduation Song...Pomp And Circumstance
34/61	Adrian Kimberly
	Graduation's Here
39/59	Fleetwoods
	Grass Is Greener
17/63	Brenda Lee
	Gravy (For My Mashed Potatoes)
9/62	Dee Dee Sharp
	Grazing In The Grass
1/68	Hugh Masekela
3/69	Friends Of Distinction
	Grease
1/78	Frankie Valli
	Great Airplane Strike
20/66	Paul Revere & The Raiders
	Great Balls Of Fire
2/57	Jerry Lee Lewis
	Great Imposter..see: (He's) The
	Great Pretender
1/56	Platters
	Greatest American Hero..see: Theme From
	Greatest Hurt
34/62	Jackie Wilson
	Greatest Love Of All
24/77	George Benson
	Green Berets..see: Ballad Of

POS/YR	RECORD TITLE/ARTIST
1/56	**Green Door** Jim Lowe
3/70	**Green-Eyed Lady** Sugarloaf
8/66	**Green Grass** Gary Lewis & The Playboys
14/63	**Green, Green** New Christy Minstrels
11/67	**Green, Green Grass Of Home** Tom Jones
39/68	**Green Light** American Breed
3/62	**Green Onions** Booker T. & The M.G.'s
2/69	**Green River** Creedence Clearwater Revival
1/68	**Green Tambourine** Lemon Pipers
21/63	**Greenback Dollar** Kingston Trio
2/60	**Greenfields** Brothers Four
7/78	**Groove Line** Heatwave
6/71	**Groove Me** King Floyd
1/67 21/67	**Groovin'** Rascals Booker T. & The M.G.'s
30/69	**Groovy Grubworm** Harlow Wilcox & the Oakies
2/66	**Groovy Kind Of Love** Mindbenders
12/70	**Groovy Situation** Gene Chandler
14/76	**Grow Some Funk Of Your Own** Elton John
9/66	**Guantanamera** Sandpipers
11/58	**Guess Things Happen That Way** Johnny Cash
31/59	**Guess Who** Jesse Belvin

POS/YR	RECORD TITLE/ARTIST
3/81	**Guilty** Barbra Streisand & Barry Gibb
5/59	**Guitar Boogie Shuffle** Virtues
11/72	**Guitar Man** Bread
28/81	**Guitar Man** Elvis Presley
	Guitar Man..see: (Dance With The)
10/55	**Gum Drop** Crew-Cuts
12/82	**Gypsy** Fleetwood Mac
24/63	**Gypsy Cried** Lou Christie
8/73	**Gypsy Man** War
20/61 3/70	**Gypsy Woman** Impressions Brian Hyland
1/71	**Gypsys, Tramps & Thieves** Cher

H

POS/YR	RECORD TITLE/ARTIST
2/69	**Hair** Cowsills
22/66	**Hair On My Chinny Chin Chin** Sam The Sham & The Pharaohs
12/63	**Half Heaven - Half Heartache** Gene Pitney
15/79	**Half The Way** Crystal Gayle
1/73	**Half-Breed** Cher
39/61 23/68	**Halfway To Paradise** Tony Orlando Bobby Vinton
33/71	**Hallelujah** Sweathog
28/73	**Hallelujah Day** Jackson 5

POS/YR	RECORD TITLE/ARTIST
	Hand Jive..see: Willie & The Hand Jive
17/70	**Hand Me Down World** Guess Who
2/60 22/64 4/77	**Handy Man** Jimmy Jones Del Shannon James Taylor
9/69	**Hang 'Em High** Booker T. & The M.G.'s
20/82	**Hang Fire** Rolling Stones
8/74	**Hang On In There Baby** Johnny Bristol
1/65 11/65	**Hang On Sloopy** McCoys Ramsey Lewis
24/58	**Hang Up My Rock And Roll Shoes** Chuck Willis
	Hangin' On..see: (You Keep Me)
38/59	**Hanging Tree** Marty Robbins
1/66	**Hanky Panky** Tommy James & The Shondells
1/67 32/67	**Happening** Supremes Herb Alpert & The Tijuana Brass
30/66	**Happenings Ten Years Time Ago** Yardbirds
11/72	**Happiest Girl In The Whole U.S.A.** Donna Fargo
30/79	**Happiness** Pointer Sisters
35/74	**Happiness Is Just Around The Bend** Main Ingredient
20/56 38/56	**Happiness Street** Georgia Gibbs Tony Bennett
22/72	**Happy** Rolling Stones
16/78	**Happy Anniversary** Little River Band
30/61	**Happy Birthday Blues** Kathy Young with The Innocents
6/61	**Happy Birthday, Sweet Sixteen** Neil Sedaka

POS/YR	RECORD TITLE/ARTIST
5/76	**Happy Days** Pratt & McClain
5/57	**Happy, Happy Birthday Baby** Tune Weavers
22/69	**Happy Heart** Andy Williams
24/67	**Happy Jack** Who
19/76	**Happy Music** Blackbyrds
1/59	**Happy Organ** Dave "Baby" Cortez
40/75	**Happy People** Temptations
34/59	**Happy Reindeer** Dancer Prancer & Nervous
25/68	**Happy Song (Dum-Dum)** Otis Redding
27/66	**Happy Summer Days** Ronnie Dove
1/67	**Happy Together** Turtles
6/56	**Happy Whistler** Don Robertson
10/60	**Happy-Go-Lucky-Me** Paul Evans
8/60	**Harbor Lights** Platters
1/64 29/66	**Hard Day's Night** Beatles Ramsey Lewis
1/58	**Hard Headed Woman** Elvis Presley
15/77	**Hard Luck Woman** Kiss
30/77	**Hard Rock Cafe** Carole King
4/55	**Hard To Get** Gisele MacKenzie
7/81	**Hard To Say** Dan Fogelberg
1/82	**Hard To Say I'm Sorry** Chicago

POS/YR	RECORD TITLE/ARTIST
3/82	**Harden My Heart** Quarterflash
39/65	**Harlem Nocturne** Viscounts
1/68	**Harper Valley P.T.A.** Jeannie C. Riley
31/73	**Harry Hippie** Bobby Womack
17/63	**Harry The Hairy Ape** Ray Stevens
13/75	**Harry Truman** Chicago
5/61	**Hats Off To Larry** Del Shannon
11/64	**Haunted House** Jumpin' Gene Simmons
31/62	**Have A Good Time** Sue Thompson
5/64	**Have I The Right?** Honeycombs
29/57	**Have I Told You Lately That I Love You** Ricky Nelson
8/71	**Have You Ever Seen The Rain** Creedence Clearwater Revival
18/63	**Have You Heard** Duprees featuring Joey Vann
24/65	**Have You Looked Into Your Heart** Jerry Vale
1/75	**Have You Never Been Mellow** Olivia Newton-John
3/71	**Have You Seen Her** Chi-Lites
9/66	**Have You Seen Your Mother, Baby, Standing In The Shadow?** Rolling Stones
14/74	**Haven't Got Time For The Pain** Carly Simon
26/79	**Haven't Stopped Dancing Yet** Gonzalez
17/62	**Having A Party** Sam Cooke
	Having My Baby..see: (You're)
4/69	**Hawaii Five-O** Ventures

POS/YR	RECORD TITLE/ARTIST
33/65	**Hawaii Tattoo** Waikikis
11/59	**Hawaiian Wedding Song** Andy Williams
13/66	**Hazy Shade Of Winter** Simon & Garfunkel
4/55 10/55 18/66	**He** Al Hibbler McGuire Sisters Righteous Brothers
7/70 20/70	**He Ain't Heavy, He's My Brother** Hollies Neil Diamond
33/81	**He Can't Love You** Michael Stanley Band
7/60 1/75	**He Don't Love You (Like I Love You)** Jerry Butler Dawn
34/62	**He Knows I Love Him Too Much** Paris Sisters
	He Will Break Your Heart..see: He Don't Love You
2/60	**He'll Have To Go** Jim Reeves
4/60	**He'll Have To Stay** Jeanne Black
36/76	**He's A Friend** Eddie Kendricks
30/81	**He's A Liar** Bee Gees
1/62	**He's A Rebel** Crystals
1/58	**He's Got The Whole World (In His Hands)** Laurie London
23/57	**He's Mine** Platters
14/61	**(He's My) Dreamboat** Connie Francis
1/63	**He's So Fine** Chiffons
3/80	**He's So Shy** Pointer Sisters
11/63	**He's Sure The Boy I Love** Crystals

POS/YR	RECORD TITLE/ARTIST
30/61	**(He's) The Great Impostor** Fleetwoods
9/79	**He's The Greatest Dancer** Sister Sledge
14/79	**Head Games** Foreigner
35/80	**Headed For A Fall** Firefall
14/77	**Heard It In A Love Song** Marshall Tucker Band
6/55 13/55	**Heart** Eddie Fisher Four Aces Featuring Al Alberts
18/61 25/61	**Heart And Soul** Cleftones Jan & Dean
3/82	**Heart Attack** Olivia Newton-John
9/65	**Heart Full Of Soul** Yardbirds
21/80	**Heart Hotels** Dan Fogelberg
15/62	**Heart In Hand** Brenda Lee
24/81	**Heart Like A Wheel** Steve Miller Band
1/79	**Heart Of Glass** Blondie
1/72	**Heart Of Gold** Neil Young
19/65	**Heart Of Stone** Rolling Stones
20/79	**Heart Of The Night** Poco
1/79	**Heartache Tonight** Eagles
7/61	**Heartaches** Marcels
1/59 35/65	**Heartaches By The Number** Guy Mitchell Johnny Tillotson
3/73	**Heartbeat - It's A Lovebeat** Defranco Family featuring Tony Defranco
1/56	**Heartbreak Hotel** Elvis Presley

POS/YR	RECORD TITLE/ARTIST
22/81	**Heartbreak Hotel** Jackson 5
38/60	**Heartbreak (It's Hurtin' Me)** Little Willie John
39/74	**Heartbreak Kid** Bo Donaldson & The Heywoods
23/80	**Heartbreaker** Pat Benatar
37/78	**Heartbreaker** Dolly Parton
	(Heartbreaker)..see: Doo Doo Doo Doo
24/78	**Heartless** Heart
5/82	**Heartlight** Neil Diamond
8/81	**Hearts** Marty Balin
1/55 15/55 20/61 37/73	**Hearts Of Stone** Fontane Sisters Charms Bill Black's Combo Blue Ridge Rangers
19/81	**Hearts On Fire** Randy Meisner
4/82	**Heat Of The Moment** Asia
4/63 5/75	**Heat Wave** Martha & The Vandellas Linda Ronstadt
29/69	**Heather Honey** Tommy Roe
39/69	**Heaven** Rascals
9/70	**Heaven Help Us All** Stevie Wonder
4/79	**Heaven Knows** Donna Summer
24/69	**Heaven Knows** Grass Roots
15/76	**Heaven Must Be Missing An Angel** Tavares
11/79	**Heaven Must Have Sent You** Bonnie Pointer
39/56	**Heaven On Earth** Platters

POS/YR	RECORD TITLE/ARTIST
6/77	**Heaven On The 7th Floor** Paul Nicholas
40/59	**Heavenly Lover** Teresa Brewer
27/71	**Heavy Makes You Happy (Sha-Na-Boom Boom)** Staple Singers
33/70	**Heed The Call** Kenny Rogers & The First Edition
10/74	**Helen Wheels** Paul McCartney
6/81	**Hello Again** Neil Diamond
1/64	**Hello, Dolly!** Louis Armstrong
1/67	**Hello Goodbye** Beatles
26/63	**Hello Heartache, Goodbye Love** Little Peggy March
26/67	**Hello Hello** Sopwith "Camel"
35/73	**Hello Hurray** Alice Cooper
1/68	**Hello, I Love You** Doors
5/73	**Hello It's Me** Todd Rundgren
9/61	**Hello Mary Lou** Ricky Nelson
2/63	**Hello Mudduh, Hello Fadduh! (A Letter From Camp)** Allan Sherman
24/76	**Hello Old Friend** Eric Clapton
3/63 15/77	**Hello Stranger** Barbara Lewis Yvonne Elliman
12/61	**Hello Walls** Faron Young
23/60	**Hello Young Lovers** Paul Anka
1/65	**Help!** Beatles
14/77	**Help Is On Its Way** Little River Band

POS/YR	RECORD TITLE/ARTIST
7/74	**Help Me** Joni Mitchell
29/66 37/66	**Help Me Girl** Animals Outsiders
8/71 33/72	**Help Me Make It Through The Night** Sammi Smith Gladys Knight & The Pips
1/65 22/75	**Help Me, Rhonda** Beach Boys Johnny Rivers
35/68	**Help Yourself** Tom Jones
6/62	**Her Royal Majesty** James Darren
11/81	**Her Town Too** James Taylor & J.D. Souther
23/77	**Here Come Those Tears Again** Jackson Browne
13/67	**Here Comes My Baby** Tremeloes
14/59	**Here Comes Summer** Jerry Keller
15/71	**Here Comes That Rainy Day Feeling Again** Fortunes
8/68 19/68	**Here Comes The Judge** Shorty Long Pigmeat Markham
24/65	**Here Comes The Night** Them
16/71	**Here Comes The Sun** Richie Havens
10/73	**Here I Am (Come And Take Me)** Al Green
5/81	**Here I Am (Just When I Thought I Was Over You)** Air Supply
37/69	**Here I Go Again** Miracles
27/65	**Here It Comes Again** Fortunes
15/67	**Here We Go Again** Ray Charles
3/78	**Here You Come Again** Dolly Parton

POS/YR	RECORD TITLE/ARTIST
12/67	**Heroes And Villains** Beach Boys
1/62	**Hey! Baby** Bruce Channel
12/67	**Hey Baby (They're Playing Our Song)** Buckinghams
19/72	**Hey Big Brother** Rare Earth
23/64	**Hey, Bobba Needle** Chubby Checker
7/78	**Hey Deanie** Shaun Cassidy
10/63	**Hey Girl** Freddie Scott
35/68	Bobby Vee
9/71	Donny Osmond
35/73	**Hey Girl (I Like Your Style)** Temptations
29/64	**Hey Harmonica Man** Stevie Wonder
3/56	**Hey! Jealous Lover** Frank Sinatra
32/64	**Hey Jean, Hey Dean** Dean & Jean
31/66	**Hey Joe** Leaves
1/68	**Hey Jude** Beatles
23/69	Wilson Pickett
35/70	**Hey Lawdy Mama** Steppenwolf
31/67	**Hey, Leroy, Your Mama's Callin' You** Jimmy Castor [Bunch]
20/62	**Hey, Let's Twist** Joey Dee & The Starliters
4/64	**Hey Little Cobra** Rip Chords
29/57	**Hey! Little Girl** Techniques
13/63	**Hey Little Girl** Major Lance
20/59	**Hey Little Girl** Dee Clark
38/61	**Hey! Little Girl** Del Shannon

POS/YR	RECORD TITLE/ARTIST
12/55	**Hey, Mr. Banjo** Sunnysiders
24/70	**Hey, Mr. Sun** Bobby Sherman
10/81	**Hey Nineteen** Steely Dan
1/63	**Hey Paula** Paul & Paula
27/63	**Hey There Lonely Girl (Boy)** Ruby & The Romantics
2/70	Eddie Holman
31/80	Robert John
16/68	**Hey, Western Union Man** Jerry Butler
1/75	**(Hey Won't You Play) Another Somebody Done Somebody Wrong Song** B.J. Thomas
21/75	**Hey You** Bachman-Turner Overdrive
10/73	**Hi, Hi, Hi** Paul McCartney
14/70	**Hi-De-Ho** Blood Sweat & Tears
11/64	**Hi-Heel Sneakers** Tommy Tucker
25/68	Jose Feliciano
33/62	**Hide & Go Seek, Part 1** Bunker Hill
20/62	**Hide 'Nor Hair** Ray Charles
29/61	**Hide Away** Freddy King
21/58	**Hideaway** Four Esquires
30/59	**High Hopes** Frank Sinatra
21/58	**High School Confidential** Jerry Lee Lewis
17/77	**High School Dance** Sylvers
28/59	**High School U.S.A.** Tommy Facenda
37/58	**High Sign** Diamonds

POS/YR	RECORD TITLE/ARTIST
22/71	**High Time We Went** Joe Cocker
	Higher & Higher..see: (Your Love Keeps Lifting Me)
4/73	**Higher Ground** Stevie Wonder
37/74	**Higher Plane** Kool & The Gang
26/79	**Highway Song** Blackfoot
14/75	**Hijack** Herbie Mann
	Hill Street Blues..see: Theme From
	Hill-Billy Heaven..see: I Dreamed Of A
6/80	**Him** Rupert Holmes
5/67	**Him Or Me - What's It Gonna Be?** Paul Revere & The Raiders
31/68	**Hip City - Pt. 2** Jr. Walker & The All Stars
37/67	**Hip Hug-Her** Booker T. & The M.G.'s
24/64	**Hippy Hippy Shake** Swinging Blue Jeans
	His Latest Flame..see: Marie's The Name
39/66	**History Repeats Itself** Buddy Starcher
9/80	**Hit Me With Your Best Shot** Pat Benatar
	(Hit Record)..see: Overnight Sensation
1/61 40/76	**Hit The Road Jack** Ray Charles Stampeders
30/63	**Hitch Hike** Marvin Gaye
34/68	**Hitch It To The Horse** Fantastic Johnny C
5/70	**Hitchin' A Ride** Vanity Fare
9/73	**Hocus Pocus** Focus
35/76	**Hold Back The Night** Trammps

POS/YR	RECORD TITLE/ARTIST
14/72	**Hold Her Tight** Osmonds
4/82	**Hold Me** Fleetwood Mac
8/65	**Hold Me, Thrill Me, Kiss Me** Mel Carter
5/68	**Hold Me Tight** Johnny Nash
15/82	**Hold On** Santana
18/79	**Hold On** Ian Gomm
38/79	**Hold On** Triumph
40/80	**Hold On** Kansas
21/66	**Hold On! I'm A Comin'** Sam & Dave
27/81	**Hold On Loosely** 38 Special
10/81	**Hold On Tight** Electric Light Orchestra
10/80	**Hold On To My Love** Jimmy Ruffin
5/79	**Hold The Line** Toto
5/65	**Hold What You've Got** Joe Tex
5/72	**Hold Your Head Up** Argent
37/82	**Holdin' On** Tane Cain
17/75	**Holdin' On To Yesterday** Ambrosia
16/67	**Holiday** Bee Gees
6/69	**Holly Holy** Neil Diamond
32/77	**Hollywood** Rufus Featuring Chaka Khan
12/78	**Hollywood Nights** Bob Seger
6/74	**Hollywood Swinging** Kool & The Gang

POS/YR	RECORD TITLE/ARTIST
23/66	**Holy Cow** Lee Dorsey
34/67	**Homburg** Procol Harum
28/79	**Home And Dry** Gerry Rafferty
25/65	**Home Of The Brave** Jody Miller
5/66	**Homeward Bound** Simon & Garfunkel
28/60	**Honest I Do** Innocents
32/57	**Honest I Do** Jimmy Reed
24/79	**Honesty** Billy Joel
1/68	**Honey** Bobby Goldsboro
6/55	**Honey Babe** Art Mooney & His Orchestra
11/67	**Honey Chile** Martha & The Vandellas
19/70	**Honey Come Back** Glen Campbell
27/74	**Honey, Honey** Abba
1/57	**Honeycomb** Jimmie Rodgers
8/72	**Honky Cat** Elton John
2/56	**Honky Tonk (Parts 1 & 2)** Bill Doggett
1/69	**Honky Tonk Women** Rolling Stones
11/63	**Honolulu Lulu** Jan & Dean
23/61	**Hoochi Coochi Coo** Hank Ballard & The Midnighters
17/64	**Hooka Tooka** Chubby Checker
5/69 1/74	**Hooked On A Feeling** B.J. Thomas Blue Swede

POS/YR	RECORD TITLE/ARTIST
10/82	**Hooked On Classics** Royal Philharmonic Orchestra
31/82	**Hooked On Swing (medley)** Larry Elgart & His Manhattan Swing Orchestra
6/66	**Hooray For Hazel** Tommy Roe
38/63	**Hootenanny** Glencoves
36/82	**Hope You Love Me Like You Say You Do** Huey Lewis & The News
13/63	**Hopeless** Andy Williams
3/78	**Hopelessly Devoted To You** Olivia Newton-John
2/68	**Horse** Cliff Nobles & Co.
1/72	**Horse With No Name** America
3/78	**Hot Blooded** Foreigner
1/78	**Hot Child In The City** Nick Gilder
1/56	**Hot Diggity (Dog Ziggity Boom)** Perry Como
2/69	**Hot Fun In The Summertime** Sly & The Family Stone
23/82	**Hot In The City** Billy Idol
28/78	**Hot Legs** Rod Stewart
5/77	**Hot Line** Sylvers
31/78	**Hot Love, Cold World** Bob Welch
21/79	**Hot Number** Foxy
15/71	**Hot Pants (She Got To Use What She Got, To Get What She Wants) (Part 1)** James Brown
11/63	**Hot Pastrami** Dartells

POS/YR	RECORD TITLE/ARTIST
36/63	**Hot Pastrami With Mashed Potatoes - Part I** Joey Dee & The Starliters
15/80	**Hot Rod Hearts** Robbie Dupree
26/60 33/60 9/72	**Hot Rod Lincoln** Johnny Bond Charlie Ryan & The Timberline Riders Commander Cody & His Lost Planet Airmen
14/69	**Hot Smoke & Sasafrass** Bubble Puppy
1/79	**Hot Stuff** Donna Summer
18/79	**Hot Summer Nights** Night
1/77	**Hotel California** Eagles
3/63	**Hotel Happiness** Brook Benton
1/56	**Hound Dog** Elvis Presley
9/59	**Hound Dog Man** Fabian
9/55	**House Of Blue Lights** Chuck Miller
1/64 7/70	**House Of The Rising Sun** Animals Frijid Pink
6/68	**House That Jack Built** Aretha Franklin
20/56	**House With Love In It** Four Lads
21/65	**Houston** Dean Martin
12/81	**How 'Bout Us** Champaign
33/60	**How About That** Dee Clark
22/58	**How Are Ya' Fixed For Love?** Frank Sinatra & Keely Smith
4/67 25/72	**How Can I Be Sure** Rascals David Cassidy
22/73	**How Can I Tell Her** Lobo

POS/YR	RECORD TITLE/ARTIST
1/71	**How Can You Mend A Broken Heart** Bee Gees
1/77	**How Deep Is Your Love** Bee Gees
	How Did..see: How'd
10/80	**How Do I Make You** Linda Ronstadt
22/80	**How Do I Survive** Amy Holland
27/67	**How Do You Catch A Girl** Sam The Sham & The Pharaohs
8/72	**How Do You Do?** Mouth & Macneal
9/64	**How Do You Do It?** Gerry & The Pacemakers
30/80	**How Does It Feel To Be Back** Daryl Hall & John Oates
7/66	**How Does That Grab You, Darlin'?** Nancy Sinatra
	How Glad I Am..see: (You Don't Know)
2/55 12/55	**How Important Can It Be?** Joni James Sarah Vaughan
13/56	**(How Little It Matters) How Little We Know** Frank Sinatra
3/75	**How Long** Ace
20/75	**How Long (Betcha' Got A Chick On The Side)** Pointer Sisters
3/78	**How Much I Feel** Ambrosia
17/77	**How Much Love** Leo Sayer
6/65 18/66 5/75	**How Sweet It Is (To Be Loved By You)** Marvin Gaye Jr. Walker & The All Stars James Taylor
11/58	**How The Time Flies** Jerry Wallace
12/78	**How You Gonna See Me Now** Alice Cooper
21/68	**How'd We Ever Get This Way** Andy Kim

POS/YR	RECORD TITLE/ARTIST
14/60	**Hucklebuck** Chubby Checker
32/58 38/58	**Hula Hoop Song** Georgia Gibbs Teresa Brewer
9/57	**Hula Love** Buddy Knox
25/62	**Hully Gully Baby** Dovells
7/55 17/55	**Hummingbird** Les Paul & Mary Ford Frankie Laine
20/73	**Hummingbird** Seals & Crofts
3/61	**Hundred Pounds Of Clay** Gene McDaniels
6/66	**Hungry** Paul Revere & The Raiders
27/65	**Hungry For Love** San Remo Golden Strings
5/81	**Hungry Heart** Bruce Springsteen
13/67	**Hunter Gets Captured By The Game** Marvelettes
5/68	**Hurdy Gurdy Man** Donovan
33/76	**Hurricane (Part 1)** Bob Dylan
4/61 28/76	**Hurt** Timi Yuro Elvis Presley
31/73	**Hurt** Cat Stevens
10/65 12/69 8/80	**Hurt So Bad** Little Anthony & The Imperials Lettermen Linda Ronstadt
2/72	**Hurting Each Other** Carpenters
2/82	**Hurts So Good** John Cougar
24/73	**Hurts So Good** Millie Jackson
26/66	**Husbands And Wives** Roger Miller

POS/YR	RECORD TITLE/ARTIST
4/68	**Hush** Deep Purple
8/65	**Hush, Hush, Sweet Charlotte** Patti Page
20/59	**Hushabye** Mystics
1/75	**Hustle** Van McCoy
21/67	**Hypnotized** Linda Jones
26/82	**I.G.Y. (What A Beautiful World)** Donald Fagen
35/76	**I.O.U.** Jimmy Dean
25/63	**I Adore Him** Angels
11/81	**I Ain't Gonna Stand For It** Stevie Wonder
36/71	**I Ain't Got Time Anymore** Glass Bottle featuring Gary Criss
24/59	**I Ain't Never** Webb Pierce
1/56	**I Almost Lost My Mind** Pat Boone
3/66	**I Am A Rock** Simon & Garfunkel
4/71	**I Am . . . , I Said** Neil Diamond
15/75	**I Am Love (Parts I & II)** Jackson 5
39/70	**I Am Somebody, Part II** Johnnie Taylor
1/72	**I Am Woman** Helen Reddy
8/58	**I Beg Of You** Elvis Presley
33/64	**I Believe** Bachelors

POS/YR	RECORD TITLE/ARTIST
22/72	**I Believe In Music** Gallery
24/80	**I Believe In You** Don Williams
11/73	**I Believe In You (You Believe In Me)** Johnnie Taylor
15/75	**(I Believe) There's Nothing Stronger Than Our Love...** Paul Anka
27/77	**I Believe You** Dorothy Moore
27/75	**I Belong To You** Love Unlimited
	I Can Dance..see: Long Tall Glasses
24/69	**I Can Hear Music** Beach Boys
1/74	**I Can Help** Billy Swan
32/66	**I Can Make It With You** Pozo-Seco Singers
6/65	**I Can Never Go Home Anymore** Shangri-Las
1/72	**I Can See Clearly Now** Johnny Nash
9/67	**I Can See For Miles** Who
	(I Can See It In Your Eyes)..see: The Circle Is Small
22/69	**I Can Sing A Rainbow** Dells
39/81	**I Can Take Care Of Myself** Billy & The Beaters
22/68	**I Can Take Or Leave Your Loving** Herman's Hermits
35/73	**I Can Understand It** New Birth
1/69	**I Can't Get Next To You** Temptations
1/65 31/66	**(I Can't Get No) Satisfaction** Rolling Stones Otis Redding
1/82	**I Can't Go For That (No Can Do)** Daryl Hall & John Oates

POS/YR	RECORD TITLE/ARTIST
34/66	**I Can't Grow Peaches On A Cherry Tree** Just Us
29/76	**I Can't Hear You No More** Helen Reddy
12/80	**I Can't Help It** Olivia Newton-John & Andy Gibb
24/62	**I Can't Help It (If I'm Still In Love With You)** Johnny Tillotson
1/65 22/72 40/80	**I Can't Help Myself (Sugar Pie, Honey Bunch)** Four Tops Donnie Elbert Bonnie Pointer
39/60	**(I Can't Help You) I'm Falling Too** Skeeter Davis
31/80	**I Can't Let Go** Linda Ronstadt
22/56	**I Can't Love You Enough** Lavern Baker
28/69	**I Can't See Myself Leaving You** Aretha Franklin
10/81	**I Can't Stand It** Eric Clapton
14/79	**I Can't Stand It No More** Peter Frampton
33/82	**I Believe** Chilliwack
28/68	**I Can't Stand Myself (When You Touch Me)** James Brown
38/73 18/78	**I Can't Stand The Rain** Ann Peebles Eruption
7/63	**I Can't Stay Mad At You** Skeeter Davis
9/68	**I Can't Stop Dancing** Archie Bell & The Drells
1/62	**I Can't Stop Loving You** Ray Charles
35/64	**I Can't Stop Talking About You** Steve & Eydie
8/80	**I Can't Tell You Why** Eagles
37/68	**I Can't Turn You Loose** Chambers Brothers

POS/YR	RECORD TITLE/ARTIST
32/66	**I Chose To Sing The Blues** Ray Charles
20/56	**I Could Have Danced All Night** Sylvia Syms
13/68	**I Could Never Love Another (After Loving You)** Temptations
18/81	**I Could Never Miss You (More Than I Do)** Lulu
9/66	**I Couldn't Live Without Your Love** Petula Clark
17/61	**I Count The Tears** Drifters
6/59	**I Cried A Tear** Lavern Baker
	I Didn't Get To Sleep At All..see: (Last Night)
35/72	**I Didn't Know I Loved You (Till I Saw You Rock And Roll)** Gary Glitter
9/67	**I Dig Rock And Roll Music** Peter Paul & Mary
37/65	**I Do** Marvelows
15/76	**I Do, I Do, I Do, I Do, I Do** Abba
26/65 20/79	**I Do Love You** Billy Stewart GQ
37/60	**(I Do The) Shimmy Shimmy** Bobby Freeman
18/71	**I Don't Blame You At All** Miracles
13/71 28/71	**I Don't Know How To Love Him** Helen Reddy Yvonne Elliman
23/79	**I Don't Know If It's Right** Evelyn King
35/82	**I Don't Know Where To Start** Eddie Rabbitt
12/61	**I Don't Know Why** Linda Scott
39/69	**I Don't Know Why** Stevie Wonder

POS/YR	RECORD TITLE/ARTIST
	I Don't Know Why..see: But I Do
8/75	**I Don't Like To Sleep Alone** Paul Anka
3/81	**I Don't Need You** Kenny Rogers
37/64	**I Don't Wanna Be A Loser** Lesley Gore
35/65	**I Don't Wanna Lose You Baby** Chad & Jeremy
20/69	**I Don't Want Nobody To Give Me Nothing (Open Up The Door, I'll Get It Myself)** James Brown
22/64	**I Don't Want To Be Hurt Anymore** Nat King Cole
	I Don't Want To Be Right..see: (If Loving You Is Wrong)
36/61	**I Don't Want To Cry** Chuck Jackson
17/71	**I Don't Want To Do Wrong** Gladys Knight & The Pips
34/64	**I Don't Want To See Tomorrow** Nat King Cole
16/64	**I Don't Want To See You Again** Peter & Gordon
39/65	**I Don't Want To Spoil The Party** Beatles
33/61	**I Don't Want To Take A Chance** Mary Wells
36/80	**I Don't Want To Walk Without You** Barry Manilow
9/57	**I Dreamed** Betty Johnson
20/61	**I Dreamed Of A Hill-Billy Heaven** Tex Ritter
12/61	**I Fall To Pieces** Patsy Cline
21/74	**I Feel A Song (In My Heart)** Gladys Knight & The Pips
1/64	**I Feel Fine** Beatles
38/56	**I Feel Good** Shirley & Lee

POS/YR	RECORD TITLE/ARTIST
F/76	**I Feel Like A Bullet (In The Gun Of Robert Ford)** Elton John
6/77	**I Feel Love** Donna Summer
5/61	**I Feel So Bad** Elvis Presley
F/71	**I Feel The Earth Move** Carole King
9/66	**I Fought The Law** Bobby Fuller Four
30/65	**I Found A Girl** Jan & Dean
32/67	**I Found A Love - Part 1** Wilson Pickett
31/82	**I Found Somebody** Glenn Frey
1/64	**I Get Around** Beach Boys
32/82	**I Get Excited** Rick Springfield
37/75	**I Get Lifted** George McCrae
34/68	**I Get The Sweetest Feeling** Jackie Wilson
7/78	**I Go Crazy** Paul Davis
9/65	**I Go To Pieces** Peter & Gordon
10/58	**I Got A Feeling** Ricky Nelson
25/69	**I Got A Line On You** Spirit
10/73	**I Got A Name** Jim Croce
24/59	**I Got A Wife** Mark IV
27/73	**I Got Ants In My Pants (and i want to dance) (Part 1)** James Brown
20/79	**I Got My Mind Made Up (You Can Get It Girl)** Instant Funk
3/67	**I Got Rhythm** Happenings

POS/YR	RECORD TITLE/ARTIST
37/75	**I Got Stoned And I Missed It** Jim Stafford
8/58	**I Got Stung** Elvis Presley
6/68	**I Got The Feelin'** James Brown
16/66	**I Got The Feelin' (Oh No No)** Neil Diamond
28/63	**I Got What I Wanted** Brook Benton
1/65	**I Got You Babe** Sonny & Cher
3/65	**I Got You (I Feel Good)** James Brown
2/72	**I Gotcha** Joe Tex
35/64	**I Gotta Dance To Keep From Crying** Miracles
20/60	**I Gotta Know** Elvis Presley
34/69	**I Guess The Lord Must Be In New York City** Nilsson
17/67	**I Had A Dream** Paul Revere & The Raiders
11/67	**I Had Too Much To Dream (Last Night)** Electric Prunes
36/63	**I Have A Boyfriend** Chiffons
1/65	**I Hear A Symphony** Supremes
30/66	**I Hear Trumpets Blow** Tokens
2/55 4/71	**I Hear You Knocking** Gale Storm Dave Edmunds
2/67 1/68	**I Heard It Through The Grapevine** Gladys Knight & The Pips Marvin Gaye
1/74	**I Honestly Love You** Olivia Newton-John
9/70	**I Just Can't Help Believing** B.J. Thomas
17/57	**I Just Don't Know** Four Lads

POS/YR	RECORD TITLE/ARTIST
26/66	**I Just Don't Know What To Do With Myself** Dionne Warwick
17/61	**I Just Don't Understand** Ann-Margret
12/79	**I Just Fall In Love Again** Anne Murray
4/78	**I Just Wanna Stop** Gino Vannelli
1/77	**I Just Want To Be Your Everything** Andy Gibb
7/71	**I Just Want To Celebrate** Rare Earth
33/77	**I Just Want To Make Love To You** Foghat
4/82	**I Keep Forgettin' (Every Time You're Near)** Michael McDonald
	I Kissed You..see: ('Til)
14/65	**I Knew You When** Billy Joe Royal
19/79	**I Know A Heartache When I See One** Jennifer Warnes
3/65	**I Know A Place** Petula Clark
8/66 7/70 24/71	**(I Know) I'm Losing You** Temptations Rare Earth Rod Stewart
3/62	**I Know (You Don't Love Me No More)** Barbara George
19/62	**I Left My Heart In San Francisco** Tony Bennett
3/77	**I Like Dreamin'** Kenny Nolan
17/64	**I Like It** Gerry & The Pacemakers
2/61 7/65	**I Like It Like That** Chris Kenner Dave Clark Five
27/64	**I Like It Like That** Miracles
25/67	**I Like The Way** Tommy James & The Shondells

POS/YR	RECORD TITLE/ARTIST
37/77	**I Like To Do It** KC & The Sunshine Band
28/74	**I Like To Live The Love** B.B. King
8/57	**I Like Your Kind Of Love** Andy Williams
38/71	**I Likes To Do It** People's Choice
12/74	**I Love** Tom T. Hall
1/81	**I Love A Rainy Night** Eddie Rabbitt
5/61 9/68	**I Love How You Love Me** Paris Sisters Bobby Vinton
	I Love Lucy..see: Disco Lucy
5/76	**I Love Music (Part 1)** O'Jays
21/57	**I Love My Baby (My Baby Loves Me)** Jill Corey
24/74	**I Love My Friend** Charlie Rich
1/82	**I Love Rock 'N Roll** Joan Jett & The Blackhearts
5/78	**I Love The Nightlife (Disco 'Round)** Alicia Bridges
9/60	**I Love The Way You Love** Marv Johnson
12/81	**I Love You** Climax Blues Band
14/68	**I Love You** People
22/62	**I Love You** Volume's
37/78	**I Love You** Donna Summer
3/63	**I Love You Because** Al Martino
39/63	**(I Love You) Don't You Forget It** Perry Como
30/66	**I Love You Drops** Vic Dana
21/71	**I Love You For All Seasons** Fuzz

POS/YR	RECORD TITLE/ARTIST
17/58	**(I Love You) For Sentimental Reasons** Sam Cooke
40/60	**I Love You In The Same Old Way** Paul Anka
28/55	**I Love You Madly** Four Coins
9/64	**I Love You More And More Every Day** Al Martino
31/66	**I Love You 1000 Times** Platters
38/62	**I Love You The Way You Are** Bobby Vinton
37/81	**I Loved 'Em Every One** T.G. Sheppard
18/59	**I Loves You, Porgy** Nina Simone
10/81	**I Made It Through The Rain** Barry Manilow
18/67	**I Make A Fool Of Myself** Frankie Valli
37/68	**I Met Her In Church** Box Tops
34/57 33/59 34/65	**I Miss You So** Chris Connor Paul Anka Little Anthony & The Imperials
19/81	**I Missed Again** Phil Collins
31/65	**I Must Be Seeing Things** Gene Pitney
28/79	**I Need A Lover** John Cougar
22/66	**I Need Somebody** ? (Question Mark) & The Mysterians
25/76	**I Need To Be In Love** Carpenters
9/72	**I Need You** America
37/82	**I Need You** Paul Carrack
4/59	**I Need Your Love Tonight** Elvis Presley
37/81	**I Need Your Lovin'** Teena Marie

POS/YR	RECORD TITLE/ARTIST
20/62	**I Need Your Loving** Don Gardner & Dee Dee Ford
12/76	**I Never Cry** Alice Cooper
9/67	**I Never Loved A Man (The Way I Love You)** Aretha Franklin
11/59 18/75	**I Only Have Eyes For You** Flamingos Art Garfunkel
22/56	**I Only Know I Love You** Four Aces Featuring Al Alberts
12/64 12/76	**I Only Want To Be With You** Dusty Springfield Bay City Rollers
25/71	**I Play And Sing** Dawn
19/80	**I Pledge My Love** Peaches & Herb
9/82	**I Ran (So Far Away)** Flock Of Seagulls
39/82	**I Really Don't Need No Light** Jeffrey Osborne
18/60 22/66 21/71	**I Really Don't Want To Know** Tommy Edwards Ronnie Dove Elvis Presley
29/61	**I Really Love You** Stereos
5/62	**I Remember You** Frank Ifield
36/64	**I Rise, I Fall** Johnny Tillotson
5/66	**I Saw Her Again** Mamas & The Papas
14/64	**I Saw Her Standing There** Beatles
14/63	**I Saw Linda Yesterday** Dickey Lee
16/72	**I Saw The Light** Todd Rundgren
4/67 10/68	**I Say A Little Prayer** Dionne Warwick Aretha Franklin
4/67	**I Second That Emotion** Miracles

POS/YR	RECORD TITLE/ARTIST
26/66	**I See The Light** Five Americans
38/74	**I Shall Sing** Art Garfunkel
1/74	**I Shot The Sheriff** Eric Clapton
15/62	**I Sold My Heart To The Junkman** Blue-Belles
6/69	**I Started A Joke** Bee Gees
39/79	**I Still Have Dreams** Richie Furay
12/67	**I Take It Back** Sandy Posey
13/67	**I Thank The Lord For The Night Time** Neil Diamond
9/68 34/80	**I Thank You** Sam & Dave ZZ Top
1/70	**I Think I Love You** Partridge Family
4/67	**I Think We're Alone Now** Tommy James & The Shondells
23/69	**I Turned You On** Isley Brothers
9/61 36/65	**I Understand (Just How You Feel)** G-Clefs Freddie & The Dreamers
33/59	**I Waited Too Long** Lavern Baker
17/56	**I Walk The Line** Johnny Cash
14/63	**I Wanna Be Around** Tony Bennett
20/59	**I Wanna Be Loved** Ricky Nelson
16/72	**I Wanna Be Where You Are** Michael Jackson
16/73	**I Wanna Be With You** Raspberries
11/80	**I Wanna Be Your Lover** Prince
23/75	**I Wanna Dance Wit' Choo (Doo Dat Dance), Part 1** Disco Tex & The Sex-O-Lettes

POS/YR	RECORD TITLE/ARTIST
10/77	**I Wanna Get Next To You** Rose Royce
36/68	**I Wanna Live** Glen Campbell
9/64	**I Wanna Love Him So Bad** Jelly Beans
39/61	**(I Wanna) Love My Life Away** Gene Pitney
20/67 36/69	**(I Wanna) Testify** Parliaments Johnnie Taylor
21/61	**I Wanna Thank You** Bobby Rydell
11/65	**I Want Candy** Strangeloves
	I Want To ..also see: I Wanna & I Wanta'
1/60	**I Want To Be Wanted** Brenda Lee
23/65	**I Want To (Do Everything For You)** Joe Tex
36/66	**I Want To Go With You** Eddy Arnold
1/64	**I Want To Hold Your Hand** Beatles
28/63	**I Want To Stay Here** Steve & Eydie
34/70 38/70	**I Want To Take You Higher** Ike & Tina Turner Sly & The Family Stone
8/59	**I Want To Walk You Home** Fats Domino
15/76	**I Want You** Marvin Gaye
20/66	**I Want You** Bob Dylan
1/70	**I Want You Back** Jackson 5
37/81	**I Want You, I Need You** Chris Christian
1/56	**I Want You, I Need You, I Love You** Elvis Presley
14/55 18/55	**I Want You To Be My Baby** Georgia Gibbs Lillian Briggs

POS/YR	RECORD TITLE/ARTIST
13/56	**I Want You To Be My Girl** Frankie Lymon & The Teenagers
7/79	**I Want You To Want Me** Cheap Trick
19/79	**I Want You Tonight** Pablo Cruise
7/79	**I Want Your Love** Chic
15/75	**I Want'a Do Something Freaky To You** Leon Haywood
29/73	**I Was Checkin' Out She Was Checkin' In** Don Covay
20/67	**I Was Kaiser Bill's Batman** Whistling Jack Smith
10/79	**I Was Made For Dancin'** Leif Garrett
11/79	**I Was Made For Lovin' You** Kiss
2/67	**I Was Made To Love Her** Stevie Wonder
22/78	**I Was Only Joking** Rod Stewart
24/62	**I Was Such A Fool (To Fall In Love With You)** Connie Francis
19/56	**I Was The One** Elvis Presley
19/66	**(I Washed My Hands In) Muddy Water** Johnny Rivers
29/63 14/70 40/79	**I (Who Have Nothing)** Ben E. King Tom Jones Sylvester
10/65	**I Will** Dean Martin
22/68	**I Will Always Think About You** New Colony Six
30/78	**I Will Be In Love With You** Livingston Taylor
1/63	**I Will Follow Him** Little Peggy March
29/78	**I Will Still Love You** Stonebolt

POS/YR	RECORD TITLE/ARTIST
1/79	**I Will Survive** Gloria Gaynor
1/77	**I Wish** Stevie Wonder
32/63	**I Wish I Were A Princess** Little Peggy March
4/68	**I Wish It Would Rain** Temptations
16/62	**I Wish That We Were Married** Ronnie & The Hi-Lites
28/64	**I Wish You Love** Gloria Lynne
13/71	**I Woke Up In Love This Morning** Partridge Family
11/74	**I Won't Last A Day Without You** Carpenters
25/63	**I Wonder** Brenda Lee
8/68	**I Wonder What She's Doing Tonight** Tommy Boyce & Bobby Hart
21/63	**I Wonder What She's Doing Tonight** Barry & The Tamerlanes
22/58	**I Wonder Why** Dion & The Belmonts
20/82	**I Wouldn't Have Missed It For The World** Ronnie Milsap
22/56	**I Wouldn't Know Where To Begin** Eddy Arnold
36/77	**I Wouldn't Want To Be Like You** Alan Parsons Project
1/76	**I Write The Songs** Barry Manilow
7/72 13/72	**I'd Like To Teach The World To Sing (In Perfect Harmony)** New Seekers Hillside Singers
40/71	**I'd Love To Change The World** Ten Years After
2/72	**I'd Love You To Want Me** Lobo
38/79	**I'd Rather Leave While I'm In Love** Rita Coolidge
2/76	**I'd Really Love To See You Tonight** England Dan & John Ford Coley

POS/YR	RECORD TITLE/ARTIST
15/69	**I'd Wait A Million Years** Grass Roots
36/73	**I'll Always Love My Mama (Part 1)** Intruders
35/65	**I'll Always Love You** Spinners
3/72	**I'll Be Around** Spinners
8/65	**I'll Be Doggone** Marvin Gaye
3/76	**I'll Be Good To You** Brothers Johnson
4/56	**I'll Be Home** Pat Boone
33/64	**I'll Be In Trouble** Temptations
20/59	**I'll Be Satisfied** Jackie Wilson
36/74	**I'll Be The Other Woman** Soul Children
1/70	**I'll Be There** Jackson 5
12/61	**I'll Be There** Damita Jo
14/65	**I'll Be There** Gerry & The Pacemakers
31/59	**(I'll Be With You In) Apple Blossom Time** Tab Hunter
40/73	**I'll Be Your Shelter (In Time Of Storm)** Luther Ingram
18/58	**I'll Come Running Back To You** Sam Cooke
25/64	**I'll Cry Instead** Beatles
40/75	**I'll Do For You Anything You Want Me To** Barry White
9/74	**I'll Have To Say I Love You In A Song** Jim Croce
34/65	**I'll Keep Holding On** Marvelettes
30/64	**I'll Keep You Satisfied** Billy J. Kramer

POS/YR	RECORD TITLE/ARTIST
21/65	**I'll Make All Your Dreams Come True** Ronnie Dove
9/71	**I'll Meet You Halfway** Partridge Family
14/62	**I'll Never Dance Again** Bobby Rydell
6/69	**I'll Never Fall In Love Again** Tom Jones
6/70	**I'll Never Fall In Love Again** Dionne Warwick
4/65	**I'll Never Find Another You** Seekers
5/79	**I'll Never Love This Way Again** Dionne Warwick
24/57	**I'll Never Say "Never Again" Again** Dinah Shore
25/61	**I'll Never Smile Again** Platters
13/55	**I'll Never Stop Loving You** Doris Day
18/75	**I'll Play For You** Seals & Crofts
23/57	**I'll Remember Today** Patti Page
34/58	**I'll Remember Tonight** Pat Boone
22/60	**I'll Save The Last Dance For You** Damita Jo
32/62	**I'll See You In My Dreams** Pat Boone
39/67	**I'll Take Care Of Your Cares** Frankie Laine
30/66	**I'll Take Good Care Of You** Garnet Mimms
25/63	**I'll Take You Home** Drifters
1/72	**I'll Take You There** Staple Singers
25/64	**I'll Touch A Star** Terry Stafford
40/67	**I'll Try Anything** Dusty Springfield

Terry Gilkyson wrote Frankie Laine's smash, "The Cry Of The Wild Goose" and performed with the Weavers on their biggest hit, "On Top Of Old Smoky," before reaching the top 10 solo with "Marianne."

The Go-Go's. In the grand girl groups tradition, the Go-Go's write their own songs, play their own instruments, select their own cover art . . . You mean girl groups never used to do those things?

Daryl Hall and John Oates are versatility personified: the pair participated in writing all their top 10 hits, and produced six of them, too.

Rolf Harris. Winning an Australian TV talent show, Rolf Harris was encouraged to give up teaching and sail to England, from where he gave the world such Down Under ditties as "Sun Arise" and "Tie Me Kangaroo Down Sport."

Brian Hyland. After his early '60s hits, Brian Hyland returned to the top 10 in 1970 with a Del Shannon-produced version of Curtis Mayfield's "Gypsy Woman."

Michael Jackson must be the only artist in chart history to reach the summit with a song about a rat. "Ben" was from the rodent movie of the same name.

Jan & Dean. "We started a band as a way to meet chicks," reminisced Dean Torrence of Jan & Dean not long ago. "Boy, did we stink."

Billy Joel backing the Shangri-Las? Some say that as a teenager, Joel worked briefly for producer George "Shadow" Morton and laid down a piano track that was used for one of the girl group's recordings.

Tom Jones was once support act for a certain Mandy Rice-Davies, a lady whose charms led to the downfall of a British cabinet minister in an early '60s sex scandal.

K.C. and the Sunshine Band. Debby Boone's "You Light Up My Life" was one of two records that kept K.C. and the Sunshine Band from taking their fifth No. 1 in two years with "Keep It Comin' Love." How would *you* feel about that?

Frankie Laine. It sounds unlikely, but Frankie Laine recorded the original version of "I'm Gonna Be Strong," the Barry Mann/Cynthia Weil song that was a '64 smash for Gene Pitney. As a B side, no less.

Steve Lawrence. Drafted by the military in 1958, Steve Lawrence was assigned as official vocalist of the Army Band at Fort Myer, Virginia, and used extensively in Army recruiting and U.S. Bonds programs. That's showbiz.

POS/YR	RECORD TITLE/ARTIST
	I'll Try Something New
39/62	Miracles
25/69	Supremes & Temptations
	I'll Wait For You
15/58	Frankie Avalon
	I'm A Believer
1/67	Monkees
	I'm A Better Man
38/69	Engelbert Humperdinck
	I'm A Fool
17/65	Dino Desi & Billy
	I'm A Fool To Care
24/61	Joe Barry
	I'm A Greedy Man (Part 1)
35/71	James Brown
	I'm A Happy Man
36/65	Jive Five Featuring Eugene Pitt
	I'm A Hog For You
38/59	Coasters
	I'm A Man
10/67	Spencer Davis Group
F/71	Chicago
	I'm A Man
17/65	Yardbirds
	I'm A Man
31/59	Fabian
	I'm A Midnight Mover
24/68	Wilson Pickett
	(I'm A) Road Runner
20/66	Jr. Walker & The All Stars
	I'm A Telling You
25/61	Jerry Butler
	I'm A Train
31/74	Albert Hammond
	I'm A Woman
12/75	Maria Muldaur
	I'm Alive
16/80	Electric Light Orchestra
	I'm Almost Ready
34/80	Pure Prairie League
	I'm Alright
7/80	Kenny Loggins
	(I'm Always Hearing) Wedding Bells
20/55	Eddie Fisher

POS/YR	RECORD TITLE/ARTIST
	I'm Available
9/57	Margie Rayburn
	I'm Blue (The Gong-Gong Song)
19/62	Ikettes
	I'm Comin' Home
40/71	Tommy James
	I'm Comin' Home, Cindy
39/66	Trini Lopez
	I'm Comin' On Back To You
19/61	Jackie Wilson
	I'm Coming Home
18/74	Spinners
	I'm Coming Out
5/80	Diana Ross
	I'm Crying
19/64	Animals
	I'm Doin' Fine Now
17/73	New York City
	I'm Easy
17/76	Keith Carradine
	I'm Every Woman
21/78	Chaka Khan
	I'm Free
37/69	Who
	(I'm Gettin') ..see: Nuttin' For Xmas
	I'm Gettin' Better
37/60	Jim Reeves
	I'm Gonna Be A Wheel Some Day
17/59	Fats Domino
	I'm Gonna Be Strong
9/64	Gene Pitney
	I'm Gonna Be Warm This Winter
18/63	Connie Francis
	I'm Gonna Get Married
3/59	Lloyd Price
	I'm Gonna Knock On Your Door
12/61	Eddie Hodges
	I'm Gonna Let My Heart Do The Walking
40/76	Supremes
	I'm Gonna Love You Just A Little More Baby
3/73	Barry White

POS/YR	RECORD TITLE/ARTIST
26/68	**I'm Gonna Make You Love Me** Madeline Bell
2/69	Supremes & Temptations
10/69	**I'm Gonna Make You Mine** Lou Christie
3/57	**I'm Gonna Sit Right Down And Write Myself A Letter** Billy Williams
28/78	**I'm Gonna Take Care Of Everything** Rubicon
27/80	**I'm Happy That Love Has Found You** Jimmy Hall
1/65	**I'm Henry VIII, I Am** Herman's Hermits
27/61	**I'm Hurtin'** Roy Orbison
19/74	**I'm In Love** Aretha Franklin
40/81	**I'm In Love** Evelyn King
3/56	**I'm In Love Again** Fats Domino
38/56	Fontane Sisters
38/61	**I'm In The Mood For Love** Chimes
2/77	**I'm In You** Peter Frampton
13/64	**I'm Into Something Good** Herman's Hermits
38/64	Earl-Jean
12/73	**I'm Just A Singer (In A Rock And Roll Band)** Moody Blues
33/61	**I'm Learning About Love** Brenda Lee
36/71	**I'm Leavin'** Elvis Presley
1/63	**I'm Leaving It Up To You** Dale & Grace
4/74	Donny & Marie Osmond
10/69	**I'm Livin' In Shame** Supremes
	I'm Losing You..see: (I Know)
40/59	**I'm Movin' On** Ray Charles

POS/YR	RECORD TITLE/ARTIST
37/73	**I'm Never Gonna Be Alone Anymore** Cornelius Brothers & Sister Rose
36/59	**I'm Never Gonna Tell** Jimmie Rodgers
27/60	**I'm Not Afraid** Ricky Nelson
14/78	**I'm Not Gonna Let It Bother Me Tonight** Atlanta Rhythm Section
2/75	**I'm Not In Love** 10cc
4/75	**I'm Not Lisa** Jessi Colter
34/70	**I'm Not My Brothers Keeper** Flaming Ember
20/67	**(I'm Not Your) Steppin' Stone** Monkees
16/75	**I'm On Fire** Dwight Twilley Band
26/75	**I'm On Fire** 5000 Volts
15/64	**I'm On The Outside (Looking In)** Little Anthony & The Imperials
16/59	**I'm Ready** Fats Domino
9/66	**I'm Ready For Love** Martha & The Vandellas
30/82	**I'm So Excited** Pointer Sisters
8/66	**I'm So Lonesome I Could Cry** B.J. Thomas
14/64	**I'm So Proud** Impressions
1/60	**I'm Sorry** Brenda Lee
1/75	**I'm Sorry** John Denver
11/57	**I'm Sorry** Platters
36/58	**I'm Sorry I Made You Cry** Connie Francis
14/57	**I'm Stickin' With You** Jimmy Bowen with the Rhythm Orchids
3/72	**I'm Still In Love With You** Al Green

POS/YR	RECORD TITLE/ARTIST
10/72	**I'm Stone In Love With You** Stylistics
1/65	**I'm Telling You Now** Freddie & The Dreamers
38/62	**(I'm The Girl On) Wolverton Mountain** Jo Ann Campbell
	I'm The One Who Loves You..see: **(Remember Me)**
	I'm The One You Need..see: (Come **'Round Here)**
27/57	**I'm Waiting Just For You** Pat Boone
4/57 17/57	**I'm Walkin'** Fats Domino Ricky Nelson
12/67	**I'm Wondering** Stevie Wonder
1/77	**I'm Your Boogie Man** KC & The Sunshine Band
6/66	**I'm Your Puppet** James & Bobby Purify
11/65	**I'm Yours** Elvis Presley
33/59	**I've Been Around** Fats Domino
35/69	**I've Been Hurt** Bill Deal & The Rhondels
27/72	**I've Been Lonely For So Long** Frederick Knight
16/67	**I've Been Lonely Too Long** Rascals
21/65	**I've Been Loving You Too Long (To Stop** **Now)** Otis Redding
9/74	**(I've Been) Searchin' So Long** Chicago
34/75	**I've Been This Way Before** Neil Diamond
28/59	**I've Come Of Age** Billy Storm
8/81	**I've Done Everything For You** Rick Springfield
5/71	**I've Found Someone Of My Own** Free Movement

POS/YR	RECORD TITLE/ARTIST
29/76	**I've Got A Feeling (We'll Be Seeing Each** **Other Again)** Al Wilson
39/74	**I've Got A Thing About You Baby** Elvis Presley
25/65	**I've Got A Tiger By The Tail** Buck Owens & His Buckaroos
20/62	**I've Got A Woman, Part I** Jimmy McGriff
18/62	**I've Got Bonnie** Bobby Rydell
5/77	**I've Got Love On My Mind** Natalie Cole
33/64	**I've Got Sand In My Shoes** Drifters
32/73	**I've Got So Much To Give** Barry White
12/74	**I've Got The Music In Me** Kiki Dee
	I've Got To ..also see: I've Gotta
38/66	**I've Got To Be Somebody** Billy Joe Royal
4/74	**I've Got To Use My Imagination** Gladys Knight & The Pips
9/66	**I've Got You Under My Skin** Four Seasons
11/69	**I've Gotta Be Me** Sammy Davis Jr.
8/68	**I've Gotta Get A Message To You** Bee Gees
25/78	**I've Had Enough** Paul McCartney
6/59	**I've Had It** Bell Notes
32/70	**I've Lost You** Elvis Presley
4/80	**I've Loved You For A Long Time** **(medley)** Spinners
3/82	**I've Never Been To Me** Charlene
40/68	**I've Never Found A Girl (To Love Me** **Like You Do)** Eddie Floyd

POS/YR	RECORD TITLE/ARTIST
	I've Passed This Way Before
17/67	Jimmy Ruffin
	I've Told Every Little Star
3/61	Linda Scott
	If
4/71	Bread
	If A Man Answers
32/62	Bobby Darin
	If A Woman Answers (Hang Up The Phone)
35/62	Leroy Van Dyke
	If Dreams Came True
7/58	Pat Boone
	If Ever I See You Again
24/78	Roberta Flack
	If I Can Dream
12/69	Elvis Presley
	If I Can't Have You
1/78	Yvonne Elliman
	If I Could Build My Whole World Around You
10/68	Marvin Gaye & Tammi Terrell
	If I Could Reach You
10/72	5th Dimension
	If I Didn't Care
22/59	Connie Francis
30/61	Platters
	If I Ever Lose This Heaven
39/75	Average White Band
	If I Give My Heart To You
34/59	Kitty Kallen
	If I Had A Girl
31/60	Rod Lauren
	If I Had A Hammer
10/62	Peter Paul & Mary
3/63	Trini Lopez
	If I Had My Wish Tonight
36/82	David Lasley
	If I Loved You
23/65	Chad & Jeremy
	If I May
8/55	Nat King Cole
	If I Ruled The World
34/65	Tony Bennett

POS/YR	RECORD TITLE/ARTIST
	If I Said You Have A Beautiful Body Would You Hold It Against Me
39/79	Bellamy Brothers
	If I Were A Carpenter
8/66	Bobby Darin
20/68	Four Tops
36/70	Johnny Cash & June Carter
	If I Were Your Woman
9/71	Gladys Knight & The Pips
	(If Loving You Is Wrong) I Don't Want To Be Right
3/72	Luther Ingram
31/79	Barbara Mandrell
	If My Pillow Could Talk
23/63	Connie Francis
	If Not For You
25/71	Olivia Newton-John
	If The Love Fits Wear It
28/82	Leslie Pearl
	If There's A Hell..see: (Don't Worry)
	If We Make It Through December
28/74	Merle Haggard & The Strangers
	If You Can Want
11/68	Miracles
	If You Could Read My Mind
5/71	Gordon Lightfoot
	(If You Cry) True Love, True Love
33/59	Drifters
	If You Don't Know Me By Now
3/72	Harold Melvin & The Bluenotes
	If You Don't Want My Love
40/55	Jaye P. Morgan
	If You Gotta Make A Fool Of Somebody
22/62	James Ray
	If You Know What I Mean
11/76	Neil Diamond
	If You Leave Me Now
1/76	Chicago
	If You Leave Me Tonight I'll Cry
38/72	Jerry Wallace
	(If You Let Me Make Love To You Then) Why Can't I Touch You?
8/70	Ronnie Dyson
	If You Love Me (Let Me Know)
5/74	Olivia Newton-John

POS/YR	RECORD TITLE/ARTIST
37/63	**If You Need Me** Solomon Burke
8/71	**If You Really Love Me** Stevie Wonder
17/79	**If You Remember Me** Chris Thompson & Night
38/80	**If You Should Sail** Nielsen/Pearson
17/74	**If You Talk In Your Sleep** Elvis Presley
1/63	**If You Wanna Be Happy** Jimmy Soul
25/74	**If You Wanna Get To Heaven** Ozark Mountain Daredevils
37/79	**If You Want It** Niteflyte
12/73	**If You Want Me To Stay** Sly & The Family Stone
9/73	**If You're Ready (Come Go With Me)** Staple Singers
20/65	**Iko Iko** Dixie Cups
6/60	**Image Of A Girl** Safaris with The Phantom's Band
7/78	**Imaginary Lover** Atlanta Rhythm Section
3/71	**Imagine** John Lennon
22/75	**Immigrant** Neil Sedaka
16/71	**Immigrant Song** Led Zeppelin
36/72	**Immigration Man** David Crosby & Graham Nash
35/66	**Impossible Dream** Jack Jones
31/69	**In A Moment** Intrigues
27/56	**In A Shanty In Old Shanty Town** Somethin' Smith & The Redheads
11/80	**In America** Charlie Daniels Band
9/67	**In And Out Of Love** Supremes

POS/YR	RECORD TITLE/ARTIST
5/65 13/65	**In Crowd** Ramsey Lewis Dobie Gray
7/63	**In Dreams** Roy Orbison
10/60	**In My Little Corner Of The World** Anita Bryant
23/63	**In My Room** Beach Boys
19/81	**In The Air Tonight** Phil Collins
	In The Chapel In The Moonlight..see: Chapel
35/81	**In The Dark** Billy Squier
3/69	**In The Ghetto** Elvis Presley
33/67	**In The Heat Of The Night** Ray Charles
27/61	**In The Middle Of A Heartache** Wanda Jackson
9/57 23/57	**In The Middle Of An Island** Tony Bennett "Tennessee" Ernie Ford
11/56 20/56	**In The Middle Of The House** Vaughn Monroe Rusty Draper
21/65 30/73	**In The Midnight Hour** Wilson Pickett Cross Country
19/64	**In The Misty Moonlight** Jerry Wallace
4/59 40/77	**In The Mood** Ernie Fields Orchestra Henhouse Five Plus Too
3/79	**In The Navy** Village People
5/72	**In The Rain** Dramatics
24/56 38/60	**In The Still Of The Nite** Five Satins Dion & The Belmonts
3/70	**In The Summertime** Mungo Jerry

POS/YR	RECORD TITLE/ARTIST
1/69	**In The Year 2525 (Exordium & Terminus)** Zager & Evans
20/81	**In Your Letter** REO Speedwagon
30/68	**In-A-Gadda-Da-Vida** Iron Butterfly
1/67	**Incense And Peppermints** Strawberry Alarm Clock
33/67	**Indescribably Blue** Elvis Presley
5/69	**Indian Giver** 1910 Fruitgum Co.
10/68	**Indian Lake** Cowsills
20/68 1/71	**Indian Reservation (The Lament Of The Cherokee Reservation Indian)** Don Fardon Paul Revere & The Raiders
5/70	**Indiana Wants Me** R. Dean Taylor
27/56 30/56	**Innamorata** Dean Martin Jerry Vale
9/71	**Inner City Blues (Make Me Wanna Holler)** Marvin Gaye
32/76	**Inseparable** Natalie Cole
34/66	**Inside-Looking Out** Animals
3/70	**Instant Karma (We All Shine On)** John Lennon
29/78	**Instant Replay** Dan Hartman
11/80	**Into The Night** Benny Mardones
15/62	**Irresistible You** Bobby Darin
	Irving..see: Ballad Of
35/60	**Is A Blue Bird Blue** Conway Twitty
34/69	**Is It Something You've Got** Tyrone Davis

POS/YR	RECORD TITLE/ARTIST
17/64	**Is It True** Brenda Lee
15/81	**Is It You** Lee Ritenour
21/79	**Is She Really Going Out With Him?** Joe Jackson
11/69	**Is That All There Is** Peggy Lee
31/60	**Is There Any Chance** Marty Robbins
1/75	**Island Girl** Elton John
25/57	**Island In The Sun** Harry Belafonte
37/82	**Island Of Lost Souls** Blondie
F/70	**Isn't It A Pity** George Harrison
13/77	**Isn't It Time** Babys
29/72	**Isn't Life Strange** Moody Blues
9/69	**Israelites** Desmond Dekker & The Aces
8/65	**It Ain't Me Babe** Turtles
13/59	**It Doesn't Matter Anymore** Buddy Holly
4/71	**It Don't Come Easy** Ringo Starr
10/70	**It Don't Matter To Me** Bread
29/64	**It Hurts Me** Elvis Presley
7/64	**It Hurts To Be In Love** Gene Pitney
23/56	**It Isn't Right** Platters
23/61	**It Keeps Rainin'** Fats Domino
3/62	**It Keeps Right On A-Hurtin'** Johnny Tillotson
37/77	**It Keeps You Runnin'** Doobie Brothers

POS/YR	RECORD TITLE/ARTIST
11/55	**It May Sound Silly** McGuire Sisters
22/62	**It Might As Well Rain Until September** Carole King
3/67	**It Must Be Him** Vikki Carr
32/79	**It Must Be Love** Alton McClain & Destiny
5/72	**It Never Rains In Southern California** Albert Hammond
38/60	**It Only Happened Yesterday** Jack Scott
11/56	**It Only Hurts For A Little While** Ames Brothers
10/75	**It Only Takes A Minute** Tavares
40/68	**It Should Have Been Me** Gladys Knight & The Pips
29/62	**It Started All Over Again** Brenda Lee
27/73	**It Sure Took A Long, Long Time** Lobo
14/67	**It Takes Two** Marvin Gaye & Kim Weston
20/66	**It Tears Me Up** Percy Sledge
28/66	**It Was A Very Good Year** Frank Sinatra
16/77	**It Was Almost Like A Song** Ronnie Milsap
11/59	**It Was I** Skip & Flip
37/77	**It's A Crazy World** Mac McAnally
3/78	**It's A Heartache** Bonnie Tyler
20/78	**It's A Laugh** Daryl Hall & John Oates
28/76	**It's A Long Way There** Little River Band
28/81	**It's A Love Thing** Whispers
8/66	**It's A Man's Man's Man's World** James Brown

POS/YR	RECORD TITLE/ARTIST
12/75	**It's A Miracle** Barry Manilow
32/70	**It's A New Day (Part 1 & Part 2)** James Brown
14/70	**It's A Shame** Spinners
7/55	**It's A Sin To Tell A Lie** Somethin' Smith & The Redheads
31/75	**It's All Down To Goodnight Vienna** Ringo Starr
1/58 25/64 24/70	**It's All In The Game** Tommy Edwards Cliff Richard Four Tops
26/64	**It's All Over Now** Rolling Stones
4/63	**It's All Right** Impressions
7/55 14/55 20/55 20/55	**It's Almost Tomorrow** Dream Weavers Featuring Wade Buff Jo Stafford David Carroll & His Orchestra Snooky Lanson
31/65	**It's Alright** Adam Faith
20/58	**(It's Been A Long Time) Pretty Baby** Gino & Gina
4/77	**It's Ecstasy When You Lay Down Next To Me** Barry White
30/69	**It's Getting Better** Mama Cass
12/72	**It's Going To Take Some Time** Carpenters
23/65	**It's Gonna Be Alright** Gerry & The Pacemakers
10/82	**It's Gonna Take A Miracle** Deniece Williams
14/61	**It's Gonna Work Out Fine** Ike & Tina Turner
18/65	**It's Growing** Temptations
10/71	**It's Impossible** Perry Como
	It's In His Kiss..see: Shoop Shoop Song

POS/YR	RECORD TITLE/ARTIST
3/59	**It's Just A Matter Of Time** Brook Benton
9/59	**It's Late** Ricky Nelson
23/65	**It's My Life** Animals
1/63	**It's My Party** Lesley Gore
4/60	**It's My Time To Cry** Paul Anka
9/81	**It's My Turn** Diana Ross
5/57	**It's Not For Me To Say** Johnny Mathis
10/65	**It's Not Unusual** Tom Jones
1/60 14/81	**It's Now Or Never** Elvis Presley John Schneider
23/67	**It's Now Winters Day** Tommy Roe
29/76	**It's O.K.** Beach Boys
20/72	**It's One Of Those Nights (Yes Love)** Partridge Family
31/66	**It's Only Love** Tommy James & The Shondells
1/58 10/70	**It's Only Make Believe** Conway Twitty Glen Campbell
16/74	**It's Only Rock 'N Roll (But I Like It)** Rolling Stones
9/64	**It's Over** Roy Orbison
37/66	**It's Over** Jimmie Rodgers
38/76	**It's Over** Boz Scaggs
11/82	**It's Raining Again** Supertramp
21/77	**It's Sad To Belong** England Dan & John Ford Coley
5/77	**It's So Easy** Linda Ronstadt

POS/YR	RECORD TITLE/ARTIST
1/80	**It's Still Rock And Roll To Me** Billy Joel
5/65 35/78	**It's The Same Old Song** Four Tops KC & The Sunshine Band
1/71	**It's Too Late** Carole King
23/66	**It's Too Late** Bobby Goldsboro
11/58	**It's Too Soon To Know** Pat Boone
6/63	**It's Up To You** Ricky Nelson
20/68	**It's Wonderful** Rascals
22/57	**It's You I Love** Fats Domino
33/78	**It's You That I Need** Enchantment
	It's You That I Need..see: (Loneliness Made Me Realize)
2/69	**It's Your Thing** Isley Brothers
25/56	**Italian Theme** Cyril Stapleton & His Orchestra
25/58	**Itchy Twitchy Feeling** Bobby Hendricks
16/68	**Itchycoo Park** Small Faces
1/60	**Itsy Bitsy Teenie Weenie Yellow Polkadot Bikini** Brian Hyland
2/56 6/56 11/56	**Ivory Tower** Cathy Carr Gale Storm Charms
18/57	**Ivy Rose** Perry Como

J

1/82	**Jack & Diane** John Cougar

POS/YR	RECORD TITLE/ARTIST
8/78	**Jack And Jill** Ray Parker Jr. & Raydio
3/75	**Jackie Blue** Ozark Mountain Daredevils
14/67	**Jackson** Nancy Sinatra & Lee Hazlewood
1/57	**Jailhouse Rock** Elvis Presley
29/62	**Jam - Part 1** Bobby Gregg & His Friends
8/69	**Jam Up Jelly Tight** Tommy Roe
14/56	**Jamaica Farewell** Harry Belafonte
30/61 16/73	**Jambalaya (On The Bayou)** Fats Domino Blue Ridge Rangers
17/62	**James (Hold The Ladder Steady)** Sue Thompson
30/62	**Jamie** Eddie Holland
14/80	**Jane** Jefferson Starship
4/64	**Java** Al Hirt
	Jaws..see: Theme From & Mr. Jaws
2/74	**Jazzman** Carole King
20/69	**Jealous Kind Of Fella** Garland Green
19/60	**Jealous Of You** Connie Francis
2/69	**Jean** Oliver
17/77	**Jeans On** David Dundas
8/58	**Jennie Lee** Jan & Arnie
40/68	**Jennifer Eccles** Hollies
26/68	**Jennifer Juniper** Donovan
36/70	**Jennifer Tomkins** Street People

POS/YR	RECORD TITLE/ARTIST
	Jenny ..see: 867-5309
10/57	**Jenny, Jenny** Little Richard
10/66	**Jenny Take A Ride!** Mitch Ryder & The Detroit Wheels
35/61	**Jeremiah Peabody's Poly Unsaturated Pills** Ray Stevens
7/65	**Jerk** Larks
11/80	**Jesse** Carly Simon
30/73	**Jesse** Roberta Flack
1/81	**Jessie's Girl** Rick Springfield
	Jesus Christ Superstar..see: Superstar
28/69	**Jesus Is A Soul Man** Lawrence Reynolds
35/73	**Jesus Is Just Alright** Doobie Brothers
7/74	**Jet** Paul McCartney
8/77	**Jet Airliner** Steve Miller Band
17/57 25/74	**Jim Dandy** Lavern Baker Black Oak Arkansas
33/73	**Jimmy Loves Mary-Anne** Looking Glass
10/67	**Jimmy Mack** Martha & The Vandellas
25/61	**Jimmy's Girl** Johnny Tillotson
6/57 35/58 36/60 21/61	**Jingle Bell Rock** Bobby Helms Bobby Helms Bobby Helms Bobby Rydell & Chubby Checker
10/70	**Jingle Jangle** Archies
1/75	**Jive Talkin'** Bee Gees
19/58	**Jo-Ann** Playmates

POS/YR	RECORD TITLE/ARTIST
17/80	**JoJo** Boz Scaggs
21/70	**Joanne** Michael Nesmith & The First National Band
28/71	**Jody's Got Your Girl And Gone** Johnnie Taylor
	John And Yoko..see: Ballad Of
1/62	**Johnny Angel** Shelley Fabares
8/58	**Johnny B. Goode** Chuck Berry
7/62	**Johnny Get Angry** Joanie Sommers
21/62	**Johnny Jingo** Hayley Mills
21/62	**Johnny Loves Me** Shelley Fabares
35/61	**Johnny Will** Pat Boone
17/72	**Join Together** Who
1/74	**Joker** Steve Miller Band
22/57 25/57	**Joker (That's What They Call Me)** Hilltoppers featuring Jimmy Sacca Billy Myles
20/66	**Joker Went Wild** Brian Hyland
4/65	**Jolly Green Giant** Kingsmen
39/81	**Jones Vs. Jones** Kool & The Gang
18/60	**Josephine** Bill Black's Combo
26/78	**Josie** Steely Dan
16/68	**Journey To The Center Of The Mind** Amboy Dukes
6/72	**Joy** Apollo 100
30/74	**Joy - Pt. 1** Isaac Hayes

POS/YR	RECORD TITLE/ARTIST
1/71	**Joy To The World** Three Dog Night
26/65	**Ju Ju Hand** Sam The Sham & The Pharaohs
22/58	**Judy** Frankie Vaughan
	Judy Blue Eyes..see: Suite
1/68	**Judy In Disguise (With Glasses)** John Fred & His Playboy Band
33/75	**Judy Mae** Boomer Castleman
5/63	**Judy's Turn To Cry** Lesley Gore
10/56	**Juke Box Baby** Perry Como
26/82	**Juke Box Hero** Foreigner
5/70	**Julie, Do Ya Love Me** Bobby Sherman
27/72	**Jump Into The Fire** Nilsson
28/60	**Jump Over** Freddy Cannon
24/82	**Jump To It** Aretha Franklin
3/68	**Jumpin' Jack Flash** Rolling Stones
21/57	**June Night** Jimmy Dorsey
4/74	**Jungle Boogie** Kool & The Gang
8/72	**Jungle Fever** Chakachas
23/77	**Jungle Love** Steve Miller Band
3/74	**Junior's Farm** Paul McCartney
9/76	**Junk Food Junkie** Larry Groce
37/61	**Jura (I Swear I Love You)** Les Paul & Mary Ford
4/58	**Just A Dream** Jimmy Clanton

POS/YR	RECORD TITLE/ARTIST
8/65	**Just A Little** Beau Brummels
40/60	**Just A Little** Brenda Lee
39/65	**Just A Little Bit** Roy Head
7/65	**Just A Little Bit Better** Herman's Hermits
23/75	**Just A Little Bit Of You** Michael Jackson
9/59	**Just A Little Too Much** Ricky Nelson
7/77	**Just A Song Before I Go** Crosby Stills & Nash
32/59 24/68	**Just As Much As Ever** Bob Beckham Bobby Vinton
7/59	**Just Ask Your Heart** Frankie Avalon
19/64	**Just Be True** Gene Chandler
29/57	**Just Because** Lloyd Price
8/57	**Just Between You And Me** Chordettes
21/81	**Just Between You And Me** April Wine
12/57	**Just Born (To Be Your Baby)** Perry Como
38/82	**Just Can't Win 'Em All** Stevie Woods
35/60	**Just Come Home** Hugo & Luigi
10/74	**Just Don't Want To Be Lonely** Main Ingredient
5/68	**Just Dropped In (To See What Condition My Condition Was In)** Kenny Rogers & The First Edition
20/61	**Just For Old Time's Sake** McGuire Sisters
18/59	**Just Keep It Up** Dee Clark
33/66	**Just Like A Woman** Bob Dylan

POS/YR	RECORD TITLE/ARTIST
11/66	**Just Like Me** Paul Revere & The Raiders
6/64	**(Just Like) Romeo & Juliet** Reflections
1/81	**(Just Like) Starting Over** John Lennon
26/58	**Just Married** Marty Robbins
1/71	**Just My Imagination (Running Away With Me)** Temptations
17/81	**Just Once** Quincy Jones Featuring James Ingram
9/65	**Just Once In My Life** Righteous Brothers
10/63	**Just One Look** Doris Troy
29/60	**Just One Time** Don Gibson
24/61	**Just Out Of Reach (Of My Two Open Arms)** Solomon Burke
11/77	**Just Remember I Love You** Firefall
40/71	**Just Seven Numbers (Can Straighten Out My Life)** Four Tops
39/81	**Just So Lonely** Get Wet
2/81	**Just The Two Of Us** Grover Washington Jr.
3/78	**Just The Way You Are** Billy Joel
7/76	**Just To Be Close To You** Commodores
26/57	**Just To Hold My Hand** Clyde McPhatter
30/75	**Just Too Many People** Melissa Manchester
2/56	**Just Walking In The Rain** Johnnie Ray
27/78	**Just What I Needed** Cars
4/79	**Just When I Needed You Most** Randy Vanwarmer

POS/YR	RECORD TITLE/ARTIST
20/65	**Just You** Sonny & Cher
4/73	**Just You 'N' Me** Chicago
27/76	**Just You And I** Melissa Manchester

K

POS/YR	RECORD TITLE/ARTIST
39/71	**K-Jee** Nite-Liters
24/56 35/56 38/56	**Ka-Ding-Dong** G-Clefs Diamonds Hilltoppers featuring Jimmy Sacca
1/59 23/63	**Kansas City** Wilbert Harrison Trini Lopez
31/65	**Kansas City Star** Roger Miller
16/58	**Kathy-O** Diamonds
16/69	**Keem-O-Sabe** Electric Indian
8/57	**Keep A Knockin'** Little Richard
2/77	**Keep It Comin' Love** KC & The Sunshine Band
37/76	**Keep Me Cryin'** Al Green
4/65	**Keep On Dancing** Gentrys
24/68	**Keep On Lovin' Me Honey** Marvin Gaye & Tammi Terrell
1/81	**Keep On Loving You** REO Speedwagon
10/64	**Keep On Pushing** Impressions
15/74	**Keep On Singing** Helen Reddy
10/74	**Keep On Smilin'** Wet Willie

POS/YR	RECORD TITLE/ARTIST
1/73	**Keep On Truckin' (Part 1)** Eddie Kendricks
9/65	**Keep Searchin' (We'll Follow The Sun)** Del Shannon
14/67	**Keep The Ball Rollin'** Jay & The Techniques
36/80	**Keep The Fire** Kenny Loggins
7/82	**Keep The Fire Burnin'** REO Speedwagon
	Keep Your Eyes On The Sparrow..see: Baretta's Theme
12/62	**Keep Your Hands Off My Baby** Little Eva
10/72	**Keeper Of The Castle** Four Tops
20/55	**Kentuckian Song** Hilltoppers featuring Jimmy Sacca
16/70	**Kentucky Rain** Elvis Presley
22/67 38/68	**Kentucky Woman** Neil Diamond Deep Purple
6/58	**Kewpie Doll** Perry Como
8/82	**Key Largo** Bertie Higgins
4/66	**Kicks** Paul Revere & The Raiders
7/60	**Kiddio** Brook Benton
25/82	**Kids In America** Kim Wilde
16/63	**Killer Joe** Rocky Fellers
12/75	**Killer Queen** Queen
28/81	**Killin' Time** Fred Knoblock & Susan Anton
1/73	**Killing Me Softly With His Song** Roberta Flack
30/77	**Killing Of Georgie (Part 1 & 2)** Rod Stewart

POS/YR	RECORD TITLE/ARTIST
1/67	**Kind Of A Drag** Buckinghams
17/63	**Kind Of Boy You Can't Forget** Raindrops
40/72	**King Heroin** James Brown
13/77	**King Is Gone** Ronnie McDowell
36/80	**King Of The Hill** `Oak
4/65	**King Of The Road** Roger Miller
30/62	**King Of The Whole Wide World** Elvis Presley
17/78	**King Tut** Steve Martin
31/74	**Kings Of The Party** Brownsville Station
21/72	**Kiss An Angel Good Mornin'** Charley Pride
1/76	**Kiss And Say Goodbye** Manhattans
25/65	**Kiss Away** Ronnie Dove
37/79	**Kiss In The Dark** Pink Lady
30/56	**Kiss Me Another** Georgia Gibbs
15/68	**Kiss Me Goodbye** Petula Clark
37/80	**Kiss Me In The Rain** Barbra Streisand
34/64	**Kiss Me Quick** Elvis Presley
29/64	**Kiss Me Sailor** Diane Renay
1/81	**Kiss On My List** Daryl Hall & John Oates
1/78	**Kiss You All Over** Exile
3/57	**Kisses Sweeter Than Wine** Jimmie Rodgers
12/64	**Kissin' Cousins** Elvis Presley

POS/YR	RECORD TITLE/ARTIST
35/61	**Kissin' On The Phone** Paul Anka
11/59	**Kissin' Time** Bobby Rydell
31/73	**Kissing My Love** Bill Withers
16/57	**Knee Deep In The Blues** Guy Mitchell
15/67	**Knight In Rusty Armour** Peter & Gordon
28/66 30/67 1/79	**Knock On Wood** Eddie Floyd Otis & Carla Amii Stewart
1/71	**Knock Three Times** Dawn
12/73	**Knockin' On Heaven's Door** Bob Dylan
14/77	**Knowing Me, Knowing You** Abba
2/55 6/55	**Ko Ko Mo (I Love You So)** Perry Como Crew-Cuts
2/73	**Kodachrome** Paul Simon
4/59	**Kookie, Kookie (Lend Me Your Comb)** Edward Byrnes
40/74	**Kung Fu** Curtis Mayfield
1/74	**Kung Fu Fighting** Carl Douglas

L

POS/YR	RECORD TITLE/ARTIST
22/65	**L-O-N-E-L-Y** Bobby Vinton
13/75	**L-O-V-E (Love)** Al Green
22/59	**La Bamba** Ritchie Valens
9/58	**La Dee Dah** Billy & Lillie

POS/YR	RECORD TITLE/ARTIST
9/69	**La La La (If I Had You)** Bobby Sherman
4/68	**La La Means I Love You** Delfonics
30/74	**La La Peace Song** Al Wilson
	La Mer..see: Beyond The Sea
20/58	**La Paloma** Billy Vaughn & His Orchestra
32/58	**La-Do-Dada** Dale Hawkins
8/80	**Ladies Night** Kool & The Gang
1/80	**Lady** Kenny Rogers
6/75	**Lady** Styx
10/79	**Lady** Little River Band
28/80	**Lady** Whispers
39/67	**Lady** Jack Jones
20/67	**Lady Bird** Nancy Sinatra & Lee Hazlewood
14/75	**Lady Blue** Leon Russell
6/66	**Lady Godiva** Peter & Gordon
24/66	**Lady Jane** Rolling Stones
24/78	**Lady Love** Lou Rawls
14/60	**Lady Luck** Lloyd Price
4/68	**Lady Madonna** Beatles
1/75	**Lady Marmalade** Labelle
2/68	**Lady Willpower** Gary Puckett & The Union Gap
8/81	**Lady (You Bring Me Up)** Commodores

POS/YR	RECORD TITLE/ARTIST
33/68	**Lalena** Donovan
	Lament Of Cherokee..see: Indian Reservation
29/66	**Land Of Milk And Honey** Vogues
30/65 6/66	**Land Of One Thousand Dances** Cannibal & The Headhunters Wilson Pickett
32/61	**Language Of Love** John D. Loudermilk
	Lara's Theme..see: Somewhere My Love
13/65	**Last Chance To Turn Around** Gene Pitney
21/76	**Last Child** Aerosmith
3/78	**Last Dance** Donna Summer
2/60 21/60	**Last Date** Floyd Cramer Lawrence Welk & His Orchestra
19/75	**Last Farewell** Roger Whittaker
18/75	**Last Game Of The Season (A Blind Man In The Bleachers)** David Geddes
2/64 34/74	**Last Kiss** J. Frank Wilson & The Cavaliers Wednesday
3/61	**Last Night** Mar-Keys
8/72	**(Last Night) I Didn't Get To Sleep At All** 5th Dimension
3/73	**Last Song** Edward Bear
9/65	**Last Time** Rolling Stones
14/74	**Last Time I Saw Him** Diana Ross
1/66	**Last Train To Clarksville** Monkees
39/80	**Last Train To London** Electric Light Orchestra
25/67	**Last Waltz** Engelbert Humperdinck

POS/YR	RECORD TITLE/ARTIST
40/66	**Last Word In Lonesome Is Me** Eddy Arnold
27/57	**Lasting Love** Sal Mineo
6/80	**Late In The Evening** Paul Simon
10/65	**Laugh At Me** Sonny
15/65	**Laugh, Laugh** Beau Brummels
10/69	**Laughing** Guess Who
15/63	**Laughing Boy** Mary Wells
1/75	**Laughter In The Rain** Neil Sedaka
14/65	**Laurie (Strange Things Happen)** Dickey Lee
3/59	**Lavender-Blue** Sammy Turner
	Laverne & Shirley Theme..see: Making Our Dreams Come True
11/70	**Lay A Little Lovin' On Me** Robin McNamara
6/70	**Lay Down (Candles In The Rain)** Melanie
3/78	**Lay Down Sally** Eric Clapton
16/56	**Lay Down Your Arms** Chordettes
7/69	**Lay Lady Lay** Bob Dylan
10/72	**Layla** Derek & The Dominos
14/67	**Lazy Day** Spanky & Our Gang
40/64	**Lazy Elsie Molly** Chubby Checker
12/58	**Lazy Mary (Luna Mezzo Mare)** Lou Monte
14/61	**Lazy River** Bobby Darin
21/58	**Lazy Summer Night** Four Preps

POS/YR	RECORD TITLE/ARTIST
1/79	**Le Freak** Chic
5/79	**Lead Me On** Maxine Nightingale
9/82	**Leader Of The Band** Dan Fogelberg
19/64	**Leader Of The Laundromat** Detergents
1/64	**Leader Of The Pack** Shangri-Las
25/62	**Leah** Roy Orbison
1/72	**Lean On Me** Bill Withers
9/66	**Leaning On The Lamp Post** Herman's Hermits
1/55	**Learnin' The Blues** Frank Sinatra
6/82	**Leather And Lace** Stevie Nicks
3/73	**Leave Me Alone (Ruby Red Dress)** Helen Reddy
21/73	**Leaving Me** Independents
1/69	**Leaving On A Jet Plane** Peter Paul & Mary
9/58	**Left Right Out Of Your Heart** Patti Page
	Legend Of Billy Jack..see: One Tin Soldier
31/80	**Legend Of Wooley Swamp** Charlie Daniels Band
35/62 20/65	**Lemon Tree** Peter Paul & Mary Trini Lopez
25/58	**Leroy** Jack Scott
31/68	**Les Bicyclettes De Belsize** Engelbert Humperdinck
34/68	**Lesson** Vikki Carr
3/76	**Let 'Em In** Paul McCartney

POS/YR	RECORD TITLE/ARTIST
	Let A Man Come In And Do The Popcorn (Parts 1 & 2)
21/69	James Brown
40/69	James Brown
	Let A Woman Be A Woman - Let A Man Be A Man
36/69	Dyke & The Blazers
	Let Her In
10/76	John Travolta
	Let It Be
1/70	Beatles
	Let It Be Me
7/60	Everly Brothers
5/64	Jerry Butler & Betty Everett
36/69	Glen Campbell & Bobbie Gentry
40/82	Willie Nelson
	Let It Out (Let It All Hang Out)
12/67	Hombres
	Let It Ride
23/74	Bachman-Turner Overdrive
	Let It Shine
30/76	Olivia Newton-John
	Let It Whip
5/82	Dazz Band
	Let Love Come Between Us
23/67	James & Bobby Purify
	Let Me
20/69	Paul Revere & The Raiders
	Let Me Be
29/65	Turtles
	Let Me Be The Clock
31/80	Smokey Robinson
	Let Me Be There
6/74	Olivia Newton-John
	Let Me Be Your Angel
21/80	Stacy Lattisaw
	(Let Me Be Your) Teddy Bear
1/57	Elvis Presley
	Let Me Belong To You
20/61	Brian Hyland
	Let Me Go
38/82	Ray Parker Jr.
	Let Me Go, Love
35/80	Nicolette Larson

POS/YR	RECORD TITLE/ARTIST
	Let Me Go, Lover!
1/55	Joan Weber
6/55	Teresa Brewer
8/55	Patti Page
17/55	Sunny Gale
	Let Me Go To Him
32/70	Dionne Warwick
	Let Me In
4/62	Sensations
	Let Me In
36/73	Osmonds
	Let Me Love You Tonight
10/80	Pure Prairie League
	Let Me Serenade You
17/73	Three Dog Night
	Let Me Tickle Your Fancy
18/82	Jermaine Jackson
	Let My Love Open The Door
9/80	Pete Townshend
	Let The Bells Keep Ringing
18/58	Paul Anka
	Let The Four Winds Blow
29/57	Roy Brown
15/61	Fats Domino
	Let The Good Times Roll
20/56	Shirley & Lee
22/67	Bunny Sigler
	Let The Little Girl Dance
7/60	Billy Bland
	Let The Music Play
32/76	Barry White
	Let The Sunshine In (medley)
1/69	5th Dimension
	Let Them..see: Let 'Em
	Let There Be Drums
7/61	Sandy Nelson
	Let Your Hair Down
27/74	Temptations
	Let Your Love Flow
1/76	Bellamy Brothers
	Let Your Love Go
28/71	Bread
	Let's All Chant
36/78	Michael Zager Band

POS/YR	RECORD TITLE/ARTIST
4/62	**Let's Dance** Chris Montez
1/75	**Let's Do It Again** Staple Singers
40/65	**Let's Do The Freddie** Chubby Checker
21/67	**Let's Fall In Love** Peaches & Herb
1/73	**Let's Get It On** Marvin Gaye
32/74	**Let's Get Married** Al Green
9/80	**Let's Get Serious** Jermaine Jackson
8/61	**Let's Get Together** Hayley Mills
	Let's Get Together..see: Get Together
14/79	**Let's Go** Cars
39/61	**Let's Go Again (Where We Went Last Night)** Hank Ballard & The Midnighters
31/66	**Let's Go Get Stoned** Ray Charles
6/60	**Let's Go, Let's Go, Let's Go** Hank Ballard & The Midnighters
19/62	**Let's Go (Pony)** Routers
26/63	**Let's Go Steady Again** Neil Sedaka
3/81	**Let's Groove** Earth Wind & Fire
3/65 32/82	**Let's Hang On!** Four Seasons Barry Manilow
37/60	**Let's Have A Party** Wanda Jackson
38/63	**Let's Kiss And Make Up** Bobby Vinton
20/63	**Let's Limbo Some More** Chubby Checker
8/67	**Let's Live For Today** Grass Roots

POS/YR	RECORD TITLE/ARTIST
35/75	**Let's Live Together** Road Apples
11/65	**Let's Lock The Door (And Throw Away The Key)** Jay & The Americans
35/73	**Let's Pretend** Raspberries
18/74	**Let's Put It All Together** Stylistics
20/66	**Let's Start All Over Again** Ronnie Dove
1/72	**Let's Stay Together** Al Green
31/74	**Let's Straighten It Out** Latimore
7/60	**Let's Think About Living** Bob Luman
20/63	**Let's Turkey Trot** Little Eva
8/61	**Let's Twist Again** Chubby Checker
26/70 32/70	**Let's Work Together** Canned Heat Wilbert Harrison
1/67 20/69 7/70	**Letter** Box Tops Arbors Joe Cocker
25/64	**Letter From Sherry** Dale Ward
19/62	**Letter Full Of Tears** Gladys Knight & The Pips
	Letter Song..see: S.Y.S.L.J.F.M.
25/58	**Letter To An Angel** Jimmy Clanton
33/73	**Letter To Myself** Chi-Lites
39/75	**Letting Go** Paul McCartney
24/72	**Levon** Elton John
7/71	**Liar** Three Dog Night
12/65	**Liar, Liar** Castaways

POS/YR	RECORD TITLE/ARTIST
	Liberty Valance..see: (Man Who Shot)
14/68	**Licking Stick - Licking Stick** James Brown
11/77	**Lido Shuffle** Boz Scaggs
13/62	**Lie To Me** Brook Benton
16/57	**Liechtensteiner Polka** Will Glahe & His Orchestra
20/66	**Lies** Knickerbockers
11/77	**Life In The Fast Lane** Eagles
8/74	**Life Is A Rock (But The Radio Rolled Me)** Reunion
34/81	**Life Of Illusion** Joe Walsh
12/78	**Life's Been Good** Joe Walsh
1/67 3/68	**Light My Fire** Doors Jose Feliciano
1/66	**Lightnin' Strikes** Lou Christie
24/67	**Lightning's Girl** Nancy Sinatra
11/67	**(Lights Went Out In) Massachusetts** Bee Gees
27/66	**Like A Baby** Len Barry
2/65	**Like A Rolling Stone** Bob Dylan
36/76	**Like A Sad Song** John Denver
40/78	**Like A Sunday In Salem (The Amos & Andy Song)** Gene Cotton
24/67	**Like An Old Time Movie** Scott McKenzie
38/61	**Like, Long Hair** Paul Revere & The Raiders
22/60	**Like Strangers** Everly Brothers

POS/YR	RECORD TITLE/ARTIST
17/68	**Like To Get To Know You** Spanky & Our Gang
2/66	**Lil' Red Riding Hood** Sam The Sham & The Pharaohs
2/62 40/62	**Limbo Rock** Chubby Checker Champs
28/63	**Linda** Jan & Dean
26/55 28/55	**Ling, Ting, Tong** Charms Five Keys
1/61 3/72	**Lion Sleeps Tonight** Tokens Robert John
17/57	**Lips Of Wine** Andy Williams
15/56	**Lipstick And Candy And Rubbersole Shoes** Julius LaRosa
5/59	**Lipstick On Your Collar** Connie Francis
1/56 19/56	**Lisbon Antigua** Nelson Riddle & His Orchestra Mitch Miller
3/66	**Listen People** Herman's Hermits
11/72	**Listen To The Music** Doobie Brothers
1/75	**Listen To What The Man Said** Paul McCartney
	Little ..also see: Lil'
16/68	**Little Arrows** Leapy Lee
21/63	**Little Band Of Gold** James Gilreath
2/67	**Little Bit Me, A Little Bit You** Monkees
11/76	**Little Bit More** Dr. Hook
2/67	**Little Bit O'soul** Music Explosion
16/65	**Little Bit Of Heaven** Ronnie Dove

POS/YR	RECORD TITLE/ARTIST
	Little Bit Of Soap
12/61	Jarmels
34/79	Nigel Olsson
	Little Bitty Girl
19/60	Bobby Rydell
	Little Bitty Pretty One
6/57	Thurston Harris
25/62	Clyde McPhatter
13/72	Jackson 5
	Little Bitty Tear
9/62	Burl Ives
	Little Black Book
29/62	Jimmy Dean
	Little Blue Man
17/58	Betty Johnson
	Little Boy Sad
17/61	Johnny Burnette
	Little Children
7/64	Billy J. Kramer
	Little Coco Palm
36/60	Jerry Wallace
	Little Darlin'
2/57	Diamonds
	Little Deuce Coupe
15/63	Beach Boys
	Little Devil
11/61	Neil Sedaka
	Little Diane
8/62	Dion
	Little Dipper
30/59	Mickey Mozart Quintet
	Little Drummer Boy
13/58	Harry Simeone Chorale
15/59	Harry Simeone Chorale
24/60	Harry Simeone Chorale
22/61	Harry Simeone Chorale
28/62	Harry Simeone Chorale
	Little Egypt (Ying-Yang)
23/61	Coasters
	Little Girl
8/66	Syndicate Of Sound
	Little Girl I Once Knew
20/65	Beach Boys
	Little Green Apples
2/68	O.C. Smith
39/68	Roger Miller

POS/YR	RECORD TITLE/ARTIST
	Little Green Bag
21/70	George Baker Selection
	Little Honda
9/64	Hondells
	Little In Love
17/81	Cliff Richard
	Little Jeannie
3/80	Elton John
	Little Latin Lupe Lu
17/66	Mitch Ryder & The Detroit Wheels
	Little Love Can Go A Long, Long Way
33/56	Dream Weavers Featuring Wade Buff
	Little Man
21/66	Sonny & Cher
	Little More Love
3/79	Olivia Newton-John
	Little Old Lady (From Pasadena)
3/64	Jan & Dean
	Little Ole Man (Uptight-Everything's Alright)
4/67	Bill Cosby
	Little Ole Wine Drinker, Me
38/67	Dean Martin
	Little Red Rented Rowboat
23/62	Joe Dowell
	Little Red Rooster
11/63	Sam Cooke
	Little Sandy Sleighfoot
32/57	Jimmy Dean
	Little Sister
5/61	Elvis Presley
	Little Space Girl
20/59	Jesse Lee Turner
	Little Star
1/58	Elegants
	Little Things
13/65	Bobby Goldsboro
	Little Things Mean A Lot
35/60	Joni James
	Little Town Flirt
12/63	Del Shannon
	Little White Lies
25/57	Betty Johnson

POS/YR	RECORD TITLE/ARTIST
3/73	**Little Willy** Sweet
3/69	**Little Woman** Bobby Sherman
2/73	**Live And Let Die** Paul McCartney
20/76	**Livin' For The Weekend** O'Jays
19/74	**Livin' For You** Al Green
40/77	**Livin' In The Life** Isley Brothers
15/79	**Livin' It Up (Friday Night)** Bell & James
13/76	**Livin' Thing** Electric Light Orchestra
22/63	**Living A Lie** Al Martino
37/75	**Living A Little, Laughing A Little** Spinners
30/59	**Living Doll** Cliff Richard
8/74	**Living For The City** Stevie Wonder
23/81	**Living In A Fantasy** Leo Sayer
22/72	**Living In A House Divided** Cher
11/72	**Living In The Past** Jethro Tull
6/81	**Living Inside Myself** Gino Vannelli
25/77	**Living Next Door To Alice** Smokie
32/73	**Living Together, Growing Together** 5th Dimension
37/75	**Lizzie And The Rainman** Tanya Tucker
14/68	**Lo Mucho Que Te Quiero (The More I Love You)** Rene & Rene
F/78	**Load-Out** Jackson Browne

POS/YR	RECORD TITLE/ARTIST
1/62 1/74	**Loco-Motion** Little Eva Grand Funk Railroad
12/63	**Loddy Lo** Chubby Checker
6/79	**Logical Song** Supertramp
9/70	**Lola** Kinks
2/58 20/58	**Lollipop** Chordettes Ronald & Ruby
39/78	**London Town** Paul McCartney
14/67	**(Loneliness Made Me Realize) It's You That I Need** Temptations
	Lonely ..also see: L-O-N-E-L-Y
6/60	**Lonely Blue Boy** Conway Twitty
1/59 F/72	**Lonely Boy** Paul Anka Donny Osmond
7/77	**Lonely Boy** Andrew Gold
6/62	**Lonely Bull** Herb Alpert & The Tijuana Brass
3/71	**Lonely Days** Bee Gees
24/59	**Lonely For You** Gary Stites
26/58	**Lonely Island** Sam Cooke
32/61	**Lonely Man** Elvis Presley
3/76	**Lonely Night (Angel Face)** Captain & Tennille
23/59	**Lonely One** Duane Eddy
5/75	**Lonely People** America
5/59	**Lonely Street** Andy Williams
39/63	**Lonely Surfer** Jack Nitzsche

Brenda Lee was discovered by country music's Red Foley via a talent contest, and appeared on his "Ozark Jubilee" show in 1956. Four years later, she was riding high with her first (and not exactly country) top 40 hit, "Sweet Nothin's."

John Lennon. October 9, 1980, saw John Lennon entering his forties in good spirits and looking forward to the release within a couple of weeks of his "comback" single, "(Just Like) Starting Over."

The Lovin' Spoonful had seven Top Ten hits in the years 1965 and 1966, but the group's leader, John Sebastian, achieved his greatest success ten years later, with his solo effort "Welcome Back," theme to the television show "Welcome Back, Kotter."

Barry Manilow worked at New York's Continental Baths in 1972, where he met Bette Midler. He became her pianist and musical director . . . and lived.

Johnny Mathis. Despite a remarkable chart career that began in 1956, Johnny Mathis had to wait more than 20 years for his second No. 1 song—and that was a duet: "Too Much, Too Little, Too Late" with Deniece Williams.

Jimmy McGriff. It was a the wedding of Jimmy McGriff's sister that he was hooked on the lectronic organ. Richard "Groove" Holmes was playing at the occasion, and invited McGriff to check out his Hammond. James never looked back.

Paul McCartney. When Beatlemania began, the group was always naming Motown artists as their personal favorites. Some 19 years later, Paul got around to recording with one of them, Stevie Wonder.

Bob & Doug McKenzie. Humor on vinyl is a difficult pursuit, and Canada's McKenzie brothers (Rick Moranis and Dave Thomas) have yet to reach the dizzying chart heights attained by Allan Sherman's "Hello Muddah, Hello Fadduh!" or Staff/Sergeant Barry Sadler's "The Ballad Of The Green Berets."

Don McLean. Several years after his "American Pie" mega-hit, Don McLean updated Roy Orbison's "Crying"—only to have it criticized (and unreleased) by his record company. Subsequent success abroad (the song went to No. 1 in the U.K.) enabled Don to secure a deal with another American label.

Sergio Mendes & Brazil '66. One of the singers in Sergio Mendes & Brasil '66 married the boss of the record label to which the group was signed. That was Lani Hall, Herb Alpert, and A&M Records respectively.

Hayley Mills. Actress Hayley Mills' only top 10 hit came from the movie soundtrack of *The Parent Trap,* in which she played the part of twin sisters. Cute Disney idea.

Rick Nelson. His career as a teen idol was demolished by the British Invasion of 1964, but he and several contemporaries (including Dion, Neil Sedaka and Brian Hyland) managed comebacks a few years later. In Rick's case, it was with the self-penned, self-produced "Garden Party."

POS/YR	RECORD TITLE/ARTIST
7/59	**Lonely Teardrops** Jackie Wilson
12/60	**Lonely Teenager** Dion
22/60	**Lonely Weekends** Charlie Rich
6/79	**Lonesome Loser** Little River Band
7/58	**Lonesome Town** Ricky Nelson
31/71	**Long Ago And Far Away** James Taylor
1/70	**Long And Winding Road** Beatles
2/72	**Long Cool Woman (In A Black Dress)** Hollies
26/72	**Long Dark Road** Hollies
38/72	**Long Haired Lover From Liverpool** Little Jimmy Osmond
33/66	**Long Live Our Love** Shangri-Las
17/65	**Long Lonely Nights** Bobby Vinton
20/70	**Long Lonesome Highway** Michael Parks
25/70	**Long Long Time** Linda Ronstadt
20/78	**Long, Long Way From Home** Foreigner
	(Long Nights)..see: Blue Collar Man
8/80	**Long Run** Eagles
9/75	**Long Tall Glasses (I Can Dance)** Leo Sayer
6/56 8/56	**Long Tall Sally** Little Richard Pat Boone
22/77	**Long Time** Boston
8/73	**Long Train Runnin'** Doobie Brothers
2/80	**Longer** Dan Fogelberg

POS/YR	RECORD TITLE/ARTIST
6/55	**Longest Walk** Jaye P. Morgan
5/74	**Longfellow Serenade** Neil Diamond
39/75	**Look At Me (I'm In Love)** Moments
16/60 19/60 26/60 29/60	**Look For A Star** Garry Miles Billy Vaughn & His Orchestra Garry Mills Deane Hawley
36/57	**Look Homeward, Angel** Johnnie Ray
14/61	**Look In My Eyes** Chantels
11/75	**Look In My Eyes Pretty Woman** Dawn
27/65	**Look Of Love** Lesley Gore
22/67 4/68	**Look Of Love** Dusty Springfield Sergio Mendes & Brasil '66
32/66	**Look Through Any Window** Hollies
24/66	**Look Through My Window** Mamas & The Papas
14/70	**Look What They've Done To My Song Ma** New Seekers
4/72	**Look What You Done For Me** Al Green
32/67	**Look What You've Done** Pozo-Seco Singers
14/80	**Look What You've Done To Me** Boz Scaggs
39/71 10/74	**Lookin' For A Love** J. Geils Band Bobby Womack
5/80	**Lookin' For Love** Johnny Lee
2/70	**Lookin' Out My Back Door** Creedence Clearwater Revival
16/72	**Lookin' Through The Windows** Jackson 5
5/58	**Looking Back** Nat King Cole

POS/YR	RECORD TITLE/ARTIST
29/76	**Looking For Space** John Denver
28/65 39/73	**Looking Through The Eyes Of Love** Gene Pitney Partridge Family
1/77	**Looks Like We Made It** Barry Manilow
4/63	**Loop De Loop** Johnny Thunder
4/74	**Lord's Prayer** Sister Janet Mead
27/76	**Lorelei** Styx
6/63	**Losing You** Brenda Lee
34/80	**Lost Her In The Sun** John Stewart
3/80	**Lost In Love** Air Supply
35/61	**Lost Love** H.B. Barnum
9/77	**Lost Without Your Love** Bread
8/79	**Lotta Love** Nicolette Larson
13/57	**Lotta Lovin'** Gene Vincent & His Blue Caps
2/63 30/66	**Louie Louie** Kingsmen Sandpipers
	Love ..also see: L-O-V-E
5/55 20/55	**Love And Marriage** Frank Sinatra Dinah Shore
20/76 18/79	**Love Ballad** L.T.D. George Benson
	Love Being Your Fool..see: **(Shu-Doo-Pa-Poo-Poop)**
25/67	**Love Bug Leave My Heart Alone** Martha & The Vandellas
10/62	**Love Came To Me** Dion
2/69	**Love (Can Make You Happy)** Mercy

POS/YR	RECORD TITLE/ARTIST
1/68	**Love Child** Supremes
17/82	**Love Come Down** Evelyn King
32/79	**Love Don't Live Here Anymore** Rose Royce
15/74	**Love Don't Love Nobody - Pt. I** Spinners
15/67	**Love Eyes** Nancy Sinatra
30/76	**Love Fire** Jigsaw
5/70	**Love Grows (Where My Rosemary Goes)** Edison Lighthouse
1/76	**Love Hangover** Diana Ross
11/71	**Love Her Madly** Doors
8/76	**Love Hurts** Nazareth
7/73	**Love I Lost (Part 1)** Harold Melvin & The Bluenotes
20/67	**Love I Saw In You Was Just A Mirage** Miracles
36/77	**Love In 'C' Minor (Part 1)** Cerrone
15/82	**Love In The First Degree** Alabama
16/76	**Love In The Shadows** Neil Sedaka
10/57	**Love Is A Golden Ring** Frankie Laine
13/66	**Love Is A Hurtin' Thing** Lou Rawls
1/55 26/55	**Love Is A Many-Splendored Thing** Four Aces Featuring Al Alberts Don Cornell
F/75	**Love Is A Rose** Linda Ronstadt
2/76	**Love Is Alive** Gary Wright
7/68	**Love Is All Around** Troggs

POS/YR	RECORD TITLE/ARTIST
15/58	**Love Is All We Need** Tommy Edwards
20/82	**Love Is Alright Tonite** Rick Springfield
1/68 22/69	**Love Is Blue** Paul Mauriat & His Orchestra Dells
1/67	**Love Is Here And Now You're Gone** Supremes
10/82	**Love Is In Control (Finger On The Trigger)** Donna Summer
7/78	**Love Is In The Air** John Paul Young
26/68	**(Love Is Like A) Baseball Game** Intruders
37/82	**Love Is Like A Rock** Donnie Iris
9/66	**Love Is Like An Itching In My Heart** Supremes
8/78	**Love Is Like Oxygen** Sweet
11/57 13/67	**Love Is Strange** Mickey & Sylvia Peaches & Herb
10/79	**Love Is The Answer** England Dan & John Ford Coley
30/76	**Love Is The Drug** Roxy Music
7/56	**(Love Is) The Tender Trap** Frank Sinatra
1/78	**(Love Is) Thicker Than Water** Andy Gibb
16/73	**Love Jones** Brighter Side Of Darkness
16/70	**Love Land** Charles Wright & The Watts 103rd Street Rhythm Band
5/62 19/66	**Love Letters** Ketty Lester Elvis Presley
1/57	**Love Letters In The Sand** Pat Boone
30/56 30/56	**Love, Love, Love** Clovers Diamonds

POS/YR	RECORD TITLE/ARTIST
1/76	**Love Machine (Part 1)** Miracles
15/68	**Love Makes A Woman** Barbara Acklin
26/63	**Love (Makes The World Go 'Round)** Paul Anka
33/58	**Love Makes The World Go 'Round** Perry Como
11/66	**Love Makes The World Go Round** Deon Jackson
2/56	**Love Me** Elvis Presley
14/76	**Love Me** Yvonne Elliman
1/64	**Love Me Do** Beatles
10/74	**Love Me For A Reason** Osmonds
24/57 25/57	**Love Me Forever** Eydie Gorme Four Esquires
19/55 20/55	**Love Me Or Leave Me** Lena Horne Sammy Davis Jr.
1/56 21/62 40/67	**Love Me Tender** Elvis Presley Richard Chamberlain Percy Sledge
11/57	**Love Me To Pieces** Jill Corey
22/82	**Love Me Tomorrow** Chicago
13/69	**Love Me Tonight** Tom Jones
25/68	**Love Me Two Times** Doors
12/62	**Love Me Warm And Tender** Paul Anka
3/64 38/66	**Love Me With All Your Heart** Ray Charles Singers Bachelors
39/71	**Love Means (You Never Have To Say You're Sorry)** Sounds Of Sunshine
	Love My Life Away..see: (I Wanna)

POS/YR	RECORD TITLE/ARTIST
40/58	**Love Of My Life** Everly Brothers
21/63	**Love Of My Man** Theola Kilgore
3/70 26/81	**Love On A Two-Way Street** Moments Stacy Lattisaw
2/81	**Love On The Rocks** Neil Diamond
36/76	**Love Or Leave** Spinners
6/70 40/82	**Love Or Let Me Be Lonely** Friends Of Distinction Paul Davis
32/78	**Love Or Something Like It** Kenny Rogers
34/79	**Love Pains** Yvonne Elliman
37/82	**Love Plus One** Haircut One Hundred
23/59 3/65	**Love Potion Number Nine** Clovers Searchers
22/68	**Love Power** Sandpebbles
22/76	**Love Really Hurts Without You** Billy Ocean
1/76	**Love Rollercoaster** Ohio Players
31/63	**Love She Can Count On** Miracles
40/63	**Love So Fine** Chiffons
3/76	**Love So Right** Bee Gees
12/74	**Love Song** Anne Murray
38/80	**Love Stinks** J. Geils Band
	Love Story..see: Theme From
11/79	**Love Takes Time** Orleans
14/71 18/71	**Love The One You're With** Stephen Stills Isley Brothers

POS/YR	RECORD TITLE/ARTIST
14/80	**Love The World Away** Kenny Rogers
21/78	**Love Theme From Eyes Of Laura Mars (Prisoner)** Barbra Streisand
34/72	**Love Theme From Godfather (Speak Softly Love)** Andy Williams
37/61	**Love Theme From One Eyed Jacks** Ferrante & Teicher
	Love Theme From One On One..see: My Fair Share
1/69	**Love Theme From Romeo & Juliet** Henry Mancini
2/76	**Love To Love You Baby** Donna Summer
1/73	**Love Train** O'Jays
30/60	**Love Walked In** Dinah Washington
30/71	**Love We Had (Stays On My Mind)** Dells
6/78	**Love Will Find A Way** Pablo Cruise
40/69	**Love Will Find A Way** Jackie DeShannon
1/75	**Love Will Keep Us Together** Captain & Tennille
13/82	**Love Will Turn You Around** Kenny Rogers
5/75	**Love Won't Let Me Wait** Major Harris
1/79	**Love You Inside Out** Bee Gees
24/81	**Love You Like I Never Loved Before** John O'Banion
26/59	**Love You Most Of All** Sam Cooke
1/70	**Love You Save** Jackson 5
7/60	**Love You So** Ron Holden with The Thunderbirds
7/82	**Love's Been A Little Bit Hard On Me** Juice Newton

POS/YR	RECORD TITLE/ARTIST
20/77	**Love's Grown Deep** Kenny Nolan
19/71	**Love's Lines, Angles And Rhymes** 5th Dimension
26/66	**Love's Made A Fool Of You** Bobby Fuller Four
1/74	**Love's Theme** Love Unlimited Orchestra
30/78	**Lovely Day** Bill Withers
12/80	**Lovely One** Jackson 5
20/56	**Lovely One** Four Voices
7/62	**Lover Please** Clyde McPhatter
2/65	**Lover's Concerto** Toys
31/68	**Lover's Holiday** Peggy Scott & Jo Jo Benson
40/80	**Lover's Holiday** Change
31/61	**Lover's Island** Blue Jays
6/59	**Lover's Question** Clyde McPhatter
36/62	**Lovers By Night, Strangers By Day** Fleetwoods
3/62	**Lovers Who Wander** Dion
2/73	**Loves Me Like A Rock** Paul Simon
25/61	**Lovey Dovey** Buddy Knox
16/79	**Lovin', Touchin', Squeezin'** Journey
1/75	**Lovin' You** Minnie Riperton
32/67	**Lovin' You** Bobby Darin
26/71	**Loving Her Was Easier (Than Anything I'll Ever Do Again)** Kris Kristofferson

POS/YR	RECORD TITLE/ARTIST
20/57	**Loving You** Elvis Presley
29/72	**Loving You Just Crossed My Mind** Sam Neely
7/75	**Low Rider** War
3/76	**Lowdown** Boz Scaggs
35/71	**Lowdown** Chicago
	Lt. Calley..see: Battle Hymn Of
5/77	**Lucille** Kenny Rogers
21/57 21/60	**Lucille** Little Richard Everly Brothers
25/77	**Luckenbach, Texas (Back To The Basics Of Love)** Waylon Jennings
25/60	**Lucky Devil** Carl Dobkins Jr.
14/59	**Lucky Ladybug** Billy & Lillie
25/57	**Lucky Lips** Ruth Brown
29/70	**Lucretia Mac Evil** Blood Sweat & Tears
1/75	**Lucy In The Sky With Diamonds** Elton John
16/56	**Lullaby Of Birdland** Blue Stars
23/61	**Lullaby Of Love** Frank Gari
2/75	**Lyin' Eyes** Eagles

M

POS/YR	RECORD TITLE/ARTIST
15/59	**M.T.A.** Kingston Trio
5/70	**Ma Belle Amie** Tee Set

POS/YR	RECORD TITLE/ARTIST

Mac Arthur Park
2/68 Richard Harris
38/71 Four Tops
1/78 Donna Summer

Machine Gun
22/74 Commodores

Macho Man
25/78 Village People

Mack The Knife
8/56 Dick Hyman Trio
11/56 Richard Hayman & Jan August
17/56 Lawrence Welk & His Orchestra
20/56 Louis Armstrong
37/56 Billy Vaughn & His Orchestra
1/59 Bobby Darin
27/60 Ella Fitzgerald

Made To Love..see: (Girls, Girls, Girls)

Mademoiselle
36/76 Styx

Madison
23/60 Al Brown('s) Tunetoppers featuring Cookie Brown

Madison Time - Part 1
30/60 Ray Bryant Combo

Maggie May
1/71 Rod Stewart

Magic
1/80 Olivia Newton-John

Magic
5/75 Pilot

Magic Bus
25/68 Who

Magic Carpet Ride
3/68 Steppenwolf

Magic Man
9/76 Heart

Magic Moments
4/58 Perry Como

Magic Touch..see: (You've Got)

Magic Town
21/66 Vogues

Magical Mystery Tour
39/77 Ambrosia

Magnet And Steel
8/78 Walter Egan

Magnificent Seven
35/61 Al Caiola & His Orchestra

Magnum P.I...see: Theme From

Mahogany..see: Theme From

Main Event
3/79 Barbra Streisand

Main Theme From Exodus..see: Exodus

Main Title And Molly-O..see: Man With The Golden Arm

Mainstreet
24/77 Bob Seger

Majestic
36/62 Dion

Make A Little Magic
25/80 Nitty Gritty Dirt Band

Make A Move On Me
5/82 Olivia Newton-John

Make Believe
28/69 Wind

Make Believe
30/82 Toto

Make It Easy On Yourself
20/62 Jerry Butler
16/65 Walker Bros.
37/70 Dionne Warwick

Make It Funky (Part 1)
22/71 James Brown

Make It With You
1/70 Bread

Make Me A Miracle
16/58 Jimmie Rodgers

Make Me Belong To You
28/66 Barbara Lewis

Make Me Smile
9/70 Chicago

Make Me The Woman That You Go Home To
27/72 Gladys Knight & The Pips

Make Me Your Baby
11/65 Barbara Lewis

Make Me Yours
21/67 Bettye Swann

POS/YR	RECORD TITLE/ARTIST
24/63	**Make The World Go Away** Timi Yuro
6/65	Eddy Arnold
36/69	**Make Your Own Kind Of Music** Mama Cass
6/55	**Make Yourself Comfortable** Sarah Vaughan
26/55	Andy Griffith
30/55	Peggy King
5/79	**Makin' It** David Naughton
20/59	**Makin' Love** Floyd Robinson
31/67	**Making Every Minute Count** Spanky & Our Gang
13/82	**Making Love** Roberta Flack
35/67	**Making Memories** Frankie Laine
25/76	**Making Our Dreams Come True** Cyndi Grecco
8/60	**Mama** Connie Francis
22/66	**Mama** B.J. Thomas
9/79	**Mama Can't Buy You Love** Elton John
14/63	**Mama Didn't Lie** Jan Bradley
11/56	**Mama From The Train** Patti Page
11/57	**Mama Look At Bubu** Harry Belafonte
4/61	**Mama Said** Shirelles
32/62	**Mama Sang A Song** Stan Kenton
38/62	Walter Brennan
34/56	**Mama, Teach Me To Dance** Eydie Gorme
1/70	**Mama Told Me (Not To Come)** Three Dog Night
30/82	**Mama Used To Say** Junior

POS/YR	RECORD TITLE/ARTIST
2/71	**Mama's Pearl** Jackson 5
17/55	**Mambo Rock** Bill Haley & His Comets
19/66	**Mame** Herb Alpert & The Tijuana Brass
32/76	**Mamma Mia** Abba
16/55	**Man Chases A Girl** Eddie Fisher
31/79	**Man I'll Never Be** Boston
14/55	**Man In The Raincoat** Marion Marlowe
16/55	Priscilla Wright
40/82	**Man On The Corner** Genesis
14/82	**Man On Your Mind** Little River Band
4/62	**(Man Who Shot) Liberty Valance** Gene Pitney
14/56	**Man With The Golden Arm (Main Title/Molly-O/Delilah Jones)** Richard Maltby
16/56	Elmer Bernstein & Orchestra
22/56	Dick Jacobs & His Orchestra
37/56	McGuire Sisters
19/68	**Man Without Love** Engelbert Humperdinck
1/75	**Mandy** Barry Manilow
1/82	**Maneater** Daryl Hall & John Oates
10/57	**Mangos** Rosemary Clooney
10/59	**Manhattan Spiritual** Reg Owen & His Orchestra
7/60	**Many Tears Ago** Connie Francis
20/58	**March From The River Kwai And Colonel Bogey** Mitch Miller
8/77	**Margaritaville** Jimmy Buffett
6/63	**Maria Elena** Los Indios Tabajaras

POS/YR	RECORD TITLE/ARTIST
	Marianne
3/57	Hilltoppers featuring Jimmy Sacca
4/57	Terry Gilkyson & The Easy Riders
	Marie
15/65	Bachelors
	(Marie's the Name) His Latest Flame
4/61	Elvis Presley
	Marina
31/59	Rocco Granata
	Marlena
36/63	Four Seasons
	Marrakesh Express
28/69	Crosby Stills & Nash
	Married Men
40/79	Bette Midler
	Martian Hop
16/63	Ran-Dells
	Mary Ann Regrets
39/62	Burl Ives
	Mary Had A Little Lamb
28/72	Paul McCartney
	Mary In The Morning
27/67	Al Martino
	Mary Lou
26/59	Ronnie Hawkins & The Hawks
	Mary's Boy Child
12/56	Harry Belafonte
	Mary's Little Lamb
39/62	James Darren
	Mashed Potato Time
2/62	Dee Dee Sharp
	Massachusetts..see: (Lights Went Out)
	Master Blaster (Jammin')
5/80	Stevie Wonder
	Master Jack
18/68	Four Jacks And A Jill
	Master Of Eyes (The Deepness Of Your Eyes)
33/73	Aretha Franklin
	Masterpiece
7/73	Temptations
	Matador
20/64	Major Lance

POS/YR	RECORD TITLE/ARTIST
	Matchbox
17/64	Beatles
	May I
39/69	Bill Deal & The Rhondels
	May The Bird Of Paradise Fly Up Your Nose
15/65	"Little" Jimmy Dickens
	May You Always
11/59	McGuire Sisters
	Maybe
15/58	Chantels
29/70	Three Degrees
	Maybe Baby
17/58	Crickets
	Maybe I Know
14/64	Lesley Gore
	Maybe I'm A Fool
22/79	Eddie Money
	Maybe I'm Amazed
10/77	Paul McCartney
	Maybe Tomorrow
20/71	Jackson 5
	Maybellene
5/55	Chuck Berry
12/64	Johnny Rivers
	Me And Baby Brother
15/74	War
	Me And Bobby McGee
1/71	Janis Joplin
40/71	Jerry Lee Lewis
	Me And Julio Down By The Schoolyard
22/72	Paul Simon
	Me And Mrs. Jones
1/72	Billy Paul
	Me And My Arrow
34/71	Nilsson
	Me And You And A Dog Named Boo
5/71	Lobo
	Me (Without You)
40/81	Andy Gibb
	Mean Woman Blues
5/63	Roy Orbison
	Mecca
12/63	Gene Pitney

POS/YR	RECORD TITLE/ARTIST
	"Medic" Theme..see: Blue Star
22/69	**Medicine Man (Part 1)** Buchanan Brothers
2/66	**Mellow Yellow** Donovan
5/57	**Melodie D'Amour** Ames Brothers
	Melody Of Love
2/55	Billy Vaughn & His Orchestra
3/55	Four Aces Featuring Al Alberts
8/55	David Carroll & His Orchestra
19/55	Frank Sinatra & Ray Anthony
30/55	Leo Diamond with Orchestra
35/69	**Memories** Elvis Presley
	Memories Are Made Of This
1/56	Dean Martin
5/56	Gale Storm
	Memories Of You
20/56	Benny Goodman Trio with Rosemary Clooney
22/56	Four Coins
	Memphis
5/63	Lonnie Mack
2/64	Johnny Rivers
33/67	**Memphis Soul Stew** King Curtis
	Men ..see: Theme From The
33/68	**Men Are Gettin' Scarce** Joe Tex
6/66	**Men In My Little Girl's Life** Mike Douglas
27/69	**Mendocino** Sir Douglas Quintet
30/69	**Mercy** Ohio Express
35/64	**Mercy, Mercy** Don Covay & The Goodtimers
4/71	**Mercy Mercy Me (The Ecology)** Marvin Gaye
	Mercy, Mercy, Mercy
5/67	Buckinghams
11/67	"Cannonball" Adderley Quintet
32/60	**Mess Of Blues** Elvis Presley

POS/YR	RECORD TITLE/ARTIST
8/66	**Message To Michael** Dionne Warwick
16/58	**Mexican Hat Rock** Applejacks
7/61	**Mexico** Bob Moore & His Orchestra
1/61	**Michael** Highwaymen
18/66	**Michelle** David & Jonathan
1/82	**Mickey** Toni Basil
8/63	**Mickey's Monkey** Miracles
6/74	**Midnight At The Oasis** Maria Muldaur
6/75	**Midnight Blue** Melissa Manchester
5/68	**Midnight Confessions** Grass Roots
10/69	**Midnight Cowboy** Ferrante & Teicher
	Midnight Hour..see: In The
2/62	**Midnight In Moscow** Kenny Ball & His Jazzmen
10/63	**Midnight Mary** Joey Powers
	Midnight Rider
27/72	Joe Cocker
19/74	Gregg Allman
24/80	**Midnight Rocks** Al Stewart
	Midnight Special
16/60	Paul Evans
20/65	Johnny Rivers
35/59	**Midnight Stroll** Revels
1/73	**Midnight Train To Georgia** Gladys Knight & The Pips
28/79	**Midnight Wind** John Stewart
34/71	**Mighty Clouds Of Joy** B.J. Thomas

POS/YR	RECORD TITLE/ARTIST
38/59	**Mighty Good** Ricky Nelson
20/74	**Mighty Love - Pt. 1** Spinners
29/74	**Mighty Mighty** Earth Wind & Fire
10/68	**Mighty Quinn (Quinn The Eskimo)** Manfred Mann
33/64	**Miller's Cave** Bobby Bare
5/60 23/73	**Million To One** Jimmy Charles & The Revelletts Donny Osmond
26/69	**Mind, Body And Soul** Flaming Ember
18/73	**Mind Games** John Lennon
38/69	**Minotaur** Dick Hyman
14/79	**Minute By Minute** Doobie Brothers
18/56	**Miracle Of Love** Eileen Rodgers
3/75	**Miracles** Jefferson Starship
10/67	**Mirage** Tommy James & The Shondells
8/82	**Mirror, Mirror** Diana Ross
22/73	**Misdemeanor** Foster Sylvers
14/81	**Miss Sun** Boz Scaggs
1/78	**Miss You** Rolling Stones
23/82	**Missing You** Dan Fogelberg
29/61	**Missing You** Ray Peterson
7/60	**Mission Bell** Donnie Brooks
32/70	**Mississippi** John Phillips

POS/YR	RECORD TITLE/ARTIST
21/70	**Mississippi Queen** Mountain
	Mister ..also see: Mr.
38/72	**Mister Can't You See** Buffy Sainte-Marie
37/81	**Mister Sandman** Emmylou Harris
12/59 21/63 14/75	**Misty** Johnny Mathis Lloyd Price Ray Stevens
3/76	**Misty Blue** Dorothy Moore
14/80	**Misunderstanding** Genesis
37/64	**Mixed-Up, Shook-Up, Girl** Patty & The Emblems
32/58	**Mocking Bird** Four Lads
7/63 5/74	**Mockingbird** Inez Foxx Carly Simon & James Taylor
20/61	**Model Girl** Johnny Maestro
18/81	**Modern Girl** Sheena Easton
21/65	**Mohair Sam** Charlie Rich
	Molly-O..see: Man With The Golden Arm
2/55	**Moments To Remember** Four Lads
25/59 29/59	**Mona Lisa** Carl Mann Conway Twitty
1/66	**Monday, Monday** Mamas & The Papas
13/73	**Money** Pink Floyd
9/76	**Money Honey** Bay City Rollers
23/60 16/64	**Money (That's What I Want)** Barrett Strong Kingsmen

POS/YR	RECORD TITLE/ARTIST
20/56	**Money Tree** Margaret Whiting
8/63	**Monkey Time** Major Lance
39/70	**Monster** Steppenwolf
1/62 10/73	**Monster Mash** Bobby "Boris" Pickett Bobby "Boris" Pickett
30/62	**Monsters' Holiday** Bobby "Boris" Pickett
8/70	**Montego Bay** Bobby Bloom
15/68	**Monterey** Animals
3/68	**Mony Mony** Tommy James & The Shondells
31/77	**Moody Blue** Elvis Presley
1/61	**Moody River** Pat Boone
24/69	**Moody Woman** Jerry Butler
11/61 11/61	**Moon River** Jerry Butler Henry Mancini
30/71	**Moon Shadow** Cat Stevens
28/58	**Moon Talk** Perry Como
38/69	**Moonflight** Vik Venus
1/56 4/56 13/56	**Moonglow And Theme From "Picnic"** Morris Stoloff George Cates & His Orchestra McGuire Sisters
3/76	**Moonlight Feels Right** Starbuck
3/57	**Moonlight Gambler** Frankie Laine
24/57 37/57	**Moonlight Swim** Tony Perkins Nick Noble
4/56	**More** Perry Como

POS/YR	RECORD TITLE/ARTIST
8/63	**More** Kai Winding & Orchestra
16/66	**More I See You** Chris Montez
23/67 10/80	**More Love** Miracles Kim Carnes
17/61	**More Money For You And Me (medley)** Four Preps
4/76	**More, More, More (Pt. 1)** Andrea True Connection
5/76	**More Than A Feeling** Boston
32/78	**More Than A Woman** Tavares
2/80	**More Than I Can Say** Leo Sayer
34/82	**More Than Just The Two Of Us** Sneaker
12/69	**More Today Than Yesterday** Spiral Starecase Featuring Pat Upton
13/59	**Morgen** Ivo Robic
	Moritat..see: Mack The Knife
14/75	**Mornin' Beautiful** Dawn
1/73	**Morning After** Maureen McGovern
24/79	**Morning Dance** Spyro Gyra
17/69	**Morning Girl** Neon Philharmonic
6/72	**Morning Has Broken** Cat Stevens
27/59 8/75	**Morning Side Of The Mountain** Tommy Edwards Donny & Marie Osmond
1/81	**Morning Train (Nine To Five)** Sheena Easton
1/73	**Most Beautiful Girl** Charlie Rich
14/55	**Most Of All** Don Cornell

POS/YR	RECORD TITLE/ARTIST
38/71	**Most Of All** B.J. Thomas
27/62	**Most People Get Married** Patti Page
31/56	**Mostly Martha** Crew-Cuts
4/72	**Mother And Child Reunion** Paul Simon
37/71	**Mother Freedom** Bread
11/69	**Mother Popcorn (You Got To Have A Mother For Me) (Part 1)** James Brown
1/61	**Mother-In-Law** Ernie K-Doe
8/66	**Mothers Little Helper** Rolling Stones
12/72	**Motorcycle Mama** Sailcat
21/60 9/64	**Mountain Of Love** Harold Dorman Johnny Rivers
2/61	**Mountain's High** Dick & DeeDee
31/69	**Move Over** Steppenwolf
	Move Two Mountains..see: (You've Got To)
14/76	**Movin'** Brass Construction
19/75	**Movin' On** Bad Company
17/78	**Movin' Out (Anthony's Song)** Billy Joel
	Mr. ..also see: Mister
16/63	**Mr. Bass Man** Johnny Cymbal
2/71	**Mr. Big Stuff** Jean Knight
1/59	**Mr. Blue** Fleetwoods
35/78	**Mr. Blue Sky** Electric Light Orchestra

POS/YR	RECORD TITLE/ARTIST
9/71	**Mr. Bojangles** Nitty Gritty Dirt Band
28/68	**Mr. Businessman** Ray Stevens
1/60	**Mr. Custer** Larry Verne
17/66	**Mr. Dieingly Sad** Critters
	Mr. Dream Merchant..see: Dream Merchant
4/75	**Mr. Jaws** Dickie Goodman
6/57	**Mr. Lee** Bobbettes
1/64	**Mr. Lonely** Bobby Vinton
21/60	**Mr. Lucky** Henry Mancini
36/66	**Mr. Spaceman** Byrds
18/69	**Mr. Sun, Mr. Moon** Paul Revere & The Raiders
1/65	**Mr. Tambourine Man** Byrds
13/56 14/56 18/56	**Mr. Wonderful** Sarah Vaughan Peggy Lee Teddi King
1/65	**Mrs. Brown You've Got A Lovely Daughter** Herman's Hermits
1/68 37/69	**Mrs. Robinson** Simon & Garfunkel Booker T. & The M.G.'s
	Muddy Water..see: (I Washed My Hands)
	Muhammad Ali..see: Black Superman
5/60	**Mule Skinner Blues** Fendermen
30/62	**Multiplication** Bobby Darin
39/59	**Mummy** Bob McFadden & Dor
39/82	**Murphy's Law** Cheri

POS/YR	RECORD TITLE/ARTIST
10/82	**Muscles** Diana Ross
39/67	**Museum** Herman's Hermits
3/79	**Music Box Dancer** Frank Mills
15/67 34/67	**Music To Watch Girls By** Bob Crewe Generation Andy Williams
4/76	**Muskrat Love** Captain & Tennille
12/74	**Must Of Got Lost** J. Geils Band
8/66	**Must To Avoid** Herman's Hermits
23/66	**Mustang Sally** Wilson Pickett
21/56	**Mutual Admiration Society** Teresa Brewer
13/78	**My Angel Baby** Toby Beau
13/65	**My Baby** Temptations
	(My Baby Don't Love Me)..see: No More
31/56	**My Baby Left Me** Elvis Presley
13/70	**My Baby Loves Lovin'** White Plains
22/66	**My Baby Loves Me** Martha & The Vandellas
17/68	**My Baby Must Be A Magician** Marvelettes
30/67	**My Back Pages** Byrds
35/78	**My Best Friend's Girl** Cars
21/56	**My Blue Heaven** Fats Domino
26/64	**My Bonnie** Beatles
11/55	**My Bonnie Lassie** Ames Brothers
21/62	**My Boomerang Won't Come Back** Charlie Drake

POS/YR	RECORD TITLE/ARTIST
20/75	**My Boy** Elvis Presley
16/55 39/55	**My Boy - Flat Top** Dorothy Collins Boyd Bennett & His Rockets
2/64	**My Boy Lollipop** Millie Small
1/63	**My Boyfriend's Back** Angels
18/58	**My Bucket's Got A Hole In It** Ricky Nelson
4/69	**My Cherie Amour** Stevie Wonder
18/63 20/63	**My Coloring Book** Kitty Kallen Sandy Stewart
8/67	**My Cup Runneth Over** Ed Ames
6/63	**My Dad** Paul Petersen
34/60	**My Dearest Darling** Etta James
1/72	**My Ding-A-Ling** Chuck Berry
24/57	**My Dream** Platters
9/61	**My Empty Arms** Jackie Wilson
1/75	**My Eyes Adored You** Frankie Valli
28/77	**My Fair Share** Seals & Crofts
1/65 35/68	**My Girl** Temptations Bobby Vee
25/82	**My Girl** Donnie Iris
12/74	**My Girl Bill** Jim Stafford
22/81	**My Girl (Gone, Gone, Gone)** Chilliwack
14/65	**My Girl Has Gone** Miracles

POS/YR	RECORD TITLE/ARTIST
14/60 29/67	**My Girl Josephine** Fats Domino Jerry Jaye
26/64	**My Girl Sloopy** Vibrations
1/64 23/82	**My Guy** Mary Wells Sister Sledge
2/59	**My Happiness** Connie Francis
4/77	**My Heart Belongs To Me** Barbra Streisand
9/64	**My Heart Belongs To Only You** Bobby Vinton
38/64	**My Heart Cries For You** Ray Charles
1/60	**My Heart Has A Mind Of Its Own** Connie Francis
3/59	**My Heart Is An Open Book** Carl Dobkins Jr.
	My Heart Reminds Me..see: (All Of A Sudden)
	My Heart Sings..see: (All Of A Sudden)
13/66	**My Heart's Symphony** Gary Lewis & The Playboys
8/60	**My Home Town** Paul Anka
18/61	**My Kind Of Girl** Matt Monro
26/61 38/61	**My Last Date (With You)** Skeeter Davis Joni James
3/78	**My Life** Billy Joel
24/56	**My Little Angel** Four Lads
9/75	**My Little Town** Simon & Garfunkel
1/66	**My Love** Petula Clark
1/73	**My Love** Paul McCartney
16/64	**My Love, Forgive Me (Amore, Scusami)** Robert Goulet

POS/YR	RECORD TITLE/ARTIST
13/67	**My Mammy** Happenings
9/73	**My Maria** B.W. Stevenson
26/59	**My Melancholy Baby** Tommy Edwards
3/74	**My Melody Of Love** Bobby Vinton
19/74	**My Mistake (Was To Love You)** Marvin Gaye & Diana Ross
39/81	**My Mother's Eyes** Bette Midler
16/73	**My Music** Loggins & Messina
24/55 28/57	**My One Sin** Nat King Cole Four Coins
33/59 13/62	**My Own True Love** Jimmy Clanton Duprees featuring Joey Vann
21/57	**My Personal Possession** Nat King Cole
14/69	**My Pledge Of Love** Joe Jeffrey Group
1/56	**My Prayer** Platters
1/79	**My Sharona** Knack
31/68	**My Song** Aretha Franklin
7/57 7/68	**My Special Angel** Bobby Helms Vogues
16/63	**My Summer Love** Ruby & The Romantics
17/74 32/77	**My Sweet Lady** Cliff DeYoung John Denver
1/70	**My Sweet Lord** George Harrison
29/74	**My Thang** James Brown
32/65	**My Town, My Guy And Me** Lesley Gore

POS/YR	RECORD TITLE/ARTIST
31/55	**My Treasure** Hilltoppers featuring Jimmy Sacca
22/63	**My True Confession** Brook Benton
3/58	**My True Love** Jack Scott
3/61	**My True Story** Jive Five Featuring Eugene Pitt
27/69 22/77	**My Way** Frank Sinatra Elvis Presley
9/69	**My Whole World Ended (The Moment You Left Me)** David Ruffin
24/63	**My Whole World Is Falling Down** Brenda Lee
12/59	**My Wish Came True** Elvis Presley
16/72	**My World** Bee Gees
5/66	**My World Is Empty Without You** Supremes
33/65	**Mystic Eyes** Them

N

POS/YR	RECORD TITLE/ARTIST
27/77	**N.Y., You Got Me Dancing** Andrea True Connection
1/69	**Na Na Hey Hey Kiss Him Goodbye** Steam
8/76	**Nadia's Theme (The Young And The Restless)** Barry Devorzon & Perry Botkin, Jr.
23/64	**Nadine (Is It You?)** Chuck Berry
25/61	**"Nag"** Halos
3/65	**Name Game** Shirley Ellis
12/78	**Name Of The Game** Abba

POS/YR	RECORD TITLE/ARTIST
8/67	**Nashville Cats** Lovin' Spoonful
16/71	**Nathan Jones** Supremes
21/78	**Native New Yorker** Odyssey
38/60	**Natural Born Lover** Fats Domino
10/73	**Natural High** Bloodstone
17/71	**Natural Man** Lou Rawls
8/67	**Natural Woman (You Make Me Feel Like)** Aretha Franklin
40/68	**Naturally Stoned** Avant-Garde
40/61	**Nature Boy** Bobby Darin
3/55 17/55	**Naughty Lady Of Shady Lane** Ames Brothers Archie Bleyer
6/64	**Navy Blue** Diane Renay
22/70	**Neanderthal Man** Hotlegs
10/58	**Near You** Roger Williams
40/58	**Nee Nee Na Na Na Na Nu Nu** Dicky Doo & The Don'ts
11/74	**Need To Be** Jim Weatherly
31/64	**Need To Belong** Jerry Butler
25/58	**Need You** Donnie Owens
13/64	**Needles And Pins** Searchers
2/73	**Neither One Of Us (Wants To Be The First To Say Goodbye)** Gladys Knight & The Pips
	Nel Blu Dipinto Di Blu..see: Volare
24/67	**Neon Rainbow** Box Tops

POS/YR	RECORD TITLE/ARTIST
6/59	**Never Be Anyone Else But You** Ricky Nelson
15/80	**Never Be The Same** Christopher Cross
28/82	**Never Been In Love** Randy Meisner
5/72	**Never Been To Spain** Three Dog Night
2/71 22/71 9/75	**Never Can Say Goodbye** Jackson 5 Isaac Hayes Gloria Gaynor
13/71	**Never Ending Song Of Love** Delaney & Bonnie & Friends
20/68	**Never Give You Up** Jerry Butler
11/76	**Never Gonna Fall In Love Again** Eric Carmen
26/70	**Never Had A Dream Come True** Stevie Wonder
6/80	**Never Knew Love Like This Before** Stephanie Mills
29/75	**Never Let Her Go** David Gates
2/67 12/71 7/74	**Never My Love** Association 5th Dimension Blue Swede
7/73	**Never, Never Gonna Give Ya Up** Barry White
19/60 13/61 37/61	**Never On Sunday** Don Costa & His Orchestra Chordettes Don Costa & His Orchestra
33/81	**Never Too Much** Luther Vandross
22/56	**Never Turn Back** Al Hibbler
37/64	**New Girl In School** Jan & Dean
1/77	**New Kid In Town** Eagles
	New Lovers..see: (Welcome)
36/63	**New Mexican Rose** Four Seasons

POS/YR	RECORD TITLE/ARTIST
6/60	**New Orleans** Gary "U.S." Bonds
39/80	**New Romance (It's A Mystery)** Spider
21/82	**New World Man** Rush
	New York ..also see: N.Y.
13/79	**New York Groove** Ace Frehley
14/67	**New York Mining Disaster 1941 Have You See My Wife Mr. Jones** Bee Gees
	New York, New York..see: Theme From
32/65	**New York's A Lonely Town** Trade Winds
5/62	**Next Door To An Angel** Neil Sedaka
17/67	**Next Plane To London** Rose Garden
F/70	**Next Step Is Love** Elvis Presley
30/76	**Nice 'N' Naasty** Salsoul Orchestra
37/82	**Nice Girls** Eye To Eye
4/72	**Nice To Be With You** Gallery
35/72	**Nickel Song** Melanie
39/81	**Nicole** Point Blank
4/60	**Night** Jackie Wilson
1/74	**Night Chicago Died** Paper Lace
1/78	**Night Fever** Bee Gees
3/63	**Night Has A Thousand Eyes** Bobby Vee
11/56	**Night Lights** Nat King Cole
4/77	**Night Moves** Bob Seger

POS/YR	RECORD TITLE/ARTIST
6/81	**Night Owls** Little River Band
1/73	**Night The Lights Went Out In Georgia** Vicki Lawrence
3/71	**Night They Drove Old Dixie Down** Joan Baez
30/66	**Night Time** Strangeloves
35/62	**Night Train** James Brown
9/75	**Nightingale** Carole King
10/76	**Nights Are Forever Without You** England Dan & John Ford Coley
2/72	**Nights In White Satin** Moody Blues
7/75	**Nights On Broadway** Bee Gees
23/67	**Niki Hoeky** P.J. Proby
1/81	**9 To 5** Dolly Parton
2/66	**19th Nervous Breakdown** Rolling Stones
1/66	**96 Tears** ? (Question Mark) & The Mysterians
7/67	**98.6** Keith
26/80	**99** Toto
11/57	**Ninety-Nine Ways** Tab Hunter
23/56	**Ninety-Nine Years (Dead Or Alive)** Guy Mitchell
33/71	**1900 Yesterday** Liz Damon('s) Orient Express
8/64 19/69	**Nitty Gritty** Shirley Ellis Gladys Knight & The Pips
23/55 26/55 27/65	**No Arms Can Ever Hold You** Georgie Shaw Pat Boone Bachelors
39/74	**No Charge** Melba Montgomery

POS/YR	RECORD TITLE/ARTIST
23/58	**No Chemise, Please** Gerry Granahan
	No Gettin' Over Me..see: (There's)
40/60	**No If's - No And's** Lloyd Price
16/71	**No Love At All** B.J. Thomas
21/57	**No Love (But Your Love)** Johnny Mathis
8/70	**No Matter What** Badfinger
3/66	**No Matter What Shape (Your Stomach's In)** T-Bones
31/69	**No Matter What Sign You Are** Supremes
35/67	**No Milk Today** Herman's Hermits
6/55 17/55	**No More** De John Sisters McGuire Sisters
25/73	**No More Mr. Nice Guy** Alice Cooper
1/79	**No More Tears (Enough Is Enough)** Barbra Streisand & Donnna Summer
23/80	**No Night So Long** Dionne Warwick
3/75	**No No Song** Ringo Starr
2/56 34/69	**No, Not Much!** Four Lads Vogues
34/61 21/63	**No One** Connie Francis Ray Charles
19/58	**No One Knows** Dion & The Belmonts
36/72	**No One To Depend On** Santana
	No Other Arms ..see: No Arms Can Ever Hold You
27/59	**No Other Arms, No Other Lips** Chordettes
10/64	**No Particular Place To Go** Chuck Berry

POS/YR	RECORD TITLE/ARTIST
29/81	**No Reply At All** Genesis
F/70	**No Sugar Tonight** Guess Who
14/79	**No Tell Lover** Chicago
5/70	**No Time** Guess Who
15/82	**Nobody** Sylvia
8/68	**Nobody But Me** Human Beinz
21/59	**Nobody But You** Dee Clark
40/69	**Nobody But You Babe** Clarence Reid
2/77	**Nobody Does It Better** Carly Simon
12/64	**Nobody I Know** Peter & Gordon
30/60	**Nobody Loves Me Like You** Flamingos
18/82	**Nobody Said It Was Easy (Lookin' For The Lights)** Le Roux
29/73	**Nobody Wants You When You're Down And Out** Bobby Womack
21/81	**Nobody Wins** Elton John
39/59	**Nola** Billy Williams
3/62	**Norman** Sue Thompson
4/60	**North To Alaska** Johnny Horton
12/63	**Not Me** Orlons
16/60	**Not One Minute More** Della Reese
25/65	**Not The Lovin' Kind** Dino Desi & Billy
34/69	**Nothing But A Heartache** Flirtations

POS/YR	RECORD TITLE/ARTIST
11/65	**Nothing But Heartaches** Supremes
12/62	**Nothing Can Change This Love** Sam Cooke
18/65	**Nothing Can Stop Me** Gene Chandler
	Nothing For Xmas..see: Nuttin'
1/74	**Nothing From Nothing** Billy Preston
20/66	**Nothing's Too Good For My Baby** Stevie Wonder
25/58	**Now And For Always** George Hamilton IV
2/59	**(Now and Then There's) A Fool Such As I** Elvis Presley
3/66	**Nowhere Man** Beatles
8/65	**Nowhere To Run** Martha & The Vandellas
9/75	**#9 Dream** John Lennon
23/62	**Nut Rocker** B. Bumble & The Stingers
22/73	**Nutbush City Limits** Ike & Tina Turner
6/55 20/55 21/55 36/55	**Nuttin' For Christmas** Barry Gordon Joe Ward Ricky Zahnd & The Blue Jeaners Fontane Sisters

POS/YR	RECORD TITLE/ARTIST
10/60	**O Dio Mio** Annette
1/67 28/67	**Ode To Billie Joe** Bobbie Gentry King Curtis
10/80	**Off The Wall** Michael Jackson
3/73	**Oh, Babe, What Would You Say?** Hurricane Smith

POS/YR	RECORD TITLE/ARTIST
23/64	**Oh Baby Don't You Weep (Part 1)** James Brown
10/57	**Oh, Boy!** Crickets
9/59	**Oh! Carol** Neil Sedaka
15/78	**Oh! Darling** Robin Gibb
1/72	**Oh Girl** Chi-Lites
4/69 40/70	**Oh Happy Day** Edwin Hawkins Singers Glen Campbell
12/66	**Oh How Happy** Shades Of Blue
5/58 23/58	**Oh Julie** Crescendos Sammy Salvo
38/82	**Oh Julie** Barry Manilow
33/73	**Oh La De Da** Staple Singers
34/60	**Oh, Little One** Jack Scott
7/58	**Oh Lonesome Me** Don Gibson
22/70	**Oh Me Oh My (I'm A Fool For You Baby)** Lulu
5/74	**Oh My My** Ringo Starr
4/81	**Oh No** Commodores
24/64	**Oh No Not My Baby** Maxine Brown
7/58	**Oh Oh, I'm Falling In Love Again** Jimmie Rodgers
1/64 12/82	**Oh, Pretty Woman** Roy Orbison Van Halen
22/55	**Oh! Susanna** Singing Dogs
10/74	**Oh Very Young** Cat Stevens

POS/YR	RECORD TITLE/ARTIST
30/79	**Oh Well** Rockets
10/69	**Oh, What A Night** Dells
	Oh, What A Night ..see: December, 1963
24/78	**Oh What A Night For Dancing** Barry White
39/66	**Oh Yeah** Shadows Of Knight
14/70	**Ohio** Crosby Stills Nash & Young
25/60	**Ol' Mac Donald** Frank Sinatra
3/57	**Old Cape Cod** Patti Page
5/75	**Old Days** Chicago
20/80	**Old Fashion Love** Commodores
37/77	**Old Fashioned Boy (You're The One)** Stallion
4/71	**Old Fashioned Love Song** Three Dog Night
5/60	**Old Lamplighter** Browns featuring Jim Edward Brown
31/72	**Old Man** Neil Young
34/56	**Old Philosopher** Eddie Lawrence
5/62	**Old Rivers** Walter Brennan
	Old Schoolyard..see: (Remember The Days Of)
15/81	**Old Songs** Barry Manilow
28/79	**Old Time Rock & Roll** Bob Seger
25/61	**Ole Buttermilk Sky** Bill Black's Combo
11/67	**On A Carousel** Hollies
5/74	**On And On** Gladys Knight & The Pips

POS/YR	RECORD TITLE/ARTIST
11/77	**On And On** Stephen Bishop
9/63 7/78	**On Broadway** Drifters George Benson
38/56	**On London Bridge** Jo Stafford
20/57	**On My Word Of Honor** Platters
	On The Dock Of The Bay..see: Sittin' On
5/80	**On The Radio** Donna Summer
4/61	**On The Rebound** Floyd Cramer
16/68	**On The Road Again** Canned Heat
20/80	**On The Road Again** Willie Nelson
38/78	**On The Shelf** Donny & Marie Osmond
4/56 18/56 28/64	**On The Street Where You Live** Vic Damone Eddie Fisher Andy Williams
27/82	**On The Way To The Sky** Neil Diamond
29/82	**On The Wings Of Love** Jeffrey Osborne
14/63	**On Top Of Spaghetti** Tom Glazer
11/61	**Once In Awhile** Chimes
19/64	**Once Upon A Time** Marvin Gaye & Mary Wells
26/61	**Once Upon A Time** Rochell & The Candles
10/75	**Once You Get Started** Rufus Featuring Chaka Khan
23/72	**Once You Understand** Think featuring Lou Stallman
5/69	**One** Three Dog Night
1/71	**One Bad Apple** Osmonds

POS/YR	RECORD TITLE/ARTIST
11/63	**One Broken Heart For Sale** Elvis Presley
37/74	**One Day At A Time** Marilyn Sellars
34/65	**One Dyin' And A Buryin'** Roger Miller
	One Eyed Jacks..see: Love Theme From
5/63 12/80	**One Fine Day** Chiffons Carole King
24/71	**One Fine Morning** Lighthouse
13/65	**One Has My Name (The Other Has My Heart)** Barry Young
11/74	**One Hell Of A Woman** Mac Davis
14/82	**One Hundred Ways** Quincy Jones Featuring James Ingram
31/57	**One In A Million** Platters
9/80	**One In A Million You** Larry Graham
14/65	**One Kiss For Old Times' Sake** Ronnie Dove
35/79	**One Last Kiss** J. Geils Band
2/70	**One Less Bell To Answer** 5th Dimension
37/73	**One Less Set Of Footsteps** Jim Croce
25/76	**One Love In My Lifetime** Diana Ross
19/70	**One Man Band** Three Dog Night
28/73	**One Man Band (Plays All Alone)** Ronnie Dyson
7/75	**One Man Woman/One Woman Man** Paul Anka
8/61	**One Mint Julep** Ray Charles
15/71	**One Monkey Don't Stop No Show - Part 1** Honey Cone

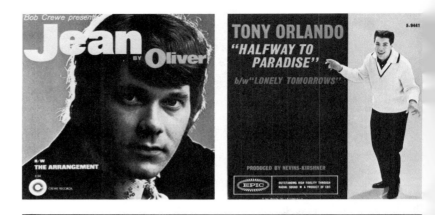

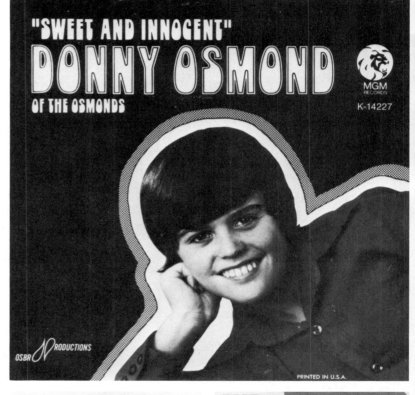

Oliver. You'll want to know that the hit-maker of "Jean" and "Good Morning Starshine" was born Oliver William Swofford, and that he wrote "Young Birds Fly" for the Cryan' Shames, which reached number 99 on *Billboard's* Hot 100 in June 1968.

Tony Orlando. The (Don) Kirshner connection saw pre-Dawn Tony Orlando record songs by many Brill Building regulars, including Carole King and Gerry Goffin, Neil Sedaka and Howard Greenfield, and Barry Mann and Cynthia Weil.

Donny and Marie Osmond collected their chart credentials—individually and together—through the shrewd choice of pop evergreens, such as "Paper Roses" (a hit for Anita Bryant in 1960), "Morning Side of The Mountain" (Tommy Edwards, 1959), "Puppy Love" (Paul Anka, 1960), "The Twelfth Of Never" (Johnny Mathis, 1957) and "Why" (Frankie Avalon, 1960). But their favorite year for oldies was 1963, as witness "Go Away Little Girl" (Steve Lawrence), "Hey Girl" (Freddie Scott), "I'm Leaving It Up To You" (Dale & Grace), and "Deep Purple" (Nino Tempo & April Stevens).

Dolly Parton. Though she wrote many of her own country hits, Dolly Parton's top 40 breakthrough came via Barry Mann and Cynthia Weil's "Here You Come Again." Barry himself first recorded the song, but his record company didn't think it good enough to release.

Paul & Paula. Paul (Ray Hildebrand) and Paula (Jill Jackson) first cut "Hey Paula" for Major Bill Smith's Le Cam Records under their original names. "Hey . . . hey . . . Jill." No, stop right there.

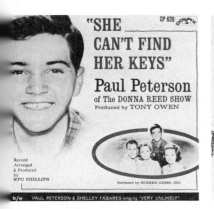

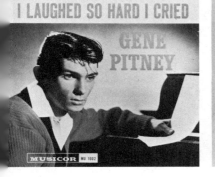

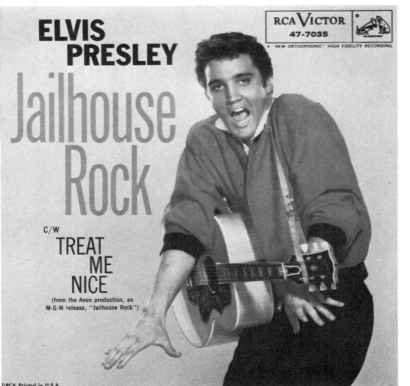

Paul Petersen. Aside from his accomplishments on "The Donna Reed Show," Paul Petersen was one of the few white pop artists to record for Motown. He waxed "Chained" in 1967, later a hit for Marvin Gaye.

Bobby Pickett. Those who only know Bobby Pickett through his two-time hit "Monster Mash" might want to hear 1963's "Simon The Sensible Surfer," 1970's "Monster Concert," 1975's "Stardrek," or 1976's "King Kong (Your Song)." On the other hand . . .

Pink Lady. It's tough for music shows of any type to survive on network television, but Pink Lady's prime time series had a particular problem: no viewers.

Gene Pitney. He spent $40 to make "I Wanna Love My Life Away," playing guitar, drums, and piano himself, as well as multi-tracking the vocals. The result was so good that the demo disc didn't need to be re-recorded for commercial release.

Sandy Posey, born Martha Sharp, sang backup on many country and pop sessions (Tommy Roe, Bobby Goldsboro, Bobby Bare, Percy Sledge, Joe Tex, Skeeter Davis) before stepping to the solo microphone for "Born A Woman" and "Single Girl," both of which she authored.

Elvis Presley had 13.8% of the 305 weeks spent at No. 1 by the top 40 chart-toppers of 1955-1982, more than any other artist or group. He also had 21.5% of the 279 weeks spent at the No. 1 spot by records from 1956 through 1959.

POS/YR	RECORD TITLE/ARTIST
29/66	**One More Heartache** Marvin Gaye
32/64	**One More Time** Ray Charles Singers
28/78	**One Nation Under A Groove (Part 1)** Funkadelic
4/58	**One Night** Elvis Presley
11/73	**One Of A Kind (Love Affair)** Spinners
1/75	**One Of These Nights** Eagles
31/60	**One Of Us (Will Weep Tonight)** Patti Page
	One On One, Love Theme From..see: **My Fair Share**
29/76	**One Piece At A Time** Johnny Cash
24/81	**One Step Closer** Doobie Brothers
7/58 22/61	**One Summer Night** Danleers Diamonds
1/81	**One That You Love** Air Supply
34/70 26/71	**One Tin Soldier [The Legend Of Billy Jack]** Original Caste Coven
10/71	**One Toke Over The Line** Brewer & Shipley
9/61	**One Track Mind** Bobby Lewis
40/80	**One Trick Pony** Paul Simon
2/65	**1-2-3** Len Barry
5/68	**1, 2, 3, Red Light** 1910 Fruitgum Co.
24/79	**One Way Or Another** Blondie
8/62	**One Who Really Loves You** Mary Wells
15/82	**One You Love** Glenn Frey

POS/YR	RECORD TITLE/ARTIST
36/80	**Only A Lonely Heart Sees** Felix Cavaliere
25/63	**Only In America** Jay & The Americans
2/62	**Only Love Can Break A Heart** Gene Pitney
33/70	**Only Love Can Break Your Heart** Neil Young
28/76	**Only Love Is Real** Carole King
33/57	**Only One Love** George Hamilton IV
28/59 6/76	**Only Sixteen** Sam Cooke Dr. Hook
24/78	**Only The Good Die Young** Billy Joel
9/82	**Only The Lonely** Motels
2/60	**Only The Lonely (Know How I Feel)** Roy Orbison
4/69	**Only The Strong Survive** Jerry Butler
17/82	**Only Time Will Tell** Asia
12/75	**Only Women** Alice Cooper
4/75	**Only Yesterday** Carpenters
5/55 8/55 9/59 6/74	**Only You** Platters Hilltoppers featuring Jimmy Sacca Franck Pourcel's French Fiddles Ringo Starr
20/71	**Only You Know And I Know** Delaney & Bonnie & Friends
23/65	**Oo Wee Baby, I Love You** Fred Hughes
34/67	**Oogum Boogum Song** Brenton Wood
25/73	**Ooh Baby** Gilbert O'Sullivan
16/65 7/79	**Ooh Baby Baby** Miracles Linda Ronstadt

POS/YR	RECORD TITLE/ARTIST
8/70	**O-o-h Child** Five Stairsteps
31/58	**Ooh! My Soul** Little Richard
28/60	**Ooh Poo Pah Doo - Part II** Jessie Hill
2/82	**Open Arms** Journey
10/67	**Open Letter To My Teenage Son** Victor Lundberg
27/66	**Open The Door To Your Heart** Darrell Banks
8/55	**Open Up Your Heart (And Let The Sunshine In)** Cowboy Church Sunday School
22/75	**Operator** Manhattan Transfer
17/72	**Operator (That's Not The Way It Feels)** Jim Croce
13/66	**Opus 17 (Don't You Worry 'Bout Me)** Four Seasons
31/67	**Other Man's Grass Is Always Greener** Petula Clark
4/82	**Other Woman** Ray Parker Jr.
1/63 11/75	**Our Day Will Come** Ruby & The Romantics Frankie Valli
30/70	**Our House** Crosby Stills Nash & Young
20/81	**Our Lips Are Sealed** Go-Go's
10/78	**Our Love** Natalie Cole
	Our Love Affair..see: Affair To Remember
9/78	**(Our Love) Don't Throw It All Away** Andy Gibb
9/63	**Our Winter Love** Bill Pursell
39/67	**Out & About** Tommy Boyce & Bobby Hart
19/80	**Out Here On My Own** Irene Cara

POS/YR	RECORD TITLE/ARTIST
15/70	**Out In The Country** Three Dog Night
3/64	**Out Of Limits** Marketts
24/63	**Out Of My Mind** Johnny Tillotson
24/64	**Out Of Sight** James Brown
23/56	**Out Of Sight, Out Of Mind** Five Keys
17/73	**Out Of The Question** Gilbert O'Sullivan
21/82	**Out Of Work** Gary "U.S." Bonds
2/72	**Outa-Space** Billy Preston
28/60	**Outside My Window** Fleetwoods
34/74	**Outside Woman** Bloodstone
1/65	**Over And Over** Dave Clark Five
20/76	**Over My Head** Fleetwood Mac
8/57 21/63	**Over The Mountain; Across The Sea** Johnnie & Joe Bobby Vinton
16/60	**Over The Rainbow** Demensions
13/66	**Over Under Sideways Down** Yardbirds
7/68	**Over You** Gary Puckett & The Union Gap
18/74	**Overnight Sensation (Hit Record)** Raspberries
16/70	**Overture From Tommy (A Rock Opera)** Assembled Multitude
13/71	**Oye Como Va** Santana

POS/YR	RECORD TITLE/ARTIST

P

POS/YR	RECORD TITLE/ARTIST
10/64	**P.S. I Love You** Beatles
8/62	**P.T. 109** Jimmy Dean
9/82	**Pac-Man Fever** Buckner & Garcia
13/58	**Padre** Toni Arden
1/66	**Paint It, Black** Rolling Stones
	Paint Me A Picture..see: You Don't Have To
34/73	**Painted Ladies** Ian Thomas
15/63	**Painted, Tainted Rose** Al Martino
	Paladin..see: Ballad Of
3/62	**Palisades Park** Freddy Cannon
26/76	**Paloma Blanca** George Baker Selection
35/66	**Pandora's Golden Heebie Jeebies** Association
31/74	**Papa Don't Take No Mess (Part 1)** James Brown
	Papa Joe's..see: (Down At)
1/72	**Papa Was A Rollin' Stone** Temptations
8/65 21/68	**Papa's Got A Brand New Bag** James Brown Otis Redding
34/67	**Paper Cup** 5th Dimension
5/60 5/73	**Paper Roses** Anita Bryant Marie Osmond
23/65	**Paper Tiger** Sue Thompson

POS/YR	RECORD TITLE/ARTIST
1/66	**Paperback Writer** Beatles
32/82	**Paperlate** Genesis
39/78	**Paradise By The Dashboard Light** Meat Loaf
38/58	**Part Of Me** Jimmy Clanton
31/75	**Part Of The Plan** Dan Fogelberg
19/63	**Part Time Love** Little Johnny Taylor
22/75	**Part Time Love** Gladys Knight & The Pips
22/78	**Part-Time Love** Elton John
1/57 5/57	**Party Doll** Buddy Knox Steve Lawrence
5/62	**Party Lights** Claudine Clark
34/81	**Party's Over (Hopelessly In Love)** Journey
5/81	**Passion** Rod Stewart
12/67	**Pata Pata** Miriam Makeba
4/70	**Patches** Clarence Carter
6/62	**Patches** Dickey Lee
1/58	**Patricia** Perez Prado & His Orchestra
13/70	**Pay To The Piper** Chairmen Of The Board
28/67	**Pay You Back With Interest** Hollies
26/74	**Payback (Part 1)** James Brown
39/68	**Paying The Cost To Be The Boss** B.B. King
	Peace In The Valley..see: (There'll Be)
38/77	**Peace Of Mind** Boston

POS/YR	RECORD TITLE/ARTIST
31/75	**Peace Pipe** B.T. Express
7/71	**Peace Train** Cat Stevens
32/70	**Peace Will Come (According To Plan)** Melanie
12/73	**Peaceful** Helen Reddy
22/73	**Peaceful Easy Feeling** Eagles
36/65	**Peaches "N" Cream** Ikettes
20/61	**Peanut Butter** Marathons
22/57	**Peanuts** Little Joe & The Thrillers
28/59	**Peek-A-Boo** Cadillacs
11/78	**Peg** Steely Dan
3/57	**Peggy Sue** Buddy Holly
18/64	**Penetration** Pyramids
24/60	**Pennies From Heaven** Skyliners
33/82	**Penny For Your Thoughts** Tavares
1/67	**Penny Lane** Beatles
5/64 39/68	**People** Barbra Streisand Tymes
12/67	**People Are Strange** Doors
14/65	**People Get Ready** Impressions
1/68	**People Got To Be Free** Rascals
22/74	**People Gotta Move** Gino Vannelli
40/77	**People In Love** 10cc

POS/YR	RECORD TITLE/ARTIST
25/72	**People Make The World Go Round** Stylistics
23/79	**People Of The South Wind** Kansas
12/64	**People Say** Dixie Cups
18/61	**"Pepe"** Duane Eddy
5/63	**Pepino The Italian Mouse** Lou Monte
12/55	**Pepper-Hot Baby** Jaye P. Morgan
1/62	**Peppermint Twist - Part 1** Joey Dee & The Starliters
10/62	**Percolator (Twist)** Billy Joe & The Checkmates
15/60	**Perfidia** Ventures
2/59	**Personality** Lloyd Price
19/82	**Personally** Karla Bonoff
8/59 27/60	**Peter Gunn** Ray Anthony & His Orchestra Duane Eddy
5/59	**Petite Fleur (Little Flower)** Chris Barber('s) Jazz Band
16/56	**Petticoats Of Portugal** Dick Jacobs & His Orchestra
1/75	**Philadelphia Freedom** Elton John
26/58	**Philadelphia U.S.A.** Nu Tornados
32/66	**Phoenix Love Theme** Brass Ring featuring Phil Bodner
1/73	**Photograph** Ringo Starr
1/81	**Physical** Olivia Newton-John
25/74	**Piano Man** Billy Joel
1/75	**Pick Up The Pieces** Average White Band

POS/YR	RECORD TITLE/ARTIST
27/68	**Pickin' Wild Mountain Berries** Peggy Scott & Jo Jo Benson
	Picnic..see: Moonglow and Theme From "Picnic"
12/68	**Pictures Of Matchstick Men** Status Quo
12/68	**Piece Of My Heart** Big Brother & The Holding Company
19/72	**Pieces Of April** Three Dog Night
4/66	**Pied Piper** Crispian St. Peters
3/73	**Pillow Talk** Sylvia
13/80	**Pilot Of The Airwaves** Charlie Dore
	(Pina Colada Song)..see: Escape
19/69 29/73	**Pinball Wizard** Who New Seekers
11/60	**Pineapple Princess** Annette
31/64	**Pink Panther Theme** Henry Mancini
3/59	**Pink Shoe Laces** Dodie Stevens
4/63	**Pipeline** Chantay's
9/66	**Place In The Sun** Stevie Wonder
38/59	**Plain Jane** Bobby Darin
19/55	**Plantation Boogie** Lenny Dee
40/73	**Plastic Man** Temptations
11/72	**Play Me** Neil Diamond
6/55	**Play Me Hearts And Flowers (I Wanna Cry)** Johnny Desmond
33/74	**Play Something Sweet (Brickyard Blues)** Three Dog Night

POS/YR	RECORD TITLE/ARTIST
1/76	**Play That Funky Music** Wild Cherry
17/82	**Play The Game Tonight** Kansas
7/62	**Playboy** Marvelettes
17/68	**Playboy** Gene & Debbe
2/73	**Playground In My Mind** Clint Holmes
21/57	**Playing For Keeps** Elvis Presley
3/67	**Pleasant Valley Sunday** Monkees
18/78	**Please Come Home For Christmas** Eagles
5/74	**Please Come To Boston** Dave Loggins
15/62	**Please Don't Ask About Barbara** Bobby Vee
1/79	**Please Don't Go** KC & The Sunshine Band
39/61	**Please Don't Go** Ral Donner
24/79	**Please Don't Leave** Lauren Wood
31/63	**Please Don't Talk To The Lifeguard** Diane Ray
8/60	**Please Help Me, I'm Falling** Hank Locklin
12/61 6/67	**Please Love Me Forever** Cathy Jean & The Roommates Bobby Vinton
3/75	**Please Mr. Please** Olivia Newton-John
1/61 1/75	**Please Mr. Postman** Marvelettes Carpenters
11/59	**Please Mr. Sun** Tommy Edwards
3/64	**Please Please Me** Beatles
26/68	**Please Return Your Love To Me** Temptations

POS/YR	RECORD TITLE/ARTIST
14/61	**Please Stay** Drifters
20/61	**Please Tell Me Why** Jackie Wilson
28/66	**Please Tell Me Why** Dave Clark Five
12/57 25/57	**Pledge Of Love** Ken Copeland Mitchell Torok
17/55 17/55	**Pledging My Love** Johnny Ace Teresa Brewer
34/62	**Pocketful Of Miracles** Frank Sinatra
2/60	**Poetry In Motion** Johnny Tillotson
5/75	**Poetry Man** Phoebe Snow
37/70	**Point It Out** Miracles
28/78	**Point Of Know Return** Kansas
21/62	**Point Of No Return** Gene McDaniels
7/59	**Poison Ivy** Coasters
8/69	**Polk Salad Annie** Tony Joe White
	Pomp & Circumstance..see: Graduation Song
1/61	**Pony Time** Chubby Checker
17/58	**Poor Boy** Royaltones
24/56	**Poor Boy** Elvis Presley
38/62	**Poor Fool** Ike & Tina Turner
22/59	**Poor Jenny** Everly Brothers
1/58	**Poor Little Fool** Ricky Nelson
27/63	**Poor Little Rich Girl** Steve Lawrence

POS/YR	RECORD TITLE/ARTIST
14/57	**Poor Man's Roses (Or A Rich Man's Gold)** Patti Page
33/81	**Poor Man's Son** Survivor
1/56 17/56 19/56	**Poor People Of Paris** Les Baxter Lawrence Welk & His Orchestra Russ Morgan & His Orchestra
31/78	**Poor Poor Pitiful Me** Linda Ronstadt
1/66	**Poor Side Of Town** Johnny Rivers
35/82	**Pop Goes The Movies, Part 1** Meco
1/79	**Pop Muzik** M
35/62	**Pop Pop Pop-Pie** Sherrys
24/72	**Pop That Thang** Isley Brothers
30/69	**Popcorn** James Brown
9/72	**Popcorn** Hot Butter
14/55	**Popcorn Song** Cliffie Stone & His Orchestra
10/62	**Popeye The Hitchhiker** Chubby Checker
21/66	**Popsicle** Jan & Dean
3/64	**Popsicles And Icicles** Murmaids
20/56	**Port Au Prince** Nelson Riddle & His Orchestra
9/61 36/67	**Portrait Of My Love** Steve Lawrence Tokens
19/56	**Portuguese Washerwomen** Joe "Fingers" Carr
	Poseidon Adventure..see: Morning After
7/65	**Positively 4th Street** Bob Dylan
24/78	**Power Of Gold** Dan Fogelberg/Tim Weisberg

POS/YR	RECORD TITLE/ARTIST
11/72	**Power Of Love** Joe Simon
11/71	**Power To The People** John Lennon
3/72	**Precious And Few** Climax featuring Sonny Geraci
19/79	**Precious Love** Bob Welch
30/71	**Precious, Precious** Jackie Moore
22/81	**Precious To Me** Phil Seymour
20/82	**Pressure** Billy Joel
	Pretty Baby..see: (It's Been A Long Time)
15/67	**Pretty Ballerina** Left Banke
9/60	**Pretty Blue Eyes** Steve Lawrence
29/66	**Pretty Flamingo** Manfred Mann
39/79	**Pretty Girls** Melissa Manchester
36/59	**Pretty Girls Everywhere** Eugene Church & The Fellows
7/61	**Pretty Little Angel Eyes** Curtis Lee
25/65	**Pretty Little Baby** Marvin Gaye
15/63	**Pretty Paper** Roy Orbison
10/63	**Pride And Joy** Marvin Gaye
8/59	**Primrose Lane** Jerry Wallace
30/61	**Princess** Frank Gari
37/65	**Princess In Rags** Gene Pitney
20/56	**Priscilla** Eddie Cooley & The Dimples

POS/YR	RECORD TITLE/ARTIST
	(Prisoner) ..see: Love Theme From "Eyes Of Laura Mars"
18/63	**Prisoner Of Love** James Brown
27/78	**Prisoner Of Your Love** Player
1/81	**Private Eyes** Daryl Hall & John Oates
2/58	**Problems** Everly Brothers
17/58	**Promise Me, Love** Andy Williams
14/74	**Promised Land** Elvis Presley
9/79	**Promises** Eric Clapton
38/81	**Promises In The Dark** Pat Benatar
19/68	**Promises, Promises** Dionne Warwick
29/63	**Proud** Johnny Crawford
2/69 4/71	**Proud Mary** Creedence Clearwater Revival Ike & Tina Turner
22/75	**Proud One** Osmonds
	Proud Ones..see: Theme From
33/78	**Prove It All Night** Bruce Springsteen
7/70	**Psychedelic Shack** Temptations
5/66	**Psychotic Reaction** Count Five
31/67	**Pucker Up Buttercup** Jr. Walker & The All Stars
2/63	**Puff The Magic Dragon** Peter Paul & Mary
20/62	**Punish Her** Bobby Vee
24/70 26/71	**Puppet Man** 5th Dimension Tom Jones

POS/YR	RECORD TITLE/ARTIST
14/65	**Puppet On A String** Elvis Presley
2/60 3/72	**Puppy Love** Paul Anka Donny Osmond
38/64	**Puppy Love** Barbara Lewis
1/58	**Purple People Eater** Sheb Wooley
27/62	**Push And Kick** Mark Valentino
	Push And Pull ..see: (Do The)
36/67	**Pushin' Too Hard** Seeds
25/63	**Pushover** Etta James
17/58	**Pussy Cat** Ames Brothers
8/57	**Put A Light In The Window** Four Lads
4/69	**Put A Little Love In Your Heart** Jackie DeShannon
32/58	**Put A Ring On My Finger** Les Paul & Mary Ford
2/71	**Put Your Hand In The Hand** Ocean
10/74	**Put Your Hands Together** O'Jays
2/59	**Put Your Head On My Shoulder** Paul Anka

Q

POS/YR	RECORD TITLE/ARTIST
1/61	**Quarter To Three** Gary "U.S." Bonds
	Que Sera Sera..see: Whatever Will Be, Will Be
2/81	**Queen Of Hearts** Juice Newton
40/76	**Queen Of My Soul** Average White Band

POS/YR	RECORD TITLE/ARTIST
9/58	**Queen Of The Hop** Bobby Darin
12/65	**Queen Of The House** Jody Miller
39/57	**Queen Of The Senior Prom** Mills Brothers
13/69	**Quentin's Theme** Charles Randolph Grean Sounde
19/60	**Question** Lloyd Price
21/70	**Question** Moody Blues
37/68	**Question Of Temperature** Balloon Farm
24/71	**Questions 67 And 68** Chicago
25/68	**Quick Joey Small (Run Joey Run)** Kasenetz-Katz Singing Orchestral Circus
8/63	**Quicksand** Martha & The Vandellas
4/59	**Quiet Village** Martin Denny
27/61	**Quite A Party** Fireballs

POS/YR	RECORD TITLE/ARTIST
16/56	**R-O-C-K** Bill Haley & His Comets
15/65	**Race Is On** Jack Jones
13/74	**Radar Love** Golden Earring
1/64	**Rag Doll** Four Seasons
F/71	**Rags To Riches** Elvis Presley
16/59	**Ragtime Cowboy Joe** Chipmunks
23/66	**Rain** Beatles

POS/YR	RECORD TITLE/ARTIST
19/71	**Rain Dance** Guess Who
10/66	**Rain On The Roof** Lovin' Spoonful
12/62	**Rain Rain Go Away** Bobby Vinton
2/67	**Rain, The Park & Other Things** Cowsills
4/57	**Rainbow** Russ Hamilton
25/79	**Rainbow Connection** Kermit
2/61	**Raindrops** Dee Clark
1/70	**Raindrops Keep Fallin' On My Head** B.J. Thomas
34/61	**Rainin' In My Heart** Slim Harpo
31/66	**Rains Came** Sir Douglas Quintet
26/75	**Rainy Day People** Gordon Lightfoot
2/66	**Rainy Day Women #12 & 35** Bob Dylan
2/71	**Rainy Days And Mondays** Carpenters
4/70	**Rainy Night In Georgia** Brook Benton
29/61	**Ram-Bunk-Shush** Ventures
21/61	**Rama Lama Ding Dong** Edsels
17/69	**Ramblin' Gamblin' Man** Bob Seger
2/73	**Ramblin' Man** Allman Brothers Band
2/62	**Ramblin' Rose** Nat King Cole
27/58	**Ramrod** Duane Eddy
2/70	**Rapper** Jaggerz
36/79	**Rapper's Delight** Sugarhill Gang

POS/YR	RECORD TITLE/ARTIST
1/81	**Rapture** Blondie
2/57 4/57 10/57	**Raunchy** Bill Justis & His Orchestra Ernie Freeman Billy Vaughn & His Orchestra
37/58	**Rave On** Buddy Holly
23/59	**Raw-Hide** Link Wray & His Ray Men
24/68	**Ray Of Hope** Rascals
15/55	**Razzle-Dazzle** Bill Haley & His Comets
20/70	**Reach Out And Touch (Somebody's Hand)** Diana Ross
20/64	**Reach Out For Me** Dionne Warwick
1/66 29/71	**Reach Out I'll Be There** Four Tops Diana Ross
10/68	**Reach Out Of The Darkness** Friend And Lover
26/75	**Ready** Cat Stevens
35/69	**Ready Or Not Here I Come (Can't Hide From Love)** Delfonics
11/78	**Ready To Take A Chance Again** Barry Manilow
5/80	**Real Love** Doobie Brothers
16/81	**Really Wanna Know You** Gary Wright
	Reaper..see: (Don't Fear) The
6/58	**Rebel-'Rouser** Duane Eddy
28/69	**Reconsider Me** Johnny Adams
37/66	**Recovery** Fontella Bass
5/59	**Red River Rock** Johnny & The Hurricanes

POS/YR	RECORD TITLE/ARTIST
37/59	**Red River Rose** Ames Brothers
10/65 11/65 23/65	**Red Roses For A Blue Lady** Vic Dana Bert Kaempfert & His Orchestra Wayne Newton
2/66	**Red Rubber Ball** Cyrkle
36/60 35/63	**Red Sails In The Sunset** Platters Fats Domino
23/65 27/73	**Reelin' And Rockin'** Dave Clark Five Chuck Berry
11/73	**Reeling In The Years** Steely Dan
2/67	**Reflections** Supremes
10/70	**Reflections Of My Life** Marmalade
15/80	**Refugee** Tom Petty & The Heartbreakers
39/73	**Relay** Who
8/62 4/67	**Release Me** "Little Esther" Phillips Engelbert Humperdinck
39/63	**Remember Diana** Paul Anka
16/71	**Remember Me** Diana Ross
26/64	**Remember Me** Rita Pavone
32/65	**(Remember Me) I'm The One Who Loves You** Dean Martin
33/77	**(Remember The Days Of The) Old Schoolyard** Cat Stevens
24/63	**Remember Then** Earls
5/64	**Remember (Walkin' In The Sand)** Shangri-Las
25/75	**Remember What I Told You To Forget** Tavares

POS/YR	RECORD TITLE/ARTIST
6/57	**Remember You're Mine** Pat Boone
3/78	**Reminiscing** Little River Band
26/75	**Rendezvous** Hudson Brothers
16/79	**Renegade** Styx
39/76	**Renegade** Michael Murphey
4/65	**Rescue Me** Fontella Bass
35/65 1/67	**Respect** Otis Redding Aretha Franklin
12/71	**Respect Yourself** Staple Singers
15/66	**Respectable** Outsiders
F/71 40/71	**Resurrection Shuffle** Tom Jones Ashton Gardner & Dyke
15/67	**Return Of The Red Baron** Royal Guardsmen
4/58	**Return To Me** Dean Martin
2/62	**Return To Sender** Elvis Presley
	Reuben..see: Ruben
1/79	**Reunited** Peaches & Herb
25/59	**Reveille Rock** Johnny & The Hurricanes
15/61	**Revenge** Brook Benton
8/63	**Reverend Mr. Black** Kingston Trio
12/68	**Revolution** Beatles
16/66	**Rhapsody In The Rain** Lou Christie
11/76	**Rhiannon (Will You Ever Win)** Fleetwood Mac

POS/YR	RECORD TITLE/ARTIST
1/75	**Rhinestone Cowboy** Glen Campbell
24/64	**Rhythm** Major Lance
3/63	**Rhythm Of The Rain** Cascades
1/77	**Rich Girl** Daryl Hall & John Oates
5/62	**Ride!** Dee Dee Sharp
23/74	**Ride 'Em Cowboy** Paul Davis
25/65	**Ride Away** Roy Orbison
4/70	**Ride Captain Ride** Blues Image
2/80	**Ride Like The Wind** Christopher Cross
37/67	**Ride, Ride, Ride** Brenda Lee
16/64	**Ride The Wild Surf** Jan & Dean
28/65	**Ride Your Pony** Lee Dorsey
	Riders In The Sky..see: Ghost
14/71	**Riders On The Storm** Doors
2/76	**Right Back Where We Started From** Maxine Nightingale
12/78	**Right Down The Line** Gerry Rafferty
23/71	**Right On The Tip Of My Tongue** Brenda & The Tabulations
29/61 14/64	**Right Or Wrong** Wanda Jackson Ronnie Dove
9/73	**Right Place Wrong Time** Dr. John
17/73	**Right Thing To Do** Carly Simon
6/77	**Right Time Of The Night** Jennifer Warnes
4/74	**Rikki Don't Lose That Number** Steely Dan

POS/YR	RECORD TITLE/ARTIST
33/65	**Ring Dang Doo** Sam The Sham & The Pharaohs
1/79	**Ring My Bell** Anita Ward
17/63	**Ring Of Fire** Johnny Cash
31/72	**Ring The Living Bell** Melanie
32/59	**Ring-A-Ling-A-Lario** Jimmie Rodgers
1/64	**Ringo** Lorne Greene
17/71	**Rings** Cymarron
10/62	**Rinky Dink** Dave "Baby" Cortez
17/56 25/56	**Rip It Up** Little Richard Bill Haley & His Comets
36/64	**Rip Van Winkle** Devotions
1/79	**Rise** Herb Alpert
14/70	**River Deep - Mountain High** Supremes & Four Tops
31/69	**River Is Wide** Grass Roots
	River Kwai March..see: March From
33/74	**River's Risin'** Edgar Winter Group
30/78	**Rivers Of Babylon** Boney M
	Road Runner..see: (I'm A)
25/59	**Robbin' The Cradle** Tony Bellus
	Rock..see: R-O-C-K
	Rock 'N' Roll ..also see: Rock And Roll, & Rockin' Roll
30/78	**Rock 'N' Roll Fantasy** Kinks
13/79	**Rock 'N' Roll Fantasy** Bad Company

POS/YR	RECORD TITLE/ARTIST
15/75	**Rock 'N' Roll (I Gave You The Best Years Of My Life)** Mac Davis
29/72	**Rock 'N' Roll Soul** Grand Funk Railroad
7/72	**Rock And Roll** Gary Glitter
	Rock And Roll ..also see: Rock 'N' Roll, & Rockin' Roll
12/76	**Rock And Roll All Nite** Kiss
32/81	**Rock And Roll Dreams Come Through** Jim Steinman
3/74	**Rock And Roll Heaven** Righteous Brothers
23/74	**Rock And Roll, Hoochie Koo** Rick Derringer
19/58	**Rock And Roll Is Here To Stay** Danny & The Juniors
28/76	**Rock And Roll Love Letter** Bay City Rollers
15/72	**Rock And Roll Lullaby** B.J. Thomas
8/57 5/76	**Rock And Roll Music** Chuck Berry Beach Boys
1/56	**Rock And Roll Waltz** Kay Starr
1/55 39/74	**Rock Around The Clock** Bill Haley & His Comets Bill Haley & His Comets
8/56	**Rock Island Line** Lonnie Donegan & His Skiffle Group
13/55	**Rock Love** Fontane Sisters
10/69	**Rock Me** Steppenwolf
34/64	**Rock Me Baby** B.B. King
38/72	**Rock Me Baby** David Cassidy
1/74	**Rock Me Gently** Andy Kim
5/74	**Rock On** David Essex

POS/YR	RECORD TITLE/ARTIST
36/56	**Rock Right** Georgia Gibbs
9/71	**Rock Steady** Aretha Franklin
1/74	**Rock The Boat** Hues Corporation
9/82	**Rock This Town** Stray Cats
1/80	**Rock With You** Michael Jackson
1/74	**Rock Your Baby** George McCrae
17/57	**Rock Your Little Baby To Sleep** Buddy Knox
10/57	**Rock-A-Billy** Guy Mitchell
10/56 37/61	**Rock-A-Bye Your Baby With A Dixie Melody** Jerry Lewis Aretha Franklin
23/62	**Rock-A-Hula Baby** Elvis Presley
38/59	**Rocka-Conga** Applejacks
6/72	**Rocket Man** Elton John
39/78	**Rocket Ride** Kiss
10/75	**Rockford Files** Mike Post
27/75	**Rockin' All Over The World** John Fogerty
14/60	**Rockin' Around The Christmas Tree** Brenda Lee
9/75	**Rockin' Chair** Gwen McCrae
7/60	**Rockin' Good Way (To Mess Around And Fall In Love)** Brook Benton & Dinah Washington
22/60	**Rockin' Little Angel** Ray Smith
1/76	**Rockin' Me** Steve Miller Band
6/72	**Rockin' Pneumonia - Boogie Woogie Flu** Johnny Rivers

POS/YR	RECORD TITLE/ARTIST
2/58	**Rockin' Robin** Bobby Day
2/72	Michael Jackson
	Rockin' Roll ..also see: Rock 'N' Roll, & Rock And Roll
14/73	**Rockin' Roll Baby** Stylistics
18/74	**Rockin' Soul** Hues Corporation
9/75	**Rocky** Austin Roberts
9/73	**Rocky Mountain High** John Denver
23/73	**Rocky Mountain Way** Joe Walsh
	Rocky, Theme From..see: Gonna Fly Now
30/79	**Rolene** Moon Martin
14/75	**Roll On Down The Highway** Bachman-Turner Overdrive
29/56	**Roll Over Beethoven** Chuck Berry
34/79	**Roller** April Wine
13/55	**Rollin' Stone** Fontane Sisters
	Rolling Stone..see: Cover Of
	Romeo & Juliet..see: Love Theme & (Just Like)
11/80	**Romeo's Tune** Steve Forbert
6/64	**Ronnie** Four Seasons
2/82	**Rosanna** Toto
3/80	**Rose** Bette Midler
6/56	**Rose And A Baby Ruth** George Hamilton IV
3/71	**Rose Garden** Lynn Anderson
	Roses And Roses..see: And Roses

POS/YR	RECORD TITLE/ARTIST
1/62	**Roses Are Red (My Love)** Bobby Vinton
24/57	**Rosie Lee** Mello-Tones
30/80	**Rotation** Herb Alpert
1/57	**Round And Round** Perry Como
21/65	**Round Every Corner** Petula Clark
13/72	**Roundabout** Yes
30/62	**Route 66** Nelson Riddle & His Orchestra
37/82	**Route 101** Herb Alpert
32/79	**Roxanne** Police
16/74	**Rub It In** Billy "Crash" Craddock
6/61	**Rubber Ball** Bobby Vee
37/79	**Rubber Biscuit** Blues Brothers
16/70	**Rubber Duckie** Ernie
2/76	**Rubberband Man** Spinners
26/69	**Ruben James** Kenny Rogers & The First Edition
28/60	**Ruby** Ray Charles
18/62	**Ruby Ann** Marty Robbins
2/63	**Ruby Baby** Dion
33/74	Billy "Crash" Craddock
6/69	**Ruby, Don't Take Your Love To Town** Kenny Rogers & The First Edition
30/60	**Ruby Duby Du** Tobin Mathews & Co.
	Ruby Red Dress..see: Leave Me Alone
1/67	**Ruby Tuesday** Rolling Stones

POS/YR	RECORD TITLE/ARTIST
21/60	**Rudolph The Red Nosed Reindeer** Chipmunks
34/56	**Rudy's Rock** Bill Haley & His Comets
16/58	**Rumble** Link Wray & His Ray Men
12/62	**Rumors** Johnny Crawford
6/69	**Run Away Child, Running Wild** Temptations
12/65	**Run, Baby Run (Back Into My Arms)** Newbeats
33/78	**Run For Home** Lindisfarne
18/82	**Run For The Roses** Dan Fogelberg
4/75	**Run Joey Run** David Geddes
36/60	**Run Red Run** Coasters
25/66	**Run, Run, Look And See** Brian Hyland
27/72	**Run Run Run** Jo Jo Gunne
28/60	**Run Samson Run** Neil Sedaka
2/61	**Run To Him** Bobby Vee
16/72	**Run To Me** Bee Gees
23/60	**Runaround** Fleetwoods
28/61	**Runaround** Regents
1/61 13/78	**Runaround Sue** Dion Leif Garrett
1/61	**Runaway** Del Shannon
12/78	**Runaway** Jefferson Starship
23/72	**Runnin' Away** Sly & The Family Stone

POS/YR	RECORD TITLE/ARTIST
1/60	**Running Bear** Johnny Preston
11/78	**Running On Empty** Jackson Browne
1/61	**Running Scared** Roy Orbison
39/72	**Runway** Grass Roots
33/65	**Rusty Bells** Brenda Lee

S

POS/YR	RECORD TITLE/ARTIST
15/75	**S.O.S.** Abba
	S.W.A.T. ..see: Theme From
39/66	**S.Y.S.L.J.F.M. (The Letter Song)** Joe Tex
20/61	**Sacred** Castells
1/79	**Sad Eyes** Robert John
29/61	**Sad Mood** Sam Cooke
5/61	**Sad Movies (Make Me Cry)** Sue Thompson
27/65	**Sad, Sad Girl** Barbara Mason
14/75	**Sad Sweet Dreamer** Sweet Sensation
5/58	**Sail Along Silvery Moon** Billy Vaughn & His Orchestra
4/79	**Sail On** Commodores
1/80	**Sailing** Christopher Cross
5/60	**Sailor (Your Home Is The Sea)** Lolita
	Saint..see: St.
18/56	**Saints Rock 'N Roll** Bill Haley & His Comets

POS/YR	RECORD TITLE/ARTIST
39/75	**Sally G** Paul McCartney
2/63	**Sally, Go 'Round The Roses** Jaynetts
20/77	**Sam** Olivia Newton-John
9/81	**Same Old Lang Syne** Dan Fogelberg
13/55	**Same Old Saturday Night** Frank Sinatra
16/60	**Same One** Brook Benton
8/61	**San Antonio Rose** Floyd Cramer
9/67	**San Franciscan Nights** Animals
	San Francisco..see: I Left My Heart In
4/67	**San Francisco (Be Sure To Wear Flowers In Your Hair)** Scott McKenzie
23/55	**Sand And The Sea** Nat King Cole
15/60	**Sandy** Larry Hall
21/63	**Sandy** Dion
27/66	**Sandy** Ronny & The Daytonas
32/57	**Santa & The Satellite (Parts 1 & 2)** Buchanan & Goodman
23/62	**Santa Claus Is Coming To Town** Four Seasons
7/80	**Sara** Fleetwood Mac
4/76	**Sara Smile** Daryl Hall & John Oates
39/80	**(Sartorial Eloquence) Don't Ya Wanna Play This Game No More?** Elton John
23/66	**Satin Pillows** Bobby Vinton
28/73	**Satin Sheets** Jeanne Pruett

POS/YR	RECORD TITLE/ARTIST
22/75	**Satin Soul** Love Unlimited Orchestra
	Satisfaction..see: (I Can't Get No)
39/66	**Satisfied Mind** Bobby Hebb
3/72	**Saturday In The Park** Chicago
28/71	**Saturday Morning Confusion** Bobby Russell
1/75	**Saturday Night** Bay City Rollers
18/64	**Saturday Night At The Movies** Drifters
27/75	**Saturday Night Special** Lynyrd Skynyrd
12/73	**Saturday Night's Alright For Fighting** Elton John
29/63	**Saturday Night** New Christy Minstrels
34/79	**Saturday Night, Sunday Morning** Thelma Houston
21/77	**Saturday Nite** Earth Wind & Fire
35/79	**Saturdaynight** Herman Brood
25/81	**Sausalito Summernight** Diesel
34/80	**Savannah Nights** Tom Johnston
22/77	**Save It For A Rainy Day** Stephen Bishop
10/64	**Save It For Me** Four Seasons
27/70	**Save The Country** 5th Dimension
1/60 18/74	**Save The Last Dance For Me** Drifters Defranco Family featuring Tony Defranco
2/65	**Save Your Heart For Me** Gary Lewis & The Playboys
27/76	**Save Your Kisses For Me** Brotherhood Of Man
37/61	**Saved** Lavern Baker

POS/YR	RECORD TITLE/ARTIST
17/81	**Say Goodbye To Hollywood** Billy Joel
3/73	**Say, Has Anybody Seen My Sweet Gypsy Rose** Dawn
21/66	**Say I Am (What I Am)** Tommy James & The Shondells
10/68	**Say It Loud - I'm Black And I'm Proud** James Brown
20/59	**Say Man** Bo Diddley
22/65	**Say Something Funny** Patty Duke
32/81	**Say What** Jesse Winchester
40/64	**Say You** Ronnie Dove
11/76	**Say You Love Me** Fleetwood Mac
20/81	**Say You'll Be Mine** Christopher Cross
15/77	**Say You'll Stay Until Tomorrow** Tom Jones
39/65	**(Say) You're My Girl** Roy Orbison
11/68 16/68	**Scarborough Fair** Simon & Garfunkel Sergio Mendes & Brasil '66
13/59	**Scarlet Ribbons (For Her Hair)** Browns featuring Jim Edward Brown
33/75	**School Boy Crush** Average White Band
3/57	**School Day** Chuck Berry
28/61	**School Is In** Gary "U.S." Bonds
5/61	**School Is Out** Gary "U.S." Bonds
7/72	**School's Out** Alice Cooper
6/71	**Scorpio** Dennis Coffey & The Detroit Guitar Band
14/59	**Sea Cruise** Frankie Ford

POS/YR	RECORD TITLE/ARTIST
21/61	**Sea Of Heartbreak** Don Gibson
2/59 33/82	**Sea Of Love** Phil Phillips with The Twilights Del Shannon
3/62 19/68 19/72	**Sealed With A Kiss** Brian Hyland Gary Lewis & The Playboys Bobby Vinton
3/57	**Searchin'** Coasters
	Searchin' So Long..see: (I've Been)
27/66	**Searching For My Love** Bobby Moore & The Rhythm Aces
1/74	**Seasons In The Sun** Terry Jacks
38/69	**Seattle** Perry Como
34/74	**Second Avenue** Art Garfunkel
40/56	**Second Fiddle** Kay Starr
7/62	**Second Hand Love** Connie Francis
32/66	**Second Hand Rose** Barbra Streisand
8/80	**Second Time Around** Shalamar
18/58	**Secret** Gordon MacRae
3/66	**Secret Agent Man** Johnny Rivers
29/66 20/75	**Secret Love** Billy Stewart Freddy Fender
3/58	**Secretly** Jimmie Rodgers
35/68	**Security** Etta James
28/80	**Seduction** James Last
27/69	**See** Rascals

POS/YR	RECORD TITLE/ARTIST
	See Me, Feel Me
12/70	Who
29/73	New Seekers
	See Saw
14/68	Aretha Franklin
	See Saw
25/56	Moonglows
	See See..see: C.C.
	See The Funny Little Clown
9/64	Bobby Goldsboro
	See You In September
23/59	Tempos
3/66	Happenings
	See You Later, Alligator
6/56	Bill Haley & His Comets
	Selfish One
11/64	Jackie Ross
	Send For Me
6/57	Nat King Cole
	Send In The Clowns
36/75	Judy Collins
19/77	Judy Collins
	Send Me Some Lovin'
13/63	Sam Cooke
	Send Me The Pillow You Dream On
17/62	Johnny Tillotson
22/65	Dean Martin
	Send One Your Love
4/79	Stevie Wonder
	Sentimental Lady
8/77	Bob Welch
	Separate Ways
20/73	Elvis Presley
	September
8/79	Earth Wind & Fire
	September In The Rain
23/61	Dinah Washington
	September Morn'
17/80	Neil Diamond
	Sequel
23/80	Harry Chapin
	Serpentine Fire
13/78	Earth Wind & Fire
	Set Me Free
23/65	Kinks

POS/YR	RECORD TITLE/ARTIST
	Set Me Free
27/80	Utopia
	7 And 7 Is
33/66	Love
	Seven Bridges Road
21/81	Eagles
	Seven Day Weekend
27/62	Gary "U.S." Bonds
	Seven Days
17/56	Dorothy Collins
18/56	Crew-Cuts
	"7-11" (Mambo No. 5)
30/58	Gone All Stars
	Seven Little Girls Sitting In The Back Seat
9/59	Paul Evans
	7 Rooms Of Gloom
14/67	Four Tops
	Seven Year Ache
22/81	Rosanne Cash
	Seventh Son
7/65	Johnny Rivers
	Seventeen
3/55	Fontane Sisters
5/55	Boyd Bennett & His Rockets
18/55	Rusty Draper
	Sexy Eyes
5/80	Dr. Hook
	Sexy Mama
17/74	Moments
	Sha La La
12/64	Manfred Mann
	Sha-La-La (Make Me Happy)
7/74	Al Green
	Shadow Dancing
1/78	Andy Gibb
	Shadows In The Moonlight
25/79	Anne Murray
	Shadows Of The Night
13/82	Pat Benatar
	Shadrack
19/62	Brook Benton
	Shaft..see: Theme From
	Shaggy Dog
38/64	Mickey Lee Lane

POS/YR	RECORD TITLE/ARTIST
7/65	**Shake** Sam Cooke
25/67	**Shake A Tail Feather** James & Bobby Purify
29/65	**Shake And Fingerpop** Jr. Walker & The All Stars
13/79	**Shake It** Ian Matthews
4/82	**Shake It Up** Cars
18/66	**Shake Me, Wake Me (When It's Over)** Four Tops
31/67	**Shake, Rattle & Roll** Arthur Conley
33/63	**Shake! Shake! Shake!** Jackie Wilson
1/76	**(Shake, Shake, Shake) Shake Your Booty** KC & The Sunshine Band
7/79	**Shake Your Body (Down To The Ground)** Jackson 5
	Shake Your Booty..see: Shake, Shake, Shake
5/79	**Shake Your Groove Thing** Peaches & Herb
23/76	**Shake Your Rump To The Funk** Bar-Kays
31/79	**Shakedown Cruise** Jay Ferguson
26/75	**Shakey Ground** Temptations
22/65	**Shakin' All Over** Guess Who
3/73	**Shambala** Three Dog Night
9/78	**Shame** Evelyn King
23/62	**Shame On Me** Bobby Bare
29/68	**Shame, Shame** Magic Lanterns
12/75	**Shame, Shame, Shame** Shirley (And Company)

POS/YR	RECORD TITLE/ARTIST
31/82	**Shanghai Breezes** John Denver
11/57 15/64 27/64	**Shangri-La** Four Coins Robert Maxwell Vic Dana
6/76	**Shannon** Henry Gross
22/68	**Shape Of Things To Come** Max Frost & The Troopers
11/66	**Shapes Of Things** Yardbirds
10/70	**Share The Land** Guess Who
13/69 14/81	**Share Your Love With Me** Aretha Franklin Kenny Rogers
6/78	**Sharing The Night Together** Dr. Hook
15/62	**Sharing You** Bobby Vee
31/79	**Shattered** Rolling Stones
30/75	**Shaving Cream** Benny Bell
23/70	**She** Tommy James & The Shondells
5/79	**She Believes In Me** Kenny Rogers
33/69	**She Belongs To Me** Ricky Nelson
30/70	**She Came In Through The Bathroom Window** Joe Cocker
19/62	**She Can't Find Her Keys** Paul Petersen
	She Comes To Me..see: (When She Needs Good Lovin')
5/62	**She Cried** Jay & The Americans
23/77	**She Did It** Eric Carmen
27/67	**She Is Still A Mystery** Lovin' Spoonful

POS/YR	RECORD TITLE/ARTIST
1/64	**She Loves You** Beatles
18/59	**She Say (Oom Dooby Doom)** Diamonds
31/64	**She Understands Me** Johnny Tillotson
40/66	Bobby Vinton
27/58	**She Was Only Seventeen (He Was One Year More)** Marty Robbins
3/67	**She'd Rather Be With Me** Turtles
22/81	**She's A Bad Mama Jama (She's Built, She's Stacked)** Carl Carlton
5/63	**She's A Fool** Lesley Gore
16/68	**She's A Heartbreaker** Gene Pitney
2/71	**She's A Lady** Tom Jones
25/68	**She's A Rainbow** Rolling Stones
4/64	**She's A Woman** Beatles
13/65	**She's About A Mover** Sir Douglas Quintet
39/71	**She's All I Got** Freddie North
17/78	**She's Always A Woman** Billy Joel
18/62	**She's Everything (I Wanted You To Be)** Ral Donner
7/76	**She's Gone** Daryl Hall & John Oates
23/82	**She's Got A Way** Billy Joel
14/62	**She's Got You** Patsy Cline
3/66	**She's Just My Style** Gary Lewis & The Playboys
15/68	**She's Lookin' Good** Wilson Pickett
14/67	**She's My Girl** Turtles

POS/YR	RECORD TITLE/ARTIST
38/58	**She's Neat** Dale Wright
11/71	**She's Not Just Another Woman** 8th Day
2/64	**She's Not There** Zombies
27/77	Santana
5/62	**She's Not You** Elvis Presley
10/80	**She's Out Of My Life** Michael Jackson
26/80	**She's So Cold** Rolling Stones
33/64	**She's The One** Chartbusters
1/62	**Sheila** Tommy Roe
17/64	**Shelter Of Your Arms** Sammy Davis Jr.
1/62	**Sherry** Four Seasons
3/55	**Shifting, Whispering Sands** Rusty Draper
5/55	Billy Vaughn & His Orchestra
24/70	**Shilo** Neil Diamond
	Shimmy, Shimmy ..see: (I Do The)
24/60	**Shimmy, Shimmy, Ko-Ko-Bop** Little Anthony & The Imperials
8/79	**Shine A Little Love** Electric Light Orchestra
40/81	**Shine On** L.T.D.
11/74	**Shinin' On** Grand Funk Railroad
1/75	**Shining Star** Earth Wind & Fire
5/80	**Shining Star** Manhattans
9/79	**Ships** Barry Manilow
10/57	**Shish-Kebab** Ralph Marterie & His Orchestra

POS/YR	RECORD TITLE/ARTIST
18/75	**Shoeshine Boy** Eddie Kendricks
9/68	**Shoo-Be-Doo-Be-Doo-Da-Day** Stevie Wonder
6/64	**Shoop Shoop Song (It's In His Kiss)** Betty Everett
31/68	**Shoot'em Up, Baby** Andy Kim
2/61 4/76	**Shop Around** Miracles Captain & Tennille
5/57	**Short Fat Fannie** Larry Williams
2/78	**Short People** Randy Newman
3/58	**Short Shorts** Royal Teens
4/65	**Shotgun** Jr. Walker & The All Stars
13/82	**Should I Do It** Pointer Sisters
19/80	**Should've Never Let You Go** Neil & Dara Sedaka
6/62	**Shout - Part 1** Joey Dee & The Starliters
31/76	**Shout It Out Loud** Kiss
6/62	**Shout! Shout! (Knock Yourself Out)** Ernie Maresca
1/74	**Show And Tell** Al Wilson
35/67	**Show Me** Joe Tex
6/76	**Show Me The Way** Peter Frampton
4/74	**Show Must Go On** Three Dog Night
28/77	**Show You The Way To Go** Jackson 5
22/76	**Shower The People** James Taylor
32/61	**Shu Rah** Fats Domino

POS/YR	RECORD TITLE/ARTIST
38/75	**(Shu-Doo-Pa-Poo-Poop) Love Being Your Fool** Travis Wammack
23/63	**Shut Down** Beach Boys
24/63	**Shutters And Boards** Jerry Wallace
22/58	**Sick And Tired** Fats Domino
8/74	**Sideshow** Blue Magic
25/64	**Sidewalk Surfin'** Jan & Dean
11/66	**Sign Of The Times** Petula Clark
3/70 18/77	**Signed, Sealed, Delivered I'm Yours** Stevie Wonder Peter Frampton
3/71	**Signs** Five Man Electrical Band
11/67	**Silence Is Golden** Tremeloes
3/57 10/57 5/65	**Silhouettes** Rays Diamonds Herman's Hermits
1/76	**Silly Love Songs** Paul McCartney
25/70	**Silver Bird** Mark Lindsay
20/55	**Silver Dollar** Teresa Brewer
38/76	**Silver Star** Four Seasons
20/62	**Silver Threads And Golden Needles** Springfields
4/68	**Simon Says** 1910 Fruitgum Co.
12/59 23/81	**Since I Don't Have You** Skyliners Don McLean
4/63	**Since I Fell For You** Lenny Welch
17/65	**Since I Lost My Baby** Temptations

Elvis Presley's death subsequently spawned more than 100 "tribute" discs, by artists of every possible description. Among them were "God Called Elvis Home," "Love Him Tender, Sweet Jesus," "From Graceland To The Promised Land," and "God Brought The Curtain Down."

Queen. When Queen secured their first hit, "Killer Queen," *Billboard* suggested that the record incorporated the "cheerfully menacing surrealism of the middle Beatles work." Which just goes to show that you can't believe everything you read.

The Ran-Dells. Rock historians have on various occasions appealed to members of the Ran-Dells to make themselves known, so that the group's story can be fully told for future generations.

The Young Rascals. What better training ground could anyone have than Joey Dee and the Starlighters at the Peppermint Lounge? Young Rascals Felix Cavaliere and Gene Cornish were in Joey's band, and that's where Felix gained experience with the electric organ—the core of the Rascal's r&b sound.

Otis Redding. Like the late Sam Cooke, whose crown he inherited and whose songs he recorded, Otis Redding was an entrepreneurial star of black music. He had his own record label (Jotis), publishing company, and management firm, and he produced protege Arthur Conley's biggest hit, "Sweet Soul Music."

Johnny Rivers. Another '60s rocker with an ear for vintage rhythm & blues, Johnny Rivers rode the top 40 with Chuck Berry's "Memphis" and "Maybelline," Huey Smith's "Rockin' Pneumonia And The Boogie Woogie Flue," and Willie Dixon's "Seventh Son," among others.

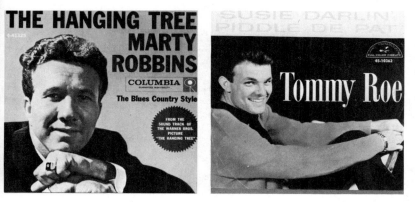

Marty Robbins. Although Elvis Presley waxed Arthur Crudup's "That's All Right" as his Sun Records debut, Marty Robbins made a version that no self-respecting rockabilly fan would be ashamed to own.

Tommy Roe was sufficiently popular in Britain in 1963—thanks to "Sheila" and another Buddy Holly soundalike, "Susie Darlin' "—that a concert promoter thought it would benefit an up-and-coming group to go on tour with the singer. That group was the Beatles.

The Rolling Stones. Their first top 10 hit was a song originally recorded by New Orleans r&b songstress Irma Thomas, and authored by Producer Jerry Ragovoy under the pseudonym of Norman Meade.

Diana Ross. *The Wiz* wasn't wonderful for Diana Ross and Michael Jackson. Their version of "Ease On Down The Road" from the movie of the Broadway show stopped one spot short of the top 40. Close, but no cigar.

Bobby Rydell. Among the huge hits associated with Philadelphia teen idol Bobby Rydell was "Nel Blu Dipinto Di Blu." Perhaps it's better remembered as "Volare."

Chubby Checker and Bobby Rydell? Not, perhaps, one of the great pairings of the rock pantheon; more on a par with Patience and Prudence, Tom and Jerrio, Steve and Eydie . . .

POS/YR	RECORD TITLE/ARTIST
12/56 34/56	**Since I Met You Baby** Ivory Joe Hunter Mindy Carson
32/67	**Since You Showed Me How To Be Happy** Jackie Wilson
38/59	**Since You've Been Gone** Clyde McPhatter
	Since You've Been Gone..see: (Sweet Sweet Baby)
1/55 20/55	**Sincerely** McGuire Sisters Moonglows
3/73	**Sing** Carpenters
5/76	**Sing A Song** Earth Wind & Fire
24/58	**Sing Boy Sing** Tommy Sands
1/56 17/56	**Singing The Blues** Guy Mitchell Marty Robbins
12/66	**Single Girl** Sandy Posey
3/60	**Sink The Bismarck** Johnny Horton
1/77	**Sir Duke** Stevie Wonder
1/75	**Sister Golden Hair** America
24/74	**Sister Mary Elephant (Shudd-Up!)** Cheech & Chong
36/67	**Sit Down, I Think I Love You** Mojo Men
37/71	**Sit Yourself Down** Stephen Stills
18/57 38/57	**Sittin' In The Balcony** Eddie Cochran Johnny Dee
1/68	**(Sittin' On) The Dock Of The Bay** Otis Redding
16/72	**Sitting** Cat Stevens
24/65	**Sitting In The Park** Billy Stewart

POS/YR	RECORD TITLE/ARTIST
32/63	**Six Days On The Road** Dave Dudley
28/59	**Six Nights A Week** Crests
18/67	**Six O'Clock** Lovin' Spoonful
13/66	**634-5789 (Soulsville, U.S.A.)** Wilson Pickett
2/59	**16 Candles** Crests
3/60	**Sixteen Reasons** Connie Stevens
1/55 17/55	**Sixteen Tons** "Tennessee" Ernie Ford Johnny Desmond
6/82	**'65 Love Affair** Paul Davis
13/74	**Skin Tight** Ohio Players
10/67	**Skinny Legs And All** Joe Tex
22/58	**Skinny Minnie** Bill Haley & His Comets
25/68	**Skip A Rope** Henson Cargill
3/75	**Sky High** Jigsaw
14/68	**Sky Pilot (Parts 1 & 2)** Animals
35/64	**Slaughter On Tenth Avenue** Ventures
13/60	**Sleep** Little Willie John
1/59	**Sleep Walk** Santo & Johnny
	Sleeping Beauty..see: To A
32/77	**Slide** Slave
6/68	**Slip Away** Clarence Carter
5/78	**Slip Slidin' Away** Paul Simon
19/75	**Slippery When Wet** Commodores

POS/YR	RECORD TITLE/ARTIST
33/56	**Slippin' And Slidin' (Peepin' And Hidin')** Little Richard
16/72	**Slippin' Into Darkness** War
3/66	**Sloop John B** Beach Boys
	Slow Dancin' ..see: Swayin' To The Music
20/77	**Slow Dancin' Don't Turn Me On** Addrisi Brothers
25/64	**Slow Down** Beatles
2/81	**Slow Hand** Pointer Sisters
20/76	**Slow Ride** Foghat
3/62	**Slow Twistin'** Chubby Checker
17/56	**Slow Walk** Sil Austin
26/56	Bill Doggett
34/77	**Slowdown** John Miles
30/70	**Sly, Slick, And The Wicked** Lost Generation
29/72	**Small Beginnings** Flash
21/61	**Small Sad Sam** Phil McLean
20/59	**Small World** Johnny Mathis
5/69	**Smile A Little Smile For Me** Flying Machine
21/55	**Smiles** Crazy Otto
3/71	**Smiling Faces Sometimes** Undisputed Truth
9/77	**Smoke From A Distant Fire** Sanford/Townsend Band
1/59	**Smoke Gets In Your Eyes** Platters
27/72	Blue Haze
4/73	**Smoke On The Water** Deep Purple

POS/YR	RECORD TITLE/ARTIST
17/60	**Smokie - Part 2** Bill Black's Combo
3/74	**Smokin' In The Boy's Room** Brownsville Station
24/81	**Smoky Mountain Rain** Ronnie Milsap
12/62	**Smoky Places** Corsairs Featuring Jay "Bird" Uzzell
27/68	**Snake** Al Wilson
8/62	**Snap Your Fingers** Joe Henderson
31/69	**Snatching It Back** Clarence Carter
2/67	**Snoopy Vs. The Red Baron** Royal Guardsmen
8/70	**Snowbird** Anne Murray
38/59	**So Close** Brook Benton
14/71	**So Far Away** Carole King
11/59	**So Fine** Fiestas
30/79	**So Good, So Right** Brenda Russell
36/69	**So Good Together** Andy Kim
39/69	**So I Can Love You** Emotions
7/77	**So In To You** Atlanta Rhythm Section
28/61	**So Long Baby** Del Shannon
6/59	**So Many Ways** Brook Benton
1/63	**So Much In Love** Tymes
2/57	**So Rare** Jimmy Dorsey
7/60	**So Sad (To Watch Good Love Go Bad)** Everly Brothers
21/62	**So This Is Love** Castells

POS/YR	RECORD TITLE/ARTIST
17/73	**So Very Hard To Go** Tower Of Power
21/74	**So You Are A Star** Hudson Brothers
29/67	**So You Want To Be A Rock 'N' Roll Star** Byrds
31/77	**So You Win Again** Hot Chocolate
14/67	**Society's Child (Baby I've Been Thinking)** Janis Ian
6/67	**Sock It To Me-Baby!** Mitch Ryder & The Detroit Wheels
35/57	**Soft** Bill Doggett
11/56 34/56	**Soft Summer Breeze** Eddie Heywood Diamonds
27/64	**Softly, As I Leave You** Frank Sinatra
29/72	**Softly Whispering I Love You** English Congregation
1/62	**Soldier Boy** Shirelles
17/75	**Solitaire** Carpenters
21/70	**Solitary Man** Neil Diamond
34/64	**Some Day We're Gonna Love Again** Searchers
36/81	**Some Days Are Diamonds (Some Days Are Stone)** John Denver
13/65	**Some Enchanted Evening** Jay & The Americans
39/73	**Some Guys Have All The Luck** Persuaders
3/75	**Some Kind Of Wonderful** Grand Funk Railroad
32/61	**Some Kind Of Wonderful** Drifters
37/59	**Some Kind-A Earthquake** Duane Eddy
30/68	**Some Things You Never Get Used To** Supremes

POS/YR	RECORD TITLE/ARTIST
26/68	**Some Velvet Morning** Nancy Sinatra & Lee Hazlewood
5/67	**Somebody To Love** Jefferson Airplane
13/77	**Somebody To Love** Queen
22/58	**Somebody Touched Me** Buddy Knox
18/56	**Somebody Up There Likes Me** Perry Como
7/82	**Somebody's Baby** Jackson Browne
8/70	**Somebody's Been Sleeping** 100 Proof Aged In Soul
33/76	**Somebody's Gettin' It** Johnnie Taylor
13/81	**Somebody's Knockin'** Terri Gibbs
32/71	**Somebody's Watching You** Little Sister
	Someday ..also see: Some Day
25/72	**Someday Never Comes** Creedence Clearwater Revival
36/82	**Someday, Someway** Marshall Crenshaw
1/69	**Someday We'll Be Together** Supremes
35/59	**Someone** Johnny Mathis
15/82	**Someone Could Lose A Heart Tonight** Eddie Rabbitt
4/75	**Someone Saved My Life Tonight** Elton John
21/80	**Someone That I Used To Love** Natalie Cole
13/55	**Someone You Love** Nat King Cole
37/77	**Somethin' 'Bout 'Cha** Latimore
1/67	**Somethin' Stupid** Nancy & Frank Sinatra
3/69	**Something** Beatles

POS/YR	RECORD TITLE/ARTIST
19/65	**Something About You** Four Tops
13/75	**Something Better To Do** Olivia Newton-John
28/76	**Something He Can Feel** Aretha Franklin
37/69	**Something In The Air** Thunderclap Newman
11/70	**Something's Burning** Kenny Rogers & The First Edition
37/62	**Something's Got A Hold On Me** Etta James
5/55 9/55	**Something's Gotta Give** McGuire Sisters Sammy Davis Jr.
12/72	**Something's Wrong With Me** Austin Roberts
31/77	**Sometimes** Facts Of Life
36/80	**Sometimes A Fantasy** Billy Joel
3/78	**Sometimes When We Touch** Dan Hill
19/64	**Somewhere** Tymes
26/66	**Somewhere** Len Barry
21/82	**Somewhere Down The Road** Barry Manilow
19/76 9/79	**Somewhere In The Night** Helen Reddy Barry Manilow
32/65	**Somewhere In Your Heart** Frank Sinatra
9/66	**Somewhere, My Love** Ray Conniff & The Singers
32/66	**Somewhere There's A Someone** Dean Martin
10/69	**Son Of A Preacher Man** Dusty Springfield
40/68	**Son Of Hickory Holler's Tramp** O.C. Smith
28/74	**Son Of Sagittarius** Eddie Kendricks

POS/YR	RECORD TITLE/ARTIST
8/56	**Song For A Summer Night (Parts 1 & 2)** Mitch Miller
14/70	**Song Of Joy** Miguel Rios
11/55	**Song Of The Dreamer** Eddie Fisher
29/79	**Song On The Radio** Al Stewart
1/72	**Song Sung Blue** Neil Diamond
25/78	**Songbird** Barbra Streisand
30/70	**Soolaimon (African Trilogy II)** Neil Diamond
9/71	**Sooner Or Later** Grass Roots
34/69	**Sophisticated Cissy** Meters
25/76	**Sophisticated Lady (She's A Different Lady)** Natalie Cole
2/59	**Sorry (I Ran All The Way Home)** Impalas
6/76	**Sorry Seems To Be The Hardest Word** Elton John
	Soul & Inspiration..see: (You're My)
	Soul Coaxing..see: Ame Caline
18/69	**Soul Deep** Box Tops
17/67	**Soul Finger** Bar-Kays
17/68	**Soul Limbo** Booker T. & The M.G.'s
35/73	**Soul Makossa** Manu Dibango
2/67 14/79	**Soul Man** Sam & Dave Blues Brothers
29/71	**Soul Power (Part 1)** James Brown
23/68	**Soul Serenade** Willie Mitchell
37/69	**Soul Shake** Peggy Scott & Jo Jo Benson

POS/YR	RECORD TITLE/ARTIST
37/73	**Soul Song** Joe Stampley
17/62	**Soul Twist** King Curtis
3/69	**Soulful Strut** Young-Holt Unlimited
36/67	**Sound Of Love** Five Americans
1/66	**Sounds Of Silence** Simon & Garfunkel
3/63	**South Street** Orlons
29/75	**South's Gonna Do It** Charlie Daniels Band
18/82	**Southern Cross** Crosby Stills & Nash
1/77	**Southern Nights** Glen Campbell
15/64	**Southtown, U.S.A.** Dixiebelles with Cornbread & Jerry
15/73	**Space Oddity** David Bowie
4/73	**Space Race** Billy Preston
23/72	**Spaceman** Nilsson
15/66	**Spanish Eyes** Al Martino
27/66	**Spanish Flea** Herb Alpert & The Tijuana Brass
10/61 2/71	**Spanish Harlem** Ben E. King Aretha Franklin
31/62	**Spanish Lace** Gene McDaniels
	(Speak Softly Love)..see: Love Theme From "The Godfather"
14/72	**Speak To The Sky** Rick Springfield
38/69	**Special Delivery** 1910 Fruitgum Co.
5/80	**Special Lady** Ray Goodman & Brown

POS/YR	RECORD TITLE/ARTIST
26/68	**Special Occasion** Miracles
17/56	**Speedo** Cadillacs
6/62	**Speedy Gonzales** Pat Boone
3/74	**Spiders & Snakes** Jim Stafford
3/70	**Spill The Wine** Eric Burdon & War
2/69	**Spinning Wheel** Blood Sweat & Tears
40/66	**Spinout** Elvis Presley
23/70	**Spirit In The Dark** Aretha Franklin
40/77	**Spirit In The Night** Manfred Mann's Earth Band
3/70	**Spirit In The Sky** Norman Greenbaum
35/75	**Spirit Of The Boogie** Kool & The Gang
11/82	**Spirits In The Material World** Police
3/58	**Splish Splash** Bobby Darin
3/68 17/79	**Spooky** Classics IV Featuring Dennis Yost Atlanta Rhythm Section
39/77	**Spring Rain** Silvetti
37/76	**Springtime Mama** Henry Gross
16/76	**Squeeze Box** Who
13/56	**St. Therese Of The Roses** Billy Ward & His Dominoes
1/59 22/67 25/71	**Stagger Lee** Lloyd Price Wilson Pickett Tommy Roe
9/60	**Stairway To Heaven** Neil Sedaka
22/69	**Stand!** Sly & The Family Stone

POS/YR	RECORD TITLE/ARTIST
	Stand By Me
4/61	Ben E. King
12/67	Spyder Turner
20/75	John Lennon
22/80	Mickey Gilley
	Stand By Your Man
19/69	Tammy Wynette
24/70	Candi Staton
	Stand Tall
10/76	Burton Cummings
	Standing At The End Of The Line
37/74	Lobo
	Standing In The Shadows Of Love
6/67	Four Tops
	Standing On The Corner
3/56	Four Lads
22/56	Dean Martin
	Star
29/74	Stealers Wheel
	Star Baby
39/74	Guess Who
	Star Is Born, Love Theme From A..see: Evergreen
	Star Wars Theme
1/77	Meco
10/77	John Williams
	Starbright
25/60	Johnny Mathis
	Stardust
12/57	Billy Ward & His Dominoes
32/64	Nino Tempo & April Stevens
	Stars On 45 [Medley]
1/81	Stars On 45
	Stars On 45 III
28/82	Stars On 45
	Start Me Up
2/81	Rolling Stones
	Start Movin' (In My Direction)
9/57	Sal Mineo
	Starting All Over Again
19/72	Mel & Tim
	Starting Over ..see: (Just Like)
	Starting Over Again
36/80	Dolly Parton

POS/YR	RECORD TITLE/ARTIST
	Stay
1/60	Maurice Williams & The Zodiacs
16/64	Four Seasons
20/78	Jackson Browne
	Stay
38/78	Rufus Featuring Chaka Khan
	Stay Awhile
7/71	Bells
	Stay Awhile
38/64	Dusty Springfield
	Stay In My Corner
10/68	Dells
	Stay With Me
17/72	Faces
	Stayin' Alive
1/78	Bee Gees
	Stayin' In
33/61	Bobby Vee
	Staying With It
37/81	Firefall
	Steal Away
17/64	Jimmy Hughes
37/70	Johnnie Taylor
	Steal Away
6/80	Robbie Dupree
	Steal The Night
25/81	Stevie Woods
	Steamroller Blues
17/73	Elvis Presley
	Steel Guitar And A Glass Of Wine
13/62	Paul Anka
	Step By Step
5/81	Eddie Rabbitt
	Step By Step
14/60	Crests
	Step By Step
37/73	Joe Simon
	Step Out Of Your Mind
24/67	American Breed
	Steppin' In A Slide Zone
39/78	Moody Blues
	Steppin' Out
6/82	Joe Jackson
	Steppin' Out
36/76	Neil Sedaka

POS/YR	RECORD TITLE/ARTIST
7/74	**Steppin' Out (Gonna Boogie Tonight)** Dawn
	Steppin' Stone..see: (I'm Not Your)
35/63	**Stewball** Peter Paul & Mary
25/61	**Stick Shift** Duals
11/71	**Stick-Up** Honey Cone
40/60	**Sticks And Stones** Ray Charles
1/79	**Still** Commodores
8/63	**Still** Bill Anderson
40/76	**Still Crazy After All These Years** Paul Simon
22/82	**Still In Saigon** Charlie Daniels Band
28/81	**Still Right Here In My Heart** Pure Prairie League
5/76	**Still The One** Orleans
4/78	**Still The Same** Bob Seger
19/82	**Still They Ride** Journey
11/70	**Still Water (Love)** Four Tops
12/73	**Stir It Up** Johnny Nash
7/80	**Stomp!** Brothers Johnson
36/78	**Stone Blue** Foghat
40/82	**Stone Cold** Rainbow
7/70	**Stoned Love** Supremes
30/73	**Stoned Out Of My Mind** Chi-Lites
3/68	**Stoned Soul Picnic** 5th Dimension

POS/YR	RECORD TITLE/ARTIST
14/71	**Stones** Neil Diamond
6/71	**Stoney End** Barbra Streisand
2/58	**Stood Up** Ricky Nelson
9/74	**Stop And Smell The Roses** Mac Davis
8/64	**Stop And Think It Over** Dale & Grace
3/81	**Stop Draggin' My Heart Around** Stevie Nicks
1/65	**Stop! In The Name Of Love** Supremes
39/71	**Stop, Look, Listen (To Your Heart)** Stylistics
7/66	**Stop Stop Stop** Hollies
36/62	**Stop The Music** Shirelles
26/71	**Stop The War Now** Edwin Starr
34/62	**Stop The Wedding** Etta James
5/68 32/79	**Stormy** Classics IV Featuring Dennis Yost Santana
23/71	**Story In Your Eyes** Moody Blues
15/57	**Story Of My Life** Marty Robbins
16/61	**Story Of My Love** Paul Anka
28/59	**Story Of My Love** Conway Twitty
16/55	**Story Untold** Crew-Cuts
39/81	**Straight From The Heart** Allman Brothers Band
36/68	**Straight Life** Bobby Goldsboro
15/78	**Straight On** Heart

POS/YR	RECORD TITLE/ARTIST
29/74	**Straight Shootin' Woman** Steppenwolf
15/56 18/56 39/56	**Stranded In The Jungle** Cadets Jayhawks Gadabouts featuring Wild Bill Putnam
14/76	**Strange Magic** Electric Light Orchestra
11/78	**Strange Way** Firefall
30/65	**Stranger In Town** Del Shannon
1/62 38/62	**Stranger On The Shore** Mr. Acker Bilk Andy Williams
1/66	**Strangers In The Night** Frank Sinatra
8/67	**Strawberry Fields Forever** Beatles
5/77	**Strawberry Letter 23** Brothers Johnson
39/68	**Strawberry Shortcake** Jay & The Techniques
1/74	**Streak** Ray Stevens
30/78	**Street Corner Serenade** Wet Willie
36/79	**Street Life** Crusaders
27/76	**Street Singin'** Lady Flash
39/60 25/63	**String Along** Fabian Ricky Nelson
1/62	**Stripper** David Rose & His Orchestra
17/81	**Stroke** Billy Squier
4/58	**Stroll** Diamonds
30/81	**Stronger Than Before** Carole Bayer Sager
22/75	**Struttin'** Billy Preston

POS/YR	RECORD TITLE/ARTIST
6/73	**Stuck In The Middle With You** Stealers Wheel
1/60	**Stuck On You** Elvis Presley
21/78	**Stuff Like That** Quincy Jones
4/79	**Stumblin' In** Suzi Quatro & Chris Norman
14/58	**Stupid Cupid** Connie Francis
18/72	**Suavecito** Malo
39/65	**Subterranean Homesick Blues** Bob Dylan
16/64	**Such A Night** Elvis Presley
26/79	**Such A Woman** Tycoon
11/65	**(Such An) Easy Question** Elvis Presley
20/81	**Suddenly** Olivia Newton-John & Cliff Richard
9/55 13/55 20/55	**Suddenly There's A Valley** Gogi Grant Jo Stafford Julius LaRosa
37/74	**Sugar Baby Love** Rubettes
10/72	**Sugar Daddy** Jackson 5
32/65	**Sugar Dumpling** Sam Cooke
30/64	**Sugar Lips** Al Hirt
5/58	**Sugar Moon** Pat Boone
22/69	**Sugar On Sunday** Clique
1/63	**Sugar Shack** Jimmy Gilmer & The Fireballs
1/69 25/70	**Sugar, Sugar** Archies Wilson Pickett
5/66	**Sugar Town** Nancy Sinatra

POS/YR	RECORD TITLE/ARTIST
1/58	**Sugartime** McGuire Sisters
21/69	**Suite: Judy Blue Eyes** Crosby Stills & Nash
1/63 3/81	**Sukiyaki** Kyu Sakamoto Taste Of Honey
4/79	**Sultans Of Swing** Dire Straits
7/76	**Summer** War
6/72	**Summer Breeze** Seals & Crofts
1/66	**Summer In The City** Lovin' Spoonful
	Summer Night..see: Song For A
5/78	**Summer Nights** Olivia Newton-John & John Travolta
24/65	**Summer Nights** Marianne Faithfull
	Summer Of '42..see: Theme From
	Summer Place..see: Theme From A
14/67	**Summer Rain** Johnny Rivers
26/66	**Summer Samba (So Nice)** Walter Wanderley
33/71	**Summer Sand** Dawn
30/60	**Summer Set** Monty Kelly & His Orchestra
7/64	**Summer Song** Chad & Jeremy
21/73	**Summer (The First Time)** Bobby Goldsboro
25/66	**Summer Wind** Frank Sinatra
11/60	**Summer's Gone** Paul Anka
10/66	**Summertime** Billy Stewart
8/58 14/68 27/70	**Summertime Blues** Eddie Cochran Blue Cheer Who

POS/YR	RECORD TITLE/ARTIST
26/58 38/62	**Summertime, Summertime** Jamies Jamies
13/66	**Sun Ain't Gonna Shine (Anymore)** Walker Bros.
18/65	**Sunday And Me** Jay & The Americans
31/67	**Sunday For Tea** Peter & Gordon
30/68 35/69	**Sunday Mornin'** Spanky & Our Gang Oliver
9/67	**Sunday Will Never Be The Same** Spanky & Our Gang
1/74	**Sundown** Gordon Lightfoot
39/77	**Sunflower** Glen Campbell
2/66	**Sunny** Bobby Hebb
14/66	**Sunny Afternoon** Kinks
34/72	**Sunny Days** Lighthouse
34/76	**Sunrise** Eric Carmen
4/72	**Sunshine** Jonathan Edwards
20/67	**Sunshine Girl** Parade
13/65	**Sunshine, Lollipops And Rainbows** Lesley Gore
5/68 36/68	**Sunshine Of Your Love** Cream Cream
1/74	**Sunshine On My Shoulders** John Denver
1/66	**Sunshine Superman** Donovan
13/70	**Super Bad (Part 1 & Part 2)** James Brown
31/73	**Super Fly Meets Shaft** John & Ernest
16/81	**Super Freak (Part 1)** Rick James

POS/YR	RECORD TITLE/ARTIST
8/72	**Superfly** Curtis Mayfield
26/79	**Superman** Herbie Mann
5/75	**Supernatural Thing - Part 1** Ben E. King
2/71	**Superstar** Carpenters
14/71	**Superstar** Murray Head With The Trinidad Singers
35/76	**Superstar** Paul Davis
18/71	**Superstar (Remember How You Got Where You Are)** Temptations
1/73	**Superstition** Stevie Wonder
33/72	**Superwoman (Where Were You When I Needed You)** Stevie Wonder
16/74	**Sure As I'm Sittin' Here** Three Dog Night
9/66	**Sure Gonna Miss Her** Gary Lewis & The Playboys
1/63	**Surf City** Jan & Dean
7/63	**Surfer Girl** Beach Boys
31/62	**Surfer's Stomp** Marketts
4/64	**Surfin' Bird** Trashmen
14/62	**Surfin' Safari** Beach Boys
3/63 36/74 20/77	**Surfin' U.S.A.** Beach Boys Beach Boys Leif Garrett
1/61	**Surrender** Elvis Presley
38/71	**Surrender** Diana Ross
11/68	**Susan** Buckinghams

POS/YR	RECORD TITLE/ARTIST
5/58 35/62	**Susie Darlin'** Robin Luke Tommy Roe
3/64	**Suspicion** Terry Stafford
13/79	**Suspicions** Eddie Rabbitt
1/69	**Suspicious Minds** Elvis Presley
27/57 11/68	**Suzie-Q** Dale Hawkins Creedence Clearwater Revival
39/73	**Swamp Witch** Jim Stafford
34/57	**Swanee River Rock (Talkin' 'Bout That River)** Ray Charles
14/60	**Sway** Bobby Rydell
10/77	**Swayin' To The Music (Slow Dancin')** Johnny Rivers
6/75	**Swearin' To God** Frankie Valli
10/55 12/55	**Sweet And Gentle** Alan Dale Georgia Gibbs
7/71	**Sweet And Innocent** Donny Osmond
19/81	**Sweet Baby** Stanley Clarke/George Duke
13/68	**Sweet Blindness** 5th Dimension
4/69	**Sweet Caroline (Good Times Never Seemed So Good)** Neil Diamond
7/69	**Sweet Cherry Wine** Tommy James & The Shondells
8/71	**Sweet City Woman** Stampeders
28/69	**Sweet Cream Ladies, Forward March** Box Tops
5/82	**Sweet Dreams** Air Supply
15/66	**Sweet Dreams** Tommy McLain

POS/YR	RECORD TITLE/ARTIST
36/75	**Sweet Emotion** Aerosmith
6/71	**Sweet Hitch-Hiker** Creedence Clearwater Revival
8/74	**Sweet Home Alabama** Lynyrd Skynyrd
18/68 37/72	**Sweet Inspiration** Sweet Inspirations Barbra Streisand
17/78	**Sweet Life** Paul Davis
2/58	**Sweet Little Sixteen** Chuck Berry
5/76	**Sweet Love** Commodores
36/79	**Sweet Lui-Louise** Ironhorse
7/71	**Sweet Mary** Wadsworth Mansion
40/75	**Sweet Maxine** Doobie Brothers
4/60	**Sweet Nothin's** Brenda Lee
7/56	**Sweet Old Fashioned Girl** Teresa Brewer
8/66	**Sweet Pea** Tommy Roe
9/72	**Sweet Seasons** Carole King
2/67	**Sweet Soul Music** Arthur Conley
33/75	**Sweet Sticky Thing** Ohio Players
13/75	**Sweet Surrender** John Denver
15/72	**Sweet Surrender** Bread
5/68	**(Sweet Sweet Baby) Since You've Been Gone** Aretha Franklin
10/66	**Sweet Talkin' Guy** Chiffons
17/78	**Sweet Talkin' Woman** Electric Light Orchestra

POS/YR	RECORD TITLE/ARTIST
5/76	**Sweet Thing** Rufus Featuring Chaka Khan
26/82	**Sweet Time** REO Speedwagon
33/73	**Sweet Understanding Love** Four Tops
40/64	**Sweet William** Millie Small
29/66	**Sweet Woman Like You** Joe Tex
9/59	**Sweeter Than You** Ricky Nelson
7/82	**Sweetest Thing (I've Ever Known)** Juice Newton
32/67	**Sweetest Thing This Side Of Heaven** Chris Bartley
10/81	**Sweetheart** Franke & The Knockouts
16/61	**Sweets For My Sweet** Drifters
39/60	**Swingin' On A Rainbow** Frankie Avalon
13/62	**Swingin' Safari** Billy Vaughn & His Orchestra
5/60	**Swingin' School** Bobby Rydell
23/58	**Swingin' Shepherd Blues** Moe Koffman Quartette
38/63	**Swinging On A Star** Big Dee Irwin
17/77	**Swingtown** Steve Miller Band
26/61	**Switch-A-Roo** Hank Ballard & The Midnighters
5/72	**Sylvia's Mother** Dr. Hook
37/76	**(System Of) Doctor Tarr And Professor Fether** Alan Parsons Project

POS/YR	RECORD TITLE/ARTIST

T

35/75	**T-R-O-U-B-L-E** Elvis Presley
1/74	**TSOP (The Sound Of Philadelphia)** MFSB
23/60	**Ta Ta** Clyde McPhatter
8/82	**Tainted Love** Soft Cell
3/78	**Take A Chance On Me** Abba
2/69	**Take A Letter Maria** R.B. Greaves
15/80	**Take A Little Rhythm** Ali Thomson
30/72	**Take A Look Around** Temptations
16/59	**Take A Message To Mary** Everly Brothers
20/69	**Take Care Of Your Homework** Johnnie Taylor
25/61	**Take Five** Dave Brubeck Quartet
7/61	**Take Good Care Of Her** Adam Wade
1/61 33/68	**Take Good Care Of My Baby** Bobby Vee Bobby Vinton
10/82	**Take It Away** Paul McCartney
12/72	**Take It Easy** Eagles
10/82	**Take It Easy On Me** Little River Band
33/76	**Take It Like A Man** Bachman-Turner Overdrive
5/81	**Take It On The Run** REO Speedwagon
4/76	**Take It To The Limit** Eagles

POS/YR	RECORD TITLE/ARTIST
16/65	**Take Me Back** Little Anthony & The Imperials
18/82	**Take Me Down** Alabama
38/68	**Take Me For A Little While** Vanilla Fudge
8/79	**Take Me Home** Cher
2/71	**Take Me Home, Country Roads** John Denver
11/75	**Take Me In Your Arms (Rock Me)** Doobie Brothers
26/79	**Take Me To The River** Talking Heads
17/81	**Take My Heart (You Can Have It If You Want It)** Kool & The Gang
16/82	**Take Off** Bob & Doug Mckenzie
10/79	**Take The Long Way Home** Supertramp
11/76	**Take The Money And Run** Steve Miller Band
8/63	**Take These Chains From My Heart** Ray Charles
11/68	**Take Time To Know Her** Percy Sledge
3/80	**Take Your Time (Do It Right) Part 1** S.O.S. Band
12/74	**Takin' Care Of Business** Bachman-Turner Overdrive
13/76	**Takin' It To The Streets** Doobie Brothers
7/63	**Talk Back Trembling Lips** Johnny Tillotson
15/66	**Talk Talk** Music Machine
34/60	**Talk That Talk** Jackie Wilson
38/59	**Talk To Me** Frank Sinatra
20/58 11/63	**Talk To Me, Talk To Me** Little Willie John Sunny & The Sunglows

POS/YR	RECORD TITLE/ARTIST
20/57	**Talkin' To The Blues** Jim Lowe
12/64	**Talking About My Baby** Impressions
18/78	**Talking In Your Sleep** Crystal Gayle
27/72	**Talking Loud And Saying Nothing** James Brown
36/59 38/64	**Tall Cool One** Wailers Wailers
	Tall Oak Tree..see: (There Was A)
7/59	**Tall Paul** Annette
6/59	**Tallahassee Lassie** Freddy Cannon
1/57 5/57	**Tammy** Debbie Reynolds Ames Brothers
18/76	**Tangerine** Salsoul Orchestra
31/75	**Tangled Up In Blue** Bob Dylan
34/68	**Tapioca Tundra** Monkees
38/66	**Tar And Cement** Verdelle Smith
7/65	**Taste Of Honey** Herb Alpert & The Tijuana Brass
18/72	**Taurus** Dennis Coffey & The Detroit Guitar Band
24/72	**Taxi** Harry Chapin
7/58	**Tea For Two Cha Cha** Tommy Dorsey Orchestra
25/62	**Teach Me Tonight** George Maharis
16/70	**Teach Your Children** Crosby Stills Nash & Young
21/58	**Teacher, Teacher** Johnny Mathis
31/61	**Tear** Gene McDaniels

POS/YR	RECORD TITLE/ARTIST
23/59	**Tear Drop** Santo & Johnny
20/57	**Tear Drops** Lee Andrews & The Hearts
5/56	**Tear Fell** Teresa Brewer
15/76	**Tear The Roof Off The Sucker (Give Up The Funk)** Parliament
20/64	**Tears And Roses** Al Martino
1/70	**Tears Of A Clown** Miracles
4/58	**Tears On My Pillow** Little Anthony & The Imperials
39/59	**Teasin'** Quaker City Boys
17/60	**Teddy** Connie Francis
40/76	**Teddy Bear** Red Sovine
	Teddy Bear ..see: Let Me Be Your
32/73	**Teddy Bear Song** Barbara Fairchild
2/57	**Teen-Age Crush** Tommy Sands
5/62	**Teen Age Idol** Ricky Nelson
6/56 19/56	**Teen Age Prayer** Gale Storm Gloria Mann
1/60	**Teen Angel** Mark Dinning
4/59	**Teen Beat** Sandy Nelson
29/59	**Teen Commandments** Paul Anka-George Hamilton IV-Johnny Nash
	Teenage Queen..see: Ballad Of
5/59	**Teenager In Love** Dion & The Belmonts
2/57	**Teenager's Romance** Ricky Nelson

POS/YR	RECORD TITLE/ARTIST
7/77	**Telephone Line** Electric Light Orchestra
18/77	**Telephone Man** Meri Wilson
6/65	**Tell Her No** Zombies
40/73	**Tell Her She's Lovely** El Chicano
4/63	**Tell Him** Exciters
8/59	**Tell Him No** Travis & Bob
17/70	**Tell It All Brother** Kenny Rogers & The First Edition
2/67 8/81	**Tell It Like It Is** Aaron Neville Heart
33/64	**Tell It On The Mountain** Peter Paul & Mary
10/67	**Tell It To The Rain** Four Seasons
7/60	**Tell Laura I Love Her** Ray Peterson
23/68	**Tell Mama** Etta James
22/62	**Tell Me** Dick & DeeDee
21/74	**Tell Me A Lie** Sami Jo
3/74	**Tell Me Something Good** Rufus Featuring Chaka Khan
37/67	**Tell Me To My Face** Keith
33/82	**Tell Me Tomorrow - Part 1** Smokey Robinson
13/64	**Tell Me Why** Bobby Vinton
18/61	**Tell Me Why** Belmonts
33/66	**Tell Me Why** Elvis Presley
24/64	**Tell Me (You're Coming Back)** Rolling Stones

POS/YR	RECORD TITLE/ARTIST
1/62	**Telstar** Tornadoes
39/70	**Temma Harbour** Mary Hopkin
27/61	**Temptation** Everly Brothers
15/71	**Temptation Eyes** Grass Roots
22/58	**Ten Commandments Of Love** Harvey & The Moonglows
24/60	**Tender Love And Care (T.L.C.)** Jimmie Rodgers
	Tender Trap..see: (Love Is)
31/61	**Tenderly** Bert Kaempfert & His Orchestra
23/70	**Tennessee Bird Walk** Jack Blanchard & Misty Morgan
35/64	**Tennessee Waltz** Sam Cooke
1/58 20/58	**Tequila** Champs Eddie Platt & His Orchestra
	Testify..see: (I Wanna)
1/75	**Thank God I'm A Country Boy** John Denver
22/78	**Thank God It's Friday** Love & Kisses
1/70	**Thank You (Falettinme Be Mice Elf Agin)** Sly & The Family Stone
25/78	**Thank You For Being A Friend** Andrew Gold
35/64	**Thank You Girl** Beatles
16/59	**Thank You Pretty Baby** Brook Benton
37/74	**Thanks For Saving My Life** Billy Paul
4/82	**That Girl** Stevie Wonder
22/80	**That Girl Could Sing** Jackson Browne
6/73	**That Lady (Part 1)** Isley Brothers

POS/YR	RECORD TITLE/ARTIST
20/64	**That Lucky Old Sun** Ray Charles
13/55 18/58 21/61	**That Old Black Magic** Sammy Davis Jr. Louis Prima & Keely Smith Bobby Rydell
21/81	**That Old Song** Ray Parker Jr. & Raydio
28/62	**That Stranger Used To Be My Girl** Trade Martin
12/63	**That Sunday, That Summer** Nat King Cole
1/57 11/76	**That'll Be The Day** Crickets Linda Ronstadt
17/56	**That's All** "Tennessee" Ernie Ford
3/55	**That's All I Want From You** Jaye P. Morgan
16/56	**That's All There Is To That** Nat King Cole
6/60	**That's All You Gotta Do** Brenda Lee
40/63	**That's How Heartaches Are Made** Baby Washington
39/58	**That's How Much I Love You** Pat Boone
31/61	**That's It-I Quit-I'm Movin' On** Sam Cooke
4/66	**That's Life** Frank Sinatra
9/62	**That's Old Fashioned (That's The Way Love Should Be)** Everly Brothers
3/77	**That's Rock 'N' Roll** Shaun Cassidy
12/64	**That's The Way Boys Are** Lesley Gore
27/72	**That's The Way I Feel About Cha** Bobby Womack
1/75	**That's The Way (I Like It)** KC & The Sunshine Band
10/71	**That's The Way I've Always Heard It Should Be** Carly Simon

POS/YR	RECORD TITLE/ARTIST
7/69	**That's The Way Love Is** Marvin Gaye
33/63	**That's The Way Love Is** Bobby Bland
12/75	**That's The Way Of The World** Earth Wind & Fire
27/61	**That's What Girls Are Made For** Spinners
35/64	**That's What Love Is Made Of** Miracles
27/75	**That's When The Music Takes Me** Neil Sedaka
29/70	**That's Where I Went Wrong** Poppy Family featuring Susan Jacks
27/76	**That's Where The Happy People Go** Trammps
13/59	**That's Why (I Love You So)** Jackie Wilson
35/60	**Theme For Young Lovers** Percy Faith & His Orchestra
1/60 16/65	**Theme From "A Summer Place"** Percy Faith & His Orchestra Lettermen
28/62	**Theme From Ben Casey** Valjean
18/73	**Theme From Cleopatra Jones** Joe Simon
13/78 25/78	**Theme From Close Encounters** John Williams Meco
39/61	**Theme From Dixie** Duane Eddy
10/62	**Theme From Dr. Kildare (Three Stars Will Shine Tonight)** Richard Chamberlain
2/81	**Theme From Greatest American Hero (Believe It Or Not)** Joey Scarbury
10/81	**Theme From Hill Street Blues** Mike Post
32/75	**Theme From Jaws (Main Title)** John Williams
9/71 13/71 31/71	**Theme From Love Story** Andy Williams Henry Mancini Francis Lai & His Orchestra

POS/YR	RECORD TITLE/ARTIST
25/82	**Theme From Magnum P.I.** Mike Post
1/76	**Theme From Mahogany (Do You Know Where You're Going To)** Diana Ross
32/80	**Theme From New York, New York** Frank Sinatra
1/76	**Theme From S.W.A.T.** Rhythm Heritage
1/71	**Theme From Shaft** Isaac Hayes
21/71	**Theme From Summer Of '42** Peter Nero
10/60	**Theme From The Apartment** Ferrante & Teicher
21/80	**Theme From The Dukes Of Hazzard (Good Ol' Boys)** Waylon Jennings
	Theme From The Man With The Golden Arm..see: Man With The Golden Arm
38/72	**Theme From The Men** Isaac Hayes
39/56	**Theme From The Proud Ones** Nelson Riddle & His Orchestra
	Theme From The Three Penny Opera..see: Mack The Knife
27/60	**Theme From The Unforgiven (The Need For Love)** Don Costa & His Orchestra
2/68	**(Theme From) Valley Of The Dolls** Dionne Warwick
21/78	**Theme Song From "Which Way Is Up"** Stargard
35/78	**Themes From The Wizard Of Oz** Meco
1/74	**Then Came You** Dionne Warwick & Spinners
6/63	**Then He Kissed Me** Crystals
6/67 27/76	**Then You Can Tell Me Goodbye** Casinos Glen Campbell
34/75	**There Goes Another Love Song** Outlaws

POS/YR	RECORD TITLE/ARTIST
2/59	**There Goes My Baby** Drifters
20/67 F/71	**There Goes My Everything** Engelbert Humperdinck Elvis Presley
19/58	**There Goes My Heart** Joni James
1/64	**There! I've Said It Again** Bobby Vinton
20/68	**There Is** Dells
11/67	**There Is A Mountain** Donovan
	There Is Love..see: Wedding Song
32/73	**There It Is** Tyrone Davis
33/59	**There Must Be A Way** Joni James
26/61	**There She Goes** Jerry Wallace
23/60	**(There Was A) Tall Oak Tree** Dorsey Burnette
36/68	**There Was A Time** James Brown
33/66	**There Will Never Be Another You** Chris Montez
18/74	**There Won't Be Anymore** Charlie Rich
25/57	**(There'll Be) Peace In The Valley (For Me)** Elvis Presley
26/69	**There'll Come A Time** Betty Everett
36/78	**There'll Never Be** Switch
20/57	**There's A Gold Mine In The Sky** Pat Boone
4/67 12/76	**There's A Kind Of Hush (All Over The World)** Herman's Hermits Carpenters
3/61	**There's A Moon Out Tonight** Capris
21/69	**There's Gonna Be A Showdown** Archie Bell & The Drells

POS/YR	RECORD TITLE/ARTIST
34/67	There's Got To Be A Word! Innocence
5/81	(There's) No Gettin' Over Me Ronnie Milsap
20/61	There's No Other (Like My Baby) Crystals
	There's Nothing Stronger Than Our Love..see: I Believe
10/58	There's Only One Of You Four Lads
31/60	There's Something On Your Mind, Part 2 Bobby Marchan
1/66	These Boots Are Made For Walkin' Nancy Sinatra
6/69 16/69	These Eyes Guess Who Jr. Walker & The All Stars
5/75	They Just Can't Stop It the (Games People Play) Spinners
1/70	(They Long To Be) Close To You Carpenters
3/66	They're Coming To Take Me Away, Ha-Haaa! Napoleon XIV
	Thicker Than Water..see: (Love Is)
15/71	Thin Line Between Love & Hate Persuaders
3/62	Things Bobby Darin
23/67	Things I Should Have Said Grass Roots
16/69	Things I'd Like To Say New Colony Six
5/77	Things We Do For Love 10cc
7/68	Think Aretha Franklin
25/64	Think Brenda Lee
33/60	Think James Brown
20/80	Think About Me Fleetwood Mac

POS/YR	RECORD TITLE/ARTIST
30/66	Think I'll Go Somewhere And Cry Myself To Sleep Al Martino
16/82	Think I'm In Love Eddie Money
27/58	Think It Over Crickets
34/78	Think It Over Cheryl Ladd
11/61	Think Twice Brook Benton
18/73	Thinking Of You Loggins & Messina
14/75	Third Rate Romance Amazing Rhythm Aces
23/80	Third Time Lucky (First Time I Was A Fool) Foghat
24/60	This Bitter Earth Dinah Washington
1/65	This Diamond Ring Gary Lewis & The Playboys
12/66	This Door Swings Both Ways Herman's Hermits
12/59	This Friendly World Fabian
9/69	This Girl Is A Woman Now Gary Puckett & The Union Gap
1/68 7/69	This Guy's (Girl's) In Love With You Herb Alpert Dionne Warwick
24/74	This Heart Gene Redding
26/59	This I Swear Skyliners
11/80	This Is It Kenny Loggins
35/78	This Is Love Paul Anka
25/68	This Is My Country Impressions
3/67	This Is My Song Petula Clark
39/77	This Is The Way That I Feel Marie Osmond

POS/YR	RECORD TITLE/ARTIST
32/65	**This Little Bird** Marianne Faithfull
11/81	**This Little Girl** Gary "U.S." Bonds
21/63	**This Little Girl** Dion
26/58	**This Little Girl Of Mine** Everly Brothers
24/58	**This Little Girl's Gone Rockin'** Ruth Brown
16/60 6/69	**This Magic Moment** Drifters Jay & The Americans
33/82	**This Man Is Mine** Heart
10/76	**This Masquerade** George Benson
19/79	**This Night Won't Last Forever** Michael Johnson
12/66	**This Old Heart Of Mine (Is Weak For You)** Isley Brothers
29/76	**This One's For You** Barry Manilow
20/59	**This Should Go On Forever** Rod Bernard
25/76	**This Song** George Harrison
6/61	**This Time** Troy Shondell
27/80	**This Time** John Cougar
10/78	**This Time I'm In It For Love** Player
6/75	**This Will Be** Natalie Cole
38/72	**This World** Staple Singers
6/63	**Those Lazy-Hazy-Crazy Days Of Summer** Nat King Cole
9/61	**Those Oldies But Goodies (Remind Me Of You)** Little Caesar & The Romans

POS/YR	RECORD TITLE/ARTIST
2/68	**Those Were The Days** Mary Hopkin
13/65	**Thou Shalt Not Steal** Dick & DeeDee
3/60	**Thousand Stars** Kathy Young with The Innocents
1/59 23/59	**Three Bells** Browns featuring Jim Edward Brown Dick Flood
35/61	**Three Hearts In A Tangle** Roy Drusky
24/67	**Three Little Fishes (medley)** Mitch Ryder & The Detroit Wheels
15/60	**Three Nights A Week** Fats Domino
33/65	**Three O'Clock In The Morning** Bert Kaempfert & His Orchestra
	Three Penny Opera..see: Mack The Knife
36/74	**Three Ring Circus** Blue Magic
11/59	**Three Stars** Tommy Dee
1/78	**Three Times A Lady** Commodores
19/80	**Three Times In Love** Tommy James
28/64	**Three Window Coupe** Rip Chords
15/70	**Thrill Is Gone** B.B. King
13/82	**Through The Years** Kenny Rogers
17/72	**Thunder And Lightning** Chi Coltrane
38/77	**Thunder In My Heart** Leo Sayer
9/78	**Thunder Island** Jay Ferguson
25/66	**Thunderball** Tom Jones
1/65	**Ticket To Ride** Beatles

POS/YR	RECORD TITLE/ARTIST
1/81	**Tide Is High** Blondie
1/73	**Tie A Yellow Ribbon Round The Ole Oak Tree** Dawn
3/63	**Tie Me Kangaroo Down, Sport** Rolf Harris
37/60	**Ties That Bind** Brook Benton
3/59	**Tiger** Fabian
11/72	**Tight Rope** Leon Russell
1/68	**Tighten Up** Archie Bell & The Drells
7/70	**Tighter, Tighter** Alive & Kicking
12/59	**Tijuana Jail** Kingston Trio
38/66	**Tijuana Taxi** Herb Alpert & The Tijuana Brass
4/59	**('Til) I Kissed You** Everly Brothers
32/75	**Til The World Ends** Three Dog Night
22/57 14/61 27/68	**Till** Roger Williams Angels Vogues
26/62	**Till Death Do Us Part** Bob Braun
20/63	**Till Then** Classics
30/59	**Till There Was You** Anita Bryant
15/81	**Time** Alan Parsons Project
36/66	**Time After Time** Chris Montez
30/60	**Time And The River** Nat King Cole
32/74	**Time For Livin'** Sly & The Family Stone
39/68	**Time For Livin'** Association

POS/YR	RECORD TITLE/ARTIST
11/68	**Time Has Come Today** Chambers Brothers
1/73	**Time In A Bottle** Jim Croce
6/64	**Time Is On My Side** Rolling Stones
6/69	**Time Is Tight** Booker T. & The M.G.'s
15/81	**Time Is Time** Andy Gibb
3/69	**Time Of The Season** Zombies
22/81	**Time Out Of Mind** Steely Dan
7/78	**Time Passages** Al Stewart
33/73	**Time To Get Down** O'Jays
5/66	**Time Won't Let Me** Outsiders
7/76	**Times Of Your Life** Paul Anka
17/71	**Timothy** Buoys
4/74	**Tin Man** America
5/55	**Tina Marie** Perry Como
17/68	**Tip-Toe Thru' The Tulips With Me** Tiny Tim
11/71	**Tired Of Being Alone** Al Green
8/80	**Tired Of Toein' The Line** Rocky Burnette
6/65	**Tired Of Waiting For You** Kinks
26/62	**To A Sleeping Beauty** Jimmy Dean
22/58	**To Be Loved** Jackie Wilson
21/60	**To Each His Own** Platters
29/68	**To Give (The Reason I Live)** Frankie Valli

POS/YR	RECORD TITLE/ARTIST
	To Know Him Is To Love Him
1/58	Teddy Bears
24/65	Peter & Gordon
34/69	Bobby Vinton
	To Know You Is To Love You
38/73	B.B. King
	To Love Somebody
17/67	Bee Gees
	To Sir With Love
1/67	Lulu
	To Susan On The West Coast Waiting
35/69	Donovan
	To The Aisle
25/57	Five Satins
	To The Door Of The Sun (Alle Porte Del Sole)
17/75	Al Martino
	To The Ends Of The Earth
25/56	Nat King Cole
	To You, My Love
27/56	Nick Noble
	Toast And Marmalade For Tea
20/71	Tin Tin
	Tobacco Road
14/64	Nashville Teens
	Today
17/64	New Christy Minstrels
	(Today I Met) The Boy I'm Gonna Marry
39/63	Darlene Love
	Today's The Day
23/76	America
	Together
6/61	Connie Francis
	Together
18/81	Tierra
	Together Again
19/66	Ray Charles
	Together Let's Find Love
37/72	5th Dimension
	Togetherness
26/60	Frankie Avalon
	Tom Cat
20/63	Rooftop Singers
	Tom Dooley
1/58	Kingston Trio

POS/YR	RECORD TITLE/ARTIST
	Tomboy
29/59	Perry Como
	Tomorrow
23/68	Strawberry Alarm Clock
	Tonight
8/61	Ferrante & Teicher
	Tonight (Could Be The Night)
26/61	Velvets featuring Virgil Johnson
	Tonight I Fell In Love
15/61	Tokens
	Tonight I'm Yours (Don't Hurt Me)
20/82	Rod Stewart
	Tonight My Love, Tonight
13/61	Paul Anka
	Tonight You Belong To Me
4/56	Patience & Prudence
15/56	Lennon Sisters
	Tonight's The Night
28/65	Solomon Burke
	Tonight's The Night (Gonna Be Alright)
1/76	Rod Stewart
	Tonights The Night
39/60	Shirelles
	Too Busy Thinking About My Baby
4/69	Marvin Gaye
	Too Close For Comfort
39/56	Eydie Gorme
	Too Hot
5/80	Kool & The Gang
	Too Hot Ta Trot
24/78	Commodores
	Too Late To Turn Back Now
2/72	Cornelius Brothers & Sister Rose
	Too Many Fish In The Sea
25/64	Marvelettes
24/67	Mitch Ryder & The Detroit Wheels
	Too Many Rivers
13/65	Brenda Lee
	Too Much
1/57	Elvis Presley
	Too Much Heaven
1/79	Bee Gees
	Too Much Of Nothing
35/67	Peter Paul & Mary

Staff/Sergeant Barry Sadler's "Ballad Of The Green Berets" was one of several records which endorsed U.S. involvement in Vietnam. It's hard to choose between that and, say, Victor Lundberg's "An Open Letter To My Teenage Son." You decide.

Frank Sinatra. Hoboken's most famous export was 50 years old when "Strangers In The Night" reached No. 1. It was just a few months after daughter Nancy, half his age, seized the summit with "These Boots Are Made For Walkin'." "Strangers" was originally written for the score of the movie "A Man Could Get Killed."

Steppenwolf. Aside from their music, Steppenwolf have given us one of the all-time great songwriter pseudonyms: Mars Bonfire. Mr. Bonfire (as The New York *Times* would have called him) composed the group's premier hit, "Born To Be Wild."

The Supremes. Nine years before the two groups teamed up for "I'm Gonna Make You Love Me," the Supremes (Primettes) were sister group to the Temptations (Primes). They performed together at parties, record hops, and school events in and around Detroit.

Survivor. Sly Stallone's cinematic exploits as "Rocky" translated into a pair of No. 1 records five years apart: Survivor's "Eye Of The Tiger" and Bill Conti's "Gonna Fly Now."

John Travolta. *Grease* must have been John Travolta's destiny. He appeared in a touring version of the musical when he was a teenager, six years before starring in the movie with Olivia Newton-John.

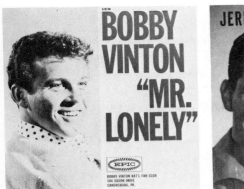

BOBBY VINTON "MR. LONELY"

JERRY WALLACE
Challenge 59060
LITTLE COCO PALM
and
MISSION BELL BLUES

F-55071
LUCINDA · · · STARDUST
LIBERTY
BILLY WARD and His Dominoes

EMPTY PLACE
Dionne Warwick
SCEPTER RECORDS

Bobby Vinton.   Enroute from teen idol to "Polish prince," Bobby Vinton sprinkled the top 40 with oldies, including songs previously recorded by the Teddy Bears, the Paris Sisters, Lee Andrews and the Hearts, Brian Hyland, Tony Orlando, Bobby Vee, and Johnnie & Joe.

Jerry Wallace.   Pop-turned-country singer Jerry Wallace secured his only top 10 hit with a song, "Primrose Lane," later employed in Henry Fonda's television series, "The Smith Family."

Billy Ward and his Dominoes.   Two of black music's finest singers emerged from Billy Ward's Dominoes: Clyde McPhatter, lead singer for the Drifters and then a solo star, and Jackie Wilson, "Mr. Excitement."

Dionne Warwick.   All but two of Dionne Warwick's top 40 hits of the '60s were written by Burt Bacharach and Hal David, who are among the top 10 songwriters of the rock era.

The Who.   Multiply the cover price of this book by 20 and you're probably getting close to the current market value of the Who's first single, "I'm The Face." At the time, they were the High Numbers, an apt description of the record's rarity value.

Glenn Yarbrough.   After several years and several big-selling albums with the Limeliters, Glenn Yarbrough went solo and achieved something that the group never did: a top 40 record.

32114
DECCA
HAPPY JACK / THE WHO
STEADman
PRINTED IN U.S.A.

45 RPM
RCA VICTOR 47-8498
BABY THE RAIN MUST FALL
I'VE BEEN TO TOWN
GLENN YARBROUGH

POS/YR	RECORD TITLE/ARTIST
19/68	**Too Much Talk** Paul Revere & The Raiders
30/60	**Too Much Tequila** Champs
9/81	**Too Much Time On My Hands** Styx
1/78	**Too Much, Too Little, Too Late** Johnny Mathis & Deniece Williams
	Too Soon To Know..see: It's Too Soon
40/81	**Too Tight** Con Funk Shun
13/68	**Too Weak To Fight** Clarence Carter
13/72	**Too Young** Donny Osmond
21/56	**Too Young To Go Steady** Nat King Cole
30/78	**Took The Last Train** David Gates
1/73	**Top Of The World** Carpenters
27/58	**Topsy I** Cozy Cole
3/58	**Topsy II** Cozy Cole
18/58 21/58	**Torero** Renato Carosone Julius LaRosa
1/77	**Torn Between Two Lovers** Mary MacGregor
39/59	**Torquay** Fireballs
20/62	**Torture** Kris Jensen
1/61	**Tossin' And Turnin'** Bobby Lewis
23/74	**Touch A Hand, Make A Friend** Staple Singers
37/80	**Touch And Go** Cars
3/69	**Touch Me** Doors
19/74	**Touch Me** Fancy

POS/YR	RECORD TITLE/ARTIST
1/73	**Touch Me In The Morning** Diana Ross
16/81	**Touch Me When We're Dancing** Carpenters
	Touch The Wind..see: Eres Tu
5/61	**Tower Of Strength** Gene McDaniels
13/62	**Town Without Pity** Gene Pitney
24/56	**Tra La La** Georgia Gibbs
35/64	**Tra La La La Suzy** Dean & Jean
2/69	**Traces** Classics IV Featuring Dennis Yost
16/65 10/67 25/76	**Tracks Of My Tears** Miracles Johnny Rivers Linda Ronstadt
9/69	**Tracy** Cuff Links
13/60	**Tracy's Theme** Spencer Ross
5/59 10/61	**Tragedy** Thomas Wayne With The Delons Fleetwoods
1/79	**Tragedy** Bee Gees
23/80	**Train In Vain (Stand By Me)** Clash
36/60	**Train Of Love** Annette
27/74	**Train Of Thought** Cher
38/79	**Train, Train** Blackfoot
22/66	**Trains And Boats And Planes** Dionne Warwick
26/67	**Tramp** Otis & Carla
38/75	**Trampled Under Foot** Led Zeppelin
8/56	**Transfusion** Nervous Norvus

POS/YR	RECORD TITLE/ARTIST
35/61	**Transistor Sister** Freddy Cannon
13/71	**Trapped By A Thing Called Love** Denise LaSalle
2/70	**Travelin' Band** Creedence Clearwater Revival
1/61	**Travelin' Man** Ricky Nelson
32/67	**Travlin' Man** Stevie Wonder
16/56	**Treasure Of Love** Clyde McPhatter
26/58	**Treasure Of Your Love** Eileen Rodgers
3/71	**Treat Her Like A Lady** Cornelius Brothers & Sister Rose
2/65	**Treat Her Right** Roy Head
18/57	**Treat Me Nice** Elvis Presley
18/81	**Treat Me Right** Pat Benatar
29/61	**Triangle** Janie Grant
25/57	**Tricky** Ralph Marterie & His Orchestra
6/72	**Troglodyte (Cave Man)** Jimmy Castor [Bunch]
9/82	**Trouble** Lindsey Buckingham
20/60	**Trouble In Paradise** Crests
33/63	**Trouble Is My Middle Name** Bobby Vinton
7/73	**Trouble Man** Marvin Gaye
35/69	**True Grit** Glen Campbell
3/56 15/56	**True Love** Bing Crosby & Grace Kelly Jane Powell
21/63	**True Love Never Runs Smooth** Gene Pitney

POS/YR	RECORD TITLE/ARTIST
	True Love, True Love..see: (If You Cry)
14/65	**True Love Ways** Peter & Gordon
1/82	**Truly** Lionel Richie
30/61	**Trust In Me** Etta James
23/69	**Try A Little Kindness** Glen Campbell
25/67 29/69	**Try A Little Tenderness** Otis Redding Three Dog Night
15/64	**Try It Baby** Marvin Gaye
33/58	**Try The Impossible** Lee Andrews & The Hearts
11/75	**Try To Remember (medley)** Gladys Knight & The Pips
12/66	**Try Too Hard** Dave Clark Five
10/76	**Tryin' To Get The Feeling Again** Barry Manilow
5/81	**Tryin' To Live My Life Without You** Bob Seger
10/77	**Tryin' To Love Two** William Bell
15/74	**Trying To Hold On To My Woman** Lamont Dozier
40/70	**Trying To Make A Fool Of Me** Delfonics
7/74	**Tubular Bells** Mike Oldfield
32/59	**Tucumcari** Jimmie Rodgers
24/68	**Tuesday Afternoon (Forever Afternoon)** Moody Blues
17/62	**Tuff** Ace Cannon
30/80	**Tulsa Time** Eric Clapton
7/72 32/78	**Tumbling Dice** Rolling Stones Linda Ronstadt

POS/YR	RECORD TITLE/ARTIST
30/58	**Tumbling Tumbleweeds** Billy Vaughn & His Orchestra
27/63	**Turn Around** Dick & DeeDee
7/68	**Turn Around, Look At Me** Vogues
3/70	**Turn Back The Hands Of Time** Tyrone Davis
16/66	**Turn-Down Day** Cyrkle
9/59	**Turn Me Loose** Fabian
35/81	**Turn Me Loose** Loverboy
28/62	**Turn On Your Love Light** Bobby Bland
10/76	**Turn The Beat Around** Vicki Sue Robinson
13/78	**Turn To Stone** Electric Light Orchestra
1/65	**Turn! Turn! Turn!** Byrds
5/82	**Turn Your Love Around** George Benson
36/80	**Turning Japanese** Vapors
36/58	**Turvy II** Cozy Cole
20/75	**Tush** ZZ Top
8/79	**Tusk** Fleetwood Mac
12/56 17/56	**Tutti' Frutti** Pat Boone Little Richard
2/55 14/55	**Tweedlee Dee** Georgia Gibbs Lavern Baker
9/57 8/73	**Twelfth Of Never** Johnny Mathis Donny Osmond
20/67	**Twelve Thirty (Young Girls Are Coming To The Canyon)** Mamas & The Papas

POS/YR	RECORD TITLE/ARTIST
15/63	**Twenty Miles** Chubby Checker
31/64	**20-75** Willie Mitchell
17/63	**Twenty Four Hours From Tulsa** Gene Pitney
6/69	**Twenty-Five Miles** Edwin Starr
4/70	**25 Or 6 To 4** Chicago
2/58	**26 Miles (Santa Catalina)** Four Preps
38/81	**Twilight** Electric Light Orchestra
1/58	**Twilight Time** Platters
30/80	**Twilight Zone/Twilight Tone** Manhattan Transfer
14/65	**Twine Time** Alvin Cash & The Crawlers
39/66	**Twinkle Toes** Roy Orbison
1/60 28/60 1/62	**Twist** Chubby Checker Hank Ballard & The Midnighters Chubby Checker
17/62 2/64	**Twist And Shout** Isley Brothers Beatles
26/62	**Twist-Her** Bill Black's Combo
25/63	**Twist It Up** Chubby Checker
9/62	**Twist, Twist Senora** Gary "U.S." Bonds
22/62	**Twistin' Matilda** Jimmy Soul
34/62	**Twistin' Postman** Marvelettes
9/62	**Twistin' The Night Away** Sam Cooke
27/60	**Twistin' U.S.A.** Danny & The Juniors
17/59	**Twixt Twelve And Twenty** Pat Boone

POS/YR	RECORD TITLE/ARTIST
16/75	**Up In A Puff Of Smoke** Polly Brown
25/69	**Up On Cripple Creek** The Band
5/63 28/79	**Up On The Roof** Drifters James Taylor
10/70	**Up The Ladder To The Roof** Supremes
7/67	**Up-Up And Away** 5th Dimension
1/82	**Up Where We Belong** Joe Cocker & Jennifer Warnes
22/67	**Ups And Downs** Paul Revere & The Raiders
1/80	**Upside Down** Diana Ross
3/66	**Uptight (Everything's Alright)** Stevie Wonder
13/62	**Uptown** Crystals
25/77	**Uptown Festival (Motown Medley)** Shalamar
4/81	**Urgent** Foreigner
2/72	**Use Me** Bill Withers
4/78	**Use Ta Be My Girl** O'Jays
34/65	**Use Your Head** Mary Wells
27/61	**Utopia** Frank Gari

V

POS/YR	RECORD TITLE/ARTIST
8/82	**Vacation** Go-Go's
9/62	**Vacation** Connie Francis
3/68	**Valleri** Monkees

POS/YR	RECORD TITLE/ARTIST
32/82	**Valley Girl** Frank Zappa
6/57	**Valley Of Tears** Fats Domino
	Valley Of The Dolls..see: Theme From
2/70	**Vehicle** Ides Of March
8/72	**Ventura Highway** America
1/59	**Venus** Frankie Avalon
1/70	**Venus** Shocking Blue
12/75	**Venus And Mars Rock Show** Paul McCartney
7/62	**Venus In Blue Jeans** Jimmy Clanton
23/58	**Very Precious Love** Ames Brothers
20/58 23/58	**Very Special Love** Debbie Reynolds Johnny Nash
11/74	**Very Special Love Song** Charlie Rich
26/64	**Very Thought Of You** Ricky Nelson
31/79	**Victim Of Love** Elton John
40/79	**Video Killed The Radio Star** Buggles
22/62	**Village Of Love** Nathaniel Mayer
7/60	**Village Of St. Bernadette** Andy Williams
12/72	**Vincent** Don McLean
29/64	**Viva Las Vegas** Elvis Presley
28/70	**Viva Tirado - Part I** El Chicano
15/81	**Voice** Moody Blues
32/80	**Voices** Cheap Trick

POS/YR	RECORD TITLE/ARTIST
	Volare (Nel Blu Dipinto Di Blu)
1/58	Domenico Modugno
12/58	Dean Martin
4/60	Bobby Rydell
33/75	Al Martino
	Voodoo Woman
27/65	Bobby Goldsboro
	Voyeur
29/82	Kim Carnes

W

POS/YR	RECORD TITLE/ARTIST
	W-O-L-D
36/74	Harry Chapin
	Wack Wack
40/67	Young-Holt Unlimited
	Wade In The Water
19/66	Ramsey Lewis
37/67	Herb Alpert & The Tijuana Brass
	Wah Watusi
2/62	Orlons
	Wait A Minute
37/61	Coasters
	Wait And See
23/57	Fats Domino
	Wait For Me
18/80	Daryl Hall & John Oates
	Wait For Me
37/60	Playmates
	Wait Til' My Bobby Gets Home
26/63	Darlene Love
	Waitin' In School
18/58	Ricky Nelson
	Waiting
19/81	Tom Petty & The Heartbreakers
	Waiting For A Girl Like You
2/81	Foreigner
	Waiting On A Friend
13/82	Rolling Stones
	Wake The Town And Tell The People
5/55	Les Baxter
13/55	Mindy Carson

POS/YR	RECORD TITLE/ARTIST
	Wake Up Everybody (Part 1)
12/76	Harold Melvin & The Bluenotes
	Wake Up Little Susie
1/57	Everly Brothers
27/82	Simon & Garfunkel
	Walk
7/58	Jimmy McCracklin
	Walk A Mile In My Shoes
12/70	Joe South
	Walk Away
23/65	Matt Monro
	Walk Away
36/80	Donna Summer
	Walk Away From Love
9/76	David Ruffin
	Walk Away Renee
5/66	Left Banke
14/68	Four Tops
	Walk-Don't Run
2/60	Ventures
	Walk-Don't Run '64
8/64	Ventures
	Walk Hand In Hand
10/56	Tony Martin
	Walk In The Black Forest
12/65	Horst Jankowski
	Walk Like A Man
1/63	Four Seasons
	Walk Like A Man
19/74	Grand Funk Railroad
	Walk On By
5/61	Leroy Van Dyke
	Walk On By
6/64	Dionne Warwick
30/69	Isaac Hayes
	Walk On The Wild Side
16/73	Lou Reed
	Walk On The Wild Side - Part 1
21/62	Jimmy Smith
	Walk On Water
17/72	Neil Diamond
	Walk Right Back
7/61	Everly Brothers
	Walk Right In
1/63	Rooftop Singers

POS/YR	RECORD TITLE/ARTIST
10/77	**Walk This Way** Aerosmith
12/57	**Walkin' After Midnight** Patsy Cline
23/64 19/70	**Walkin' In The Rain** Ronettes Jay & The Americans
14/72	**Walkin' In The Rain With The One I Love** Love Unlimited
	Walkin' In The Sand..see: Remember
37/67	**Walkin' In The Sunshine** Roger Miller
12/63	**Walkin' Miracle** Essex Featuring Anita Humes
22/66	**Walkin' My Cat Named Dog** Norma Tanega
29/58	**Walking Along** Diamonds
6/75	**Walking In Rhythm** Blackbyrds
26/63	**Walking Proud** Steve Lawrence
10/63	**Walking The Dog** Rufus Thomas
	Walking The Floor..see: I'm Walking
6/60	**Walking To New Orleans** Fats Domino
32/80	**Walks Like A Lady** Journey
2/62	**Wanderer** Dion
3/80	**Wanderer** Donna Summer
1/71	**Want Ads** Honey Cone
38/55	**Wanting You** Roger Williams
1/70	**War** Edwin Starr
17/66	**Warm And Tender Love** Percy Sledge
39/78	**Warm Ride** Rare Earth

POS/YR	RECORD TITLE/ARTIST
25/62	**Warmed Over Kisses (Left Over Love)** Brian Hyland
2/63	**Washington Square** Village Stompers
37/81	**Wasn't That A Party** Irish Rovers
8/75	**Wasted Days And Wasted Nights** Freddy Fender
9/82	**Wasted On The Way** Crosby Stills & Nash
40/79	**Watch Out For Lucy** Eric Clapton
30/67	**Watch The Flowers Grow** Four Seasons
11/71	**Watching Scotty Grow** Bobby Goldsboro
10/81	**Watching The Wheels** John Lennon
40/61	**Water Boy** Don Shirley Trio
4/59	**Waterloo** Stonewall Jackson
6/74	**Waterloo** Abba
10/63	**Watermelon Man** Mongo Santamaria
25/61	**Watusi** Vibrations
18/77	**Way Down** Elvis Presley
3/60	**Way Down Yonder In New Orleans** Freddy Cannon
24/77	**Way I Feel Tonight** Bay City Rollers
35/59	**Way I Walk** Jack Scott
4/75	**Way I Want To Touch You** Captain & Tennille
7/72	**Way Of Love** Cher
1/74 11/75	**Way We Were** Barbra Streisand Gladys Knight & The Pips

POS/YR	RECORD TITLE/ARTIST
11/64	**Way You Do The Things You Do** Temptations
20/78	Rita Coolidge
13/61	**Way You Look Tonight** Lettermen
24/58	**Ways Of A Woman In Love** Johnny Cash
1/56	**Wayward Wind** Gogi Grant
28/56	Tex Ritter
5/67	**(We Ain't Got) Nothin' Yet** Blues Magoos
	We All Shine On..see: Instant Karma
2/79	**We Are Family** Sister Sledge
4/78	**We Are The Champions** Queen
32/58	**We Belong Together** Robert & Johnny
21/68	**We Can Fly** Cowsills
1/66	**We Can Work It Out** Beatles
13/71	Stevie Wonder
36/76	**We Can't Hide It Anymore** Larry Santos
7/80	**We Don't Talk Anymore** Cliff Richard
6/59	**We Got Love** Bobby Rydell
35/69	**We Got More Soul** Dyke & The Blazers
2/82	**We Got The Beat** Go-Go's
13/65	**We Gotta Get Out Of This Place** Animals
20/71	**We Gotta Get You A Woman** Todd Rundgren
12/77	**We Just Disagree** Dave Mason
27/80	**We Live For Love** Pat Benatar
39/64	**We Love You Beatles** Carefrees

POS/YR	RECORD TITLE/ARTIST
21/73	**We May Never Pass This Way (Again)** Seals & Crofts
31/80	**We Were Meant To Be Lovers** Jim Photoglo
F/78	**We Will Rock You** Queen
9/78	**We'll Never Have To Say Goodbye Again** England Dan & John Ford Coley
4/64	**We'll Sing In The Sunshine** Gale Garnett
14/68	**We're A Winner** Impressions
7/77	**We're All Alone** Rita Coolidge
1/73	**We're An American Band** Grand Funk Railroad
40/72	**We're Free** Beverly Bremers
34/74	**We're Getting Careless With Our Love** Johnnie Taylor
	(We're Gonna) ..see: Rock Around The Clock
25/65	**We're Gonna Make It** Little Milton
15/81	**We're In This Love Together** Al Jarreau
25/72	**We've Got To Get It On Again** Addrisi Brothers
13/79	**We've Got Tonite** Bob Seger
2/70	**We've Only Just Begun** Carpenters
2/58	**Wear My Ring Around Your Neck** Elvis Presley
23/67	**Wear Your Love Like Heaven** Donovan
32/56	**Weary Blues** McGuire Sisters
10/64	**Wedding** Julie Rogers
1/69	**Wedding Bell Blues** 5th Dimension

POS/YR	RECORD TITLE/ARTIST
	Wedding Bells ..see: (I'm Always Hearing)
24/71	**Wedding Song (There Is Love)** Paul Stookey
35/58	**Week End** Kingsmen
29/79	**Weekend** Wet Willie
10/77	**Weekend In New England** Barry Manilow
19/69	**Weight** Aretha Franklin
1/76	**Welcome Back** John Sebastian
22/62	**Welcome Home Baby** Shirelles
18/60	**(Welcome) New Lovers** Pat Boone
29/61	**Well, I Told You** Chantels
13/66	**Well Respected Man** Kinks
21/78	**Werewolves Of London** Warren Zevon
37/62	**West Of The Wall** Miss Toni Fisher
24/70	**Westbound # 9** Flaming Ember
8/58	**Western Movies** Olympics
5/67	**Western Union** Five Americans
24/63	**Wham!** Lonnie Mack
16/76	**Wham Bam (Shang-A-Lang)** Silver
	What A Beautiful World..see: I.G.Y.
8/59 20/75	**What A Diff'rence A Day Makes** Dinah Washington "Little Esther" Phillips
1/79	**What A Fool Believes** Doobie Brothers
22/61	**What A Party** Fats Domino

POS/YR	RECORD TITLE/ARTIST
22/61	**What A Price** Fats Domino
33/61	**What A Surprise** Johnny Maestro
31/67	**What A Woman In Love Won't Do** Sandy Posey
	(What A) Wonderful World..see: Wonderful World
39/72	**What Am I Crying For?** Classics IV Featuring Dennis Yost
8/75	**What Am I Gonna Do With You** Barry White
9/58 26/60	**What Am I Living For** Chuck Willis Conway Twitty
14/81	**What Are We Doin' In Love** Dottie West
39/71	**What Are You Doing Sunday** Dawn
7/66	**What Becomes Of The Brokenhearted** Jimmy Ruffin
	What Cha..see: Whatcha
38/65	**What Color (Is A Man)** Bobby Vinton
4/69	**What Does It Take (To Win Your Love)** Jr. Walker & The All Stars
29/65	**What Have They Done To The Rain** Searchers
5/60	**What In The World's Come Over You** Jack Scott
10/71	**What Is Life** George Harrison
15/59	**What Is Love?** Playmates
19/70	**What Is Truth** Johnny Cash
10/81	**What Kind Of Fool** Barbra Streisand & Barry Gibb
17/62	**What Kind Of Fool Am I** Sammy Davis Jr.
21/82	**What Kind Of Fool Am I** Rick Springfield

POS/YR	RECORD TITLE/ARTIST
	What Kind Of Fool Do You Think I Am
9/64	Tams
23/69	Bill Deal & The Rhondels
	What Kind Of Love Is This
18/62	Joey Dee & The Starliters
	What Now
40/65	Gene Chandler
	What Now My Love
14/66	Sonny & Cher
24/66	Herb Alpert & The Tijuana Brass
30/67	Mitch Ryder
	What The World Needs Now Is Love
7/65	Jackie DeShannon
8/71	Tom Clay
	What Will Mary Say
9/63	Johnny Mathis
	What You ..also see: Whatcha
	What You Won't Do For Love
9/79	Bobby Caldwell
	What'd I Say
6/59	Ray Charles
30/61	Jerry Lee Lewis
24/62	Bobby Darin
21/64	Elvis Presley
	What's A Matter Baby (Is It Hurting You)
12/62	Timi Yuro
	What's Easy For Two Is So Hard For One
29/64	Mary Wells
	What's Forever For
19/82	Michael Murphey
	What's Going On
2/71	Marvin Gaye
	What's New Pussycat?
3/65	Tom Jones
	What's So Good About Good-By
35/62	Miracles
	What's The Matter With You Baby
17/64	Marvin Gaye & Mary Wells
	What's The Use Of Breaking Up
20/69	Jerry Butler
	What's Your Name
7/62	Don & Juan
	What's Your Name
13/78	Lynyrd Skynyrd

POS/YR	RECORD TITLE/ARTIST
	Whatcha Gonna Do With My Lovin'
22/79	Stephanie Mills
	Whatcha Gonna Do?
6/77	Pablo Cruise
	Whatcha See Is Whatcha Get
9/71	Dramatics
	Whatever Gets You Thru The Night
1/74	John Lennon
	Whatever Lola Wants
6/55	Sarah Vaughan
12/55	Dinah Shore
	Whatever Will Be, Will Be (Que Sera, Sera)
2/56	Doris Day
	Whatever You Got, I Want
38/74	Jackson 5
	Wheel Of Hurt
26/66	Margaret Whiting
	Wheels
3/61	String-A-Longs
28/61	Billy Vaughn & His Orchestra
	When
5/58	Kalin Twins
	When A Man Loves A Woman
1/66	Percy Sledge
35/80	Bette Midler
	When All Is Said And Done
27/82	Abba
	When He Shines
30/82	Sheena Easton
	When I Die
18/69	Motherlode
	When I Fall In Love
7/62	Lettermen
	When I Grow Up (To Be A Man)
9/64	Beach Boys
	When I Need You
1/77	Leo Sayer
	When I See You
29/57	Fats Domino
	When I Wanted You
20/80	Barry Manilow
	When I Was Young
15/67	Animals

POS/YR	RECORD TITLE/ARTIST
25/65	**When I'm Gone** Brenda Holloway
26/82	**When It's Over** Loverboy
18/66	**When Liking Turns To Loving** Ronnie Dove
19/56	**When My Blue Moon Turns To Gold Again** Elvis Presley
14/56	**When My Dreamboat Comes Home** Fats Domino
28/62	**When My Little Girl Is Smiling** Drifters
37/66	**(When She Needs Good Lovin') She Comes To Me** Chicago Loop
11/81	**When She Was My Girl** Four Tops
10/61	**When The Boy In Your Arms (Is The Boy In Your Heart)** Connie Francis
19/58	**When The Boys Talk About The Girls** Valerie Carr
23/64	**When The Lovelight Starts Shining Through His Eyes** Supremes
	When The Saints Go Marching In..see: Saints Rockin' Roll
12/56 18/56	**When The White Lilacs Bloom Again** Helmut Zacharias Billy Vaughn & His Orchestra
10/61	**When We Get Married** Dreamlovers
8/60 2/75	**When Will I Be Loved** Everly Brothers Linda Ronstadt
2/74	**When Will I See You Again** Three Degrees
33/55	**When You Dance** Turbans
32/72	**When You Say Love** Sonny & Cher
35/64	**When You Walk In The Room** Searchers
30/60	**When You Wish Upon A Star** Dion & The Belmonts

POS/YR	RECORD TITLE/ARTIST
9/71	**When You're Hot, You're Hot** Jerry Reed
6/79	**When You're In Love With A Beautiful Woman** Dr. Hook
23/67	**When You're Young And In Love** Marvelettes
39/64	**Whenever He Holds You** Bobby Goldsboro
5/78	**Whenever I Call You "Friend"** Kenny Loggins
38/76	**Whenever I'm Away From You** John Travolta
32/60	**Where Are You** Frankie Avalon
36/62	**Where Are You** Dinah Washington
1/64 15/71	**Where Did Our Love Go** Supremes Donnie Elbert
33/71	**Where Did They Go, Lord** Elvis Presley
	(Where Do I Begin)..see: Theme From Love Story
25/65	**Where Do You Go** Cher
21/62 26/65	**Where Have All The Flowers Gone** Kingston Trio Johnny Rivers
5/72	**Where Is The Love** Roberta Flack & Donny Hathaway
3/60	**Where Or When** Dion & The Belmonts
28/73	**Where Peaceful Waters Flow** Gladys Knight & The Pips
	Where The Action Is..see: Action
4/61	**Where The Boys Are** Connie Francis
23/59	**Where Were You (On Our Wedding Day)?** Lloyd Price
28/66	**Where Were You When I Needed You** Grass Roots

POS/YR	RECORD TITLE/ARTIST
23/79	**Where Were You When I Was Falling In Love** Lobo
21/67	**Where Will The Words Come From** Gary Lewis & The Playboys
40/71 37/72	**Where You Lead** Barbra Streisand Barbra Streisand
26/69	**Where's The Playground Susie** Glen Campbell
2/70	**Which Way You Goin' Billy?** Poppy Family featuring Susan Jacks
7/81	**While You See A Chance** Steve Winwood
14/80	**Whip It** Devo
11/64 27/77	**Whispering** Nino Tempo & April Stevens Dr. Buzzard's Original "Savannah" Band
9/57	**Whispering Bells** Dell-Vikings
11/66	**Whispers (Gettin' Louder)** Jackie Wilson
7/55 34/57 26/60 12/61 38/62	**White Christmas** Bing Crosby Bing Crosby Bing Crosby Bing Crosby Bing Crosby
19/76	**White Knight** Cledus Maggard & The Citizen's Band
28/71	**White Lies, Blue Eyes** Bullet
9/64	**White On White** Danny Williams
8/67	**White Rabbit** Jefferson Airplane
6/68	**White Room** Cream
7/57 18/57 22/57 9/60	**White Silver Sands** Don Rondo Owen Bradley Quintet Dave Gardner Bill Black's Combo
2/57	**White Sport Coat (And A Pink Carnation)** Marty Robbins

POS/YR	RECORD TITLE/ARTIST
5/67	**Whiter Shade Of Pale** Procol Harum
21/66	**Who Am I** Petula Clark
14/78	**Who Are You** Who
33/64	**Who Can I Turn To (When Nobody Needs Me)** Tony Bennett
1/82	**Who Can It Be Now?** Men At Work
25/64	**Who Do You Love** Sapphires
15/74	**Who Do You Think You Are** Bo Donaldson & The Heywoods
40/81	**Who Do You Think You're Foolin'** Donna Summer
33/68	**Who Is Gonna Love Me?** Dionne Warwick
3/75	**Who Loves You** Four Seasons
9/57	**Who Needs You** Four Lads
7/61	**Who Put The Bomp (In The Bomp, Bomp, Bomp)** Barry Mann
19/68	**Who Will Answer?** Ed Ames
18/76	**Who'd She Coo?** Ohio Players
29/80	**Who'll Be The Fool Tonight** Larsen-Feiten Band
34/65	**Who'll Be The Next In Line** Kinks
F/70	**Who'll Stop The Rain** Creedence Clearwater Revival
4/81	**Who's Crying Now** Journey
27/73	**Who's In The Strawberry Patch With Sally** Dawn
5/68 39/81	**Who's Making Love** Johnnie Taylor Blues Brothers

POS/YR	RECORD TITLE/ARTIST
	Who's Sorry Now
4/58	Connie Francis
40/75	Marie Osmond
	Who's Your Baby?
40/70	Archies
	Whodunit
22/77	Tavares
	Whole Lot Of Shakin' Going On
3/57	Jerry Lee Lewis
	Whole Lotta Love
4/70	Led Zeppelin
	Whole Lotta Loving
6/59	Fats Domino
	Why
1/60	Frankie Avalon
13/72	Donny Osmond
	Why Baby Why
5/57	Pat Boone
	Why Can't I Touch You..see: (If You Let Me Make Love)
	Why Can't We Be Friends?
6/75	War
	Why Can't We Live Together
3/73	Timmy Thomas
	Why Do Fools Fall In Love
6/56	Frankie Lymon & The Teenagers
9/56	Gale Storm
12/56	Diamonds
7/81	Diana Ross
	Why Do Lovers Break Each Other's Heart?
38/63	Bob B. Soxx & The Blue Jeans
	Why Don't They Understand
10/58	George Hamilton IV
	Why Don't You Believe Me
37/63	Duprees featuring Joey Vann
	Why Me
16/73	Kris Kristofferson
	Why Me
26/80	Styx
	Why Not Me
18/80	Fred Knoblock
	Wichita Lineman
3/68	Glen Campbell
	Wiggle Wobble
22/62	Les Cooper & The Soul Rockers

POS/YR	RECORD TITLE/ARTIST
	Wild!
33/63	Dee Dee Sharp
	Wild Cherry
29/56	Don Cherry
	Wild Honey
31/67	Beach Boys
	Wild Horses
28/71	Rolling Stones
	Wild In The Country
26/61	Elvis Presley
	Wild Is The Wind
22/57	Johnny Mathis
	Wild Night
28/71	Van Morrison
	Wild One
2/60	Bobby Rydell
	Wild One
34/65	Martha & The Vandellas
	Wild Thing
1/66	Troggs
20/67	Senator Bobby
14/74	Fancy
	Wild Weekend
8/63	Rebels
	Wild World
11/71	Cat Stevens
	Wildfire
3/75	Michael Murphey
	Wildflower
9/73	Skylark
	Wildwood Days
17/63	Bobby Rydell
	Wildwood Weed
7/74	Jim Stafford
	Will It Go Round In Circles
1/73	Billy Preston
	Will You Be Staying After Sunday
32/69	Peppermint Rainbow
	Will You Love Me Tomorrow
1/61	Shirelles
24/68	Four Seasons
39/78	Dave Mason
	Willie And The Hand Jive
9/58	Johnny Otis Show
26/74	Eric Clapton

POS/YR	RECORD TITLE/ARTIST
15/65	**Willow Weep For Me** Chad & Jeremy
22/58	**Win Your Love For Me** Sam Cooke
1/66	**Winchester Cathedral** New Vaudeville Band
31/69	**Windmills Of Your Mind** Dusty Springfield
32/67	**Windows Of The World** Dionne Warwick
1/67	**Windy** Association
12/61	**Wings Of A Dove** Ferlin Husky
8/81	**Winner Takes It All** Abba
21/76	**Winners And Losers** Hamilton Joe Frank & Reynolds
17/81	**Winning** Santana
16/70	**Winter World Of Love** Engelbert Humperdinck
2/63 16/66	**Wipe Out** Surfaris Surfaris
35/57	**Wisdom Of A Fool** Five Keys
17/64	**Wish Someone Would Care** Irma Thomas
38/67	**Wish You Didn't Have To Go** James & Bobby Purify
6/64	**Wishin' And Hopin'** Dusty Springfield
18/58	**Wishing For Your Love** Voxpoppers
11/74	**Wishing You Were Here** Chicago
1/58	**Witch Doctor** David Seville
21/72	**Witch Queen Of New Orleans** Redbone
6/58	**Witchcraft** Frank Sinatra

POS/YR	RECORD TITLE/ARTIST
32/63	**Witchcraft** Elvis Presley
9/72	**Witchy Woman** Eagles
29/66	**With A Girl Like You** Troggs
1/78	**With A Little Luck** Paul McCartney
15/57	**With All My Heart** Jodie Sands
39/59	**With Open Arms** Jane Morgan
35/69	**With Pen In Hand** Vikki Carr
21/59	**With The Wind And The Rain In Your Hair** Pat Boone
27/65	**With These Hands** Tom Jones
14/67	**With This Ring** Platters
4/80	**With You I'm Born Again** Billy Preston & Syreeta
30/57	**With You On My Mind** Nat King Cole
12/76	**With Your Love** Jefferson Starship
28/58	**With Your Love** Jack Scott
19/57 29/63 5/70	**Without Love (There Is Nothing)** Clyde McPhatter Ray Charles Tom Jones
1/72	**Without You** Nilsson
7/61	**Without You** Johnny Tillotson
24/82	**Without You (Not Another Lonely Night)** Franke & The Knockouts
20/80	**Without Your Love** Roger Daltrey
14/63	**Wives And Lovers** Jack Jones
	Wizard Of Oz..see: Themes From The

POS/YR	RECORD TITLE/ARTIST
40/75	**Wolf Creek Pass** C.W. McCall
6/62	**Wolverton Mountain** Claude King
2/81	**Woman** John Lennon
14/66	**Woman** Peter & Gordon
15/60	**Woman, A Lover, A Friend** Jackie Wilson
14/55	**Woman In Love** Four Aces Featuring Al Alberts
19/55	Frankie Laine
1/80	**Woman In Love** Barbra Streisand
4/81	**Woman Needs Love (Just Like You Do)** Ray Parker Jr. & Raydio
22/74	**Woman To Woman** Shirley Brown
4/68	**Woman, Woman** Gary Puckett & The Union Gap
29/65	**Woman's Got Soul** Impressions
36/71	**Women's Love Rights** Laura Lee
15/71	**Won't Get Fooled Again** Who
19/60	**Won't You Come Home Bill Bailey** Bobby Darin
11/61	**Wonder Like You** Ricky Nelson
25/59	**Wonder Of You** Ray Peterson
9/70	Elvis Presley
22/62	**Wonderful Dream** Majors
14/63	**Wonderful Summer** Robin Ward
4/58	**Wonderful Time Up There** Pat Boone
16/78	**Wonderful Tonight** Eric Clapton
14/57	**Wonderful! Wonderful!** Johnny Mathis
7/63	Tymes

POS/YR	RECORD TITLE/ARTIST
12/60	**Wonderful World** Sam Cooke
4/65	Herman's Hermits
17/78	Art Garfunkel with James Taylor & Paul Simon
25/70	**Wonderful World, Beautiful People** Jimmy Cliff
40/59	**Wonderful You** Jimmie Rodgers
12/57	**Wondering** Patti Page
21/80	**Wondering Where The Lions Are** Bruce Cockburn
25/80	**Wonderland** Commodores
1/61	**Wonderland By Night** Bert Kaempfert & His Orchestra
15/61	Louis Prima
18/61	Anita Bryant
16/59	**Woo-Hoo** Rock-A-Teens
1/61	**Wooden Heart** Joe Dowell
11/70	**Woodstock** Crosby Stills Nash & Young
23/71	Matthews' Southern Comfort
2/65	**Wooly Bully** Sam The Sham & The Pharaohs
11/67	**Words** Monkees
15/68	**Words** Bee Gees
5/67	**Words Of Love** Mamas & The Papas
13/57	**Words Of Love** Diamonds
18/66	**Work Song** Herb Alpert & The Tijuana Brass
32/74	**Workin' At The Car Wash Blues** Jim Croce
33/62	**Workin' For The Man** Roy Orbison
20/69	**Workin' On A Groovy Thing** 5th Dimension
29/82	**Working For The Weekend** Loverboy

POS/YR	RECORD TITLE/ARTIST
8/66	**Working In The Coal Mine** Lee Dorsey
9/66 2/80	**Working My Way Back To You** Four Seasons Spinners
33/63	**Workout Stevie, Workout** Stevie Wonder
37/69	**World** James Brown
7/73	**World Is A Ghetto** War
19/65	**World Of Our Own** Seekers
21/58	**World Outside** Four Coins
30/67	**World We Knew (Over And Over)** Frank Sinatra
1/64	**World Without Love** Peter & Gordon
37/64	**Worried Guy** Johnny Tillotson
20/59	**Worried Man** Kingston Trio
3/69	**Worst That Could Happen** Brooklyn Bridge
8/66	**Wouldn't It Be Nice** Beach Boys
38/81	**Wrack My Brain** Ringo Starr
2/76	**Wreck Of The Edmund Fitzgerald** Gordon Lightfoot
12/57 33/57	**Wringle, Wrangle** Fess Parker Bill Hayes
5/61	**Writing On The Wall** Adam Wade
34/64	**Wrong For Each Other** Andy Williams
32/57	**Wun'erful, Wun'erful! (Parts 1 & 2)** Stan Freberg

X

POS/YR	RECORD TITLE/ARTIST
8/80	**Xanadu** Olivia Newton-John/Electric Light Orchestra

Y

POS/YR	RECORD TITLE/ARTIST
2/79	**Y.M.C.A.** Village People
7/61	**Ya Ya** Lee Dorsey
35/63	**Yakety Sax** Boots Randolph
1/58	**Yakety Yak** Coasters
8/77	**Year Of The Cat** Al Stewart
35/80	**Years** Wayne Newton
37/61	**Years From Now** Jackie Wilson
21/65	**Yeh, Yeh** Georgie Fame
25/67	**Yellow Balloon** Yellow Balloon
4/61	**Yellow Bird** Arthur Lyman Group
23/70	**Yellow River** Christie
1/55 3/55 16/55	**Yellow Rose Of Texas** Mitch Miller Johnny Desmond Stan Freberg
2/66	**Yellow Submarine** Beatles
30/59	**"Yep!"** Duane Eddy

POS/YR	RECORD TITLE/ARTIST
5/65	**Yes, I'm Ready** Barbara Mason
2/80	Teri DeSario with K.C.
34/60	**Yes Sir, That's My Baby** Ricky Nelson
12/57	**Yes Tonight, Josephine** Johnnie Ray
11/73	**Yes We Can Can** Pointer Sisters
31/68	**Yester Love** Miracles
7/69	**Yester-Me, Yester-You, Yesterday** Stevie Wonder
1/65	**Yesterday** Beatles
25/67	Ray Charles
2/73	**Yesterday Once More** Carpenters
19/69	**Yesterday, When I Was Young** Roy Clark
21/64	**Yesterday's Gone** Chad & Jeremy
11/82	**Yesterday's Songs** Neil Diamond
3/71	**Yo-Yo** Osmonds
8/60	**Yogi** Ivy Three
20/75	**You** George Harrison
21/58	**You** Aquatones
25/78	**You** Rita Coolidge
34/68	**You** Marvin Gaye
1/74	**You Ain't Seen Nothing Yet** Bachman-Turner Overdrive
12/61	**You Always Hurt The One You Love** Clarence "Frog Man" Henry
13/78	**You And I** Rick James
9/77	**You And Me** Alice Cooper

POS/YR	RECORD TITLE/ARTIST
9/74	**You And Me Against The World** Helen Reddy
9/72	**You Are Everything** Stylistics
26/62	**You Are Mine** Frankie Avalon
7/58	**You Are My Destiny** Paul Anka
6/55	**You Are My Love** Joni James
27/76	**You Are My Starship** Norman Connors
7/62	**You Are My Sunshine** Ray Charles
5/75	**You Are So Beautiful** Joe Cocker
25/61	**You Are The Only One** Ricky Nelson
1/73	**You Are The Sunshine Of My Life** Stevie Wonder
9/76	**You Are The Woman** Firefall
20/66	**You Baby** Turtles
9/62	**You Beat Me To The Punch** Mary Wells
6/78	**You Belong To Me** Carly Simon
7/62	**You Belong To Me** Duprees featuring Joey Vann
37/59	**You Better Know It** Jackie Wilson
24/62	**You Better Move On** Arthur Alexander
20/66	**You Better Run** Rascals
9/67	**You Better Sit Down Kids** Cher
18/81	**You Better You Bet** Who
6/61	**You Can Depend On Me** Brenda Lee
37/79	**You Can Do It** Dobie Gray

POS/YR	RECORD TITLE/ARTIST
8/82	**You Can Do Magic** America
12/61 34/74	**You Can Have Her** Roy Hamilton Sam Neely
36/58	**You Can Make It If You Try** Gene Allison
18/63	**You Can Never Stop Me Loving You** Johnny Tillotson
9/79	**You Can't Change That** Ray Parker Jr. & Raydio
1/66	**You Can't Hurry Love** Supremes
40/66	**You Can't Roller Skate In A Buffalo Herd** Roger Miller
20/56	**You Can't Run Away From It** Four Aces Featuring Al Alberts
29/61 3/63	**You Can't Sit Down** Philip Upchurch Combo Dovells
12/77	**You Can't Turn Me Off (In The Middle Of Turning Me On)** High Inergy
12/58	**You Cheated** Shields
32/72	**You Could Have Been A Lady** April Wine
15/82	**You Could Have Been With Me** Sheena Easton
32/81	**You Could Take My Heart Away** Silver Condor
7/79	**You Decorated My Life** Kenny Rogers
10/66	**You Didn't Have To Be So Nice** Lovin' Spoonful
1/78	**You Don't Bring Me Flowers** Barbra Streisand & Neil Diamond
3/63	**You Don't Have To Be A Baby To Cry** Caravelles
1/76	**You Don't Have To Be A Star (To Be In My Show)** Marilyn McCoo & Billy Davis, Jr.
15/66	**(You Don't Have To) Paint Me A Picture** Gary Lewis & The Playboys

POS/YR	RECORD TITLE/ARTIST
4/66 11/70	**You Don't Have To Say You Love Me** Dusty Springfield Elvis Presley
11/64	**You Don't Know How Glad I Am** Nancy Wilson
14/56 2/62	**You Don't Know Me** Jerry Vale Ray Charles
4/61	**You Don't Know What You've Got (Until You Lose It)** Ral Donner
8/72	**You Don't Mess Around With Jim** Jim Croce
10/57	**You Don't Owe Me A Thing** Johnnie Ray
2/64	**You Don't Own Me** Lesley Gore
16/82	**You Don't Want Me Anymore** Steel Breeze
31/82	**You Dropped A Bomb On Me** Gap Band
24/69	**You Gave Me A Mountain** Frankie Laine
38/79	**You Gonna Make Me Love Somebody Else** Jones Girls
11/74	**You Got The Love** Rufus Featuring Chaka Khan
18/67	**You Got To Me** Neil Diamond
10/60 7/67	**You Got What It Takes** Marv Johnson Dave Clark Five
40/69	**You Got Yours And I'll Get Mine** Delfonics
1/74	**You Haven't Done Nothin** Stevie Wonder
24/69	**You, I** Rugbys
1/66 6/68	**You Keep Me Hangin' On** Supremes Vanilla Fudge
25/68	**(You Keep Me) Hangin' On** Joe Simon
38/82	**You Keep Runnin' Away** 38 Special

POS/YR	RECORD TITLE/ARTIST
19/67	**You Keep Running Away** Four Tops
35/80	**You Know That I Love You** Santana
12/67	**You Know What I Mean** Turtles
1/77	**You Light Up My Life** Debby Boone
12/74	**You Little Trustmaker** Tymes
22/63	**You Lost The Sweetest Boy** Mary Wells
10/77	**You Made Me Believe In Magic** Bay City Rollers
9/77	**You Make Loving Fun** Fleetwood Mac
2/74	**You Make Me Feel Brand New** Stylistics
1/77	**You Make Me Feel Like Dancing** Leo Sayer
36/79	**You Make Me Feel (Mighty Real)** Sylvester
5/81	**You Make My Dreams** Daryl Hall & John Oates
7/80	**You May Be Right** Billy Joel
17/60	**You Mean Everything To Me** Neil Sedaka
35/68	**You Met Your Match** Stevie Wonder
15/64	**You Must Believe Me** Impressions
5/61 35/67	**You Must Have Been A Beautiful Baby** Bobby Darin Dave Clark Five
40/79	**You Need A Woman Tonight** Captain & Tennille
11/58	**You Need Hands** Eydie Gorme
25/70	**You Need Love Like I Do (Don't You)** Gladys Knight & The Pips
1/78	**You Needed Me** Anne Murray

POS/YR	RECORD TITLE/ARTIST
14/64	**You Never Can Tell** Chuck Berry
10/78	**You Never Done It Like That** Captain & Tennille
3/72	**You Ought To Be With Me** Al Green
7/64 36/78	**You Really Got Me** Kinks Van Halen
27/65	**You Really Know How To Hurt A Guy** Jan & Dean
37/81	**You Saved My Soul** Burton Cummings
1/57 8/57	**You Send Me** Sam Cooke Teresa Brewer
3/76	**You Sexy Thing** Hot Chocolate
35/80	**You Shook Me All Night Long** AC/DC
1/76	**You Should Be Dancing** Bee Gees
39/64	**You Should Have Seen The Way He Looked At Me** Dixie Cups
5/82	**You Should Hear How She Talks About You** Melissa Manchester
6/69	**You Showed Me** Turtles
10/79	**You Take My Breath Away** Rex Smith
3/60	**You Talk Too Much** Joe Jones
38/65	**You Tell Me Why** Beau Brummels
40/79	**You Thrill Me** Exile
39/78	**You Took The Words Right Out Of My Mouth** Meat Loaf
8/65	**You Turn Me On (Turn On Song)** Ian Whitcomb & Bluesville
25/73	**You Turn Me On, I'm A Radio** Joni Mitchell

POS/YR	RECORD TITLE/ARTIST
36/72	**You Want It, You Got It** Detroit Emeralds
13/72	**You Wear It Well** Rod Stewart
12/60	**(You Were Made For) All My Love** Jackie Wilson
21/65	**You Were Made For Me** Freddie & The Dreamers
39/58	**You Were Made For Me** Sam Cooke
21/59	**You Were Mine** Fireflies Featuring Ritchie Adams
3/65 36/67	**You Were On My Mind** We Five Crispian St. Peters
30/65	**You Were Only Fooling (While I Was Falling In Love)** Vic Damone
22/62	**You Win Again** Fats Domino
8/74	**You Won't See Me** Anne Murray
22/65	**You'd Better Come Home** Petula Clark
14/80	**You'll Accomp'ny Me** Bob Seger
8/62 32/76	**You'll Lose A Good Thing** Barbara Lynn Freddy Fender
2/76	**You'll Never Find Another Love Like Mine** Lou Rawls
34/64 23/73	**You'll Never Get To Heaven (If You Break My Heart)** Dionne Warwick Stylistics
11/56	**You'll Never Never Know** Platters
34/64	**You'll Never Walk Alone** Patti LaBelle & The Blue Belles
	You're ..also see: Your
36/78	**You're A Part Of Me** Gene Cotton with Kim Carnes
12/73	**You're A Special Part Of Me** Marvin Gaye & Diana Ross

POS/YR	RECORD TITLE/ARTIST
15/64	**You're A Wonderful One** Marvin Gaye
7/68 19/71 34/75	**You're All I Need To Get By** Marvin Gaye & Tammi Terrell Aretha Franklin Dawn
25/57	**You're Cheatin' Yourself (If You're Cheatin' On Me)** Frank Sinatra
39/66	**(You're Gonna) Hurt Yourself** Frankie Valli
34/59	**You're Gonna Miss Me** Connie Francis
1/74	**(You're) Having My Baby** Paul Anka
4/78	**You're In My Heart (The Final Acclaim)** Rod Stewart
16/76	**You're My Best Friend** Queen
6/67	**You're My Everything** Temptations
27/81	**You're My Girl** Franke & The Knockouts
	You're My Girl ..see: (Say)
14/57	**You're My One And Only Love** Ricky Nelson
1/66 38/78	**(You're My) Soul And Inspiration** Righteous Brothers Donny & Marie Osmond
26/64 18/77	**You're My World** Cilla Black Helen Reddy
1/75	**You're No Good** Linda Ronstadt
25/65	**You're Nobody Till Somebody Loves You** Dean Martin
7/79	**You're Only Lonely** J.D. Souther
8/60 1/74	**You're Sixteen** Johnny Burnette Ringo Starr
17/59	**You're So Fine** Falcons
1/73	**You're So Vain** Carly Simon

POS/YR	RECORD TITLE/ARTIST
29/72	**You're Still A Young Man** Tower Of Power
34/80	**You're Supposed To Keep Your Love For Me** Jermaine Jackson
	You're The Best Thing..see: Best Thing
3/63	**(You're The) Devil In Disguise** Elvis Presley
2/74	**You're The First, The Last, My Everything** Barry White
18/78	**You're The Love** Seals & Crofts
4/65	**You're The One** Vogues
22/70	**You're The One - Part I** Little Sister
1/78	**You're The One That I Want** Olivia Newton-John & John Travolta
13/80	**You're The Only Woman (You & I)** Ambrosia
11/61	**You're The Reason** Bobby Edwards
3/63	**You're The Reason I'm Living** Bobby Darin
33/65	**You've Been Cheatin'** Impressions
36/65	**You've Been In Love Too Long** Martha & The Vandellas
	(You've Got) ..see: Personality
1/71 29/71	**You've Got A Friend** James Taylor Roberta Flack & Donny Hathaway
38/70	**(You've Got Me) Dangling On A String** Chairmen Of The Board
33/77	**You've Got Me Runnin'** Gene Cotton
4/56	**(You've Got) The Magic Touch** Platters
28/71	**You've Got To Crawl (Before You Walk)** 8th Day
10/65	**You've Got To Hide Your Love Away** Silkie

POS/YR	RECORD TITLE/ARTIST
20/60	**(You've Got To) Move Two Mountains** Marv Johnson
	(You've Got What It Takes)..see: Baby
7/65	**You've Got Your Troubles** Fortunes
1/65 16/69 12/80	**You've Lost That Lovin' Feelin'** Righteous Brothers Dionne Warwick Daryl Hall & John Oates
39/67 2/69	**You've Made Me So Very Happy** Brenda Holloway Blood Sweat & Tears
22/73	**You've Never Been This Far Before** Conway Twitty
8/63	**You've Really Got A Hold On Me** Miracles
25/55	**Young Abe Lincoln** Don Cornell
28/75	**Young Americans** David Bowie
17/63	**Young And In Love** Dick & DeeDee
	Young And The Restless..see: Nadia's Theme
23/58	**Young And Warm And Wonderful** Tony Bennett
8/57 20/76	**Young Blood** Coasters Bad Company
40/79	**Young Blood** Rickie Lee Jones
12/60	**Young Emotions** Ricky Nelson
2/68	**Young Girl** Gary Puckett & The Union Gap
20/76	**Young Hearts Run Free** Candi Staton
1/57 1/57 17/57 F/73	**Young Love** Tab Hunter Sonny James Crew-Cuts Donny Osmond
38/82	**Young Love** Air Supply
6/63	**Young Lovers** Paul & Paula

POS/YR	RECORD TITLE/ARTIST
	Young Lovers..see: Theme For
5/81	**Young Turks** Rod Stewart
5/62	**Young World** Ricky Nelson
	Your ..also see: You're
24/75	**Your Bulldog Drinks Champagne** Jim Stafford
29/62	**Your Cheating Heart** Ray Charles
34/61	**Your Friends** Dee Clark
18/69	**Your Good Thing (Is About To End)** Lou Rawls
33/82	**Your Imagination** Daryl Hall & John Oates
15/77	**Your Love** Marilyn McCoo & Billy Davis, Jr.
38/75	**Your Love** Graham Central Station
6/67 2/77	**(Your Love Keeps Lifting Me) Higher And Higher** Jackie Wilson Rita Coolidge
24/61	**Your Ma Said You Cried In Your Sleep Last Night** Kenny Dino
4/73	**Your Mama Don't Dance** Loggins & Messina
40/71	**Your Move** Yes
14/62	**Your Nose Is Gonna Grow** Johnny Crawford
40/63	**Your Old Stand By** Mary Wells
40/61	**Your One And Only Love** Jackie Wilson
28/63	**Your Other Love** Connie Francis
5/67	**Your Precious Love** Marvin Gaye & Tammi Terrell
20/77	**Your Smiling Face** James Taylor

POS/YR	RECORD TITLE/ARTIST
8/71	**Your Song** Elton John
40/71	**Your Time To Cry** Joe Simon
33/67	**Your Unchanging Love** Marvin Gaye
32/63	**Your Used To Be** Brenda Lee
20/57	**Your Wild Heart** Joy Layne
	(Yowsah, Yowsah, Yowsah)..see: Dance, Dance, Dance
4/68	**Yummy Yummy Yummy** Ohio Express

Z

POS/YR	RECORD TITLE/ARTIST
8/63	**Zip-A-Dee Doo-Dah** Bob B. Soxx & The Blue Jeans
36/67	**Zip Code** Five Americans
16/57	**Zip Zip** Diamonds
11/66	**Zorba The Greek** Herb Alpert & The Tijuana Brass
17/58	**Zorro** Chordettes

THE RECORD HOLDERS

TOP ARTIST AND RECORD ACHIEVEMENTS

THE TOP 40 RECORDS 1955-1982

YR	WKS	#1	TITLE/ARTIST
56	24	11	1. DON'T BE CRUEL/HOUND DOG Elvis Presley
55	26	10	2. CHERRY PINK AND APPLE BLOSSOM WHITE Perez Prado
56	22	10	3. SINGING THE BLUES Guy Mitchell
81	21	10	4. PHYSICAL Olivia Newton-John
77	21	10	5. YOU LIGHT UP MY LIFE Debby Boone
55	21	10	6. SINCERELY McGuire Sisters
57	22	9	7. ALL SHOOK UP Elvis Presley
59	22	9	8. MACK THE KNIFE Bobby Darin
81	20	9	9. BETTE DAVIS EYES Kim Carnes
81	19	9	10. ENDLESS LOVE Diana Ross & Lionel Richie
68	19	9	11. HEY JUDE Beatles
60	17	9	12. THE THEME FROM "A SUMMER PLACE" Percy Faith
55	25	8	13. ROCK AROUND THE CLOCK Bill Haley & His Comets
56	22	8	14. THE WAYWARD WIND Gogi Grant
56	22	8	15. HEARTBREAK HOTEL Elvis Presley
55	19	8	16. SIXTEEN TONS Tennessee Ernie Ford
78	18	8	17. NIGHT FEVER Bee Gees
57	24	7	18. LOVE LETTERS IN THE SAND Pat Boone
57	19	7	19. JAILHOUSE ROCK Elvis Presley
78	19	7	20. SHADOW DANCING Andy Gibbs
57	18	7	21. (Let Me Be Your) TEDDY BEAR Elvis Presley
58	18	7	22. AT THE HOP Danny & The Juniors
61	17	7	23. TOSSIN' AND TURNIN' Bobby Lewis
76	17	7	24. TONIGHT'S THE NIGHT (Gonna Be Alright) Rod Stewart
82	16	7	25. I LOVE ROCK 'N ROLL Joan Jett & The Blackhearts
82	15	7	26. EBONY AND IVORY Paul McCartney & Stevie Wonder
68	15	7	27. I HEARD IT THROUGH THE GRAPEVINE Marvin Gaye
64	14	7	28. I WANT TO HOLD YOUR HAND Beatles
67	13	7	29. I'M A BELIEVER Monkees
55	21	6	30. LOVE IS A MANY-SPLENDORED THING Four Aces
82	20	6	31. CENTERFOLD J. Geils Band
56	20	6	32. ROCK AND ROLL WALTZ Kay Starr
56	20	6	33. THE POOR PEOPLE OF PARIS Les Baxter
57	19	6	34. APRIL LOVE Pat Boone
80	19	6	35. CALL ME Blondie
80	19	6	36. LADY Kenny Rogers
56	19	6	37. MEMORIES ARE MADE OF THIS Dean Martin
58	19	6	38. IT'S ALL IN THE GAME Tommy Edwards
55	19	6	39. THE YELLOW ROSE OF TEXAS Mitch Miller
82	18	6	40. EYE OF THE TIGER Survivor

YR : Year of peak popularity
WKS: Total weeks in the top 40
#1 : Weeks record held the No. 1 spot

Records are ranked according to the number of weeks they held #1. Ties are then broken in the following order:
1. Weeks in the top 40
2. Weeks on the top 100

RECORDS OF LONGEVITY

Records making the top 40 for 23 or more weeks

YR	POS	WKS	TITLE/ARTIST
60	1	33	1. THE TWIST Chubby Checker
55	2	27	2. MELODY OF LOVE Billy Vaughn
55	1	26	3. CHERRY PINK AND APPLE BLOSSOM WHITE Perez Prado
55	1	26	4. AUTUMN LEAVES Roger Williams
77	1	26	5. HOW DEEP IS YOUR LOVE Bee Gees
57	2	26	6. SO RARE Jimmy Dorsey
55	1	25	7. ROCK AROUND THE CLOCK Bill Haley & His Comets
55	2	25	8. MOMENTS TO REMEMBER Four Lads
78	7	25	9. I GO CRAZY Paul Davis
56	1	24	10. DON'T BE CRUEL/HOUND DOG Elvis Presley
57	1	24	11. LOVE LETTERS IN THE SAND Pat Boone
56	1	24	12. LISBON ANTIGUA Nelson Riddle
62	1	24	13. MONSTER MASH Bobby ''Boris'' Pickett & The Crypt-Kickers
57	1	23	14. TAMMY Debbie Reynolds
77	1	23	15. I JUST WANT TO BE YOUR EVERYTHING Andy Gibb
57	1	23	16. HONEYCOMB Jimmie Rodgers
56	2	23	17. CANADIAN SUNSET Hugo Winterhalter with Eddie Heywood
56	2	23	18. JUST WALKING IN THE RAIN Johnnie Ray
57	5	23	19. IT'S NOT FOR ME TO SAY Johnny Mathis
55	7	23	20. IT'S A SIN TO TELL A LIE Somethin' Smith & The Redheads

1. Re-charted '62 (Pos #1)
7. Re-charted '74 (Pos #39)
13. Re-charted '73 (Pos #10)

YR : Year of peak popularity
POS: Highest position reached
WKS: Total weeks in top 40

Ties are broken by the following criteria:
   1. Highest charted position
   2. Weeks at highest position
   3. Weeks on Hot 100

THE TOP 40 ARTISTS 1955-1982

ARTISTS	POINTS	ARTISTS	POINTS
1. ELVIS PRESLEY	3556	21. JAMES BROWN	951
2. BEATLES	2033	22. PERRY COMO	950
3. STEVIE WONDER	1478	23. EVERLY BROTHERS	942
4. PAT BOONE	1371	24. CHICAGO	906
5. ROLLING STONES	1369	25. OLIVIA NEWTON-JOHN	876
6. RICKY NELSON	1287	26. BOBBY VINTON	862
7. SUPREMES	1221	27. SAM COOKE	842
8. NEIL DIAMOND	1195	28. CARPENTERS	834
9. TEMPTATIONS	1165	29. RAY CHARLES	833
10. CONNIE FRANCIS	1137	30. THREE DOG NIGHT	813
11. BEE GEES	1129	31. NAT KING COLE	806
12. ELTON JOHN	1125	32. MIRACLES	803
13. ARETHA FRANKLIN	1113	33. JACKSON 5	799
14. MARVIN GAYE	1108	34. FRANK SINATRA	794
15. BEACH BOYS	1089	35. DIANA ROSS	788
16. FATS DOMINO	1053	36. BARRY MANILOW	779
17. FOUR SEASONS	1048	37. GLADYS KNIGHT & THE PIPS	769
18. PAUL McCARTNEY	1039	38. DIONNE WARWICK	756
19. PAUL ANKA	1036	39. PLATTERS	752
20. BRENDA LEE	952	40. FOUR TOPS	749

Artist's points are calculated using the following formula:

1. Each artist's top 40 records are given points based on their highest charted position (#1=40 points; #2=39, etc.), and added together.
2. Total weeks charted are added in.
3. Total weeks an artist held the #1 position are also added in.

When two artists combine for a hit record (Ex.: Paul McCartney/Stevie Wonder; Supremes/Temptations), these points are divided by two and split between the artists.

Artists such as 'Simon & Garfunkel,' 'Sonny & Cher' and 'Loggins & Messina' are considered regular recording teams and are not split or shared by either of the artists individually.

The above point system is a good measure of the real top artists of 'all-time' and of each decade, as those artists who continually chart in the higher positions will naturally accumulate more points than an artist, such as James Brown, who may have a lot of charted hits, but only a very few in the top 10.

TOP ARTISTS BY DECADE

ARTISTS	POINTS

FIFTIES ('55-'59)

	ARTISTS	POINTS
1.	ELVIS PRESLEY	1431
2.	PAT BOONE	1195
3.	PERRY COMO	808
4.	RICKY NELSON	709
5.	FATS DOMINO	698
6.	PLATTERS	592
7.	NAT KING COLE	586
8.	FRANK SINATRA	497
9.	JOHNNY MATHIS	476
10.	EVERLY BROTHERS	475

SIXTIES ('60-'69)

	ARTISTS	POINTS
1.	BEATLES	1844
2.	ELVIS PRESLEY	1559
3.	SUPREMES	1013
4.	BRENDA LEE	952
5.	BEACH BOYS	945
6.	FOUR SEASONS	935
7.	CONNIE FRANCIS	850
8.	TEMPTATIONS	796
9.	RAY CHARLES	761
10.	BOBBY VINTON	746

SEVENTIES ('70-'79)

	ARTISTS	POINTS
1.	ELTON JOHN	953
2.	PAUL McCARTNEY	907
3.	BEE GEES	857
4.	CHICAGO	819
5.	CARPENTERS	800
6.	STEVIE WONDER	736
7.	JACKSON 5	734
8.	THREE DOG NIGHT	657
9.	BARRY MANILOW	619
10.	OLIVIA NEWTON-JOHN	592

EIGHTIES ('80-'82)

	ARTISTS	POINTS
1.	DARYL HALL & JOHN OATES	434
2.	AIR SUPPLY	375
3.	KENNY ROGERS	345
4.	DIANA ROSS	323
5.	NEIL DIAMOND	301
6.	OLIVIA NEWTON-JOHN	284
7.	DAN FOGELBERG	273
8.	KOOL & THE GANG	266
9.	JUICE NEWTON	250
10.	RICK SPRINGFIELD	238

TOP ARTIST ACHIEVEMENTS

ARTISTS	NO.

MOST CHARTED RECORDS

	ARTISTS	NO.
1.	ELVIS PRESLEY	107
2.	BEATLES	48
3.	JAMES BROWN	43
4.	STEVIE WONDER	39
5.	MARVIN GAYE	39
6.	PAT BOONE	38
7.	TEMPTATIONS	37
8.	NEIL DIAMOND	36
9.	ROLLING STONES	36
10.	FATS DOMINO	36

MOST TOP 10 RECORDS

	ARTISTS	NO.
1.	ELVIS PRESLEY	38
2.	BEATLES	33
3.	STEVIE WONDER	24
4.	ROLLING STONES	20
5.	SUPREMES	20
6.	PAUL McCARTNEY	18
7.	RICKY NELSON	18
8.	ELTON JOHN	17
9.	MARVIN GAYE	17
10.	PAT BOONE	16

MOST #1 RECORDS

	ARTISTS	NO.
1.	BEATLES	20
2.	ELVIS PRESLEY	18
3.	SUPREMES	12
4.	BEE GEES	9
5.	ROLLING STONES	8
6.	PAUL McCARTNEY	8
7.	STEVIE WONDER	7
8.	ELTON JOHN	6
9.	DIANA ROSS	6
10.	PAT BOONE	6

MOST WEEKS HELD #1 POSITION

	ARTISTS	NO.
1.	ELVIS PRESLEY	80
2.	BEATLES	59
3.	BEE GEES	27
4.	PAUL McCARTNEY	24
5.	SUPREMES	22
6.	PAT BOONE	21
7.	DIANA ROSS	20
8.	FOUR SEASONS	18
9.	OLIVIA NEWTON-JOHN	18
10.	ROLLING STONES	17

THE TOP RECORDS — BY DECADE

YR	WKS	#1	TITLE/ARTIST
			## FIFTIES ('55-'59)
56	24	11	1. DON'T BE CRUEL/HOUND DOG Elvis Presley
55	26	10	2. CHERRY PINK AND APPLE BLOSSOM WHITE Perez Prado
56	22	10	3. SINGING THE BLUES Guy Mitchell
55	21	10	4. SINCERELY McGuire Sisters
57	22	9	5. ALL SHOOK UP Elvis Presley
59	22	9	6. MACK THE KNIFE Bobby Darin
55	24	8	7. ROCK AROUND THE CLOCK Bill Haley & His Comets
56	22	8	8. THE WAYWARD WIND Gogi Grant
56	22	8	9. HEARTBREAK HOTEL Elvis Presley
55	19	8	10. SIXTEEN TONS Tennessee Ernie Ford
			## SIXTIES ('60-'69)
68	19	9	1. HEY JUDE Beatles
60	17	9	2. THE THEME FROM "A SUMMER PLACE" Percy Faith
61	17	7	3. TOSSIN' AND TURNIN' Bobby Lewis
68	15	7	4. I HEARD IT THROUGH THE GRAPEVINE Marvin Gaye
64	14	7	5. I WANT TO HOLD YOUR HAND Beatles
67	13	7	6. I'M A BELIEVER Monkees
69	16	6	7. AQUARIUS/LET THE SUNSHINE IN 5th Dimension
60	14	6	8. ARE YOU LONESOME TO-NIGHT? Elvis Presley
69	12	6	9. IN THE YEAR 2525 Zager & Evans
60	16	5	10. IT'S NOW OR NEVER Elvis Presley
			## SEVENTIES ('70-'79)
77	21	10	1. YOU LIGHT UP MY LIFE Debby Boone
78	18	8	2. NIGHT FEVER Bee Gees
78	19	7	3. SHADOW DANCING Andy Gibb
76	17	7	4. TONIGHT'S THE NIGHT (Gonna Be Alright) Rod Stewart
79	16	6	5. MY SHARONA Knack
72	15	6	6. THE FIRST TIME EVER I SAW YOUR FACE Roberta Flack
72	15	6	7. ALONE AGAIN (Naturally) Gilbert O'Sullivan
71	15	6	8. JOY TO THE WORLD Three Dog Night
70	13	6	9. BRIDGE OVER TROUBLED WATER Simon & Garfunkel
79	19	5	10. LE FREAK Chic
			## EIGHTIES ('80-'82)
81	21	10	1. PHYSICAL Olivia Newton-John
81	20	9	2. BETTE DAVIS EYES Kim Carnes
81	19	9	3. ENDLESS LOVE Diana Ross & Lionel Richie
82	16	7	4. I LOVE ROCK 'N ROLL Joan Jett & The Blackhearts
82	15	7	5. EBONY AND IVORY Paul McCartney & Stevie Wonder
82	20	6	6. CENTERFOLD J. Geils Band
80	19	6	7. CALL ME Blondie
80	19	6	8. LADY Kenny Rogers
82	18	6	9. EYE OF THE TIGER Survivor
81	19	5	10. (JUST LIKE) STARTING OVER John Lennon

SONGS WITH MOST CHARTED VERSIONS

The following 2 songs each had
4 versions make the top 10:

UNCHAINED MELODY
Les Baxter 1/55
Al Hibbler 3/55
Righteous Brothers 4/65
Roy Hamilton 6/55

ONLY YOU
Platters 5/55
Ringo Starr 6/74
Hilltoppers 8/55
Franck Pourcel 9/59

The following song had 7
versions make the top 40:

MACK THE KNIFE
(Moritat - A Theme From "The Threepenny Opera")
Bobby Darin 1/59
Dick Hyman Trio.8/56
Richard Hayman & Jan August 11/56
Lawrence Welk 17/56
Louis Armstrong 20/56
Ella Fitzgerald 27/60
Billy Vaughn 37/56

The songs highest position and year are shown after the artist's name.

Not including medleys, there have been 20 songs that have had at least four versions to make the top 40 since 1955.

#1 RECORDS LISTED CHRONOLOGICALLY 1955-1982

For the years 1955 through 1958, when more than one pop chart was published each week, special columns are shown here to show the weeks each #1 record spent on each of these pop charts.

The date shown is the earliest date that a record hit #1 on any of the four pop charts. The weeks column (next to date) is the most total weeks each record held the #1 position from any *one* of the four charts. This total is *not* a combined total from the four charts.

Because of the four charts used in my research, some dates are duplicated, as different records peaked at #1 on the same week on different charts. *Billboard* also showed ties at #1 on some of these charts, therefore the total weeks for each year may calculate out to more than 52.

Lines are drawn in on the charts column to show when any of the four pop charts were not published. See the introduction of this book for more details about researching the four pop charts.

DATE: Date record first hit the #1 position.

WKS : Total weeks record held the #1 position.

*   : Consensus #1 record - hit #1 on all pop charts published ('55-'58)

†   : Indicates record hit #1, dropped down, then returned to the #1 spot.

CHARTS COLUMN:

BS : Best Sellers
JY : Jockeys
JB : Juke Box
TP : Top 100
HT : Hot 100

592 records have hit the #1 position on *Billboard's* pop charts from 1955 through 1982. "The Twist", even though it hit #1 in 1960 and again in 1962, is counted only once. There have been 526 #1 records since the Hot 100 chart began in 1958.

DATE	WKS	RECORD TITLE	ARTIST	BS	JY	JB	TP	HT
		1955						
1/1	4	* 1. LET ME GO LOVER	Joan Weber	2	4†	4	—	—
2/5	3	2. HEARTS OF STONE	Fontane Sisters	1	—	3	—	—
2/12	10	* 3. SINCERELY	McGuire Sisters	6	10	7	—	—
3/26	5	* 4. THE BALLAD OF DAVY CROCKETT	Bill Hayes	5	3	3	—	—
4/30	10	* 5. CHERRY PINK AND APPLE BLOSSOM WHITE	Perez Prado	10	6†	8	—	—
5/14	2	6. UNCHAINED MELODY	Les Baxter	—	2†	—	—	—
5/14	3	7. DANCE WITH ME HENRY	Georgia Gibbs	—	—	3	—	—
7/9	2	8. LEARNIN' THE BLUES	Frank Sinatra	—	2†	—	—	—
7/9	8	* 9. ROCK AROUND THE CLOCK	Bill Haley & His Comets	8	6†	7	—	—
9/3	6	*10. THE YELLOW ROSE OF TEXAS	Mitch Miller	6†	6	6	—	—
9/17	2	11. AIN'T THAT A SHAME	Pat Boone	—	—	2	—	—
10/8	6	*12. LOVE IS A MANY-SPLENDORED THING	Four Aces	2†	6	3	3	—
10/29	4	13. AUTUMN LEAVES	Roger Williams	4	—	—	—	—
11/26	8	*14. SIXTEEN TONS	Tennessee Ernie Ford	7	6	8	6	—
		1956						
1/7	6	* 1. MEMORIES ARE MADE OF THIS	Dean Martin	5	6	4	5	—
2/18	2	2. THE GREAT PRETENDER	Platters	—	2	1	2	—
2/18	6	* 3. ROCK AND ROLL WALTZ	Kay Starr	1	1	6	4	—
2/25	4	4. LISBON ANTIGUA	Nelson Riddle	4	2†	—	—	—
3/17	6	* 5. THE POOR PEOPLE OF PARIS	Les Baxter	4	6†	3	6	—
4/21	8	* 6. HEARTBREAK HOTEL	Elvis Presley	8	3	8	7	—
5/5	1	7. HOT DIGGITY	Perry Como	—	1	—	—	—
6/2	3	8. MOONGLOW AND THEME FROM "PICNIC"	Morris Stoloff	—	3	—	—	—

DATE	WKS	RECORD TITLE	ARTIST	CHARTS				
				BS	JY	JB	TP	HT
		1956 CONTINUED						
6/16	8	* 9. THE WAYWARD WIND	Gogi Grant	6	8	4	7	—
7/28	1	10. I WANT YOU, I NEED YOU, I LOVE YOU	Elvis Presley	1	—	—	—	—
7/28	4	11. I ALMOST LOST MY MIND	Pat Boone	—	—	4	2	—
8/4	5	*12. MY PRAYER	Platters	2	3	1	5	—
8/18	11	*13. DON'T BE CRUEL/ 14. HOUND DOG	Elvis Presley	11	8	11	7	—
11/3	3	15. THE GREEN DOOR	Jim Lowe	—	—	3	3	—
11/3	5	*16. LOVE ME TENDER	Elvis Presley	5	5	1	4†	—
12/8	10	*17. SINGING THE BLUES	Guy Mitchell	9	9	10	9	—
		1957						
2/9	1	1. DON'T FORBID ME	Pat Boone	—	—	1	1	—
2/9	3	2. TOO MUCH	Elvis Presley	3	—	1	—	—
2/9	1	3. YOUNG LOVE	Sonny James	—	1	—	—	—
2/16	6	* 4. YOUNG LOVE	Tab Hunter	4	6	5†	6	—
3/30	1	5. PARTY DOLL	Buddy Knox	1	—	—	—	—
3/30	3	6. BUTTERFLY	Andy Williams	—	2	—	3	—
4/6	2	7. BUTTERFLY	Charlie Gracie	—	—	2	—	—
4/6	2	8. ROUND AND ROUND	Perry Como	1	2	—	1	—
4/13	9	* 9. ALL SHOOK UP	Elvis Presley	8	7	9	8	—
6/3	7	*10. LOVE LETTERS IN THE SAND	Pat Boone	5	7	—	5	—
7/8	7	*11. LET ME BE YOUR TEDDY BEAR	Elvis Presley	7	3	—	7	—
8/19	5	*12. TAMMY	Debbie Reynolds	3†	5	—	5	—
9/9	1	13. DIANA	Paul Anka	1	—	—	—	—
9/23	1	14. THAT'LL BE THE DAY	Crickets	1	—	—	—	—
9/23	4	*15. HONEYCOMB	Jimmie Rodgers	2	4	—	2	—
10/14	4	*16. WAKE UP LITTLE SUSIE	Everly Brothers	1	4	—	2	—
10/21	1	17. CHANCES ARE	Johnny Mathis	—	1	—	—	—
10/21	7	*18. JAILHOUSE ROCK	Elvis Presley	7†	2	—	6	—
12/2	3	*19. YOU SEND ME	Sam Cooke	2	1	—	3	—
12/16	6	*20. APRIL LOVE	Pat Boone	2	6	—	1	—
		1958						
1/6	7	* 1. AT THE HOP	Danny & The Juniors	5	3	—	7	—
2/10	5	* 2. DON'T	Elvis Presley	5	1	—	1	—
2/17	4	3. SUGARTIME	McGuire Sisters	—	4	—	—	—
2/24	2	4. GET A JOB	Silhouettes	—	—	—	2	—
3/17	5	* 5. TEQUILA	Champs	5	2	—	5	—
3/24	1	6. CATCH A FALLING STAR	Perry Como	—	1	—	—	—
4/14	4	7. HE'S GOT THE WHOLE WORLD IN HIS HANDS	Laurie London	—	4	—	—	—
4/21	1	* 8. TWILIGHT TIME	Platters	1	1	—	1	—
4/28	3	9. WITCH DOCTOR	David Seville	2	—	—	3	—
5/12	5	*10. ALL I HAVE TO DO IS DREAM	Everly Brothers	4	5	—	3	—
6/9	6	*11. THE PURPLE PEOPLE EATER	Sheb Wooley	6	4	—	6	—
7/21	1	12. YAKETY YAK	Coasters	—	—	—	1	—
7/21	2	13. HARD HEADED WOMAN	Elvis Presley	2	1	—	—	—
7/28	1	14. PATRICIA	Perez Prado	—	1	—	1	—
8/4	2	*15. POOR LITTLE FOOL	Ricky Nelson	2	—	—	—	2

DATE	WKS	RECORD TITLE	ARTIST	CHARTS				
		1958 CONTINUED		BS	JY	JB	TP	HT
8/18	5	*16. NEL BLU DIPINTO DI BLUE (VOLARE)	Domenico Modugno	5†	—	—	—	5†
8/25	1	17. BIRD DOG	Everly Brothers	1	—	—	—	—
8/25	1	18. LITTLE STAR	Elegants	—	—	—	—	1
9/29	6	*19. IT'S ALL IN THE GAME	Tommy Edwards	3	—	—	—	6
11/10	2	20. IT'S ONLY MAKE BELIEVE	Conway Twitty	—	—	—	—	2†
11/17	1	21. TOM DOOLEY	Kingston Trio	—	—	—	—	1
12/1	3	22. TO KNOW HIM, IS TO LOVE HIM	Teddy Bears	—	—	—	—	3
12/22	4	23. THE CHIPMUNK SONG	Chipmunks	—	—	—	—	4

DATE	WKS	RECORD TITLE	ARTIST
		1959	
1/19	3	1. SMOKE GETS IN YOUR EYES	Platters
2/9	4	2. STAGGER LEE	Lloyd Price
3/9	5	3. VENUS	Frankie Avalon
4/13	4	4. COME SOFTLY TO ME	Fleetwoods
5/11	1	5. THE HAPPY ORGAN	Dave 'Baby' Cortez
5/18	2	6. KANSAS CITY	Wilbert Harrison
6/1	6	7. THE BATTLE OF NEW ORLEANS	Johnny Horton
7/13	4	8. LONELY BOY	Paul Anka
8/10	2	9. A BIG HUNK O' LOVE	Elvis Presley
8/24	4	10. THE THREE BELLS	Browns
9/21	2	11. SLEEP WALK	Santo & Johnny
10/5	9	12. MACK THE KNIFE	Bobby Darin†
11/16	1	13. MR. BLUE	Fleetwoods
12/14	2	14. HEARTACHES BY THE NUMBER	Guy Mitchell
12/28	1	15. WHY	Frankie Avalon
		1960	
1/4	2	1. EL PASO	Marty Robbins
1/18	3	2. RUNNING BEAR	Johnny Preston
2/8	2	3. TEEN ANGEL	Mark Dinning
2/22	9	4. THE THEME FROM "A SUMMER PLACE"	Percy Faith
4/25	4	5. STUCK ON YOU	Elvis Presley
5/23	5	6. CATHY'S CLOWN	Everly Brothers
6/27	2	7. EVERYBODY'S SOMEBODY'S FOOL	Connie Francis
7/11	1	8. ALLEY-OOP	Hollywood Argyles
7/18	3	9. I'M SORRY	Brenda Lee
8/8	1	10. ITSY BITSY TEENIE WEENIE YELLOW POLKADOT BIKINI	Brian Hyland
8/15	5	11. IT'S NOW OR NEVER	Elvis Presley
9/19	1	12. THE TWIST (re-entered #1 on 1/13/62)	Chubby Checker
9/26	2	13. MY HEART HAS A MIND OF ITS OWN	Connie Francis
10/10	1	14. MR. CUSTER	Larry Verne
10/17	3	15. SAVE THE LAST DANCE FOR ME	Drifters†
10/24	1	16. I WANT TO BE WANTED	Brenda Lee
11/14	1	17. GEORGIA ON MY MIND	Ray Charles
11/21	1	18. STAY	Maurice Williams & The Zodiacs
11/28	6	19. ARE YOU LONESOME TO-NIGHT?	Elvis Presley

DATE	WKS	RECORD TITLE	ARTIST
1961			
1/9	3	1. WONDERLAND BY NIGHT	Bert Kaempfert
1/30	2	2. WILL YOU LOVE ME TOMORROW	Shirelles
2/13	2	3. CALCUTTA	Lawrence Welk
2/27	3	4. PONY TIME	Chubby Checker
3/20	2	5. SURRENDER	Elvis Presley
4/3	3	6. BLUE MOON	Marcels
4/24	4	7. RUNAWAY	Del Shannon
5/22	1	8. MOTHER-IN-LAW	Ernie K-Doe
5/29	2	9. TRAVELIN' MAN	Ricky Nelson†
6/5	1	10. RUNNING SCARED	Roy Orbison
6/19	1	11. MOODY RIVER	Pat Boone
6/26	2	12. QUARTER TO THREE	U.S. Bonds
7/10	7	13. TOSSIN' AND TURNIN'	Bobby Lewis
8/28	1	14. WOODEN HEART	Joe Dowell
9/4	2	15. MICHAEL	Highwaymen
9/18	3	16. TAKE GOOD CARE OF MY BABY	Bobby Vee
10/9	2	17. HIT THE ROAD JACK	Ray Charles
10/23	2	18. RUNAROUND SUE	Dion
11/6	5	19. BIG BAD JOHN	Jimmy Dean
12/11	1	20. PLEASE MR. POSTMAN	Marvelettes
12/18	3	21. THE LION SLEEPS TONIGHT	Tokens
1962			
1/13	2	1. THE TWIST (formerly #1 on 9/19/60)	Chubby Checker
1/27	3	2. PEPPERMINT TWIST	Joey Dee & The Starliters
2/17	3	3. DUKE OF EARL	Gene Chandler
3/10	3	4. HEY! BABY	Bruce Channel
3/31	1	5. DON'T BREAK THE HEART THAT LOVES YOU	Connie Francis
4/7	2	6. JOHNNY ANGEL	Shelley Fabares
4/21	2	7. GOOD LUCK CHARM	Elvis Presley
5/5	3	8. SOLDIER BOY	Shirelles
5/26	1	9. STRANGER ON THE SHORE	Mr. Acker Bilk
6/2	5	10. I CAN'T STOP LOVING YOU	Ray Charles
7/7	1	11. THE STRIPPER	David Rose
7/14	4	12. ROSES ARE RED	Bobby Vinton
8/11	2	13. BREAKING UP IS HARD TO DO	Neil Sedaka
8/25	1	14. THE LOCO-MOTION	Little Eva
9/1	2	15. SHEILA	Tommy Roe
9/15	5	16. SHERRY	4 Seasons
10/20	2	17. MONSTER MASH	Bobby "Boris" Pickett & The Crypt Kickers
11/3	2	18. HE'S A REBEL	Crystals
11/17	5	19. BIG GIRLS DON'T CRY	4 Seasons
12/22	3	20. TELSTAR	Tornadoes

DATE	WKS	RECORD TITLE	ARTIST
1963			
1/12	2	1. GO AWAY LITTLE GIRL	Steve Lawrence
1/26	2	2. WALK RIGHT IN	Rooftop Singers
2/9	3	3. HEY PAULA	Paul & Paula
3/2	3	4. WALK LIKE A MAN	4 Seasons
3/23	1	5. OUR DAY WILL COME	Ruby & The Romantics
3/30	4	6. HE'S SO FINE	Chiffons
4/27	3	7. I WILL FOLLOW HIM	Little Peggy March
5/18	2	8. IF YOU WANNA BE HAPPY	Jimmy Soul
6/1	2	9. IT'S MY PARTY	Lesley Gore
6/15	3	10. SUKIYAKI	Kyu Sakamoto
7/6	2	11. EASIER SAID THAN DONE	Essex
7/20	2	12. SURF CITY	Jan & Dean
8/3	1	13. SO MUCH IN LOVE	Tymes
8/10	3	14. FINGERTIPS - PT 2	Little Stevie Wonder
8/31	3	15. MY BOYFRIEND'S BACK	Angels
9/21	3	16. BLUE VELVET	Bobby Vinton
10/12	5	17. SUGAR SHACK	Jimmy Gilmer & The Fireballs
11/16	1	18. DEEP PURPLE	Nino Tempo & April Stevens
11/23	2	19. I'M LEAVING IT UP TO YOU	Dale & Grace
12/7	4	20. DOMINIQUE	Singing Nun
1964			
1/4	4	1. THERE! I'VE SAID IT AGAIN	Bobby Vinton
2/1	7	2. I WANT TO HOLD YOUR HAND	Beatles
3/21	2	3. SHE LOVES YOU	Beatles
4/4	5	4. CAN'T BUY ME LOVE	Beatles
5/9	1	5. HELLO, DOLLY!	Louis Armstrong
5/16	2	6. MY GUY	Mary Wells
5/30	1	7. LOVE ME DO	Beatles
6/6	3	8. CHAPEL OF LOVE	Dixie Cups
6/27	1	9. A WORLD WITHOUT LOVE	Peter & Gordon
7/4	2	10. I GET AROUND	Beach Boys
7/18	2	11. RAG DOLL	4 Seasons
8/1	2	12. A HARD DAY'S NIGHT	Beatles
8/15	1	13. EVERYBODY LOVES SOMEBODY	Dean Martin
8/22	2	14. WHERE DID OUR LOVE GO	Supremes
9/5	3	15. THE HOUSE OF THE RISING SUN	Animals
9/26	3	16. OH, PRETTY WOMAN	Roy Orbison
10/17	2	17. DO WAH DIDDY DIDDY	Manfred Mann
10/31	4	18. BABY LOVE	Supremes
11/28	1	19. LEADER OF THE PACK	Shangri-Las
12/5	1	20. RINGO	Lorne Greene
12/12	1	21. MR. LONELY	Bobby Vinton
12/19	2	22. COME SEE ABOUT ME	Supremes†
12/26	3	23. I FEEL FINE	Beatles

DATE	WKS	RECORD TITLE	ARTIST
1965			
1/23	2	1. DOWNTOWN	Petula Clark
2/6	2	2. YOU'VE LOST THAT LOVIN' FEELIN'	Righteous Brothers
2/20	2	3. THIS DIAMOND RING	Gary Lewis & The Playboys
3/6	1	4. MY GIRL	Temptations
3/13	2	5. EIGHT DAYS A WEEK	Beatles
3/27	2	6. STOP! IN THE NAME OF LOVE	Supremes
4/10	2	7. I'M TELLING YOU NOW	Freddie & The Dreamers
4/24	1	8. GAME OF LOVE	Wayne Fontana & The Mindbenders
5/1	3	9. MRS. BROWN YOU'VE GOT A LOVELY DAUGHTER	Herman's Hermits
5/22	1	10. TICKET TO RIDE	Beatles
5/29	2	11. HELP ME, RHONDA	Beach Boys
6/12	1	12. BACK IN MY ARMS AGAIN	Supremes
6/19	2	13. I CAN'T HELP MYSELF	Four Tops†
6/26	1	14. MR. TAMBOURINE MAN	Byrds
7/10	4	15. (I CAN'T GET NO) SATISFACTION	Rolling Stones
8/7	1	16. I'M HENRY VIII, I AM	Herman's Hermits
8/14	3	17. I GOT YOU BABE	Sonny & Cher
9/4	3	18. HELP!	Beatles
9/25	1	19. EVE OF DESTRUCTION	Barry McGuire
10/2	1	20. HANG ON SLOOPY	McCoys
10/9	4	21. YESTERDAY	Beatles
11/6	2	22. GET OFF MY CLOUD	Rolling Stones
11/20	2	23. I HEAR A SYMPHONY	Supremes
12/4	3	24. TURN! TURN! TURN!	Byrds
12/25	1	25. OVER AND OVER	Dave Clark Five
1966			
1/1	2	1. THE SOUNDS OF SILENCE	Simon & Garfunkel†
1/8	3	2. WE CAN WORK IT OUT	Beatles†
2/5	2	3. MY LOVE	Petula Clark
2/19	1	4. LIGHTNIN' STRIKES	Lou Christie
2/26	1	5. THESE BOOTS ARE MADE FOR WALKIN'	Nancy Sinatra
3/5	5	6. THE BALLAD OF THE GREEN BERETS	Ssgt. Barry Sadler
4/9	3	7. (YOU'RE MY) SOUL AND INSPIRATION	Righteous Brothers
4/30	1	8. GOOD LOVIN'	Young Rascals
5/7	3	9. MONDAY, MONDAY	Mama's & Papa's
5/28	2	10. WHEN A MAN LOVES A WOMAN	Percy Sledge
6/11	2	11. PAINT IT, BLACK	Rolling Stones
6/25	2	12. PAPERBACK WRITER	Beatles†
7/2	1	13. STRANGERS IN THE NIGHT	Frank Sinatra
7/16	2	14. HANKY PANKY	Tommy James & The Shondells
7/30	2	15. WILD THING	Troggs
8/13	3	16. SUMMER IN THE CITY	Lovin' Spoonful
9/3	1	17. SUNSHINE SUPERMAN	Donovan
9/10	2	18. YOU CAN'T HURRY LOVE	Supremes
9/24	3	19. CHERISH	Association
10/15	2	20. REACH OUT I'LL BE THERE	Four Tops

DATE	WKS	RECORD TITLE	ARTIST
10/29	1	21. 96 TEARS	? (Question Mark) & The Mysterians
11/5	1	22. LAST TRAIN TO CLARKSVILLE	Monkees
11/12	1	23. POOR SIDE OF TOWN	Johnny Rivers
11/19	2	24. YOU KEEP ME HANGIN' ON	Supremes
12/3	3	25. WINCHESTER CATHEDRAL	New Vaudeville Band†
12/10	1	26. GOOD VIBRATIONS	Beach Boys
12/31	7	27. I'M A BELIEVER	Monkees

1967

DATE	WKS	RECORD TITLE	ARTIST
2/18	2	1. KIND OF A DRAG	Buckinghams
3/4	1	2. RUBY TUESDAY	Rolling Stones
3/11	1	3. LOVE IS HERE AND NOW YOU'RE GONE	Supremes
3/18	1	4. PENNY LANE	Beatles
3/25	3	5. HAPPY TOGETHER	Turtles
4/15	4	6. SOMETHIN' STUPID	Nancy Sinatra & Frank Sinatra
5/13	1	7. THE HAPPENING	Supremes
5/20	4	8. GROOVIN'	Young Rascals†
6/3	2	9. RESPECT	Aretha Franklin
7/1	4	10. WINDY	Association
7/29	3	11. LIGHT MY FIRE	Doors
8/19	1	12. ALL YOU NEED IS LOVE	Beatles
8/26	4	13. ODE TO BILLY JOE	Bobbie Gentry
9/23	4	14. THE LETTER	Box Tops
10/21	5	15. TO SIR WITH LOVE	Lulu
11/25	1	16. INCENSE AND PEPPERMINTS	Strawberry Alarm Clock
12/2	4	17. DAYDREAM BELIEVER	Monkees
12/30	3	18. HELLO GOODBYE	Beatles

1968

DATE	WKS	RECORD TITLE	ARTIST
1/20	2	1. JUDY IN DISGUISE (WITH GLASSES)	John Fred & His Playboy Band
2/3	1	2. GREEN TAMBOURINE	Lemon Pipers
2/10	5	3. LOVE IS BLUE	Paul Mauriat
3/16	4	4. (SITTIN' ON) THE DOCK OF THE BAY	Otis Redding
4/13	5	5. HONEY	Bobby Goldsboro
5/18	2	6. TIGHTEN UP	Archie Bell & The Drells
6/1	3	7. MRS. ROBINSON	Simon & Garfunkel
6/22	4	8. THIS GUY'S IN LOVE WITH YOU	Herb Alpert
7/20	2	9. GRAZING IN THE GRASS	Hugh Masekela
8/3	2	10. HELLO, I LOVE YOU	Doors
8/17	5	11. PEOPLE GOT TO BE FREE	Rascals
9/21	1	12. HARPER VALLEY P.T.A.	Jeannie C. Riley
9/28	9	13. HEY JUDE	Beatles
11/30	2	14. LOVE CHILD	Diane Ross & The Supremes
12/14	7	15. I HEARD IT THROUGH THE GRAPEVINE	Marvin Gaye

DATE	WKS	RECORD TITLE	ARTIST
1969			
2/1	2	1. CRIMSON AND CLOVER	Tommy James & The Shondells
2/15	4	2. EVERYDAY PEOPLE	Sly & The Family Stone
3/15	4	3. DIZZY	Tommy Roe
4/12	6	4. AQUARIUS / LET THE SUNSHINE IN	5th Dimension
5/24	5	5. GET BACK	Beatles
6/28	2	6. LOVE THEME FROM ROMEO & JULIET	Henry Mancini
7/12	6	7. IN THE YEAR 2525	Zager & Evans
8/23	4	8. HONKY TONK WOMEN	Rolling Stones
9/20	4	9. SUGAR, SUGAR	Archies
10/18	2	10. I CAN'T GET NEXT TO YOU	Temptations
11/1	1	11. SUSPICIOUS MINDS	Elvis Presley
11/8	3	12. WEDDING BELL BLUES	5th Dimension
11/29	1	13. COME TOGETHER	Beatles
12/6	2	14. NA NA HEY HEY KISS HIM GOODBYE	Steam
12/20	1	15. LEAVING ON A JET PLANE	Peter, Paul & Mary
12/27	1	16. SOMEDAY WE'LL BE TOGETHER	Diana Ross & The Supremes
1970			
1/3	4	1. RAINDROPS KEEP FALLIN' ON MY HEAD	B. J. Thomas
1/31	1	2. I WANT YOU BACK	Jackson 5
2/7	1	3. VENUS	Shocking Blue
2/14	2	4. THANK YOU FALETTINME BE MICE ELF AGIN	Sly & The Family Stone
2/28	6	5. BRIDGE OVER TROUBLED WATER	Simon & Garfunkel
4/11	2	6. LET IT BE	Beatles
4/25	2	7. ABC	Jackson 5
5/9	3	8. AMERICAN WOMAN	Guess Who
5/30	2	9. EVERYTHING IS BEAUTIFUL	Ray Stevens
6/13	2	10. THE LONG AND WINDING ROAD	Beatles
6/27	2	11. THE LOVE YOU SAVE	Jackson 5
7/11	2	12. MAMA TOLD ME (NOT TO COME)	Three Dog Night
7/25	4	13. (THEY LONG TO BE) CLOSE TO YOU	Carpenters
8/22	1	14. MAKE IT WITH YOU	Bread
8/29	3	15. WAR	Edwin Starr
9/19	3	16. AIN'T NO MOUNTAIN HIGH ENOUGH	Diana Ross
10/10	1	17. CRACKLIN' ROSIE	Neil Diamond
10/17	5	18. I'LL BE THERE	Jackson 5
11/21	3	19. I THINK I LOVE YOU	Partridge Family
12/12	2	20. THE TEARS OF A CLOWN	Smokey Robinson & The Miracles
12/26	4	21. MY SWEET LORD	George Harrison

DATE	WKS	RECORD TITLE	ARTIST
1971			
1/23	3	1. KNOCK THREE TIMES	Dawn
2/13	5	2. ONE BAD APPLE	Osmonds
3/20	2	3. ME AND BOBBY McGEE	Janis Joplin
4/3	2	4. JUST MY IMAGINATION (RUNNING AWAY WITH ME)	Temptations
4/17	6	5. JOY TO THE WORLD	Three Dog Night
5/29	2	6. BROWN SUGAR	Rolling Stones
6/12	1	7. WANT ADS	Honey Cone
6/19	5	8. IT'S TOO LATE	Carole King
7/24	1	9. INDIAN RESERVATION	Raiders
7/31	1	10. YOU'VE GOT A FRIEND	James Taylor
8/7	4	11. HOW CAN YOU MEND A BROKEN HEART	Bee Gees
9/4	1	12. UNCLE ALBERT / ADMIRAL HALSEY	Paul & Linda McCartney
9/11	3	13. GO AWAY LITTLE GIRL	Donny Osmond
10/2	5	14. MAGGIE MAY	Rod Stewart
11/6	2	15. GYPSYS, TRAMPS, & THIEVES	Cher
11/20	2	16. THEME FROM SHAFT	Isaac Hayes
12/4	3	17. FAMILY AFFAIR	Sly & The Family Stone
12/25	3	18. BRAND NEW KEY	Melanie
1972			
1/15	4	1. AMERICAN PIE	Don McLean
2/12	1	2. LET'S STAY TOGETHER	Al Green
2/19	4	3. WITHOUT YOU	Nilsson
3/18	1	4. HEART OF GOLD	Neil Young
3/25	3	5. A HORSE WITH NO NAME	America
4/15	6	6. THE FIRST TIME EVER I SAW YOUR FACE	Roberta Flack
5/27	1	7. OH GIRL	Chi-Lites
6/3	1	8. I'LL TAKE YOU THERE	Staple Singers
6/10	3	9. THE CANDY MAN	Sammy Davis, Jr.
7/1	1	10. SONG SUNG BLUE	Neil Diamond
7/8	3	11. LEAN ON ME	Bill Withers
7/29	6	12. ALONE AGAIN (NATURALLY)	Gilbert O'Sullivan†
8/26	1	13. BRANDY (YOU'RE A FINE GIRL)	Looking Glass
9/16	1	14. BLACK & WHITE	Three Dog Night
9/23	3	15. BABY DON'T GET HOOKED ON ME	Mac Davis
10/14	1	16. BEN	Michael Jackson
10/21	2	17. MY DING-A-LING	Chuck Berry
11/4	4	18. I CAN SEE CLEARLY NOW	Johnny Nash
12/2	1	19. PAPA WAS A ROLLING STONE	Temptations
12/9	1	20. I AM WOMAN	Helen Reddy
12/16	3	21. ME AND MRS. JONES	Billy Paul

DATE	WKS	RECORD TITLE	ARTIST
		1973	
1/6	3	1. YOU'RE SO VAIN	Carly Simon
1/27	1	2. SUPERSTITION	Stevie Wonder
2/3	3	3. CROCODILE ROCK	Elton John
2/24	5	4. KILLING ME SOFTLY WITH HIS SONG	Roberta Flack†
3/24	1	5. LOVE TRAIN	O'Jays
4/7	2	6. THE NIGHT THE LIGHTS WENT OUT IN GEORGIA	Vicki Lawrence
4/21	4	7. TIE A YELLOW RIBBON ROUND THE OLE OAK TREE	Dawn
5/19	1	8. YOU ARE THE SUNSHINE OF MY LIFE	Stevie Wonder
5/26	1	9. FRANKENSTEIN	Edgar Winter Group
6/2	4	10. MY LOVE	Paul McCartney & Wings
6/30	1	11. GIVE ME LOVE (GIVE ME PEACE ON EARTH)	George Harrison
7/7	2	12. WILL IT GO ROUND IN CIRCLES	Billy Preston
7/21	2	13. BAD, BAD LEROY BROWN	Jim Croce
8/4	2	14. THE MORNING AFTER (SONG FROM THE POSEIDON ADVENTURE)	Maureen McGovern
8/18	1	15. TOUCH ME IN THE MORNING	Diana Ross
8/25	2	16. BROTHER LOUIE	Stories
9/8	2	17. LET'S GET IT ON	Marvin Gaye†
9/15	1	18. DELTA DAWN	Helen Reddy
9/29	1	19. WE'RE AN AMERICAN BAND	Grand Funk
10/6	2	20. HALF-BREED	Cher
10/20	1	21. ANGIE	Rolling Stones
10/27	2	22. MIDNIGHT TRAIN TO GEORGIA	Gladys Knight & The Pips
11/10	2	23. KEEP ON TRUCKIN'	Eddie Kendricks
11/24	1	24. PHOTOGRAPH	Ringo Starr
12/1	2	25. TOP OF THE WORLD	Carpenters
12/15	2	26. THE MOST BEAUTIFUL GIRL	Charlie Rich
12/29	2	27. TIME IN A BOTTLE	Jim Croce

DATE	WKS	RECORD TITLE	ARTIST
		1974	
1/12	1	1. THE JOKER	Steve Miller Band
1/19	1	2. SHOW AND TELL	Al Wilson
1/26	1	3. YOU'RE SIXTEEN	Ringo Starr
2/2	3	4. THE WAY WE WERE	Barbra Streisand†
2/9	1	5. LOVE'S THEME	Love Unlimited Orchestra
3/2	3	6. SEASONS IN THE SUN	Terry Jacks
3/23	1	7. DARK LADY	Cher
3/30	1	8. SUNSHINE ON MY SHOULDERS	John Denver
4/6	1	9. HOOKED ON A FEELING	Blue Swede
4/13	1	10. BENNIE AND THE JETS	Elton John
4/20	2	11. TSOP (THE SOUND OF PHILADELPHIA)	MFSB featuring The Three Degrees
5/4	2	12. THE LOCO-MOTION	Grand Funk
5/18	3	13. THE STREAK	Ray Stevens
6/8	1	14. BAND ON THE RUN	Paul McCartney & Wings
6/15	2	15. BILLY, DON'T BE A HERO	Bo Donaldson & The Heywoods
6/29	1	16. SUNDOWN	Gordon Lightfoot
7/6	1	17. ROCK THE BOAT	Hues Corporation
7/13	2	18. ROCK YOUR BABY	George McCrae
7/27	2	19. ANNIE'S SONG	John Denver
8/10	1	20. FEEL LIKE MAKIN' LOVE	Roberta Flack
8/17	1	21. THE NIGHT CHICAGO DIED	Paper Lace
8/24	3	22. (YOU'RE) HAVING MY BABY	Paul Anka
9/14	1	23. I SHOT THE SHERIFF	Eric Clapton
9/21	1	24. CAN'T GET ENOUGH OF YOUR LOVE, BABE	Barry White
9/28	1	25. ROCK ME GENTLY	Andy Kim
10/5	2	26. I HONESTLY LOVE YOU	Olivia Newton-John
10/19	1	27. NOTHING FROM NOTHING	Billy Preston
10/26	1	28. THEN CAME YOU	Dionne Warwicke & Spinners
11/2	1	29. YOU HAVEN'T DONE NOTHIN	Stevie Wonder
11/9	1	30. YOU AIN'T SEEN NOTHING YET	Bachman-Turner Overdrive
11/16	1	31. WHATEVER GETS YOU THRU THE NIGHT	John Lennon with the Plastic Ono Nuclear Band
11/23	2	32. I CAN HELP	Billy Swan
12/7	2	33. KUNG FU FIGHTING	Carl Douglas
12/21	1	34. CAT'S IN THE CRADLE	Harry Chapin
12/28	1	35. ANGIE BABY	Helen Reddy

DATE	WKS	RECORD TITLE	ARTIST
		1975	
1/4	2	1. LUCY IN THE SKY WITH DIAMONDS	Elton John
1/18	1	2. MANDY	Barry Manilow
1/25	1	3. PLEASE MR. POSTMAN	Carpenters
2/1	1	4. LAUGHTER IN THE RAIN	Neil Sedaka
2/8	1	5. FIRE	Ohio Players
2/15	1	6. YOU'RE NO GOOD	Linda Ronstadt
2/22	1	7. PICK UP THE PIECES	AWB
3/1	1	8. BEST OF MY LOVE	Eagles
3/8	1	9. HAVE YOU NEVER BEEN MELLOW	Olivia Newton-John
3/15	1	10. BLACK WATER	Doobie Brothers
3/22	1	11. MY EYES ADORED YOU	Frankie Valli
3/29	1	12. LADY MARMALADE	Labelle
4/5	1	13. LOVIN' YOU	Minnie Riperton
4/12	2	14. PHILADELPHIA FREEDOM	Elton John Band
4/26	1	15. (HEY WON'T YOU PLAY) ANOTHER SOMEBODY DONE SOMEBODY WRONG SONG	B. J. Thomas
5/3	3	16. HE DON'T LOVE YOU (LIKE I LOVE YOU)	Tony Orlando & Dawn
5/24	1	17. SHINING STAR	Earth, Wind & Fire
5/31	1	18. BEFORE THE NEXT TEARDROP FALLS	Freddy Fender
6/7	1	19. THANK GOD I'M A COUNTRY BOY	John Denver
6/14	1	20. SISTER GOLDEN HAIR	America
6/21	4	21. LOVE WILL KEEP US TOGETHER	Captain & Tennille
7/19	1	22. LISTEN TO WHAT THE MAN SAID	Wings
7/26	1	23. THE HUSTLE	Van McCoy & The Soul City Symphony
8/2	1	24. ONE OF THESE NIGHTS	Eagles
8/9	2	25. JIVE TALKIN'	Bee Gees
8/23	1	26. FALLIN' IN LOVE	Hamilton, Joe Frank & Reynolds
8/30	1	27. GET DOWN TONIGHT	K.C. & The Sunshine Band
9/6	2	28. RHINESTONE COWBOY	Glen Campbell
9/20	2	29. FAME	David Bowie†
9/27	1	30. I'M SORRY	John Denver
10/11	3	31. BAD BLOOD	Neil Sedaka
11/1	3	32. ISLAND GIRL	Elton John
11/22	2	33. THAT'S THE WAY (I LIKE IT)	K.C. & The Sunshine Band†
11/29	3	34. FLY, ROBIN, FLY	Silver Convention
12/27	1	35. LET'S DO IT AGAIN	Staple Singers

DATE	WKS	RECORD TITLE	ARTIST
		1976	
1/3	1	1. SATURDAY NIGHT	Bay City Rollers
1/10	1	2. CONVOY	C. W. McCall
1/17	1	3. I WRITE THE SONGS	Barry Manilow
1/24	1	4. THEME FROM MAHOGANY (DO YOU KNOW WHERE YOU'RE GOING TO)	Diana Ross
1/31	1	5. LOVE ROLLERCOASTER	Ohio Players
2/7	3	6. 50 WAYS TO LEAVE YOUR LOVER	Paul Simon
2/28	1	7. THEME FROM S.W.A.T.	Rhythm Heritage
3/6	1	8. LOVE MACHINE (PART 1)	Miracles
3/13	3	9. DECEMBER, 1963 (OH, WHAT A NIGHT)	Four Seasons
4/3	4	10. DISCO LADY	Johnnie Taylor
5/1	1	11. LET YOUR LOVE FLOW	Bellamy Brothers
5/8	1	12. WELCOME BACK	John Sebastian
5/15	1	13. BOOGIE FEVER	Sylvers
5/22	5	14. SILLY LOVE SONGS	Wings†
5/29	2	15. LOVE HANGOVER	Diana Ross
7/10	2	16. AFTERNOON DELIGHT	Starland Vocal Band
7/24	2	17. KISS AND SAY GOODBYE	Manhattans
8/7	4	18. DON'T GO BREAKING MY HEART	Elton John & Kiki Dee
9/4	1	19. YOU SHOULD BE DANCING	Bee Gees
9/11	1	20. (SHAKE, SHAKE, SHAKE) SHAKE YOUR BOOTY	KC & The Sunshine Band
9/18	3	21. PLAY THAT FUNKY MUSIC	Wild Cherry
10/9	1	22. A FIFTH OF BEETHOVEN	Walter Murphy & The Big Apple Band
10/16	1	23. DISCO DUCK (PART 1)	Rick Dees & His Cast Of Idiots
10/23	2	24. IF YOU LEAVE ME NOW	Chicago
11/6	1	25. ROCK'N ME	Steve Miller
11/13	7	26. TONIGHT'S THE NIGHT (GONNA BE ALRIGHT)	Rod Stewart
		1977	
1/8	1	1. YOU DON'T HAVE TO BE A STAR (TO BE IN MY SHOW)	Marilyn McCoo & Billy Davis, Jr.
1/15	1	2. YOU MAKE ME FEEL LIKE DANCING	Leo Sayer
1/22	1	3. I WISH	Stevie Wonder
1/29	1	4. CAR WASH	Rose Royce
2/5	2	5. TORN BETWEEN TWO LOVERS	Mary MacGregor
2/19	1	6. BLINDED BY THE LIGHT	Manfred Mann's Earth Band
2/26	1	7. NEW KID IN TOWN	Eagles
3/5	3	8. LOVE THEME FROM "A STAR IS BORN" (EVERGREEN)	Barbra Streisand
3/26	2	9. RICH GIRL	Daryl Hall & John Oates

DATE	WKS	RECORD TITLE	ARTIST
1977 CONTINUED			
4/9	1	10. DANCING QUEEN	Abba
4/16	1	11. DON'T GIVE UP ON US	David Soul
4/23	1	12. DON'T LEAVE ME THIS WAY	Thelma Houston
4/30	1	13. SOUTHERN NIGHTS	Glen Campbell
5/7	1	14. HOTEL CALIFORNIA	Eagles
5/14	1	15. WHEN I NEED YOU	Leo Sayer
5/21	3	16. SIR DUKE	Stevie Wonder
6/11	1	17. I'M YOUR BOOGIE MAN	KC & The Sunshine Band
6/18	1	18. DREAMS	Fleetwood Mac
6/25	1	19. GOT TO GIVE IT UP	Marvin Gaye
7/2	1	20. GONNA FLY NOW (THEME FROM "ROCKY")	Bill Conti
7/9	1	21. UNDERCOVER ANGEL	Alan O'Day
7/16	1	22. DA DOO RON RON	Shaun Cassidy
7/23	1	23. LOOKS LIKE WE MADE IT	Barry Manilow
7/30	4	24. I JUST WANT TO BE YOUR EVERYTHING	Andy Gibb†
8/20	5	25. BEST OF MY LOVE	Emotions†
10/1	2	26. STAR WARS THEME/CANTINA BAND	Meco
10/15	10	27. YOU LIGHT UP MY LIFE	Debby Boone
12/24	3	28. HOW DEEP IS YOUR LOVE	Bee Gees
1978			
1/14	3	1. BABY COME BACK	Player
2/4	4	2. STAYIN' ALIVE	Bee Gees
3/4	2	3. (LOVE IS) THICKER THAN WATER	Andy Gibb
3/18	8	4. NIGHT FEVER	Bee Gees
5/13	1	5. IF I CAN'T HAVE YOU	Yvonne Elliman
5/20	2	6. WITH A LITTLE LUCK	Wings
6/3	1	7. TOO MUCH, TOO LITTLE, TOO LATE	Johnny Mathis/ Deniece Williams
6/10	1	8. YOU'RE THE ONE THAT I WANT	John Travolta & Olivia Newton-John
6/17	7	9. SHADOW DANCING	Andy Gibb
8/5	1	10. MISS YOU	Rolling Stones
8/12	2	11. THREE TIMES A LADY	Commodores
8/26	2	12. GREASE	Frankie Valli
9/9	3	13. BOOGIE OOGIE OOGIE	Taste Of Honey
9/30	4	14. KISS YOU ALL OVER	Exile
10/28	1	15. HOT CHILD IN THE CITY	Nick Gilder
11/4	1	16. YOU NEEDED ME	Anne Murray
11/11	3	17. MacARTHUR PARK	Donna Summer
12/2	2	18. YOU DON'T BRING ME FLOWERS	Barbra Streisand & Neil Diamond†
12/9	5	19. LE FREAK	Chic†

DATE		RECORD TITLE	ARTIST
		1979	
1/6	2	1. TOO MUCH HEAVEN	Bee Gees
2/10	4	2. DA YA THINK I'M SEXY?	Rod Stewart
3/10	3	3. I WILL SURVIVE	Gloria Gaynor†
3/24	2	4. TRAGEDY	Bee Gees
4/14	1	5. WHAT A FOOL BELIEVES	Doobie Brothers
4/21	1	6. KNOCK ON WOOD	Amili Stewart
4/28	1	7. HEART OF GLASS	Blondie
5/5	4	8. REUNITED	Peaches & Herb
6/2	3	9. HOT STUFF	Donna Summer†
6/9	1	10. LOVE YOU INSIDE OUT	Bee Gees
6/30	2	11. RING MY BELL	Anita Ward
7/14	5	12. BAD GIRLS	Donna Summer
8/18	1	13. GOOD TIMES	Chic
8/25	6	14. MY SHARONA	The Knack
10/6	1	15. SAD EYES	Robert John
10/13	1	16. DON'T STOP 'TIL YOU GET ENOUGH	Michael Jackson
10/20	2	17. RISE	Herb Alpert
11/3	1	18. POP MUZIK	M
11/10	1	19. HEARTACHE TONIGHT	Eagles
11/17	1	20. STILL	Commodores
11/24	2	21. NO MORE TEARS (ENOUGH IS ENOUGH)	Barbra Streisand/ Donna Summer
12/8	2	22. BABE	Styx
12/22	2	23. ESCAPE (THE PINA COLADA SONG)	Rupert Holmes†
		1980	
1/5	1	1. PLEASE DON'T GO	KC & The Sunshine Band
1/19	4	2. ROCK WITH YOU	Michael Jackson
2/16	1	3. DO THAT TO ME ONE MORE TIME	Captain & Tennille
2/23	4	4. CRAZY LITTLE THING CALLED LOVE	Queen
3/22	4	5. ANOTHER BRICK IN THE WALL (PART II)	Pink Floyd
4/19	6	6. CALL ME	Blondie
5/31	4	7. FUNKYTOWN	Lipps, Inc.
6/28	3	8. COMING UP (LIVE AT GLASGOW)	Paul McCartney & Wings
7/19	2	9. IT'S STILL ROCK AND ROLL TO ME	Billy Joel
8/2	4	10. MAGIC	Olivia Newton-John
8/30	1	11. SAILING	Christopher Cross
9/6	4	12. UPSIDE DOWN	Diana Ross
10/4	3	13. ANOTHER ONE BITES THE DUST	Queen
10/25	3	14. WOMAN IN LOVE	Barbra Streisand
11/15	6	15. LADY	Kenny Rogers
12/27	5	16. (JUST LIKE) STARTING OVER	John Lennon

DATE	WKS	RECORD TITLE	ARTIST
1981			
1/31	1	1. THE TIDE IS HIGH	Blondie
2/7	2	2. CELEBRATION	Kool & The Gang
2/21	2	3. 9 TO 5	Dolly Parton†
2/28	2	4. I LOVE A RAINY NIGHT	Eddie Rabbitt
3/21	1	5. KEEP ON LOVING YOU	REO Speedwagon
3/28	2	6. RAPTURE	Blondie
4/11	3	7. KISS ON MY LIST	Daryl Hall & John Oates
5/2	2	8. MORNING TRAIN (NINE TO FIVE)	Sheena Easton
5/16	9	9. BETTE DAVIS EYES	Kim Carnes†
6/20	1	10. STARS ON 45 MEDLEY	Stars on 45
7/25	1	11. THE ONE THAT YOU LOVE	Air Supply
8/1	2	12. JESSIE'S GIRL	Rick Springfield
8/15	9	13. ENDLESS LOVE	Diana Ross & Lionel Richie
10/17	3	14. ARTHUR'S THEME (BEST THAT YOU CAN DO)	Christopher Cross
11/7	2	15. PRIVATE EYES	Daryl Hall & John Oates
11/21	10	16. PHYSICAL	Olivia Newton-John
1982			
1/30	1	1. I CAN'T GO FOR THAT (NO CAN DO)	Daryl Hall & John Oates
2/6	6	2. CENTERFOLD	J. Geils Band
3/20	7	3. I LOVE ROCK 'N ROLL	Joan Jett & The Blackhearts
5/8	1	4. CHARIOTS OF FIRE — TITLES	Vangelis
5/15	7	5. EBONY AND IVORY	Paul McCartney/ Stevie Wonder
6/19	3	6. DON'T YOU WANT ME	Human League
7/24	6	7. EYE OF THE TIGER	Survivor
9/4	2	8. ABRACADABRA	Steve Miller Band†
9/11	2	9. HARD TO SAY I'M SORRY	Chicago
9/18	4	10. JACK & DIANE	John Cougar
10/30	1	11. WHO CAN IT BE NOW?	Men At Work
11/6	3	12. UP WHERE WE BELONG	Joe Cocker & Jennifer Warnes
11/27	2	13. TRULY	Lionel Richie
12/11	1	14. MICKEY	Toni Basil
12/18	4	15. MANEATER	Daryl Hall & John Oates

NOW GET THE BOOK THAT GETS TO THE BOTTOM OF THE "HOT 100."

If you like to stay on top of charted pop music, tracking the Top 40 is a great way to start.

But it's only the beginning. Because beyond the Top 40 lie the sixty other chart positions that comprise *Billboard*'s *"Hot 100,"* the most influential chart in the history of music.

Joel Whitburn's Top Pop 1955–1982 is the only book that gets to the bottom of the *"Hot 100."*

Not only does it include all of the Top 40 singles and artists listed in the book you now hold, it picks up where the Top 40 leaves off—with the more than 8,700 additional titles that have appeared in the "Bottom 60" of the *"Hot 100"* throughout the years.

Over 875 pages long, this fascinating hard-bound volume chronicles the full range and diversity of pop music, from the big hits by obscure artists, to the obscure singles by some of pop's biggest stars and superstars. All in a concise, easy-to-use format that's the same as that of *The Billboard Book of Top 40 Hits*, but with additional features that make it even more useful.

So, take an in-depth look at pop music with the book that delves deeper into the *"Hot 100"* than any other work ever published. For complete information on *Joel Whitburn's Top Pop 1955–1982*, as well as *Joel Whitburn's Pop Annual* and the entire line of *Record Research* books on charted music, please write for a free catalog.

Record Research

P.O. BOX 200
MENOMONEE FALLS, WISCONSIN 53051